Surveillance, Crime and Social Control

International Library of Criminology, Criminal Justice and Penology – Second Series
Series Editors: Gerald Mars and David Nelken

Titles in the Series:

Gender and Prisons
Dana M. Britton

Quantitative Methods in Criminology
Shawn Bushway and David Weisburd

Detecting Deception
David Canter and Donna Youngs

Offender Profiling
David Canter and Michael Davis

Insurgent Terrorism
Gerald Cromer

Criminal Courts
Jo Dixon, Aaron Kupchik and
Joachim Savelsberg

Crime and Immigration
Joshua D. Freilich and Graeme Newman

Crime and Security
Benjamin Goold and Lucia Zedner

Crime and Regulation
Fiona Haines

Recent Developments in Criminological Theory
Stuart Henry

Gun Crime
Richard Hobbs and Robert Hornsby

The Criminology of War
Ruth Jamieson

The Impact of HIV/AIDS on Criminology and Criminal Justice
Mark M. Lanier

Burglary
Robert Mawby

Domestic Violence
Mangai Natarajan

Women Police
Mangai Natarajan

Crime and Immigration
Graeme Newman and Joshua Freilich

Surveillance, Crime and Social Control
Clive Norris and Dean Wilson

Crime and Social Institutions
Richard Rosenfeld

The Death Penalty, Volumes I and II
Austin Sarat

Gangs
Jacqueline Schneider and Nick Tilley

Corporate Crime
Sally Simpson and Carole Gibbs

Green Criminology
Nigel South and Piers Beirne

Crime and Deviance in Cyberspace
David Wall

Surveillance, Crime and Social Control

Edited by

Clive Norris and Dean Wilson

University of Sheffield, UK and Monash University, Australia

ASHGATE

Published by
Ashgate Publishing Limited
Gower House
Croft Road
Aldershot
Hampshire GU11 3HR
England

Ashgate Publishing Company
Suite 420
101 Cherry Street
Burlington, VT 05401-4405
USA

Ashgate website: http://www.ashgate.com

British Library Cataloguing in Publication Data
Surveillance, crime and social control. - (International
    library of criminology, criminal justice and penology.
    Second series)
    1. Electronic surveillance 2. Social control 3. Crime
    prevention
    I. Norris, Clive II. Wilson, Dean
    363.2'52

Library of Congress Control Number 2006932214

ISBN 0 7546 2460 9
ISBN 978-0-7546-2460-8

Printed in Great Britain by TJ International Ltd, Padstow, Cornwall

Contents

PART III   UNDERCOVER POLICE SURVEILLANCE

PART IV   BODIES, DATABASES AND TECHNOLOGIES

PART V   SURVEILLANCE FUTURES

Acknowledgements

The editors and publishers wish to thank the following for permission to use copyright material.

Blackwell Publishing for the essays: Kevin D. Haggerty and Richard V. Ericson (2000), 'The Surveillant Assemblage', *British Journal of Sociology*, **51**, pp. 605–22. Copyright © 2000 London School of Economics and Political Science; Steven Greer (1995), 'Towards a Sociological Model of the Police Informant', *British Journal of Sociology*, **46**, pp. 509–27. Copyright © 1995 London School of Economics; Richard Rosenfeld, Bruce A. Jacobs and Richard Wright (2003), 'Snitching and the Code of the Street', *British Journal of Criminology*, **43**, pp. 291–309. Copyright © 2003 Centre for Crimes and Justice Studies; Mike Nellis (2003), 'News Media, Popular Culture and the Electronic Monitoring of Offenders in England and Wales', *Howard Journal of Criminal Justice*, **42**, pp. 1–31. Copyright © 2003 Blackwell Publishing.

Criminal Justice Press for the essays: Jason Ditton and Emma Short (1999), 'Yes, it Works, No, it Doesn't: Comparing the Effects of Open–Street CCTV in Two Adjacent Scottish Town Centres', *Crime Prevention Studies*, **10**, pp. 201–23. Copyright © 1999 Criminal Justice Press; Clive Norris and Gary Armstrong (1999), 'CCTV and the Social Structuring of Surveillance', *Crime Prevention Studies*, **10**, pp. 157–78.

Foundation for the Study of Independent Social Ideas for the essay: Gary T. Marx (1985), 'I'll be Watching You: Reflections on the New Surveillance', *Dissent*, Winter, pp. 26–34.

MIT Press Journals for the essay: Gilles Deleuze (1992), 'Postscript on the Societies of Control', *October*, **59**, pp. 3–7.

Oxford University Press for the essay: Emma Short and Jason Ditton (1998), 'Seen and Now Heard: Talking to the Targets of Open Street CCTV', *British Journal of Criminology*, **38**, pp. 404–28.

Pion Ltd for the essay: S. Graham (1999), 'The Eyes Have It: CCTV as the "Fifth Utility"', *Environment and Planning B: Planning and Design*, **26**, pp. 639–42.

Irma van der Ploeg (1999), 'Written on the Body: Biometrics and Identity', *Computers and Society*, **29**, pp. 37–44. Copyright © 1999 Irma van Der Ploeg.

Queen's Quarterly for the essay: David Lyon (1991), 'Bentham's Panopticon: From Moral Architecture to Electronic Surveillance', *Queen's Quarterly*, **98**, pp. 596–617.

Preface to the Second Series

The first series of the International Library of Criminology, Criminal Justice and Penology has established itself as a major research resource by bringing together the most significant journal essays in contemporary criminology, criminal justice and penology. The series made available to researchers, teachers and students an extensive range of essays which are indispensable for obtaining an overview of the latest theories and findings in this fast changing subject. Indeed the rapid growth of interesting scholarly work in the field has created a demand for a second series which like the first consists of volumes dealing with criminological schools and theories as well as with approaches to particular areas of crime criminal justice and penology. Each volume is edited by a recognised authority who has selected twenty or so of the best journal articles in the field of their special competence and provided an informative introduction giving a summary of the field and the relevance of the articles chosen. The original pagination is retained for ease of reference.

The difficulties of keeping on top of the steadily growing literature in criminology are complicated by the many disciplines from which its theories and findings are drawn (sociology, law, sociology of law, psychology, psychiatry, philosophy and economics are the most obvious). The development of new specialisms with their own journals (policing, victimology, mediation) as well as the debates between rival schools of thought (feminist criminology, left realism, critical criminology, abolitionism etc.) make necessary overviews that offer syntheses of the state of the art.

GERALD MARS
Visiting Professor, Brunel University, Middlesex, UK

DAVID NELKEN
Distinguished Professor of Sociology, University of Macerata, Italy;
Distinguished Research Professor of Law, University of Cardiff, Wales;
Honourary Visiting Professor of Law, LSE, London, UK

Introduction

This volume draws together a range of contemporary writings to explore how the surveillance gaze has been directed in the name of crime control. In delimiting what constitutes surveillance we have drawn on Dandeker's observation that, although 'surveillance activities are features of all social relationships', it generally involves one or more of the following:

(1) The collection and storage of information presumed to be useful about people or objects;
(2) The supervision of the activities of people or objects through the issuing of instructions or the physical design of the natural and built environments...
(3) The application of information gathering activities to the business of monitoring the behaviour of those under supervision, and, in the case of subject persons, compliance with instructions (Dandeker, 1990, p. 37).

In this sense, surveillance is nearly always implicated in the formal response of the modern nation-state's desire to control crime. It is no accident that, in Britain at least, the precursors to the modern police emerged from a system of citizen 'watches'. Similarly, the transformation of the medieval jail as a place of containment to a site of punishment and reformation entailed the development of an architecture of surveillance epitomized, if never fully realized, in Bentham's design for the Panopticon prison.

By way of introduction we want to briefly sketch the development of surveillance practice in the British criminal justice system: first, as a means of confirming identity; second as a means of locating bodies in space; and third, as a means of uncovering hidden states of the body and mind.

Surveillance and Identity

The medieval system of policing largely rested on the voluntary participation of all householders in a community in periodically undertaking the duty of the 'Watch', the purpose of which was to keep watch over the town, particularly after nightfall, and challenge those acting suspiciously or in a disorderly manner (Rawlings, 2003). Over the course of the next 600 years responsibility for staffing the watch was shifted to paid functionaries and, between 1829 and 1856, throughout England and Wales, it was replaced by the establishment of a full-time professional police force. Thus the principle was established that, in the public realm at least, the citizenry, particularly the urban poor, could expect to be monitored by state functionaries who had the right to intervene and arrest if they found evidence of crime or disorder.

Even at its inception the politics of surveillance was a major factor in shaping the nature of English policing. One of the foremost objections to the establishment of a centralized professional police force was that it would lead to a Napoleonic system of political policing based on a network of spies and informers. As a result, a compromise was brokered by Sir

Robert Peel, the founder of London's Metropolitan Police: the new police would have no plain-clothes detective branch but a body of men sporting a distinctive non-militarist uniform, crowned with a top hat so they would be visible to all (Critchley, 1978). Although a detective branch was finally set up in 1842, for the next quarter of a century it was limited to 15 men serving the whole of the Metropolitan Police (Wright, 2002, p.74).

As Foucault (1977) reminds us, the mere ability to watch over someone provides only one element of the panoptic power of surveillance. The true power of surveillance is unleashed when the face can be named and the name can be used to link an individual to their official record. For then an individual is unable to escape their officially codified past and they can be judged and disciplined on the basis of accumulated information. So, while early police surveillance primarily entailed monitoring the movements and activities of bodies in public space through the physical presence of the constable, in the absence of a formal system of records, the panoptic power of surveillance was limited.

In the context of the massive social and economic changes that were unleashed by the Industrial Revolution, the urban population became increasingly mobile, transitory and anonymous. This meant that the ability to identify those on the street based on a constable's knowledge of a stable community was increasingly undermined. Moreover nineteenth-century social administrators were particularly concerned to differentiate the petty criminal from the habitual criminal and this required a means of linking a person with their criminal history. To this end, in 1869 The Habitual Criminals Act mandated the Metropolitan Police to establish a centralized register of all convicted criminals in England and, by 1874, the register contained 117 568 names and was growing at a rate of 30 000 per year (Hastings, 1875, p. 13).

However, a system that was based on matching records by name was soon found to be inadequate. In an age where many people could not read or write, when the spelling of a name was subject to phonetic interpretation and the more experienced criminal could falsify their name, the register was inherently unreliable for the purposes of identification. So much so that in the words of one contemporary commentator 'registration is of no use, and might as well be got rid of at once' (Hastings, 1875, p. 13).

Thus even as late as the 1890s, one of the primary means of identifying the habitual criminal was still based on the local constable's face-to-face knowledge. Lambourne describes the procedure carried out at Holloway prison:

> To this prison were sent all persons committed for trial or remanded in custody by magistrates in the Metropolitan Police District. Here three times a week prison warders from Wormwood Scrubs, Pentonville, Wandsworth and Chelmsford prison, together with detectives for the then twenty-two Metropolitan Police Divisions, an inspector from New Scotland Yard, and six officers from the City of London Police, viewed the unconvicted prisoners as they exercised. In this way a prisoner (whose identity was unknown) would often be recognized. ... During 1893 1,949 such identifications were made (Lambourne, 1984, p. 47).

In France, the same problem was exercising Alphonse Bertillon: how to devise a system that was not dependent on a person's name or a police officer's memory? Although the French records contained a photograph, the task of trying to match an individual photograph with the tens of thousands of records held in the files was formidable and could take weeks. Bertillon solved this problem by utilizing a series of anthropometrical measurements which, when combined, would allow the calculation of an individual reference point based on bodily dimensions. As Bertillon had estimated that the chance of two people sharing the same series of measurements was 1 in 4 million, this came close to providing a unique identification number. This number would be used to position the record in the system nearest to those who shared similar physical dimensions. To determine whether a person already had an entry in the archive, the identification number on their new record could be checked against a small subset of existing entries, and a final comparison made between the photographs (Sekula, 1986, pp. 25–34).

At last there was an efficient means of linking an individual to their record, which could now be used to differentiate the habitual from the petty criminal and, by 1893, about a dozen countries around the world had introduced the system. Nevertheless, the system was not without its problems. First, as many convicted criminals were youths, as they advanced from adolescence to adulthood, their measurements would change, thus undermining the value of a reference system based on anthropometric measurement. Second, the system required accurate measurements to be taken, something that could not always be relied upon. Finally, as the number of records held grew ever larger, the subset needed for manual comparison increased from around a dozen to several hundred, considerably reducing the efficiency of the system (Browne and Brock, 1953; Cole, 2001).

It was the pioneering work of Francis Galton, among others, which demonstrated that each individual carries with them a unique and unchanging token of identity, and one that could be easily recorded – the fingerprint. By devising a simple system of classification he made it amenable to systematic description and comparison. By 1901, in England, the fingerprint had replaced the Bertillon system of measurement and rapidly became adopted across the world as the primary means for the police to establish a suspect's identity (Critchley, 1978, p. 162).

The birth of the criminal record and the subsequent means of linking it with certainty to a named individual provided the cornerstone of the development of routine bureaucratic surveillance. But the fingerprint has one other advantage: if left at the scene of a crime it enables an individual to be fixed at a specific spatial location even after they have fled, thus expanding the surveillance gaze in both space and time. By 1918 the fingerprints of 300 000 criminals were filed in the national archive. Yet in the same year, not one crime in London was solved by fingerprint identification (Lambourne, 1984, p. 96). Herein lies the irony of mass surveillance systems. Their theoretical efficiency increases as the number of files in the system expands – but their practical efficiency decreases as the paper-based system is overwhelmed by the sheer volume of files.

Over the next 50 years the manual system was improved with new processing routines, but it is only when records can be digitalized and stored in electronic form that their potential can be fully unleashed, for then they can be processed automatically. Thus it is the development of computerized record systems in the 1970s that marks the decisive break from information recording and retrieval practices rooted in the nineteenth century to the emerging surveillance practices of the twenty-first century. However, change did not occur overnight. The so-called 'information revolution' of the 1970s relied on more than computerization alone – a point well illustrated by the development of the Police National Computer. Launched in 1974 it started modestly enough with an index of stolen vehicles, but quickly expanded to include indices of: fingerprints (1976), criminal names (1977), wanted and missing persons (1978), disqualified drivers (1980) and sex offenders (1997). It was, however, merely an electronic filing cabinet, with a very limited capacity for searching and cross-referencing (Povey, 2000, p. 74). It was only in the 1990s, after the development and application of advanced relational database software and automated processing routines that enable real-time processing, complex searching and the almost instantaneous distribution of information to any points in the system, that we were able to talk about the information society being transformed into the surveillance society.

Surveillance and Locating Bodies in Space

While DNA and fingerprinting have been the primary means for establishing identity, they also have the additional capacity of determining an association between an individual and a specific spatial location. Historically, the juridical means of associating the criminal body with a specific locale has been through the use of fingerprint and eyewitness testimony. Both suffer from inherent weaknesses. Eyewitness identification suffers from the problem of memory, fingerprints from problem of localism and the quality of the samples. Localism meant that the print was generally only searched against a locally held database rather than a national archive. As a consequence of the increased mobility of the criminal, the chances of finding a successful match were greatly reduced (Blakey, 2000). With the creation of a centrally held national database of fingerprints capable of automated searching, there has been a major drive to increase the number of fingerprint and DNA samples collected at crime scenes. However, fingerprint identification is, of course, limited to the extent that a print can be successfully lifted from a scene. DNA, on the other hand, is much more accommodating – traces of blood, sweat, saliva, semen, skin and hair can all contain sufficient DNA to enable a profile to be obtained, greatly increasing the chance that a crime scene will reveal the identity of the transgressor. In 1995 the UK government set up the world's first national DNA database and, between 2000 and 2005, it invested an additional £240 million in the DNA expansion programme. The aim, according to the prime minister, was to ensure that the entire active criminal population would be recorded on the database by 2005 (FSPU, 2005, p. 3). In December 2005 the database held profiles on 3.45 million individuals – roughly 5.2 per cent of the population. This has meant a huge rise in the number of suspects being connected to a crime scene. In 2004 fingerprint matches had increased to 4,500 per month and DNA matches to 40 000 per year (MHB, 2004).

The advent of wide-scale CCTV surveillance has also expanded the scope of the surveillance gaze, facilitating the extensive monitoring of the population at large as they move through public and semi-public space. With estimates putting the number of CCTV cameras in excess of 4 million (McCahill and Norris, 2003) it is now difficult for the average UK citizen to avoid being caught on cameras as they go about their daily business. Indeed, one report suggests that a busy Londoner may be captured on over 300 cameras each day (Norris and Armstrong, 1999, p. 42). CCTV not only facilitates the active monitoring of the population, it also provides an historical record of their activities so that, at some future time, a person may be located in time and space. Thus, in high-profile incidents such as the 7 July terrorist attacks in London, CCTV footage provided a major investigative resource for tracking the movement of the suicide bombers from their home town to their final moments on the London Underground (House of Commons, 2006). However, in more routine cases, the problem of identity remains, as the citizenry is largely anonymous to those observing them, and, despite advances in facial recognition software, the chance of identifying a face in a crowd is still elusive (Norris, 2003).

If faces are difficult to identify, vehicle licence plates are not, as they provide a link to a named record of the registered owner held by the national Drivers and Vehicle Licensing Centre. Since 1996 there has been a dramatic increase in the camera-based enforcement of speed restrictions, which has been facilitated by the ability to digitally extract the licence plate details from a photograph and automatically process the data. This enables a real-time match against the computerized records held by the DVLC. The effect has been an exponential growth in the camera-based enforcement of traffic violations from just over 300 000 in 1996 to over 2 million in 2004, raising an estimated revenue of £113 million in fines per annum (Wilkins and Additcott, 1998; Ransford *et al.*, 2005).

The ability to use the licence plate to both identify and track individuals has now become a central plank of policing strategy. In March 2005 the Association of Chief Police Officers published their strategic report on the development of ANPR, entitled 'Denying Criminals the Use of the Roads' (ACPO, 2005). Their vision is to create a national network of licence plate readers, often integrated with public CCTV systems, which identify the registered owner, and check whether the vehicle or owner are wanted in connection with any outstanding offences or are subject to intelligence reports. ACPO aims to have the ability to deploy an instant response unit to any vehicle coming under suspicion, and to hold the details of vehicle movements for two years.

> The digital image is converted into data, which is processed through the ANPR system. This system is able to cross reference the data against a variety of databases including the Police National Computer (PNC), Local Force Intelligence Systems and other related databases, for example DVLA. Once the data has been cross checked against these databases – a process that takes around 1.5 seconds to complete – information about the vehicle, its registered owner and driver appears on a computer where it is evaluated by ANPR officers. If the information supplied via the ANPR system alerts officers to an offence or relevant intelligence on a vehicle, the vehicle will be stopped to allow officers to investigate further. ... ANPR systems are able to check up to 3,000 number plates per hour, per lane, even at speeds of up to 100mph (Cambridgeshire Constabulary, 2006).

The significance of ANPR is that it integrates a surveillance device, the camera, with the Police National Computer and all of its associated databases. Like open-street CCTV it targets all under its gaze, but greatly enhances its surveillance capacity as it creates a permanent investigative resource of a vehicle's movements and locations, regardless of the status of the driver.

If vehicles can now be routinely located in space and time, it is only by proxy that an individual can be located. However, the last decade has witnessed the expansion of individually targeted surveillance through the electronic monitoring of an ever-expanding range of criminals: those subject to home detention orders as part of early release from prison, (1999) to children sentenced to curfew orders (2001) and to those remanded on bail (2002). As a result, the numbers subjected to electronic monitoring regimes have increased from around 3,500 in 1998–99 to 53 000 in 2004–05 (NAPO, 2005; NPS, 2006a). Although current tagging technology enables a known offender to be located in space and time, it is limited in that it merely records their physical proximity at specific times to a device located in their home. It is therefore not continuous monitoring. In 2004 the UK government announced plans of a £3 million pilot scheme to assess the potential tracking of persistent and serious offenders by satellite. Satellite-tracking has the capacity to continuously monitor a person's movements, not only providing the ability to determine a person's whereabouts in real-time but also creating a permanent record of an offender's location in space and time (NPS, 2006b).

Interrogating the Body and Mind

In the rhetoric of English law the maxim that 'no one can be required to be his own betrayer', popularly understood as 'the right to silence', is enshrined as a fundamental element of the presumption of innocence (Ashworth, 1994, p. 113). However, while the law does not compel an accused to speak, and may only in certain circumstances draw adverse inferences from silence, it increasingly requires that suspects and offenders offer samples of bodily fluids and tissues to reveal underlying pharmacological states.

The most familiar of these is the roadside breath test, introduced in 1967, which requires suspected drink-drivers to blow into a breathalyser to determine the level of alcohol present in the body. If the roadside test is positive the suspect is required to attend the police station to provide a further blood or urine sample to determine a more accurate measure of alcohol levels. By 1970 around 73 000 roadside tests has been carried out; this had increased to 577,000 in 2004, resulting in 105 000 prosecutions (Wilkins and Additcott, 1998; Ransford *et al.*, 2005).

Mandatory drug testing was introduced into all prisons in 1996 with an expectation that between 5 and 10 per cent of the prison population would be subject to a random test each month (Singleton *et al.*, 2005). In 2004–05 a total of 51 484 tests were carried out, of which 11.6 per cent were positive (HMPS, 2005, p. 110). Having introduced testing into the prison system, it has since been extended throughout the criminal justice system. In 2000 The Criminal Justice and Courts Services Act gave probation officers the power to test prisoners released on licence. In 2003 a new community sentence was established, the Drug Treatment and Testing Order, which made a non-custodial sentence conditional on submitting to a treatment and testing regime. In 2004–05 some 7,500 offenders were subject to the order (Home Office, 2005a). In 2006, after extensive trials (see Sondhi *et al.*, 2004), mandatory drug testing of all people arrested for certain trigger offences, including theft, robbery, burglary, begging and taking a vehicle without consent, was introduced (Home Office, 2006). Put simply, at all stages of the criminal justice process, from arrest through to release from prison, the putative and convicted criminal is increasingly likely to be coerced, through the threat of negative sanctions, into providing samples to determine whether they have used illegal drugs.

Routine alcohol and drug testing have extended the surveillance gaze from the surface of the body to its interior, and the Home Office is now seeking to use surveillance technologies to reveal mental, as well as physical, states. One measure is the proposed introduction of a mandatory polygraph test, administered by probation officers, to determine whether sex offenders are lying about the extent to which they are complying with the conditions of their licence (Home Office, 2005b). Second, to determine whether sex offenders can be safely returned to the community, the probation and prison service has been recommended to investigate the use of the Penile Plethysmography Test. This test measures the erectile state of the penis to determine whether a sex offender shows an arousal response to inappropriate stimuli, such as scenes depicting non-consensual sex (Bridges, 2006).

The examples we have outlined of the development of surveillance and crime control in the British context are paralleled in various forms in other jurisdictions of the northern hemisphere. In the 1990s Feeley and Simon (1994) argued that a paradigm shift was taking place in which the Old Penology was being replaced by the New Penology. The Old Penology was preoccupied with the identification of the individual offender for the purpose of assigning guilt and blame and imposing punishment and treatment. The New Penology, by contrast, was concerned with the classification and management of groups by levels of ascribed dangerousness. The capacity of these new forms of actuarial justice, based on risk assessment, is significantly amplified by the vast technological processing, matching and searching facilities of contemporary criminal record databases. However, as developments in the surveillance of offenders in the British case make clear, the individual is also subject to increasingly fine-grained and technologized forms of surveillance. Thus the power of contemporary crime control surveillance practices rests both in the amplified capacity of the state to classify and categorize aggregate populations and simultaneously monitor and control the individual. The essays in this volume, which are discussed in the following five sections of this Introduction, all contribute in various ways to our understanding of the complex ways in which surveillance practices aimed at crime control have emerged in particular historical, social and political environments.

Theory

While James Rule's groundbreaking study, *Private Lives and Public Surveillance*, was published in 1973, it was not until Michel Foucault published his influential historical studies of surveillance and discipline that social theorists began to treat surveillance seriously as a subject in its own right. Foucault's theory of disciplinary power rested upon the metaphor of Bentham's Panopticon, where the promise of observation was equally as important as observation itself. For Foucault (1977), the Panopticon was the model for new configurations of discipline and power. These configurations relied on reshaping individual subjectivities through inculcating a belief in the unbridled surveillance capacity of the state. Equally as influential as the Panopticon has been the metaphor of 'Big Brother' drawn from George Orwell's imagined totalitarian regime envisaged in his novel, *Nineteen Eighty Four*. Orwell's dystopian vision, in which telescreens continuously monitor all activities, has wielded a considerable influence on surveillance theory, particularly in the concept of 'surveillance capacities' developed by Rule (1973) in which Orwell's vision represented a worst case 'total surveillance society'. Orwell's ideas have thus migrated into the academic lexicon, and form a framework of continuing influence for both popular and scholarly interpretation (Lyon, 1994, p. 55–62). Although the metaphors of the Panopticon and 'Big Brother' continue to exert a powerful sway over our understandings of surveillance, it is vital that scholars continue to question the utility of these paradigms in the contemporary context. The authors whose essays are included in Part I of this volume all engage with these central metaphors but, importantly, also seek to transcend their limitations and, in so doing, carve out new conceptual terrain. They have therefore contributed to the formation of new modes of interpretation that acknowledge the historically contingent nature of both surveillance practices and the theoretical language used to describe them.

The first essay, by Gary Marx, reflects the central concerns of this volume in crime and social control. Marx expands upon the observations of others that surveillance is intrinsically bound to social transformation. The 'new surveillance', Marx suggests, transcends time, distance and physical barriers, shifts from targeting a specific subject to a broader 'categorical suspicion', encourages self-policing, and is decentralized, intensive and ever more extensive. He suggests that society needs to be vigilant against the totalitarian tendencies of these developments.

The remaining essays in Part I all engage with the continuing relevance of the panopticon as the dominant metaphor for understanding contemporary surveillance practices. In Chapter 2 David Lyon emphasizes the enduring legacy of Bentham's original formulation and of Michel Foucault's subsequent analysis. Then, Gilles Deleuze (Chapter 3) extends Foucault's analysis from the role of surveillance in disciplinary societies to the emergence, in the contemporary context, of societies of control based on massive decentralized flows of data and computerization. For Deleuze, contemporary surveillance has increasingly become uncoupled from the process of discipline and is far more concerned with the distribution of rights on the basis of identity. In Chapter 4 Thomas Mathiesen offers a challenging reinterpretation of panopticism, suggesting that it has become synoptic. Contemporary surveillance is characterized by the many observing the few, which is facilitated by an increasingly intrusive mass media. Similarly, Kevin Haggerty and Richard Ericson (Chapter 5) also suggest that, in the panopticon, power is centralized and hierarchical, but this no longer adequately captures the nature of contemporary surveillance. Drawing upon the work of Félix Guattari and Gilles Deleuze, they suggest that surveillance is 'rhizomatic' and fractured. Surveillance is exercised not by a single disciplinary machine, but through an 'assemblage' of local discrete systems, with different rationales.

CCTV

In some future time, when historians come to write the history of the early twenty-first century, the rise of camera-mediated visual surveillance is likely to be seen as one of the key transformations in the form of social control. In Britain it has been estimated that there are now over 4 million cameras watching over public space (McCahill and Norris, 2003), and, although Britain was the first country to engage in a massive publicly funded expansion of CCTV, there is now a worldwide proliferation of video surveillance. Countries as diverse as the USA and China are now embarking on rapid expansion (Norris, Wood and McCahill, 2004). Although CCTV was initially heralded as a panacea to spiralling crime rates, two recent Home Office-funded studies have concluded that its impact in reducing crime is rather modest. Welsh and Farrington's meta review concluded 'that CCTV had a significant desirable effect on crime, although the overall reduction in crime was a rather small 4%' (2003, pp. 42–3).

The second study, conducted by Gill and Spriggs, reported:

The most obvious conclusion to be drawn from the analysis in this chapter is that CCTV is an ineffective tool if the aim is to reduce overall crime rates and make people feel safer. The CCTV systems installed in 14 areas mostly failed to reduce crime (with a single exception), mostly failed to allay public fear of crime (with three exceptions) and the vast majority of specific aims set for the various CCTV schemes were not achieved (Gill and Spriggs, 2005, p. 61).

In the light of these studies, in Part II, we have not dwelt on the issues of effectiveness, although we have included Short's and Ditton's important analysis of the impact of CCTV in two Scottish locations, which illustrates the complexities of undertaking evaluations in this area and the difficulty of interpreting contradictory findings. Instead, drawing primarily from British sources, we have selected essays that address the wider implications of what Stephen Graham, in Chapter 9, prophetically describes as the emerging 'Fifth Utility'. First, however, Clive Norris and Gary Armstrong (Chapter 6) draw our attention to the discriminatory potential of CCTV surveillance: far from being a neutral gaze, CCTV surveillance can all too easily exacerbate discriminatory police practices and, as Hille Koskela, reminds us in Chapter 12, the meaning of surveillance for those under the camera's gaze is not gender-neutral. The experience of being under surveillance is also taken up in Chapter 10 by James Ditton and Emma Short, who explore how those most likely to be a target of surveillance perceive and adapt to the camera's presence.

As with all forms of surveillance, CCTV also arises within specific political and legal contexts. The political context is explored in Roy Coleman's and Joe Sim's essay (Chapter 7) that demonstrates how the deployment of urban surveillance operates in conjunction with broader processes of spatial and social exclusion and results in the criminalization of particular populations. Of course, such practices do not occur in a legal vacuum, but are constrained or facilitated by the legal framework. This is the subject of Nick Taylor's essay (Chapter 11), which explores the emergent British regulatory regime in the context of the European Human Rights Act, and argues for extending the concept of privacy to facilitate the control and regulation of overt surveillance in public space.

Undercover Police Surveillance

The criminological literature on the police use of informants is, perhaps unsurprisingly, sparse. The necessary secrecy surrounding the police–informer relationship inevitably renders it difficult for the researcher to enter the subterranean world of detectives and their 'snouts'. But there is more to it than that. In general, the utility of a police informer is related to the degree to which they are enmeshed in the criminal underworld and probably an active player themselves (Dunnighan and Norris, 1999). In the police world, where a binary dualism of right and wrong, us and them, hero and villain pervades, a detective who associates with informers is always in danger of being seen as having crossed the line: as being more like 'them' than 'us'. And the informal and formal strategies that detectives deploy to facilitate the use of informers only serve to compound the morally ambiguous nature of the relationship: informal payments; gifts; official monetary rewards; the turning of a blind eye to past and ongoing offences; bail, charge and sentencing bargaining; enrolment on witness protection programmes and so forth. Not only does the informer gain from acts of treachery against associates, they often evade the judicial consequences of their own criminal activities. Nowhere is this ambiguity more apparent than in the use of 'participating informers' where the marginal role the informer is supposed to play in the commission of the offence is often questionable, leading to accusations that they are agent provocateurs, engaging in entrapment.

In this context, then, we have selected four essays for Part III. The first two are conceptual in that they help us define an informer and consider the consequences of their use. In Chapter 14 Steven Greer, drawing on his work documenting the rise and fall of the supergrass system during the 'Troubles' in Northern Ireland, provides an insightful analysis and helps us conceptualize the varieties of the police informant, from the causal, one-off informant, who may be motivated by a sense of public duty, to the fully-fledged supergrass concerned with how to most profitably save their own skin.

Jean-Paul Brodeur's essay (Chapter 13), drawing on the work of Gary Marx (1988) and written in the context of scandal surrounding political surveillance by the Royal Canadian Mounted Police, develops a fourfold typology to classify the consequences of the police use of informants. For Brodeur, the consequences are either intended or unintended and may, from a law enforcement perspective, have both desirable and undesirable consequences. And this typology provides a useful and enduring framework for critically assessing the role of the police informant. This is taken up by Clive Norris's and Colin Dunnighan's essay (Chapter 15), which explores, on the basis of extensive interviews with police informant handlers in the UK, one such unintended and undesirable consequence of the police use of informers: the generation of organizational conflict. Finally, in a corrective to much criminological research which neglects the offender's perspective, Richard Rosenfield, Bruce Jacobs and Richard Wright examine the meaning of snitching for a group of active criminals. On the basis of interviews with 20 American street criminals, they explore the paradox of how, although no one will admit to being a 'snitch', there is a belief that all one's criminal associates are secretly talking to the police.

Bodies, Databases and Technologies

Surveillance was implicated in the birth of modern nation-states through their expanded capacity to generate and collate files and dossiers on individuals. Nowhere was this more evident than in the area of criminal justice, where those designated 'criminal' were subject to increasingly close scrutiny through the expanding web of files compiled by police, courts and prison authorities. Increasingly, also, the body of the criminal was subject to technologies of identification – initially photography, then fingerprinting, and more recently electronic tagging and DNA sampling. Such technologies have sought not only to file, but also to locate and restrain. With the advance of computerization in the 1970s, and more recent advances in digital algorithms, criminal records are increasingly searchable and 'networked' between agencies. Developments in techniques of identification and database collation initiated in the area of crime control have a tendency to prefigure wider application. For this reason the essays we have assembled in Part IV should be of considerable interdisciplinary interest. They are all centrally concerned with the complex interaction between identity, databases, technology and the exercise of power.

In a pivotal essay, Alan Sekula (Chapter 17) elegantly traces the dialectic relationship between photography and bureaucratic surveillance, noting how the technology of the camera was embedded within a more pervasive bureaucratic-clerical-statistical system of 'intelligence'. Sekula's finely grained historical account alerts us to the genealogy of the extensive and intensive surveillance that characterizes contemporary Western societies. In Chapter 18, Diane Gordon focuses on the FBI's National Crime Information Centre (NCIC) in order to discuss the implications of a national criminal records system. For Gordon, this database is a panoptic 'machinery of power'. She notes that the dynamic of system expansion is extremely powerful and, moreover, that there is a strong tendency at junctures where the state is predisposed to exercise power for databases of criminal records to be used for purposes beyond crime control. Gordon suggests that this 'electronic panopticon' contains within it its own self-perpetuating mechanism: as the number of records and the data they contain increase, more and more subjects become included within the web of data surveillance, and simultaneously the range of 'authorized users' of the system expands.

The essays by Ronald Corbett and Gary Marx (Chapter 19) and by Mike Nellis (Chapter 20) deal with the issue of the electronic monitoring of offenders. However, although both essays focus on this single development within the corrections field, they have broader implications for the study of surveillance. Indeed both essays indicate the importance of symbolism in any critique of surveillance, be that within criminal justice or more broadly. Corbett and Marx note some of the commonly made assumptions surrounding technological modes of surveillance which they categorize in terms of ten 'techno-fallacies'. Analysing technological measures of surveillance provides a more critical perspective as an antidote to the 'idolatrous dream of omniperception' so frequently articulated by purveyors of surveillance technologies and relayed by their clients – whether they be in the government or private sector. Nellis's essay also alerts us to the importance of representation and imagery in the analysis of surveillance. Through examining representations of electronic monitoring in popular culture, he notes a 'matrix of mutual stimulation' through which new technologies can be conceived and generated, as well as received and filtered.

The final chapters of Part IV deal with the profound societal and political implications of biometric technologies. Biometric technology involves the collection of digital representations of physiological features unique to an individual, such as fingerprints, iris patterns, and retina and voice patterns: it may also include typical behavioural patterns such as typing or writing a signature. This digital representation is then usually transformed via algorithm to produce a template which is stored in a centralized database that is accessed when the finger, hand, face, eye or voice is later presented to the system (see p. 461). In Chapter 21 Irma van der Ploeg theorizes the significance of these developments. Unlike recent theoretical writings that posit information technologies as instrumental in the formation of 'virtual identities' detached from the corporeal body, van der Ploeg suggests that physical bodies will become more, not less, important in the construction of identities. The identities generated will, she argues, amplify certain tendencies inherent in the social and cultural milieu within which biometric technology is deployed. Current trends indicate that biometrics will be implicated in the shaping of social order through regulating access to services, spaces and privileges. As van der Ploeg concludes, 'through biometrics bodies may be inscribed with identities shaped by longstanding social and political inequalities' (p. 468).

In the post 9/11 environment, where there is what Mike Davis (2001) describes as a 'globalisation of fear', hi-tech solutions to problems of security have proven incredibly persuasive and ascendant. This proliferation of biometric technologies in particular has been most evident at the borders between nation-states, where the use of biometric passports matched with surveillance tools such as face and iris recognition technologies are being rapidly deployed at airports and other land and sea border posts. Coterminous with heightened concerns surrounding borders and mobility is an increased securitization of societies *within* the boundaries of the nation-state. The desire of nation-states to maintain greater surveillance over internal populations is evident in the expanding number of states either establishing or contemplating national ID cards embedded with personal identifiers (Stalder and Lyon, 2003).

In Chapter 22 Elia Zureik and Karen Hindle note that, in high modernity, technology is increasingly positioned as the ultimate guarantor of security. They argue that, post 9/11, notions of security have continued to shift from a conception of personal security dependent on interpersonal relationships and communal life to a military–technological conception of 'national' or 'state' security. The preoccupation with 'state security' rather than 'citizen security' has resulted in the monopolization of security by experts and professionals who bypass public participation and advance 'top-down' solutions (see Valverde, 2002). Biometrics are, Zureik and Hindle argue, precisely such a 'top-down' solution, claiming the technological capacity to assuage anxieties over national security. Advocates of biometrics have been increasingly successful in presenting the technology as integral in the identification and categorization of people, including welfare recipients, immigrants and travellers. Pressures for national ID cards would extend this classificatory power to entire populations. As Zureik and Hindle caution, biometric technology facilitates social profiling on a hitherto unforseen scale – a development which would exacerbate social division, rather than provide 'security'.

Surveillance Futures

The concluding observations of Zureik and Hindle provide an appropriate link with the final Part of this volume, concerned, as it is, with future directions in surveillance. In Chapter 23 Clive Norris, Jade Moran and Gary Armstrong chart current developments in visual surveillance technologies, particularly the development of algorithms that facilitate ever more complex calculations of scenes. The linking of these systems to databases of suspects or potential suspects has, they suggest, significant consequences for social control. Automated surveillance systems linked to databases will inevitably tend to widen, thin and strengthen the net of social control. Automated surveillance thus becomes instrumental in the process that Cohen (1985) termed 'net-widening'. Not only does automated surveillance extend the reach of policing, however; it also changes its very nature. Automation may erase the margin of police discretion, in the process transforming the relationship between police and public. Importantly, this essay alerts us to the exclusionary and discriminatory potential of surveillance. Looking at trends in the UK, the authors suggest that the ultimate result of automated surveillance may be to 'intensify an already unequal pattern of policing'. What they term 'algorithmic justice' has powerful exclusionary potential.

The potential of surveillance technologies to exacerbate patterns of spatial and social division and exclusion is further explored by Richard Jones in Chapter 24 where he develops the theoretical concept of 'digital rule'. Drawing upon the insights of Deleuze (see Chapter 3, this volume) Jones argues that controlling societies may increasingly be subjected to a form of 'digital rule' by which decisions are automated. Moreover, he points out, punishment is increasingly defined by euphemistic phrases such as 'the removal of access privileges'. Stephen Graham and David Wood (Chapter 25) develop similar themes to indicate possible surveillance futures based on the present. They note, as have others (for example, McCahill, 2002), the danger of technological determinism, pointing out that even automated systems are embedded within social contexts that shape surveillance practices. A characteristic of digital surveillance technologies, they suggest, is their ambivalence. Systems can socially exclude people, based on automated decisions of social or economic value, but these same systems can also be programmed to ameliorate processes of social marginalization. Despite this, however, the pervasiveness of neo-liberal market-based ideologies has seen digital technologies deployed in a manner that increases social disadvantage. In such a context, affluent citizens attain heightened advantage and mobility while marginalized groups experience intensified stigmatization and exclusion.

In the final chapter David Lyon traces the trend towards globalizing surveillance. Lyon notes that surveillance has become increasingly globalized since the 1980s with the intensification of what Giddens (1990) terms 'time-space distanciation'. The events of 11 September 2001 catalysed globalized surveillance. Lyon notes, however, that the experience of surveillance is still contingent on the local and regional social and political environment. Electronic tagging, for example, is more frequently deployed in the US than in Europe. As other authors have noted (for example, Sutton and Wilson, 2004), the extensive installation of CCTV systems evident in the UK is not necessarily mirrored in other jurisdictions.

Post-9/11 both government and private enterprise have increasingly articulated the need for an expansion of surveillance and greater expenditure on technological surveillance capacities. Although it is the spectre of the terrorist that has provided the rationale, the incorporation of surveillance technologies into the routine practice of criminal justice is also gathering pace. We hope that the assembled essays provide a foundation for those wanting to analyse contemporary surveillance practices in the name of crime control.

References

ACPO (Association of Chief Police Officers) (2002), *Infinet: A National Strategy for Mobile Information*, available at: http://www.acpo.police.uk/policies.asp.

ACPO (Association of Chief Police Officers) (2005), 'ANPR Strategy for the Police Service – 2005/2008 ANPR Steering Group: Denying Criminals the Use of the Roads', March, available at: http://www.acpo.police.uk/asp/policies/Data/anpr_strat_2005-08_march05_12x04x05.doc (accessed July 2006)

Ashworth, A. (1994), *The Criminal Process, an Evaluative Study*, Oxford: Oxford University Press.

Blakey, D. (2000), *Under the Microscope, Thematic Inspection Report on Scientific and Technical Support*, London: HMIC, Home Office.

Bridges, A. (2006), An Independent Review of a Serious Further Offence Case: Anthony Rice' London: Her Majesty's Inspectorate of Probation.

Browne, D.G. and Brock, A. (1953), *Fingerprints*, London: Harrap.

Cambridgeshire Constabulary (2006), ANPR – What is ANPR?', available at: http://www.cambs.police.uk/camops/anpr/what.asp (accessed May 2006).

Cohen, S. (1985), *Visions of Social Control*, Cambridge: Polity Press.

Cole, S. (2001), *Suspect Identities: A History of Fingerprinting and Criminal Identification*, Boston, MA: Harvard University Press.

Critchley, T. (1978), *A History of Police in England and Wales*, London: Constable.

Dandeker, C. (1990), *Surveillance, Power and Modernity*, Cambridge: Polity Press.

Davis, M. (2001), 'The Flames of New York', *New Left Review*, **12**, pp. 34–50.

Dunnighan, C. and Norris, C. (1999), 'The Detective, The Snout, and the Audit Commission: The Real Costs in Using Informants', *The Howard Journal*, **38**(1), pp. 67–86.

Feeley, M. and Simon, J. (1994), 'Actuarial Justice: The Emerging New Criminal Law', in D. Nelken (ed.), *The Futures of Criminology*, London: Sage.

Foucault, M. (1977), *Discipline and Punish*, New York: Vintage.

FSPU (Forensic Science and Pathology Unit) (2005), *DNA Expansion Programme 2000–2005: Reporting Achievement*, London Home Office.

Giddens, A. (1987), *The Nation-State and Violence: Volume Two of A Contemporary Critique of Historical Materialism*, Berkeley: University of California Press.

Giddens, A. (1990), *The Consequences of Modernity*, Stanford, CA: Stanford University Press.

Gill, M. and Spriggs, A. (2005), *Assessing the Impact of CCTV*, London: Home Office Research, Development and Statistics Directorate.

Hastings, G.W. (1875), *Address on the Repression of Crime*, London: Spottiswoode and Co.

HMPS (Her Majesty's Prison Service) (2005), *Her Majesty's Prison Service Annual Report and Accounts, Annex 1: Statistical Information*, London: Stationery Office.

Home Office (2004), *Eye in the Sky Launched to Monitor Offenders*, press release, 2 September, London: Home Office.

Home Office (2005a), *Sentencing Statistics 2004, England and Wales*, Home Office Statistical Bulletin 15/05, London: Home Office.

Home Office (2005b), *Making Provision in the Management of Offenders and Sentencing Bill for the Mandatory Polygraph Testing of Certain Sexual Offenders: Regulatory Impact Assessment*, London, Home Office.

Home Office (2006), *Operational Process Guidance for Implementation of Testing on Arrest, Required Assessment and Restrictions on Bail*, London: Home Office.

House of Commons (2006), *Report of the Official Account of the Bombings in London on 7th July 2005*, HC 1087, London: Stationery Office.

Hucklesby, A. and Wilkinson C. (2001), 'Drug Misuse in Prison: Some Comments on the Prison Service Drug Strategy', *The Howard Journal*, 40(4), November, pp. 347–63.

Lambourne, G. (1984), *The Fingerprint Story*, London: Harrap.

Lyon, D. (1994), *The Electronic Eye: The Rise of Surveillance Society*. Minneapolis, MN: University of Minnesota Press.

Lyon, D. (2001), *Surveillance Society: Monitoring Everyday Life*, Milton Keynes: Open University Press.

Lyon, D. (2002), 'Surveillance Studies: Understanding Visibility, Mobility and the Phonetic Fix', *Surveillance and Society*, **1**, pp. 1–7.

McCahill, M. (2002), *The Surveillance Web: The Rise of Visual Surveillance in an English City*, Cullompton: Willan.

McCahill, M. and Norris, C. (2003), 'Estimating the Extent, Sophistication and Legality of CCTV in London', in M. Gill (ed.), *CCTV*, Leicester: Perpetuity Press.

Marx, Gary (1988), *Under Cover: Police Surveillance in America*, Los Angeles: University of California Press.

Matrix (MHA) and Nacro (2003), *Evaluation of Drug Testing in the Criminal Justice System In Nine Pilot Areas*, Home Office Research Findings 180, London: Home Office.

MHB (Morgan Harris Burrows) (2004), *The Processing of Fingerprint Evidence after the Introduction of the National Automated Fingerprint Identification (NAFIS)*, Home Office Online Report 23/04, London: Home Office.

NAPO (National Association of Probation Officers) (2005), *Electronically Monitored Curfew Orders: Time for a Review* April, available at: http://www.napo.org.uk/cgi bin/dbman/db.cgi?db=default&uid =default&ID=111&view_records=1&ww=1 (accessed May 2006).

NPS (National Probation Service) (2006a), *Electronic Monitoring*, available at: http://www.probation. homeoffice.gov.uk/output/Page137.asp#Current%20Programmes (accessed May 2006).

NPS (National Probation Service) (2006b), 'Satellite Tracking', available at: http://www.probation. homeoffice.gov.uk/output/Page251.asp (accessed May 2006).

Norris, C. (2003), 'From Personal to Digital: CCTV, the Panopticon and the Technological Mediation of Suspicion and Social Control', in D. Lyon (ed.), *Surveillance and Social Sorting: Privacy Risk and Automated Discrimination*, London: Routledge.

Norris, C. and Armstrong, G. (1999), *The Maximum Surveillance Society: The Rise of CCTV*, Oxford: Berg.

Norris, C. and Dunnighan, C. (2000), 'Subterranean Blues – Conflict as an Unintended Consequence of the Police Use of Informers', *Policing and Society*, **9**(4), pp. 385–412.

Norris, C. and McCahill, M. (2006), 'CCTV: Beyond Penal Modernism?', *British Journal of Criminology*, **46**, pp. 97–118.

Norris, C., Wood, D. and McCahill, M. (2004), 'The Growth of CCTV: A Global Perspective on the International Diffusion of Video Surveillance in Publicly Accessible Space', *Surveillance and Society. The Politics of CCTV in Europe and Beyond*, special edn, **2**(2–3), pp. 110–35.

Northrop Grumman (2004), *United Kingdom Police Information Technology Organisation Selects Northrop Grumman for Identification Services Contract*, press release, available at: http://www.northropgrumman.co.uk/IT/media_centre/ press_releases/police_services (accessed May 2006).

PITO (2005), *Police Information Technology Organisation Annual Report 2004–2005*, London: Stationery Office.

Povey, K. (2000), *On the Record: Thematic Inspection Report Police Crime Recording and the Police National Computer and Phoenix Intelligence System Data Quality*, London: Her Majesty's Inspectorate of Constabulary.

Ransford, F., Perry, D. and Murray, L. (2005), *Motoring Offences and Breath Test Statistics: England and Wales 2003*, Home Office Statistical Bulletin, London: Home Office.

Rawlings, P. (2003), 'Policing Before the Police', in T. Newburn (ed.), *Handbook of Policing*, Cullompton: Willan.

Rule, J. (1973), *Private Lives and Public Surveillance: Social Control in the Computer Age*, London: Allen-Lane.

Sekula, A. (1986), 'The Body and the Archive', *October*, (39), Winter, pp. 3–64.

Singleton, N. *et al.* (2005), *The Impact and Effectiveness of Mandatory Drug Testing in Prisons*, Home Office Research Findings 223, London: Home Office.

Sondhi, A., O'Shea, J. and Williams K. (2004), *Arrest Referral: Emerging Findings from the National Monitoring and Evaluation Programme*, London: Home Office.

Stalder, F. and Lyon, D. (2003), 'Electronic Identity Cards and Social Classification', in D. Lyon (ed.), *Surveillance as Social Sorting: Privacy, Risk, and Digital Discrimination*, London: Routledge.

Sutton, A. and Wilson, D. (2004), 'Open-Street CCTV in Australia: Politics, Resistance and Expansion', *Surveillance and Society*, **2**(2/3), pp. 310–22.

Valverde, M. (2002), 'Governing Security, Governing through Security', in R.J. Daniels, P. Macklem and K. Roach (eds), *The Security of Freedom: Essays on Canada's Anti-Terrorism Bill*, Toronto: University of Toronto Press.

Wilkins, G. and Additcott, C. (1998), *Motoring Offences England and Wales 1996*, Home Office Statistical Bulletin, London: Home Office.

Wright, A. (2003), *Policing: An Introduction to Concepts and Practice*, Cullompton: Willan.

Part I
Theory

[1]

I'll Be Watching You

Reflections on the New Surveillance

Gary T. Marx

Popular culture is sometimes far ahead of academic analysis in identifying important social currents. This is true of the hit song *Every Breath You Take*, sung by a celebrated rock group known as The Police. It contains these lines:

every breath you take	[breath analyzer]
every move you make	[motion detector]
every bond you break	[polygraph]
every step you take	[electronic anklet]
every single day	[continuous monitoring]
every word you say	[bugs, wiretaps, mikes]
every night you stay . . .	[light amplifier]
every vow you break . . .	[voice stress analysis]
every smile you fake	[brain wave analysis]
every claim you stake . . .	[computer matching]
I'll be watching you	[video surveillance].

From this song we can draw hints of what can be called "the new surveillance." The surveillance component of social control is changing radically. The rationalization of crime control, which began in the 19th century, has crossed a critical threshold as a result of broad changes in technology and social organization. Surveillance has become penetrating and intrusive in ways that previously were imagined only in fiction.

The information-gathering powers of the state and private organizations are extending ever deeper into the social fabric. The ethos of social control has expanded from focused and direct coercion used after the fact and against a particular target to anticipatory actions entailing deception, manipulation, planning, and a diffuse panoptic vision.

I shall attempt here to (1) describe some of the major types of this new surveillance; (2) indicate how contemporary forms differ from traditional ones; (3) consider some undesirable consequences of these changes.

The gigantic data banks made possible by computers raise important surveillance questions. Many basic facts about the computerization of credit, banking, medical, educational, employment, tax, welfare, telephone, and criminal-justice records are well known. But beyond the increased amount of information they make available, computers have altered the very nature of surveillance. Record surveillance is routinized, broadened and deepened, and, for practical purposes, records become eternal. Bits of scattered information that in the past did not threaten the individual's privacy and anonymity are now joined. Organizational memories are extended over time and across space. Observations have a more textured, dimensional quality. Rather than focusing on the discrete individual at one point in time and on static demographic data such as date of birth, surveillance increasingly involves more complex transactional analysis, interrelating persons and events (for instance, the timing of phone calls, travel, bank deposits).[1]

A thriving new computer-based, data-scavenging industry now sells information gleaned from such sources as drivers' licenses, vehicle- and voter-registration lists, birth, marriage, and death certificates, land deeds, telephone and organizational directories, and census-tract records.

Many issues—such as privacy, civil liberties, uses of and control over information, unauthorized access, errors, and the rights of the person about whom information is gathered— are raised by the computer-matching and -profiling operations that have come into increased prominence in the last decade.[2]

Matching involves the comparison of information from two or more distinct data sources. In the United States, more than 500 computer-matching programs are routinely carried out by government at state and federal levels, and the matching done by private interests is far more extensive. Profiling involves an indirect and inductive logic. Often, clues are sought that will increase the probability of discovering violations. A number of distinct data items are correlated in order to assess how close an event or person comes to a predetermined model of known violations or violators. Consider the following examples:

• A Massachusetts nursing-home resident lost her eligibility for government medical assistance because of a match of bank and welfare records. The computer match discovered that she had more than the minimum amount welfare recipients are permitted in a savings account. What the computer did not know was that the money was held in trust for a local funeral director, to be used for her burial expenses. Regulations exempt burial contracts from asset calculations.

• The Educational Testing Service uses profiling to help discover cheating. In 1982 it sent out about 2,000 form letters alleging "copying" to takers of its scholastic aptitude test based partly on computer analysis. A statistical review had "found close agreement of your answers with those on another answer sheet from the same test center. Such agreement is unusual and suggests that copying occurred." Students were told that in two weeks their scores would be canceled and colleges notified, unless they provided "additional information" to prove they had not cheated.

• In New York City, because of computer matching, persons cannot purchase a marriage license or register a deed for a new home if they have outstanding parking tickets.

Some of fiction's imaginary surveillance technology, like the two-way television that George Orwell described, is now reality. According to some observers, video-telephone communication is likely to be widespread in private homes by the year 2000. One-way video surveillance has expanded rapidly, as anyone who ventures into a shopping mall or uses an electronic bank teller should realize. The inte-

rior of many stores is monitored by closed-circuit TV. The camera is often inside a ceiling globe with complete 360-degree movement and the ability to tape-record. Amber or mirrored surfaces hide where the cameras are aimed.

Among the new techniques that permit intrusions that only recently were in the realm of science fiction, or not even envisioned there, are new or improved lasers, parabolic mikes and other bugs with still more powerful transmitters, subminiature tape recorders, remote-camera and videotape systems; means of seeing in the dark, detecting heat or motion; odor, pressure, and contraband sensors; tracking devices and voice stress analyzers.

The last decade has seen the increased use of supposedly scientific "inference" or "personal truth technology" based on body clues (such as the polygraph, voice stress analysis, the stomach pump, the "passive alcohol detector," and blood or urine analysis for drugs). These highly diverse forms of detection have at least one thing in common—they seek to verify an implicit or explicit claim put forth by an individual regarding identity, attitudes, and behavior.

"Mini-Awacs" and satellites that can spot a car or a person from 30,000 feet up have been used for surveillance of drug traffickers. The CIA has apparently used satellite photographs for "domestic coverage" to determine the size and activities of antiwar demonstrations and civil disorders. The "starlight scope" light amplifier, developed for the Vietnam War, can be used with a variety of cameras and binoculars. When it amplifies light 85,000 times it turns night settings into daylight. Unlike the infrared devices developed earlier, it does not give off a tell-tale glow.

The highly secretive National Security Agency—using 2,000 staffed interception posts throughout the world, and satellites, aircraft, and ships—monitors all electronic communication from and to the United States. Its computer system permits simultaneous monitoring of about 54,000 telephone calls and cables. The agency is beyond the usual judicial and legislative controls and can disseminate its information to other government agencies without a warrant.[3]

The 1968 wiretap law makes it a felony for a third party to place an electronic listening device on a telephone or in a room. Government agents can do this only under strictly defined conditions with a warrant. Yet this law refers only to aurally transmitted "conversations." It says nothing about nonvoice and video communications. No restrictions are placed on the interception of information transmitted in digital microwave form. As a result of recent technical developments, more than half of all long-distance telephone calls are now transmitted from point to point in digital form and then converted back to a familiar voice sound. Telephone voice communications will increasingly be sent this way. Much computer information is also sent via microwaves. Even if laws were to be passed granting this information the same protection as voice conversations, the information can easily be picked up without leaving a trace by anyone with even modest snooping equipment.

Another surveillance use of the telephone involves the expansion of hot lines for anonymous reporting. One of the largest programs is TIP (Turn-in-a-Pusher). The video equivalent of the old reward posters, a program found in hundreds of communities, is called Crime Stoppers USA, Inc. It uses televised reenactments ("The Crime of the Week") to encourage witnesses to unsolved crimes to come forward. There are also radio and newspaper versions. Many companies maintain an internal hot line for anonymous reporting. WeTiP, Inc., a nonprofit organization, offers a general, nationwide 24-hour toll-free hot line for reporting suspicious activities. All 19 federal inspector-generals and some state and local agencies have hot lines for receiving allegations.

THE REAL ACTION, in the future, will be with nonhuman informers: a 400-pound, bulletproof mobile robot "guard" has been developed. It is equipped with a sonar range finder, sonic and infrared sensors, and an odor detector for locating humans. The robot can find its way through a strange building. Should it encounter an intruder, it can say in a stern, synthesized voice, "You have been detected." Another "mobile robotic sentry," resembling a miniature tank, patrols an area and identifies intruders. Users can choose the robot's weaponry and whether or not human permission (from a re-

mote monitoring station) is needed before it opens fire. But not to worry. The manufacturer assures us that in the U.S. the device will not be "armed with lethal weapons"; or if it is, "there will always be a human requirement in the loop."

Telemetric devices attached to a subject use radio waves to transmit information on the location and/or physiological condition of the wearer and permit continuous remote measurement and control. Such devices, along with new organizational forms based on theories of diversion and deinstitutionalization (such as halfway houses and community treatment centers), diffuse the surveillance of the prison into the community.

After over a decade of discussion, telemetric devices are now being tried in the criminal-justice system. Offenders in at least four experimental jurisdictions are serving court-supervised sentences that stipulate wearing a monitoring anklet containing an electronic transmitter. The radio signal it emits is picked up by a receiver connected to the telephone in the wearer's home. This receiver relays the signal to a central computer. If the wearer goes beyond 150 feet from this telephone or tries to remove or unplug the device, the interruption of the signal is displayed on the computer. The judge receives a daily copy of the printout, and any errant behavior must be explained.

In other proposed systems subjects are not restricted to their residence; however, their whereabouts are continuously known. The radio signal is fed into a modified missile-tracking device that graphs the wearer's location and can display it on a screen. In some police departments, an automatic car-locator system has been tried to help supervisors know exactly where patrol cars are at all times. There also are various hidden beepers that can be attached to vehicles and other objects to trace their movements.

The Hong Kong government is testing an electronic system for monitoring where, when, and how fast a car is driven. A small radio receiver in the car picks up low-frequency signals from wire loops set into streets and then transmits back the car's identification number. The system was presented as an efficient means for applying a road tax to the many cars in Hong Kong's concentrated traffic areas. It can, of course, also be used to enforce speed limits and for surveillance. In the U.S., a parking meter has recently been patented that registers inserted coins and then radios police when the time has run out.

Surveillance of workers, whether on assembly lines or in offices or stores, has become much more severe with computerized electronic measures. Factory outputs and mistakes can be more easily counted and work pace, to a degree, controlled. Employee theft of expensive components or tools may be deterred by embedded sensors that emit a signal when taken through a barrier. Much has been written about the electronic office, where the data-processing machine serves both as a work tool and monitoring device. Productivity and employee behavior thus are carefully watched, and even executives are not exempt. In some major American corporations communication flows (memo circulation, use of internal phone systems) now are closely tracked.

In some offices, workers have to inform the computer when they are going to the bathroom and when they return. Employees may be required to carry an ID card with a magnetic stripe and check in and out as they go to various "stations."

Integrated "management systems" offer visual, audio, and digital information about the behavior of employees and customers. Information may be recorded from cash-register entries, voices, motion, or when standing on a mat with a sensor. Audiovisual recordings and alarms may be programmed to respond to a large number of "triggering devices."

Means of personal identification have gone far beyond the rather easily faked signature or photo ID. Thus one new employee security-checking procedure involves retinal eye patterns. Before gaining access, or a benefit, a person's eyes are photographed through a set of binoculars, and an enlarged print of the retina pattern is compared to a previous print on file. Retinal patterns are said to be more individual than thumbprints, offering greater certainty of identification.

FINALLY, UNDERCOVER PRACTICES—those old, traditional means of surveillance and investigation—have drastically changed in form and expanded in scale during the last decade. The new devices and techniques have enabled police and federal agencies to penetrate criminal, and sometimes noncriminal, milieus in utterly new ways.[4]

In the United States, the federal agency that is most affected is the Federal Bureau of Investigation. In the past, the FBI viewed undercover operations as too risky and costly (for both individuals and the agency's reputation) for use in routine investigations of conventional criminal activity. Now, however, in the words of an agent, "Undercover operations have become the cutting edge of the FBI's efforts to ferret out concealed criminal activity." In the mid-1970s the FBI began using undercover agents in criminal investigations. The number of such investigations has steadily increased from 53 in 1977, to 239 in 1979, to 463 in 1981.

Beyond well-known cases—such as Abscam, the fake consulting firm run jointly by IBM and the FBI that sold "stolen" data to Japanese companies, the John DeLorean case, police posing as derelicts with exposed wallets or as fences purchasing stolen property—recent cases have involved policewomen posing as prostitutes and then arresting the men who propositioned them; tax agents stationed in banks and businesses posing as prospective buyers or clients to gain information; phony cases entered into the criminal-justice system to test if prosecutors and judges would accept bribes; "bait sales" in which undercover agents offer to sell, at a very low price, allegedly stolen goods to merchants or persons they meet in bars; agents acting as guides for big game hunters and then arresting them for killing protected species or animals out of season. These examples—and we could add many more—surely make clear that it is a new ball game, and that its players are sometimes beyond meaningful restraint.

II

Although the causes, nature, and consequences of the various new surveillance methods I have described differ from each other, they do share, to varying degrees, nine characteristics that distinguish them from traditional ones.

The New Surveillance:

(1) *It transcends distance, darkness, and physical barriers.* As many observers have noted, the historic barriers to the old, Leviathan state lay in the sheer physical impossibility of extending the rulers' ideas and surveillance to the outer regions of vast empires; through closed doors; and into the inner intellectual, emotional, and physical regions of the individual. Technology, however, has gradually made these intrusions easier. Technical impossibility and, to some extent, inefficiency have lost their roles as unplanned protectors of liberty. Sound and video can be transmitted over vast distances, infrared and light-amplifying technologies pierce the dark, intrusive technologies can "see" through doors, suitcases, fog. Truth-seeking technologies claim to be capable of going beneath surface reality to deeper, subterranean truths.

(2) *It transcends time;* its records can easily be stored, retrieved, combined, analyzed, and communicated. Surveillance information can be "socially freeze-dried."[5] When stored, it is available for instant analysis many years after the fact and in totally different interpretive contexts. Computer records, video and audio tapes and discs, photos, and various "signatures"—like workers or parts used in mass production—have become increasingly standardized and interchangeable. Information can be converted into a form that makes it portable, easily reproducible, and transferable across vast distances. Thus data sharing, on an immense scale, becomes possible.

(3) *It is capital- rather than labor-intensive.* It has become much less expensive per unit watched, because technical developments have dramatically altered the economics of surveillance. Information is easily sent back to a central source. A few persons can monitor a great many things (in contrast to traditional forms, such as the gumshoe tailing a suspect at a discreet distance for many days or manually searching records). The monitor need not literally be attending at the instant of transmission to be able to use it. Economy is further enhanced because persons have become voluntary and involuntary consumers of much of this surveillance—and are participating in their own monitoring. Many of the points that follow relate to these economic changes that facilitate expanded surveillance.

(4) *It triggers a shift from targeting a specific suspect—to categorical suspicion.* In the technical implementation of Kafka's nightmare, modern society suspects everyone. The camera, the tape recorder, the identity card, the metal detector, the obligatory tax form that must be filled out even if one has no income, and, of course, the computer make all who come within their province reasonable targets for surveillance. The new, softer forms of control are helping to create a society in which people are permanently under suspicion and surveillance. Everyone is assumed to be guilty until proven innocent. As Michel Foucault observed, what is central here is not physical coercion—but never-ending "judgments, examinations, and observation."

(5) *One of its major concerns is the prevention of violations.* Thus control is extended to ever more features of society and its surroundings. Rather than simply reacting to what is served up around us, anticipatory strategies seek to reduce risk and uncertainty. Publicity about omnipresent and omnipowerful surveillance is to deter violations. And "target hardening" (for instance, better locks) is to make committing violations more difficult. Where violations cannot be prevented, the surroundings may be so structured that violators are either caught in the act or leave strong evidence of their identity and guilt.

(6) *It is decentralized—and triggers self-policing.* In contrast to the trend of the last century, information can now in principle flow as freely from the center to society's periphery as the reverse. Surveillance is decentralized in the sense that national data resources are available to widely dispersed local officials. (The power of national elites, in turn, may also increase as they obtain instant information on those in the farthest reaches of the network.)

Those watched become (willingly and knowingly or not) active participants in their own monitoring, which is often self-activated and automatic. One aspect of this process is that persons are motivated to report themselves to government agencies and large organizations and corporations in return for some benefit or to avoid a penalty; another is the direct triggering of surveillance systems by its subjects when, for instance, a person walks, talks on the telephone, turns on a TV set, checks a book out from the library, enters or leaves a controlled area.

(7) *It either has low visibility or is invisible.* Thus it becomes ever more difficult to ascertain when and whether or not we are being watched and who is doing the watching. There is a distancing (both socially and geographically) between watchers and watched, and surveillance is increasingly depersonalized. Its instruments are often difficult to discover, either because they are something other than they appear to be or, as with snooping into microwave transmissions, there often are few indications of surveillance. (Contrast this with traditional wire-tapping, which changes electrical currents, or hidden voice analysis with the traditional polygraph, which requires the subject's cooperation.)

(8) *It is ever more intensive—probing beneath surfaces, discovering previously inaccessible information.* Like drilling technology boring ever deeper into the earth, today's surveillance can prod ever deeper into physical, social, and personal areas. It hears whispers, penetrates clouds, walls, and windows. It "sees" into the body—and attempts to "see" into the soul, claiming to go beneath ostensible meanings and appearances to real meanings.

(9) *It grows ever more extensive—covering not only deeper, but larger areas.* Previously unconnected surveillance threads now are woven into gigantic tapestries of information. Or, in Stan Cohen's imagery, the mesh of the fishing net has not only become finer and more pliable, the net itself now is wider.[6] Broad new categories of persons and behavior have become subjects for information collection and analysis, and as the pool of persons watched expands, so does the pool of watchers. Not only might anyone be watched; everyone is also a potential watcher. And the creation of uncertainty about whether or not surveillance is present is an important strategic element. Mass surveillance has become a reality. The increased number of watchers (whether human or electronic) and self-monitoring devices have recreated, in today's metropolis, some of the dense controls characteristic of the small, closely watched village.

The awesome power of the new surveillance lies in the paradoxical, never before possible combination of decentralized and centralized forms. We are also witnessing an expansion and joining of intensive forms of monitoring traditionally used only in the investigation and surveillance of criminal and espionage suspects, or prisoners, with the more shallow forms of categorical monitoring directed at broad populations.

III

The new surveillance has been generally welcomed by those in business, government, and law enforcement. It does have many attractive features. Stirring examples of its effectiveness are readily available. For example, the life of an elderly heart-attack victim who lived alone was saved when her failure to open the refrigerator sent an alarm through her telephone to a centralized monitor; a corrupt judge was caught when he took a bribe from a police agent pretending to be a criminal; serious crimes have been solved as a result of tips received on hot lines. Consider also the ease of obtaining consumer goods with a credit card; the saving of taxpayers' dollars because of computer-matching programs; citizens' increased feeling of safety when video surveillance is installed. Indeed, Americans seem increasingly willing, even eager, to live with intrusive technologies because of the benefits they expect to result.

Problems concerning errors, data tampering and misuse can be lessened by government legislation and policies, good program design and sensitive and intelligent management. Furthermore, in a free-market economy, some surveillance can be neutralized (by, for instance, the proliferation of antiradar, debugging, and encryption devices).

My point is not to advance some romantic neo-Luddite world view, or to deny the complexity of the moral judgments and trade-offs

31

involved. Yet in our eagerness to innovate and our infatuation with technical progress and the gimmickry of surveillance, it is easy to miss the time bombs that may be embedded therein. The negative aspects of these new trends have not received sufficient attention.

There is nowhere to run or to hide. A citizen's ability to evade this surveillance is diminishing. There is no escape from the prying eyes and ears and whirring data-processing machines of government and business. To participate in the consumer society and the welfare state, we must provide personal information. To venture into a shopping mall, bank, subway, sometimes even a bathroom, is to perform before an unknown audience. To apply for a job may mean having to face lie-detector questioning about intimate details of one's life. Requests for parts of one's personal biography (for birth, marriage, and death certificates, driver's licenses, vehicle and voter registration, information for phone, occupational, educational, and special-interest directories) are invitations to comply with more finely tuned manipulative efforts by a new breed of government and marketing researchers, who combine the enormous quantities of available data with the advantages of computerization.

The new surveillance goes beyond merely invading privacy, as this term has been understood; it makes many of the constraints that made privacy possible irrelevant. Traditionally, privacy depended on certain technically or socially inviolate physical, spatial, or temporal barriers—varying from distance to darkness to doors, to the right to remain silent. To invade privacy required crossing an intact barrier. With much of the new technology, however, many of these simply cease to be barriers. As we discussed, information becomes accessible without the need to resort to traditional coercive forms of intrusion. There is no longer the need to enter a room surreptitiously to plant a bugging device, when a microphone aimed at a window a hundred yards away can accomplish the same end; when microwave phone and computer transmissions can simply be plucked from the air without bothering with direct wire-tapping. Without being opened, mail can be read, purses and briefcases viewed through X-rays or sniffed. Alcohol intake can

be assessed without a suspect's consent, and voice stress analysis administered without the subject's awareness.

What of Privacy & Autonomy?

IN THE FACE OF THESE CHANGES, we must rethink the nature of privacy and create new supports for it. Some of these, ironically, will rely in part on products of the system's technologies (such as coded or scrambled communications, antiradar and debugging devices).

The most desirable support of our individual privacy and autonomy surely is public awareness. At this point, less than one state in five has laws requiring binding standards for the collection, maintenance, and dissemination of personal information.

Yet more is at stake than privacy. Some of the positive anonymity involving the right to be left alone and unnoticed, so characteristic of modern society, is diminished. The easy computer-bank combining and mining of vast publicly available data to yield precise lists (whether of suspects or targets for sales pitches and solicitations) generate a sense of vulnerability that is very different from the feeling experienced on receipt of junk mail addressed to "occupant." Aside from the annoyance factor, the somewhat "personalized" yet standardized word-processed solicitations can leave one asking "How do they know this about me? How did they find this out? What else do they know? Who are they?" One need not be a Franz Kafka character to feel uneasy.

TO MENTION, BRIEFLY, some other, major negative aspects of the new surveillance:

It may violate the spirit of the Fourth Amendment. For it can trigger fishing expeditions and searches where there is no specific evidence of wrongdoing. Thus it might transform the presumption of innocence into one of guilt—shifting the burden of proof from the state to the target of surveillance, the accused. There also is a danger of presumption of guilt by association or statistical artifact. And, because of the technical nature of the surveillance and its distancing aspects, the accused may (at least initially) be unable to face the accuser. The legal basis of some of the new surveillance's crime-prevention actions is also questionable.

The system's focus on prevention can entail the risk of sparking violations that would otherwise not occur. And powerful new mechanisms may invite overloading the system. Far more violations may be uncovered and added to the data banks than can be acted upon. This overabundance of violations in turn may lead to the misuse of prosecutorial discretion, the demoralization of control agents and, perhaps, to favoritism and corruption. And, as our examples suggest, the new surveillance has the potential of fostering repression. The system is, invariably, less effective and certain, and more subject to manipulation and error, than advocates admit. (Computer matching, for instance, can be no better than the data it is fed, which may be dated or wrong, and is often blunt and acontextual. Chemical analysis, which can detect drugs in a person's body, cannot determine how they got there—if a person, for instance, smoked marijuana or simply was around others who did—or whether a drug was taken on or off the job.)

While deterring or discovering some offenders, the routinization of surveillance, ironically, may grant an almost guaranteed means for successful violations and theft to those who gain knowledge of the system and take action to neutralize and exploit it. This suggests that, over time, it seems likely that many of these systems will disproportionately net the marginal, amateur, occasional violator rather than the master criminal.

The proliferation of the new techniques may create a lowest-denominator morality, which may even affect those who will actively protect privacy and autonomy, who thus will use—indiscriminately—the very tactics of those who seek to lessen them.[7]

The new surveillance increases the power of large organizations (whether governmental or private) over the individual.

Individual freedom and liberty prosper when detailed information about a person's life, for the most part, is private. The permanence and accessibility of computerized records mean that we are all tailed by electronic tale-bearers. As there is the possibility of locking in erroneous or sabotaged data, this may have the unintended consequence of permanent, unjust stigmatization. Thus persons may never cease paying for earlier, or never committed, misdeeds. The issues here go far beyond criminal records and faulty computer banks. As records of education, work, health, housing, civil suits, and the like become ever more important in administering the society, persons may decline needed services (as for mental health), avoid conflictual or controversial action (filing a grievance against a boss or a landlord), shun taking risks and experimenting for fear of what it will look like on the record. Conformity and uniformity may increase—squashing diversity, innovation, and vitality.

The fragmentation and isolation characteristic of totalitarian societies result not only from the state's banning or absorption of private organizations, but because individuals mistrust each other and organizations: trust, the most sacred and important element of the social bond, is damaged.

To be sure, we are far from such a society, but the direction in which the new surveillance points is clear. Making the means of anonymous denunciation easily available can lead to false and malicious accusations, and efforts to create a "myth of surveillance" may backfire and create a degree of inhibition, fear, and anxiety unbecoming a democratic society. The potential for harm may be so great, should social conditions change, that we must hesitate before creating even apparently justified surveillance systems (such as linkages between all federal and state data banks, or a mandatory national identification system). From this perspective, framing the policy debate around how to reform such systems is misguided. The issue, instead, is, Should the system be there to begin with?[8] Once these new surveillance systems are institutionalized and taken for granted in a democratic society, they can be used for harmful ends. With a more repressive government and a more intolerant public—perhaps upset over severe economic downturns, large waves of immigration, social dislocations, or foreign policy setbacks—these devices could easily be used against those with the "wrong" political beliefs, against racial, ethnic, or religious minorities, and those with life styles that offend the majority.

Yet should totalitarianism ever come to the United States it would more likely be by accretion than by cataclysmic events. As Sinclair Lewis argued in *It Can't Happen Here*, it would come in traditional American guise, with the gradual erosion of liberties.

Voluntary participation, beneficent rationales, changes in cultural definition and language hide the onerous aspects of the new surveillance. But as Justice Brandeis warned:

> Experience should teach us to be most on our guard when the government's purposes are beneficent. Men born to freedom are naturally

alert to repel invasion of their liberty by evil-minded rulers. The greatest dangers to liberty lurk in insidious encroachment by men of zeal, well-meaning, but without understanding.[9]

The first task of a society that would have liberty and privacy is to guard against the misuse of physical coercion by the state and private parties. The second task is to guard against the softer forms of secret and manipulative control. Because these are often subtle, indirect, invisible, diffuse and deceptive and shrouded in benign justifications, this is clearly the more difficult task.

Notes

This article is drawn from a longer paper available from the author prepared for meetings on George Orwell held by the Council of Europe and the American Sociological Association.

[1] David Burnham, *The Rise of the Computer State* (New York: Random House, 1983) offers a useful discussion of this and other salient themes.

[2] See, for example, G. Marx and N. Reichman, "Routinizing the Discovery of Secrets: Computers as Informants," *American Behavioral Scientist*, March 1984.

[3] J. Bramford, *The Puzzle Palace* (New York: Penguin Books, 1983); K. Krajick, "Electronic Surveillance Makes a Comeback," *Police Magazine*, March 1983.

[4] For example, see G. Marx, "Who Really Gets Stung? Some Issues Raised by the New Police Undercover Work," *Crime and Delinquency*, April 1982; see also U.S. Congress, Select Committee to Study Undercover Activities of Components of the Department of Justice, 97th Congress, Second Session, *Final Report, December 1982* (Washington, D.C.: Government Printing Office, 1982). U.S. Congress, Subcommittee on Civil and Constitutional Rights of the Committee on the Judiciary, House of Representatives, 98th Congress, Second Session, *Report: FBI Undercover Operations* (Washington, D.C.: G.P.O., 1984).

[5] See, for example, G. Goodwin and L. Humphreys, "Freeze-Dried Stigma: Cybernetics and Social Control," *Humanity and Society*, November 1982.

[6] S. Cohen, "The Punitive City: Notes on the Dispersion of Social Control," *Contemporary Crisis*, 1979, no. 3, pp. 339-63.

[7] A large array of control and countercontrol devices, through mail-order catalogues and ads in major national periodicals, are now available for the mass market. One large company offers a "secret-connection briefcase," which among other things includes a "pocket-sized tape-recorder detector that lets you know if someone is secretly recording your conversation," a "micro-minature hidden bug-detection system, which lets you know if you're being bugged," a "miniature voice stress analyzer, which lets you know when someone is lying," a "built-in scrambler for total telephone privacy," an "incredible 6-hour tape recorder—so small it fits in a cigarette pack." Ready for use—or misuse. . . .

[8] See, for example, the thoughtful discussion in J. Rule, D. McAdam, L. Stearns, and D. Uglow, *The Politics of Privacy* (New York: New American Library, 1980).

[9] *Olmstead vs. U.S.*, 277 U.S. [Supreme Court] 438 (1927).   □

[2]

Bentham's Panopticon: From Moral Architecture to Electronic Surveillance

DAVID LYON

While Jeremy Bentham's ambitious blueprints for penitentiary construction were never wholly embraced, many elements of his "Panopticon" concept have gradually been incorporated into prisons, schools, and workplaces. But it is the idea of moulding human behaviour through constant surveillance, as opposed to Bentham's architectural innovation, that has left a mark on societal organization. David Lyon gauges the extent to which our modern world – of data banks and electronic surveillance – has been shaped by the eighteenth century Panopticon.

EXACTLY TWO HUNDRED YEARS AGO, in 1791, Jeremy Bentham published plans for a new concept in prison architecture, the Panopticon. In the Panopticon we find physical expression of Bentham's utilitarian philosophy, which came to dominate Victorian capitalism. Today, the influential idea of Panopticon lives on, but in a new context. Electronic technologies monitor our everyday lives so intimately, it is said, that society itself is like a panoptic prison. A disturbing thought, indeed. But is it true?

DAVID LYON is an associate professor of sociology at Queen's University. Author of *The Information Society: Issues and Illusions* (1988) Blackwell, he is presently writing a book on electronic surveillance.

The Greek-based neologism "Panopticon," in which Bentham
delighted, summed up the key idea of the prison: all-seeing. From an
"inspection lodge" observers would be able to keep an eye on prisoners, whose cells fanned out in a circular pattern around the central
tower. Through careful use of lighting, prisoners' every movement
would be clearly visible to the guards, although they, skilfully concealed behind wooden blinds, would be out of the prisoners' sight.
Moral architecture, indeed.

Highly controversial in his lifetime, Bentham's plans failed to find
acceptance with the British government, despite decades of argument
and badgering. Bentham himself regarded the Panopticon as a crucial
component of his rationalist social reform agenda. His commitment
to it even survived changes in his political allegiance. Though now
regarded – ironically, as we shall see – as playing a vital role in the
development of modern democratic polity, Bentham was unable to
sell his prize product.

Yet the principles expressed in the Panopticon persisted. They
found their way to other European countries and also to North
America. They actually formed the design basis not only of many nineteenth century prisons – including Canada's oldest, Kingston
Penitentiary – but also of numerous schools, factories, workshops, barracks and hospitals.

In his classic study of the birth of the prison, French historian
Michel Foucault gives the Panopticon pride of place. For him, it epit-
omizes the new disciplines of modern social control. The break with
past modes of punishment that frequently were public and brutal was
made symbolically in the Panopticon. After this watershed, the emphasis would be on putting prisoners away – isolating, categorizing, and
monitoring them, and keeping their records on file. Indeed, argues
Foucault, social control in general took on panoptic features.

What Foucault's work antedated, however, was the so-called computer revolution of the later twentieth century. While various
Victorian social institutions picked up panoptic principles, until the
advent of computer power the technical realization of Bentham's
dream remained out of reach. Today, via massive police computers,
government databases and commercial monitoring of consumers, the
electronic Panopticon appears as a potential inheritor of Bentham's
scheme. Some already speak of the emerging "maximum security
society."

This article traces the fortunes of Bentham's Panopticon, from moral architecture to electronic surveillance. The story takes us across eras, from the novel methods of social control characteristic of modernity to the digital disciplines of what some see as postmodernity. The idea of the "inspection house" actually gives us a unique vantage point from which to view social and cultural change. But we can not only view it; we can also question how far the electronic Panopticon already encloses us, so as to evaluate its effects and to assess our chances of escape.

The Panopticon: Utilitarian Utopia

BENTHAM BELIEVED that his "Inspection House," the Panopticon, offered a solution to some of the most pressing concerns of his day. Although his precious plans may be read as a fantastic cure-all scheme for reordering society along rational lines, he proposed them as a practical possibility. The promise held out was not modest: "Morals reformed – health preserved – industry invigorated – instruction diffused – public burthens lightened – Economy seated, as it were upon a rock – the gordian knot of the Poor Laws not cut but untied – all by a simple idea in Architecture!"

Many reasons may be adduced to account for Bentham's apparently immoderate enthusiasm for the Panopticon. Its intrinsic elegance as a rational panacea, its adaptability to changes in his own philosophical position, and personal interests vested in its success are three significant ones. The idea of inspection, however, appealed particularly to Bentham as a clever means of contributing to his society's political controversy about prisons. Famous for its anti-slavery campaign, the "evangelical party" in the Church of England already included in its humanitarian agenda the reform of filthy, corrupt, overcrowded, unsanitary, and brutal jails. Some politicians favoured deportation to Australia as an alternative. Bentham's Panopticon promised prison reform, without a religious base, on British soil.

The Panopticon's inspector could see at a glance everything going on. Nothing could be hidden from his penetrating, comprehensive gaze. As Bentham observed, "To be incessantly under the eyes of the inspector is to lose in effect the power to do evil and almost the thought of wanting to do it." We may be forgiven for imagining that in a work by a self-proclaimed secularist we hear echoes of religion. Bentham actually quoted from the biblical Psalm 139 in a preface:

Thou art about my path, and about my bed: and spiest out all my ways. If I say, peradventure the darkness shall cover me, then shall my night be turned into day.

Though he avoided having a cleric read the French version of his manuscript because it was too irreligious (Halevy 86), Bentham drew freely on his understanding of God's omniscience in his outline of the Panopticon. Realizing that constant supervision was out of the question, he contrived to ensure that at least prisoners would always *conceive* themselves to be under inspection. Indeed, Bentham's truly original contribution was just this, to make subordination rest on uncertainty. Hence the need for elaborate measures guaranteeing the invisibility of the inspector, plus artificial lighting and reflectors to turn the prisoners' night into day.

Like many utopian plans, then, the Panopticon fed on religious sources. Yet like many eighteenth century social thinkers, Bentham sought to devise alternatives to what he saw as theologically dominated theories of society. Bentham's quest for a society founded upon Reason rather than religion rejected the central core of Christianity but retained some of the content. If religion performed some useful social functions, why not transpose them into a secular key? Divine omniscience, suitably shorn of its fleece of faith, appeared as a handy tool for the social reformer.[1]

Certainty without blood

THE INSPECTION PRINCIPLE, argued Bentham, would simply make redundant the old regime of physical – and often arbitrary – punishment of the body and also the paraphernalia of restraints such as chains. At the same time, it would obviate potentially rebellious communication between prisoners; the unruly crowd could be tamed. Indeed, the prisoners' belief that they were watched would make them impose a discipline on themselves, making them active participants in their own supervision. As Bentham saw it, the Panopticon was irresistibly superior to rival schemes and could not fail to work.

Alongside the central principle of inspection, Bentham recommended solitary cells. (Later, bowing to economy, he conceded that shared cells might work.) Moreover, prisoners had to be clearly classified and segregated by category to avoid the dangers of association. In one of his plans, Bentham accommodated in separate areas "Thoroughbred Housebreakers, Quiet Old Offenders, Decent Females, Dissolute Females" and so on. The wearing of prisoner numbers followed logically in this progression.

Bentham anticipated objections to his scheme, scathingly dismissing many such as misguided liberalism. He produced reassurance for those worried about the despotic potential of a prison whose inspector was modelled on a rigidly moral and coldly calculating unseen deity. Addressing the anxiety that he might be constructing a set of "machines under the similitude of men," he asserted that the key criterion was not liberty or rights but the greatest happiness of the majority. And this foolproof system of discipline would meet that criterion. Contrasted with Addison's mind-boggling proposal to "try virginity with lions," for instance, Bentham proclaimed the Panopticon a clear winner. "There you saw blood and uncertainty: here you see certainty without blood."

In the event, the Panopticon was not a winner, at least politically. It finally failed to gain parliamentary approval in 1810, to Bentham's disgust and chagrin. Its downfall came, not on account of the inspection principle, but because, as we shall see, Bentham had advocated running it as a private enterprise. The idea of inspection, together with the rules of a formal bureaucracy, lived on, even flourished in the new penitentiaries of industrializing Europe. As Michael Ignatieff comments, the Panopticon was "a symbolic caricature of the characteristic features of disciplinary thinking in his age" (Ignatieff 113).

The Panopticon concept profoundly influenced institutions such as Millbank Penitentiary in London, England, and, despite Bentham's official rejection in France as well, the penitentiary at Mettray. On the walls at Mettray, prisoners read the ominous words inscribed in black, "Dieu vous voit." Across the Atlantic, the principles of the Panopticon – though not always the precise plan – found willing acceptance both in Canada and the United States.

For instance, the successful plan for Kingston Penitentiary was drawn up in a Report dated 1832, the year Bentham died. It made persistent reference to the need for inspection, or "undetected surveillance." As C. J. Taylor notes, the "moral architecture" at Kingston was "planned far in excess of any conceivable needs for the incarceration of prisoners, it was a model society, a laboratory for controlled behaviour, a visible panacea for many of Upper Canada's real or imagined ills." Bentham would have been gratified.

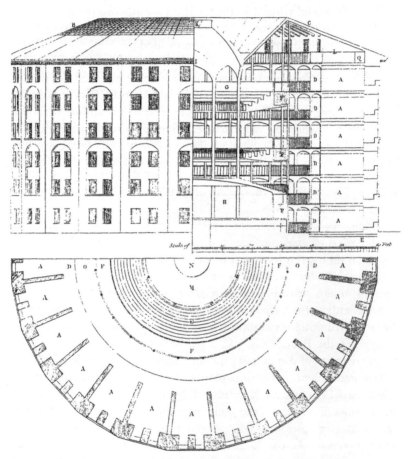

A general idea of a penitentiary panopticon (from J. Bentham Collected Works, Vol. IV, 1843.)

The spider in the web

THE BRITISH PARLIAMENT dashed Bentham's hopes of having the Panopticon adopted into official correctional policy because he wanted it managed as a profit-making venture. Alongside the inspection principle lay a commitment to contract as a means of ensuring efficiency. The "rule of economy" whereby the state would have no financial responsibility for the Panopticon, promised both incentives to the governor and, of course, "public burthens lightened." But parliamentary objections prevailed.

Bentham planned to correct the disorder of idleness with a prison regime of hard labour. Among the most suitable tasks, he listed making ropes, weaving sacks, spinning yarn and knitting nets, though he was not averse to wheel-treading. He wished to streamline the common practice whereby manufacturers contracted with magistrates to use workhouse and prison labour. The problem, as he saw it, was that the system hung uneasily between state and economy. Much better,

Bentham's wish was fulfilled. His auto-icon is kept at University College, London. Photo courtesy of UCL.

he claimed, for the whole institution to be run on capitalist lines, so that market interest could regulate both prisoners and governors. The latter would find it in their interest to keep prisoners fit and healthy, would open their doors for casual public inspection, and would discover their own status rising steadily. In short, Bentham's Panopticon was also a factory.

While the inspection principle would eventually be enshrined in numerous institutions, the contract principle fell foul of criticism. The purpose of "reformation by seclusion" was paramount, insisted Bentham's opponents.[2] He had allowed economic criteria too much play. Prison labour was not to be exploited for profit. Bentham neglected religious instruction, they charged, and even subordinated his principle of seclusion to the sway of market forces. No, the counter-argument ran, the state should control punishment, uncontaminated by commercial gain. Authority was better lodged with bureaucratic rules and inspection than with a profit-seeking entrepreneur.

However, there was another reason why the Panopticon was so roundly rejected in Parliament; Bentham himself aspired to be its first contractor. He offered his services both to see to prisoners' needs, keep watch over them, and to receive the "produce of their labour." For Gertrude Himmelfarb, this explains at last the huge scale of Bentham's ambitious enthusiasm and untiring campaigning for its acceptance. Perhaps it also helps explain why, deprived of a monument in the Panopticon, Bentham required that a wax model be created over his skeleton after death, to be seated next to his mummified head. At any rate, Bentham's intentions were public knowledge at the time. Confronted with the Panopticon plans, Edmund Burke exclaimed, "There's the keeper, the spider in the web!" (Himmelfarb 59)

It seems that this "spider" saw no contradictions within his plans, or indeed, within his overall position of Philosophical Radicalism. The greatest happiness of the greatest number could cheerfully be obtained through the greatest power of that majority. The rights of the minority did not enter the equation. Only interests exist. When it came to the state, Bentham saw no problem with illimitable sovereignty, as in the Panopticon. A curious conclusion, this, for someone whose work commonly has been viewed as contributing to modern democracy. Yet as we shall see, modern democracy has yet to shake off the clinging contribution of Bentham. For the spider left behind his web.

The Panopticon in Foucault: Discipline and Modernity

ENTHAM HAD HIS EYE ON FRANCE as a potential customer for the Panopticon. In a poetic twist, the full significance of his plans was first recognized by a French historian, Michel Foucault. It is no exaggeration to say that the Panopticon forms the centrepiece of Foucault's *Discipline and Punish*, although whether it deserves that dubious honour is another question. Foucault discerned in the Panopticon a "marvellous machine" for producing "homogeneous effects of power" in any given setting. It was also a "laboratory ... to alter behaviour, to train or correct individuals."

Foucault's genius lay in situating the Panopticon historically at the watershed between the old regime and modernity. Indeed, the prison was for Foucault what the factory had been for Marx, the epitome of the modern era. Prior to this time, prisoners could expect to be chained, whipped, tortured, and abused – all of which marked the body and smelled of vengeance. The new penology aimed to change behaviour, to alter conduct by calculated human intervention. It assumed that people would respond to subtle switches in the pain-pleasure calculus. Such discipline became an achievable goal in the Panopticon, which induced "in the inmate a state of conscious and permanent visibility that assures the automatic functioning of power." Thus, at a stroke, it dispensed with the straitjacket in the asylum, the shackles in the prison, and the personal tyranny of the workhouse master. The Panopticon was an impersonal, automatic machine, appropriate to modernity.

Bentham's social engineering ambitions led him to promise relevance in the Panopticon for diverse social spheres. Foucault showed how Bentham's hopes had been realized: many modern institutions – whether directly indebted to Bentham or not – definitely display panoptic features. Others, such as Aldous Huxley, have done this in a fairly trivial fashion, remarking on the likeness between today's efficient offices or up-to-date factories and the Panopticon (Huxley 203-6, quoted in Himmelfarb 34). But Foucault saw "factories, schools, barracks and hospitals" all reflecting the Panopticon in their detailed regimes of examination, classification and "individualizing observation ... with the analytical arrangement of space." The aim, as Foucault observed, is consistent – the production of "docile bodies," disciplined to do the bidding of whatever institution surrounds them.

One strong merit of Foucault's work has been to highlight something only dimly perceived before him, that in modern societies surveillance is a source of power in its own right. It cannot, in other words, be reduced to a reflex of capitalism, industrialism, urbanism or the state, even if they are implicated in its operation in specific ways. As older methods of social control were disrupted and destroyed by the coming of industrial factories and cities, new means of disciplining mobile populations emerged. They involved both the supervision of labour in workshops and the gathering of data by administrators, which together may be thought of as surveillance. The Panopticon is surveillance-power, as Bentham would have said, "perfected."

From L'Homme Machine to Gradgrind and beyond

THE FRENCH CONNECTION with the Panopticon does not simply follow Bentham to Foucault. Several of Bentham's intellectual ancestors were French as well, which is not surprising, considering his father had him read Voltaire's *Candide* at age ten! From Helvetius, for instance, Bentham took the notion of a pleasure-pain calculus, that supposedly governs all our actions. And with La Mettrie, notes Foucault, originated the doctrine of *L'Homme Machine* – that human beings are machines, to be understood, controlled, and used. This meshes nicely with Bentham's belief that reforming people is a "species of manufacture" (in Ignatieff 68).

La Mettrie's *L'Homme Machine* is symptomatic, suggests Foucault, of the materialist mood of optimism prevailing in late eighteenth century France. It neatly draws together both the idea, derived from Descartes, of anatomical description of bodies, and the "technico-political" by which bodies could be manipulated. The analytical and the manipulable together yield "docility." This convergence is illustrated neatly in the development of army drill. Close to the previously mentioned Kingston Penitentiary lies Old Fort Henry, a British outpost where present-day students dressed as red-coated soldiers parade nineteenth century discipline before applauding tourists. To achieve coordination, soldiers' movements were analyzed, producing regulations specifying so many steps to raise the rifle, extend it, and so on. Here in the drill-yard docile bodies are produced; *L'Homme Machine* epitomized.

Thus the Newtonian world-view, based on the universal laws of nature, was applied in society: a new "social physics" for a new era. For Foucault, this is "political anatomy" engaged in a constant quest for new techniques to discipline and dominate bodies, making them function as required, with maximum efficiency. Bentham and the Utilitarians prided themselves on their concern with material value, with facts alone, which earned them Charles Dickens' biting scorn in *Hard Times*. Gradgrind the schoolmaster accepted no answer to the question "what is a horse?" but that it is a hard-hoofed graminivorous quadruped. But the facts did not exist on their own. To focus on facts was also to find a means of altering social reality. The Victorian school room could equally pass muster as a laboratory, where children's activities were timed, their location in class predetermined.

Utilitarianism encouraged the vast expansion of government fact-gathering during the nineteenth century. Census, police reports, voters' lists, and registers of marriages and deaths – all these meant burgeoning bureaucracy, collection of data, and storage of files. By the mid-Victorian era, Karl Marx was poring over the government "Blue Books" in the British Museum. They formed the empirical foundation, laid by Bentham and his cadre of officials, for yet more social science (although, ironically, Marx's writings excoriate Bentham's "economic man"). Bentham, and to a greater extent, Foucault, recognized that the accumulation of these facts spells power.

Analogously, docile bodies could be produced in factories. In fact, Bentham got his initial inspiration for the Panopticon from his brother Samuel's workshop at Critchoff in Tsarist Russia. A ragged but continuous line may be traced from there to the automobile assembly lines of Henry Ford and the scientific management practices of Frederick Winslow Taylor. Although much has been made of the increased technical efficiency of the early factories over cottage industry, much evidence suggests that employers' belief in the need for regularized labour discipline played just as important a part in their genesis. The serfs of feudalism eventually found their "freedom" as contracted workers under the eye of managers, and within buildings that were, to use Foucault's phrase, "architectures of power."

What for Bentham was a dream, for Foucault is the social reality *par excellence* of modernity. The specific architecture of the Panopticon recedes as panoptic discipline diffuses throughout modern society. Handling human beings with the effective instrument of technical rationality becomes part of our taken-for-granted world. Who needs a governor in an inspection lodge when the high school record, the doctor's report, the police dossier, the social worker's file, the factory clock-in card, and the marriage certificate each classify us, treat us as analyzable individual atoms, and set out for us the parameters of everyday life?

The absent governor, the empty inspection lodge

A S BENTHAM triumphantly pointed out, it does not matter if there is no one in the Panopticon inspection lodge. The discipline is automatic, not least because inmates *think* there is someone watching and regulate their *own* conduct accordingly. Foucault takes up this point repeatedly. Once the monarch ensured he or she was visible to subjects; now the subjects find themselves in the spotlight. The ruler has disappeared. The panoptic mechanism operates anonymously, neutrally, flexibly. It shapes its subjects to the norm without reference to outside scales of value. It represents strategies of power rather than any identifiable locus of power. It is, in fact, a web without a spider.

Foucault accepts this vacuum at the centre, even revels in it. It fits his own intellectual stance and his approach to history. If Bentham's prophetic voice rang with tones of modernity, Foucault's captures the new mood, often dubbed postmodernity. Human beings as conscious agents play little part in his dramas. Indeed, subjectivity is constituted by the disciplines he describes. Individuality is an invention. While some important insights reside here, Foucault's approach is not only idiosyncratic as history, it hints that history before Foucault was a mistake. If Bentham rid himself of God acting in history, Foucault dispenses with humanity as well.

It is hardly surprising, then, that Foucault's work is dashed by the waves of controversy. I mention three examples. Firstly, Foucault paid little attention to the ways that other dimensions of modernity accompany the rise of surveillance, such as the right to vote, join labour unions, or claim welfare benefits – each of which paradoxically confers power on the subjects of surveillance.[3] *Discipline and Punish* focuses on subordination by rational means and says precious little about resistance or about the cooperation and care that also characterizes social life.

Secondly, though he criticized those who seek a "total" explanation of events, *Discipline and Punish* exudes the impression that panopticism is a generalized form of social power, creeping into every capillary of the social organism. Yet are not factories, schools, and hospitals just as distinct from prisons as they are similar? Is modern rational discipline really the same everywhere?·

Thirdly, while Foucault fulminated against the Panopticon, he winds up with a form of fatalism. He discloses neither the basis for his attack nor any potential remedial action. I shall return to this three-pronged critique in a moment. It will help us assess the salience of the Panopticon to electronic surveillance.

Just as Bentham opened the door to the house of modernity, Foucault ushers us into its remodelled postmodern version. Bentham bequeathed his Panopticon to a world seeking to apply science to society in the belief that if the appropriate laws were observed, all manner of diverse ends could be met. In Foucault's commentary on panopticism, however, the promise of automatic functioning is fulfilled. Forget the reformation of character, or any other Enlightenment enterprise. The prisons failed at that. What lives on is the panoptic production of docile deviants.

Towards the electronic panopticon?

YESTERDAY, only a few weeks after passing an Ontario driver's test, I received, unsolicited, a membership form for the Canadian Automobile Association. How did they know? Actually, it was coincidence. CAA buys name-and-address lists from Infomart, who in turn get them from Bell Canada. I simply showed up as a non-member in a computer matching process called "merge-purge." Recently, I talked with a student about my social insurance card, and she told me without seeing it what its first three digits are. How did she know?

Simple. She happened to work in an Employment and Immigration Office and knew the number sequence for temporary residents in Canada. Different numbers indicate birthplace, refugee status, and so on.

Today, the tremendous technical power of computers and telecommunications has been harnessed to process personal data. The garnering of facts and the supervising of activities are now facilitated by new technologies undreamed of by Bentham and unremarked by Foucault. When stopped by police, instant checks can be made on you and your car using massive databanks networked by satellite. When you purchase with a credit card, immediate verification is available to indicate creditworthiness. Is this the Panopticon, electronically recycled?

A casual glance at popular media suggests that it is. Paul Simon sings,

These are the days of miracle and wonder, this is the long-distance call. The way the cameras follow us in slo-mo, the way we look to us all ... " (Paul Simon, *Graceland*)

Even the spider reappears, now as Spiderman. An American judge got the idea of electronic tagging of offenders from the strip cartoon. We do not have to look far, it seems, to find evidence of electronic panopticism in the popular media!

Research into electronic monitoring in the workplace, computerized commercial invasion of the home, and administrative or police surveillance reveals similar processes at work. In each case the depth of penetration into the minutiae of everyday life is greater, whether through the pacing of tasks, itemized phone billing, or cross-checking between different departmental databases. In each case also, Foucault's criteria for classic Benthamite panopticism reappear; electronic surveillance is invisible and unverifiable. It proceeds automatically though it simultaneously requires our participation; it is we who leave the ubiquitous traces of transactional information – Social Insurance and credit card numbers – in our trail.

Mark Poster, discerning in electronic surveillance a "Superpanopticon," hears echoes of the postmodern motifs of Foucault's analysis. While highly disciplinary, no power-centre is discernible. Electronic panopticism pervades all but parades no monarch. The subject, or the self, is now constituted not by anything as grand as history – unless you count credit-history or medical-history – but by mere electronic impulses. Fragments of personal information now circulate in a weird world (a virtual reality?) of data fields and digital switches, constantly disconnected then reconnected in new patterns and arrangements.

This elusive electronic realm has real enough effects in the other world, however. Which of us would have thought up schemes such as those proposed in New York – denying marriage licenses to parking ticket defaulters, or in Australia – the withholding of medical assistance from ID card refuseniks? Only the perverse magic of computer-matching makes feasible the creation of such categories and classifications. So the disciplines embedded in this putative panoptic system are as effectual as ever, only more so, courtesy of electronic enhancement.

Care is called for at this point, however. The unseen observer is indeed electronically present, prying ever more profoundly into the routines of daily life, categorizing and classifying us with ever finer precision. But this does not necessarily mean that society itself is becoming more prison-like, or that in those specific organizations that exhibit panoptic traits, people are less capable of recognizing them and responding appropriately. The mistake is to imagine that this epitome of modern social control – the Panopticon – is still with us in its (electronic) entirety. Equally erroneous, however, is the complacent belief that Bentham's influence - or Foucault's commentary on it – is merely a matter of historical interest.

The return of Bentham's ghost

IT IS ONE THING to rediscover Bentham's inspection principle in the computer age, but even more salutary to realize that his other key principle, contract, is also making a comeback. What was Bentham's undoing in 1810 now reemerges as a workable solution to problems of social control and the containment of deviance. Recall that the age of the computer is also the age of the consumer. There are at least two aspects to this, but each relates anew social discipline and market forces.

First, the doctrine that the state should control the means of policing, prisons, and punishment has fallen on hard times. The phenomenon of private policing has mushroomed over recent years. From industrial sites to housing complexes, universities to shopping malls, the commercially-run security force is in evidence. They most obviously use the whole panoply of electronic aids; video cameras, bar-coded entry cards and so on, which simultaneously facilitate coopera-tion with "official" police and with intelligence agencies, through the cross-checking of databases.

It is equally plausible to see the growth of treatments "in the com-munity" as a response both to fiscal constraint and to technological potential. Experiments with the electronic tagging of offenders is a case in point. The central criteria offered have been that this method, by relying on technological surveillance, is supposedly far cheaper than using prison personnel and facilities. Remember "... a machine ... public burthens lightened ... ?"[4]

Secondly, given earlier references to commercial surveillance via credit cards, telephone-billing, direct mail and so on, could we not conceive the whole high-tech apparatus of the consumer society as panoptic? When one considers how the difficulties of stimulating and maintaining consumer demand is increasingly viewed as a "social man-agement" problem, this interpretation starts to make sense. The capi-talist enterprise, having applied management and technological tech-niques to production, now turns its attention to the next slow-to-respond and unpredictable area, the marketplace.

Massively complex computer-power produces careful distinctions between potential consumers, the more accurately to focus sales of the latest goods. "Smart" telephone networks can now identify callers, so that when a commercial toll-free number is dialled, the representa-tive knows as you speak whether or not you are in a "desirable" – "Pools and Patios" – category. For those thus participating in their own commercial surveillance, the process is even experienced as plea-surable. It is flattering to be known, convenient to read out the credit card number. And with such systems in place, who needs the state to reproduce social order?

But what exactly is going on here? Which "system" is now the agent of social control? Clearly, with commercial surveillance some of the strict and severe elements of panoptic discipline fall away, though clas-sification and inspection continue. Not only do the more rigid con-straints – the "carcerality" – of the Panopticon dissolve in this world of consumer discipline, however; it seems that in reality another set of principles is steadily supplanting the Panopticon.

If pain was once the instrument for achieving social order, which Bentham and his cadre replaced with (panoptic) discipline, then today the key principle is pleasure. Granted, consumer "choices" are often a commercially-engineered mirage, and granted, our preferences have been unwittingly disclosed to marketeers to a discomforting degree (that is, discomforting when we know it); nonetheless, the social order of consumer society is not carceral in the sense that the Panopticon was. Today we are seduced into conformity, not coerced into compliance.

None of the above should be taken as an excuse for complacency, however. Bentham's ghost may return to haunt us in more than one respect. The systems we have just been discussing raise acute questions of democracy. The social challenge of information technology is often thought of in terms of conventional political discourse: does it contribute to dissemination of, or restricting access to, information, on which democracy depends? Does it tend to increase invasions of privacy? What happens if these powerful machines fall into the wrong – read despotic – hands?

However, if the kind of analysis suggested in the panoptic concept holds any water at all, these may well turn out to be the wrong questions. Bentham's soul-training Panopticon retained the vestiges of moral categories, which is why parliamentarians said it should not be sullied by commerce. But the apparatus itself was almost entirely instrumental, flexibly suited to the goals of any and all interests. I shall return in a moment to the question of computers and instrumentality, but note here that once commercial criteria become paramount – as in private policing or electronic tagging – the moral categories fade. The new surveillance is preventative. The supermarket security guard's task is to protect his employer from loss of profit. The question of theft, of lawbreaking, is virtually unaddressed.

Protests about privacy are often heard when some new system is introduced, be it machine-readable health-care numbers, electronic ID cards or whatever. Privacy is not only notoriously slippery to define, but by concentrating our concern on this issue, we may miss more fundamental dangers. With electronic technologies, the totalitarian tendencies of large organizations are more pronounced, even without evil intent, without a malign dictator, without a spider in the web. Once new technology systems are installed, it becomes easier to merge the databases of commerce and government, easier to classify political, sexual or religious deviants, easier, in short, to establish panoptic control. The more this occurs through "technical" decisions about what software to buy, the more policy is made by default.

Of course, the advent of information technology serves to reinforce the neo-Benthamite obsession with facts – now data – and technical decisions. Administrative departments develop insatiable appetites for data. Computers are marketed as solutions to the information over-load problems of burdened bureaucracy. They appear in the nick of time, to aid statistical analysis, to facilitate communication, to lubri-cate the system, to centralize control. The person brandishing the print-out speaks with authority. Utilitarianism is very much at home in the computer age.

The Panopticon: maturing with modernity?

F IN BENTHAM'S PANOPTICON we read modernity, and in Foucault's, postmodernity, then the computer neatly connects the two together. Indeed, computer-power lends weight to the argument that "post-modernity" is no such thing; today's cultural landscape is simply modernity matured. In this version, no rift with the modern era has occurred. Rather, some of its basic principles and practices are repro-duced in starker form, others are modified or atrophy over time. Consider two aspects of this duality.

Firstly, with respect to new technology and surveillance we could say this: information technology facilitates the continued quest for certainty – and the elimination of alternative certainties – and still contributes to the subordination of certain social groups via its "invisi-ble inspection" capacity. The lust for complete control still forms a major motivation for acquiring and accumulating computer-power. In this sharpening and fine-tuning of modern practice lurk dangers for democratic involvement in several spheres which, if uncontested, could severely limit the conditions of political life. It also raises questions about personal freedom and dignity, insofar as this rests on our ability to choose when, what, and to whom we disclose data about ourselves (see further, Fortner 1986, 1989). Thus panoptic principles persist.

However, it is one thing to resist totalitarian tendencies within spe-cific situations, another to adopt a paranoid position that regards contemporary social conditions as irremediably panoptic. This is simply to fall headlong into the Foucaldian trap, mentioned above, of "totalizing" the partial. While contemporary societies continue to repress their underclass of non-consumers, and while individual citizens still stand little chance against the growing might of big organizations, the main vehicle for maintaining social order today is probably not panoptic power but seduction by consumerism.[5] The *societal* Panopticon is a chimera.

Secondly, the more general issue of instrumental approaches to social problems is highlighted by new technology and the Panopticon. This again puts the computer at the cultural interface between the modern and the "postmodern." The instrumental appears to oust moral orientation. In his report for the Conseil des Universités de Québec Jean-François Lyotard reviews regretfully the demise of the grand "metanarratives" of modernity; Reason, Democracy, Justice, Peace. And he predicts that, having once cut the tissue connecting knowledge to such ends, nothing will be left to define knowledge but computer-based criteria. Naked instrumental technique alone will rule, automatically, flexibly, ubiquitously.

As we have seen, Bentham's project, though originally rooted in the moral categories of criminal justice, contained no safeguards against merely mechanical application. Modern instrumentality, bolstered by bureaucratic organization, is today electronically extended. For example, we become police computer "suspects" or commercial surveillance "targets" because of the categories into which we fall, irrespective of our actions or intentions. Which illustrates Lyotard's position nicely.

T HE ANALYSES mentioned thus far, however, seem to push us towards either Lyotard's pessimism or Foucault's fatalism. Are these the only alternatives available? Emphatically not! As I indicated above with regard to Foucault's followers, it is not so much that we are already enclosed in the cells of the electronic Panopticon, but that certain contemporary institutions display panoptic features. Panopticism is one tendency among others, albeit one augmented technologically today. It is ominous, but not overwhelming.

Within modernity, such panoptic tendencies seem to have grown in a symbiotic relationship with countervailing trends – the emergence of civil, political, economic, and welfare rights. This does not, of course, justify smugness or relaxed vigilance! Rather, if the threat is adequately to be met, the struggles that gave birth to those oppositional tendencies should be rejoined in a manner appropriate to present conditions. Already some labour unions question new monitoring devices, civil liberties groups press for "privacy" concerns, and courageous computer professionals collectively resist unethical practice.[6]

Returning to Lyotard, we could argue that it makes more sense to see instrumentality against a bigger backdrop. His account bemoans the loss of modernity's metanarratives, whereas one could equally see this as the eclipse of morally guided orientation in general. To re-read the account as secularization: Modernity, having ripped the roots of social order from Revelation, was unable to prevent their being severed from Reason as well. Thus the Panopticon, for instance, slides easily from the discourse of justice and morality to that of mere calculation and instrumentality, thus also rendering it a prime candidate for computerization.

Viewed from this more distant – pre-modern – horizon, however, Lyotard's narrative takes on another complexion. Recall, if you will, Bentham's initial inspiration for the panoptic principle of inspection: divine omniscience. Recall his epigraph, Psalm 139. The oscillating dialectic of control that gives us first the Panopticon, then human rights or democracy, then electronically amplified aspects of the Panopticon once more could equally be seen against the backdrop of that Psalm.

Undoubtedly the psalmist feels the eye of God upon him. Just as surely, his sensitivity to moral failure is heightened thereby. But simultaneously, that same eye protects and enables. It may constrain, but never incarcerate. Bentham conveniently ignored the antinomy involved in divine omniscience – not to mention in English usage – that to "watch over" may be as much for loving care as for control. Thus the knowledge he sought was merely classificatory, objectifying, empirical, not – as for the psalmist – personal, relational, and mutual.

Elements for a radical critique of electronic surveillance lie right here. Such a critique would recognize realistically the need for and the benefits of surveillance – the potential for limiting violence or abuse for instance – but would advocate or judge them according to moral categories. Simultaneously, it would be acutely aware of the inherent dangers, including the panoptic and instrumental tendencies of all surveillance techniques, but especially the electronic. It would refuse, in short, the Benthamite reduction of "knowing" to

merely accurate, empirical classification for the purpose of subordination by uncertainty. And it would embrace the new technologies
only insofar as their use is compatible with democratic participation
and free personhood.

Bentham's Panopticon still has its adherents today, two centuries
on. Though the penchant for moral architecture is giving way to social
control by consumer seduction, a residual element of deeply invasive
electronic surveillance remains. Bentham's ghost is not easily exor-
cised. Silicon technocrats, seeking new strategies, unwittingly celebrate
its efficiency and follow its instrumental logic. Democratically-minded
critics, on the other hand, complain about its inhumanity and the sinister threat of social management. But the activities of both groups
are illuminated in the longer time-frame: the pre-modern, the modern, and the mature modern. The Panopticon straddles all three. We
forget its origins at our own expense. It was a secular Utopia.

Notes

My thanks are due to colleagues who kindly commented on earlier drafts of this article,
Peter Bramham, Rob James, Gayle MacDonald, Bob Pike, Rebecca Sutherns and
anonymous *Queen's Quarterly* reviewers. Zygmunt Bauman also encouraged me and
offered crucial guidance for understanding the Panopticon.

1 Bentham may also have been influenced indirectly by Greek sceptical philosophy.
   Critias, a "tyrant of Athens" (404 B.C.) claimed that "Some shrewd man first, a
   man in counsel wise, Discovered unto men the fear of Gods, Thereby to frighten
   sinners should they sin E'en secretly in deed, or word, or thought..." See *Sextus
   Empiricus*, 31
2 In fact prisoners often feared solitary confinement the most. At least labour and
   treadmills offered the hope of surreptitious sociability.
3 I elaborate this in Lyon 1991
4 Tagging remains a highly controversial issue, of course. Some American evidence
   suggests that, in the long term, it is more expensive than its more labour-inten-
   sive equivalents. British studies show that a high proportion of experimentally
   tagged "volunteers" have managed to dupe the system.
5 This is elaborated most effectively in the work of Zygmunt Bauman.
6 The group known as "Computer Professionals for Social Responsibility," for
   instance, was involved in the successful bid to prevent a major software company
   from marketing a highly invasive marketing tool early in 1991.

Works Cited

Bauman, Zygmunt. *Modernity and Ambivalence*. Cambridge: Polity Press, 1991.

_____. *Legislators and Interpreters: On Modernity, Postmodernity and Intellectuals*, Cambridge: Polity Press, 1987.

Bentham, Jeremy. *Collected Works* volume IV, edited by John Bowring. London, 1843.

Fortner, Robert. "Physics and Metaphysics in an Information Age: Privacy, Dignity and Identity." *Communication*. 9 (1986): 151-72.

_____. "Privacy is not enough: Personhood and High Technology." *The Conrad Grebel Review*. (Spring 1989): 159-77.

Foucault, Michel. *Discipline and Punish: The Birth of the Prison*. New York: Vintage, 1977. ET of *Surveiller et Punir*. Paris: Gallimard, 1977, by Alan Sheridan.

Halevy, Elie. *The Growth of Philosophic Radicalism*. London: Faber, 1926, revised 1972.

Himmelfarb, Gertrude. "The haunted house of Jeremy Bentham", *Victorians Minds*. New York: Knopf, 1952, 1968.

Huxley, Aldous. *Themes and Variations*. London: Chatto, 1950.

Ignatieff, Michael. *A Just Measure of Pain: The Penitentiary in the Industrial Revolution*. New York: Pantheon, 1978.

Lyon, David. *Citizenship and Surveillance in the Information Age*. Kingston: Queen's University, Studies in Communication and Information Technology Working Paper. 1991.

Lyotard, Jean-Francois. *The Postmodern Condition: A Report on Knowledge*. Minneapolis: University of Minnesota Press, 1984. ET of *La Condition Postmoderne: Rapport sur le Savoir*. Paris: Editions de Minuit, 1979.

Poster, Mark. *The Mode of Information*. Cambridge: Polity Press, 1990.

Sextus Empiricus. volume III, (Loeb Classical Library), Cambridge, MA: Harvard University Press, 1933.

Taylor, C. J. "The Kingston, Ontario, Penitentiary as Moral Architecture." *Histoire Sociale - Social History* 12 (1979): 385-408

[3]

Postscript on the Societies of Control*

GILLES DELEUZE

1. Historical

Foucault located the *disciplinary societies* in the eighteenth and nineteenth centuries; they reach their height at the outset of the twentieth. They initiate the organization of vast spaces of enclosure. The individual never ceases passing from one closed environment to another, each having its own laws: first, the family; then the school ("you are no longer in your family"); then the barracks ("you are no longer at school"); then the factory; from time to time the hospital; possibly the prison, the preeminent instance of the enclosed environment. It's the prison that serves as the analogical model: at the sight of some laborers, the heroine of Rossellini's *Europa '51* could exclaim, "I thought I was seeing convicts."

Foucault has brilliantly analyzed the ideal project of these environments of enclosure, particularly visible within the factory: to concentrate; to distribute in space; to order in time; to compose a productive force within the dimension of space-time whose effect will be greater than the sum of its component forces. But what Foucault recognized as well was the transience of this model: it succeeded that of the *societies of sovereignty*, the goal and functions of which were something quite different (to tax rather than to organize production, to rule on death rather than to administer life); the transition took place over time, and Napoleon seemed to effect the large-scale conversion from one society to the other. But in their turn the disciplines underwent a crisis to the benefit of new forces that were gradually instituted and which accelerated after World War II: a disciplinary society was what we already no longer were, what we had ceased to be.

We are in a generalized crisis in relation to all the environments of

*   This essay, which first appeared in *L'Autre journal*, no. 1 (May 1990), is included in the forthcoming translation of *Pourparlers* (Paris: Editions Minuit, 1990), to be published by Columbia University Press.

enclosure—prison, hospital, factory, school, family. The family is an "interior," in crisis like all other interiors—scholarly, professional, etc. The administrations in charge never cease announcing supposedly necessary reforms: to reform schools, to reform industries, hospitals, the armed forces, prisons. But everyone knows that these institutions are finished, whatever the length of their expiration periods. It's only a matter of administering their last rites and of keeping people employed until the installation of the new forces knocking at the door. These are the *societies of control*, which are in the process of replacing the disciplinary societies. "Control" is the name Burroughs proposes as a term for the new monster, one that Foucault recognizes as our immediate future. Paul Virilio also is continually analyzing the ultrarapid forms of free-floating control that replaced the old disciplines operating in the time frame of a closed system. There is no need here to invoke the extraordinary pharmaceutical productions, the molecular engineering, the genetic manipulations, although these are slated to enter into the new process. There is no need to ask which is the toughest or most tolerable regime, for it's within each of them that liberating and enslaving forces confront one another. For example, in the crisis of the hospital as environment of enclosure, neighborhood clinics, hospices, and day care could at first express new freedom, but they could participate as well in mechanisms of control that are equal to the harshest of confinements. There is no need to fear or hope, but only to look for new weapons.

2. Logic

The different internments or spaces of enclosure through which the individual passes are independent variables: each time one is supposed to start from zero, and although a common language for all these places exists, it is *analogical*. On the other hand, the different control mechanisms are inseparable variations, forming a system of variable geometry the language of which is *numerical* (which doesn't necessarily mean binary). Enclosures are *molds*, distinct castings, but controls are a *modulation*, like a self-deforming cast that will continuously change from one moment to the other, or like a sieve whose mesh will transmute from point to point.

This is obvious in the matter of salaries: the factory was a body that contained its internal forces at a level of equilibrium, the highest possible in terms of production, the lowest possible in terms of wages; but in a society of control, the corporation has replaced the factory, and the corporation is a spirit, a gas. Of course the factory was already familiar with the system of bonuses, but the corporation works more deeply to impose a modulation of each salary, in states of perpetual metastability that operate through challenges, contests, and highly comic group sessions. If the most idiotic television game shows are so successful, it's because they express the corporate situation with great precision. The factory constituted individuals as a single body to the double advantage of the boss who surveyed each element within the mass and the unions who mobilized a mass resistance; but the corporation constantly presents the brashest rivalry as a healthy form of emulation, an excellent motivational force that opposes individuals against one another and runs through each, dividing each within. The modulating principle of "salary according to merit" has not failed to tempt national education itself. Indeed, just as the corporation replaces the factory, *perpetual training* tends to replace the *school*, and continuous control to replace the examination. Which is the surest way of delivering the school over to the corporation.

In the disciplinary societies one was always starting again (from school to the barracks, from the barracks to the factory), while in the societies of control one is never finished with anything—the corporation, the educational system, the armed services being metastable states coexisting in one and the same modulation, like a universal system of deformation. In *The Trial*, Kafka, who had already placed himself at the pivotal point between two types of social formation, described the most fearsome of juridical forms. The *apparent acquittal* of the disciplinary societies (between two incarcerations); and the *limitless postponements* of the societies of control (in continuous variation) are two very different modes of juridical life, and if our law is hesitant, itself in crisis, it's because we are leaving one in order to enter into the other. The disciplinary societies have two poles: the signature that designates the *individual*, and the number or administrative numeration that indicates his or her position within a *mass*. This is because the disciplines never saw any incompatibility between these two, and because at the same time power individualizes and masses together, that is, constitutes those over whom it exercises power into a body and molds the individuality of each member of that body. (Foucault saw the origin of this double charge in the pastoral power of the priest—the flock and each of its animals—but civil power moves in turn and by other means to make itself lay "priest.") In the societies of control, on the other hand, what is important is no longer either a signature or a number, but a code: the code is a *password*, while on the other hand the disciplinary societies are regulated by *watchwords* (as much from the point of view of integration as from that of resistance). The numerical language of control is made of codes that mark access to information, or reject it. We no longer find ourselves dealing with the mass/individual pair. Individuals have become "*dividuals*," and masses, samples, data, markets, or "*banks*." Perhaps it is money that expresses the distinction between the two societies best, since discipline always referred back to minted money that locks gold in as numerical standard, while control relates to floating rates of exchange, modulated according to a rate established by a set of standard currencies. The old monetary mole is the animal of the spaces of enclosure, but the serpent is that of the societies of control. We have passed from one animal to the other, from the mole to the serpent, in the system under which we live, but also in our manner of living and in our relations with others. The disciplinary man was a discontinuous producer of energy, but the man of control is undulatory, in orbit, in a continuous network. Everywhere *surfing* has already replaced the older *sports*.

Types of machines are easily matched with each type of society—not that machines are determining, but because they express those social forms capable of generating them and using them. The old societies of sovereignty made use of simple machines—levers, pulleys, clocks; but the recent disciplinary societies equipped themselves with machines involving energy, with the passive danger of entropy and the active danger of sabotage; the societies of control operate with machines of a third type, computers, whose passive danger is jamming and whose active one is piracy and the introduction of viruses. This technological evolution must be, even more profoundly, a mutation of capitalism, an already well-known or familiar mutation that can be summed up as follows: nineteenth-century capitalism is a capitalism of concentration, for production and for property. It therefore erects the factory as a space of enclosure, the capitalist being the owner of the means of production but also, progressively, the owner of other spaces conceived through analogy (the worker's familial house, the school). As for markets, they are conquered sometimes by specialization, some-times by colonization, sometimes by lowering the costs of production. But, in the present situation, capitalism is no longer involved in production, which it often relegates to the Third World, even for the complex forms of textiles, metallurgy, or oil production. It's a capitalism of higher-order production. It no longer buys raw materials and no longer sells the finished products: it buys the finished products or assembles parts. What it wants to sell is services and what it wants to buy is stocks. This is no longer a capitalism for production but for the product, which is to say, for being sold or marketed. Thus it is essentially dispersive, and the factory has given way to the corporation. The family, the school, the army, the factory are no longer the distinct analogical spaces that converge towards an owner—state or private power—but coded figures—deformable and transformable—of a single corporation that now has only stockholders. Even art has left the spaces of enclosure in order to enter into the open circuits of the bank. The conquests of the market are made by grabbing control and no longer by disciplinary training, by fixing the exchange rate much more than by lowering costs, by transformation of the product more than by specialization of production. Corruption thereby gains a new power. Marketing has become the center or the "soul" of the corporation. We are taught that corporations have a soul, which is the most terrifying news in the world. The operation of markets is now the instrument of social control and forms the impudent breed of our masters. Control is short-term and of rapid rates of turnover, but also continuous and without limit, while discipline was of long duration, infinite and discontinuous. Man is no longer man enclosed, but man in debt. It is true that capitalism has retained as a constant the extreme poverty of three quarters of humanity, too poor for debt, too numerous for confinement:

control will not only have to deal with erosions of frontiers but with the explo-
sions within shanty towns or ghettos.

3. Program

The conception of a control mechanism, giving the position of any element
within an open environment at any given instant (whether animal in a reserve
or human in a corporation, as with an electronic collar), is not necessarily one
of science fiction. Félix Guattari has imagined a city where one would be able
to leave one's apartment, one's street, one's neighborhood, thanks to one's
(dividual) electronic card that raises a given barrier; but the card could just as
easily be rejected on a given day or between certain hours; what counts is not
the barrier but the computer that tracks each person's position—licit or illicit
—and effects a universal modulation.

The socio-technological study of the mechanisms of control, grasped at
their inception, would have to be categorical and to describe what is already in
the process of substitution for the disciplinary sites of enclosure, whose crisis is
everywhere proclaimed. It may be that older methods, borrowed from the
former societies of sovereignty, will return to the fore, but with the necessary
modifications. What counts is that we are at the beginning of something. In the
prison system: the attempt to find penalties of "substitution," at least for petty
crimes, and the use of electronic collars that force the convicted person to stay
at home during certain hours. For the *school system*: continuous forms of control,
and the effect on the school of perpetual training, the corresponding abandon-
ment of all university research, the introduction of the "corporation" at all levels
of schooling. For the *hospital system*: the new medicine "without doctor or patient"
that singles out potential sick people and subjects at risk, which in no way attests
to individuation—as they say—but substitutes for the individual or numerical
body the code of a "dividual" material to be controlled. In the *corporate system*:
new ways of handling money, profits, and humans that no longer pass through
the old factory form. These are very small examples, but ones that will allow
for better understanding of what is meant by the crisis of the institutions, which
is to say, the progressive and dispersed installation of a new system of domination. One of the most important questions will concern the ineptitude of the
unions: tied to the whole of their history of struggle against the disciplines or
within the spaces of enclosure, will they be able to adapt themselves or will they
give way to new forms of resistance against the societies of control? Can we
already grasp the rough outlines of these coming forms, capable of threatening
the joys of marketing? Many young people strangely boast of being "motivated";
they re-request apprenticeships and permanent training. It's up to them to
discover what they're being made to serve, just as their elders discovered, not
without difficulty, the telos of the disciplines. The coils of a serpent are even
more complex than the burrows of a molehill.

[4]

The viewer society

Michel Foucault's 'Panopticon' revisited

THOMAS MATHIESEN
University of Oslo, Norway

Abstract

The article takes its point of departure in one limited and consciously selected aspect of Michel Foucault's use of Jeremy Bentham's concept of 'Panopticon': in his book *Discipline and Punish*, the aspect of surveillance, and the emphasis on a fundamental change and break which presumably occurred in the 1800s from social and theatrical arrangements, where the many saw the few, to modern surveillance activities where the few see the many. It is maintained that Foucault contributes in an important way to our understanding of and sensitivity regarding modern surveillance systems and practices, which are expanding at an accelerating rate, but that he overlooks an opposite process of great significance which has occurred simultaneously and at an equally accelerated rate: the mass media, and especially television, which today bring the many — literally hundreds of millions of people at the same time — with great force to see and admire the few. In contrast to Foucault's panoptical process, the latter process is referred to as synoptical. Together, the processes situate us in a viewer society in a two-way and double sense. This article explores the developmental parallels and relationships between Panopticon and Synopticon, as well as their reciprocal functions. It is maintained that the control and discipline of the 'soul', that is, the creation of human beings who control themselves through self-control and who thus fit neatly into a so-called democratic capitalist society, is a task which is actually fulfilled by modern Synopticon, whereas Foucault saw it as a function of Panopticon.

Key Words

• Foucault • mass media • Panopticon • surveillance • Synopticon

In 1975 Michel Foucault published his widely acclaimed and important book *Surveiller et punir: Naissance de la prison*. The book was quickly translated into a number of languages, and was first published in English by Allen Lane in 1977 under the title *Discipline and Punish: The Birth of the Prison* (Vintage edition, 1979). Through the 1970s and 1980s it exerted a strong influence on the sociology and philosophy of social control in a number of western countries. It also initiated important debates over the issues involved.

The concept and idea of 'panopticon', which Foucault borrowed from Jeremy Bentham, is among the most important in the book. It is also a concept which strongly needs to be supplemented.

Panopticism

The opening chapter of *Discipline and Punish* gives a dramatic and terrifying account of an execution in Paris. The year was 1757, and the man who was executed was a certain Robert Francois Damiens, who had attempted to murder the King of France, Louis XV. Those who have read the book will remember the account. The execution was brutal to say the least, Damiens was kept alive for a long time and tortured in the most painful manner, and finally torn apart by horses tied to his arms and legs. The horses had to be helped by the executioner to complete the task. The spectacle was attended by large crowds. What Foucault does not tell us is that members of the Court also attended, and that the ladies of the Court wept, not in pity with the culprit, but over the toil of the horses.[1]

This was, to repeat, 1757. The next account in Foucault's presentation — and again this is well known to his readers — implies a complete change of scene. Three-quarters of a century has past. The year is 1838, and Foucault's source now is the rules for 'the house of young prisoners in Paris'. The life of the young prisoners is regulated by rules down to the most minute details, from the first drum roll in the morning, making the prisoners rise and dress in silence, through prayer, working hours, meals, education, rest, the washing of hands, the inspection of clothes, and finally order, silence and sleep 'at half-past seven in the summer, half-past eight in the winter'. Gone is the open brutality and uncontrolled infliction of physical pain so characteristic of Damiens' execution; instead, there is a carefully developed system of rules regulating life in full and complete detail.

What does Foucault want to illustrate by contrasting the two scenes?

First, he wants to say something about the change in the nature of punishment, from physical punishment to prison. Second, and more importantly, he wants to say something about a change in the content of punishment, from the torture of the body to the transformation of the soul. 'At the beginning of the nineteenth century', Foucault states, 'the great spectacle of physical punishment disappeared; the tortured body was avoided; the theatrical representation of pain was excluded from punishment' (Foucault, 1979: 14). Surely, prison was and is a 'corporal' kind of punishment. But in this context, the body is a tool or a link: 'During the 150 or 200 years that Europe has been setting up its new penal systems, the judges have gradually ... taken to judging something other than crimes, namely, the "soul" of the criminal' (p. 19). As a correlate, the public character of punishment has disappeared: 'Punishment, then, will tend to become the most hidden part of the penal process' (p. 9).

Third, Foucault wants to say something about a broad historical change of social order. Apparently, this is his most essential point. 'This book is intended', he says, 'as a correlative history of the modern soul and of a new power to judge' (p. 23). Modern penal leniency is actually a technique of power, and by an analysis of it 'one might understand both how man, the soul, the normal or abnormal individual have come to duplicate crime as objects of penal intervention' (p. 24). By the control of the soul, vis-a-vis the control of the body, I understand him to mean the creation of human beings who control themselves through self-control, thus fitting neatly into a so-called democratic capitalist society.

The new prisons had, with variations, an important common form: they were organized so that a few could supervise or survey a large number. They were, in this sense, 'panoptical', from the Greek word *pan*, meaning 'all', and *opticon*, which represents the visual. To Foucault, however, the movement towards the panoptical form was not only a characteristic feature of the modern prison. A new kind of society was implied in the transformation. 'In appearance', he says, panopticism 'is merely the solution of a technical problem, but, through it, a whole new type of society emerges' (p. 216). To Foucault, panopticism represents a fundamental movement or transformation *from the situation where the many see the few to the situation where the few see the many.*

He lets the German prison reformer M.H. Julius describe the transformation. Antiquity had been the civilization of spectacle. 'To render accessible to a multitude of men the inspection of a small number of objects'; this was the problem to which the architecture of the temples, theatres and circuses responded. This was the age of public life, intensive feasts, sensual proximity. The modern age poses the opposite problem: 'To procure for a small number, or even for a single individual, the instantaneous view of a great multitude' (Julius, 1831, in Foucault, 1979: 216). Foucault formulates it this way: 'Our society is one not of spectacle, but of surveillance . . . We are much less Greeks than we believe. We are neither in the amphitheatre, nor on the stage, but in the panoptical machine, invested by its effects of power, which we bring to ourselves since we are a part of its mechanism' (p. 217).

On this background, Foucault describes how panopticism has been transported 'from the penal institution to the entire social body' (p. 298). A carceral society has been developed, in which the principle of panopticism gradually and imperceptibly has invaded ever-larger segments. 'At the moment of its full blossoming', Foucault admits, the new society 'still assumes with the Emperor the old aspect of power of spectacle'. The old monarch may be kept in the new state. But the tendency is that 'the pomp of sovereignty, the necessarily spectacular manifestations of power', gradually yield to 'the daily exercise of surveillance, in a panopticism in which the vigilance of the intersecting gazes was soon to render useless both the eagle and the sun' (p. 217). It is the normalizing gaze of panopticism which presumably produces that subjectivity, that self-control, which disciplines people to fit into a democratic capitalist society.

Synopticism

In what follows, I shall touch on the wider ramifications of Foucault's thesis, notably his perspective — as I understand it — on the control of the 'soul', but rather than providing a full discussion and interpretation of Foucault, which numerous others have provided anyway, I will largely and explicitly limit myself to putting the magnifying glass on one selected aspect of his book: the emphasis on panoptical surveillance as such. There are several good reasons for doing this. For one thing, that aspect is surely there in *Discipline and Punish* as one important component or ingredient; indeed, the French title — *Surveiller et punir* — in itself alludes to it. Second, the same aspect has in a decisive way influenced parts of criminology, notably the study of and debate about the 'widening of the net' of formal control around the prison (Cohen, 1985; McMahon, 1992). Third, recent historical developments suggest the increasing and politically extremely great importance of the modern surveillance machines as such.

As an observer of the development of modern control systems in Norway and other western countries, I find the panoptical principle, where the few see the many, to be a pronounced aspect of various systems and parts of society. First, in the immediate circle around the prison, organized systems of surveillance of those who are released from prison have grown. Second, further away from the prison, but still within the realm of the criminal control system in a broad sense of the word, organized computerized surveillance of whole categories of people rather than just individuals, with a view towards possible future crimes rather than past acts, has grown enormous. In Europe, the recent enormous systems of computerized police cooperation — the Europol Information System, the Schengen Information System, the so-called Sirenes and the European Information System — are cases in point. Third, still further away from the prison, and outside the realm of the police and other formal control systems, it may be said that important social institutions have surveillance functions. It may be maintained that the school system, the medical services, the psychiatric and social systems through their classificatory and diagnostic techniques and scales, are panoptical systems with carceral functions. We certainly live in a society where the few see the many.

Yet, something of crucial importance is missing. Acceleration of surveillance where the few see the many, yes. But is Foucault right in saying that we have developed *from* a situation where the many see the few *to* a situation where the few see the many?

As a striking parallel to the panoptical process, and concurring in detail with its historical development, we have seen the development of a unique and enormously extensive system enabling *the many to see and contemplate the few*, so that the tendency for the few to see and supervise the many is contextualized by a highly significant counterpart.

I am thinking, of course, of the development of the total system of the modern mass media. It is, to put it mildly, puzzling that Michel Foucault, in a large volume which explicitly or implicitly sensitizes us inter alia to surveillance in modern society, does not mention television — or any other mass media — with a single word. It is more than just an omission; its inclusion in the analysis would necessarily in a basic way have changed his whole image of society as far as surveillance goes.

Corresponding to panopticism, imbued with certain basic parallels in structure, vested with certain reciprocal supplementary functions, and — during the past few years — merged with panopticism through a common technology, the system of modern mass media has been going through a most significant and accelerating development. The total time span of this development — the past 150 to 200 years — coincides most remarkably with the period of the modern growth of panopticism. Increasingly, the few have been able to see the many, but also increasingly, the many have been enabled to see the few — to see the VIPs, the reporters, the stars, almost a new class in the public sphere.

Formulated in bold terms, it is possible to say that not only panopticism, but also *synopticism* characterizes our society, and characterized the transition to modernity.[2] The concept is composed of the Greek word *syn* which stands for 'together' or 'at the same time', and *opticon*, which, again, has to do with the visual. It may be used to represent the situation where a large number focuses on something in common which is condensed. In other words, it may stand for the *opposite* of the situation where the few see the many. In a two-way and significant double sense of the word we thus live in a *viewer society*.

As I have said, the panoptical and the synoptical structures show several conspicuous parallels in development, and they together, precisely together, serve decisive control functions in modern society. Let us first look at some of the parallels, and, by way of conclusion, the control functions.

Parallels

I want to emphasize three parallels:

1. The first one has been alluded to already and strikes the eye immediately: *the acceleration which synopticism as well as panopticism has shown in modern times, that is, during the period 1800–2000.*

The story and history of the media is well known, but has to be sketched briefly in order to place the panoptical development in perspective. Foucault takes the modern prison, which came between 1750 and 1830, as his point of departure for panopticism. Precisely at the same time, between 1750 and 1830, the mass press was born — the first wave of mass media after the printed book. Though we had newspapers in the 1700s, the 1800s was the seminal century, and the 1830s was a seminal decade in what was to become the mass media society par excellence, the USA. In 1833 Benjamin Day founded the *New York Sun*. Two months later, on 3 September 1833, the circulation was 3000, and after five years it was 30,000. James Gordon Bennett's *Herald*, also of New York, was the main competitor. In 1836, Bennett wrote:

> Books have had their day — the theatres have had their day — the temple of religion has had its day. A newspaper can be made to take the lead in all of these in the great movements of human thought and of human civilization. A newspaper can send more souls to heaven, and save more from Hell, than all of the churches or chapels in New York — besides making money at the same time.
>
> (quoted in De Fleur and Ball-Rokeach, 1989: 54)

The growth of the newspaper presupposed a comprehensive scientific and technical development which took place about the same time — the train and the steam ship, which facilitated the distribution of newspapers as well as the interchange of news, and the telegraph, which made rapid communication of news possible. It also presupposed important social conditions: a changed political role of the citizens and the development of a large middle class followed by the growth of trade and consequently of large markets. In a peripheral country like Norway, the same development took place, only a little later.

And, as we know, then came the other media, in a neatly packed row (for details of the development, see De Fleur and Ball-Rokeach, 1989; for Norway, see Mathiesen, 1993), as striking parallels to the development of panopticism. The second wave was the film, also founded on a complex set of technological innovations and social conditions. First silent film, then film with a sound track added, black-and-white film, and finally colour film. The enormous popularity of the film implied the gathering of large crowds of people in large film theatres, blatantly contradicting Foucault's thesis that in modern times we have moved away from the situation where the many see the few, away from synopticism. The popularity of the film presupposed a social structure where mobility, especially out of the family, was possible. In turn, the film probably also facilitated such mobility.

Then came the radio, followed by television, as the third and fourth wave. Television shared the history of the radio as well as its financial basis, its traditions and talents. A large number of complex social circumstances established a need and a search for new communication media which could communicate instantaneous messages over very great distances. An understanding of electricity in the 1900s constituted the foundation of instantaneous communication in its modern form (instantaneous communication was not unknown in earlier times — drum signals and smoke signals in so-called primitive societies, the semaphore stations in Napoleon's France, and so on). The radio was in many ways a by-product of a long, continuous and basic chain of investigations into electrical energy. The 1920s was the great decade for the establishment of regular broadcasting from a number of stations in the United States and other parts of the world.

And, finally, from 1945 in the United States and 1960 in Norway, television, based on a technology developed before and during the Second World War. The basic synoptical character of the media was in a fundamental way enhanced by television. As television developed, millions, hundreds of millions, of people could see the few on the stage, first by the aid of the camera after the event, and more recently on the spot and directly. We may speak of a fifth wave, from the 1980s on, with the enormous technological advances in the form of video, cables and satellites, in Norway and other countries accompanied by privatization of radio and television, as well as digital technology and entirely new pathways of communication. With the plethora of television channels, a decentralization has also taken place, so that there are many synopticons. But there are certainly also many panopticons, many surveillance systems. The decentralized, narrowly oriented panopticons may quickly be combined into large broad-ranging systems by simple technological devices, covering large categories of people in full detail. So may, on given important occasions, the various decentralized synopticons, and in terms of general content the synopticons are strikingly similar.

In his account of society as developing *from* a situation where the many see the few *to* a situation where the few see the many, Foucault fails to take into account all of the major waves of synoptical development briefly outlined above. Perhaps he could not foresee the developments in the 1980s and 1990s, but the major trends were certainly visible in 1975.

To some extent the media waves have supplemented or added on to each other. For example, the radio has adjusted to television and become the medium of the kitchen, the car and the beach, and in Norway the local newspapers have so far survived despite television. But the media waves have also replaced each other. Norway as well as Sweden have very recently seen a downward trend in newspaper circulation, probably partly caused by competition from television and other modern media. At the same time the older media, like the newspapers (at least the tabloid papers) and the radio, have changed form (large headlines, large pictures, short texts) as well as content (entertainment), bringing them within the orbit of the culture of television. It appears that television has become a model for the old media (Mathiesen, 1993: 296–7). The most typical medium where the many see the few, the clearest contrast to Foucault's panopticism, has in other words developed dramatically, either directly or through its influence on the older media.

2. Second, the panoptical surveillance structure and the media structure
are parallel in that they are archaic, or 'ancient', as means or potential
means of power in society.

Clearly it is Foucault's view that the history of the panoptical structure as
a main model commenced in the late 1700s and the early 1800s, though he
also mentions historical lines going further back, and he does mention that
the panoptical techniques taken 'one by one' have 'a long history behind
them' (1979: 224). This historical understanding is expressed through the
dramatic *break*, which Foucault emphasized so strongly, from the control
policy of the mid-1700s to that of the mid-1800s.

This historical understanding must be wrong. It seems closer to the facts
that a panoptical system, though strongly developed during the most recent
two centuries, has ancient historical roots; that not only individual surveillance techniques, but the very model of the panoptical surveillance system,
goes back to the early Christian era or before. Indeed, in the Gospel of
Luke (Luke 2:1) it is stated: 'And it came to pass in those days that there
went out a decree from Caesar Augustus that all the world shall be taxed.
And this taxing was first made when Cirenius was governor of Syria. And
all went to be taxed, everyone into his own city.' The Roman State, in other
words, undertook such a large task as to tax, and thereby register, what
was at the time 'all the world' in the archives of the state. The surveillance
was hardly always successful as a control measure; Herod failed in his
search for at least one first-born male child. But this is not the last time
surveillance systems have failed to 'hit'; it is indeed a characteristic also of
modern data systems. Probably all great state structures in history have had
such systems, at least in elementary form. In our own more recent history,
three institutions have been particularly important: the church, the Inquisition and the military. I will return to them shortly.

Synopticism is equally ancient, with the emphasis on maximum diffusion
from a few leading figures of visual impressions, sound impressions and
other impressions. Foucault emphasizes the ancient nature of this structure,
though he does not relate it to the media — his point is that it *is* the old
form. The older institutions of spectacle differed in several respects from
the modern ones. In the older context, people were gathered together; in
the modern media context, the 'audience' has increasingly been delocalized
so that people have become isolated from each other. In the older context,
'sender' and 'receiver' were in each other's proximity, be it in the ancient
theatre or the festivals and image-building of the Colosseum; in the modern
media context, distance between the two may be great. Such differences,
and especially the general fragmentation which is alluded to here, may have
consequences for persuasion as well as protest. Yet, the similarity and
continuity is also striking.

The main point here is that the models of both systems go back far
beyond the 1700s, and that they have historical roots in central social and
political institutions. What has happened in the 1800s, and especially in the
1900s, is that organizational and technological changes have advanced the

use of *both models* by leaps and bounds, thus making them into two basic characteristics of modernity.

3. Third, and most importantly, panopticism and synopticism *have developed in intimate interaction, even fusion, with each other.* The same institutions have often been panoptical as well as synoptical. Historically we have many examples of this.

The Roman Catholic Church, with the confession during which many isolated individuals confide their secrets one by one to the unseen representative of the Church, has functioned panoptically as a setting in which the few — the priests — have seen and surveyed the many — the people of the town. Simultaneously, the Catholic Church has definitely functioned synoptically, with its enormous cathedrals intentionally placed in very visible locations for synoptical admiration, drawing large masses of people to listen to the sermon, and with the Pope speaking from the balcony of St Peter's on Easter Day.

The Inquisition was panoptical; indeed, panopticism was its very purpose in relation to heresy and witchcraft from the 1200s on: 'As a spider it sat there on guard, watching so that catholicism was not exposed to harmful influences from abroad or from corrupted souls within the country itself' (Henningsen, 1981: 28; translated from the Danish by the present author). But it was also synoptical, with its manifestations of great authority through its many visitations, with the highly visible Inquisitor up front, throughout the communities of the enormous Spanish empire.

The military has always had a strict disciplinary hierarchy providing possibilities for hidden surveillance from the upper echelons of the system. But it has also been synoptical with highly visible military leaders victoriously entering the city after the battle.

Even more clearly the interaction — indeed, fusion — of panopticism and synopticism may be seen in the old prison chapels from the 1800s. They were panoptical in that the minister could see all of the prisoners sitting isolated in their booths, but they were at the same time synoptical in that the prisoners, from their booths, could see only one person — the minister in the pulpit.

In modern times, the interaction has taken new form, and concrete fusion is even more pronounced. First of all, in our century, panopticism and synopticism have developed on the basis of a joint technology. The telegraph and the radio have, as I have already mentioned, been methods on both sides. In our own time, television, video, satellites, cables and modern computer development are joint technological features. In his book *1984* George Orwell described panopticism and synopticism in their ultimate form as completely merged: through a screen in your living room you saw Big Brother, just as Big Brother saw you. We have not come this far, but we clearly see tendencies for panopticism and synopticism to merge into one. A fusion takes place between the two structures in the 'electronic super highway'. Today it is technologically entirely possible to have a large number of consumers synoptically watch television and order and pay for the commodities advertised, as well as undertaking a number of other economic transactions, while the producers of the commodities panoptically survey everyone, controlling the consumers' ability to pay, ensuring that payment takes place, or interrupting the transaction if solvency does not obtain.

Great emphasis has recently been placed on various forms of interactive mass media. The Norwegian author and lawyer Jon Bing has described the 'interactive novel', where the receiver participates with active inputs, thus creating the novel in cooperation and interaction with the original author. His book on the topic has the suggestive title *The Book is Dead! Long Live the Book!* (Bing, 1984). The Internet, World Wide Web and the numerous video games which have entered the market are further cases in point. The receiver actively enters the system and takes out the information needed, combines it with still other pieces of information in numerous novel ways, and actively transmits his own information to others through the Web pages, or, in the case of games, activates actors in various ways through the game. However, two points should be kept in mind, especially in connection with the Internet as the most advanced point-to-point interactive system:

First, contrary to what academics in the universities (who have relatively free access to the Internet and the Web) tend to trust and believe, the Internet and the Web are hardly for 'everyone'. For one thing, installation and use of the Internet costs money. This in itself makes its distribution skewed in terms of class and status. Furthermore, the use of the Internet is predominantly a male preoccupation. In Norway, about 75 percent of the users are men, in spite of the fact that access is more evenly distributed. In addition, there is a center–periphery dimension involved – in Norway, an industrialized and urbanized society, the use of the Internet is heavily located in the capital city and immediate surroundings: 35 percent of the inhabitants of Oslo have access to the Internet in one capacity or another, while the percentages in the regions are far lower. All of this points towards a new class division in terms of information and communication.

Second, capital increasingly sees the Internet as a source of profit, and economic and political control of the Internet is currently becoming an issue. This goes to the heart of the matter. In Norway, the media company Schibsted, small by international standards but a giant within Scandinavia, has recently launched a new Internet 'concept'. In cooperation with Norway's largest cable owner, the company offers access to the Internet though the TV-cable. With a special, high velocity modem connecting the cable to the computer, the speed with which the Internet is activated and used is increased between 70 and 100 times compared with an ordinary modem. It is also cheaper. Transmission of video, television, as well as far more advanced Web pages than we have at present are made possible. This makes the Internet commercially extremely interesting. Schibsted's plan, which the company has made fully public, is not to make the customers publish their own material on the Internet. The idealistic initial period of the truly interactive Internet with a 'flat' point-to-point structure is thus coming to an end, and the Internet is rapidly and in the near future developing into what may be called *an interactive one-way medium*: it is interactive in the sense that you may choose what you would like to see, but it is one-way in the sense that Schibsted bars you from sending information for others to see. Schibsted provides you with especially designed and politically determined commercial entertainment and information services, and invites you to spend time and money choosing between and in the numerous packages they offer. The Telenor Company (a state-owned and capitalistic, highly competitive version of the earlier Government Administration of Telephone, Telegraph, Radio and Broadcasting Services) has not yet launched a similar offer. Instead, it merged with Schibsted early in 1997 (in addition to swallowing some 80 small private companies in the area). Under the new common name, Scandinavia Online, the two companies plan to own and run most of the Internet in Norway. In developing from a 'flat' point-to-point *grunder* phase to a commercial monopolized one-way structure in relation to the general public, the Internet resembles the developmental process of other media. In short, even in the most modern interactive media, the basic conditions are increasingly and in the near future being set from above rather than from below, from the level of capital rather than from the level of the participants, though they may still contain *an illusion* of two parties on an equal footing. One of the parties, the party with economic and political power, systematically and increasingly defines the criteria or frames of reference for the information which is to be stored, which is to be available, and which subsequently may be selected, combined and recombined. The human actor in this context is a chooser and not a creator. The Norwegian sociologist Tom Johansen has formulated it in general terms as follows, and his formulation is highly relevant to the modern mass media:

> When I have now demonstrated that the actions of daily life increasingly constitute choices among given alternatives, and that *the choice* as action is becoming predominant, it is implied that action life is dislocated: Homo Creator yields to Homo Elector. It is a question of choice actions: not to manufacture things yourself or produce, but to select, to choose among the most handy utility articles, such is our time.
>
> (Johansen, 1981: 112, translated from the Norwegian by the present author)

What about power?

Before concluding, an elaboration is necessary as far as synopticism goes: is *power* actually represented in the media? This is an important question. To repeat, Foucault wrote that 'the pomp of sovereignty, the necessarily spectacular manifestations of power', have today gradually yielded to 'the daily exercise of surveillance, in a panopticism in which the vigilance of the intersecting gazes was soon to render useless both the eagle and the sun'.

The power of visible and concrete rulers was and is fading away. This perspective fits nicely with Foucault' s view of power in modern society: the visible actors' power in central institutions of state and society is blurred, indistinct and even unimportant; instead, power is a phenomenon permeating society as invisible micropower.

If this is true, and if those we meet and see in the media are just ornamental figures without power, Foucault's omission of synopticism might not be so serious.

I do not think it is true, and find reason to give an affirmative answer to the question of whether power — indeed, great power — is located in concrete individuals and concrete delimited groups as represented in our mass media. The eagle and the sun have not been extinguished, but are expressed in a different way. This is probably especially so in the most visible media. It does not mean that Foucault's micropower, which cannot be delimited to definite performers but which silently permeates the social fabric, is unimportant. Both perspectives, the perspective of micropower but also that of *the actor's* power, are necessary.

In synoptic space, particular news reporters, more or less brilliant media personalities and commentators who are continuously visible and seen are of particular importance. To understand them just as ornamental figures is to underestimate them. They actively filter and shape information; as has been widely documented in media research, they produce news (for an early documentation, see Cohen and Young, 1973; see also Tuchman, 1978); they place topics on the agenda and avoid placing topics on the agenda (Protess and McCombs, 1991). To be sure, all of this is performed within the context of a broader hidden agenda of political or economic interests, so to speak behind the media (Curran and Seaton, 1988; Murdock, 1988). But this does not detract from the importance and role of the visible actors, on the stage. Stage setters also operate behind and outside the scene. But the visible personalities cooperate with them, contributing significantly in their way — as creative mouthpieces — to the collective and enormously important staging of the great moments in the nation and the world, such as the staging of the Gulf War, so favourable to American interests, in 1991 (see Johnsen and Mathiesen, 1991, 1992; Ottosen, 1992), and the Olympic Games in Atlanta and the Republican Party Convention, both in 1996.

It is interesting to see what public opinion polls tell us about people's *confidence* in media personalities. Two nationwide representative Norwegian studies from 1991 and 1993 revealed very great confidence throughout the Norwegian population in prominent television personalities — particular charismatic reporters, commentators and so on. As far as it may be measured through opinions polls of this kind, these reporters and commentators did not only compete effectively, in people's minds, with very central and internationally known and popular politicians. They were even partly ahead in terms of confidence. This brings us to the core of their importance: it appears that the classical and greatly influential 'two step hypothesis' about the influence of the media, in which opinion leaders in outside society are seen as links and transmitters of media messages from the media to the larger population (Lazarsfeld et al., 1948), must be revised. As the Norwegian sociologist Ole Kristian Hjemdal has pointed out,[3] television has produced television personalities who *themselves*, from the screen, function as opinion leaders and links between the media message and people — well known, dear to us, and on the face of it close to us.

But this does not end the story of power. Second, we must add what we know about who are allowed to enter the media from the outside to express their views. A number of international and Norwegian studies have shown that they systematically belong to *the institutional elites*. Those who are allowed to enter are systematically men — not women — from the higher social strata, with power in political life, private industry and public bureaucracy (a summary of the findings is provided in Mathiesen, 1993: 152–8). From a democratic point of view, the dominance of the television personalities is serious enough through the filtering of information and so on which we know they perform. The problem of democracy is in a decisive way enlarged by the dominance of the institutional elites.

But do not many people with power actively try to avoid the limelight of public attention? Certainly, today as in former times. Nevertheless, they are in an interesting and important way represented by hired information professionals. This point of view has been forcefully presented by the Norwegian sociologist and journalist Sigurd Allern (1992, quotes translated from the Norwegian by the present author). Allern writes that

> . . . the point is not only that the media and journalists *choose* sources. The roles may also be reversed, so that the sources choose the media; they operate professionally and in a goal-oriented way to establish the premises for news production. *The sources* have become constantly more professionalized.

In business, public administration and large-scale organizations there has taken place during the past few decades 'a systematic organizational development to meet the bureaucratic quest for news on the part of the press' (p. 94). 'Information', which in actual fact is influence, has 'become an integrated part of the activity of industrial companies, financial institutions, ministries, police, municipal services and professional organizations' (p. 94). The information professionals have become highly visible and valuable sources of information for the media; informational activity has become an occupation. The information professionals are trained to filter information, and to present images which are favourable to the institution or organization in question.

Take business life as a concrete example. 'Norwegian Hydro' [a large and, from a business point of view, successful Norwegian company with many international investments], Allern writes, 'has on a nationwide basis about 60 employees engaged, Statoil [the Norwegian Oil Company, owned by the state] has fewer, but both have a larger number of employees in this sector than the editorial staff of the *Labourer* [*Arbeiderbladet*, the main newspaper of the Labour Party, currently in power in Norway]' (p. 100). In 1991 the Norwegian Bank Association and the four largest commercial banks reported that they had 32 information professionals. Also in 1991, the Norwegian Insurance Association and the 7 largest insurance companies had 41 employees in their information departments. If those who are partly engaged in other tasks as well as those working in industrial trade organizations are included, the total number of information professionals in Norwegian industry and business may be estimated to be over 1000 (p. 100). This figure is very large for a small country like Norway; comparable British and American figures are of course much larger still. A number of key posts as information professionals are filled by people who earlier were employees in the Norwegian Broadcasting Company and by people from the press. 'The situation', Allern writes, 'at times resembles how people are bought in the upper divisions of soccer'.

Control functions

Finally, I arrive at the question of control functions. I use the concept here in its simplest possible form, as change in behaviour or attitude in a wide sense, following from the influence of others. 'Control', then, is something more than 'surveillance'; it implies the regulation of behaviour or attitude which may follow for example from surveillance. I use the concept of 'discipline', Foucault's term, as a synonym.

There is an ongoing discussion of whether panopticism and synopticism, surveillance and the media, in fact have the effect of control or discipline (Bottoms, 1983; Waldahl, 1989). The discussion should be taken beyond the effects of isolated, single measures or messages, which has characterized media research in particular. The question is the effects of the total pattern of surveillance measures or media messages. Thus, with regard to the media, the total Gestalt produced by the messages of television is much more important than the individual programme or even type of programme. The American media researcher George Gerbner and associates have pointed to this in a number of empirical works. As they succinctly put it:

> '[The point is a concept of] broad enculturation rather than of narrow changes in opinion or behavior. Instead of asking what communication 'variables' might propagate what kinds of individual behavior changes, we want to know what types of common consciousness whole systems of messages might cultivate. This is less like asking about preconceived fears and hopes and more like asking about the 'effects' of Christianity on one's views of the world or — as the Chinese *had* asked — of Confucianism on public morality.
>
> (Gerbner and Gross, 1976: 180)

The question is, then, the control or discipline of behaviour and attitude. That aspect of *panopticism* which consists of the growth of a modern veiled and secret surveillance industry, and which preoccupies us here, first of all controls or disciplines our *behaviour*. In this respect the modern surveillance systems are very different from the old panoptical prisons, which are also growing by leaps and bounds. The latter inflict great pain on those who inhabit them. But a vast amount of research shows that they have no effect, or at most a marginal effect, in terms of controlled behaviour (Mathiesen, 1990). Rather, I am thinking of the vast hidden apparatus, and the effect of this apparatus on people in usual or unusual political situations. Well aware of 'the intersecting gazes' of panopticism, but unable to point concretely to them — this is the nature of their secrecy — we arrange our affairs accordingly, perhaps without being fully aware of it. We remain, in our attitude, communists, left-oriented, or what have you, but adjust in terms of behaviour.

Two major examples come to mind. First, the McCarthy period in the US in the 1950s. I experienced the 1950s in McCarthy's own state, at the University of Wisconsin. Communists remained communists, but they became cautious, secretive and partly silent. Second, the activities of the Norwegian secret police from 1945 until the mid-1980s. Extensive unacceptable and illegal surveillance activities have recently been uncovered in an authoritative report delivered by a commission appointed by Parliament (The Lund Report, 1996). The report only verified what communists and other left-oriented groups had said for years. It contains numerous accounts of how communists remained communists and Marxist-Leninists remained Marxist-Leninists, but also of how they adjusted in terms of behaviour, became cautious and secretive, using cover names even for their children when attending political summer camps (it was documented that children down to the age of 11 had been registered). Psychological breakdowns, with repercussions throughout whole families, ensued. The argument that surveillance has negligible effect on behaviour was dramatically contradicted.

Other features of the political situation at the time were no doubt also important in both instances — the Cold War in the wake of the Second World War being one of them. But in the Norwegian case, widespread surveillance as well as the behavioural effects of it continued through the 1970s and 1980s, and to some extent even in the 1990s, and the effects on behaviour are concretely demonstrated.

What I have said here is, as far as it goes, in line with Foucault: to him, the fact that the torture of the docile body came to an end did not mean that the body ceased to be an object of attention. It just took place in a different way: 'The human body was entering a machinery of power that explores it, breaks it down and rearranges it' (1979: 138). But at the same time, as I have said before, he saw his book as 'a correlative history of the modern soul'. To repeat, by the control of the soul, vis-a-vis the control of the body, I understand him to mean the creation of human beings who control themselves through self-control.

My guess is that the souls in our time, and precisely in Foucault's sense as I understand it, above all belong to the other machinery, that of *synopticism,* and that James Gordon Bennett in fact was right when in 1836 he said just that about the mass media. My point is that synopticism, through the modern mass media in general and television in particular, first of all directs and controls or disciplines our *consciousness.* The concept of 'consciousness industry' (Enzenberger, 1974; Tuchman, 1981) is suggestive: to Enzenberger, the modern media encourage the 'industrialization of mind', 'they foster a consciousness conducive to advanced industrialism, just as some fifty years ago, earlier industrialists and efficiency experts transformed the body into an extension of the machine' (Tuchman, 1981: 84), thus — in my words — inducing self-control and making us fit into the requirements of modernity. Max Horkheimer and Theodor Adorno pointed to this process, in the context of their time, half a century ago in their analysis of the culture industry (Horkheimer and Adorno, 1947/1969), and their presentation seems all the more relevant today.

To repeat, it is the total pattern or Gestalt rather than the individual programme or type of programmes which functions this way, à la Gerbner, like Christianity 'on one's views of the world'. Surely, there are variations which are obvious topics for research, and which have been extensively researched: when people have first-hand knowledge, when the issues are close to people's everyday life, and when people have access to alternative information, and so on, the effects are smaller. Indeed, this is also how Christianity worked and continues to work. But the variations should not make us overlook the effect of the total message system. The total message inculcates or produces a general understanding of the world, a *world paradigm* if you like, which emphasizes personal and individual, the deviant, the shuddering, the titillating — as alluded to already, the entertaining in a wide sense (Postman, 1985). The paradigm is successful because it is received in the context of a need — satisfies a need — for escape from the concrete misery of the world, very much like the Church which offered rescue and salvation in the hereafter. It is by satisfying the need for escape that people are made to acquiesce, accept and fit into the requirements of our society. In this sense, the Church and television are real functional alternatives, a relationship which has been explored in such detail and so eloquently by James Curran (1988).

Each from their side, like a pincer, panopticon and synopticon thus subdue or even make silent what Pierre Bourdieu calls 'the heterodox debate' (Bourdieu, 1977: Chapter 4), that is, the debate which raises the basic critical questions concerning the very foundation of our life and existence. We are left, again in Bourdieu's terminology, with 'the orthodox debate', where the answers to the basic questions are taken for granted, and the debate concerns details and remains on the surface. In bold relief: surveillance, panopticon, makes us silent about that which breaks fundamentally with the taken-for-granted because we are made afraid to break with it. Modern television, synopticon, makes us silent because we do not have anything to talk about that might initiate the break.

It does not improve matters that panopticon and synopticon reciprocally feed on each other. Those parts of modern panopticon which I am concerned with here, the secret apparatuses of surveillance, try to keep synopticon at arm's length. After all, they wish to live under cover. But this is precisely where other parts of panopticon, in and close to the old prison, have their function. News from these parts of panopticon — news about prisoners, escapes, robberies, murder — are the best pieces of news which synopticon — television and the tabloid newspapers — can find. Inside synopticon, which devours this news, the material is purged of everything but the purely criminal — what was originally a small segment of a human being becomes the whole human being — whereupon the material is hurled back into the open society as stereotypes and panic-like, terrifying stories about individual cases, thus completely contradicting Foucault's thesis that punishment tends to become the most hidden part of the penal process. The execution in Paris in 1757 becomes, as a spectacle, peanuts compared to the executions (real or metaphoric) on the screens of modern television. This way, a basis is established for more resources to be given not only to the expansion of prisons, but also to the concealed panoptical surveillance systems: the modern European computerized registration and surveillance systems mentioned earlier are, on the formal level, motivated by crime prevention. But empirically we can safely say that they hardly prevent much crime. The 'hit' figures as far as official crime goes are extremely low (Mathiesen, 1996: 28–9). In the light of the mass media image of crime, the low 'hit' figures are taken as a sign that still more resources are needed. And so it continues in a circle.

Taken as a whole, things are much *worse* than Michel Foucault imagined. The total situation clearly calls for political resistance (Mathiesen, 1982). But to muster such double resistance is a difficult task, because the call for resistance may — in line with what I have argued in this article — be silenced by the very panopticon and synopticon which we wish to counteract. In the years to come, much effort and lots of time should therefore be devoted to the search for the roads to resistance.

Notes

1. Oral information from the Swedish historian Erik Anners.
2. The concept was first used by the Danish sociologist Frank Henriksen, in a review of a book I had written on the topic I deal with here (Henriksen, 1985; Mathiesen, 1985).
3. Oral communication to the author.

References

Allern, Sigurd (1992) *Kildenes makt. Ytringsfrihetens politiske økonomi* (The Power of the Sources. The Political Economy of the Freedom of Expression). Oslo: Pax Publishers.

Bing, Jon (1984) *Boken er død! Leve boken! og andre essays om informasjonspolitikk* (The Book is Dead! Long Live the Book! and Other Essays in the Politics of Information). Oslo: Norwegian Universities Press.

Bottoms, Anthony E. (1983) 'Neglected Features of Contemporary Penal Systems', in D. Garland and P. Young (eds) *The Power to Punish. Contemporary Penality and Social Analysis*, pp. 166–202. London: Heinemann.

Bourdieu, Pierre (1977) *Outline of a Theory of Practice*. Cambridge: Cambridge University Press.

Cohen, Stanley (1985) *Visions of Social Control. Crime, Punishment and Classification*. Cambridge: Polity Press.

Cohen, Stanley and Jock Young (eds) (1973) *The Manufacture of News. Social Problems, Deviance and the Mass Media*. London: Constable.

Curran, James (1988) 'Communications, Power and Social Order', in Michael Gurevitsch, Tony Bennett, James Curran and Janet Woollacott (eds) *Culture, Society and the Media*, pp. 202–35. London: Methuen.

Curran, James and Jean Seaton (1988) *Power Without Responsibility. The Press and Broadcasting in Britain*. London: Routledge.

De Fleur, Melvin and Sandra Ball-Rokeach (1989) *Theories of Mass Communication*. New York: Longman.

Enzenberger, Hans Magnus (1974) *The Consciousness Industry*. New York: Seabury Press.

Foucault, Michel (1979) *Discipline and Punish. The Birth of the Prison*. New York: Vintage.

Gerbner, George and Larry Gross (1976) 'Living with Television. The Violence Profile', *Journal of Communication* 26 (2): 173–98.

Henningsen, Gustav (1981) *Heksenes advokat* (The Witches' Advocate). Copenhagen: Delta Publishers.

Henriksen, Frank (1985) Anmeldelse av T. Mathiesen: *Seer-samfundet* (Review of T. Mathiesen: The Viewer Society), *Sociolog-nyt* 96: 35–6.

Horkheimer, Max and Theodor Adorno (1947/1969) 'Kulturindustrie. Aufklärung als Massenbetrug', in *Dialektik der Aufflärung*. Frankfurt: S. Fischer Verlag.

Johnsen, Jan and Thomas Mathiesen (eds) (1991) *Mediekrigen. Søkelys på massemedienes dekning av Golfkrigen* (The Media War. The Media Coverage of the Gulf War under Scrutiny). Oslo: Cappelen.

Johnsen, Jan and Thomas Mathiesen (1992) 'A War in the Name of Freedom', *The Nordicom Review of Nordic Mass Communication Research* 2: 3–19.

Johansen, Tom (1981) 'Kulissenes regi' (The Effects of Staging), in K. Andenæs, T. Johansen and T. Mathiesen (eds) *Maktens ansikter. Perspektiver på makt og maktforskning* (The Faces of Power. Perspectives on Power and Power Research), pp. 104–46. Oslo: Gyldendal Publishers.

Lazarsfeld, Paul F., Bernard Berelson and Hazel Gaudet (1948) *The People's Choice. How the Voter makes up his Mind in a Presidential Campaign*. New York: Columbia University Press.

McMahon (1992) *The Persistent Prison? Rethinking Decarceration and Penal Reform*. Toronto: Toronto University Press.

Mathiesen, Thomas (1982) *Makt og motmakt* (Power and Counter-Power). Oslo: Pax Publishers.

Mathiesen, Thomas (1985) *Tittarsamhället. Om medier och kontrol i det moderna samhället* (The Viewer Society. On Media and Control in Modern Society). Göteborg: Korpen Publishers.

Mathiesen, Thomas (1990) *Prison on Trial. A Critical Assessment*. London: Sage Publications.

Mathiesen, Thomas (1993) *Makt og medier. En innføring i mediesosiologi* (Power and the Media. An Introduction to Media Sociology). Oslo: Pax Publishers.

Mathiesen, Thomas (1996) *Er Schengen noe for Norge? Et bidrag til europeisk politiforskning* (Is Schengen Something for Norway? A Contribution to European Police Research). Oslo: Institute for Sociology of Law Series No. 54.

Murdock, Graham (1988) 'Large Corporations and the Control of the Communications Industries', in Michael Gurevitsch, Tony Bennett, James Curran and Janet Woollacott (eds) *Culture, Society and the Media*, pp. 118–50. London: Methuen.

Ottosen, Rune (1992) 'The Allied Forces' "Media Victory" in the Gulf. Waterloo for Journalism?', *The Nordicom Review of Nordic Mass Communication Research* 2: 31–47.

Postman, Neil (1985) *Amusing Ourselves to Death. Public Discourse in the Age of Show Business*. London: Heinemann.

Protess, David and Maxwell McCombs (eds) (1991) *Agenda Setting: Readings on the Media, Public Opinion and Policy Making*. Hillsdale, NJ: Lawrence Erlbaum.

The Lund Report (1996) *Rapport til Stortinget fra kommisjonen som ble nedsatt av Stortinget for å granske påstander om ulovlig overvåking av norske borgere (Lund-rapporten)* (Report to Parliament from the Commission Appointed by Parliament to Investigate Allegations Concerning Illegal Surveillance of Norwegian Citizens.) Document No. 15, 1995–96, delivered to Parliament 28 March 1996.

Tuchman, Gaye (1978) *Making News. A Study in the Construction of Reality*. New York: The Free Press.

Tuchman, Gaye (1981) 'Myth and the Consciousness Industry: A New Look at the Effects of the Mass Media', in Elihu Katz and Tamás Szecskö (eds) *Mass Media and Social Change*, pp. 83–100. London: Sage.

Waldahl, Ragnar (1989) *Mediepåvirkning* (Media Influence). Oslo: Ad Notam Publishers.

234   *Theoretical Criminology*

THOMAS MATHIESEN is Professor of Sociology of Law at the University of Oslo, Norway, and the author of numerous books and other publications on prisons, criminal policy, social and political control systems and the mass media. Many of his books have been translated into English, German, Italian, Swedish and Danish. He was one of the founders of KROM — Norwegian Association for Penal Reform, where he is still an active participant.

[5]

The surveillant assemblage

Kevin D. Haggerty and Richard V. Ericson

ABSTRACT

George Orwell's 'Big Brother' and Michel Foucault's 'panopticon' have dominated discussion of contemporary developments in surveillance. While such
metaphors draw our attention to important attributes of surveillance, they also
miss some recent dynamics in its operation. The work of Gilles Deleuze and Félix
Guattari is used to analyse the convergence of once discrete surveillance systems.
The resultant 'surveillant assemblage' operates by abstracting human bodies
from their territorial settings, and separating them into a series of discrete flows.
These flows are then reassembled in different locations as discrete and virtual
'data doubles'. The surveillant assemblage transforms the purposes of surveillance and the hierarchies of surveillance, as well as the institution of privacy.

KEYWORDS: Surveillance; assemblage; Deleuze; panopticon; social theory

INTRODUCTION

One of the most recognizable figures in cultural theory is the flâneur as
analysed by Walter Benjamin (1983). A creature of nineteenth-century
Paris, the flâneur absorbs himself in strolling through the metropolis
where he is engaged in a form of urban detective work. Concealed in the
invisibility of the crowd, he follows his fancies to investigate the streets and
arcades, carving out meaning from the urban landscape. Possessing a 'sovereignty based in anonymity and observation' (Tester 1994: 5), the flâneur
characterizes the urban environment and the experience of modernity.

There has been an exponential multiplication of visibility on our city
streets. Where the flâneur was involved in an individualistic scrutiny of the
city's significations, the population itself is now increasingly transformed
into signifiers for a multitude of organized surveillance systems. Benjamin

recognized the importance of even the earliest prototypes of such tech-nologies, observing how the development of photography helped under-mine the anonymity which was central to the flâneur by giving each face a single name and hence a single meaning (Benjamin 1983: 48).

Surveillance has become a salient topic for theoretical reflection, and this interest coincides with the quantitative increase in surveillance in western societies. However, this paper does not propose to provide a com-prehensive overview of these systems of observation. A number of other authors have documented developments in this rapidly changing area (Staples 1997; Bogard 1996; Dandecker 1990; Lyon 1994; Gandy 1993). Instead, we view surveillance as one of the main institutional components of late modernity (Giddens 1990). Our aim is to reconsider some of the more familiar theoretical preoccupations about this topic. We do so by drawing from the works of Gilles Deleuze and Félix Guattari to suggest that we are witnessing a convergence of what were once discrete surveillance systems to the point that we can now speak of an emerging 'surveillant assemblage'. This assemblage operates by abstracting human bodies from their territorial settings and separating them into a series of discrete flows. These flows are then reassembled into distinct 'data doubles' which can be scrutinized and targeted for intervention. In the process, we are witnessing a rhizomatic leveling of the hierarchy of surveillance, such that groups which were previously exempt from routine surveillance are now increas-ingly being monitored.

THEORIZING SURVEILLANCE: ORWELL AND FOUCAULT

Writing well in advance of the contemporary intensification of surveillance technologies, Orwell (1949) presented a prescient vision. In his futuristic nation of Oceana, citizens are monitored in their homes by a telescreen, a device which both projects images and records behaviour in its field of vision. The 'thought police' co-ordinate this extensive monitoring effort, operating as agents of a centralized totalitarian state which uses surveil-lance primarily as a means to maintain social order and conformity. Not all citizens, however, are singled out for such scrutiny. The upper and middle classes are intensely monitored, while the vast majority of the population, the underclass 'proles', are simply left to their own devices.

The fact that we continue to hear frequent cautions about '1984' or 'Big Brother' speaks to the continued salience of Orwell's cautionary tale. In the intervening decades, however, the abilities of surveillance technologies have surpassed even his dystopic vision. Writing at the cusp of the develop-ment of computing machines, he could not have envisioned the remark-able marriage of computers and optics which we see today. Furthermore, his emphasis on the state as the agent of surveillance now appears too restricted in a society where both state and non-state institutions are involved in massive efforts to monitor different populations. Finally, Orwell's prediction that the 'proles' would largely be exempt from surveillance seems simply wrong in light of the extension and intensification of surveillance across all sectors of society.

Michel Foucault's (1977) analysis of the panopticon provides the other dominant metaphor for understanding contemporary surveillance. In part, Foucault extends Orwell's fears, but his analysis also marks a significant departure, as it situates surveillance in the context of a distinctive theory of power. The panopticon was a proposed prison design by eighteenth-century reformer Jeremy Bentham (1995). What distinguished this structure was an architecture designed to maximize the visibility of inmates who were to be isolated in individual cells such that they were unaware moment-to-moment whether they were being observed by guards in a central tower. More than a simple device for observation, the panopticon worked in conjunction with explicitly articulated behavioural norms as established by the emerging social sciences, in efforts to transform the prisoner's relation to him or her self. This disciplinary aspect of panoptic observation involves a productive soul training which encourages inmates to reflect upon the minutia of their own behaviour in subtle and ongoing efforts to transform their selves. Foucault proposed that the panopticon served as a diagram for a new model of power which extended beyond the prison to take hold in the other disciplinary institutions characteristic of this era, such as the factory, hospital, military, and school.

Foucault's analysis improves on Orwell's by reminding us of the degree to which the proles have long been the subject of intense scrutiny. In fact, Foucault accentuates how it was precisely this population – which was seen to lack the self-discipline required by the emerging factory system – that was singled out for a disproportionate level of disciplinary surveillance. Foucault also encourages us to acknowledge the role surveillance can play beyond mere repression; how it can contribute to the productive development of modern selves. Unfortunately, Foucault fails to directly engage contemporary developments in surveillance technology, focusing instead on transformations to eighteenth and nineteenth century total institutions. This is a curious silence, as it is these technologies which give his analysis particular currency among contemporary commentators on surveillance. Even authors predisposed to embrace many of Foucault's insights believe that rapid technological developments, particularly the rise of computerized databases, require us to rethink the panoptic metaphor. For example, Mark Poster (1990: 93) believes that we must now speak of a 'superpanopticon' while Diana Gordon (1987) suggests the term 'electronic panopticon' better captures the nature of the contemporary situation. But even these authors are in line with a general tendency in the literature to offer more and more examples of total or creeping surveillance, while providing little that is theoretically novel. For our purposes, rather than try and stretch Foucault's or Orwell's concepts beyond recognition so that they might better fit current developments, we draw from a different set of analytical tools to explore aspects of contemporary surveillance.

THE SURVEILLANT ASSEMBLAGE

The philosopher Gilles Deleuze only occasionally wrote directly on the topic of surveillance, usually in the context of his commentaries on Foucault's work (Deleuze 1986; 1992). In conjunction with his colleague Félix Guattari, however, he has provided us with a set of conceptual tools that allow us to re-think the operation of the emergent surveillance system, a system we call the 'surveillant assemblage'.

While Deleuze and Guattari were prolific inventors of concepts, we embrace only a few of their ideas. Undoubtedly, this means that we are not fully representing their thought. However, our approach is entirely in keeping with their philosophy which animates one to 'think otherwise': to approach theory not as something to genuflect before, but as a tool kit from which to draw selectively in light of the analytical task at hand (Deleuze and Foucault 1977: 208).

Deleuze and Guattari introduce a radical notion of multiplicity into phenomena which we traditionally approach as being discretely bounded, structured and stable. 'Assemblages' consist of a 'multiplicity of heterogeneous objects, whose unity comes solely from the fact that these items function together, that they "work" together as a functional entity' (Patton 1994: 158). They comprise discrete flows of an essentially limitless range of other phenomena such as people, signs, chemicals, knowledge and institutions. To dig beneath the surface stability of any entity is to encounter a host of different phenomena and processes working in concert. The radical nature of this vision becomes more apparent when one realizes how any particular assemblage is itself composed of different discrete assemblages which are themselves multiple.

Assemblages, for Deleuze and Guattari, are part of the state form. However, this notion of the state form should not be confused with those traditional apparatuses of governmental rule studied by political scientists. Instead, the state form is distinguished by virtue of its own characteristic set of operations; the tendency to create bounded physical and cognitive spaces, and introduce processes designed to capture flows. The state seeks to 'striate the space over which it reigns' (Deleuze and Guattari 1987: 385), a process which involves introducing breaks and divisions into otherwise free-flowing phenomena. To do so requires the creation of both spaces of comparison where flows can be rendered alike and centres of appropriation where these flows can be captured.

Flows exist prior to any particular assemblage, and are fixed temporarily and spatially by the assemblage. In this distinction between flows and assemblages, Deleuze and Guattari also articulate a distinction between forces and power. Forces consist of more primary and fluid phenomena,

and it is from such phenomena that power derives as it captures and striates such flows. These processes coalesce into systems of domination when
otherwise fluid and mobile states become fixed into more or less stable and
asymmetrical arrangements which allow for some to direct or govern the
actions of others (Patton 1994: 161).

It is desire which secures these flows and gives them their permanence
as an assemblage. For psychoanalysts, desire is typically approached as a
form of lack, as a yearning that we strive to satisfy. In contrast, Deleuze and
Guattari approach desire as an active, positive force that exists only in
determinate systems. Desire is a field of immanence, and is a force 'without
which no social system could ever come into being' (May 1993: 4). As such,
desire is the inner will of all processes and events; what Nietzsche refers to
as the 'will to power'. As we demonstrate below, a range of desires now
energize and serve to coalesce the surveillant assemblage, including the
desires for control, governance, security, profit and entertainment.

The remainder of this paper documents attributes of the surveillant
assemblage. Some caution is needed, however, at this point. To speak of *the*
surveillant assemblage risks fostering the impression that we are concerned
with a stable entity with its own fixed boundaries. In contrast, to the extent
that the surveillant assemblage exists, it does so as a potentiality, one that
resides at the intersections of various media that can be connected for
diverse purposes. Such linkages can themselves be differentiated according
to the degree to which they are *ad hoc* or institutionalized. By accentuating
the emergent and unstable characteristic of the surveillant assemblage we
also draw attention to the limitations of traditional political strategies that
seek to confront the quantitative increase in surveillance. As it is multiple,
unstable and lacks discernible boundaries or responsible governmental
departments, the surveillant assemblage cannot be dismantled by prohibiting a particularly unpalatable technology. Nor can it be attacked by
focusing criticism on a single bureaucracy or institution. In the face of multiple connections across myriad technologies and practices, struggles
against particular manifestations of surveillance, as important as they
might be, are akin to efforts to keep the ocean's tide back with a broom –
a frantic focus on a particular unpalatable technology or practice while the
general tide of surveillance washes over us all.

Perhaps we risk having something still more monumental swept away in
the tide. Recall Foucault's (1970: 387) controversial (and frequently misunderstood) musings at the end of *The Order of Things*. In this conclusion
to his archaeology of how the understanding of Man has been transformed
in different epochs as humanity came into contact with different forces,
Foucault suggests that

> If those arrangements were to disappear as they appeared, if some event
> of which we can at the moment do no more than sense the possibility . . .
> were to cause them to crumble, as the ground of classical thought did, at
> the end of the eighteenth century, then one can certainly wager that

man would be erased, like a face drawn in sand at the edge of the sea. (Foucault 1970: 387)

Among the proliferation of late-modern forces which are candidates for contributing to such a radical transformation we can include the intensification of technologized forms of observation.

COMPONENT PARTS

The analysis of surveillance tends to focus on the capabilities of a number of discrete technologies or social practices. Analysts typically highlight the proliferation of such phenomena and emphasize how they cumulatively pose a threat to civil liberties. We are only now beginning to appreciate that surveillance is driven by the desire to bring systems together, to combine practices and technologies and integrate them into a larger whole. It is this tendency which allows us to speak of surveillance as an assemblage, with such combinations providing for exponential increases in the degree of surveillance capacity. Rather than exemplifying Orwell's totalitarian state-centred Oceana, this assemblage operates across both state and extra-state institutions.

Something as apparently discrete as the electronic monitoring of offenders increasingly integrates a host of different surveillance capabilities to the point that

> no one is quite sure any longer what [Electronic Monitoring] is. Voice, radio, programmed contact, remote alcohol testing, and automated reporting station ('kiosk') technologies proliferate and are used both singly and in a dizzying array of combinations. (Renzeman 1998: 5)

The police are continually looking for ways to integrate their different computer systems and databases, as exemplified by ongoing efforts by the FBI forensics section to link together databases for fingerprints, ballistics and DNA (Philipkoski 1998). Still another example of such combinations is the regional police computer system in Central Scotland

> Phone conversations, reports, tip-offs, hunches, consumer and social security databases, crime data, phone bugging, audio, video and pictures, and data communications are inputted into a seamless GIS [geographic information system], allowing a relational simulation of the time-space choreography of the area to be used in investigation and monitoring by the whole force. The Chief Constable states: 'what do we class as intelligence in my new system in the force? Everything! The whole vast range of information that comes into the possession of a police force during a twenty four hour period will go on to my corporate database. Everything that every person and vehicle is associated with'. (Norris and Armstrong (1997) quoted in Graham 1998: 492)

In situations where it is not yet practicable to technologically link surveillance systems, human contact can serve to align and coalesce discrete systems. For example, various 'multi-agency' approaches to policing are institutionalized. Originally, such efforts were wedded to a welfarist ideology of service delivery, but in recent years social service agencies have been drawn into the harder edge of social control (O'Malley and Palmer 1996; Ericson and Haggerty 1999). The coming together (face-to-face, or through electronic mediation) of social workers, health professionals, police and educators to contemplate the status of an 'at risk' individual combines the cumulative knowledge derived from the risk profiling surveillance systems particular to each of these institutions.

THE BODY

A great deal of surveillance is directed toward the human body. The observed body is of a distinctively hybrid composition. First it is broken down by being abstracted from its territorial setting. It is then reassembled in different settings through a series of data flows. The result is a decorporealized body, a 'data double' of pure virtuality.

The monitored body is increasingly a cyborg; a flesh-technology-information amalgam (Haraway 1991). Surveillance now involves an interface of technology and corporeality and is comprised of those 'surfaces of contact or interfaces between organic and non-organic orders, between life forms and webs of information, or between organs/body parts and entry/projection systems (e.g., keyboards, screens)' (Bogard 1996: 33). These hybrids can involve something as direct as tagging the human body so that its movements through space can be recorded, to the more refined reconstruction of a person's habits, preferences, and lifestyle from the trails of information which have become the detritus of contemporary life. The surveillant assemblage is a visualizing device that brings into the visual register a host of heretofore opaque flows of auditory, scent, chemical, visual, ultraviolet and informational stimuli. Much of the visualization pertains to the human body, and exists beyond our normal range of perception.

Rousseau opens *The Social Contract* with his famous proclamation that 'Man was born free, and he is everywhere in chains'. To be more in keeping with the human/machine realities of the twenty-first century, his sentiment would better read: 'Humans are born free, and are immediately electronically monitored'. If such a slogan seems unduly despairing, one might consider the new electronic ankle bracelet for infants, trademarked HUGS, which is being marketed to hospitals as

> a fully supervised and tamper-resistant protection system that automatically activates once secured around an infant's ankle or wrist. Staff [are] immediately alerted at a computer console of the newly activated tag, and can enter pertinent information such as names and medical

conditions. Password authorization is needed to move infants out of the designated protection area and – if an infant is not readmitted within a predetermined time limit – an alarm will sound. An alarm also sounds if an infant with a Hugs tag is brought near an open door at the perimeter of the protected area without a password being entered. The display console will then show the identification of the infant and the exit door on a facility map. Alternatively, doors may also be fitted with magnetic locks that are automatically activated. As well, Hugs can be configured to monitor the progress and direction of the abduction within the hospital. Weighing just 1/3 of an ounce, each ergonomically designed infant tag offers a number of other innovative features, including low-battery warning, the ability to easily interface with other devices such as CCTV cameras and paging systems and time and date stamping. (Canadian Security 1998)

Professor Kevin Warwick of Reading University is the self-proclaimed 'first cyborg,' having implanted a silicon chip transponder in his forearm (Bevan 1999). The surveillance potential of this technology has been rapidly embraced to monitor pets. A microchip in a pet's skin can be read with an electronic device which connects a unique identifying number on the microchip to details of the pet's history, ownership and medical record. Warwick has proposed that implanted microchips could be used to scrutinize the movement of employees, and to monitor money transfers, medical records and passport details. He also suggests that

> anyone who wanted access to a gun could do so only if they had one of these implants . . . Then if they actually try and enter a school or build-ing that doesn't want them in there, the school computer would sound alarms and warn people inside or even prevent them having access. (Associated Press 1998)

These examples indicate that the surveillant assemblage relies on machines to make and record discrete observations. As such, it can be con-trasted with the early forms of disciplinary panopticism analysed by Foucault, which were largely accomplished by practitioners of the emer-gent social sciences in the eighteenth and nineteenth centuries. On a machine/human continuum, surveillance at that time leaned more toward human observation. Today, surveillance is more in keeping with the technological future hinted at by Orwell, but augmented by technologies he could not have even had nightmares about.

The surveillant assemblage does not approach the body in the first instance as a single entity to be molded, punished, or controlled. First it must be known, and to do so it is broken down into a series of discrete sig-nifying flows. Surveillance commences with the creation of a space of com-parison and the introduction of breaks in the flows that emanate from, or circulate within, the human body. For example, drug testing striates flows of chemicals, photography captures flows of reflected lightwaves, and lie detectors align and compare assorted flows of respiration, pulse and electricity. The body is itself, then, an assemblage comprised of myriad component parts and processes which are broken-down for purposes of observation. Patton (1994: 158) suggests that the concept of assemblage 'may be regarded as no more than an abstract conception of bodies of all kinds, one which does not discriminate between animate and inanimate bodies, individual or collective bodies, biological or social bodies'.

It has become a commonplace among cultural theorists to acknowledge the increasing fragmentation of the human body. Such an appreciation is evidenced in Grosz's (1995: 108) schematic suggestion that we need to think about the relationship between cities and bodies as

> collections of parts, capable of crossing the thresholds between substances to form linkages, machines, provisional and often temporary sub- or micro-groupings . . . their interrelations involve a fundamentally disunified series of systems, a series of disparate flows, energies, events, or entities, bringing together or drawing apart their more or less temporary alignments.

Likewise, the surveillant assemblage standardizes the capture of flesh/information flows of the human body. It is not so much immediately concerned with the direct physical relocation of the human body (although this may be an ultimate consequence), but with transforming the body into pure information, such that it can be rendered more mobile and comparable.

Such processes are put into operation from a host of scattered centres of calculation (Latour 1987) where ruptures are co-ordinated and toward which the subsequent information is directed. Such centres of calculation can include forensic laboratories, statistical institutions, police stations, financial institutions, and corporate and military headquarters. In these sites the information derived from flows of the surveillant assemblage are reassembled and scrutinized in the hope of developing strategies of governance, commerce and control.

In the figure of a body assembled from the parts of different corpses, Mary Shelly's *Frankenstein* spoke to early-modern anxieties about the potential consequences of unrestrained science and technology. Contemporary fears about the implications of mass public surveillance continue to emphasize the dark side of science. Today, however, we are witnessing the formation and coalescence of a new type of body, a form of becoming which transcends human corporeality and reduces flesh to pure information. Culled from the tentacles of the surveillant assemblage, this new body is our 'data double', a double which involves 'the multiplication of the individual, the constitution of an additional self' (Poster 1990: 97). Data doubles circulate in a host of different centres of calculation and serve as markers for access to resources, services and power in ways which are often unknown to its referent. They are also increasingly the objects toward which governmental and marketing practices are directed (Turow

1997). And while such doubles ostensibly refer back to particular individuals, they transcend a purely representational idiom. Rather than being accurate or inaccurate portrayals of real individuals, they are a form of pragmatics: differentiated according to how useful they are in allowing institutions to make discriminations among populations. Hence, while the surveillant assemblage is directed toward a particular cyborg flesh/technology amalgamation, it is productive of a new type of individual, one comprised of pure information.

RHIZOMATIC SURVEILLANCE

Deleuze and Guattari (1987) outline how 'rhizomes' are plants which grow in surface extensions through interconnected vertical root systems. The rhizome is contrasted with arborescent systems which are those plants with a deep root structure and which grow along branchings from the trunk. The rhizome metaphor accentuates two attributes of the surveillant assemblage: its phenomenal growth through expanding uses, and its leveling effect on hierarchies.

Rhizomatic Expansion

Rhizomes grow across a series of interconnected roots which throw up shoots in different locations. They 'grow like weeds' precisely because this is often what they are. A rhizome 'may be broken, shattered at a given spot, but it will start up again on one of its old lines, or on new lines' (Deleuze and Guattari 1987: 9). Surveillance has comparable expansive and regenerative qualities. It is now estimated that there are 500,000 surveillance cameras operating in Britain (Freeman 1999), where a city dweller can now expect to be caught on film every five minutes (Duffy 1999). Paul Virilio argues that this growth in observation has transformed the experience of entering the city: 'Where once one necessarily entered the city by means of a physical gateway, now one passes through an audiovisual protocol in which the methods of audience and surveillance have transformed even the forms of public greeting and daily reception' (Virilio 1997: 383). Resounding echoes of his point can be heard in the effusive boastings of an operation's director for a British surveillance firm who recounts how 'The minute you arrive in England, from the ferry port to the train station to the city centres, you're being CCTV'd' (Freeman 1999). The study by Norris and Armstrong (1999) of British CCTV also demonstrates how this ostensibly unitary technology is in fact an assemblage that aligns computers, cameras, people and telecommunications in order to survey the public streets

Deleuze and Guattari emphasize how 'the rhizome operates by variation, expansion, conquest, capture, offshoots' (1987: 21). No single technological development has ushered in the contemporary era of surveillance.

Rather, its expansion has been aided by subtle variations and intensifications in technological capabilities, and connections with other monitoring and computing devices. Some of the rhizomatic offshoots of the surveillant assemblage derive from efforts to seek out new target populations that ostensibly require a greater degree of monitoring. The list of such populations is limited only by imagination, and currently includes, for example, the young, caregivers, commuters, employees, the elderly, international travelers, parolees, the privileged and the infirm. Much of this expansion is driven by the financial imperative to find new markets for surveillance technologies which were originally designed for military purposes (Haggerty and Ericson 1999).

For Orwell, surveillance was a means to maintain a form of hierarchical social control. Foucault proposed that panoptic surveillance targeted the soul, disciplining the masses into a form of self-monitoring that was in harmony with the requirements of the developing factory system. However, Bauman (1992: 51) argues that panopticism in contemporary society has been reduced in importance as a mechanism of social integration. Instead of being subject to disciplinary surveillance or simple repression, the population is increasingly constituted as consumers and seduced into the market economy. While surveillance is used to construct and monitor consumption patterns, such efforts usually lack the normalized soul training which is so characteristic of panopticism. Instead, monitoring for market consumption is more concerned with attempts to limit access to places and information, or to allow for the production of consumer profiles through the *ex post facto* reconstructions of a person's behaviour, habits and actions. In those situations where individuals monitor their behaviour in light of the thresholds established by such surveillance systems, they are often involved in efforts to maintain or augment various social perks such as preferential credit ratings, computer services, or rapid movement through customs.

Foucault's larger body of work displays an appreciation for the multiple uses and targets of surveillance. Most discussions of surveillance fixate on his analysis of the panopticon, with its individualized disciplinary form of bodily scrutiny. However, Foucault also analysed aggregate forms of surveillance. Institutions are involved in the production and distribution of knowledge about diverse populations for the purpose of managing their behaviour from a distance (Foucault 1991). In this way, surveillance also serves as a vital component of positive population management strategies.

The concept of 'surplus value' has traditionally been associated with Marxism. For Marx, it designated how the owners of the means of production profit from workers' excess labour power for which they are not financially compensated. Surveillance plays an important role in this process, as it allows managers to establish and monitor production norms at previously unheard of levels. Today, however, surplus value has escaped from a purely labour-oriented discourse and can now also be located in the language of cybernetics. Increasingly important to modern capitalism is the value that is culled from a range of different transaction and interaction points between individuals and institutions. Each of these transactions is monitored and recorded, producing a surplus of information. The monetary value of this surplus derives from how it can be used to construct data doubles which are then used to create consumer profiles, refine service delivery and target specific markets. There is a growing trade in the corporate sale of such information. Governments are also keen to profit from the sale of information stored in scattered official databases. Millions of dollars are already being made through the sale of data from license bureaus, personal income data and employment records (Kanaley 1999). In a cybernetic world, surplus value increasingly refers to the profit that can be derived from the surplus information that different populations trail behind them in their daily lives.

The public is slowly awakening to the profits that are being made from the sale of their data doubles. One consequence of this recognition has been the further commodification of the self. Parallel to how the emergence of the wage economy necessitated the fixing of monetary prices to labour power, citizens and economists are now contemplating what, if any, compensation individuals should receive for the sale of their personal information. Dennis (1999) reports on a recent study which found that 70 per cent of Britons were happy to have companies use their personal data, on the condition that they receive something in return, such as more personal service or rewards. Privacy is now less a line in the sand beyond which transgression is not permitted, than a shifting space of negotiation where privacy is traded for products, better services or special deals.

In addition to a desire for order, control, discipline and profit, surveillance has voyeuristic entertainment value. Clips from CCTV's are now a staple of daytime talk shows while programmes such as *America's Dumbest Criminals* have helped soften the authoritarian overtones of mass public surveillance (Doyle 1998). The proliferation of hand-held video cameras has also given rise to *America's Funniest Home Videos*, as well as the more morbid *Faces of Death* videos which portray a procession of accidental fatalities which have been captured on film.

As the surveillant assemblage transcends institutional boundaries, systems intended to serve one purpose find other uses. In his early analysis of paper-based records, Stanton Wheeler (1969) pointed out that it is a characteristic of such records that they can be combined to serve new purposes. The computerization of record-keeping has greatly expanded this ability. For example, police organizations have secured routine, and often informal, access to a host of non-police databases, such as those from insurance companies and financial institutions. Research by Northrop, Kramer and King (1995) indicates that the police have become the primary users of many systems originally established for other governmental purposes, and Gordon (1990) reports on proposals to link the US federal NCIC police database to computers from Social Security, Internal Revenue, Passport, Securities and Exchange and the State Department. Davis (1998:

381) recounts how in some Southern California communities the police now have direct computerized access to school records.

In surveying the informational horizon for ever more potentially useful sources, police organizations have recently recognized the surveillance and investigative potential of corporate databases. Files from telephone and utilities companies can be used to document an individual's lifestyle and physical location (Ericson and Haggerty 1997), and marketing firms have developed consumer profiling techniques that contain precise information on a person's age, gender, political inclinations, religious preferences, reading habits, ethnicity, family size, income, and so on (Gandy 1993; Turow 1997). When these sources are combined through computerized data matching, they allow for exponential increases in the amount of information the police have at their disposal. Burnham (1997: 164–7) relates that the FBI has employed commercial databases for undisclosed investigative purposes, and that the US Drug Enforcement Agency has developed its own in-house registry with information culled from mailing and telephone listings, direct marketers, voters records, and assorted commercial sources. Although cloaked in secrecy, this registry was expected to contain 135,000,000 records as of its inception in 1991 and would subsequently receive regular updates of corporate and residential data.

Ostensibly non-criminal justice institutions are being called upon to augment the surveillance capacities of the criminal justice surveillance system. In Canada, for example, in an effort to deter money laundering, financial institutions are compelled to monitor and report 'suspicious' transactions. More recently, regulations have been introduced to require American banks to compare the financial holdings of their clients against an electronic list of parents who owe child support. Educators and medical practitioners are already legally compelled to report suspected instances of child abuse, and the police have started to request or confiscate media tapes of public disturbances in efforts to identify lawbreakers.

Rhizome and Hierarchy

For both Orwell and Foucault, surveillance is part of a regime where comparatively few powerful individuals or groups watch the many, in a form of top-down scrutiny. Contemporary studies of surveillance continue to emphasize this hierarchical aspect of observation. For example, Fiske concludes his insightful analysis of the surveillance of American Blacks (particularly Black men), by proclaiming that 'although surveillance is penetrating deeply throughout our society, its penetration is differential. The lives of the white mainstream are still comparatively untouched by it' (Fiske 1998: 85). And while the targeting of surveillance is indeed differential, we take exception to the idea that the mainstream is 'untouched' by surveillance. Surveillance has become rhizomatic, it has transformed hierarchies of observation, and allows for the scrutiny of the powerful by both institutions and the general population.

All contemporary institutions subject their members to forms of bureaucratic surveillance. Individuals with different financial practices, education and lifestyle will come into contact with different institutions and hence be subject to unique combinations of surveillance. The classifications and profiles that are entered into these disparate systems correspond with, and reinforce, differential levels of access, treatment and mobility. Hence, while poor individuals may be in regular contact with the surveillance systems associated with social assistance or criminal justice, the middle and upper classes are increasingly subject to their own forms of routine observation, documentation and analysis. The more institutions they are in contact with, the greater the level of scrutiny to which they are subjected. In the case of the powerful, this can include the regular monitoring of consumption habits, health profile, occupational performance, financial transactions, communication patterns, Internet use, credit history, transportation patterns, and physical access controls.

It is not exclusively powerful social groups and institutions which observe the powerful. Mathiesen (1997) accentuates the tendency toward 'bottom-up' forms of observation in his claim that a process of *synopticism* is now at work which parallels Foucault's panopticism. Synopticism essentially means that a large number of individuals are able to focus on something in common. New media, particularly television, allow the general public to scrutinize their leaders as never before (Meyrowitz 1985). We need only consider the media circus which surrounds Britain's royal family to acknowledge this point. Furthermore, the monitoring of the powerful has been eased by the proliferation of relatively inexpensive video cameras. These allow the general public to tape instances of police brutality, and have given rise to inner-city citizen response teams which monitor police radios and arrive at the scene camera-in-hand to record police behaviour. Such monitoring culminates in those surreal situations of labour unrest where picketing workers film the police while the police film the strikers. While not a complete democratic leveling of the hierarchy of surveillance, these developments cumulatively highlight a fractured rhizomatic criss-crossing of the gaze such that no major population groups stand irrefutably above or outside of the surveillant assemblage.

A further distinction is needed, however, if we are to fully appreciate the distinctive form that the observation of the powerful now assumes. Such surveillance is often a mile wide but only an inch deep. The depth, or intensity, of the surveillance directed at the powerful generally exists as a potentiality of connections of different technologies and institutions. It is activated, or intensified, when there is some perceived *ex post facto* or prospective need to profile their movements, consumption patterns, reading preferences, tastes in erotica, personal contacts, such that they coalesce into a remarkably detailed data double. The O. J. Simpson case provides a telling example of the intensity that this potentiality can assume when put into motion. Included among the reams of information that the L. A. P. D. were able to collect about O. J. Simpson were details about which pornographic movie he watched in his hotel a few days prior to the murders. The police also approached a private company which sells satellite surveillance photographs to try and discern whether Simpson's now (in)famous white Bronco was in the driveway of Nicole Brown Simpson's home on the night of the murders (Fiske 1998).

CONCLUSION: THE DISAPPEARANCE OF DISAPPEARANCE

Premodern living arrangements typically consisted of individuals residing in rural villages where they knew and were known by their neighbours. The mass movements of individuals into cities ruptured these long-standing neighbourly and familial bonds. Individuals in cities became surrounded by streams of unknown strangers. Sociologists have drawn a wide range of implications from this social transformation. Anonymity allowed for new possibilities in self-creation: the freedom to partake in experiments with identities and life projects. Simmel believed that the metropolis 'grants to the individual a kind and an amount of personal freedom which has no analogy whatsoever under other conditions' (1950: 416). Others have accentuated the darker side of these possibilities for self-creation, cautioning how this new found 'freedom' could also be experienced as a daunting obligation, as modern individuals are now compelled to be free, to establish identities and life projects in the face of radical uncertainty about correct courses of action. Bauman (1997: 20–1) observes that modernity transformed 'identity from the matter of ascription into the achievement [*sic*] – thus making it an individual task and the individual's responsibility,' and these 'individual life-projects find no stable ground in which to lodge an anchor'.

From the beginning, however, this general narrative of anonymity and invisibility contained a subplot, one which involved countervailing efforts by institutions. The rise in credentials and surveillance systems was a way to create institutional reputations and provide for ways to differentiate among unknown strangers (Nock 1993). These new forms of reputation lack the deep subjective nuances which characterized familial and neighbourly relations in the idealized premodern rural village. Instead, knowledge of the population is now manifest in discrete bits of information which break the individual down into flows for purposes of management, profit and entertainment. While such efforts were originally a footnote to the historical rise of urban anonymity, they now constitute an important force in their own right.

The coalescence of such practices into the surveillant assemblage marks the progressive 'disappearance of disappearance' – a process whereby it is increasingly difficult for individuals to maintain their anonymity, or to escape the monitoring of social institutions. Efforts to evade the gaze of different systems involves an attendant trade-off in social rights and benefits. Privacy advocates bring this point home in their facetious advice that individuals who are intent on staying anonymous should not use credit, work, vote, or use the Internet. Two quite different historical examples accentuate the extent to which the possibilities for disappearance have narrowed.

A recent biography of a female activist recounted how she was followed in the 1950s by secret service agents. Unbeknownst to her, at one point she managed to evade her pursuers by simply taking an ocean cruise which rendered her beyond the reach of their abilities to track her movements. Clearly, this would not be the case today. Even on the ocean a person's whereabouts could still be discerned through the monitoring of credit card transactions, computer connections, travel arrangements and telephone calls.

Our second example also concerns ship travel, but this time it involves the greatest naval armada ever assembled – the allied invasion of Normandy in 1944. At that time the Germans were reasonably certain that an invasion of France was imminent, but it was not until the fog lifted on the morning of June 6th to reveal a fleet of over 5,000 ships off the coast that they knew the invasion had truly begun. Again, the contrast between yesterday and today is telling. With advanced military sensing devices that now include globe-scanning satellites and submarines equipped with sensors that can detect the propeller of a ship traveling on the opposite side of the ocean, the surprise appearance of such a massive military grouping is simply inconceivable.

The invisible armada and elusive activist have faded into historical memories. From now on, such matters will be readily captured by a surveillant assemblage devoted to the disappearance of disappearance.

(Date accepted: May 2000)

Kevin D. Haggerty
Department of Sociology
University of Alberta
and

Richard V. Ericson
Principal of Green College
Professor of Law and Sociology
University of British Columbia

BIBLIOGRAPHY

Associated Press 1998 'Professor Gets First Chip Implant', August 27.
Bauman, Z. 1992 *Intimations of Postmodernity*, London: Routledge.
—— 1997 *Postmodernity and Its Discontents*, New York: New York University Press.
Benjamin, W. 1983 *Charles Baudelaire: A*

Lyric Poet in the Era of High Capitalism, London: Verso.
Bentham, J. 1995 *The Panopticon Writings*, London: Verso.
Bevan, S. 1999 'Chips May Dip into Workplace Sanity', *The Windsor Star*, May 10.
Bogard, W. 1996 *The Simulation of*

Surveillance: Hypercontrol in Telematic Societies, Cambridge: Cambridge University Press.

Burnham, D. 1997 *Above the Law: Secret Deals, Political Fixes, and Other Misadventures of the U. S. Department of Justice*, New York: Scribner.

Canadian Security 1998 'The Importance of Hugs', November/December.

Dandecker, C. 1990 *Surveillance, Power and Modernity: Bureaucracy and Discipline from 1700 to the Present Day*, Cambridge: Polity.

Davis, M. 1998 *Ecology of Fear: Los Angeles and the Imagination of Disaster*, New York: Henry Holt.

Deleuze, G. 1986 *Foucault*, Minneapolis: University of Minnesota Press.

—— 1992 'Postscript on the Societies of Control', *October* 59(Winter): 3–7.

Deleuze, G., and Foucault, M. 1977 'Intellectuals and Power,' in M. Foucault *Language, Counter-Memory, Practice: Selected Essays and Interviews*, (edited by D. Bouchard and translated by D. Bouchard and S. Simon), New York: Cornell University Press.

Deleuze, G. and Guattari, F. 1987 *A Thousand Plateaus*, Minneapolis: University of Minnesota Press.

Dennis, S. 1999 '75% of Brits Happy to Give Firms Their Personal Data', *YAHOO News Asia*, May 18.

Doyle, A. 1998 '"Cops": Television Policing as Policing Reality', in M. Fishman and G. Cavendar (eds) *Entertaining Crime: Television Reality Programs*, New York: Aldine de Gruyter.

Duffy, J. 1999 'Something to Watch Over Us', *BBC News Online*, May 04.

Ericson, R., and Haggerty, K. 1997 *Policing the Risk Society*, Toronto: University of Toronto Press and Oxford: Oxford University Press.

—— 1999 'Governing the Young' in R. Smandych (ed.) *Governable Spaces: Readings on Governmentality and Crime Control*, Dartmouth: Ashgate.

Fiske, J. 1998 'Surveilling the City: Whiteness, the Black Man and Democratic Totalitarianism', *Theory, Culture and Society* 15(2): 67–88.

Foucault, M. 1970 *The Order of Things: An Archeology of the Human Sciences*, New York: Vintage.

—— 1977 *Discipline and Punish: The Birth of the Prison*, New York: Vintage.

—— 1991 'Governmentality', in G. Burchell, C. Gordon, and P. Miller (eds) *The Foucault Effect*, Chicago: University of Chicago Press.

Freeman, A. 1999 'Big Brother Turning into a Big Bother', *The Globe and Mail*, May 25.

Gandy, O. 1993 *The Panoptic Sort: A Political Economy of Personal Information*, Boulder: Westview.

Giddens, A. 1990 *The Consequences of Modernity*, Stanford: Stanford University Press.

Gordon, D. 1987 'The Electronic Panopticon: A Case Study of the Development of the National Crime Records System', *Politics and Society* 15(4): 483–511

—— 1990 *The Justice Juggernaut: Fighting Street Crime, Controlling Citizens*, New Brunswick: Rutgers University Press.

Graham, S. 1998 'Spaces of Surveillant Simulation: New Technologies, Digital Representations, and Material Geographies', *Environment and Planning D: Society and Space* 16(4): 483–504.

Grosz, E. 1995 *Space, Time and Perversion*, New York: Routledge.

Haggerty, K., and Ericson, R. 1999 'The Militarization of Policing in the Information Age', *The Journal of Political and Military Sociology* 27(2): 233–45.

Haraway, D. 1991 *Simians, Cyborgs and Women: The Reinvention of Nature*, New York: Routledge.

Kanaley, R. 1999 'States' Sale of Data: At What Price?' *Philadelphia Inquirer*, June 13.

Latour, B. 1987 *Science in Action*, Cambridge, Mass.: Harvard University Press.

Lyon, D. 1994 *The Electronic Eye: The Rise of Surveillance Society*, Minneapolis: University of Minnesota Press.

Mathiesen, T. 1997 'The Viewer Society: Michel Foucault's "Panopticon" Revisited', *Theoretical Criminology* 1(2): 215–33.

May, T. 1993 'The System and Its Fractures: Gilles Deleuze on Otherness', *Journal of the British Society for Phenomenology* 24(1): 3–14.

Meyrowitz, J. 1985 *No Sense of Place*, New York: Oxford University Press.

Nock, S. 1993 *The Costs of Privacy: Surveillance and Reputation in America*, New York: Aldine De Gruyter.

Norris, C., and Armstrong, G. 1997 'Categories of Control: The Social

Construction of Suspicion and Intervention in CCTV Systems', Report to ESRC; Department of Social Policy, University of Hull.

—— 1999 *The Maximum Surveillance Society*, Oxford: Berg

Northrop, A., Kramer, K. and King, J. L. 1995 'Police Use of Computers', *Journal of Criminal Justice* 23(3): 259–75.

O'Malley, P., and Palmer, D. 1996 'Post-Keynesian Policing', *Economy and Society* 25(2): 137–55.

Orwell, G. 1949 *Nineteen Eighty-Four*, New York: Penguin.

Patton, P. 1994 'MetamorphoLogic: Bodies and Powers in *A Thousand Plateaus*', *Journal of the British Society for Phenomenology* 25(2): 157–69.

Philipkoski, K. 1998 'A Crime-Sniffing Network', *Wired News*, 11 August.

Poster, M. 1990 *The Mode of Information*, Chicago: University of Chicago Press.

Renzeman, M. 1998 'GPS: Is Now the Time to Adopt?' *Journal of Offender Monitoring* 11(2): 5.

Simmel, G. 1950 'The Metropolis and Mental Life' in G. Simmel *The Sociology of Georg Simmel*, New York: The Free Press.

Staples, W. 1997 *The Culture of Surveillance: Discipline and Social Control in the United States*, New York: St. Martin's Press.

Tester, K. 1994 'Introduction' in K. Tester (ed.) *The Flâneur*, London: Routledge.

Turow, J. 1997 *Breaking Up America: Advertisers and the New Media World*, Chicago: University of Chicago Press.

Virilio, P. 1997 'The Overexposed City', in N. Leach (ed.) *Rethinking Architecture*, London: Routledge.

Wheeler, S. 1969 'Problems and Issues in Record Keeping' in S. Wheeler (ed.) *On Record*, New York: Russell Sage Foundation.

Part II
CCTV

[6]

CCTV AND THE SOCIAL STRUCTURING OF SURVEILLANCE

by

Clive Norris
University of Hull

and

Gary Armstrong
University of Reading

Abstract: The installation of Closed Circuit Television Cameras (CCTV) on British streets has been the crime prevention initiative of the century. However, little attention has been paid to who and what the cameras actually watch and how operators select their targets. This paper draws on a two-year study in the operation of CCTV control rooms to examine how target selection is socially differentiated by age, rage and gender and asks whether this leads to discrimination.

INTRODUCTION

There is now a growing body of literature that has attempted to evaluate the effectiveness of closed circuit television (CCTV). These studies have shed considerable light on the complexity of measuring the impact of CCTV on the crime rate, and have led to a far more sober assessment of its reductionist potential (Tilley, 1993; Bulos and Grant, 1996; Short and Ditton, 1996; Squires and Measor, 1996; Ditton and Short, 1998; Skinns, 1998). However, one consequence of this concern with effectiveness has been to concentrate attention almost solely on outcomes rather than process. This is perhaps unsurprising: those who have commissioned evaluations have, to a large extent, been concerned with the bottom-line; i.e., does CCTV reduce crime? Evaluators have therefore concentrated their efforts on describing the correlation between the crime rate and the introduction

158 — Clive Norris and Gary Armstrong

of CCTV. They have then tried to isolate CCTV as the cause of the correlation by ruling out other factors. The time-consuming task of analysing trend data, displacement, and "halo effects" has left little time to explore the more general, but in our view, equally important question of how CCTV operates in practice. CCTV is about far more than just the reduction of crime. It is about the power to watch and potentially intervene in a variety situations, whether or not they be criminal. But who and what gets watched and the extent to which this is socially differentiated has largely been ignored by existing research.

This is important because CCTV has been portrayed, to use the words of one Home Office Minister, as a "Friendly Eye in the Sky" (*Guardian*, 1st January 1995) benignly and impartially watching over the whole population and targeting only those deemed as acting suspiciously. As one code of practice for a northern city centre system states, "CCTV is not a 'spy system.' There will be no interest shown or deliberate monitoring of people going about their daily business." Similarly, Graham (1998:99) writing of the North Shields system, states that the CCTV operators "have strict guidelines for the operation of the system. For example, guards are not permitted to 'track' people around the town unless they are acting suspiciously." However, what constitutes "suspicious behaviour" is not addressed by codes of conduct or by training, as Bulos and Sarno (1996:24) note: "The most neglected area of training consists of how to identify suspicious behaviour, when to track individuals or groups and when to take close-up views of incidents or people. This was either assumed to be self evident or common sense."

It is unpacking this "common sense" that is the aim of this paper: we want to know who and what gets targeted, and by what criteria they are selected. This issue of selectivity is central to any discussion of CCTV operational practice, because the sheer volume of information entering a CCTV system threatens to swamp the operators with information overload. Consider how much incoming information there is in a medium-sized 24-hour city centre system with 20 cameras.

The answer, as we can see from Table 1, is a quite staggering 43 million "pictures" per day. Inevitably, operators cannot focus their attention on every image from every camera — somehow they must narrow down the range of images to concentrate on. This problem could, of course, be solved entirely randomly, so that each person on the street has an equal chance of being selected for initial surveillance but only a small proportion have a chance of actually being sampled. However, this would still leave operators with the problem of whom to pay prolonged attention to once initial selection had taken place. For some the answer is obvious: those behaving suspiciously. But this begs the question as to what, in practice, constitutes suspicious behaviour?

Table 1: Incoming Information as Measured by Individual Frames of Video Footage in a 20-Camera, 24-Hour, City Centre System

25-frames per second per camera		25
x 20 cameras in system	Total number of frames entering the system per second	500
x 60 frames per minute	Total number of frames entering the system per minute	30,000
x 60 frames per hour	Total number of frames entering the system per hour	1,800,000
x 24 frames per day	Total number of frames entering the system per day	43,200,000

It is instructive here to draw on the writings of Harvey Sacks (1978) on the police construction of suspicion. For Sacks (1978:190), the key problem for a police patrol officer was how he or she could use a person's appearance as an indicator of their moral character and, thus, "maximise the likelihood that those who turn out to be criminal and pass into view are selected, while minimising the likelihood that those who do not turn out to be criminal and pass into view are not selected."

The problem is identical for the CCTV operator. Bombarded by a myriad of images from dozens of cameras, and faced with the possibility of tracking and zooming in on literally thousands of individuals, by what criteria can operators try to maximise the chance of choosing those with criminal intent? Camera operators and street patrol officers are at both an advantage and a disadvantage. Because the "presence" of operatives is remote and unobtrusive, there is less likelihood that people will orient their behaviour in the knowledge that they are being watched, and, by virtue of the elevated position and telescopic capacity of the camera, operators have a greater range of vision than the street-level patrol officer. However, these advantages must be offset against their remoteness, which means they are denied other sensory input — particularly sound —that can be essential in contextualising visual images. Unlike the patrol officer, the CCTV operative is both deaf and dumb: he simply cannot ask citizens on the street for information, nor can they hear what is being said.

Faced with such an avalanche of images, and a limited range of sensory data, how then does the CCTV operator selectively filter these images to decide what is worthy of more detailed attention? The problem is that operatives do not have prior knowledge that would enable them to determine which persons are going to engage in criminal activity. It is therefore an occupational necessity that they develop a set of working rules to narrow down the general population to the suspect population. To shed light on this, we now draw on our two-year study, funded by the Economic and Social Research Council, of the operation of CCTV control rooms, and we briefly outline our methodology below.

METHODOLOGY

Observations were carried out in three sites between May 1995 and April 1996. One was in the commercial centre of a major metropolitan city with a total population in excess of 500,000. During the day it was a bustling shopping and business district and as darkness fell supported a thriving night life based on clubs, pubs and eateries. Another site centred on the market square of an affluent county town with a population of nearly 200,000. It was thronged with shoppers during the day but at night was fairly quiet until the weekends, when it would attract revellers from the surrounding area for a night on the town. The third site focussed on a run down but busy high street in a poor inner-city borough with an ethnically diverse population of nearly 250,000. We have named these three sites Metro City, County Town, and Inner City, to reflect their contrasting features.

The systems also differed in other ways. Metro City, cost over £1 million to install, consisted of 32 cameras and had running costs of over £200,000 per annum. Although the system was located in the control room of the local police station, it was run by an independent trust responsible for all aspects of its day-to-day operation, including the staffing of the control room and maintenance of the system. In contrast, the County Town system cost around £500,000 to install and had annual running costs in the region of £120,000. It consisted of over 100 cameras, although the main monitors generally only displayed the pictures from the 25 or so cameras focused on the town centre. The Inner City system cost around £450,000 with annual running costs of about £100,000, and had 16 cameras focussing on the busy high street and surrounds. County Town and Inner City were run by their respective local authorities, were housed in purpose-built control rooms in local authority premises, and subcontracted the staffing of the controls rooms to private security firms. All three systems had 24-hour-a day monitoring. In County Town and Metro City this involved three eight-hour shifts; in Inner City, two 12-hour shifts.

In total, 592 hours of monitoring — the equivalent of 74 eight-hour shifts — were observed. All days of the week were covered, as were early, late and night shifts. On each shift the observer would "attach" himself to one operative and shadow that individual's work. In total, 25 different operatives were shadowed. A small notebook was used in the field when appropriate, and full field notes were written up at the end of each shift. These included full descriptions of any targeted surveillance. We defined targeted surveillance as one that lasted more than one minute on an individual or group of individuals, or where the surveillance was initiated from outside the system, for example, by police or private security, regardless of whether a target was identified. The field notes recorded key data for each targeted surveillance based on a checklist of salient features. Field notes were also recorded for general observations on the operation and control of the system, as well as operatives' beliefs and values, work tensions, interactions with visitors to the system, and included informal interviews with operators and managers.

The field notes of targeted surveillances also formed the basis for filling in the quantitative observation schedule. This recorded four types of data: (1) shift data, including the number of operatives on each shift, the time screens were left unattended, who visited the system, and whether and how many tapes were borrowed for inspection and for what purpose; (2) targeted suspicion data, including the reason for the suspicion, type of suspicion, how the surveillance was initiated, how many cameras were used, and whether the incident was brought to somebody else's attention; (3) person data, detailing the age, race sex and appearance of up to four people for each targeted surveillance; and (4) deployment data, recording all deployments initiated by the system operatives, how the system was used during the deployment and what the outcome was.

In total, this yielded data on 888 targeted surveillances. In 711 of these surveillances, a person was identified for whom basic demographic data (age, race, sex, and appearance) was recorded, as it was on another 966 people who were the second, third or fourth person in a group being surveilled.

THE SOCIAL STRUCTURING OF SURVEILLANCE

As Table 2 shows, selection for targeted surveillance appears, at the outset, to be differentiated by the classic sociological variables of age, race, and gender. Nine out of ten target surveillances were on men (93%), four out of ten on teenagers (39%) and three out of ten on black people (31%).

Table 2: Age and Sex of All People and Primary Person Surveilled

Sex		
Male	660	(93%)
Female	49	(7%)
Total	709	(100%)
Age		
Teenagers	270	(39%)
In their twenties	320	(46%)
Thirties plus	107	(15%)
Total	697	(100%)
Race		
White	483	(69%)
Black	210	(30%)
Asian	5	(0%)
Total	698	(99%)

In terms of the general population, men were nearly twice as likely to be targeted than their presence in the population would suggest. Similarly, teenagers — who account for less than 20% of the population — made up 40% of targeted surveillances. Of course, the street population (i.e., those available for targeting) is not the same as the general population. However, all three of our sites were busy commercial areas that during the day were populated by shoppers and workers, both male and female, many of whom were middle aged.

It is more difficult to estimate how a person's race affected the chance of being selected for targeting, since the proportion of ethnic minorities varied dramatically from site to site. However, we have calculated that black people were between one-and-a-half and two-and-a-half times more likely to be targeted for surveillance than their presence in the population would suggest (for further details, see Norris and Armstrong, 1997, 1999).

On their own, however, these findings do not indicate that CCTV operators are selecting targets for surveillance merely on the basis of observable social characteristics, since this distribution may relate to the behaviour of those targeted that initially prompted operator suspicion. To examine this we classified each surveillance as: "crime related," "order related," occurring for "no obvious reason," or "other." For instance, a youth crouching down by the side of a car would be classified as "crime related," a group of men involved in revelry at pub closing time as "order related," and surveying the scene of a traffic accident as "other." This "crime related" category does not imply that the person was involved in any criminal behaviour, merely that the operator had some explicit grounds for targeting the person or incident. A youth crouching by the side of a car is, in all probability, tying his or her shoelaces rather than removing hub caps, and the targeted surveillance may well confirm this. All the same, this action will still be coded as "crime related" since the operator is treating the behaviour as indicative of theft. Similarly, if the operator tracks a known shoplifter this would also be classified as crime related because the operator has explicit grounds for their suspicion. If there were no signs from a person's behaviour or he was not a "known offender," then we recorded the surveillance as for "no obvious reason."

Three out of ten people (30%) were surveilled for crime-related matters, two out of ten (22%) for forms of disorderly conduct, but the largest category — nearly four out of ten (36%) — were surveilled was for "no obvious reason." This was echoed when we examined the basis of suspicion, with one quarter (24%) of people subject to targeted surveillance because of their behaviour. But the most significant type of suspicion was categorical; one-third (31%) of people were surveilled merely on the basis of belonging to a particular social or subcultural group. The extent to which the reason for the surveillance was socially differentiated is shown in Table 3.

As Table 3 shows, the reason for the surveillance and the suspicion on which it was based was also found to be highly differentiated. Thus, we can see that two-thirds (65%) of teenagers — compared with only one in five (21%) of those aged over 30 — were surveilled for "no obvious reason." Similarly, black people were twice as likely (68%) to be surveilled for "no obvious reason" than whites (35%), and men three times (47%) more likely than women (16%). The young, the male and the black were systematically and disproportionately targeted, not because of their involvement in crime or disorder, but for "no obvious reason" and on the basis of categorical suspicion alone.

If we cannot explain the patterning of target selection on the basis of observable difference in behaviour, it is necessary to examine the influence of the values and attitudes of the operators and how they relate to age, race and gender.

Table 3: Reason for Surveillance by Age, Race and Gender in Numbers and Percentages

Age						
	Teenagers		In their twenties		Thirties plus	
Crime Related	59	(22%)	80	(26%)	17	(17%)
Public Order	30	(11%)	83	(27%)	46	(45%)
No Obvious	173	(65%)	115	(38%)	21	(21%)
Other	4	(2%)	29	(9%)	18	(18%)
Total	266	(100%)	307	(100%)	102	(101%)
Gender						
	Male		Female			
Crime Related	138	(22%)	19	(43%)		
Public Order	150	(24%)	12	(27%)		
No Obvious	302	(47%)	7	(16%)		
Other	49	(8%)	6	(14%)		
Total	639	(101%)	44	(100%)		
Race						
	White		Black			
Crime Related	115	(25%)	42	(20%)		
Public Order	148	(32%)	13	(6%)		
No Obvious	163	(35%)	141	(68%)		
Other	41	(9%)	12	(6%)		
Total	467	(101%)	208	(100%)		

Age

As we have seen, young men were the main targets of surveillance. This is not surprising given the attitudes that operators displayed towards youths in general and particularly those identified — by attire, location, or body language — as poor or belonging to the underclass. Further, like police, CCTV operators often referred to such categories as "toe-rags," "scumbags," "yobs," "scrotes," and "crapheads." As the following two examples illustrate, operatives need no special reason to ascribe malign intent merely on the basis of age, particularly if youths are in a group.

13.45: The operator sees and zooms in on four boys walking through a pedestrian precinct. Aged between 10 and 12 and casually, but fashionably, dressed, the four, — combining age, appearance, location and numbers — are suspects for a variety of possibilities. The four gather around in a form of "conference," and 30 seconds later walk a few yards to their left and enter a shop well known for selling toys. What the operator sees is not kids entering a shop meant for kids, but something else: they are all up to no good and, in his opinion, have probably just plotted to steal and will come running out any minute with stolen merchandise. In anticipation, he fixes a camera onto the shop door and tells the other operator to put the cameras onto the street he presumes they will run into.

Using two cameras and two operators, the surveillance lasts six minutes before the boys leave the shop — slowly and orderly and without any apparent stolen goods. Now, the operator informs me, he will zoom in on the four as they walk through town in a search for bulges under their clothing, particularly around the waistline — this according to him, is where stolen toys would be concealed. But the boys have jeans and T-shirts on and no bulges are apparent. Still, however, the four are followed by both operators to see if they will pull items out of their pockets; they don't. The four then disappear from view as they enter another department store. The operator looks elsewhere, but comments to his colleague, "They're definitely up to no good."

While youths are generally seen as suspicious and warranting of targeted surveillance, this would still leave CCTV operators with far too many candidates to choose from on the basis of the images alone. Two additional features — attire and posture — become salient for further subdividing youths into those who are worthy of more intensive surveillance and those who are not.

The following garments were thought by operatives to be indicative of the criminal intent of the wearer: "puffer" coats (ski-style fashion), track suit bottoms, designer training shoes, baseball caps (ponytail hairstyles only compounded suspicion), and anything that may conceal the head (a woolly hat, hood or cap) and football shirts or supporter paraphernalia. Any type of loose-fitting jacket could also provoke suspicion because in the operators' eyes it may conceal stolen items or weapons; a jacket or head gear worn in warm weather only compounded suspicion. The following field note extracts illustrate the manner in which a person's visual identity is used to further stigmatise and subclassify the youth population:

01.46: Surveilling the car park the operator finds a suspicious person. This is a white male in his early 20s, dressed casually but expensively. The object of suspicion is the sunglasses he wears. The operator asks himself why a man needs them on at night. Furthermore, the targeted person is leaning against a good (i.e., sporty) car talking to another male. The first male compounds his suspicion further by wearing a leather zip-up bomber jacket, designer trainers and a fashionable haircut. The camera is fixed on him and his colleague as they get into the car and drive away. As they do so, the vehicle registration number is zoomed in on and noted on a pad the operator has with him. The operator keeps his own dossier on "flash cars" and their occupants, and believes such people are all potential drug dealers. (2 minutes, 1 camera)

03.01: A male and a female are noted walking across the car park. Both are white and in their mid-20s. Whilst she is smartly dressed, it is her male companion who arouses the operator's suspicion. The companion has about him the stigmata of criminality — he has a coat on with a hood up. The operator knows it is not raining so cannot understand why (the possibility that it is because it is bitterly cold outside does not appear in his logic). The couple are carefully surveilled as they walk to the railway station, check a railway timetable board, and then retrace their steps and walk out of sight. (4 minutes, 4 cameras)

11.50: A black male, aged around 16, attracts the attention of the operator because of his white cloth cap. Followed and zoomed in on, he has no apparent criminal characteristics, but as the operator states, his attire makes him appear to be a "wide-boy " and therefore worth following. (2 minutes, 1 camera)

00.42: The operator follows two white males, aged 16, dressed casually but with hoods covering their heads on this cold winter night. The operator's suspicion is founded on two things: firstly, they have the ever-incriminating hood up, and secondly, they are walking through an open-air car park whilst apparently too young to drive. The operator sees in them a "result," and as they pass a cluster of parked cars mutters to the screen they are visible on "have a go, have a go". They disappoint him. Whilst followed, they merely walk out of the car park and towards a Council estate. (2 minutes, 1 camera)

There are two issues to note from these examples. First, suspicion is not unidimensional. The background assumptions concerning youths are refined by utilising other visual clues that can be inferred from the clothes of a potential suspect, and this is read in conjunction with temporal and spatial features of a locale. In the surveillance of the couple in the car park, attire is also compounded by place and time — a young man in a car park with his face obscured at three in the morning is unambiguously read as a potential car thief. In the first example, involving the young man with the sunglasses, attire was compounded by accoutrements — a flashy car, and the hour. Implicitly, this form of reasoning is based on a reading of the Protestant work ethic: who can afford to buy an expensive car by the fruits of an honest day's work if they are out enjoying themselves at nearly two o'clock in the morning?

The second point is that wearing headgear is particularly stigmatising in the view of CCTV operators. This has two components. First baseball caps, woolly hats, and hooded parkas were seen as indicative of subcultural affiliation, and thus helped to single out respectable from "deviant" youths. Indeed, sometimes the only distinguishing feature that could justify why one youth, as opposed to another, was targeted for extended surveillance was the presence of baseball caps, particularly if worn with the peak facing backwards. But, more importantly, operators know that hats can potentially deprive them of recording a clear image of a person's face. Knowing this, they act on the assumption that citizens do as well. Operators believe they have a right to surveille any person's face who appears in their territory. Anyone who supports a visible means of denying them this opportunity immediately places himself in the category of persons of questionable intent and worthy of extended surveillance. Moreover, in the eyes of the operator, moving the headgear to deliberately obscure the face merely compounds suspicion, as the following incident reveals:

> 13.13: *Three youths are zoomed in on outside Santana's. One has a baseball cap on and elicits suspicion when, in the interpretation of the operator, he adjusts it so as to conceal his identity from the cameras. Whilst standing talking, the three are zoomed in on and when they walk down the street they are followed until out of sight. (3 minutes, 2 cameras).*

It is not just attire that provides a warrant for narrowing down the suspect population. In all sites operators believed in a practise known as the "scrote walk," which was a rather fluid concept reduced to a series of seemingly contradictory clichés:

- Too confident for their own good
- Head up, back straight, upper body moving too much
- Chin down, head down, shuffling along

- Swaggering, looking hard

Suspicion was compounded when a "scrote haircut" was evident. This could be very short, very long, or medium length with hair gel. But to make identification easier, "scrotes" generally could be identified because they hung around in groups.

> *21.45: The operator notices a character who has come to his attention before. Believed to be involved in all sorts of criminal activities, the suspect and his two mates are surveilled and zoomed in on as they stand outside McDonald's. The operators discuss with contempt the characteristics of these three males reserving particular venom for their "swaggering" and "scrote way of walking." However, they have done no wrong for the moment, bar offending the operator with their presence, and so are left alone after they walk through the town. (5 minutes, 1 camera)*

As Kenan Malik (1995:5) reported, in the March 3 edition of *Independent* on the operation of the CCTV in the West End of Newcastle, the selection of youth was also based on such categorisation. The operators told him: " ... we keep an eye on them to see if they're up to something. They're the type you see ... They're all scrotes round here - petty thieves, vandals, druggies, there's not much that you can do but keep an eye on them" *(Independent, 9th March, 1995:5)*.

The selection of youths as potential candidates for targeting rests on the background assumption as to their overpropensity for criminality. This is then refined through the use of visual clues that enable some youths to be identified as belonging to commonsense categories of moral waywardness, and this then gives the warrant for targeted and extended surveillance.

This selective targeting of youth is not just a product of operator assumptions and values; it is also a consequence of operational policy. In Metro City, the police liaison officer informed us that the system was not to be used to target traffic offences or vehicle tax evasion, because this would mitigate against the "feel-good" factor that CCTV was supposed to promote amongst the town centre consumers. This was even echoed in the official codes of practice drafted for another scheme, which stated: "Police...may seek and take control of the system in respect of the following...to prevent or mitigate interruptions to traffic flow (not to enforce minor breaches of traffic law)." In this way, the underrepresentation of older, relatively affluent offenders is enshrined in the system's operating procedures, as they are protected from the full impact of the cameras' gaze. Thus, despite those over age 30 making up around half of the population, they represented only 15% of those subject to targeted surveillance. When they did become targets, in nearly two thirds (62%) of cases it was because of their overt behaviour directly indicating involvement in crime or disorder, and only 21% were targeted for "no obvious reason."

So far we have talked about the processes that make youths the disproportionate targets of surveillance. But, as we have seen, it is not only youths, but black youths in particular who are oversurveilled.

Race

Racist language was not unusual to hear among CCTV operators. Although only used by a minority, the terms "Pakis," "Jungle Bunnies" and "Sooties" when used by some operatives did not produce howls of protests from their colleagues or line managers. Stereotypical negative attitudes towards ethnic minorities and black youths in particular were more widespread. These attitudes ranged from more extreme beliefs, held by a few operators, about these groups' inherent criminality to more general agreement as to their being "work-shy," or "too lazy" to get a job, and in general, "trouble."

Given these assumptions, the sighting of a black face on the streets of either Metro City or County Town would almost automatically produce a targeted surveillance.

10.48: Whilst surfing the cameras and streets, the operator sees two young men standing in a pedestrian shopping precinct, both looking into a hold-all bag one of them is carrying. Whilst this scene is not remarkable, what is unusual is that one of the two is black — a rare sight in the city centre. The two are in their early 20s and smartly dressed. After a minute or so, one hands to the other a piece of paper that most onlookers would presume was an address or phone number. Finally, when going their separate ways, the two indulge in a fashionable "high-five" handshake. This alerts both operators.

To these two, the "high-five" is suspicious because it was not done with flat hands and it "wasn't firm enough." In fact, according to the second operator, one of the men had a distinctly cupped hand. Whilst this was explainable by his holding the piece of paper just given him by the other, the operators see only criminality — this could be a surreptitious yet overtly public exchange of drugs. The youth with the bag is surveilled closely as he continues his walk. He not only has a bag possibly containing the merchandise, but he is also black — a potential drug dealer. The suspect enters a men's fashion store, which means that the camera is now trained on the doors whilst the operator awaits a possible hasty reappearance complete with stolen items in shoulder bag. After a few minutes, the camera is zoomed into the store and the suspect is visible in a capacity the operators did not consider — he is a sales assistant.

As the next example demonstrates, this colour-coded suspicion was intensified when combined with cars or headgear, and when people were in places the operators presumed they should not be.

15.00: A black male with dreadlocks, wearing sports gear and in his mid-20s invites the operators' suspicion and surveillance because he is in the wrong place doing the wrong thing. He is, in fact, crouched by a bicycle rack fiddling about with a bike. Zooming in, the operator looks for evidence of a theft — is he looking around him as he fiddles? No. Is he forcing something that won't move? No. He gets something out of his back pocket that happens to be a bicycle rear lamp. Fitting it on, he rides the bicycle, which is obviously his, safely and legally. (4 minutes, 1 camera)

23.05: A group of 12 black youths, all in their late teens and casually dressed, is noted outside a fast-food outlet. Whilst doing nothing more than eating and talking to various youths — male and female, white and black — who approach them, the operator surveilles them. She is encouraged by the manager of the CCTV system, who instructs her to "watch that lot...our ethnic problem." So the operator follows them for the next 20 minutes as they move up the street. (20 minutes, 1 camera)

14.34: As a former police officer of 10 years' experience, the operator "knows" that young black men are "trouble." When she catches sight of a white escort convertible, complete with wheel trims/spoilers and with its hood down, driven by a black male aged in his mid to late 20s she is alerted enough to zoom in on him. The vehicle is parked and he is chatting to his passenger, a white girl with blonde hair aged in her early 20s. This combination of colour and technology is all too much for the operator. She phones the police controller, explaining that "men of that age and that colour only get their money one way and it's not through hard work," and puts the image onto his monitor. On suspicion of being a drug dealer the operator zooms in on the registration plate whilst police do a PNC [Police National Computer] on the vehicle. Whilst not disclosing fully what he did or is suspected of doing, the controller gets back to the operator to tell her that the driver is "of police interest." The suspect drives away out of sight, unaware of who has been watching and talking about him. (8 minutes, 2 cameras)

The overrepresentation of black youths cannot be simply understood as white operators selecting young black men on the basis of second hand stereotypes. However, as we have seen, some of the white operators targeted blacks with a relish that implied a deep prejudice. Black operators similarly targeted young blacks, but their comments directed at the screen were not usually so venomous. The following example goes some way towards illustrating the point.

19.20: The night shift has inherited a job from the day shift; namely, a group of 15 to 20 black males and females, all in their teens and casually/subculturally dressed, who are standing in a group outside an off-licence and general store called Santana's that is adjacent to a series of bus stops. Zooming in on this group the operator can see nine black males and four black females. The operator, Victor, a black man in his late 50s, is not impressed by this assortment, saying for my and the other operator's benefit that the police should round 'em up and get their mums and dads to come and fetch 'em and shame them. The group is generally standing, talking, and flirting, with the occasional bout of horseplay and dancing. The youths harass no one. Nearby are standing dozens of people awaiting one of the 12 bus routes that pick up at this point. Even so, the camera remains on the group for 30 minutes and then notices a group of eight black males in their early 20s who walk through the gathering and continue elsewhere. Two of this group then split off, and the operator decides to follow the remaining six but is thwarted when they walk out of range of the cameras. (51 minutes, 4 cameras)

02.00: Standing outside the all-night shop are three black males in their 30s. One has the stigma of being a Rastafarian and having a woolly hat balancing on long dreadlocks. The operator is confused and tells his co-operator of his dilemma: why are they still out at night and not buying anything? The answer: they don't work, they just sleep all day. With mutual disgust the two black operators watch these black men as they stand and talk and then drive away in a car. (5 minutes, 1 camera)

However, in Inner City, the selection of black youths was not just a matter of operator discretion but a deliberate matter of policy. The first weeks of operation saw the police officer responsible for setting up the scheme give advice to both shifts on where and what to watch. The priority target was stated to be black youths and the priority

172 — Clive Norris and Gary Armstrong

crimes drug dealing and street robbery. This effectively meant that the majority of the cameras were never really monitored, since they covered the more general shopping area. Instead, for the purposes of target selection, attention was focussed almost solely on a junction that housed a row of bus stops and a number of small shops that daily after school closing saw a congregation of black youths alighting from and awaiting buses to take them home.

Male youths, particularly if black or stereotypically associated with the underclass, represent the fodder of CCTV systems. But this overrepresentation is not justified on the basis of those subsequently arrested. While teenagers accounted for 39% of targeted surveillance, they only made up 18% of those arrested, whereas those in their 20s accounted for 46% of targeted surveillance but made up 82% of all arrests. Similarly, black people accounted for 32% of targeted surveillance but only 9% of those arrested.

Gender

While women make up 52% of the general population they only accounted for 7% of primary persons surveilled. Women were almost invisible to the cameras unless they were reported as known shoplifters by store detectives (33%) or because of overt disorderly conduct (31%). Nor were women more likely to became targets by virtue of a protectional gaze. Indeed, in nearly 600 hours of observation only one woman was targeted for protectional purposes — as she walked to and from a bank cash dispenser. Moreover, there was evidence that the same attitudes that have traditionally been associated with the police occupational culture surrounding domestic violence continue to inform the operation of CCTV.

Shortly after 01.00 a.m. the operator notices a couple in the street having an animated row. Both are white, in their late 20s and stylishly dressed as if returning from a night out. This quiet Monday night has produced nothing of interest, and these two arguing is the most interesting event of the past three hours. This and the fact that the woman in view is blond and good looking has added to the attraction. The operator tells the Comm Room staff (two men) to have a look at the event unfolding.

After a two-minute argument the woman storms off up the street, but does not go out of the man's sight and slumps against a wall looking miserable. The man, meanwhile, climbs into a nearby car, closes the door and waits in the driver's seat, lights off. The impasse lasts five minutes, the female walks slowly towards the car and begins to talk to the man via the driver's window, only to storm off again after a minute. This time the male follows her on foot to continue the row. The operators and police enter into a commentary urging the man not to chase after her. Having decided she is hot-tempered and sulky, the operator says aloud "You hit her and we'll be your witnesses."

The couple continue their debate and this time the female decides to walk off past the man. but as she does so he attempts to restrain her by holding her arm. She pulls back. In the stand-off further words are exchanged, and a blow is aimed from the male to the female that strikes her around the upper chest and causes her to stumble. The blow does not look to be a hard one and she picks herself up and walks away. Meanwhile the male returns to his car and once again sits and waits. This time the female walks down the street past the car and continues for 20 yards only to stop, walk back to the car and stand looking into it.

After a couple of minutes of her looking and him pretending not to notice the pair resume their chat, this time via the passenger door. The drama continues when she walks away again. This time the distance is only 10 yards. Then she does an about-turn and, returning to the car, opens the front passenger door. Whilst she sits in the car she leaves the door wide open. After a mutual silence (seen by zooming the camera into the car's windscreen), the pair decide to talk again. This time she lasts three minutes before getting out and storming off.

By now other personnel have appeared to watch this drama. Two other officers have entered the room so that six men can now, in pantomime mode, boo and cheer good moves and bad moves. One boo is reserved for the male when he starts up the car, does a three-point turn, drives up to where she is sulking, and, parking, tries to persuade her to get it. A cheer goes up when he has seemingly failed in this effort and so drives away. But cheers turn to boos when he reverses to resume his persuasion. His words work and, to boos, she climbs into the car. After a four-minute discussion, the stationary car drives away into the distance. (25 minutes, 2 cameras).

As this incident makes clear, there is no simple correspondence between the discovery of criminal activity and the resulting deployment and arrest. Lesser assaults, when perpetrated by men on men outside nightclubs, resulted in police officers being deployed and arrests being made. However, the images from the screen are filtered through an organisational lens that accords meaning, status, and priority to events. It will come as no surprise to critics of the police handling of domestic violence (Edwards, 1989; Stanko, 1985) that the existence of "objective" evidence led to neither a protective response in the first instance to prevent the assault from occurring nor, once it had occurred, a legalistic response to arrest the perpetrator. As Edwards has argued, the police have always concerned themselves more with public order than private violence, and this was deemed as essentially a private matter, albeit occurring in public space.

Moreover, this example gives credence to Brown's (1998) assertion that the essentially male gaze of CCTV has little relevance for the security of women in town centres, and may indeed undermine it by offering the rhetoric of security rather than providing the reality. CCTV also fosters a male gaze in the more conventional and voyeuristic sense: with its pan-tilt and zoom facilities, the thighs and cleavages of scantily clad women are an easy target for those male operators so motivated. Indeed, 10% of all targeted surveillances on women and 15% of operator-initiated surveillance on women were for voyeuristic reasons, which outnumbered protective surveillance by five to one. Moreover, the long-understood relationship between cars and sex provides operators and police with other chances for titillation, as illustrated by the following example.

> *01.00: On the first night shift the operator is keen to show me all his job entails. Eventually I am taken, via the camera, to "Shaggers Alley," an area of a car park near the railway station used by local prostitutes and their punters (customers). Whilst this location is out of the way to passers-by, many a punter and indeed a happy couple not involved in a financial transaction are unaware of the reach of the all-seeing camera, whose job is facilitated by a large and powerful car park light that does not leave much to the imagination of the observer.*

> *Clearly visible on this night thanks to the cameras' ability to zoom in and look into cars, is a male in his late 20s sitting in the driver's seat with what can only be described as an expression of glee as a female, kneeling on the passenger seat performs fellatio on him. Her hair and head are noticeably bouncing up and down for around two minutes. When the performance is over the woman is clearly visible, topless, in the front seat. From beginning to end this scenario is put onto the police monitor, with the operator informing me that the police officers in the communications office enjoy such scenarios and, when bored, will sometimes phone to ask him to put the cameras on Shaggers Alley for their titillation. (11 minutes, 1 camera).*

In one of our sites, the "appreciation" of such public displays was a regular feature of the night shift and not just confined to those with access to the monitors. Many such encounters could be found on the "Shaggers Alley greatest hits tape," which was compiled and replayed for the benefit of those who had missed the "entertainment."

DISCRETION, DIFFERENTIATION AND DISCRIMINATION

The power of CCTV operators is highly discretionary as they have extraordinary latitude in determining who will be watched, for how long and whether to initiate deployment. The sum total of these individual discretionary judgments produces, as we have shown, a highly differentiated pattern of surveillance leading to a massively disproportionate targeting of young males, particularly if they are black or visibly identifiable as having subcultural affiliations. As this differentiation is not based on objective behavioural and individualised criteria, but merely on being categorised as part of a particular social group, such practices are clearly discriminatory.

Of course, it may be argued that since those officially recorded as deviant — young, male, black, and working class — are disproportionately represented, targeting such groups merely reflects the underlying reality of the distribution of criminality. Such an argument is, however, circular: the production of the official statistics is also based on preconceived assumptions as to the distribution of criminality, which itself leads to the particular configuration of formal and informal operational police practice. As self-report studies of crime reveal, offending is, in fact, far more evenly distributed throughout the population than reflected in the official statistics (Coleman and Moynihan, 1996). Indeed, race and class differentials, so marked in the official statistics, disappear when self-reported offending behaviour of juveniles is examined (Bowling et al., 1994). Thus, McConville et al. (1991:35) argue, the convicted population "is a subset of the official suspect population. Whilst convicted criminals may be broadly representative of suspects, there is good reason to believe that they are very dissimilar to the 'real criminal population.' The make up of the convicted population is, therefore, like the make up of the suspect population: a police construction."

Another argument is that even if there is differentiation in target selection, it is irrelevant because it does not result in actual intervention and therefore no "real" discrimination occurs. As our own results clearly show, even though teenagers make up 39% of those targeted they constitute only 23% of those deployed against and 18% of the arrested population. Thus, we would respond that on effectiveness measures alone, such targeting is inefficient, but we would also challenge the notion that it is irrelevant. Just because no intervention or arrest results does not mean that a significant social interaction, albeit remote and technologically mediated, has not taken place. Imagine two youths who, on entering city centre space, are immediately picked up by the cameras. They notice the first camera moving to track them as they move through the streets and go out of range of one camera. At the same time, another camera is seen altering its position to bring them into view. In fact, wherever they go they can see cameras being repositioned to monitor their every movement. How do these youths feel? They have done nothing wrong, they have not drawn attention to themselves by their behaviour and they are not "known offenders." But they are being treated as a threat, as people who cannot be trusted, as persons who do not belong, as unwanted outsiders. The guarantee that such systems will show no interest or engage in deliberate monitoring of people going about their daily business is empty rhetoric.

This technologically mediated and distanced social interaction is, then, loaded with meaning. Moreover, for literally thousands of black and working-class youths, however law-abiding, it transmits a wholly negative message about their position in society. But it has wider consequences than just its impact on individual psychology. The central tenet of policing by consent — that policing is viewed as legitimate by those who experience it — is undermined. If social groups experience CCTV surveillance as an extension of discriminatory and unjust policing, the consequential loss of legitimacy may have disastrous consequences for social order. As Brogden et al. (1988:90) have argued, it was precisely this experience of unjust policing that was both the "underlying cause and the trigger of all the urban riots of the 1980s."

Acknowledgements: We gratefully acknowledge the support of the Economic and Social Research Council who gave substance to the first author's initial interest in CCTV by funding a project on CCTV, Surveillance and Social Control (Grant no: L210252023) under its Crime and Social Order Programme. This enabled the second author to work full-time studying the operation of CCTV control rooms. We would also like to thank the various colleagues who have helped in bringing this project to fruition, especially Keith Bottomley, Clive Coleman, Jason Ditton, Jade Moran, Nigel Norris and Malcolm Young.

Address correspondence to: Clive Norris, Centre for Criminology and Criminal Justice, University of Hull, Hull, HU6 7RX, United Kingdom.

REFERENCES

Bowling, B., J. Graham and A. Ross (1994). "Self-Reported Offending among Young People in England and Wales." In: J. Junger-Tas, G. J. Terlouw and M. Klein (eds.), *Delinquent Behaviour Among Young People in the Western World*. Amsterdam, NETH: Kugler.

Brogden, M., T. Jefferson and S. Walklate (1988). *Introducing Policework*. London, UK: Unwin Hyman.

Brown, S. (1998). "What's the Problem, Girls? CCTV and the Gendering of Public Safety." In: C. Norris, J. Moran and G. Armstrong (eds.), *Surveillance, Closed Circuit Television and Social Control*. Aldershot, UK: Ashgate.

Bulos, M. and D. Grant (1996). *Towards a Safer Sutton? CCTV One Year On*. London, UK: London Borough of Sutton.

—— and C. Sarno (1996). *Codes of Practice and Public Closed Circuit Television Systems*. London, UK: Local Government Information Unit.

Coleman, C. and J. Moynihan (1996). *Understanding Crime Data*. Milton Keynes, UK: Open University Press.

Ditton, J. and E. Short (1998). "Evaluating Scotland's First Town Centre CCTV Scheme." In: C. Norris, J. Moran, and G. Armstrong (eds.), *Surveillance, Closed Circuit Television and Social Control*. Aldershot, UK: Ashgate.

Edwards, S. (1989). *Policing "Domestic" Violence*. London, UK: Sage.

Graham, S. (1998). "Towards the Fifth Utility? On the Extension and Normalisation of Public CCTC." In: C. Norris, J. Moran and G. Armstrong (eds.), *Surveillance, Closed Circuit Television and Social Control*. Aldershot, UK: Ashgate.

McConville, M., A. Sanders and R. Leng (1991). *The Case for the Prosecution*. London, UK: Routledge.

Norris, C. and G. Armstrong (1997). *The Unforgiving Eye: CCTV Surveillance in Public Space.* Mimeo. Hull, UK: Centre for Criminology and Criminal Justice, University of Hull.

—— and G. Armstrong (1999). *The Maximum Surveillance Society.* Oxford, UK: Berg.

Sacks, H. (1978). "Notes on Police Assessment of Moral Character." In: J. Maanen and P.K. Manning (eds.), *Policing: A View from the Street.* New York, NY: Random House.

Short, E. and J. Ditton (1996). *Does Closed Circuit Television Prevent Crime?* Edinburgh, SCOT: Central Research Unit, Scottish Office.

Skinns, D. (1998). "Crime Reduction, Diffusion and Displacement: Evaluation of the Effectiveness of CCTV". In: C. Norris, J. Moran and G. Armstrong (eds.), *Surveillance, Closed Circuit Television and Social Control.* Aldershot, UK: Ashgate.

Squires, P. and L. Measor (1996). *Closed Circuit TV Surveillance and Crime Prevention in Brighton: Half Yearly Report.* Brighton, UK: University of Brighton.

Stanko, E. (1985). *Intimate Intrusions: Women's Experience of Male Violence.* London, UK: Routledge and Kegan Paul.

Tilley, N. (1993). *Understanding Car Parks, Crime and CCTV.* (Crime Prevention Unit Series Paper, #42.) London, UK: Home Office.

[7]

'You'll never walk alone': CCTV surveillance, order and neo-liberal rule in Liverpool city centre[1]

Roy Coleman and Joe Sim

ABSTRACT

This paper is concerned to chart the establishment and uses of CCTV within the location of Liverpool city centre. In doing this the paper seeks to contextualize CCTV within contemporary 'partnership' approaches to regeneration which are reshaping the material and discursive form of the city. Thus CCTV schemes along with other security initiatives are understood as social ordering strategies emanating from within locally powerful networks which are seeking to define and enact orderly regeneration projects. In focusing on the normative aspects of CCTV, the paper raises questions concerning the efficacy of understanding contemporary forms of 'social ordering practices' primarily in terms of technical rationalities while neglecting other, more material and ideological processes involved in the construction of social order.

KEYWORDS: CCTV; crime; regeneration; order; state

Liverpool's trades union leaders of 1991 crowing atop piles of stinking rubbish like cockerels on dung heaps, its welfare mentality growing upon the destruction of wealth producing jobs ... poverty and crime nourished on the thin gruel of welfare, the whole mess financed by borrowing whose costs choke any tentative growth of industry or commerce, was the world's image and terrible reality of Britain in the 1970s. (Tebbit 1991: 23)

The city is reinventing itself and tuning in with the requirements of modern learning curves. Morphocity is now informed by a new and different set of values: openness, meritocracy, social diversity, plurality of skills, youth culture, transparency, vision, change, experimentation and cosmopolitanism. (Humphreys and MacDonald 1995: 50)

For many political and media commentators the views expressed by

Norman Tebbit identified the malaise that had gripped Liverpool since the 1970s: a political, economic and cultural backwater, a disorderly city at odds with the cutting edge of neo-liberal discourse and the maker of its own demise. In contrast the notion of 'Morphocity' emerges from a document that speaks of a 'new' Liverpool: a city in renaissance, forward looking, replete with the latest technologies of urban management which for some contemporary commentaries is expressive of an urban space that is creative, spontaneous and 'playful' (Christopherson 1994: 409). The contemporary regeneration of Liverpool encapsulates these two contrasting positions. There is currently a struggle to re-image the city and to invoke a sense of 'place' that coheres with broader strategies concerned with managing a range of problems which could potentially disqualify the city from its share in the national and international market place. Within these strategic problems of urban governance, debates about crime, insecurity and social anxiety are central to 'a very contemporary political struggle over notions of the public as well as private interest' (Taylor 1997: 70).

This paper analyses the development of Closed Circuit Television Cameras (CCTV) and their place within the construction of Liverpool as 'Morphocity'. In developing our argument we build on the work of a number of writers who have been particularly concerned with questions of the state and state power. What Foucault (1991: 103) identified as the 'the excessive value attributed to the problem of the state' has encouraged a shift in the analysis of power under 'neo-liberal' conditions towards multiple centres of government, autonomous forms of expertise and localized technologies and mechanisms of rule (Rose and Miller 1992; Barry et al. 1996). Thus contemporary forms of crime control and, more broadly social control, are understood as phenomena exercised and nurtured through neo-liberal rule within dense networks and alliances acting 'at a distance' from central and national 'public powers' (Rose 1996: 58).

We wish to challenge some of these assumptions. If, as Norris and Armstrong (1997: 8) argue, CCTV surveillance is to be understood critically, as 'a form of power with a number of dimensions' we will focus on how this power is to be understood, its sites of exercise and contextualization, and its role in both constructing and circumscribing the meaning of urban governance, 'order' and 'regeneration'. Thus in seeking to understand technologies of urban rule the paper draws attention to and argues for an analysis of the normative discourses that underpin techniques and strategies for the maintenance of order as articulated by those involved in initiating these strategies. The paper is divided into three sections. Section one discusses the interests that have shaped the consolidation of the camera network in the city; section two provides a broader theoretical consideration of the issues involved; finally section three offers some concluding thoughts on the future direction of crime control and the role of CCTV in the process of criminal justice.

PARTNERSHIP AND REVITALIZATION IN LIVERPOOL

Regenerating the City

Regeneration in Liverpool is built around retailing, consumption, commerce, leisure and tourism, culture and the arts (The City of Liverpool 1996). As in other cities it is underpinned by a partnership approach to governance that has consolidated the involvement of a 'new business elite', encouraged by European and central government funding criteria, in local economic and political development strategies (Bassett 1996). Established in 1992 the Liverpool City Centre Partnership (LCCP) is part of a network of local bodies loosely connected to local government which is concerned with the promotion and regeneration of the city. The LCCP has a team of seconded personnel who have an annual administration budget of £72,000. It is involved in various schemes orientated 'towards maximising the city centre's potential as a regional centre, and enhancing its attractiveness to all those who use it' (LCCP 1996: 5).

The Partnership makes decisions about, and acts as a catalyst and facilitator for, generating funds for city centre developments including transport, area ownership schemes, re-development projects, anti-litter campaigns, and street security. Much of this work is centred on an Action Group involving Merseytravel, the city's two universities, Liverpool Stores' Committee and the Chamber of Commerce. Outside interests are targeted by the Group as potential investors in local projects including CCTV (Coleman and Sim 1998: 30).

The LCCP was therefore established as a local initiative and was chaired by the (un-elected) City Centre Manager. Its work runs parallel with the government sponsored Merseyside Development Corporation and City Challenge, both of whom emphasize a partnership and more business-like approach to governing urban centres. 'Efficiency' is stressed through the neo-liberal strategy of 'flexible' institutional arrangements and fragmented service provision which address specific issues and problems rather than providing universally agreed services (Cochrane 1993: 95). Such entrepreneurial governance not only involves business but the application of management techniques espousing expert-technical 'solutions' which appear 'neutral' and provide a claim to legitimacy outside of the electoral process. The City Centre Manager in Liverpool is invariably described in the local press as 'city centre supremo' who in 'getting done what needs to be done' (Research Interview) is constructed as a dynamic destroyer of the 'red tape mentality' which is invariably associated with local democratic politics.

The Liverpool City Centre Plan published in 1993 (The City of Liverpool 1993: 4–6) outlines its vision for the city. It noted that 'competition is intense' and that the public and private sectors must work 'to a common purpose' to develop 'the strategies, policies and proposals needed to help create Liverpool as an international city'. The instigation of 'proper management' through harnessing public and private is the prescribed role of the LCCP (op.cit.: 30). A distinctive city image has been marketed: 'Liverpool – A Maritime City', 'A Pool of Talent' and 'Local and Proud' are three examples of this marketing. The Albert Dock complex, which claims 5 million visitors a year, contains the city's bid for 'cultural differentiation', the Tate Gallery. In attracting 'capital and people of the right sort' local partnerships have planned and funded improved telecommunications, infrastructural support, tourist attractions and leisure services involving Beatles tours, cafe-bars and sports (Coleman and Sim 1998: 31). Private developments in retail and leisure are underpinned by Merseyside's Objective One funding status whereby £630 million has already been claimed from the European Community for investments in technology, exports, marketing and small businesses (*The Times* 5th March 1995). The attempts to expand the service based economy built on the initiatives above have been hailed as a success for the city and its people in creating investment and jobs. Tales of success have been trumpeted through the local press with headlines such as 'Mersey Partners Doing the Business' (*Liverpool Echo* 20 May 1998); 'Mersey fortunes in the hands of experts' (*Liverpool Echo* 12 September 1996) and 'Progress – Here and Now' (*Liverpool Echo* 11 September 1995). Such strategies of 'place marketing' attempt to positively promote aspects of the city's 'quality of life' – its health, heritage, culture, infrastructure, leisure and other amenities. Included in these promotional campaigns are the discourses of 'safety' and 'security' that seek to re-image locations as 'safe places to do business'. One such promotional document jointly produced by Merseyside Police and Business in the Community is titled *Merseyside: A Safe Place to do Business?* and addresses potential investors in an effort to counter negative images of the region and the city. It states

> If Merseyside is to become a hotbed of industrial activity it is essential that we can effectively attract new businesses here. All forms of grant assistance to Merseyside are allowing companies to make considerable improvements to their premises, to not only make them more appealing but much more secure against crime. Most of our major town centres now have comprehensive CCTV systems and many businesses are participating in various schemes that upgrade their security. (Merseyside Police Community Strategy Department 1998: 1)

A survey (shown to one of the researchers) conducted through the Government Office indicated that decisions to invest in the city depended (in order of importance) on perceptions of crime, poor industrial relations and political instability. For urban managers these perceptions inform 'the client pool of our potential inward investment' (Research Interview) and the regeneration work they undertake. These developments have simultaneously been underpinned by the drive to create a safe, consumer orientated environment in the city centre, a drive which has been legitimated by a number of academic contributions towards the creation of 'safer city centres' (Oc and Tiesdell 1997). One survey has suggested that potential city centre users are deterred by fear of car crime, litter, vagrants/ beggars and gangs of youths (in descending order of perceived seriousness). A majority preferred to consume and pursue leisure activities in enclosed malls containing CCTV and a visible private security presence. Therefore in order to reverse the move away from the city centres it has been argued that public and private interests will need to fund 'safe shopping strategies' (Beck and Willis 1995). It is against this background that CCTV cameras emerged and have become consolidated in Liverpool.

CCTV in Liverpool

Liverpool's camera network was launched in July 1994 with total capital funding of £396,000. Central government and the European Regional Development Fund contributed £100,000 and £158,000 respectively while £138,000 came from the private sector. Twenty high resolution pan, tilt and zoom cameras with full night-time capability were initially installed within an area of the two square miles which covered the central shopping and office districts. David McClean the then Home Office Minister for Crime Prevention highlighted the murder of local two-year-old James Bulger at the network's high-profile launch to illustrate the need for CCTV. National media coverage also focussed on the preventative capacity of CCTV in protecting children in public (Coleman and Sim 1998: 31).

Although the police contributed neither capital funding nor maintenance costs, monitor and audio links have subsequently been installed at Merseyside Police Headquarters and in the Police Shop located in the city's central shopping street. Cameras have been placed on police advice in 'recognised trouble spots and escape routes' (LCCP 1996: 1). By 1998 the network had 40 cameras and was monitored by a private security firm from a secret control room located in one of Liverpool's shopping malls. The system forms part of an extensive network which links the police, private security and in-house store security via a radio 'early warning' system which makes possible the monitoring of persons in both open public space and private shop space.

However, while official discourses highlight and amplify the particular risks which it is contended CCTV can manage, these discourses tell us very little about the deeper political struggles and the shifts in urban governance that informed the consolidation of the network. The trajectory of CCTV in Liverpool demonstrates the particularities of its emergence within specific elite partnerships whose powerful discursive interventions have been central to the development of a local social ordering strategy. Through the LCCP, the private sector has played a central role in constructing definitions of risk and danger in the city and who should be targeted to avoid these risks and dangers. Their hegemonic ascendance was fought for within the context of fiscal constraints on both local police and local government and in the spaces created by the developments towards entrepreneurial governance. Since the middle of the 1970s Merseyside Police has maintained one of the highest recorded crime rates and costs of any police force in the UK (Brogden 1982). Today the force is the second most expensive in the country and takes 11 per cent of its income from local council tax which through the 1990s has been set at the highest national level (Merseyside Police Authority Annual Report 1998: 4). This situation, coupled with the perception that Liverpool has a particularly negative image, led to local businesses mobilizing and pushing for cameras in the city. Thus, 'the Bulger case served to focus attention but was not the prime cause in establishing CCTV – it's a much longer term thing than that' (Research Interview). Furthermore business perceptions of police 'ineffectiveness' and falling 'morale' underpinned the drive towards the network's development.

Within this context a 'siege mentality' developed among local retailers who felt let down by public authorities and who therefore identified advantages in a privately funded and managed security network

> We were the leading advocate of CCTV. We had been pursuing the issue for 4 or 5 years before the establishment of the City Centre Partnership but when the Partnership was formed the number one priority of the City Manager was to establish a CCTV system which he did successfully . . . housed in the city centre and run predominantly by the private sector. (Research Interview)

Thus the cameras developed out of longer term struggles at the local level to managing the negative image of the city as a 'dangerous place' and in the need to counter the 'horrendous losses' from shop theft (Research Interview).

Private interests were lobbied to fund the scheme. Local interests were 'pretty sold on the idea' as 'they all had the same problems, previously outlined and there was a general move toward this' (ibid.). At the same time, the development of the system was not unproblematic. Collecting revenue for the network was a key problem for the LCCP who had 'to go cap in hand' to maintain funding. This was derided as 'no way to run a business' (Research Interview).

Tensions also existed between the police, who were 'at arms length with CCTV in the early years' (ibid.), and the LCCP. It was felt that the police should be more involved in managing and funding the system

> One of the reasons I was unwilling to push forward with it was I and others felt very strongly that Merseyside Police should have accepted long term liabilities for the maintenance and management of the system. Okay, it's an expensive system . . . but realistically it [is] a policing tool. (Research Interview)

For other private agencies the 'arms length' approach of the police enhanced the system's credibility amongst the local population

> We make the point – and I think it's very healthy – that this is a separate and independent body. I think the worst thing is if the police had

control of the system. I'm not saying anything improper would happen ... but I think public perception and credibility is everything. Whilst we've got Mr and Mrs Bloggs on board, great. (Research Interview)

Despite these contradictions the system was quickly hailed as a success by all of those involved. Importantly the notion of 'success' was ubiquitously expressed in a context whereby 'it would be difficult to produce accurate and meaningful figures relating to the CCTV system' (LCCP 1996: 1). At the same time the system was deemed to be an effective tool in targeting those who had long been identified as problematic in the city centre: 'that is what is most effective about CCTV ... It is effective when you know *who* you are looking for' (Research Interview, emphasis in the original). Thus while senior corporate managers could point to the 'reassurance' that the network gave to 'potential investors' *(Liverpool Echo* 13 June 1996), the secure, regenerated city was also based on a moral vision in which 'people feel happy to come and shop on a family basis ... people are preoccupied with shopping and that's how it should be' (Research interview). The cameras' role was about generating 'an appropriate police response' and sending out a clear message to those targeted by the system so that 'known shoplifters and people who are banned cannot walk around the city centre with impunity' (ibid.). The police were also clear in their support

The system is like having 20 more officers on duty 24 hours a day, who make a note of everything, never take a holiday and are rarely off sick. (City Centre Commander, *The Times* 6 July 1994)

Thus the impetus behind the establishment of CCTV was complex involving the desire to reconstruct Liverpool's deviant image, the bolstering of consumer and business confidence and the concern to counter particular forms of crime. The cameras were therefore crucial to what Norris and Armstrong (1998: 10) have termed 'the social construction of suspicion' – a process that was increasingly left to emergent 'primary definers' from the private sector. This involved an instrumental drive that prioritized profit and loss underpinned by the construction of a preferred and particular moral order built on the politics of inclusionary respectability and exclusionary otherness.

CCTV cameras were and are pivotal to this process. In the next part of the paper, we want to situate the network in a broader theoretical context and to consider how a materialist perspective can help to explain CCTV as a strategy for what Nicola Lacey has called 'social ordering practices' (Lacey 1994: 28).

RE-THINKING CCTV: THEORETICAL CONSIDERATIONS

Recent work in criminological and sociological theory appears to provide the explanatory framework necessary for understanding the changing nature of crime control in advanced capitalist states and the place of CCTV within that control. In particular the work of writers such as Peter Miller and Nikolas Rose has been important in utilizing key themes in Foucault's analysis of governmentality for dissecting 'the rationalities and technologies that are currently emerging in the field of crime control' (Garland 1997: 173). These themes include: first, that the 'apparatus of a State have neither the unity nor functionality ascribed to them' (Rose 1996: 42–3); second, that the power of the state is a 'resultant not a cause, an outcome of the composition and assembling of actors, flows, buildings, relations of authority . . . towards the achievement of particular objectives by common means' (ibid.: 43); third, that sociological analysis must focus on 'governmentalities' defined as 'complex processes of negotiation' between 'loose and mobile networks that can bring persons, organisations and objectives into alignment' (Miller and Rose 1990: 1); fourth, that under neo-liberal conditions, public authorities 'seek to employ forms of expertise in order to govern society at a distance, without recourse to any direct forms of repression or intervention' (Barry et al. 1996: 14). Finally, the development of electronic communications and technologies while increasing the 'quantity and rapidity of the flow of information between spatially dispersed points' has done so without 'the need for an extensive system of surveillance controlled by the state' (ibid.).

While there is much that we would agree with in this literature, particularly the emphasis on the non-homogeneity of state structures and the contingency of state action, the assumption that the alignments which have materialized under neo-liberal conditions constitute 'action-at-a-distance' prioritizes the technical and instrumental over the ideological and normative aspects of local crime control policy. The governmentality literature also neglects the complex relationship between the local and the national in the formulation of crime control policy. We wish to illustrate these points by exploring four dimensions that have been central to the development of CCTV.

The New Networks of State Power

Partnership in Liverpool involves the re-working of established local elite interests. This process raises analytical questions around the nature of state formation and power particularly in relation to the individuals involved and the ideologies they bring to this involvement. Personal links between individuals in the state and civil society at local and national levels and the coincidence of interests on which these links have been built and reproduced have been central to a materialist analysis of the state since it assumed its modern form at the beginning of the nineteenth century (Miliband 1969; Corrigan 1977).

For our purposes the notion of 'the catalytic state' (Weiss 1997: 26) is useful in understanding how the state remains and retains an active power centre both in ideological terms and policy setting. The consolidation of

CCTV cameras in Liverpool illustrates how such links operate at local and national levels through a variety of agencies, partnerships, formal and informal networks and traditional state structures. The official aim of the Government Office for Merseyside which employs some 300 staff is to bring coherence to the regeneration programme and to strategically develop partnerships in the region. The Assistant Chief Constable attends meetings of the CBI in order to inform and reassure potential investors as to the effectiveness of policing strategies on levels of crime. Businesses, police and private security firms have agreed a strategy for 'Town Watch' personnel in the city. Initially pushed by the Stores' Committee, its most notable early supporter was Marks and Spencer who not only work closely with the Government Office but whose directors hold regular meetings with Home Office Ministers of State. Furthermore the role of 'Town Watch' has been agreed by the Association of Chief Police Officers. Its aims are: to trigger an 'appropriate' police response; check the validity of Big Issue sellers; encourage people not to drop litter; and offer help to tourists. The plan is to recruit from the long term unemployed and to train them in 'non-aggressive communication skills' (Research Interview). As one interviewee has expressed it

> [Town Watch is] only part of the solution. Town Watch feeds in with an agreed strategy between city centre occupiers, it involves linking in with CCTV, it involves linking in with the police. It also involves a significant publicity campaign so people know why they are there – its got to be marketed right. (ibid.)

As was noted above, the Government Office is central to the co-ordination process. In Liverpool it utilizes a Superintendent seconded from the police and links the local with the national

> I think it is a method for delivering on a local basis but the policies, the significant policies, are still set nationally by central government but it's left to local government and other organisations . . . to actually deliver things on the ground and to feed back to the central policy making machinery about what works, what doesn't and why. (Ibid.)

Thus crime control initiatives such as CCTV, the criteria for establishing such systems and their uses are decided centrally with local feedback mechanisms reporting back to the policy centre. Furthermore, the co-ordinating role of the Government Office not only establishes links between the centre and the local but provides a platform for established powerful actors – namely the police – at the local level. The work of such bodies is concerned with building a consensus among local elite agencies regarding the 'good governance' and strategic rule of a particular locality which for the police and other institutions means experimenting with new cross-agency roles. As one interviewee expressed it

> The police organization wants to be involved in the regeneration process as partners and we want to see the place as a vibrant region which is

attractive to inward investors and supports a high quality of life for citizens and visitors. Having a police officer in here has been able to make a change in the bid approval process and help deliver policy objectives around quality of life and freedom from crime. It is actually a good thing for the police as an organisation as well as a good thing for the people of Merseyside. It's an example of good practice.

Ideologically, therefore, the 'old' and the 'new' managers of social control stand on the same discursive terrain. It is a terrain, which although it contains contradictions and contingencies, is none the less constructed around who and what is problematic for the social order of the city. The ideological distance in relation to the problematic other is therefore minimal, a key point which is neglected in the governmentality literature discussed earlier. This point is elaborated in the next section of the paper.

Defining Risk and the Objects of Power

The emphasis within the governmentality literature on *how* government is possible – its techniques and procedures – has downplayed questions of *why* forms of rule have been adopted – their normative and value laden underpinnings. Thus the formal and informal networks described above raise significant theoretical questions about 'government-at-a-distance'. Linked to these networks are the definitions of crime and insecurity articulated by those involved in groups such as the Stores' Committee which often cut across and blur tensions and contradictions between them and the organizations involved in the networks. During the course of our research, findings from observational data were accrued from regular attendance at one meeting point for public and private police – *Crime Alert.* It is here that the police, crime prevention and operational support, private security and store security meet on a monthly basis to discuss intelligence and the targeting of activities in the city centre. These meetings provide a central focus for local business, police and private security in defining risks, gaps in the network and policing objectives. Such closed forums it could be argued constitute the development of local 'security networks' within which the police are but one component in a broader reconfiguration of local governance. Such a network defines the role and use of CCTV in Liverpool. The activities targeted, the gathering of intelligence and its dissemination is focused on recurring categories: youth, 'known and potential' shoplifters, the homeless and licensed and unlicensed street traders. These problem categories and those involved in their primary definition reinforce and consolidate the discourses around who and what are problematic for social order.

Partnership has opened up political spaces for new 'primary definers' (Schlesinger and Tumber 1995: 17) to articulate a strategy for urban, social and political regeneration while simultaneously identifying those who pose a danger to that regeneration. It is within these spaces that notions of the 'public interest' are being recast around discourses of crime and insecurity. Ideologically, the individuals actively participating in this process operate as 'constructor, organiser "permanent persuader" and not just [as] simple orator[s]' (Gramsci 1971: 10). They not only legitimate new technologies such as CCTV but they also provide an ideological and political space where traditional state servants such as the police who have suffered a severe crisis of legitimacy can reassert their credibility by supporting a strategy which appears to be impacting on the crime rate (Coleman and Sim 1998: 40). There are therefore important continuities between those involved in the new networks and traditional state servants and the definitions of crime, risk and danger which underpin the operationalization of CCTV.

Women have been particularly targeted within this discourse. The aims and objectives of the Liverpool system make special reference to a safer environment being created for women and children (LCCP 1996). However, the notion that CCTV promotes women's safety in public spaces is problematic. Indeed, the cameras may reinforce the masculinization of those spaces (Brown 1997). Furthermore, the needs of women conflict with official discourses surrounding security and insecurity built as they often are on alternative definitions of reality relating to adequate toilet provision, crèche facilities and transportation (Creed 1994). Feminist research continues to maintain that the risk of violence towards women and the actuality of that violence, remain in the private sphere (Mooney 1997). Thus the masculine definition of risk and insecurity continues to dominate debates around crime prevention (Walklate 1997). More broadly, the interests behind CCTV operationalize particular conceptions of order and danger in the city and marginalize alternative definitions of danger and insecurity which do not fit easily within a traditional crime prevention framework. These other definitions which would also challenge the notion of the city centre as a 'safe' place include: sexual and racial harassment on the streets and in workplaces, homophobic violence, insecurities generated by homelessness, city centre pollution and local white-collar crime such as fraud and income tax evasion (Coleman and Sim 1998: 35).

Militarization and Authoritarianism

In a recent collection which exemplifies the theoretical and political underpinnings of the 'government-at-a-distance' literature the editors argued that 'public authorities seek to employ forms of expertise in order to govern society at a distance without recourse to direct forms of repression or intervention' (Barry et al.1996: 14). The appearance of CCTV seems to provide a clear example of the authors' arguments. They have been taken up by other authors who have maintained that CCTV is underpinned by 'chains of enrolment' and loose coalitions at the local level which is indicative of a 'new penology' concerned with managing 'risk' (McCahill 1997: 53–7). However in making these arguments these authors ignore a central development in relation to the state, namely the intensification in the militaristic and authoritarian capabilities that state servants have at their disposal and the range of practices initiated towards the 'policing of social boundaries' that characterize 'the militarization of street life' (Davis 1990: 223). In the UK the intensification in the coercive capabilities of the state across a range of criminal justice areas has been profound in the last two decades and has fallen disproportionately on the powerless to the further detriment of the policing of the powerful (Hillyard and Percy-Smith 1988; Scraton et al. 1991; Ryan and Sim 1995). We do not wish to enter into the full complexities of the debate about the nature of the UK state here. However, as Nicos Poulantzas and Bob Jessop have argued, discourse theory in general and Foucault's work in particular is theoretically and politically compromised by its failure to deal with the materiality of violence and coercion in securing compliance (Poulantzas 1978; Jessop 1990). Thus in Liverpool (and in the UK in general) the network of cameras reinforce and are reinforced by a heavily militarized police force which is not only taking to the streets but in doing so is militarizing city spaces under the watchful gaze of those who operate the network. In the city, 72 police officers are trained and regularly deployed in armed response techniques, the local prison is now one of the biggest in Europe, a new private prison has been opened, there is the possibility that a third institution will open in the near future and there is an increasing emphasis on intelligence gathering to the point where *Crime Alert* which meets every month and which consists of local business people and undercover police discuss who should be targeted and kept under surveillance. In and around the city centre the police are initiating 'zero tolerance' strategies in an 'all out war on street crimes' financed by £30 million from the Home Office 'Crime Hotspot' fund (*Liverpool Echo* 13 November 1998). Furthermore, a senior police officer and council officials visited New York in 1998 to observe the experiments in 'quality of life policing' in Liverpool's twin city (*Liverpool Echo* 30 September 1998). Other initiatives include 'Operation Tranquility' which is committed to 'keeping unruly youngsters off the streets' (*Liverpool Echo* 17 October 1997). These and other examples point to a dialectical relationship between the 'old' style of policing with its emphasis on responding quickly and coercively to designated deviants and trouble-spots and the new technologies of surveillance which CCTV represents. The deployment of militarized police officers to targeted hot spots and the racialized use of stop and search powers (Statewatch 1999) provide indications of continuities of state control practices and of the need to analyse CCTV not as a benign alternative to such practices but in dialectical inter-relation to them. The cameras can be understood as part of a social ordering strategy which although not always coherent designates who can legitimately use public space, where and when. Thus governmentality theorists have ignored the centrality of coercive aspects of power directed at dissenters from neo-liberal rule (Frankel 1997; Stenson 1997).

CCTV, The New Governance and Securing Consent

Some have argued that surveillance technologies and electronic communications can be understood not simply as instruments of state surveillance but rather as technologies of freedom (Barry 1996: 138). Within this
discourse CCTV cameras can be understood as helping to create public
spaces for 'free', 'responsible', consumer-oriented individuals who independently choose their autonomous role in the life of the city. Thus CCTV
is constructed around the idea of 'empowerment' and 'freedom', particularly the 'freedom and safety to shop' (Home Office 1994: 9).

Central to these processes is the desire to promote consumer confidence
and participation in the city centre. This in turn is built on very specific
ideas about the legitimate use of the city centre and the *moral* order which
underpins it. Thus one interviewee has described the camera system as

> a people's system . . . it is very important that we get over the feeling they
> are in a safe city and that hopefully generates and sustains the pedestrian
> flow of traffic . . . people feel happy to come and shop on a family basis.
> *It affects everybody where there is criminal activity in town centres.* (Research
> Interview, emphasis added)

The deployment of such discursive representations pertaining to the uses
of the city centre form part of a larger orchestration concerned to construct a consensualized ideal of a benign authoritative power over territory.
In Liverpool, co-ordinating agencies such as the Government Office underpinned by 'advanced liberal strategies of rule' have brought together
police, developers, regeneration managers, businesses and elected
officials. However, in scrutinizing the work of these networks it is important to critically analyse their role in securing legitimacy and consent from
the wider populace – in 'convincing local peoples as to the benevolence of
entrepreneurial strategies' (Hall and Hubbard 1996: 162). Included here
are an abundance of 'place marketing' strategies through local and
national media that seek to promote generalized images of 'crime' whilst
at the same time promising a 'safer city for all' and thereby, and in conjunction with the other processes we have mentioned, serve to promote
particular interests in city centre regeneration. Partnership in Liverpool
has realigned agencies of governance and put to the fore issues of leadership and strategic direction.

'Partnership' involves constructing alliances that contribute towards 'the
focusing of minds', the 'negotiation of sensible terms of reference' and the
'commitment of resources to agreed packages' (Research Interview).
These processes are re-drawing notions of the public and private interest.
The attempts to build a 'collective will' are not without their contradictions
but neither do such strategies involve a collective 'free for all' where every
opinion carries equal weight in the construction of the consensus around
the 'proper' use of city spaces. As one interviewee pointed out

One of the biggest problems has been around consultation in Liverpool

636   *Roy Coleman and Joe Sim*

and the transparency of the process itself. The temptation is when you
are setting something up you go and talk to somebody who you know will
respond to your need. You take the easy way around. (Research Interview)

As we have indicated the local media play a crucial role in the regeneration
process as a whole and in its representation of Liverpool regarding issues
around crime, safety and policing. As well as supporting and sponsoring
local regeneration projects the local press in particular has been involved
in the re-negotiation of protocols with Merseyside Police regarding policing in the city and levels of crime. One interviewee described these negotiations as 'about building trust with the media' after a series of 'damaging
articles for Liverpool'. These stories

> were basically along the lines of 'crime is out of hand and the police are
> unable to cope with it'. At the end of the day it is as much in the interest
> of the Echo's Editor as it is in the interest of Merseyside Police that we
> repopulate, have prosperity and vibrancy. I mean he'll sell more news-
> papers if there are more people living here, working and with money to
> spend. (Research Interview)

While forging an alliance between key players in the locality has not been
unproblematic in reality this alliance has been central to the construction
of a consensual world-view and the powerful definitions of the 'public
interest' and the 'collective will' that underpin it. The process of coalition-
building has therefore increasingly endeavoured to link the notions of
'good business practice' with the proactive management of crime and its
incidence.

   Thus the security network is not simply to be understood as a mechanism of crime prevention technology but as an important alliance of interests that have emerged in the gaps left by a series of legitimation deficits
around policing and in urban governance generally. The security network
works at constructing a consensus through generating images and categories of dangerousness which target the economically marginalized, the
homeless and petty thieves as groups who consistently appear 'unable to
learn the lesson that neo-liberalism now expects of its subjects' (Pratt 1997:
181). It is therefore in the regenerated city with its not so subtle lessons for
proper conduct in public space – its re-emphasis on spectacle, consumption and 'leisure' – that neo-liberal governance has successfully sustained
economic polarization as well as assumed a greater role in managing its
'fall out' through the deployment of authoritative categories that define
the unreconstituted other.

3. CONCLUSION

At the present historical moment CCTV cameras remain effectively unchal-
lenged in the repertoire of responses to crime in Liverpool and nationally.

The advent of New Labour (NL) into government in May 1997 has seen little critique of the discourses of success which surround the camera network. The Home Secretary, while not blindly pursuing the retributive path of his predecessor (Downes 1998) is none the less showing few signs of deviating from the reductionist explanations of criminal conduct which dominate government, state and popular thinking about crime (Brownlee 1998; Sim 1999). The government's unswerving embrace of new technology across the social landscape and its support for private sector involvement in partnership with the public sector is likely to provide further opportunities for camera networks to flourish. NL's focus on a range of contemporary folk-devils particularly the young as exemplified in the 1998 Crime and Disorder Act (Sim op. cit.) will generate an intensification of surveillance strategies in civil and political society via the rejuvenated nuclear family, the idealized community, the state welfare system and in the institutions of the criminal justice system. CCTV can therefore be seen as part of a surveillance continuum which while not homogenous and cut through with contingencies and contradictions is none the less a key ideological and political player in the construction and reproduction of particular categories of crime and visions of social order. The continuum with its gaze turned almost continuously downwards can be contrasted with the lack of upward surveillance of the powerful whose often socially detrimental and harmful activities remain effectively beyond scrutiny and regulation. Those at the centre of this downward gaze can be understood as the contemporary equivalents of Foucault's leper whose identification and targeting reinforces 'the constant division between the normal and the abnormal' (Foucault 1979: 199–200).

Thus the surveillance continuum along with the coercive apparatus at the state's disposal are being refined within neo-liberal strategies of rule. Unless subjected to serious sociological and political scrutiny then it is likely that CCTV cameras will remain central to sustaining the divisive colonization inherent in advanced capitalist societies which the contemporary equivalents of the leper unconsciously help to reproduce.

(Date accepted: May 2000)

Roy Coleman
and
Joe Sim
Centre for Criminal Justice
Liverpool John Moores University

NOTES

1. The funding for this research was provided by the Research Strategy and Funding Committee, Liverpool John Moores University. The data were gathered through conducting semi-structured interviews with 28 of the key individuals involved in the establishment of the CCTV network in Liverpool as well as attending 8 meetings of those involved in *Crime Alert* (from which field notes were taken). Interviewees were

selected using snowball or network sampling. This was necessary given the 'invisibility' of much partnership work and the difficulties in identifying local nodal points and local actors (particularly from the private sector). Of those interviewed two were from the City Council; eight from local businesses; two developers; three police officers; eight private security and five from quangos. The data from interviews were analysed thematically around the meaning attributed to 'orderly' regeneration, problems perceived to hinder this process and the rationalization for security technologies. All the interviewees have been guaranteed anonymity.

BIBLIOGRAPHY

Barry, A. 1996 'Lines of Communication and spaces of rule', in A. Barry, T. Osborne, and N. Rose (eds) *Foucault and Political Reason: Liberalism, Neo-liberalism and Rationalities of Government*, London: UCL Press.

Barry, A. Osborne, T. and Rose, N. (eds) 1996 'Introduction', in A. Barry, T. Osborne, and N. Rose (eds) *Foucault and Political Reason: Liberalism, Neo-liberalism and Rationalities of Government*, London: UCL Press.

Bassett, K. 1996 'Partnerships, Business Elites and Urban Politics: New Forms of Governance in an English City', *Urban Studies* 33(3) 539–55.

Beck, A. and Willis, A. 1995 *Crime and Security: Managing the Risk to Safe Shopping*, Leicester: Perpetuity Press.

Brogden, M. 1982 *The Police: Autonomy and Consent*, London: Academic Press.

Brown, S. 1997 'What's the problem, girls? CCTV and the gendering of public safety', in C. Norris, J. Moran, and G. Armstrong (eds) *Surveillance, Closed Circuit Television and Social Control*, Aldershot: Ashgate.

Brownlee, I. 1998 'New Labour – New Penology? Punitive Rhetoric and the Limits of Managerialism in Criminal Justice Policy', *Journal of Law and Society* 25(3): 313–35.

Christopherson, S. 1994 'The Fortress City: Privatized Spaces, Consumer Citizenship', in A. Amin (ed.) *Post-Fordism: A Reader*, Oxford: Blackwell.

The City of Liverpool 1993 *Liverpool City Centre Plan*, The City of Liverpool, Planning and Transport Services.

—— 1996 *Ambitions For The City Centre: Liverpool's Draft City Centre Strategy for the Next Five Years*, The City of Liverpool, Planning and Transport Services.

Cochrane, A. 1993 *Whatever Happened to Local Government?*, Buckingham: Open University Press.

Coleman, R. and Sim, J. 1998 'From the Dockyards to the Disney Store: Surveillance, Risk and Security in Liverpool City Centre', *International Review of Law Computers and Technology* 12(1): 27–45.

Corrigan, P. 1977 *State Formation and Moral Regulation in Nineteenth Century Britain: Sociological Investigations*, Unpublished PhD thesis, University of Durham.

Creed, C. H. 1994 *Women and Planning: Creating Gendered Realities*, London: Routledge.

Davis, M. 1990 *City of Quartz: Excavating the Future in Los Angeles*, London: Verso.

Downes, D. 1998 'From Labour Opposition to Labour Government', paper presented at the conference on New Labour and Crime, University of Hull, July.

Foucault, M. 1979 *Discipline and Punish: The Birth of the Prison*, Harmondsworth: Peregrine.

—— 1991 'Governmentality', in G. Burchill, C. Gordon and P. Miller (eds) *The Foucault Effect: Studies in Governmentality*, London: Harvester Wheatsheaf.

Frankel, B. 1997 'Confronting Neoliberal Regimes: The Post-Marxist Embrace of Populism and Realpolitick', *New Left Review* 226 (November/December): 57–92.

Garland, D. 1997 'Governmentality and the problem of crime: Foucault, criminology, sociology', *Theoretical Criminology* 1(2): 173–214.

Gramsci, A. 1971 *Selections from Prison Notebooks*, London: Lawrence and Wishart.

Hall, T. and Hubbard, P. 1996 'The entrepreneurial city: new urban politics new urban geographies?', *Progress in Human Geography* 20(2): 153–174.

Hillyard, P. and Percy-Smith, J. 1998 *The Coercive State*, London: Fontana.

Home Office 1994 *CCTV: Looking For You*, London: HMSO.

Humphries, J. and McDonald, R. 1995 *Morphocity: Architectural Odyssey*, Centre for

Architecture, Liverpool John Moores University.

Jessop, B. 1990 *State Theory: Putting Capitalist States in their Place*, Cambridge: Polity Press.

Lacey, N. 1994 'Introduction: Making Sense of Criminal Justice', in N. Lacey (ed.) *Criminal Justice*, Oxford: Oxford University Press.

Liverpool City Centre Partnership 1996 *CCTV in Liverpool City Centre: A Partnership Approach to a Safer City*.

Liverpool Echo 1996 'Spy at Night', 13 June.
—— 1997 'Caught on Camera', 17 October.
—— 1998 'All Out War On Street Crimes', 13 November.
—— 1998 'NYPD Blueprint For Crime Fight', 30 September.

McCahill, M. 1997 'Beyond Foucault: towards a contemporary theory of surveillance', in C. Norris, J. Moran and G. Armstrong (eds) *Surveillance, Closed Circuit Television and Social Control*, Aldershot: Ashgate.

Merseyside Police Authority 1998 *Annual Report 1997–1998*.

Merseyside Police Community Strategy Department 1998 *Merseyside: A Safe Place to do Business?*, Community Strategy Department – Merseyside Police

Miller, P. and Rose, N. 1990 'Governing economic life', *Economy and Society* 19(1): 1–30.

Miliband, R. 1969 *The State in Capitalist Society: The Analysis of the Western System of Power*, London: Quartet Books.

Mooney, J. 1997 'Violence, Space and Gender: The Social and Spatial Parameters of Violence Against Women and Men', in N. Jewson and S. MacGregor *Transforming Cities: Contested Governance and New Spatial Divisions*, London: Routledge.

Norris, C. and Armstrong, G. 1997 'Introduction: power and vision', in C. Norris, J. Moran and G. Armstrong (eds) *Surveillance, Closed Circuit Television and Social Control*, Aldershot: Ashgate.
—— 1998 'The suspicious eye', *Criminal Justice Matters*, 33 (Autumn): 10–11.

Oc, T. and Tiesdell, S. (eds) 1997 *Safer City Centres: Reviving the Public Realm*, London: Paul Chapman Publishing.

Poulantzas, N. 1978 *State, Power, Socialism*, London: Verso.

Pratt, J. 1997 *Governing the Dangerous*, Sydney: The Federation Press.

Rose, N. 1996 'Governing "advanced" liberal democracies', in A. Barry, T. Osborne, and N. Rose (eds) *Foucault and Political Reason: Liberalism, Neo-liberalism and Rationalities of Government*, London: UCL Press.

Rose, N. and Miller, P. 1992 'Political power beyond the state: problematics of government', *British Journal of Sociology* 43(2): 173–205.

Ryan, M. and Sim, J. 1995 'The Penal System in England and Wales: Round up the Usual Suspects', in V. Ruggiero, M. Ryan and J. Sim (eds) *Western European Penal Systems: A Critical Anatomy*, London: Sage

Schlesinger, P. and Tumber, H. 1995 *Reporting Crime: The Media Politics of Criminal Justice*, Oxford: Clarendon

Scraton, P. Sim, J. and Skidmore, P. 1991 *Prisons Under Protest*, Buckingham: Open University Press.

Sim, J. 1999 'New Labour and Social Harm', paper presented to the conference on Zemiology: Beyond Criminology? Darlington Hall, February.

Stenson, K. 1997 'Rethinking Liberal Government – The Case of Crime Prevention', paper presented to the conference on The Displacement of Social Policies, University of Jyvaskyla, Finland, January 15–16th.

Statewatch 1999 'The cycle of UK racism' 9(1) (January–February): 1–2.

Taylor, I. 1997 'Crime, anxiety and locality: responding to the "condition of England" at the end of the century', *Theoretical Criminology* 1(1): 53–75.

Tebbit, N. 1991 *Unfinished Business*, London: Weidenfeld and Nicolson.

The Times 1994 'Security cameras zoom in on crime', 6 July.
—— 1995 'Merseyside to benefit from European fund', 5 March .

Walklate, S. 1997 'Risk and criminal victimization: a modernist dilemma' *British Journal of Criminology* 37(1): 35–45.

Weiss, L. 1997 'Globalisation and the Myth of the Powerless State', *New Left Review* 225 (September–October): 5–27.

[8]

SEEN AND NOW HEARD

Talking to the Targets of Open Street CCTV

EMMA SHORT and JASON DITTON*

The presence of closed circuit television cameras (CCTV) in town and city centres, mostly with Home Office or Scottish Office support, has grown enormously in the past few years. Analysis of their effectiveness in preventing crime is infrequent, and then usually relies only on comparing police recorded or otherwise reported criminal victimization rates before and after camera installation. It is difficult for this approach to tackle convincingly the possibility of camera-induced crime displacement. This article tries an alternative approach to displacement: asking offenders. To test the efficacy of the approach, an area whose criminal statistical profile had previously been studied intensely—Airdrie, a small town near Glasgow which has one of the first CCTV schemes to be installed in Scotland—was revisited. Thirty offenders (most were then on probation or doing community service) were interviewed and their attitudes to the cameras and to reoffending recorded. Few, if any, clear patterns emerged. Indeed, what is more remarkable is the rich and broad diversity of views, which, in turn, serve to defy any obvious or common-sense categorization of offender reaction to CCTV surveillance.

Background

Open street surveillance Closed Circuit TeleVision (CCTV) has seen explosive growth in the UK, with one estimate concluding that '300,000 security cameras are sold every year and that the annual spend on video surveillance is £300 million' (Bulos, quoted in Groombridge and Murji 1994: 9). A survey conducted by Bulos and Sarno (1994) demonstrated extensive installation of open street CCTV (in a sample containing all London Boroughs and Metropolitan Authorities and 10 per cent of District Councils) with a large proportion of those currently without such schemes intending to install them.

Most recently, in April 1995, the Home Office announced financial support for a further 105 open street CCTV schemes in England and Wales; and even these are unlikely to be the last. Home Office committed funding is now expected to exceed £20m in four years. Scotland has 12 operational open street surveillance CCTV schemes, with Scottish Office funding (on a pound-for-pound basis) for a further 32 schemes announced in August, 1996. More are to be considered for funding in future years.

There are two key concerns relating to the effectiveness of open street surveillance CCTV schemes as crime prevention measures. One, do they reduce crime? Two, if so, is this at the cost of displacing it elsewhere?

SEEN AND NOW HEARD

Hitherto, neither question has been answered satisfactorily. First, there is no agreement on the general effect of CCTV on crime, with some studies claiming it reduces offending (Hancox and Morgan 1975; Burrows 1979; Tilley 1993), others that it has no effect (Musheno *et al*. 1978), and still others that CCTV's ability to reduce crime even spreads outside the area covered by the cameras (Poyner 1988, 1991). That different studies offer contradictory findings may well indicate that CCTV sometimes 'works' and sometimes doesn't. Areas—such as Airdrie, a small town in Scotland which is the subject of this article—where CCTV seems to have had an effect, are worthy of further study oriented to discovering the conditions under which it does 'work', what side effects it might have, and why it might 'work' differentially for different groups, precisely as such areas are in the best position to illustrate these key issues.

Previous analysis of police-recorded crime data for Airdrie indicated that, after seasonal factors and other underlying trends are eliminated, crime fell by 21 per cent in the two years after CCTV cameras were originally installed in the town centre in November 1992 (Short and Ditton 1996).

This cannot be counted as a success until it can be demonstrated that these apparently saved crimes have not simply been displaced elsewhere. In general, various types of displacement are believed possible. First, 'temporal' displacement (moving offending to a different time of day), second, 'tactical' displacement (a change in methods of continuing to offend in the same way); third, 'target' displacement (committing the same crime, but now on different targets); fourth, 'functional' displacement (a move to a different crime), and finally, 'geographical' displacement (offender moving to a different area) (Repetto 1976). Barr and Pease (1990: 279) add a sixth, 'perpetrator' displacement, wherein 'a crime opportunity is so compelling that different offenders are always available to commit the crime. The most obvious example of this type of displacement is international drug trafficking'.

The earlier statistical study did not permit a check for temporal, tactical or target displacement. A check for functional and geographical displacement was conducted by analysing statistical data from policing areas adjacent to those areas with cameras. None was found.

Crimes which had been reduced in the CCTV area (chiefly burglary and car crime) were not found to have increased elsewhere. However, other crimes (mostly drugs offences) had increased both there and elsewhere. This might have been functional displacement, or it might have reflected a general increase in such crimes.

Also, the check (and non-discovery) of geographical displacement was confined to adjacent areas: offenders may well be choosing to move very much further afield to continue offending. Various studies conducted in other countries have found that burglars will travel long distances, and for many hours, to reach their targets (Gabor 1978: 105); but that some, although not all, will be dissuaded from offending by such crime prevention measures (Bennett 1986).

Interviewing offenders is clearly a necessary stage if anything even faintly conclusive is to be said about displacement. Such a strategy is in line with the findings of professional research in crime displacement. Repetto's seminal work was based on interviews with offenders (Repetto 1976); and Gabor (1978: 104) indicates that analyses of statistics 'may constitute necessary, but not sufficient components of a displacement study ... the recognition of the subjective element involved [in offending] necessitates the investigation of offenders' motives and rationale for target selection', because, as he

EMMA SHORT AND JASON DITTON

later claims, 'our inability to detect displacement [from statistics] does not mean that the phenomenon is not present' (Gabor 1990; 60).

Cornish and Clarke (1987: 934–5) add that 'evidence of displacement may lie concealed within . . . crime statistics. Moreover, such research on its own fails to provide an adequate explanation for the occurrence or absence of displacement . . . additional ways of investigating displacement are needed and, in particular, studies which focus upon the offender's own explanations for his decisions and choices.' There is no apparent disagreement with this general position in other key texts (Clarke and Weisburd 1994; Barr and Pease 1990, 1992; Pease 1994).

Accordingly, funds were secured to return to Airdrie, and interview a small number of local offenders.[1] The study reported here was conducted in early mid-1996. Airdrie's CCTV cameras were installed nearly four years earlier. Interviews were conducted with those on probation or on community service in 1996. Probation term lengths are typically 12 months, and never more than three years in Scotland (Ditton and Ford, 1994). Hence our sampling strategy inevitably excludes those offenders that CCTV had persuaded to retire from offending, and concentrates on those determined to continue (or, unaware of the cameras). Such a skew would not be acceptable in a full study.

Sample

A total of 30 offenders was interviewed between early April and the end of May, 1996. Most had appeared in the Airdrie Sheriff Court, and 16 were serving a term of probation at the time, 11 were on community service, and the remaining three were fully at liberty.[2] The youngest was 16 and the oldest 41. Most of them were in their late teens or early twenties. Only three of the 30 were female, and all three were on probation.

Offending History

Most had been involved in the sort of fairly trivial public order offences that town centre CCTV cameras can expect to film (not that this was necessarily how their own cases had come to court). Seventeen had been charged with a variety of non-property offences (breach of the peace, assault, being drunk and disorderly, possession of drugs), nine with theft offences (car theft, shoplifting, housebreaking, shop breaking, loitering with intent, and so on), and the final four with a mixture of non-property and property offences.

---

[1] The authors are grateful to the Nuffield Foundation for funding this pilot study; and to Ken Pease, Nick Tilley and anonymous reviewers for constructive comments on earlier drafts.

[2] Probation is administered by Social Work departments in Scotland, and is not a separate service (see Ditton and Ford 1994). It was intended initially to interview at least 25 probationers contacted through the local social work office, with the hope that more might be contacted via 'snowballing'. In the event, 28 were recruited by the first method, and only two by snowballing. Both the latter were fully at liberty when interviewed; the third was an ex-probationer who had maintained contact with his social worker, who brokered the interview.

SEEN AND NOW HEARD

However, their offending histories confirm that most cannot simply be classified as either property or non-property offenders. Of the 17 classifiable as non-property offenders in terms of their last offence, only eight had a prior offending history just relating to non-property offences. The other nine had previously been involved in property offences or in a mixture of property and non-property offending. Four of the nine with immediately previous property offences had been non-property offenders prior to that. Two of the four with mixed immediately previous offending had only had convictions for property offending before that.

In summary, most are from poor areas and are trapped in low (or, more typically, non-existent) earned incomes. As one 20-year-old man currently on probation for car theft put it, boredom and poverty account for a great deal: '. . . Aye . . . you know . . . make money . . . sittin' skint aw the time[3] . . . living aff a Giro. Can steal a motor, take the motor . . . dae anythin' . . .' A 19-year-old currently on probation for housebreaking (not his first offence) claimed only to have done it during '. . . a spell, 3 or 4 month period, where I wasnae workin' . . . I'm at University . . . I've been waitin' for University to start, that's what I've been waitin' for, aw the summer'n that . . . for that tae start, but I just . . .'

Fifteen of the 30 claim that drink or drugs (mostly drink) play a part in their offending, and whether or not they become involved in assaults or in thefts of one or other kind often appears to be a minor decision, made spontaneously. A 20-year-old man currently on community service for breach of the peace and assault put it like this:

Well, that was the first time . . . it was ma pal, I was wi' ma pal. It was him that was really doin' it all, 'cause I didn't know what to do'n that . . . I was drunk at the time, and he just asked me if I wanted to do it. I just says, 'Aye' . . . Well, I was drunk at the time, and it just . . . he just asked me if I wanted to do it, I just says, 'Aye'. He says, 'You don't need to do anything, I'll just do it all' . . .

The idea that any of the 30 are in any sense specialized 'career' criminals is misplaced. Yet they are not necessarily mere occasional offenders. A 25-year-old male currently on community service for possession of drugs, claimed his offending history included, 'house-breaking, car theft, police assault, a load of breaches . . .', and two men, both on probation for breach of the peace and assault (the first one was 17-years old, the second one 30), said that they had in the past been 'done' for 'caught hittin' people, lifted aff the streets for drink,[4] drunk and disorderly, breaches, shoutin', abuse'n that . . . the usual . . . Aye, I've got a bad tamper'n aw, it's the temper, just, everytime I'm caught, but I've always been drinkin' . . .' and the other claimed a history of a '. . . lotta breakin' intae places, lotta theft and assaults, breach of the peaces, drunk . . . lotta drunk stuff . . .'

Some claimed that their offending was only prompted by drink or drugs (or both, as in the following case, a 25-year-old man currently doing community service for car theft):

. . . I've been in trouble since 1990, or something like that . . . mostly it was drinking when I did things, breach of the peaces, and that . . . assault, basically I was being a drunk.

---

[3] 'Skint' = being without money. It is a convention amongst researchers working with qualitative data in Scotland to retain the 'Scottishness' of the original, rather than translate it into a foreign tongue (e.g. English). Most Scots would be angry if they knew that most English people think that the Scots speak English. However, to ease international understanding, some passages have been ethnically cleansed, and elsewhere, such as here, translations are attempted.

[4] To lift: to arrest (not citizens' arrest).

EMMA SHORT AND JASON DITTON

So, why did you steal a car this time?

. . . Because it progressed, see? . . . from drink . . . went on to harder drugs, using the car to steal from other cars . . . I was getting into harder drugs at the time, so I needed more money . . . to finance it.

Most seem to be co-involved in a local drink and drug culture, separated by the fact that they live in different areas, and stitched together by regular fighting in the town centre. As one 26-year old, currently on probation for breach of the peace and assault, put it, '. . . since I was about 14, started drinkin' an' that, that's aw there is tae dae in this wee village . . . know? . . . everybody was always steamin'.[5] Once a year, regular as clockwork, I'd be lifted . . . I've always been fighting . . .'

Attitudes to CCTV

Awareness of the cameras

How did this group come to know about the CCTV cameras in Airdrie? The system was originally launched in early November 1992, and this was publicized in the local paper. This did not pass unnoticed, with 14 of the 30 claiming that they had first heard of the cameras in this way. As one put it (correctly) 'Oh . . . it was in all the papers, because it was the first town in Scotland . . .' Another said:

. . . The cameras? . . . they were always in the local paper, the Coatbridge Advertiser.[6] Soon as they got put up, there was a big thing in the paper, then every time ye went intae Airdrie after that, you were always lookin' to see where they were . . .

Actually, the considerable advance publicity may well have backfired. As one 24-year old male probationer put it:

. . . Well, it was always in the papers . . . that they knew they were coming, so everybody was tryin' tae break intae things afore they got them put up . . . they knew they couldnae dae it wi' the cameras there . . .

Some even attended the police station 'open day' where, reputedly, thousands of local inhabitants showed up, queuing for hours to see the monitors. One of the 30 wasn't keen ('. . . Naw, I didnae go, naw. It's no' my favourite place! . . .'), but two of the 30 tried to join the queue. One found that '. . . aye, it was mobbed, couldnae get in . . .' The other remembered that:

. . . they had an open day'n aw, showed everybody how it works. I went doon there, was lookin' at it, they were showin' ye the zoom lens from Milton Court. Milton Court, that's that high flat doon there . . . can see like, intae yer hame, and I wis like that![7] Phew! Cannae dae nuthin' noo! . . . Aye, the place was full, [you] wantae seen it. I just got in for five minutes for a quick look, just to be nosey . . . plus when I got lifted'n that, takin' ye to the cells, the charge desk, they've moved the charge desk noo, but it used to be next tae where the camera place is, just dae a wee nosey in the door, look in . . .

---

[5] 'Steaming' = drunk.
[6] Coatbridge is a nearby town.
[7] 'I was like that!' is a local west of Scotland expression meaning, 'I was flabbergasted'.

SEEN AND NOW HEARD

Those who missed (or forgot) the publicity found out the hard way. As one 30-year-old male on probation for breach of the peace and assault charges put it:

. . . Aye, I'm aware of where they are noo! I wisnae aware tae I got caught the very first time. As I say, I just forgot aw aboot it. Remember readin' the Advertiser, it had been on the telly'n aw that. Once yer lifted, ye become very very aware of where they are, know? . . .

Of those who were asked specifically, all knew that the monitors were housed in the local police station, and most that the pictures were in black and white, although two thought they were in colour. Another commented:

. . . Aye, well I think they should be able to see at night if they're spendin' aw this money. Should be colour cause I've seen black and white cameras in action, quality of picture, an' that, it's no' very . . . you can make oot people an' that, but it's hard to say it's him . . . ye know . . . so I reckon [they] should be in colour and be able to see at night.

Apart from that, they were all rather vague. Four of the 18 specifically questioned knew that there were 12 cameras in operation (other guesses ranged from 3 to 33); most thought that the police (or '. . . whoever is in the building . . .') watched the monitors, and only one guessed the inauguration date correctly (three and a half years previously, or November 1992) with estimates ranging from 'ages' ago, to 'six months ago'. Twelve of them were shown a street map of the town centre, and asked to shade in the bits that the cameras could see.[8] Most seemed to have quite a clear idea of which bits of the town were in vision, even if, for some (particularly those who thought there were far fewer than 12 cameras in operation) this wasn't particularly accurate. Still, most were quite specific, even indicating which parts of which streets were visible. One 30-year-old male on probation for theft was typical:

. . . I would say I've got a pretty good idea . . . cannae see the whole of Broomhill Street, only see aboot half of it . . . Can't even really see half it . . . can only see a wee bit of it, cause the camera's roon the corner, wherever this is. If this is meant to be . . . right? Stirling Street? Can see aw the way up there, that's like Airdrie sort town centre in there . . . can see in there. Bank Street, can see doon Bank Street, cause there's one at the . . . can see up there, Mummm, can see right up there'n aw.

One or two respondents were aware of blind spots in coverage, not calculated through technical knowledge of the system so much as by recalling incidents that they knew had occurred, but which had not incurred police action. Most assumed from this that, rather than, for example, inattentiveness in the control room, the area wasn't ever in vision. Most also assumed (correctly) that 'wee lanes' were not visible on camera. Here are two, a 24-year-old male probationer, and an 18-year-old on community service for breach of the peace:

. . . Behind the new social work department that's gettin' built, there's a camera up on the roof, an' it swings roon the bus station'n that, but it cannae see right roon like the back'ae the shops, like John Menzies. There's a lotta people still standin' there, an' they drink . . .

. . . I think they can see everywhere, just a wee lane, that's aboot it, you could get a good fight in there, or whatever . . . Aye, like just say there was three of us, and three of them, like that, 'C'mon, in this wee

---

[8] The capability of the camera network is illustrated on Map 4, Annex B, of Short and Ditton (1996).

EMMA SHORT AND JASON DITTON

bit and we'll see who's sayin' this'n whatever' . . . set aboot them in there, cause the camera cannae see ye at the social, and the two cameras in the main street cannae see ye, 'cause it's just a wee tunnel.

The value of the cameras

Most were quite clear what the cameras were for. Here is a good summary, from a 41-year-old woman on probation for fraud:

. . . Oh, I think they're mostly there for the public's protection, the shopkeepers' protection, and to make life a wee bit easier for the police, a wee bit more simple . . .

A 25-year-old male doing community service for drugs offences added:

. . . I suppose the public gains, an' the people that own the pubs and shops and that . . . because they put the money into it, didn't they? Partly the public and mostly, I'd say, the shop owners . . .

Some accounts are quite perceptive. Consider this 30-year-old male on probation for theft:

. . . Well, probably a deterrent to crime a lot . . . 'cause you know you're gettin' watched, but it's only gonnie affect different offenders in different ways, likesa car crime. Probably help stop a lot of car crime, 'cause it's targeting aw the car parks, and things like that, so no doubt it would affect car thieves. I don't see it affecting shoplifters much either cause they're ootside the shops, aw the shoplifting gets done in the shops, so only maybe affect people that's maybe drunk on the street, as I say, fighting an' making a nuisance of themselves, causing damage, damage to property . . . it would affect them 'cause they get seen . . .

Two others were rather more cynical. Both are 20-year-old males on probation for breach of the peace and police assault:

. . . They're supposed to make everybody feel safer, but the only thing I've really seen them getting used for is to convict people . . . I don't think they're saving anybody from trouble . . . [they're] just for catching people committing petty offences . . .

. . . Who they're for? . . . Who they're for! The Government! Aye, cause they'll go . . . they gie ye cameras an' people'll go, 'Oh, Wow! Thanks!' . . . and vote for them 'cause they're gettin' a lotta protection. That's what it's aw aboot init? . . . Aye, it works, it does work. Depends on what you're talking about. People still go shopliftin' in Airdrie aw the time, disnae matter if the cameras are there or no', but they'll know no' tae—there's been people stabbed in Airdrie in front ae they cameras'n everything, so I don't know if it stops it . . . just calms it doon a wee bit, cuts it down . . .

In sum, most are neither idealistic nor cynical: just realistic about the intended 'consumers' of the cameras, and the likely effects that they will have.[9] Some (like this 20-year-old male on probation for breach of the peace and police assault) even had ideas for improving the system:

. . . they shouldnae be targetting people, petty offenders, they should be looking mair towards stopping muggings and people getting battered and the rest of that. They should be targetting that

---

[9] To be fair, most didn't know whether the system 'worked' or not (and in this sense they are no less informed than anybody else). Consider these careful remarks from a 25-year-old male on community service for car theft: '. . . No, I don't know if it's working or no', but what I know about it, it's no' working . . .'

SEEN AND NOW HEARD

way and all, and not just daft petty crimes . . . taking that to court just to show that somebody kicked over a bin in the precinct . . . committed a breach of the peace, that's the kind of thing that they're doing . . . I mean they should be doing it mair[10] for to help people, or making people feel safer . . .

Perhaps surprisingly (given their criminal records) most of this group are reasonably positive about CCTV. Of 17 who were overtly asked whether they thought the CCTV installation 'good' or 'bad',[11] 11 thought it good, five were indifferent, and only one thought it bad, and in this way the Airdrie offenders are rather like those researched by French (1994, 1996). Yet most of the problems they have are not so much because they follow specialized criminal career paths, as get into 'trouble'. Here, they may emerge formally as 'offender' or 'victim', although most seem to have an informal view of themselves as either blameless at the outset of 'trouble' or as blameworthy as the other party. Possibly, formal labelling as an 'offender' may well add to their feelings of being 'victims'. In this context, their appreciation of the cameras becomes less overtly paradoxical. One in particular (a 30-year-old male on probation for breach of the peace and assault) got the balance just right:

. . . Aye, as I say, it's no' . . . it'll stop a lotta doins gettin' gied oot,[12] so it will, especially wi' the young ones in Airdrie the noo, know? Aye, it's a good thing . . . wouldn't want mair o' them, but . . .

Some have as many reservations as official civil libertarians, but also see that this might well be balanced with a concern about crime. As this male 29-year-old former probationer put it:

No, I'm not bothering about it. I've got no' problem with somebody watching me, and things like that . . . because it does give you a slight thingummy, you know, you're OK, you know there's somebody watching over you, you know what I mean. You get other ones, right enough, you see these ones, you hear 'Oh, fucking cameras!' watching, you know what I mean . . . my mum, she says there's somebody watching you all the time, I says, 'Ah, I think it's a good thing, to be honest with you . . . prevent a lot of crime' . . . you know what I mean? . . .

Others feign indifference (or really feel it): '. . . the cameras, they don't bother me being there. They didn't bother me if they weren't there. You know, not too much interested in them . . .' and '. . . doesnae make things any worse anyway. Maybe makes things better . . .'

Another, when asked what he thought, said '. . . I don't actually think I thought anything. A lot of people said it goes intae their privacy and all that, but I don't see how it goes into their privacy . . . They don't bother me, being there, as I say I'd be quite happy if they did stop a crime that was going to be caused towards me . . .' Only one was antagonistic, and even he added that they '. . . helped me a bit, but still don't like them, man . . .'

As well as giving relative vague judgments as to whether the CCTV system was 'good' or 'bad', 27 of the 30 were specifically asked whether or not the system made them 'feel safer'. Here the balance was reversed, with ten claiming it made them feel safer, and 17 that it either made no difference or, in a few cases, worse. Most of those feeling safer

---

[10] 'Mair' = more.

[11] Interviews were non-directive, which is why this question did not occur every time.

[12] (trans.) Prevent a lot of beatings being given out.

justified their view by referring to their status as possible victims of minor public order offences. One 30-year-old male probationer with a history of breach of the peace and assault offending himself claimed:

... Aye, sometimes. I'd be a liar tae say naw. It's no, sortae ... no feart[13] or nothin' ... it's ... I've had a lotta doins ... It can happen, know? ... but it cuts the chances down. I wouldnae be someone that gied somebody a doin' doon the street wi' the cameras there. If I'm no' willin' tae dae it, there'll be a lotta other people no' willin' tae dae it; whereas I wid've ... but no' wi' the cameras there ...

Most of the others agreed: '... Aye, in a way, aye. Means you can go up the street an' nobody gonnie be assaulted or whatever ...' or: '... Aye, 'cause I've got a lotta enemies ... up here, there's folk that if I bumped intae them, it would be 'square go' material ... doon there, wi' the cameras ... I just go the other way ...'[14] and:

... sometimes, like, if there [is] a crowda guys walkin' aboot the street, and I'm [by] maself ... before the cameras went up, I'd be a wee bit wary case they started attackin' me ... if yer from somewhere else ... it's just the way they operate ... an' noo that the cameras are up ... don't get bother so much ... still watch what they're up tae, just in case, but ...

Indeed, for several, the installation of the cameras made them feel safer rather than more threatened. A 25-year-old male on community service for drugs offences claimed:

... It's a ... it's a lot safer ... if you're going out at night, you know you can walk down the street with your girlfriend, and see. Look ... Airdrie before was a bad place ... see? At night time, you used to see guys getting kickings all over the place ... there was about 20 minutes before the polis[15] would reach ... whereever it was happening. But now, wi' the cameras, if there are any fighting, the polis are there within seconds ...

Another (a 35-year-old male doing community service for assaulting the police and breach of the peace) agreed that the cameras had made a difference:

... Aye, oh aye, definitely. Because you don't get everybody standing in the street drinking in doorways, things like that, you know what I mean? ... Likes of that pizza shop, there was fightings outside it every night at the weekend. Slashings, you know, things like that. The polis, they were never awae from it. Everybody coming out of the disco went into that shop, and they were always arguing in the queues and what not, you know what I mean? There was fighting in the street. But the cameras are going all that way now, and they go up the side of the street, naw, so it's dead at the weekend now, you know? Everybody's into taxis and away hame ...

Appreciation of the cameras for other reasons was unusual. However, one 41-year-old woman on probation for fraud implied that the cameras simultaneously made her feel safer, although they also curtailed her interactions with known shoplifters:

... I've a cheek tae talk ... aye! ... But, honestly, it does [make her feel safer]. The other thing about it as well ... I hate anybody tae talk to me in Airdrie if I know they've been shopliftin' an' ye maybe get a

---

[13] 'Feart' = afraid.
[14] Historically, a 'square go' is a fair (if bloody and illegal) public fight. Patrick (1973: 235) defines it as 'a fight without weapons'. In Airdrie, such subtle nuances may be lost to some, who just seemed to use the phrase for a fight. The most recent descriptions of fighting in the Glasgow *environs* are to be found in Uildriks and van Mastrigt (1991) and in MacCallum (1994).
[15] 'Polis' = police. This is spelt this way in the west of Scotland, and pronounced as it is spelt (with heavy emphasis on the 'o').

SEEN AND NOW HEARD

lotta wee kids comin' up and sayin' 'D'you want tae buy something?' . . . yer like this, 'Go away!' . . .
'cause you know they cameras are there, so it makes ye a wee bit feart as well . . .

One 34-year-old male (on probation for car theft) didn't feel safer in Airdrie, but might
do in other places with town centre CCTV systems. He said: '. . . Normally . . . well, I'm
from Airdrie, so doesn't bother me, cameras there. Go somewhere else, likes of
Motherwell, cameras does make you feel safer, aye . . .' Yet others were either
indifferent, or had come to terms with what they felt was a future of endless surveillance.
A 36-year-old male on community service for drugs offences:

. . . Honestly, it's something that doesn't bother me, you know. It doesn't bother us, because I think
they've got them in most places now . . . Coatbridge, most of the flats. You just . . . I think they'll be
everywhere soon, anyway . . .

Rather more respondents felt no safer, and did so for a wide variety of reasons. One (a
19-year-old male doing community service for shop breaking) felt impervious to
trouble anyway: '. . . Don't bother . . . naebody touches me anyway. I know everybody,
I'm well known . . .', and another (a 26-year-old male doing community service for
breach of the peace) had never experienced any of the problems that CCTV cameras
are supposed to alleviate:

Doesnae make me feel any safer. It's no' as if I've ever been attacked or anything like that . . . up the
street . . . know what I mean? Up in Airdrie? Never had any problems that way, but no, they've no'
really, no' changed me feelin' safer . . .

At least one felt that if you were going to be attacked, then fate could not be bypassed
with CCTV: '. . . can't make you feel safe. If somebody's going to do something,
somebody's going to do [it] . . .' Another felt that, for him, the cameras were just in the
wrong place to make him feel safe: '. . . see? I've never really been in trouble down in
Airdrie town centre, it's been the outskirts where I've been in trouble . . .' and another
that numbers, rather than cameras, made for safety (although he did appreciate that
cameras might help those alone, or in pairs): '. . . Wouldnae say it makes me feel safer.
Always feel safe, anyway, 'cause . . . usually 8 or 9 of us oot at the one time. Suppose it
makes other people feel safer . . . one or two . . . [but] I know if somebody attack me, they
[cameras] would be there, sort of thing . . .'

For several others, their own experience indicated that while CCTV cameras might
be good at identifying attackers, they do not necessarily prevent the attack. One didn't
even think that the cameras could, necessarily, spot an attack. He (a 20-year-old male
on probation for assault and breach of the peace) said: '. . . Naw [doesn't feel any safer]
. . . somebody could just walk up to ye, an' stab ye, an' be away, and the polis'll go: 'Whit?
What happened?' . . . it's that simple . . .' Others thought the CCTV system was just
inefficient. First a 25-year-old male on community service for drugs offences, and then
a 20-year-old male on probation for breach of the peace and assaulting the police. Both
thought the cameras poor at dealing with public order victimization:

. . . For instance, I've seen me coming out of discos at 3 o'clock in the morning, getting into fights.[16]
Right beside the cameras, and getting really hurted . . . and the polis don't come anywhere near you. I

---

[16] Another local linguistic construction. Consider the popular west of Scotland way of saying, for example, 'my male partner is a
vegetarian', which usually emerges as, 'See me? See ma man! See meat? Hates it!'.

mean, they're supposed to come round, you can actually see the camera! . . . [The] camera staring straight at you, you can see it . . . it still takes the polis 10–15 minutes to get there. Whereas that camera should be telling the polis where to go . . . they must turn it off . . .

. . . No [when asked if he felt any safer] . . . No. I've been attacked in Airdrie since they put the cameras up. Right underneath one! It was five feet above my head. I was attacked and I was underneath it, and nothing was done about it. And there was another camera, just doon the street, and we're talking about just round the corner by the police station. There was nothing done about it . . . . They didn't use it, or they didn't have it taped. Somebody doesn't watch one area all the time . . . I was underneath that one . . . And if that didnae see us, and it probably didnae, we were right underneath it . . . the other one could have seen us . . .

In sum, feelings on the germane aspects of awareness of CCTV held by these respondents—whether they concern pre-knowledge of camera installation, how many cameras (of what type) there were, where they were located, how far (and where) they could see, who or what they were 'for', whether or not they were a 'good' or 'bad' thing, whether or not they increased perceptual safety, and what the cameras could do—were mixed and variable. No obvious patterns (across or within) individuals were clearly discernible. A more extensive qualitative or quantitative study could attempt to establish any such perceptual patternings—if such exist.

Experience of the cameras

Many were aware that the cameras picked up on, and followed people 'like' them. One (a 20-year-old male on probation for assault and breach of the peace) recognized that this was more or less what they were supposed to do. He said:

. . . Aye, they can, aye. Well, that's what they're meant to be there for. They think you're dodgy, they'll follow you to see what's happening . . .

Doesn't that bother you?

. . . Naw. Why should it if you're no' daein' anything? . . .

"Well, that's true. But, I mean, some folk think it's a bit unfair that they're getting followed around.

. . . They were probably daein' something in the first place! . . .

One thought he was under scrutiny when stationary in the town centre ('. . . Anytime I go down to Airdrie, I've been standing on the street corner, maybe waiting on someone coming out of a shop, or something, you just look up and the camera's right on you . . . it follows you about . . . looking at you as though you're one of these shoplifters, or something . . .'), but most of those who objected felt that surveillance was unnecessary when they were moving around. Two (a 19-year-old male on probation for housebreaking and a 17-year-old male on probation for breach of the peace and assault) both claimed:

. . . Aye, yer walkin' roon aboot the streets . . . just at a certain bit, just ootside the discos'n that, yer always lookin' to see where the cameras are, 'cause they move aboot, point in different directions, and yer always lookin' tae see if they're lookin' at ye . . . they're watching in case you start fighting . . .

SEEN AND NOW HEARD

. . . Aye, if, just, say yer walkin' doon from the thingmy, cameras facin' that way, see if ye look suspicious or that, it'll follow ye right roon, yer walkin' doon, then the other one'll turn an' catch ye here. One'll turn roon there, catch ye there. Either way, if yer no' daein' nothin', nothin' tae worry aboot . . . failing that, if yer daein anthin' . . .

Two others felt that they were not only followed when behaving innocently, but that this could also lead to an arrest for no reason. The first is a 16-year-old male on supervision for breach of the peace and car theft; the second, a 19-year-old male doing community service for shop breaking:

. . . I don't like the cameras. Know what I mean? Hate them, man! . . . Just cannae go doon the street. Cannae dae the things you used to be able tae dae man. Don't get me wrang [I] kept oota trouble quite a long . . . get jobs'n that . . . but still no, cameras see you doon the street, man. Yer just gettin' lifted for nothin' a lot . . . just the polis see me on the cameras, and they'll just lift me for nothin' 'cause I'm a well-known face. I've been up for a few breach of the peaces for nothin' just because the cameras are there . . . clock[17] me walkin' doon the street, just following me everywhere . . .

. . . Polis always stop you for nothin'n aw . . . always following us aw the time, getting searched. Coupla weeks ago . . . 15 of us got stopped. Goes like that tae me, 'Gie's yer name and address again' . . . I was the only one gonnie get lifted . . . [*Why?*] . . . 'cause thingmy, I'm a known thief . . .

Another (an 18-year-old male doing community service for breach of the peace) thought, rather gloomily, that things were getting worse, and he was barely able to break the law any more:

. . . Aye, you could. Even when the cameras just got put up, you could still go doon the street, hunners ae yiz,[18] just sit in the town centre an' get a good drink, a good laugh'n that. Sometimes, things would happen'n aw that, but none ae us went aboot lookin' for fights or anythin' like that. Always people walkin' by, things like that . . . used tae get a good swally[19] . . . noo, ye just, ye cannae go doon the street any mair, just jailbait. Get followed everywhere wi' the cameras for nuthin' . . . I mean, if yer were doon wi' yer Ma, ye get followed wi' the cameras . . . [*Really? Does that bother you?*] . . . A bit . . . 'cause ye cannae dae nothin' . . . cannae even get a joint[20] in peace doon the street withoot a camera on ye . . .

Some are less defeatist. One claimed that when he walked through the town, he was always '. . .tryin' tae dodge them, aye, tryin' know? . . . Tryin' just tae pretend they're no' there, ye know . . .', and another took more active evasion:

. . . Sometimes . . . see, it aw depends man, sometimes I go doon the street'n it might no' clock me. See, if I'm wi' a coupla people . . . walkin' away, maybe, maybe it's like my way, and just walk roon the corner, it'll no' follow you . . . but a lottae the times, I've taken the mick wi' the cameras, man . . . clocked it followin' us, and I've just went under a [camera] pole with the cameras tryin' tae follow me aboot where I'm goin'. I just take the mick right oot them . . .[21]

---

[17] Clock = see.

[18] Trans. 'Hundreds of you'.

[19] Alcoholic beverage (probably brewed by the good monks of Buckfast Abbey). Buckfast wine ('Bucky') is the default drink of an alarming proportion of the local population.

[20] Marihuana cigarette.

[21] Another interviewee recalled that he was once prosecuted, and convicted of breaching the peace for 'giein' the fingers to the cameras'n that' on one occasion.

EMMA SHORT AND JASON DITTON

None knew for sure that there was any abuse of the cameras (although one thought that the police used the cameras for 'perving'[22]), but a few were suspicious, not least because, as one put it, 'nobody can see them doing it, can they?' However, the majority didn't suspect any abuse of the cameras by the operators, or by the police of the evidence generated thereby. A 25-year-old on community service for car theft was fairly typical:

... What? ... Oh, I see. For prying on people's privacy, and things like that? I don't think so. I think they just basically watch what's happening on the main street, and things like that. I don't see them prying on anybody's ... any person's house, or anything ...

Further, those who didn't suspect any misuse had ideas as to how, to put it frankly, they, and others like them, might be more easily prosecuted in future. The 41-year-old woman on probation for fraud, again, but now with a rather touching faith in the police (and impressive ignorance of the law):

... Well, I don't see how they can, really [police using the cameras in ways that they shouldn't] ... I don't see how they can turn it round tae suit theirselves, if the evidence is in front of all in black and white. I do believe that they should, if they've got ye on camera, sit ye down an' show it. 'Look, there yer are, there ye've done it' ... know what I mean? I do believe that if they've got you on camera they should show you it, shouldn't say, 'Oh, look. We've got ye on camera, just sign this' ... they should say, 'Right, come on, stand there. There, it's there. Is that you?' ... Well, ... it would save a lotta court's time as well ... steada goin' up tae court'n pleadin' not guilty ... [where they say] 'Why's you plead not guilty? There yer there on the camera' ...

One way of summarizing what appeared to be a common feeling was that they knew they were sometimes on camera, and some even thought that they were rightfully so (with a few more being quite happy in case the cameras prevented them from becoming victims). So, they expected to be video-followed, and there were more complaints about the inadequacy of the cameras than about the invasion of civil liberties that their presence implied. Testifying to this, some even objected to 'ordinary people' being surveyed. Here is an 18-year-old male doing community service for loitering with intent to steal, who has been asked whether or not he thinks being surveyed is an invasion of his privacy:

... No, not I think ... Causing crime, man, it's not invading your privacy, but everybody else's. How many people in Airdrie? Not all of them steal or anything like that: they're getting watched everywhere they go. Shouldn't be allowed ...

Yet, one reasonably common source of objection (even from those who recognized the legitimacy of tracking them when with their friends and/or late at night) was of being obviously followed when that was highly unlikely to reap any benefit. As one put it (an 18-year-old male on probation for assault):

... I suppose that's what they get the cameras for ... to sit an' watch what people are up tae ... but I don't like it walkin' aboot the street ... even if yer doon wi' yer girl friend, or doon wi' yer Ma ... like they see yer face an' they'll sit'n follow ye aw ower the street ... Been doon the street wi' ma Ma a coupla times ... the cameras have followed us ... followin' me ...

---

[22] Undefined, but we infer 'salacious surveillance'.

SEEN AND NOW HEARD

In total, 26 were asked if they had ever been caught on camera. Twelve had been caught themselves, four knew other people that had, for three it had been a case of mistaken identity, and seven had not, as far as they knew, been caught on camera at all.

Some indicated that the experience of being caught doing something illegal on camera didn't persuade them to plead guilty (one claimed that he '. . . just plead guilty all the time . . .' because '. . . I couldnae be bothered goin' doon tae court aw the time . . .', but he was possibly unusual). Another recalled that being caught on camera didn't necessarily lead to having to plead at all. He is a 25-year-old male currently doing community service for drugs offences, but this was a previous occasion:

. . . Once [caught on camera] . . . but I never got charged or anything . . . it was just like larking about, breach of the peace, I wasnae damaging anything like that, and they come up and warned us. They says, 'You're getting watched, so you'd better watch what you're doing' . . . that settled us down . . . we just went up the road peacefully . . .

One other knew he was caught on camera, but can remember little. His subsequent story is fairly typical of the responses of several (and many of those with no direct experience have heard similar stories from their friends):

. . . I knew there was a camera at the bottom of the hill, but was aw . . . it wisnae as if I wanted tae . . . it was a furniture shop . . . it wisnae as if I wanted tae put the slab through the windie[23] . . . tae steal or anything like that, it was just a moment of madness. It was after the Celtic/Rangers game at New Year[24] . . . that's when it happened. It was just a moment of madness . . . think it was just through drink and anger as, well, more than anything else . . .

Did you know the cameras were watching?

. . . To be honest wi'ye, I didnae. I wasnae really thinkin' 'cause, as I say, I cannae really remember much. Can just remember wakin' up in the polis station, and asking what I'd done! . . . I pled not guilty at first. An' then I pled guilty 'cause the PF[25] and the judge watched it on tape, an' I pled guilty . . .

Is that when you changed your plea? So did you not see it before it got to court, then?

. . . No, I never seen nothin' . . . Ma lawyer told me. Ma lawyer seen it as well. Ma lawyer told me that they had it [breaking the window] on tape, an' I just changed ma mind, I pleaded guilty. I said I'd plead guilty 'cause there's nae use goin' up and pleadin' not guilty if they've got the evidence in front of them, is there? . . .

Naturally, he, like the others with similar stories, never got to see the alleged tape as there is never any need to show it to the defendant after a plea of guilty has been entered. Here, CCTV experience seems to add to the mood of fatalism which accompanies so much youthful delinquency. However, stories also circulate about the fallibility of CCTV, including from one woman, that of alibi:

. . . I got arrested at ma house, and took tae Coatbridge, but it wasn't me that done it anyway. But they said it was me that done it, an' they said 'Right, come on, we've got ye on camera. The shop was

---

[23] 'Windie' = window.

[24] Glasgow Celtic and Glasgow Rangers, both football teams, are fierce rivals, with the usual religious basis for such rivalry.

[25] Procurator Fiscal. The long-established independent Scottish prosecution agency.

camera'd when you were in it, doin' this'n that, an' the next thing, and you were identified' . . . I said, 'I've no' been out the door' . . . and then they told me what day it was, and I was lucky 'cause I was in the hospital that day, so I knew I'd been . . . so when they told me the day, I says, 'Well, on ye go then, let me see . . . take me tae court, let me see' . . . I said, 'Show me yer film then, prove it was me' . . .

They refused. She engaged a lawyer, and nothing more was heard. Another was, perhaps, more endearing, and certainly more convincing, as he claimed to be wrongfully innocent. Here is his story (he is a 34-year-old male doing community service for breach of the peace and assaulting the police):

. . . I got caught in a shop, I was arguing with the shopkeeper . . . got caught on camera . . . and then the polis came. But they never charged me with that, they charged another guy, my brother, and it was me on the camera. He was the wrongfully arrested [one] . . . through the camera . . . It was clear enough. You could tell. Everybody else could tell it was me, but the polis said it was definitely my brother. Even the judge said it was me. He told one of the lawyers later. He says, 'I knew it was the other one'. He had to acquit my brother . . .

And does your brother look like you?

. . . No, he's a lot thinner on top, man. He's a lot taller. You know what I mean? He was wearing different clothes and everything . . .

In terms of their own experience of being on camera, most of these respondents thought they were targeted regularly, sometimes without good reason. Some accepted this passively: some tried to 'dodge' being in vision. Nearly half of those asked had been caught doing something illegal by the cameras. Practically all of those asked had great faith in the legal power of the resulting videotapes, especially when used in court.

Effects of CCTV

The effect on individuals

Some—8 of the 30—claim that the CCTV cameras have no effect on their pattern of offending. One for example (a 17-year-old currently at liberty, but with a history of breach of the peace, shoplifting and breaking and entering) claimed that you could always offend outwith the sight of the cameras:

. . . Cameras just don't bother me. What we used tae do doon the street, we just do somewhere else. Simple as that. We used tae drink doon the street aw the time, aw we do noo is just go doon the park. If they put cameras doon the park, we'll just move somewhere else. They cannae put the cameras everywhere, ye know . . . cost too much money to dae that, put them everywhere . . . know what I mean?
. . .

Another (a 25-year-old man doing community service for car theft) thought offenders could be careful enough to avoid camera-capture:

. . . They don't bother me because I don't think I'll get caught. Because I've got away with it in the past too often for to have to worry about it. I've never been caught through the evidence of the cameras . . .

SEEN AND NOW HEARD

However, he went on to suggest that, bravado aside, he might now not consider some other types of offending:

> . . . They never . . . once we got away with it the first time, they never caught us the . . . it was obvious we thought, 'They're not really watching all the time' . . . We've done it two or three times, and got away with it, no bother . . . the cameras didnae put me aff stealing a car in Airdrie . . . The only thing it would ever stopped me from doing is maybe snatching a bag on the main street or anything. That's all; but it's not stopped me stealing motors or anything to do with cars. You just ignore them. It takes too long . . . by the time they get to the polis, you've done what you've done, and you're away. They cannae follow you everywhere . . .

He may well be claiming to be restrained from committing illegal acts he had no intention of committing, but this is difficult to tell. Thinking the cameras are competent, but possible to dodge, is another way of neutralizing the moral consequences of continuing to offend. One 19-year-old male (currently on community service for shop breaking) commented that:

> . . . you just wait until the camera looks the other way . . . most of the times, the cameras are lookin' the other way anyway . . . right up the main street, just smash the windie, just grab a loada stuff . . . would just stand doon under the camera an' that . . . watch the camera turnin' roon . . . just run ower. The camera always points the one way for a while . . .

Others, too, believed that the cameras somehow followed fixed rotational patterns which could be calculated with enough effort. An 18-year-old male on probation for assault claimed that: '. . . if somebody wanted tae tan a shop,[26] need tae sit and suss out the camera for ages, camera's watchin' . . . need tae wait on it movin' 'fore they could dae whit they were doin' . . .'

Seven others claimed that yes, they had stopped offending, but not because of the cameras: they have decided to desist anyway. For several of these, desistance seems to be, at most, an aim rather than a reality. Some confessed that if the right sort of opportunity irresistibly presented itself, they would have to, with regret, renew an offending career. First an 18-year-old male on community service for breach of the peace (who claimed not nowadays to be stealing all the time), and secondly, a 30-year-old male on probation for theft. The first considers theft opportunities:

> . . . You could go away intae . . . cannae go intae Coatbridge, that's cameras noo, you could go away intae Lanark or somewhere'n tan a shop if ye wanted . . .

Do you do that? Would you go that far?

> . . . Naw, aye, I would if I wis still stealing at the time . . . I like a ram raid, go an' dae a ram raid . . . that's aboot it . . . they've stopped stealing mostae us . . . [I get my money from] the b'reau[27] . . . but like if a

---

[26] 'Tan'—to break into a shop, or to shoplift. Unhappily, which meaning is intended when the word is used is, on most occasions, difficult (if not impossible) to decipher.

[27] Pronounced 'broo' or (for the English) 'brew'. Contraction of 'bureau', itself a shortened form of Public Assistance Bureau, an earlier form of the DHS. Patrick (1973: 231) has it as 'buroo', but also as a version of bureau, in his case (mystifyingly) from the 'Ministry of Social Security'.

EMMA SHORT AND JASON DITTON

quick chance came along . . . just a car 'turned up' . . . I'd dae it if I knew there was a good chance of me no' gettin caught . . . Like a wee grab'n run or whatever . . .

The second is more concerned with public order non-offending:

. . . 'cause it depends what you're daein' . . . I'm no' offending anymore, anyway, so it disnae affect me . . . the cameras being there. But it probably widnae [put anybody off] because it depends what you're gonnie dae. If you're talkie' about fighting, or something, sometimes you get into a fight, so you're involved in a fight . . . cameras are no' gonnie to stop you because you're no' gonnie stand and let somebody batter you, or assault you in any way . . .

Rather more—12 of the 30—confessed that the CCTV cameras had indeed affected their behaviour. For most, this resulted in a sense of increased wariness when in camera range. For some, awareness of the cameras didn't prevent offending—it just made them more careful. First an 18-year-old male doing community service for breach of the peace:

. . . ye can dae a lotta things when the cameras are there . . . Aye, set aboot people'n that. Set aboot a few people doon the street an' the cameras are there 'cause they only face one way, know what I mean? . . . an' then ye see them turnin' roon . . . 'cause I've stood, an' the camera's been right on me, an' they it's just turned roon . . . then just smackin' somebody . . . an' it turn roon again an' that'd be it . . . know what I mean? . . .

Now, another, this time a 29-year-old male, currently at liberty, but with a history of assault and breach of the peace, who had become much more wary:

. . . Oh, aye, aye. It's stopped me, and all a few times . . . coming out of pubs with my pals, right, and years ago, right? we used to go . . . squaring up to guys ootside pubs an' that and have a go at them . . . we'd have a go at them, right? . . . by the time the polis come, we're away. But now you're like that. Cameras is watching, so you're watching all the time, know what I mean? . . . watching in case you're carrying anything, and you're watching and you cannae dae anything against them, because you get caught on camera . . . know what I mean? So you always watch anything, because you're that scared, so you don't bother at all, you just got straight home, you know what I mean? . . . just jump in the first black[28] and away home . . .

Increased wariness was the most common attitude among those who had noticed the cameras, as these slight quotations illustrate: '. . . I do, it has worked, aye. If you walk down the street now, you go like that, you say to yourself, 'The camera's there, don't do anything stupid' . . . and: '. . . [we] still go doon the street, but just watch what we're daein' . . . or: '. . . you're wary to dae anything cause ye know the cameras are there . . .' and: '. . . Aye, wi' these new cameras an' that, maybe think twice aboot doin' it in the streets, an' that . . .'

For a small minority, the only option was to stay away or give up offending entirely. For example, one 20-year-old male currently on probation for housebreaking had subsequently tried shoplifting, but claimed that after '. . . only aboot three or four times, or somethin' then I just thought, "Forget that!" . . . every corner ye were goin roon, there was another camera there . . . No intae this" . . .'

---

[28] Local slang for public-hire, but not private-hire taxi (contraction of black cab—hackney cab).

The effect on public order offences

Many felt that the CCTV cameras had affected the fighting, but none felt that it had actually prevented it from happening entirely. Here is a 30-year-old male on probation for breach of the peace and assault:

... Eh ... there's a big difference noo, I think. [When] I was younger, big gangs of us runnin' aboot doon the street, know? ... aboot 30 at a time ... The odd time I've been doon the street late at night [recently], it's no' the same, know? There's no' as much police presence, but, I think they rely on the cameras a lot. I don't know if they're on 24 hours a day, or no', or if they're only on sometimes, but I think it's cut oot a lotta stuff, I think ... I'd say so. Especially since I was maybe 17, 18 ... or even younger than that, 'cause we just roamed aw ower Airdrie ... never got caught fur it ... Disnae happen much noo, very rare, I think for it happening so much, big teams aw hangin' aboot together. It's happened a couple of times, mostly only maybe three or four intae it altogether, or two ontae the one, but no' so much ...

One claimed (he was an 18-year-old male currently on probation for armed robbery and assault) that fighting had certainly been reduced:

... Few year ago, used tae be a tribe'ae like people from up here that wid go oot drinkin'. If they bump intae anybody ... like sat an' talked to them'n that ... pals, and things like from school ... but if somebody started growlin' ... know, like if I say somethin', they say somethin' tae me, just like me fighting ... next minute everybody just jumpin' in. Like if it happened in the main street, cameras'd be watchin' just get the polis comin' from everywhere. [Nowadays] no' as much fightin' doon the street. Still fights doon the street, but it's just like ... cameras watchin' or whatever. It's no' big fights any mair. It's just a quick fight, hopefully get it over with quick, an' away up the road ...

Another claimed that CCTV: '... certainly stops crime, unless you've had too many drinks, you don't really give a toss about whether the camera's there or not ...' and, finally, yet another male probationer (aged 24) added, rather forlornly, 'Well, I think it does have a lotta effect on the fights up the street ... 'cause there used to be hunners'a fights a night up there ... noo, you're lucky if there's one every weekend ...' Indeed, most thought that it had, in the words of one, '... stopped it a wee bit ...' if not entirely eradicated it.

Others claimed that fighting continued, but either out of sight of the cameras, or out of range of the whole CCTV system. One, a 25-year-old male doing community service for drugs offences, thought that fighting could still continue, even in front of the cameras, if the timing was right:

... Aye, when they just come out, people were always saying, 'Watch out! There's the camera. Watch what you're doing' ... But a lot of people know where they can still get away with things. Because some of them, they look down one street, and as soon as they turn away to look down the next street, then you know you've got about four or five minutes, before the camera'll come back round ... You know, if it's three or two boys, and they see the camera, they'll say, 'Right, we'll wait a minute' ... As soon as the camera turns away, then the two of them have their square go ... and it's broke up before the camera comes back round ...

Another (a 29-year-old male, currently free, but with a history of assault and breach of the peace) added that if somebody had been identified as a target for assault, the cameras were just a minor problem. He said, '... Oh, if you want to get somebody, you

EMMA SHORT AND JASON DITTON

know where the cameras are, you can pinpoint where the cameras are, so you say, "If he goes up this street, there's no cameras there, so you can get him there" . . .' However, another (a 20-year-old male on probation for assault and breach of the peace) thought that most would fight out of sight of the cameras when sober, but might forget to do so when drunk. He said:

. . . What's the cameras gonnie dae? They're no' gonnie stop it. They just wait till the guys are oot the town centre, an' do it . . . when they're drunk they still fight in the town centre. I've seen somebody stabbed in the town centre when the cameras were up. Just don't bother, if you're drunk, you don't bother . . . anyway, until ye wake up the next day . . .

Another (a 19-year-old male doing community service for shop breaking) thought there were parts of the town that the cameras couldn't reach. He said that people '. . . still fight, just get oot the way of the camera, just go roon the car park . . . camera cannae see ye, that wee bit at ——— (supermarket) . . . camera cannae see right doon there . . .' He added that you can still fight in front of the cameras without any retribution: '. . . I seen a fight on Saturday when I was doon. Polis never done nothin'. Cameras right on it, too . . .'

Finally, here, another male probationer (a 30-year-old who had been convicted of breach of the peace and assault) claimed that much fighting had been displaced to areas outwith the town centre, which itself had become somewhat calmer:

. . . I was never ever feart tae go doon the street . . . but . . . Airdrie was awfully menacin' at one time . . . maybe 10 aw together . . . Just hang aboot their ain schemes[29] noo. It's kept people oot the main streets, but they've aw just hit the schemes like ———, ———, maybe not so much ———, it's aw tight-knit up there . . . the ones that go doon the street causin' the trouble just go to the schemes noo, so they do . . .

This was a quite common assertion. Two more claimed: '. . . they [cameras] just . . . it's preventin' people from goin' doon the street'n drinkin' 'cause they're just daein' it up the schemes'n an' that, but it would cost too much money to get the cameras in aw the schemes . . .' and: '. . . well, I daresay there's no' gonnie be much gang fights up Airdrie. There isnae really much gang fights any mair anyhow, sorta quiet. Wi' the cameras there, aw the trouble's been forced back into the schemes again . . .'

A 19-year-old male on probation for housebreaking was asked whether or not things had changed since the cameras were installed:

. . . Bit quieter . . . no' as much fighting. Used to be a fight on every street corner afore they were up, but stopped it a bit . . . quite a lot . . .

So who was it that was fighting?

. . . Just everybody . . . anybody . . . just aboot everybody goes intae the discos, an' that. Roon aboot Airdrie, everybody knows each other, they've aw got grudges against each other . . . Naw, I wouldnae really say there's gangs, but if you were oot wi' a crowd, say . . . with all the ——— ones, it would just take somebody fae ——— to throw a punch at somebody fae anywhere else . . . that would be it . . . Probably if you could avoid the cameras, ye wid. But if I was standin' an' I knew a camera was watchin' me, somebody came up and tried tae make punches, or something like that . . . wouldnae stop me . . .

---

[29] Public housing estates.

SEEN AND NOW HEARD

He added that he would '. . . maybe try and avoid it if I could, try an' tell them to go somewhere else tae fight, or something like that, roon the corner . . .'

So, in sum, their view was that CCTV had reduced large fights, but not necessarily that it had stopped fighting altogether. Smaller fights in the town centre might be arranged out of sight of the cameras (drunkenness tended to interfere with the ability to arrange this), but the more traditional fights would be staged out of vision of the whole CCTV system (although there was no sign that these large gang fights were common). However, this had not necessarily made things safer. There was something of a feeling that the large gang-type fights of the past were fuelled by alcohol, but that the more individual fighting of the present might be unpredictably affected by drugs, and that this could be more dangerous. One 29-year-old male (a former probationer) claimed:

. . . Now it's a lot of young ones, the now . . . and they don't care . . . the Dutch courage we got was from drink, right? I'm talking as if I'm an old man! . . . Know what I mean? Wi' us, it was mainly drink because we werenae really into [drugs], alright, maybe an odd joint and things like that . . . but now you don't know what they're firing down their neck[30] . . . you don't know what's going through their brain, so you don't know what they're capable of, you know, so you're always that wary. It could be a wee daft 17-year-old kid, know what I mean? . . . One minute stuck up . . . plunged[31] you in the chest . . . you don't know, just don't risk it any more. It's got a lot worse, I think, in Airdrie . . .

Overall, the effect of CCTV on public order offending seems to be to change its character (from large fracas to small affrays), to deflect its location (the former to outwith the town centre; the latter to side streets) and to reduce its actual—as opposed to recorded—incidence. If this is displacement, then it is 'benign' in the sense that potential victims of such offending will find it easier to avoid being victimized.

The effect on theft

The believed effects of CCTV on property offending are similarly ambiguous, although rather more respondents believed that CCTV had changed things. Some didn't. First, a 20-year-old male currently on probation for breach of the peace and police assault, but who had once had more than a passing interest in other people's cars. He was asked initially whether or not he thought that shoplifting had been affected by the CCTV cameras:

. . . Oh, no . . . far from it. There's still a lot of shoplifting going on, and that . . . Now, car crime. I used to be into a wee bit of car crime myself when I was younger and all . . . and when I done it, I didnae take any notice of the cameras. I just did it anyway, and I wasnae caught once. Not with the car crime, anyway . . . well, once the camera on top of the —— (supermarket) building . . . and we were wanting to take a motor from the car park. We just waited until [the camera] couldn't see us . . . it was facing the other way . . . I used to take Cavaliers and Astras, and I could take them in 30 seconds to a minute . . . Aye, it only takes less than a minute, less time than it takes for the camera to come round again . . . And I could be away with one . . .

---

[30] What drugs they were taking.
[31] Stabbed.

EMMA SHORT AND JASON DITTON

Another agreed that the cameras could be fooled. This time it is an 18-year-old male on community service for loitering with intent to steal, and talking about shoplifting, after being asked what effect the cameras have had:

. . . No' really much. Still know people that'll go shoplifting. Still get off with as much as they used to get off with . . . because you canna see much with the cameras. I've seen shops with cameras, all you can see is the precinct. All people going about their own business, that's all you can see. You cannae see shoplifters, cannae see anybody breaking into cars into the car parks either, because it just shows you up the precinct. They [cameras] always face the same way, well, more or less the same way . . .

Another (a 25-year-old male on community service for car theft) knew somebody who had been recently caught shoplifting, but nevertheless didn't think that the cameras were much of a deterrent:

. . . he's caught actually shoplifting, lifting a couple of jumpers out of the shop and ran down the main street, they got him on the camera . . . plus a woman picked him out on ID, so he's done even without the cameras anyway, so . . . it doesn't matter whether they're [cameras] there or not. If they're going to do it, they're [offenders are] going to do it . . . there's far too many people I meet that come from Glasgow, Cumbernauld, and all that, intae Airdrie, to go shoplifting, because they're easy pickings, because I don't know whether the shops in Airdrie are led into a false sense of security because the CCTV's there. But a lot of shoplifters and that do come to Airdrie, just for the sake of easy pickings. That's just what I know, people I talk to . . .

While most had been quite forthcoming about public-order matters (and the effect that the cameras had had on them) they were vague about theft. Common were diluted versions of the much publicized police success story ('. . . crime's fell. Helped a lotta people. Not been as much shops broke intae . . .' and '. . . they [cameras] definitely stop crime in the centre of Airdrie . . . and I think a lot of women and young people and that, be able tae walk safer without getting mugged or something like that . . .') with one (the 25-year-old male on community service for drugs offences) actually citing statistics!

. . . they reckoned it was a 70 per cent decrease in crime, so that will be breaking, break-ins, and that, shops and everything . . . fighting, people come out wi' a drink in them and just smashing windaes for nothing, you know . . .

Some, however, claimed that they could carry on much as in the past. First a 29-year-old male, currently free, but with a history of assault and breach of the peace, and then an 18-year-old male doing community service for loitering with intent to steal:

. . . they just go elsewhere, to be honest with you. They just go to different car parks that haven't got cameras in them . . . or . . . they would stay within the Airdrie area, you know what I mean? . . . down a side street or something, you know, they know it's no' thingmaed wi' cameras. Not getting watched from a camera . . .

. . . The mair cameras on in Airdrie, it's stopping places getting broken into in Airdrie, they'll go elsewhere, break into other people's motors . . .[32]

[32] Estimates of how far those intent on stealing cars or from houses ranged from half a mile to 15 miles. Quite a few mentioned travelling to Glasgow (15 miles away), and one mentioned Dumbarton (about 30 miles away). See Rengert (1992) on this.

Surveillance, Crime and Social Control

As for their response to being under surveillance, some continued unaffected, some desisted. Knowledge of how the cameras had worked was rudimentary (and usually inaccurate). Most claimed that CCTV had changed their behaviour, but more often towards wariness than desistance. Public-order offending was felt to be somewhat decreased (although police recorded public offending had increased to 133 per cent of that recorded before camera installation), and also channelled into geographical areas out of camera vision. Large town centre gang set-tos were agreed to be mostly a thing of the past. Theft offending was also felt to have been affected variously, although opinions were less specific and fulsome. Being a more private matter than public-order offending (in the sense that the latter typically involves more than one person), interviewees could offer no common consensus of the effect.

The effect overall

The initial statistical study indicated that the 21 per cent overall fall in recorded crime in Airdrie concealed variations for different types of crimes. More specific data indicates that crimes of dishonesty fell to 48 per cent,[33] but public-order crimes rose to 133 per cent.[34]

The qualitative interviews conducted with offenders in Airdrie offer a rich background to these statistical findings. With crimes of dishonesty, displacement seems to account for some, but not all of the decreases in discovered crime rates. Some respondents—but only a few—admitted to travelling elsewhere (the 15 miles to Glasgow was often mentioned) where the depredations of a few now mobile Airdrie inhabitants would not have been noticeable in Glasgow's recorded crime rates, and thus not traced in our original statistical analysis of local crime rates. Some others claimed to have given up committing such crimes,[35] and still others (but none of the interviewed) are believed to have originally travelled from Glasgow to Airdrie (particularly to shoplift), and these have been persuaded now to travel even further (being now doubly displaced).[36]

Somewhat curiously, the impact of the CCTV cameras on public order offending seemed greater in qualitative than in quantitative analysis. Most of the interviewed group claimed considerable reductions, but the percentage statistical decline was small. However, it should be recognized that many of those who spoke of the effect of the cameras on public-order offending (and who claimed that they would be more careful in future) were caught on camera, and this alone will have swelled the public-order offence statistics after the cameras were installed, and implied that the cameras were

---

[33] Crimes of dishonesty are collated as Group 3 crimes. Major subcategories are: theft by housebreaking; theft of motor vehicle; theft from motor vehicle; theft; taking and driving away motor vehicle; and shoplifting. Full and further detail to be found in Short, Ditton and Phillips (1995: Table 2.1, p. 27).

[34] Group 6 offences include: petty assault, breach of the peace, drunkenness offences, public urination, and other offences. (Possession of offensive weapons and serious assault are Group 1 crimes, and are not included in the statistics quoted here. In total, Group 1 crimes constituted only 3 per cent of all crimes and offences recorded in Airdrie. For further detail, see ibid. Table 2.4, p. 29.)

[35] The respondents interviewed can be expected to include more apparent age-based desistors than would constitute the 'active' population, and in this sense the group interviewed may be atypical.

[36] Airdrie police intelligence (and, apparently, local court records) indicates that shoplifters from residential rather than central parts of Glasgow certainly used to visit Airdrie's shops before camera installation.

EMMA SHORT AND JASON DITTON

not effective (as measured by reducing the crime rate). In any event, public order offending has certainly changed, partly because of the presence of the cameras. The cameras, specifically, persuaded potential aggressors to use the back lanes (within the CCTV area, but out of vision) or to return to public housing estates and continue hostilities well out of the CCTV vision area.

That the response to CCTV is varied, complex and unpredictable (rather than a uniformly simple case of predictable mono-causal crime prevention) may seem logical—particularly with the benefit of hindsight—but is nevertheless hard to establish in the face of the populist, and chiefly amateur, onslaught that CCTV 'works' (Tilley 1997).

Conclusion

Good qualitative research is often tantalising. If sufficiently persuasive, readers regularly crave more. Particularly if the appetite is whetted, satiety can only come from knowing more of the various attitudes, opinions, reactions, and so on, that research has brought to the surface, and the relative frequencies that one might expect of each in a representative population. Research on the issue of displacement of offending currently cannot offer a calibration of the latter, although future work might well attempt to do so.

This slight but helpful pilot study indicates that offenders are knowledgeable about and will talk relatively freely about open street CCTV and their reactions and responses to it. Further, offenders possess a wide variety of attitudes (not all of them, perhaps surprisingly, negative) and utilize many different responses to CCTV. Nevertheless, a simple answer to the critical displacement issue still eludes research. The issue is critical because the simplistic demonstrations of crime rate decreases that typically accompany the installation of open street CCTV systems are normally used to justify the original and ongoing system expenditure. If offending can be shown to be merely displaced elsewhere, then these demonstrations of apparent effectiveness would be revealed as worthless.

Offenders' accounts still seem to be the most fruitful way to understand displacement; to which end a sophisticated analysis of police recorded criminal statistics still seems to be a necessary precursor. The interview material gathered to date indicates that CCTV can reduce offending, even when police recorded crime and offence rates register little or no effect. It has to be remembered that this set of respondents are 'hardened' offenders (in the sense that they continued to offend after CCTV installation), and that by definition they thus understate the power of CCTV to foster desistance.

This is starkly the case with public-order offending in Airdrie. Installation of CCTV was followed by a noticeable rise in recorded public-order offences. Most of those interviewed claimed that public-order offending had declined markedly in general, and that what persisted had been displaced—relatively benignly—into smaller fracas in back streets, or larger affrays away from the town centre. This may be an example of CCTV reducing and displacing offending, and then permitting a very much larger proportion of a markedly diminished residual to be recorded. This suggested, perhaps erroneously, that there had been a rise in public-order offending.

SEEN AND NOW HEARD

What can this study add to the theoretical appreciation of displacement? Referring again to the Repetto typology outlined earlier, there was, firstly, no indication of any 'temporal', 'tactical', 'target' or 'functional' displacement. When interviewees confessed to any change in behaviour consequential on CCTV installation, it seemed to refer to a mixture of desistance and one or more of several varieties of 'geographical' displacement. When property offending continued, it was sometimes continued in Airdrie, and sometimes in other towns. There were hints that those who previously travelled to Airdrie to, for example, shoplift, no longer did so. With public-order offending, it was felt that there had been an overall decline, but that continued offending moved away from the major camera-surveilled town centre streets.

However, if the issue of CCTV in particular, and displacement in general, is to be taken any further, then we suggest that this can only usefully be done via a full offender study. Such a study would take at least four years to complete as it is essential to collect data during both the two years before, and the two years after the installation of an open street CCTV scheme in a town centre.[37] The focus of such a study would be on a greater variety of offenders than this pilot was able to contact. A full study should take care to research 'retired' and 'active' offenders, as well as 'potential' ones. The latter may well be the younger brothers, or even the sons, of the former. Initial points of contact may well have to be formal, but time spent snowballing from these to offenders not in current contact with the criminal justice system would be time well spent. Offender histories should be detailed and built into career life history cases, of a sort which, in principle, could be tied to police, court, prison and probation records. Participant observation—where possible and legal—would be a solid background against which to conduct repeated qualitative interviews and even group discussions.

REFERENCES

BARR, R. and PEASE, K. (1990), 'Crime Placement, Displacement, and Deflection', in M. Tonry and N. Morris, eds., *Crime and Justice: A Review of Research*, vol. 12: 277–317. Chicago: University of Chicago Press.

—— (1992) 'A Place for Every Crime and Every Crime in its Place: An Alternative Perspective on Crime Displacement', in D. J. Evans *et al.*, eds., *Crime, Policing and Place: Essays in Environmental Criminology*, ch. 10. London: Routledge.

BENNETT, T. (1986), 'Situational Crime Prevention from the Offenders' Perspective', in K. Heal and G. Laycock, eds., *Situational Crime Prevention: From Theory to Practice*, ch. 4: 41–54. London: HMSO.

BULOS, M. and SARNO, C. (1994), *Closed Circuit Television and Local Authority Initiatives: The First National Survey*, Research Monograph RM1/1994. South Bank University.

BURROWS, J. N. (1979), 'The impact of closed circuit television on crime in the London Underground', in P. Mayhew, R. G. V. Clarke, J. N. Burrows, J. M. Hough and S. W. C. Winchester, *Crime in Public View*, Home Office Research Study, No. 49, Ch. 3. London: HMSO.

---

[37] Four years of data are necessary (six would be ideal as this would include all four pre-installation years' data from which to construct a seasonal effect pattern without having to co-opt the post-installation years, and thus contaminate the possible effect with post-experimentation data). So, four years' data are a minimum: not a maximum. Somewhere as big as a city would probably be unmanageable. Basing a study in one of the now proliferating small residential schemes is unlikely to generate enough data. Accordingly, a town centre seems to be an appropriately sized locale.

EMMA SHORT AND JASON DITTON

CLARKE, R. V. and WEISBURD, D. (1994), 'Diffusion of Crime Control Benefits: Observations on the Reverse of Displacement', in R. V. Clarke, ed., *Crime Prevention Studies*, vol. 2: 165–83.

CORNISH, D. and CLARKE, R. V. (1987), 'Understanding Crime Displacement: An Application of Rational Choice Theory', *Criminology*, 25/4: 933–47.

DITTON, J. and FORD, R. (1994), *The Reality of Probation: A Formal Ethnography of Process and Practice*. Aldershot: Gower.

FRENCH, P. W. (1994), The Opinions of the Public and Offenders Concerning the Use of Closed Circuit Television Surveillance in Public Places, MA Dissertation. Bramshill Police Staff College.

—— (1996), 'Inside the Offender's Mind', *CCTV Today*, 3/3: 16–19.

GABOR, T. (1978) 'Crime Displacement: The Literature and Strategies for its Investigation', *Crime and Justice*, 6/2: 100–107.

—— (1990) 'Crime Displacement and Situational Prevention: Toward the Development of some Principles', *Canadian Journal of Criminology*, 32: 41–74.

GROOMBRIDGE, N. and MURJI, K. (1994), 'Obscured by Cameras? CCTV and Policing', *Criminal Justice Matters*, 17, Autumn.

HANCOX, P. D. and MORGAN, J. B. (1975), 'The Use of CCTV for Police Control at Football Matches', *Police Research Bulletin*, 25: 41–44.

MACCALLUM, R. G. (1994), *Tongs Ya Bas*, Glasgow: New Glasgow Press.

MUSHENO, M. C., LEVINE, J. P. and PALUMBO, D. J. (1978), 'Television Surveillance and Crime Prevention: Evaluating an Attempt to Create Defensible Space in Public Housing', *Social Science Quarterly*, 58/4: 647–56.

PATRICK, JAMES [Pseud.] (1973), *A Glasgow Gang Observed*. London: Methuen.

PEASE, K. (1994), 'Crime Prevention', in M. Maguire, *et al.*, eds., *The Oxford Handbook of Criminology*, ch. 14: 659–703. Oxford: Oxford University Press.

POYNER, B. (1988), 'Video Cameras and Bus Vandalism', *Journal of Security Administration*, 11: 44–51.

—— (1991), 'Situational crime prevention in two parking facilities', *Security Journal*, 2: 96–101.

RENGERT, G. F. (1992), 'The Journey to Crime: Conceptual Foundations and Policy Implications', in D. J. Evans, N. R. Fyfe and D. T. Herbert, *Crime, Policing and Place: Essays in Environmental Criminology*, Ch. 6: 109–17. London: Routledge.

REPETTO, T. A. (1976), 'Crime Prevention and the Displacement Phenomenon', *Crime and Delinquency*, 22: 166–7.

SHORT, E. and DITTON, J. (1995), 'Does CCTV Affect Crime?', *CCTV Today*, 2/2: 10–12.

—— (1996), *Does Closed Circuit Television Prevent Crime? An Evaluation of the Use of CCTV Surveillance Cameras in Airdrie Town Centre*. Scottish Office, Central Research Unit.

SHORT, E., DITTON, J. and PHILLIPS, S. (1995), *Closed Circuit Television in Small Towns in Scotland*. Final Report to Scottish Office.

SHOVER, N. and HONAKER, D. (1992), 'The Socially Bounded Decision Making of Persistent Property Offenders', *Howard Journal of Criminal Justice*, 31/4: 276–93.

TILLEY, N. (1993), *Understanding Car Parks, Crime and CCTV: Evaluation Lessons from Safer Cities*, Crime Prevention Unit Paper No. 42. London: Home Office.

—— (1997), 'Whys and Wherefores in Evaluating the Effectiveness of CCTV', *International Journal of Risk, Security and Crime Prevention*, 2/3: 175–85.

ULDRIKS, N. and VAN MASTRIGT, H. (1991), *Policing Police Violence*, London: Aberdeen University Press.

[9]

The Eyes Have It: CCTV As The 'Fifth Utility'

S Graham

"You're on CCTV Surveillance" signs are everywhere these days. But these might soon be replaced by signs that say "Warning! You are entering an area which is NOT covered by CCTV!" So widespread is closed-circuit television (CCTV) coverage becoming, and so reliant are we now on the gaze of millions of electronic eyes, that we may soon start to treat the *absence* or *collapse* of CCTV systems with the sort of fear and anxiety with which we treat electricity cuts or the collapse of the telephone network. We might soon have a fear of unwatched spaces. CCTV, in short, looks set to become a fifth utility, to join electricity, gas, water, and telephone networks as ubiquitous infrastructures that we expect to cover all places and therefore largely take for granted.

How can we tell that CCTV is on the verge of being virtually omnipresent? I would point to four early signs. The first and simplest is its widening geographical coverage. CCTV now covers so many of our town and city centres, shopping malls, petrol garages, leisure centres, stadia, car parks, transport networks, residential and public spaces that, soon, virtually every part of our waking hour will be watched, somewhere, by someone.

Over 500 British towns and cities now have public CCTV systems—up from 74 three years ago—and the expansion rate is remarkable. The UK market for CCTV equipment is currently the biggest in Europe, at over £385 million per year. Once established, CCTV systems generally add cameras to cover larger areas on a continuous basis to make the most of the investment in people and a monitoring office to take advantage of new technology. Within cities like Newcastle, for example, separate CCTV systems now cover the city centre, main shopping malls, district centres, business parks, transport networks, stadia, and a growing range of housing and residential districts. The uncovered space between these areas is diminishing fast.

In smaller towns, CCTV control centres in one town are being linked to new CCTV systems covering other market towns in the surrounding region to save money. Beyond the main towns and cities, there is a notable shift of CCTV towards smaller places in more remote rural areas. Smaller settlements, worried by fear of crime and potential overspill from larger urban areas with CCTV, are increasingly installing their own systems. In Wales, a progressive diffusion of the systems had led to Cardigan, with 4000 people, and Newcastle Emlyn (with 1500), now having CCTV. Even very small villages are now considering investing in the technology. Bassenthwaite, a village of 400 residents near Keswick in the Lake District, is keen to install a system, with residents arguing it would deter car crime and burglaries.

The second sign is that the growth of CCTV seems to be fuelling itself in a spiral of self-reinforcement. This is happening through its symbiotic relationship with television. More and more of the nation's, indeed the world's, criminal acts are caught directly on camera as they happen. Soon after, they are beamed direct to our living rooms through the countless news reports and cheap crime TV shows that flood the proliferating cable, satellite, and terrestrial channels, from *Police Stop!* and *Crime Watch* to *America's Dumbest Criminals*. Even local newspapers are now trying to print CCTV images of convicted criminals' faces. The deputy editor of one such paper, the *Portsmouth Evening News*, believes this is "part of what makes CCTV effective".

But why does this link fuel the further growth of CCTV? Ade Thomas, an ex-researcher for the civil liberties group Liberty, argues that the close connection between

TV, local news, and CCTV is likely to foster a feedback loop supporting the shift to ubiquitous surveillance. Viewers are likely to react to the crime TV shows by developing further anxieties about the risks of crime on the street and in their homes. In response to these anxieties, they are likely to support further extension of CCTV. Thus, more crime events will be captured to be relayed onto TV programmes. And so the spiral continues.

The third sign of the shift towards ubiquitous surveillance is more subtle. Over the past few years, attention in the British media has started to shift from watched places to unwatched ones. As part of this process of what sociologists call 'normalisation', every murder, school break-in, or terrorist act seems to intensify the spiral of demands for ubiquitous surveillance. The question, especially in the local and tabloid press, has shifted from "Are these new CCTV schemes a good thing?" to "Why can't we have cameras everywhere?"

Take a couple of examples. The recent installation of CCTV in Chapeltown, Leeds, was prompted by the murder there of Stefan Popvich in 1996. Local councillors were widely criticised for not installing the system before the murder, either to deter it in the first place, or to help in detecting the culprit. Likewise, when cameras were removed from Ladyton shopping centre in Scotland, a few months before a murder there in 1996, the local press reported this scandalous 'video blunder' in more detail than the murder itself.

Soon, it seems, the newsworthy events will emerge not when another CCTV system is installed or when CCTV images are used by the police or private security personnel (that much will be assumed as given). Rather, media and public attention will be on the dangers and threats that lurk in unwatched places, either when camera systems fail, or when serious crime occurs in the interstitial uncovered spaces between existing CCTV systems.

The fourth and final ominous sign of the shift to ubiquitous surveillance comes from the remarkable technological changes underway in CCTV which seem likely to support strongly its shift towards a fifth utility. In particular, CCTV is starting to be computerised. Video surveillance is now moving from the use of analogue video systems, like the ones we use at home, to digital computerised systems.

This shift to digital CCTV will have two crucial consequences for its spread. First, it will remove barriers to geographical expansion. This is because digital CCTV systems can be programmed to search automatically for specified events and people within much larger CCTV systems than are currently possible, rather than relying on the built-in limits of the 'Mk1 eyeball' of the human operator.

Second, it is very easy to link computerised CCTV automatically to image databases of car number plates and human face scans. In other words, technologies for crude visual tracking quickly become automatic tracking systems of people and cars which can memorise their movements in time and space as well as tracking them in 'real time'.

In digital CCTV systems computer programs stipulate what an 'unusual' event is— say a person walking past at night, a person running, or the presence of a specified individual car or face. It then sets the cameras recording automatically when such an event is detected. Early trials for these sorts of technologies are already in operation, with Britain leading the world. Around the City of London's 'Ring of Steel', which automatically scans car number plates, linking instantaneously to the computerised car number-plate records of the Driving and Vehicle Licensing Authority, cars moving the 'wrong way' down a street automatically trigger cameras to monitor and record the scene. Attention is also alerted if cars entering the zone do not leave within a specified time.

In Newham in East London, meanwhile, a recently unveiled system actively scans for the 'target faces' of 60 – 100 suspected criminals 24 hours a day through 140 fixed and 11 mobile cameras by using a software system called Mandrake. But the real potential for linking databases to digital CCTV will be realised when the many local CCTV networks start to interconnect into bigger, national or even international systems (as is already happening with the UK's national recognition system for car number plates). With an effective national CCTV system, linked to facial and car number-plate databases, it will be very simple for law and order authorities to track the movements of all cars and people continuously and in real time.

Suspect individuals and cars will be instantly tracked down. Those who are not registered within the system—illegal immigrants, for example—will be easy to isolate and track. Long-mooted national identity cards, with their digital facial images, might provide the organising database for individuals. Movements of low-level convicted criminals with electronic tags will be tracked and scrutinised. People's movements, activities, and behaviours might be archived to support later analysis of 'suspicious' activities. And incidences of crime might be correlated with people's movements to identify suspects through 'proactive policing'.

So, what emerges in the bigger picture when we take all these points together? CCTV is geographically spreading over more and more of the country. It is linking to TV to fuel ever-further extension. We are starting to notice unwatched places more than watched ones. And CCTV is starting to be computerised. Continuing these trends over, say, 15 years, we can envisage a position where visual surveillance is so woven into the fabric of daily life that it becomes, in effect, a fifth utility. CCTV will be expected, everywhere, all the time, like telephone access or water or electricity supply is today. Middle-class house and car owners and parents will expect to be able to watch remotely over their homes, cars, and children while away or on holiday (in fact, small CCTV cameras can already be used for this purpose over phone networks and the Internet). There will be an increasing expectation by many people to be under the reassuring scrutiny of CCTV at all times and places (over the Internet, cable systems, the telephone networks, or whatever). For many, ubiquitous coverage will in fact be taken for granted.

Paradoxically, though, CCTV will become less rather than more visible in this shift towards ubiquitous surveillance. CCTV cameras will become much smaller (at present, colour CCTV cameras of size less than 32 mm^2 are available). They will also become more covert. But the very ubiquity of the cameras will render them so utterly banal and normal that few will bother to take much notice (the way we treat telephones, computer screens, flushing toilets, and electricity sockets now). Soon, as cameras become so small, we will begin to assume that they are there, embedded in everything from lamp posts to clocks, doors, street lights, and bus stops.

These trends seem convincing. But what finally makes me believe that CCTV is a proto-fifth utility is the remarkable similarity between its current development and the early history of the four traditional utilities—electricity, water, gas, and telecommunications—in the 19th century city.

In the 19th century, these services first emerged as small specialised networks, geared towards a myriad of separate uses. They utilised a wide variety of technologies and covered only small parts of Victorian cities. The networks sprang up through complex patchworks of both public and private entrepreneurship. Industries started their own electricity and water networks. Town gas networks were built by ambitious municipalities for lighting their streets. And the first telephone and telegraph networks were used mainly by large businesses and emergency services. There was much confusion and many different technologies were in use. London, for example, had many separate electricity generators all covering their small areas and using differing voltages. And, initially, many places in between these areas of coverage remained without electricity, telephone, and water services for a considerable period of time, to their considerable annoyance.

Just like CCTV today, in fact. These utility networks, of course, have long since merged and extended. They have become technologically standardised. They are multipurpose and nationally regulated. And they have virtually universal coverage. Indeed, since the 1940s the government has regulated the four main utilities to ensure that they cover everyone and every area of the country. Such requirements have remained in place even with privatisation and the onset of competition.

CCTV coverage seems set to extend towards ubiquity in a similar way. Like the earlier utilities it will merge into a national integrated system. It will become more multipurpose. It will be regulated nationally. And it will gradually adopt standardised packages of technologies. In fact, the CCTV industry itself recognises the likely emergence of a nationally integrated CCTV infrastructure for real-time face and car tracking, forged out of the gradual merging of the thousands of individual CCTV 'islands' which currently exist. Jon Fassenbender (1997), a commentator in *CCTV Today* magazine, admitted recently that the full usefulness of CCTV and facial recognition will only come "when a national database is established to provide instant image analysis". In a recent commentary in *CCTV Today* magazine, he argued that "at the moment, CCTV is very much flavour of the month. But what might happen in perhaps ten years time when most individual surveillance systems have been gradually integrated towards providing total coverage, as part of a larger, integrated scheme?"

The more CCTV coverage becomes the norm, the more excluded areas will fight to gain coverage. As with the extension of gas, electricity, telephone, and water networks towards national coverage earlier this century, the rush to ubiquity will be on. State regulatory mechanisms will also be necessary to oversee the process, minimise abuses, and maximise the value of the collective CCTV systems in tracking down suspects in serious crimes. Already, police forces in London have started to look into a London-wide registration system for CCTV cameras to aid their antiterrorist investigations. National efforts to regulate and standardise CCTV will intensify, not only to help allay public fears of abuse of the systems, but so that they can be used to correlate crime and behaviour patterns in real time.

It is extremely unlikely, though, that some single, national 'Big Brother' CCTV system will develop, in the model of the water boards or gas boards of the postwar era. Since privatisation, utilities are now made up of a myriad of competing private companies covering different areas, offering different technologies and services, and geared to different niche markets. Such services are superimposed on the technological grids of the infrastructure networks. The key support to this situation is the use of information technology (IT) to support the interconnection of all these competing different networks.

I suspect that CCTV will emerge in the same way. There will probably be some form of national regulator and a myriad of service providers from the telecoms, cable, media, security, and IT industries, offering many different types of service, from simple 'watch your home while away' to enormous networks covering all the premises of a multinational or multisite organisation, perhaps across continental or even global scales, from a single point. Telephone lines, cable networks, the Internet, and wireless links will all be used. Smaller TVs will monitor smaller cameras over increasingly powerful communications grids. It has even been suggested that 'Global Neighbourhood Watch' might emerge. In this scenario, affluent neighbourhoods in, say, San Francisco, London, and Hong Kong would use small CCTV cameras on the Internet to monitor each other overnight in a curious parallel to the 8-hour separation between the three major stock exchanges of the world.

One thing, though, is clear. Given the huge costs of wiring the nation with electronic eyes, it might not be long before you have another quarterly bill landing on your doormat or being electronically debited from your bank account.

S Graham

Reference
Fassenbender J, 1997, "A vision of the future" *CCTV Today* March issue, page 51

[10]

YES, IT WORKS, NO, IT DOESN'T: COMPARING THE EFFECTS OF OPEN-STREET CCTV IN TWO ADJACENT SCOTTISH TOWN CENTRES

by

Jason Ditton

and

Emma Short
Scottish Centre for Criminology

Abstract: *This paper reports the evaluation of two contrasting open-street closed circuit television (CCTV) installations in Scotland. Twelve cameras were installed in a small town called Airdrie in 1992, and 32 cameras were installed in Glasgow, a large city, in 1994. After controlling for extraneous factors, it was discovered that, overall, recorded crime fell (and detections rose) in Airdrie after camera installation, but in Glasgow recorded crime rose (and detections fell). However, in both locations, some more specific types of recorded crimes fell and some others rose. It cannot simply be concluded that CCTV "works" in small towns, but not in large cities. In part this is because the goals of open-street CCTV installations are usually developed at a somewhat slower pace than are the systems themselves, and are often incompatible. For example, proponents claim that CCTV will both reduce crime (by deterring potential offenders) and increase it (by capturing more illegal acts on camera). Accordingly, in both locations studied, CCTV has been a different sort of success.*

INTRODUCTION

There has been substantial investment in closed circuit television (CCTV) schemes in Britain since the early 1990s. Central and local government investment in open-street CCTV in the U.K. between the years 1994 and 1997 has been estimated to have been in excess of £100 million (Norris and Armstrong, 1998). Before this, some small-scale research had indicated that CCTV had had an impact in various closed locations, such as: in shops (Van Straelen, 1978; Burrows, 1991; Gill and Turbin, 1997); on buses (Poyner, 1988); in car parks (Poyner, 1991; Tilley, 1993); on the London Underground (Mayhew et al., 1979); and in small businesses (Hearnden, 1996). However, in general, instances of fully independent professional evaluation of open-street CCTV schemes has been rare,[1] a gap which the research reported here hopes partly to fill.

Scotland differs slightly from England and Wales insofar as, in the main, partially government-backed schemes were not introduced until slightly later, and not substantially before the results of independent professional evaluation were available. Flying in the face of its legendary fiscal caution, Scotland has since adopted town and city centre CCTV schemes with uncharacteristic abandon. There have been two distinctly different investment phases. Prior to 1996, the 12 schemes that were in operation in January 1996 were all the result of the handiwork of sharp-eyed solitary moral entrepreneurs working in different locations and occupying different roles.[2] Since 1996, funding has become institutionalised, with the Scottish Office playing a key role in encouraging the spread of CCTV by mounting two CCTV Challenge competitions. In the 1996-97 round, 32 additional schemes were partially funded by the Scottish Office (the total capital cost of the 32 successful schemes amounted to £4.859 million, of which the Scottish Office contributed £1.851 million). In the 1997-98 round, 30 more schemes were partially funded by the Scottish Office (the total capital cost of these schemes amounted to £4.953 million, of which the Scottish Office contributed £1.861 million).

Twelve open-street CCTV cameras were installed in Airdrie's town centre in 1992, and became operational in November of that year. This was the first multi-camera CCTV installation in Scotland. Almost exactly two years later, in November 1994, 32 cameras were installed in Glasgow's city centre. Glasgow is Scotland's biggest city, and Airdrie is a small town located some 15 miles east of Glasgow. We were responsible for the independent professional evaluation of both installations. Details of the governmental and other publications stemming from this endeavor are given at the end of this paper. This is the first time the effects of CCTV in the two places have been considered together.

THE EFFECT IN AIRDRIE

The area of the centre of Airdrie actually visible from one or more of the cameras represents parts of six separate police patrol beats. Crime and offence data were collected for the period November 1990 to October 1994. This represents exactly 24 months before installation of the cameras, and 24 months afterwards. Considerable care was taken to plot areas visible to the cameras, so as to be able to distinguish those crimes and offences recorded in areas visible to the cameras from those recorded in the remainder of the six beats.

Recorded crime and offence and detection data were also collected for six increasingly sized areas of comparison: the CCTV vision area, the rest of those six beats, the rest of the subdivision, the rest of the division, the rest of the police force area, and the rest of Scotland. These data were collected to allow both a comparison of rates of change in the commission of crimes and offences in the CCTV area and other comparable areas, and to allow a check to be made for possible displacement of criminal activity from the CCTV area to other areas, and/or for possible diffusion of benefits of CCTV to such areas.

Recorded Crime in Airdrie

The overall effect on recorded crime and offence rates of installing CCTV cameras in Airdrie can be seen in Figure 1.

The "before" segment represents the 24 months prior to installation, and the "after" segment, the two years following. The curved line represents the total recorded crime and offence rate derived from data that have been both seasonally adjusted and controlled for underlying trends.[3]

It is hard to determine visually a periodic trend from a curved line. To calculate the trend (in effect to straighten the line), the "line of best fit" (the regression line)[4] has been calculated separately for the before and after periods. For each line, the angle of slope indicates the trend (both before and after CCTV installation, recorded crimes were decreasing); and the position of the line from the baseline indicates the magnitude of the effect. The dashed line represents the line of best fit before installation, and the solid black one, the line of best fit afterwards.

Clearly, the installation of CCTV has had a beneficial effect. This is indicated in Figure 1 by the area between the dashed and solid sloped lines of best fit after CCTV installation. One way of looking at

204 — Jason Ditton and Emma Short

this area is to see it as representing 772 recorded crimes and offences that CCTV installation has prevented.

Figure 1: Recorded Crimes and Offences in Airdrie's CCTV Area, Lines of "Best Fit" Before and After Camera Installation
November 1990 – October 1994

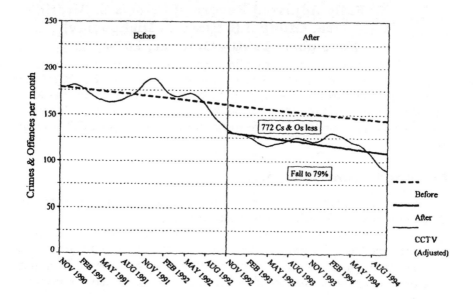

CCTV seems to have had a variable effect on the rates of different types of recorded crimes and offences. Recorded crimes and offences are divided into seven general groups by the Scottish Office, and it seems sensible to use identical aggregations. These groups vary in direction and the degree to which they are affected by the installation of CCTV. The first five groups are crimes; the last two, offences.[5]

It is not possible to analyse changes in recorded crimes from Group 1 (violence) and Group 2 (indecency), as too few were recorded.[6] Recorded crimes of dishonesty (Group 3 crimes) fell to 48% in the 24 months after installation of CCTV. This represents 1,231 fewer recorded crimes in the area of Airdrie covered by the cameras in the 24 months following installation (see Figure 2).

Figure 2: Fully Adjusted Recorded Crimes in Airdrie's CCTV Area, Group 3 (Crimes of Dishonesty) November, 1990 – October, 1994

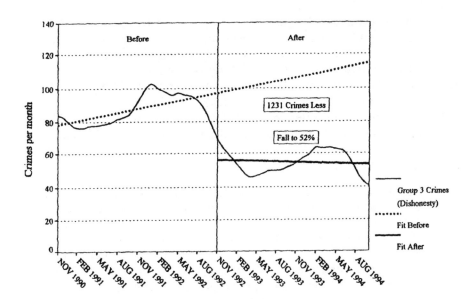

Group 4 crimes (fire-raising and vandalism) fell by 19% in the 24 months after installation of CCTV. This decrease is based on relatively small numbers of recorded crimes and translates into just 42 fewer crimes in the 24 months following CCTV installation. Recorded crimes in Group 5 (other) crimes rose by 1,068% (when compared to previously recorded levels) in the 24 months following installation. Again, the numbers are small in this group with this percentage representing 180 more crimes in the 24 months after CCTV was operational.

Similarly, 194 more Group 6 (miscellaneous) offences were recorded in the 24 months following CCTV installation — a rise to 133% of previously recorded levels in the 24 months. Finally, Group 7 offences (motor vehicle-related) increased by a total of 58, to 126% of previously recorded levels, in the 24 months following CCTV installation.[7]

Increases in recorded crimes in Group 5, and in recorded offences in Groups 6 and 7 are not necessarily indicative of the failure of CCTV. Within Group 5, an increase in drug offences may reflect well on the surveillance ability of CCTV to detect crimes that might otherwise have gone unnoticed. The same could be said of "breach of the peace" offences (Group 6) and minor traffic violations (Group 7).

Overall, crimes and offences fell to 79% of previously recorded levels in the two years following the installation of CCTV in Airdrie.

Detections in Airdrie

In the two years after CCTV installation, detections[8] improved to 116% of previously recorded levels. To put this another way, the clear-up rate improved from 50% to 58% of recorded crimes and offences. This is illustrated in Figure 3.

The improvement in detections varied by crime and offence group. Group 3 crimes of dishonesty did not play such a big role in the overall improvement in detections as they played in the reduction in recorded crimes, maintaining a 31% clearance rate both before and after CCTV installation. (Again, it is not possible to consider changes in detections for Group 1 and Group 2 crimes, as even fewer were recorded in each group than was the case for recorded crimes in these two groups.)

Most impressive were Group 4 crimes, which showed a detection improvement from a 20% to a 27% clear-up rate (itself, a 35% improvement). Detections in Group 5 crimes (from 95% to 97%), and Group 6 miscellaneous offences (from 82% to 87%) both show a slight

Figure 3: Adjusted Recorded Crimes, Offences and Detentions in Airdrie's CCTV Area, All Crimes and Offences November 1990 – October 1994

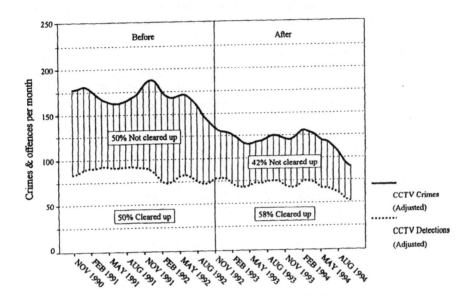

improvement. Group 7 motor vehicle offences saw a slight deterioration (from 98% to 94%). It should be recalled that Group 7 offences have a very high detection rate anyway, one that would be difficult to improve substantially.

Overall, detections improved to 116% of previously recorded levels in the two years following the installation of CCTV in Airdrie.

Displacement or Diffusion from Airdrie?

It is possible that at least some of the crimes and offences apparently prevented by the installation of CCTV were not prevented at all, but instead will have been "displaced" from that area and committed elsewhere or in other ways.

The areas surrounding the parts of Airdrie in camera vision generally saw an increase in recorded crimes. Much of this increase in criminal activity in adjacent areas was due to an increase in Group 5 (other) crimes, which include drug-related offences. These increased to 161% and 215%, respectively, of previously recorded levels in the 24 months after installation of CCTV in the rest of the CCTV visible beats and in the rest of the subdivision. This gives some sort of context to the finding that recorded Group 5 crimes also increased in the area covered by the cameras (to 145% of previously recorded levels in the 24 months after installation of CCTV).

A breakdown of Group 5 crimes in the CCTV area shows that Bail Act offences (something of a "phantom" crime)[9] and drug offences accounted for the majority of the increase. The same pattern holds in the potential displacement areas (both in the rest of the CCTV visible beats and in the rest of the subdivision). The best interpretation we can offer is that Bail Act offences and drug offences were increasing across the board and are relatively impervious to CCTV intervention.

There is no statistical evidence, therefore, to suggest that the crimes "prevented" in the CCTV area — mainly crimes of dishonesty (Group 3) — have been "geographically" displaced to either of the two immediately adjacent and larger areas. Nor is it likely that they have been displaced "functionally" to these areas, as displacement cannot explain the increase in Group 5 Bail Act and drug-related offences. Rather, as noted above, Bail Act and drug-related offences have increased in all areas.

This tentative conclusion seems to be borne out by attempting to "find" crimes apparently prevented in the CCTV area, in both the rest of the CCTV beats and the rest of the subdivision. Statistical evidence suggests that 772 crimes have been prevented in the CCTV area following installation of cameras. (This is calculated by projecting expected totals to the two years following camera installation in the CCTV area and then subtracting the actual adjusted recorded crime total). As it was not possible to trace any of these crimes to the immediately adjacent areas, it may be justifiable to treat them as having been prevented rather than merely displaced.

However, this cannot be treated as "proof" that displacement did not occur. Our check of geographical displacement was confined to adjacent areas; offenders may well be choosing to move very much further afield to continue offending. Various studies conducted in other countries have found that some burglars (Gabor, 1978) and some robbers (van Koppen and Jansen, 1998) will travel long distances and for many hours to reach their targets, while some, although not all, will be dissuaded from offending by such crime prevention measures (Bennett, 1986). Since conducting the main statistical study in Airdrie, we have piloted the idea of interviewing offenders in the area. This proved instructive, and these initial enquiries have been published as Short and Ditton,1998; and Ditton and Short, 1998a, 1998b. However, a full-scale study has not been undertaken.

THE EFFECT IN GLASGOW

Glasgow's city centre is covered by Strathclyde Police Force's "A" Division, which is itself divided into two subdivisions: "AB" and "AC." The CCTV cameras cover most, but not all of the beats in "AB" subdivision (21 of the 25), and some of the beats in "AC" subdivision (7 of the 24). Thus, the CCTV cameras cover, to some degree or other,[10] 28 separate beats in "A" Division.

Data were collected for the periods: 1st November, 1992 through 31st October, 1993; 1st November, 1993 through 31st October, 1994; and 1st November, 1994 through 31st October, 1995. This represents the first year after CCTV installation, compared with the identical calendar periods one year and two years before.

Equivalent data were also collected from: the beats in "A" Division that do not have any camera coverage (beats 1, 2, 5 and 6 from "AB" sub-division, and beats 26, 28-31, and 38-49 from "AC" subdivision, referred to henceforth as the rest of "A" Division); the surrounding police Divisions (Divisions "B," "C," "D," "E," "F," and "G"); and the rest of Strathclyde Police Force (Divisions "K," "L," "N," "P," "Q," "R," "U" and "X").

These additional data were collected, first, to establish a yardstick from which an underlying trend rate could be calculated. Then, after initial analysis ruled out alternative choices, the rest of "A" Division was chosen. In earlier work in Airdrie, a broadly similar aggregation (in that case, the rest of "N" Division) was chosen as the underlying trend yardstick.

Recorded Crime in Glasgow

The overall effect of installing CCTV cameras in Glasgow's city centre can be seen in Figure 4. The "before" segment represents the 24 months prior to installation, and the "after" segment the year following. The curved line represents the total recorded crime rate derived from data that have been both seasonally adjusted and controlled for underlying trends. A technical description of these processes is given in Annex Two of Ditton, et al. (1999). Apart from one slight but necessary modification, exactly the same analytic processes were used here as in the evaluation of the CCTV installation in Airdrie.[11]

Again, the line of best fit (the regression line) has been calculated separately for the before and after periods. For each line, the angle of slope indicates the trend (before CCTV installation, recorded crimes were decreasing); and the position of the line from the baseline indicates the magnitude of the effect. The dashed line represents the line of best fit before installation, and the solid black one, the line of best fit afterwards.

In Airdrie, it was calculated that recorded crimes and offences fell to 79% of previously recorded and adjusted totals. In Glasgow, contrarily, recorded crimes and offences rose to 109% of previously recorded and adjusted totals. CCTV seems to have had a variable effect on the rates of different types of recorded crimes and offences. The same Scottish Office groups that were used to aggregate data in Airdrie were used again in the Glasgow part of the study.

The pattern is by no means consistent, even if the overall effect is a slight rise. Recorded crimes in Groups 1 and 4, and recorded offences in Groups 6 and 7, all fell, but recorded crimes in Groups 2, 3 and 5 all rose.[12] Group 1 crimes fell to 78% of their previous amount (amounting to 230 fewer crimes); Group 2 crimes and offences rose to 117% (equivalent to 120 more crimes); Group 3 crimes rose to 123% (2,185 more crimes, as illustrated in Figure 5); Group 4 fell to 92% (57 fewer crimes); Group 5 rose to 132% (464 more crimes); Group 6 fell to 93% (272 fewer offences); and Group 7 fell to 88% (318 fewer offences).

Detections in Glasgow

Overall, the clearance rate (detections expressed as a percentage of recorded crimes and offences) fell slightly from 64% to 60% (Figure 6). In Airdrie, the clearance rate improved from 50% to 58% over all.

Comparing the Effects of Open-Street CCTV — 211

In Glasgow, crimes and offences in Groups 1, 4 and 6 fell, and those in Groups 2 and 3 rose. The clearance rates in Groups 5 and 7 remained virtually unchanged. Specifically, detections in Group 1 fell from 74% to 46%; in Group 2, they rose from 92% to 98%; in Group 3, they rose from 39% to 44%; in Group 4, they fell from 39% to 30%; in Group 5, they fell from 100% to 99%; in Group 6, they fell from 86% to 82%; and in Group 7, they rose from 99% to 100%.

Figure 4: Recorded Crimes and Offences in Glasgow's CCTV Area, Lines of "Best Fit" Before and After Camera Installation November 1992 – October 1995

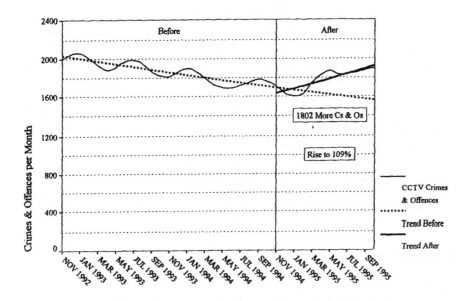

Complacency or Confusion in Glasgow?

It is only thus at an ambitious and unrealistic level (i.e., affecting *all* recorded crimes and offences positively) that CCTV in Glasgow can be said not to have "worked." Even after the undertaking of various statistical procedures (seasonal adjustment, smoothing, controlling for underlying trends) — each of which depressed the effect of CCTV when used on data from the first part of this study in Airdrie — there have been reductions in recorded instances of violence (Group 1), vandalism, etc. (Group 4), petty personal offences such as breach of the peace and petty assault (Group 6), and offences involving vehicles (Group 7). Because there was no recorded fall in the overall number of crimes and offences reported in Glasgow's CCTV area, no search for displacement could logically be undertaken.

DISCUSSION

Put at its starkest, after the installation of open-street CCTV in Airdrie, recorded crimes and offences fell to 79% of their previously recorded levels, and detections rose from 50% to 58%. Conversely, after the installation of open-street CCTV in Glasgow, recorded crimes and offences rose to 109% of their previously recorded levels, and detections fell from 64% to 60%.[13] Rather crudely, it could be concluded that CCTV worked in Airdrie, but not in Glasgow. This interpretation should be resisted firmly.

Why? Because there are a series of interrelated problems that preclude simplistic judgements like this. These may be grouped into concerns relating to the adequacy of the *test* of effectiveness; the *type* of situation in which CCTV was "tested," and the *timing* of the introduction of CCTV in different locations.

Adequacy of Tests of Effectiveness

First, then, concerns relating to the adequacy of the *test* of CCTV's effectiveness. A major difficulty here is confusion to the point of contradiction as to what, precisely, open-street CCTV cameras are supposed to do. From one point of view, their ability to see criminal events unfolding when there are no police officers physically present should increase logically the number of crimes and offences thus recorded. From another point of view, their sheer presence should deter offenders from offending, and should decrease the number of crimes and offences thus recorded. If such cameras prove better at the first goal than the second, then the crime rate should rise, and this would be counted as a "success." If, contrarily, they prove to be better at the second than at the first, then the crime rate should fall, and this would be counted as a "success."

We might, at this point, turn to the history of the two CCTV schemes to see what the goals of each actually were. In Airdrie, CCTV began as the imaginative response to a specific local crime problem (teenage shoplifters disappearing into the massed ranks of dancing teenagers at a local youth club). An energetic local police officer had confronted the youth club members, and at one point in these discussions, a young girl suggested to him, "you should put a camera in

Figure 5: Group 3 Recorded Crimes in Glasgow's CCTV Area, Lines of "Best Fit" Before and After Camera Installation November 1992 – October 1995

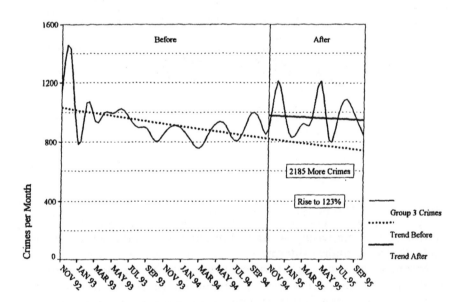

Figure 6: All Recorded Crimes, Offences and Detections in Glasgow's CCTV Area
November 1992 – October 1995

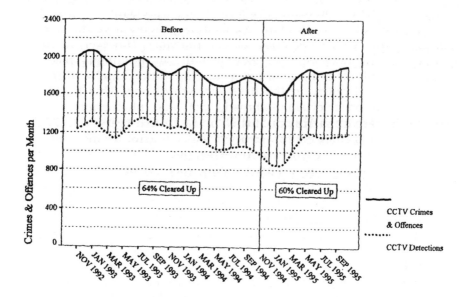

the youth club." Once germinated, the idea proliferated with speed: by the end of the week, he had planned the whole town centre network (Ditton & Short, 1998b).

In Glasgow, the CCTV scheme began life as an idea designed to have a positive impact on the erroneous image of the city as a "dangerous" place in the minds of inward investors based in other countries. In the early days, CCTV was actively promoted by the local development agency in terms that indicated that it was expected to increase inward investment to the city by £43 million per year, generate 1,500 new jobs, and bring an additional 225,000 visitors to the city every year. Within 18 months, CCTV was "about" reducing criminal victimisation to locally resident visitors to the city centre.

Indeed, there seem to have been a succession of goals, and with the benefit of hindsight, it is now clear that the original objectives have been regularly replaced to the point where, in a two-year period, current goals bear no resemblance to initial ones. However, by which goal achievement should Glasgow's cameras be judged?

In Airdrie, CCTV's "mission creep" (from policing a youth club to policing a town centre) was not self-contradictory. However, in Glasgow it was distinctly so. For example, the most famous piece of CCTV-captured offending is of two young men attacking, and finally jumping up and down on the head of, a third one. This has been widely shown on television (abroad, too), and photographic stills taken from it are frequently published in the British press.

No doubt this confirms the ability of CCTV to capture incidents on camera, and helps to justify the presence of the system, particularly in its endless search for annual running costs. It may also be good for employee morale. Indeed, the operators are justifiably proud of having noticed the incident unfold, of having alerted the police, and of having rushed medical assistance to the scene. But what has this publicity done to either calm the fears of foreign investors or reassure locally resident visitors that Glasgow is a safe place to visit?

These problems aside, a related issue is the vastly inflated expectations of the effect of open-street CCTV. It is really just some video cameras pointing either up or down a handful of city streets. Glasgow has 32 cameras, and Airdrie has 12, but each network has only two relatively untrained persons watching them at any one time. One person can really only watch one screen at a time, and our observation in the Glasgow control room indicated that there were occasions when nobody was watching anything. There were also many other occasions when operators were watching the screens, but nothing apparently was happening. Camera vision is impressive, yet occasionally obscured (by trees in leaf, by snow on the lens), and therefore ultimately limited. In addition, there is no sound.

Overall, in the first year of operation, Glasgow's CCTV system was linked to 290 arrests, although it is unclear how many of these would have been made without the cameras. Even if all 290 would not have occurred without the cameras in place, this is still a strike rate of one arrest per camera for every 967 hours of operation, or one every 40 days. Put another way, the cameras "saw" under 5% of the total number of crimes and offences that resulted in arrests in the area they surveilled during the first year of operation. Why, thus, should

CCTV there have more than a 5% effect in either reducing or increasing recorded offending?[14]

Types of Testing Situations

A second main concern relates to the *type* of situation into which open-street CCTV is being introduced. Glasgow has a "centre": so does Airdrie. There the similarity ends. Glasgow is a huge port city, and Airdrie is a sleepy little town. The people of Airdrie are very proud of their cameras. We have been told that when the control room first became operational there, thousands of local inhabitants queued for hours to get a quick glimpse of the monitors in the police station. A year or two later, when the budget was low and the survival of the whole installation under threat, these same local residents held coffee mornings to raise money to keep it going.

For Airdrionians, the middle of the town is "their" town centre. For Glaswegians, the middle of the city is "the" city centre. Only an insignificant number of people actually live in Glasgow's city centre, and most of those who visit it cannot get there on foot. More people actually live in the middle of Airdrie, and those who live in the rest of the town can easily walk to the centre. One year after camera installation in Glasgow (a year that saw frequent mentions of the cameras in the local media), only between a quarter and a third of the ambulatory population were even aware of their existence (Ditton et al., 1999). No satisfactory general population poll has been conducted in Airdrie, but when we interviewed a small group of offenders, most claimed to have first heard about the cameras from the local media.[15]

Timing of CCTV Introduction

Finally, and perhaps most crucially, the *timing* of the introduction of cameras in the two centres may well have had the biggest effect on relative success, when the latter is conceived narrowly in terms of reductions in the overall rate of recorded offending. It should be recalled — and this is unusual given the history of implementation of most crime prevention initiatives (see Campbell and Ross, 1968) — that CCTV was introduced into Glasgow's city centre at a point when recorded crime had been on the decline for at least two years. It is unclear why recorded crime rates oscillate over the long term. But, when they are on the rise, there is more inclination to experiment with ways of reversing this than when they are on the decline.

Had Glasgow's CCTV system been installed at a relative recorded crime zenith, it would have been a simple matter to predict an independent downturn thereafter. Being, as it was, installed at a nadir, an upturn thereafter was always the most likely consequence. Equally plausibly, had Airdrie's cameras been introduced two years later, then, after a probable period of decline in recorded offending, crime rates might well have begun to rise.

CONCLUSION

It should be noted that CCTV has had an impact very different in Glasgow than in Airdrie.[16] In both, some occasional yet noteworthy success was obtained in capturing emerging incidents on camera. Yet, in Airdrie recorded crime declined as a whole, and no displacement effect could be discovered. In Glasgow, on the other hand, recorded crime as a whole rose slightly (although it fell in some categories), and thus no search for displacement could be undertaken.

However, in Glasgow, the CCTV system seems gradually to be finding a different role for itself, particularly in the relatively recently developed reviewing of tapes to retrospectively investigate major crimes.[17] Here, rather than base the evaluated utility of the system on its ability to spot contemporary offending (or even prevent it), the videotape library is used as an archive. After the notification of a major criminal incident, tapes for the day and time in question are examined minutely, frame by frame, for anything that might help the police with their enquiries. Although this may be no more than a new and cost-effective way of conducting an age-old police activity, it is one job that police officers claim that CCTV can do well.[18] Given the alleged cost of conventional major criminal enquiries, and the apparent capability of CCTV networks to succeed at conducting them at little cost, this latterly discovered benefit may well be the real use of open-street CCTV systems in the centres of major cities. The use of the tape archive has been of great use in retrospectively investigating major crimes in Glasgow; but there has been little scope for this in Airdrie, which suffers few, if any, crimes of this seriousness.

It appears, then, that open-street CCTV works differently in different situations. Airdrie is a small town: Glasgow a major city. Many of those seen on screen in Airdrie were well-known to the local police as residents. In Glasgow, this was far less likely to be the case. For this and other reasons, instead of asking blandly "does CCTV work?" we need, following the advice of Tilley (1997), to ask what works, in what circumstances, and how.

We conclude: open-street CCTV can "work" in limited ways, but is not a universal panacea. It works in different ways in different situa-

218 — Jason Ditton and Emma Short

tions, and future evaluation might choose wisely to concentrate on "how" rather than "if." In both locations studied, Airdrie and Glasgow, CCTV has been a different sort of success.

Address correspondence to: Jason Ditton, Scottish Centre for Criminology, Charing Cross Clinic, 8 Woodside Crescent, Glasgow, G3 7UY, United Kingdom.

REFERENCES

Bennett, T. (1986). "Situational Crime Prevention from the Offenders' Perspective." In: K. Heal and G. Laycock (eds.), *Situational Crime Prevention: From Theory to Practice*. London, UK: Her Majesty's Stationery Office.

Brown, B. (1995). *CCTV in Town Centres: Three Case Studies*. (Crime Detection and Prevention Series Paper, #68.) London, UK: Home Office.

Burrows, J. (1991). *Making Crime Prevention Pay: Initiatives from Business*. (Crime Prevention Unit Paper, #27.) London, UK: Home Office.

Campbell, D. and H. Ross (1968). "The Connecticut Crackdown on Speeding: Time-Series Data in Quasi-Experimental Analysis." *Law & Society Review* 3(1):33-53.

Ditton, J. and E. Short (1998a). "When Open Street CCTV Appears to Reduce Crime — Does it Just Get Displaced Elsewhere?" *CCTV Today* 5(2):13-16.

—— (1998b). "Evaluating Scotland's First Town Centre CCTV Scheme: Airdrie's Crime Data and Airdrie's Offenders." In: C. Norris and G. Armstrong (eds.), *Surveillance, CCTV and Social Control — The Rise of Closed Circuit Televisual Surveillance in Britain*. Avebury, UK: Gower.

—— S. Phillips, C. Norris and G. Armstrong (1999). *The Effect of the Introduction of Closed Circuit Television on Recorded Crime Rates and on Concern about Crime in Glasgow*. Edinburgh, SCOT: Central Research Unit, Scottish Office.

Gabor, T. (1978). "Crime Displacement: The Literature and Strategies for its Investigation." *Crime and Justice* 6(2):100-107.

Gill, M. and V. Turbin (1997). "CCTV and Shop Theft: Towards a Realistic Evaluation." Paper presented at the British Criminology Conference, Belfast, July.

Hearnden, K. (1996). "Small Businesses' Approach to Managing CCTV to Combat Crime." *International Journal of Risk, Security and Crime Prevention* 1(1):19-31.

Mayhew, P., R. Clarke, J. Burrows, J. Hough and S. Winchester (1979). *Crime in Public View.* (Home Office Research Study, #49.) London, UK: Home Office.

Norris, C. and G. Armstrong (1998). "CCTV and the Rise of the Mass Surveillance Society." In: R. Morgan and P. Carlen (eds.), *Crime Unlimited.* London, UK: Macmillan.

Poyner, B. (1988). "Video Cameras and Bus Vandalism." In: R.V. Clarke (ed.), *Situational Crime Prevention Successful Case Studies.* Albany, NY: Harrow and Heston.

—— (1992). "Situational Crime Prevention in Two Parking Facilities." In: R.V. Clarke (ed.), *Situational Crime Prevention Successful Case Studies (2nd ed.).* Albany, NY: Harrow and Heston.

Short, E. and J. Ditton (1996). *Does Closed Circuit Television Prevent Crime? An Evaluation of the Use of CCTV Surveillance Cameras in Airdrie Town Centre.* Edinburgh, SCOT: Central Research Unit, Scottish Office.

—— (1998) "Seen and Now Heard: Talking to the Targets of Open Street CCTV." *British Journal of Criminology* 38(3):404-428.

Skinns, D. (1997). *Annual Report of the Safety in Doncaster Evaluation Project.* Doncaster, UK: Doncaster Council and South Yorkshire Police Partnership.

Tilley, N. (1993). *Understanding Car Parks, Crime and CCTV: Evaluation Lessons from Safer Cities.* (Crime Prevention Unit Paper #42.) London, UK: Home Office.

—— (1997). "Whys and Wherefores in Evaluating the Effectiveness of CCTV." *International Journal of Risk, Security and Crime Prevention* 2(3):175-85.

van Koppen, P. and R. Jansen (1998). "The Road to the Robbery: Travel Patterns in Commercial Robberies." *British Journal of Criminology* 38(2):230-246.

Van Straelen, F. (1978). "Prevention and Technology." In: J. Brown (ed.), *Cranfield Papers.* London, UK: Peel Press.

220 — Jason Ditton and Emma Short

NOTES

1. Brown (1995) is something of an exception, although it is more of an attempt professionally to reanalyse locally collected data from three very different areas.

2. These schemes are detailed in Annex A of Short & Ditton (1996). This report also contains a fuller analysis of the crime and offence and detection data discussed below. The collection and analysis of this statistical data was funded by the Scottish Office, to whom we are grateful.

3. Recorded crime and offence rates exhibit mostly inexplicable, but noticeable, seasonal patterns. These were extracted, in a formal sense, from the four years of data, and then deleted, leaving a seasonally adjusted residue. The underlying trend is the direction in which the recorded crime and offence "line" could have been expected to have gone if CCTV cameras had not been introduced. This underlying trend was calculated from trends in locally comparable areas where there were no cameras. This, too, was factored into the calculations.

4. These are standard regression lines, i.e., straight lines that minimise the *sums* of the *squared* vertical distances from the observed data points to the line.

5. Crimes are, generally speaking, more serious than offences. The groups are:

   Group 1: Crimes of violence, etc. This group contains the most serious crimes; for example, murder, attempted murder, serious assault, handling of offensive weapons and robbery. Group 1 crimes total about 1% of all crimes and offences recorded by the police in Scotland.

   Group 2: Crimes of indecency. This group contains sex crimes of violence (rape, attempted rape and indecent assault), lewd and libidinous practices, and prostitution. Group 2 crimes total about ½% of all crimes and offences recorded by the police in Scotland.

   Group 3: Crimes of dishonesty. This is the largest group, and contains housebreaking, theft of (and from) motor vehicles, etc., shoplifting, fraud, and other crimes of dishonesty. Group 3 crimes total about 38% of all crimes and offences recorded by the police in Scotland.

   Group 4: Fire-raising, malicious mischief, etc. Group 4 only includes fire-raising and vandalism. Group 4 crimes total about 9% of all crimes and offences recorded by the police in Scotland.

   Group 5: Other crimes. Group 5 includes crimes against public justice, drug-related offences, and other miscellaneous crimes. Group 5 crimes total about 5% of all crimes and offences recorded by the police in Scotland.

Group 6: Miscellaneous offences. Miscellaneous offences include petty assault, breach of the peace, and drunkenness. Group 6 crimes total about 12% of all crimes and offences recorded by the police in Scotland.

Group 7: Offences relating to motor vehicles. Motor vehicle offences include reckless and careless driving, drunk driving, speeding, unlawful use of vehicles, and various vehicle defect offences. Group 7 crimes total about 34% of all crimes and offences recorded by the police in Scotland.

6. One hundred eleven Group 1 crimes of violence were recorded in the 24 months prior to CCTV installation in the area surveyed by the cameras, with 99 being recorded in 24 months following installation. Six Group 2 crimes of indecency were recorded in the 24 months prior to CCTV installation in the area surveyed by the cameras, with 4 being recorded in 24 months following installation.

7. The net reduction in recorded crimes and offences is, calculating by this method, 841 fewer crimes and offences, which seems at odds with the reduction of 772 mentioned earlier. Of this difference of 69, 43 are accounted for procedurally, i.e., by one method totalling raw data and then adjusting for seasonality and controlling for underlying trends, and by the other method adjusting for seasonality and controlling for underlying trends and then totalling. This leaves 26 unaccounted for. These are probably accounted for by not including Groups 1 and 2 in the group totalling exercise. (Although both fell slightly in raw terms, this does not mean that adjusting and controlling might not have predicted increases.)

8. A crime or offence is detected, or, more properly, cleared up, "if one or more offenders is apprehended, cited, warned or traced for it."

9. If someone commits an offence while on bail, this is also recorded as a further offence of bail abuse.

10. Data for one test month (March 1994) were examined, and all crimes and offences recorded were classified in terms of whether or not they were in CCTV vision. There are two ways of looking at each beat: first, the degree of geographical camera coverage; and second, the percentage of recorded crime occurring in the areas in vision. Beats were classified in terms of the second into those with very low penetration (beats 3, 7, 8, 9, 11, 36 and 37), those with low penetration (beats, 4, 19, 25, 27, 32, 33, and 34), those with high penetration (beats 10, 16, 20, 22, 23, 24, and 35) and those with very high penetration (beats 12, 13, 14, 15, 17, 18 and 21). These four areas together are henceforth referred to as the

222 — Jason Ditton and Emma Short

CCTV visibility area. On analysis, no relationship was found between degree of CCTV penetration and either changes in recorded crimes and offences, or detections. This offers slight confirmation of the overall finding that CCTV has not had a noticeable effect on crime in Glasgow.

11. See Short and Ditton (1996). The one exception relates to the fact that in Glasgow, only three rather than four years' data were available. This was dealt with by reverse-extrapolating data for a fictitious preliminary year, which were then used to construct a model for seasonal deconstruction before the fictitious year was dropped from all further calculations. In fact, two fictitious preliminary years were constructed (one maximising the level of recorded crime that might have occurred, the other minimising it). Both were used independently before being discarded. There was no significant difference in the results obtained whichever fictitious year was used.

12. When calculated as a single total, the trend effect for the CCTV visibility area is of 1,802 more recorded crimes and offences (a 9% increase). When calculated separately, the sum of the group changes amounts to 1,892 additional recorded crimes and offences. The difference of 90 additional recorded crimes and offences is a procedural artifact created by, in the first exercise, totalling raw data and then adjusting for seasonality and controlling for underlying trends; and in the second, adjusting for seasonality and controlling for underlying trends and then totalling.

13. To some degree, changes in recorded crimes and offences and changes in detections may not be independent measures. Given relatively fixed police manpower, a reduction in rates of offending presumably frees more time to concentrate upon detections. Conversely, an increase in rates of offending leaves less time to concentrate upon detections. This may in part explain the difference between the outcomes in Airdrie and Glasgow.

14. A separate query relating to the adequacy of the test of CCTV's effectiveness is the conventional analyst's lament: it is simply impossible to be sure that one has ever had all the relevant data at hand, and that analysis has not missed the operation of some ignored variable. An anecdote might suffice. Camera 12 in Glasgow (which saw more than three times as many arrests as any other camera) has been the success story of the whole installation. It is positioned overseeing a popular disco, which was a known trouble spot. Prior to installation, we have been told, a police van full of uniformed officers would be parked at the exit at the end of each evening. Nearby, an informal rank of taxis waited to take revellers home. After installation, the police van parked instead around the corner, and stayed in radio contact with the CCTV control room.

Thereafter, they could be alerted not only to any trouble, but also could be given descriptions of the offenders before appearing on the scene to arrest those thus implicated. Apparently to facilitate both recognition and tracking of offenders, the taxi rank was disbanded, allegedly on police advice. So, here, two simple crime and disorder prevention measures (the visible presence of police; and taxis in which the exuberant may leave peacefully) were discontinued, effectively encouraging offending for the camera to see. Is it any wonder that crime rates rose?

15. These interviews, reported in Short and Ditton (1998), were made possible by a small grant from the Nuffield Foundation, for which we are grateful.

16. Skinns (1997) suggests an impact somewhere between the two in his preliminary analysis of the effects of CCTV on crime in Doncaster. Doncaster is bigger than Airdrie and smaller than Glasgow. This suggests that town/city size may well affect the efficacy of open-street CCTV.

17. It is understood that this emerged relatively spontaneously in Glasgow. Apparently, an officer on light duties was given the task of searching for those attempting robberies at automated teller machines, with the expectation that any success, if any resulted, would take weeks to materialise. Again apparently, this officer identified those responsible in a day.

18. Glasgow's police have indicated that between April 1995 and June 1996, the CCTV archive has been used effectively in resolving 10 major incidents (including five murders and one attempted murder).

[11]

State Surveillance and the Right to Privacy

Nick Taylor[1]

Abstract

The influence of Article 8 of the European Convention on Human Rights on domestic law has ensured that the state's use of technical covert surveillance equipment has become legally regulated over the past twenty years, albeit in a somewhat piecemeal fashion. The passage of the Human Rights Act 1998 will see the development of the 'right to respect for private life' in UK law. This paper seeks to reflect upon the impact that the European Convention has had on the regulation of covert surveillance, and whether there is a theoretical justification for developing the 'right to respect for private life' beyond traditional private spheres and into the public arena. It is argued that overt surveillance in the form of closed circuit television cameras (CCTV) should thus be legally regulated according to the principles established by the European Convention, and that such an extension of the 'right to respect for private life' need not be detrimental to the common good.

Introduction

Throughout the history of policing in Britain, the response to social disorder and rising crime rates has been to adopt the most modern equipment and techniques available. Over the past thirty years in particular, considerable advances in technology have dramatically increased the powers of the state to carry out surveillance upon its citizens. This inevitably brings with it the dystopic vision of an Orwellian society, where citizens are constantly under the vigilant gaze and attentive ear of 'Big Brother'.

Though the allusion to 'Big Brother' is a popular modern metaphor for the role of the State in social control, it ignores the numerous benefits increased surveillance has brought about. Surveillance does, undoubtedly, have two faces. It can act to curtail rights through, for example, reinforcing divisions within society, or it can be a vital tool in preventing and detecting crime. For citizens to accept and consent to certain forms of surveillance, that is to say its positive face, the state should be accountable for its actions. It cannot be left with an unfettered discretion to determine why and where it carries out surveillance on, and on behalf of, its citizens, without some form of legal responsibility. The governors and the governed should be subject to the law.

---

[1] Centre for Criminal Justice Studies, Department of Law, University of Leeds, Leeds LS2 9JT, UK.
Tel: 0113 233 5033 (ext. 35027), Email: N.W.Taylor@Leeds.ac.uk

In the UK the massive growth in state surveillance directed towards crime prevention and detection has been largely unencumbered by the law, legislation often developing later to legitimise practices found to be in breach of human rights standards by the European Court of Human Rights. The aim of this paper is to reflect upon how the right to respect for private life as contained in the European Convention on Human Rights has impacted upon the regulation of various forms of covert surveillance by the police in the UK, and to consider the question of whether reliance on a concept of privacy can provide an adequate basis for laws governing overt surveillance by way of closed circuit television systems.

Privacy and Covert Surveillance

Despite (or perhaps because of) the vast literature surrounding 'privacy', it has proved to be a somewhat nebulous concept. Wacks has argued, "Privacy has been so devalued that it no longer warrants if it ever did serious consideration as a legal term of art." (Wacks, 1980a: 10). He continues, "the long search for a definition of "privacy" has produced a continuing debate that is often sterile, and, ultimately futile." (ibid.). It is partly the difficulty of providing an adequate definition that has seen reluctance on the part of both Parliament and the courts to develop a domestic concept of privacy. Thus, despite the pertinent comment in the Canadian case, R v Duarte (1990 65 DLR (4th) 240, at 249), that 'one can scarcely imagine a state activity more dangerous to individual privacy than electronic surveillance', such activities have been lawful within the UK even in the absence of legal regulation.

Despite the apparent difficulties of finding an adequate definition, a right to privacy is enshrined in many international documents and national constitutions. For example, Article 8 of the European Convention on Human Rights provides a right to "respect for private and family life", which has affected, and continues to affect, UK law. Therefore, despite the lack of protection for privacy in domestic courts, a relatively comprehensive regulatory regime for state surveillance practices has developed over the past twenty years. The next section will reflect upon the influence of the Convention on the regulation of police surveillance techniques to date, to be followed by a consideration of how this influence might be developed and extended to the regulation of overt public space surveillance.

European Convention on Human Rights
The European Convention on Human Rights sets out a minimum statement of rights to be protected in each signatory state, and provides a mechanism to allow individuals to enforce it against the state where the state has infringed their rights under the Convention and domestic law has failed to provide a remedy. In the context of state surveillance, the right most obviously under threat is the right to respect for private life contained in Article 8, which states:

8(1). Everyone has the right to respect for his private and family life, his home and his correspondence.

8(2). There shall be no interference by a public authority with the exercise of this right except such as is in accordance with the law and is necessary in a democratic society in the interests of national security, public safety or the economic well being of the country, for the prevention of disorder or crime, for the protection of health or morals, or for the protection of the rights and freedoms of others.

Before considering its particular application to the regulation of surveillance by the police, it is worth noting a number of general principles that have derived from the interpretation of the exceptions to the general right.

- In Accordance with the Law

European Convention jurisprudence has interpreted Article 8(2) to mean that, regardless of the end to be achieved, no right guaranteed by the Convention should be interfered with unless a citizen knows the basis for the interference through an ascertainable national law (Malone v UK (1984) 7 EHRR 14, Leander v Sweden (1987) 9 EHRR 433). In Kruslin v France ((1990) 12 EHRR 546), a case concerning surveillance techniques, the European Court commented, "it is essential to have clear, detailed rules on the subject, especially as the technology available for use is continually becoming more sophisticated". More recently the Court has expressed the view that as the interception of communications represents a 'serious interference' with private life the law must be particularly precise (Kopp v Switzerland (1999) 27 EHRR 91). With regard to interferences with private life in the 'prevention of crime' context, it appears that the European Court is demanding increasingly rigorous legal provisions (Valenzuela v Spain (1998) 28 EHRR 483).

- Legitimate Objective

If the primary right is engaged in a particular case then any interference with that right must be directed towards a legitimate aim. In terms of the right to private life, restrictions that may be justified are found in Article 8(2). The restrictions on the primary right are numerous and widely drawn and it is not overly burdensome to require state conduct to remain within such boundaries.

- Necessary in a Democratic Society.

This is essentially a test of proportionality. It has to be shown that any interference with a Convention right is both necessary to fulfil a pressing social need and is a proportionate response to that need. The importance of the aim in question and the actual situation through which the aim is being secured are factors to be taken into account (Silver v UK (1983) 5 EHRR 347). As stated by Harris et al, "action for the prevention of crime may be directed against homicide or parking offences: the weight of each compared with the right sought to be limited is not the same" (Harris, O'Boyle and Warbrick, 1995: 297).

The lack of any legal regulation governing the use of electronic surveillance devices by the police in the UK would inevitably be problematic in light of the above principles. Attention was specifically drawn to this fact by the well-documented case of Malone v Metropolitan Police Commissioner No.2 ([1979] 2 WLR 700). The defendant was prosecuted for allegedly handling stolen property and it became apparent during the trial that the prosecution had tapped Malone's telephone. He challenged the legality of the tap only to find that there had been no violation of English law. Megarry V-C recognised that the interception of the defendant's telephone calls was not a crime and as such 'it was not a subject on which it [was] possible to feel any pride in English law' (ibid: 732). Malone took his case to the European Court in Strasbourg who held that his right to respect for private life under Article 8 had been infringed (Malone v UK (1984) 7 EHRR 14). The interception of a telephone call fell within the definition of both 'private life' and 'correspondence' in Article 8(1) (Klass v Germany (1978) 2 EHRR 214). The Court acknowledged that although Home Office guidelines governed the use of the telephone tap this did not satisfy the requirement that an infringement of a person's right to respect for their private life could only be legitimised if there was a legal rule directed towards one of the legitimate exceptions.

> [T]he requirement of foreseeability cannot mean that an individual should be enabled to foresee when the authorities are likely to intercept his communications so that he can adapt his conduct accordingly. Nevertheless, the law must be sufficiently clear in its terms to give citizens an adequate indication as to the circumstances in which and the conditions on which the [police] are empowered to resort to this secret and potentially dangerous [measure]. (Malone v UK: para. 67)

Largely in response to this decision (and the privatisation of the telecommunications service), the Government introduced the Interception of Communications Act 1985 (IOCA) (Lustgarten and Leigh, 1994: ch.3). Through the 1985 Act the Government sought to provide a statutory framework for legitimate interception. Regrettably the Act went no further than the Malone judgment demanded and, as such, the misleadingly named Act regulated merely public telephone interceptions and the metering of telephone calls. During its passage through Parliament, the Act was criticised as "setting out to regulate canal traffic in the age of the high speed train and the motorway" (H.C. Debs, vol. 75, col. 241). To govern the use of public telephone interceptions whilst ignoring other forms of aural electronic surveillance was indefensible (see, Leigh, 1986). Subsequent caselaw also suggested that the Act failed to regulate the interception of cordless telephones (Effick [1994] 99 Cr. App. R. 312) or non-public networks (Halford v UK [1997] EHRLR 540). The number of warrants issued and those in force under IOCA increased virtually year on year until the Act was repealed by the Regulation of Investigatory Powers Act 2000 (Akdeniz, Taylor and Walker, 2001). Whilst a legal basis for interception was formulated (albeit rather loosely drafted), it was questionable whether clear limits and remedies were created (Taylor and Walker, 1996). With regard to interceptions based on national security grounds it has been suggested that an adequate legal basis had been established (Christie v UK (1994) DR 78-A, 119, but see, Fenwick, 2000: 331) though in relation to the prevention of crime it is doubtful that the 1985 Act was sufficiently clear as to when an interception might occur (see, Valenzuela v Spain (1998) 28 EHRR 483).

Given the lack of comprehensive legislation to govern all forms of interception, the emphasis was very much on reflecting the specific demands of the adverse Malone judgment than any real concern to protect privacy. As Fenwick suggests, "since the driving force behind the response of the UK government in the [Act] was a need to provide a statutory basis for interception, it can be termed a largely procedural rather than substantive reform" (Fenwick, 2000: 346).

It would take a further expensive and arduous journey to the Strasbourg Court to challenge the use of other covert surveillance techniques. In 1992 the police placed an aural surveillance device on the property of Mr. Bashforth who was, at the time, under investigation for dealing in heroin. Mr. Khan visited the house, and, by means of the surveillance device, the police obtained recordings of a conversation in the course of which Khan admitted that he had been involved in the earlier importation of drugs by Newab. He was arrested as a result. At Khan's trial the judge admitted evidence from the tape recording and Khan was sentenced to three years' imprisonment. The House of Lords rejected an appeal stating that even if they were to take into account a possible breach of Article 8 of the Convention (which they were not obliged to do prior to the Human Rights Act) this did not necessitate exclusion of the evidence gained as a result. Lord Nolan said:

> It would be a strange reflection on our law if a man who has admitted his participation in the illegal importation of a large quantity of heroin should have his conviction set aside on the grounds that his privacy has been invaded (R v Khan [1996] 3 WLR 162 at 175).

At Strasbourg the case presented a relatively straightforward breach of Article 8 (Khan v UK (2001) 31 EHRR 1016). Though the breach of privacy arguably could have been justified by reference to the 'prevention of disorder or crime' exception, as in Malone the lack of clear legal regulation of the surveillance practices in question failed the test of being 'in accordance with law'. A further question for the Court was whether evidence gathered in breach of Article 8 thereby infringed an individual's right to a fair trial under Article 6. If the fairness of the trial would be affected, the evidence gained as a result of the breach of Article 8 should be excluded from the trial. Taking into account the proceedings as a whole the Court found that there would be no unfairness in admitting the evidence. Such a decision has implications for future evidence gathering. Despite the recent developments towards a comprehensive regulatory framework for surveillance, evidence gathered in breach of the framework, which would thereby be likely to infringe Article 8, could still be admitted in criminal proceedings.

One of the effects of the Human Rights Act 1998 (HRA) is that it gives domestic judges the opportunity to interpret the Convention in a domestic context. Whilst taking into account Strasbourg jurisprudence, there is no necessity to follow it as binding precedent. Therefore, if the courts were to take an active interpretation of their role under the HRA, the conclusion of the inter-play between Article 6 and 8 could be different, thereby granting greater respect for the private life of citizens. However, given the current interpretation by the courts of their discretion to exclude unfairly obtained evidence, this appears unlikely (Fitzpatrick and Taylor, 2001).

It has been argued that Part III of the Police Act 1997 was passed when it became clear to the Government that they would lose the case of Khan v UK in Strasbourg (Starmer et al, 2001: 36, see also, Govell v UK (1997) 4 EHRR 438). Indeed, when the case was in the House of Lords, Lord Nolan had recommended that the Government legislate in the area to satisfy the Convention standards (R v Khan [1996] 3 WLR 162 at 175). Senior police officers too expressed a desire for electronic surveillance to be legally regulated given that the powers of the security services to carry out similar actions had already been given express legal approval in the Security Services Act 1989 (ironically, itself in part a response to Harman and Hewitt v UK (1992) 14 EHRR 657), and that the Intelligence Services Act 1994 and the Security Services Act 1996, had expanded the role of MI5 to aiding the police with preventing and detecting serious crime (Home Affairs Committee, 1995: 124, para. 4.11; 136, para. 3.8).

Part III of the Act was designed to regulate surveillance techniques that would otherwise involve unlawful conduct on the part of the police such as trespass or criminal damage. Article 8 was the obvious driving force behind the legislation. It would ensure that the regulatory scheme for surveillance techniques was widened, with respect for private life being the overall context. However, as with IOCA, significant gaps in the law remained. The legislation failed to regulate techniques involving, for example, long range microphones, telescopic lenses or other 'remote' techniques. Devices installed with the consent of the person in a position to give such consent for the premises were also left unregulated, entirely failing to respect the privacy of persons who are on the premises but do not know of the surveillance operation. The basis for allowing surveillance was unduly broad and appeared to be wider than the administrative guidelines they replaced. The lack of mandatory judicial supervision of authorisation procedures has been viewed as a 'great weakness' (Uglow, 1999: 296) and at best marginally satisfies the criteria for authorisation laid down in Klass (Klass v Germany (1978) 2 EHRR 214, paras.55-6), which views supervision by the judiciary as desirable though other independent safeguards might suffice. The Act represented an opportunity missed to provide a comprehensive framework for the regulation of all technical surveillance operations. Again, though it could be argued that the impetus for the legislation was the European Convention, the Act appeared to represent an attempt to head off future adverse rulings from Strasbourg rather than being a meaningful attempt to respect the private life of the individual. Though Article 8 reflects a minimum standard to be achieved, the Police Act appeared to be a minimalist attempt to achieve it.

Taylor: State Surveillance and the Right to Privacy

The Regulation of Investigatory Powers Act 2000 (RIPA) finally represented a legislative attempt to provide comprehensive regulation. The Human Rights Act 1998 (HRA) was designed to give the European Convention a more central role in domestic law. A requirement of the HRA was that all legislation, past and present, wherever possible should be read and given effect in a way compatible with Convention rights (s.3) and where relevant to proceedings before them, the courts must take into account jurisprudence from the European Court (s.2). Furthermore, all public authorities are required to act in compliance with the Convention unless they are prevented from doing so by statute (s.6). This would have the effect of ensuring that the target of any unregulated surveillance practice by the state would have a right to a remedy in a domestic court. Arguably RIPA is, therefore, a further example of legislation in this field being driven by the demands of the Convention: certainly the timing would suggest so. However, it too has been criticised for its procedural rather than substantive compliance with the Convention. Despite the statements by the Home Secretary, Jack Straw, that RIPA is Convention compatible and that it is "a significant step forward for the protection of human rights in this country" (HC Debs. vol.345 col.767), Fenwick argues, "[I]n certain respects the RIPA realises the worst fears of those who viewed the HRA as likely to lead to a diminution in the protection for liberty in the UK" (Fenwick, 2000: 345).

Part I of the Act supersedes IOCA 1985 and extends the definitions of interception to include most forms of telecommunication including email. Judicial authorisation of warrants was not adopted in the legislation which still allows for executive authorisation. Part II of RIPA provides a regulatory framework for the use of three types of covert surveillance, namely, directed surveillance, intrusive surveillance and the use and conduct of covert human intelligence sources. However, the different authorisation standards applicable to intrusive and directed surveillance are difficult to justify and might not satisfy Convention standards. Part II also allows for a considerable amount of detail to be determined through the use of delegated legislation that does little for the clarity of the law. In Amman v. Switzerland ((2000) 30 EHRR 843) the European Court re-iterated the need for clear and precise rules governing covert surveillance techniques. Whether Part II of the Act meets those standards is open to debate.

Part III was seen as one of the more controversial aspect of the Act. It relates to the power to issue notices requiring the disclosure of encrypted material and the creation of an offence of failure to comply with such a notice. It is in such instances where a minimal interpretation of the Convention has led to the statutory rubber stamp for somewhat illiberal state action.

On the positive side, the Act is comprehensive and places many previously legally unregulated surveillance techniques on a statutory basis. However, the law remains fragmented – it does not offer a single legal regulatory system (Justice, 1998: 15) though one was promised by the Home Office (Home Office, 1999: para 4.1) – and the law remains weak in terms of the protection for privacy in electronic communications and the imposition of regulation. It is an Act that is not so much directed at the protection of privacy, as a measure designed to ensure that the HRA has little impact upon the area. As Fenwick has argued:

> Under the rhetoric about protecting human rights ... lies an unadmitted concern – to keep scrutiny of such matters outside the courts ... whereas had powers of surveillance remained on a non-statutory basis they would have been vulnerable to challenge under Article 8 of the Convention ... .
> (Fenwick, 2000: 345)

In summary, one could argue that the effect of Article 8 has been to ensure the development of a comprehensive statutory regime governing covert surveillance techniques. Unfortunately, the minimalist interpretation of Article 8 by the legislators has had a detrimental effect upon the quality of those laws. Successive pieces of legislation appear to simply rubber stamp or extend existing practice. However, the Convention is a living instrument and in recent years has been requiring ever-stricter standards in relation to state surveillance. Given this, and the input of the domestic courts' interpretation of Article 8, it could mean that the regulatory system will have to evolve to meet more exacting standards. Whether those standards will apply to overt surveillance techniques in the form of public space CCTV remains a matter of interpretation. However, if one wishes to influence the debate about the extent of privacy rights in the public arena an attempt must be made to justify that position by reference to theoretical foundations.

Privacy and Public Space Surveillance

Given that the use of covert technical surveillance now has a comprehensive regulatory framework, albeit one that is heavily criticised, could the Convention also place similar demands on the use of the now ubiquitous public space visual surveillance schemes? If one could assert a claim to privacy in public, or a claim to privacy regarding the collection and retention of images recorded, legislation would have to follow. However, would the notion of asserting privacy claims in public lead to the common good being systematically neglected, as some would argue? In this section I will use Feldman's construct of privacy to establish that privacy can operate in the public arena. Following this, Etzioni's claims that privacy rights in the US have adversely affected the common good will be addressed to illustrate how this can be avoided in the development of domestic law.

The influence of the European Convention has not yet been fully realised in the area of public space surveillance. Firstly, there has been very little discussion of overt public space surveillance to date and, secondly, now that the Convention rights can be interpreted in domestic courts one might anticipate such interpretation to be more liberal, without the need to remain within the parameters of international consensus, thus jurisprudence from Strasbourg is not determinative of an issue. How then, might the concept of privacy be utilised in public space?

Taylor: State Surveillance and the Right to Privacy

In the US, which has developed its notion of privacy over a century, the seminal Supreme Court decision in Katz v United States (1967, 389 U.S. 347; Shattuck, 1977: 16) determined that the test of privacy was not dependant wholly on location but where one would have a 'reasonable expectation of privacy'. Justice Harlan expanded on the test thus:

> ...there is a twofold requirement, first that a person have exhibited an actual (subjective) expectation of privacy, and, second, that the expectation be one that society is prepared to recognise as 'reasonable'. Thus, a man's home is, for most purposes, a place where he expects privacy, but objects, activities, or statements that he exposes to the plain view of outsiders are not protected because no intention to keep them to himself has been exhibited.

Subsequent cases have indicated that what is already in the public domain can be recorded and disseminated since it would amount to no more than exposing what could already be seen. For example, in California v Greenwood ((1988) 486 US. 35), the Supreme Court ruled that citizens could have no reasonable expectation of privacy in items they discarded in the dustbin for the express purpose of having strangers take it away.

Despite this US interpretation, it could be argued that we all carry out acts in public that we would consider to be of a 'private' nature, where subjectively, we might have exhibited an expectation of privacy. Furthermore, though we may have exposed certain actions to public gaze, this does not necessarily mean that we would be happy for many different actions, in different locations, to be recorded and collated into a permanent record of behaviour over a particular period. In open, publicly accessible spaces "ordinary people expect to remain anonymous. ... scrutiny of more than a casual character would seem to offend reasonable expectations of being able to remain anonymous" (Von Hirsch, 2000: 61). Norris and Armstrong have argued that although the law does not recognise a right to privacy in public "it is clear that rules governing the production and reproduction of order in public space are finely attuned to its micro-sociological dimensions." (Norris and Armstrong, 1998: 4). In co-presence the watcher and the watched can read signals from each other, such as a threatening look, and can challenge or question each other accordingly. CCTV surveillance modifies this relationship. The watcher and the watched are 'distanciated'. The potential subject of surveillance does not know the extent to which he is being watched, if at all, but may modify his behaviour nevertheless. Whilst no one would anticipate a casual look to be a threat to privacy, how might prolonged visual surveillance fare?

Feldman's analysis of the right to privacy is instructive here (Feldman, 1994). He asserts that every individual will be part of a multitude of different interlocking spheres within society, such as through their workplace, membership of social clubs, family and so on. Each sphere represents an area marked off from those outside it, whilst inside, individuals have relatively little privacy against others in that sphere for the purposes of that sphere. For example, whilst those in the family home may enjoy a significant degree of privacy

Taylor: State Surveillance and the Right to Privacy

from the outside world, they enjoy considerably less privacy as regards each other for the purposes of living in the communal environment. An appeal to privacy thus assumes a conflict of interests, differing according to the circumstances. Such an analysis offers an alternative to the idea that what occurs in public cannot, as a matter of fact, be private. Privacy in each sphere operates in four dimensions: space, time, action and information (ibid. 52). In relation to the use of public space CCTV one cannot control the spatial element of who can watch, or set time limits on when people can watch, but arguably there can be an active element and an information element. For example, though limited, one could have a claim not to be the subject of intensive surveillance without due cause, and a stronger claim to control the diffusion of information about what has occurred there. Though the expectation of privacy may be considerably reduced in a public setting, this does not automatically mean that all privacy is lost. The operation of public space CCTV might be justified on crime control grounds, but that incursion into privacy does not therefore mean that the CCTV operator can intensively focus on individuals without good cause or do as he or she wishes with the recorded images:

> If the surveillance is overt, it carries with it a clearly implied threat that the fruits of the surveillance may be used for purposes adverse to the interests of the person being watched. This is calculated to undermine people's commitments to their own plans and values. It thus represents a failure of respect for people's dignity and autonomy (ibid.: 61).

Nissenbaum argues that a theory of privacy in public has never fully developed because until the advent of modern technology it has never really been an issue Nissenbaum, 2000). As such traditional theories have reflected the dichotomy that privacy refers to intimate areas and public to non-intimate areas. Feldman's construct is not wholly bound to the ideas of the intimate and the non-intimate. To stray from the traditional theories might be to produce another ingredient to an already complex dish but:

> ... although an important purpose of philosophical theory is to introduce greater conceptual rigour, a normative theory that strays too far from ordinary usage and popular sentiment is thereby rendered unhelpful, or worse, irrelevant (ibid.: 19).

Whilst it can be seen that overt CCTV surveillance could theoretically impinge upon a right to privacy, does Article 8 itself currently demand practical measures to uphold privacy in this respect?

The European Court has never sought to give a conclusive definition of privacy, considering it neither necessary nor desirable. However, in Niemietz v Germany ((1992) 16 EHRR 97) the Court stated:

> it would be too restrictive to limit the notion to an 'inner circle' in which the individual may live his own personal life as he chooses and to exclude therefrom entirely the outside world not encompassed within that circle. Respect for private life must also comprise to a certain degree the right to

establish and develop relationships with other human beings. There appears, furthermore, to be no reason of principle why this understanding of the notion of 'private life' should be taken to exclude activities of a professional or business nature since it is, after all, in the course of their working lives that the majority of people have a significant, if not the greatest opportunity of developing relationships with the outside world. (ibid.: 29)

The 'right to establish and develop relationships with others' reinforces the idea that privacy vests in people not places, and as such could be capable of being exercised when in a public environment. Harris et al comment, "the expanding understanding of private life set out in the Niemietz case indicates that a formal public/private distinction about the nature of the location will not always be decisive" (Harris, O'Boyle, and Warbrick, 1995: 309). A pertinent factor should, perhaps, be the subjective behaviour of the individual rather than their location. A homeless person living his life in public spaces still has a right to have his private life respected. Prolonged or regular visual surveillance of them is arguably a failure to respect that right, if it is not based on justifiable grounds. However, the Strasbourg Court has not yet moved to a position of accepting visual surveillance per se as an affront to privacy, albeit one capable of legitimisation under the appropriate circumstances outlined in Article 8(2).

In Friedl v Austria ((1995) 21 EHRR 88) the applicant took part in a demonstration causing an obstruction to the highway. When the police broke up the demonstration they took photographs of the participants, including the applicant. The Austrian Government gave assurances that the photographs were taken solely to record the nature of the incident and no names were recorded, or action taken to identify the persons photographed by means of data processing. The Commission attached weight to these assurances and, noting that there had been no intrusion into the 'inner circle' of the applicant's private life; that the demonstration was public; and the applicant was there voluntarily, found that the taking and retention of the photographs did not breach Article 8. The questioning of the applicant to establish his identity and the recording of these personal data was an interference requiring justification under Article 8(2). This is consistent with the idea that; '[P]rivacy involves a bundle of interests, rather than a single right, so loss of part of the bundle does not entail loss of the whole'. (Feldman, 1994: 61)

The decision is also in line with the case of X v United Kingdom (App. No. 5877/72), where, similarly, the taking and storage of photographs of a woman taking part in a demonstration was not a prima facie breach of Article 8. Fenwick, aligned with other authors, argues that there is an identifiable trend within the European Court for a broadening scope of Article 8, and this is an area where one should look to the evolutive nature of the Convention rather than to individual decisions (Fenwick, 2002: 704). However, to find that CCTV surveillance in public spaces is a breach of privacy per se would be to broaden Article 8 in a way that, it appears, the European Court is not prepared to do. In 1996 Pierre Herbecq, a Belgian national and secretary-general of the 'Human Rights League', argued before the Commission on Human Rights that the use of public space CCTV interfered with his right to privacy (Herbecq v Belgium, App No.

32200/96). He was concerned that the cameras were not regulated by law thus depriving citizens of the knowledge of when they might be surveilled and by whom. As such people would censure their behaviour in order to avoid being conspicuous, effectively producing a 'chilling effect'. Herbecq did not complain about the recording of the images or their possible dissemination. The Commission declared the application inadmissible. As nothing was recorded, there wasn't any material that could have been made available to the general public, or used for anything more than keeping watch on places. What was being watched was simply public behaviour.

From the above cases it would appear that a dominant theme is the control of personal information. If the use of public space CCTV involves the collection and storage of information relating to identifiable individuals then this is more likely to engage Article 8. A case involving the legally unregulated use of CCTV surveillance is currently awaiting determination in Strasbourg. In August 1995 Geoffrey Peck, suffering from depression, allegedly attempted to kill himself using a kitchen knife. He had walked through the centre of Brentwood, Essex, with the knife in his hand and the incident was recorded by the CCTV operator. The police were alerted and Mr. Peck was detained under the Mental Health Act 1983. This incident was later included by the Council in a positive press release about the benefits of its CCTV system. Subsequently, a regional television company obtained a copy of the footage for broadcast. Although Mr. Peck's face was masked by the television company at the Council's request, a number of viewers still recognised him. Following a complaint by Mr. Peck the Independent Television Commission decided that the footage breached their privacy requirements. An unmasked photograph of the incident later appeared in a local newspaper, and the footage was also shown on national television by the BBC, again unmasked. The Broadcasting Standards Commission also held that an unwarranted infringement of privacy had occurred. Mr. Peck's application to Strasbourg regarding a potential breach of Article 8 is not based on the existence of the cameras, but on the disclosure of recorded material to the media. In support are a number of cases from the European Court that emphasise that Article 8 can be engaged when public authorities store and use personal information.

It is evident that domestic common law is also moving towards a position of protecting such information. In the High Court hearing of the Peck case in 1997 Harrison J. stated:

> I have some sympathy with the applicant who has suffered an invasion of his privacy ... Unless and until there is a general right of privacy recognised by English law... reliance must be placed on effective guidance being issued by Codes of Practice or otherwise, in order to try and avoid such undesirable invasions of a person's privacy ([1998] CMLR 697).

It has been suggested that such a general right to privacy is beginning to emerge. Over the past decade the law of confidence has developed into what some would argue is a de facto privacy law. In Hellewell v Chief Constable of Derbyshire ([1995] 1 WLR 804) Laws LJ said:

> ... the disclosure of a photograph may, in some circumstances, be
> actionable as a breach of confidence. If someone with a telephoto lens
> were to take from a distance and with no authority a picture of another
> engaged in some private act, his subsequent disclosure of the photograph
> would ... as surely amount to a breach of confidence as if he had found or
> stolen a letter or diary in which the act was recounted and proceeded to
> publish it.

Cases such as this had to be treated cautiously, however, being an application for an interim injunction it meant that the plaintiff only had to make out an arguable case. However, the passing of the HRA has given the courts the impetus they needed to continue the development of the law. Fenwick states that the HRA "provides the normative impetus for the consolidation of the radical developments" in cases such as Hellewell (Fenwick, 2002: 581). In the recent case Douglas v Hello! ([2001] 2 WLR 992) which involved the prohibited taking of photographs at a wedding, Sedley LJ stated that the law of confidence had now developed to the point at which it could provide a right to privacy as distinct from confidence. Privacy extended to:

> those who simply find themselves subjected to an unwarranted intrusion
> into their private lives. The law no longer needs to construct an artificial
> relationship of confidentiality between intruder and victim: it can
> recognise privacy itself as a legal principle drawn from the fundamental
> value of personal autonomy (ibid: 1025).

Undoubtedly the parameters of this common law action will develop only after much debate and legal activity. However, the recording and dissemination of CCTV material, such as in the Peck case, may well fall within those parameters. Though Mr. Peck's actions were carried out in a public place, it could be argued that to broadcast the footage on national television represented an unwarranted intrusion into his private life.

With the reducing cost of CCTV systems there are few publicly owned schemes that do not have the capacity to record information. Therefore, if such publicly owned schemes can engage the right to privacy, such surveillance should be in accordance with law, aimed at a legitimate objective, and be necessary and proportionate.

The recent enactment of the Data Protection Act 1998 may prove to be a satisfactory form of domestic regulation as far as the Convention's relatively limited demands require, but arguably it will fail to have a significant impact in this area. The Act requires that those who operate CCTV systems (data controllers) and who record images from which individuals can be identified, must register with the Information Commissioner and ensure that the system is operated in accordance with the data protection principles. The extent to which they impact on CCTV systems is made explicit through the guidance given in the CCTV Code of Practice published by the Information Commissioner (Data Protection Commissioner, 2000).

The first principle requires that data be processed fairly and lawfully. One aspect of this is that the CCTV system must be operated for a 'legitimate reason'. The prevention and detection of crime would satisfy this. The 'fair' processing of images would also require, in many instances, that adequate signage give the public notice of who collects the data and for what purpose. The second principle requires that data should be obtained only for specified and lawful purposes, and should not be processed in any manner incompatible with that purpose. This would help to ensure the confidentiality of information obtained. Thirdly, data should be adequate, relevant and not excessive. This would have implications for privacy in terms of ensuring that cameras were not monitoring individuals in private spaces. The fourth and fifth principles necessitates that personal data should be accurate and, where necessary, kept up to date, and should not be kept longer than is necessary. Finally, adequate measures should be taken against unlawful processing. This would include satisfactory security arrangements in terms of who could access the recorded material. These requirements could ensure that at least the privacy of recorded information could be maintained.

However, the statute does have a number of drawbacks. Firstly, one would have to question how many data controllers are aware that the new DPA applies to recorded CCTV images. Furthermore, even if the data controller is aware, are the day-to-day CCTV operators aware of the requirements of the Act? Given the widespread adoption of CCTV surveillance there has been relatively little publicity or education about how the law applies to CCTV. The 1984 version of the Act was criticised as a "paper tiger" (Davies, 1996: 104) and Flaherty suggested, in 1989, that;

> Data protection agencies are, in many ways, functioning as legitimators of
> new technology. ... [T]hey act rather as shapers of marginal changes in
> the operating rules for such instruments of public surveillance. (Flaherty,
> 1989: 384)

Similarly, it could be argued that the DPA has failed to have any significant impact upon the public. If the public are not aware that they have the right to see data that a CCTV operator may hold on them, how will they be in any position to challenge abuse except in the most obvious of situations? The role of the Information Officer has grown in recent years but the Office lacks the powers and resources to actively ensure CCTV is effectively regulated, though it may technically be 'in accordance with law'.

To be a justifiable incursion upon the right to privacy, CCTV surveillance must satisfy a legitimate aim. The most obvious legitimising factor from Article 8(2) is the prevention of disorder or crime. The claims in support of CCTV as a crime prevention tool are many and given considerable media attention (Norris and Armstrong, 1999: 60). The Home Secretary of the day, Michael Howard, was quoted as saying, 'I am absolutely convinced that CCTV has a major part to play in helping to detect, and reduce crimes and to convict criminals'. (ibid. 63)

Yet there has been relatively little reliable evidence to support this view. What evidence exists has been referred to as "post hoc shoestring efforts by the untrained and self interested practitioner."(Pawson and Tilley, 1994: 291). As a crime detection tool, CCTV has been shown to work in specific instances though the effect of its wholesale use is rather more ambiguous. Though crime detection is not included in a literal reading of Article 8(2) it is likely that the courts would adopt a more purposive interpretation. Whether widespread use of CCTV in public spaces is a proportionate response to an identified problem is perhaps more debateable. Rather than being a well-directed measure aimed at a particular target CCTV arguably is sometimes installed in public locations as part of a domino effect:

> CCTV is now seen as the fashionable solution to everything. Councils are saying we need CCTV, either for political reasons, or because the town next door has got it... (quoted in Clarke, 1994: 28).

The right to privacy in public is a relatively weak right whilst the prevention of crime is an important social objective. However, there is arguably an element of arbitrariness in the proliferation of CCTV schemes to areas that provide little evidence of a need for mass surveillance. One could argue that by their very nature crime prevention measures are necessary before a real problem arises, and it is the flexibility of the language in the Convention that can be problematic when seeking to buttress rights. Of course, a reliance on privacy should not become a cloak for criminal activity, but arguably what is absent in the CCTV context is a system whereby schemes can only operate under licence in areas only where a legitimate need can be identified. This should require evidence to be provided as to when, where and how CCTV is seen to be an appropriate response to an identifiable problem. Once operational, the controls placed by the DPA on the collection, storage and dissemination of data (including images) are, in principle, sound policies and would be adequate when coupled with greater powers of enforcement. However, would legislation with its roots in privacy be detrimental to the common good?

The Limits of Privacy

Within a liberal political framework privacy rights are principally and undeniably individualistic, and are, of course, not without their critics. Restricting the activity of the state reduces its ability to intervene to ensure that society is organised more equitably for the weakest groups, or to ensure that a greater balance is struck between individual rights and social responsibilities. Etzioni, for example, argues that in the US privacy is treated as a highly privileged value but that it is not an unmitigated good (Etzioni, 1999). "In several important matters of public safety and public health, the common good is being systematically neglected out of excessive deference to privacy." (Ibid: 4). In the UK the position has not been replicated. The US has developed its concept of privacy over a century to the extent that it now holds a place as an implied constitutional right. In the UK the courts have only just begun to develop the concept of privacy. However, if privacy were extended in limited circumstances to public spaces, or the DPA was not considered to be an adequate response in privacy terms to public space CCTV, would such a development be detrimental to the common good? Having established that an assertion of privacy in public is possible, this section seeks to ascertain that this claim need not necessarily adversely affect the common good.

Etzioni suggests a number of criteria to help determine whether the balance between individual rights, in this case privacy, and the common good has been achieved (Ibid. 10). His analysis obviously concerns the state of US law but can nonetheless be illuminating for the future development of UK privacy. Firstly, he claims that society should only take steps to limit privacy if it faces a well-documented and macroscopic threat to the common good. Arguably the European Convention takes such concerns into account through the exceptions outlined in Article 8(2). Disorder and crime are certainly well documented threats but before privacy is limited an evaluation should be carried out to determine whether CCTV really could be a solution to a particular problem. In essence, this is similar to the requirements of proportionality outlined earlier. The relatively weak status of privacy in public (or the collection of 'data' in the public domain) should therefore only be a bar to the arbitrary introduction of CCTV schemes in public spaces. If it could be established that a CCTV scheme was justifiable, a second issue must be considered. Can the common good be supported without privacy-destructing measures? From a political perspective CCTV is a very useful tool of crime prevention in that it is a highly visible response that invariably has the support of the media and the commercial sector. In the UK where 'rights' have traditionally been of a residual character, crime control has considerably over-shadowed concerns for individual liberties. As the then Prime Minister, John Major stated;

> 'Closed-circuit television cameras have proved they can work, so we need more of them where crime is high ... I have no doubt that we will hear some protest about a threat to civil liberties. Well, I have no sympathy whatsoever for so-called liberties of that kind.' (quoted in Groombridge and Murji, 1994).

If Article 8 were to apply to public visual surveillance systems it would at least ensure a debate about whether or not CCTV surveillance could be justified in an individual situation, or whether other methods of crime prevention might be equally, or more, successful with less intrusion. Indeed, as Etzioni points out (Etzioni, 1999: 213), it is social scrutiny of the community by the community that leads to the best crime prevention policy, namely, the community's own moral and informal enforcement mechanisms. This would lead to a reduction in the need for formal state surveillance. Whilst Etzioni uses this point to argue for less privacy, it may also support the case for increased privacy where the balance has tipped away from privacy. For example, to arbitrarily introduce CCTV into areas that do not necessarily support such a measure may be at the cost of community scrutiny, where individuals feel they no longer need to watch over each other as Big Brother is doing it anyway!

Thirdly, if privacy is to be curbed, is it to a minimal extent? For example, consideration should be given to the placement and number of cameras. A camera to monitor traffic flow would not necessarily require full pan, tilt and zoom facilities; indeed, the ability to record images might not be crucial. If Article 8 were engaged the issue of proportionality would require that the least obtrusive means necessary should be undertaken, thus not barring surveillance, but ensuring it is appropriate and justifiable.

Finally, measures that treat the adverse effects of privacy-destroying methods are to be favoured over those that ignore such effects. The Data Protection Act attempts to ensure this in relation to the CCTV operators' collection and storage of personal data. For example, by placing limits on the duration images can be held for, and limiting the class of people to whom disclosure can be made, the Act is engaging measures that limit the privacy intrusion. However, as stated earlier, without stronger enforcement mechanisms much of the intention behind the Act might be lost.

In the US Etzioni argues for a reformulation of privacy to ensure that a more appropriate balance is found with the common good. In the UK it could be argued that the position is reversed. Privacy has long been a stranger to domestic courts, and the concept of privacy imported from the European Convention is far from an inalienable right. To extend the Convention's interpretation of privacy to the public sphere, or to apply its standards in regard to the collection of personal data in the public sphere, does not necessarily entail short-changing the common good. Privacy can be an essential element of a functioning community. Without privacy people might feel inhibited from forming close relationships within the family, or outside in social groups. It allows the social spheres to function and as a result a degree of privacy helps the community to function. Privacy need not displace the common good and whilst the European Convention can provide a framework for legislation, it is a matter for Parliament and the courts to determine exactly where the balance lies.

Conclusion

It has been argued that a reliance on such a nebulous concept as privacy is not the long-term solution to resisting surveillance (Lyon, 2001). Paradoxically, it is a demand for privacy that drives the need for surveillance and therefore greater privacy and so on. However, a practical reality in relation to overt public space surveillance is that Article 8 already provides a context within which covert state surveillance takes place, and that reality recognises that privacy is not an inalienable right and that surveillance can be a necessity. Article 8 has ensured that the UK has, over the past twenty years, introduced a degree of legal accountability for covert police surveillance practices where none existed before. Arguably, successive governments have responded to the demands of Article 8 by introducing minimalist legislative responses, but without the impact of the Strasbourg Court very little would have happened in terms of privacy protection.

If it is accepted that privacy does not end when entering public spaces, at least to the extent of recording personal data, then the state should similarly be able to justify their reasons for infringing such a right, and should have their powers to do so explicitly detailed. Furthermore, once legislation is in place drawing on the principles derived from the European Convention, it could be applied to private operators, with necessity and proportionality being determined accordingly. The DPA, almost inadvertently rather than by design, presents a reasonably sound ethical basis for CCTV operators to work from, and the proactive regulation of data collection and privacy protection has to be better than resorting to court action to develop the law. However, the enforcement mechanisms in the DPA arguably represent a rather weak response to the ubiquitous gaze of the surveillance camera. There are situations when the state has to intervene in the lives of its citizens, such as to prevent crime, but such intervention must be based on, and restricted by, principled legislation. Article 8 has played a major role in the development of comprehensive statutory regulation of surveillance practices, but as an international instrument it is inevitably imprecise and malleable. The development of a domestic concept of privacy through the Human Rights Act, based on the principles from Article 8, might ensure that not only are covert surveillance practices more tightly controlled, but that overt practices are also adequately regulated.

Acknowledgments

I am grateful to my colleague Ben Fitzpatrick, and the anonymous referees, for their helpful comments on an earlier draft of this piece. Responsibility for errors remains my own.

References

Akdeniz, Y., N. Taylor, and C. Walker (2001) Regulation of Investigatory Powers Act 2000: Bigbrother.gov.uk: State Surveillance in the Age of Information and Rights *Criminal Law Review*, February: 73-90

Clarke, M. (1994) Blind Eye on the Street. *Police Review*,5 (August): 28-30

Cooley, T. (1888) *The Law of Torts*.Ch icago: Callaghan

Data Protection Commissioner (2000) CCTV Code of Practice. Available at: http://www.dataprotection.gov.uk/dpr/dpdoc.nsf

Davies, S. (1996) *Big Brother: Britain's Web of Surveillance and the New Technological Order*. London: Pan

Etzioni, A. (1999) *The Limits of Privacy*. New York: Basic Books.

Feldman, D. (1994) Secrecy, Dignity or Autonomy? Views of Privacy as a Civil Liberty. *Current Legal Problems*,4 7(2): 41-71.

Fenwick, H. (2000) *Civil Rights: New Labour, Freedom and the Human Rights Act*. Harlow: Longman

Fenwick, H. (2002) *Civil Liberties and Human Rights*. (3rd ed.) London: Cavendish

Fitzpatrick, B., and N. Taylor, (2001) Human Rights and the Discretionary Exclusion of Evidence. *Journal of Criminal Law*, 65(4): 349-359.

Flaherty, D. (1989*) Protecting Privacy in Surveillance Societies: The Federal Republic of Germany, Sweden, France, Canada, and the United States*. Chapel Hill: University of North Carolina Press.

Groombridge, N. and Murji, K. (1994b) As Easy as AB and CCTV? *Policing*, 10(4): 283-290.

Harris, D.J., M. O'Boyle, and C. Warbrick, (1995) *Law of the European Convention on Human Rights*. London: Butterworths.

Home Office (1999) *Interception of Communications in the United Kingdom* Cm.4368.

JUSTICE (1998) *Under Surveillance*. London.

Leigh, I. [1986] A Tapper's Charter? *Public Law*,S pring: 8-18

Lustgarten, L., and I. Leigh (1994) *In From The Cold: National Security and Parliamentary Democracy*. Oxford: Clarendon Press.

Lyon, D. (2001) *Surveillance Society: Monitoring Everyday Life*. Buckingham: Open University Press.

Nissenbaum, H. (1998) Protecting Privacy in an Information Age: The Problem of Privacy in Public. *Law and Philosophy*, 17: 559-596.

Norris, C., and Armstrong, G. (1998) Introduction: Power and Vision, in C. Norris, J. Moran and G. Armstrong, (eds.) *Surveillance, Closed Circuit Television and Social Control*. Aldershot: Ashgate,3 -20.

Norris, C. and G. Armstrong (1999) *The Maximum Surveillance Society: The Rise of CCTV*. Oxford: Berg.

Pawson, R. and Tilley, N. (1994) What Works in Evaluation Research? *British Journal of Criminology*,3 4(3), 291-306.

Shattuck, J.H.F. (1977) *Rights of Privacy*. Skokie: National Textbook Company.

Starmer, K., M. Strange and W. Whitaker (2001) *Criminal Justice, Police Powers and Human Rights*. London: Blackstone.

Taylor, N., and C. Walker (1996) Bugs in the System. *Journal of Civil Liberties*, 1: 105-124.

Uglow, S. [1999] Covert Surveillance and the European Convention on Human Rights. *Criminal Law Review*, April: 287-299

Von Hirsch, A. (2000) The Ethics of Public Television Surveillance, in Von Hirsch, A. D. Garland and K. Wakefield (eds.) *Ethical and Social Perspectives on Situational Crime Prevention*. Oxford: Hart, 59-76.

Wacks, R. (1980a) *The Protection of Privacy*. London: Sweet and Maxwell.

Wacks, R. (1980b) The Poverty of Privacy. *Law Quarterly Review*,9 6: 73-89.

Westin, A. (1967) *Privacy and Freedom*. New York: Atheneum.

[12]

VIDEO SURVEILLANCE, GENDER, AND THE SAFETY OF PUBLIC URBAN SPACE: "PEEPING TOM" GOES HIGH TECH?

Hille Koskela[1]

Department of Geography
University of Helsinki

Abstract: The obsession with security has been claimed to be the master narrative of contemporary urban design. This paper explores some of the complex relationships between security, space and gender. The paper shows how gender is linked in various ways to the practices of video surveillance and to how it is executed and experienced. First, links to sexual harassment are examined. Technical surveillance is not only insensitive to possible cases of harassment but also opens up new opportunities for the offenders. There clearly is a temptation to abuse the equipment for voyeuristic purposes. Second, some empirical interview material is used to discuss how women perceive surveillance. The accountability of the operators is of great importance. Concealed surveillance, either the cameras or the control rooms, erodes confidence. What is of concern to women is not just whether a particular space is monitored or not but rather the more widespread politics of surveillance. [Key words: video surveillance, gender, fear of crime, urban planning, public space.]

> When I am on the street I don't wonder whether people look at me
> or not—so how come I was so uneasy in front of that camera?
>
> —Elisa, Helsinki

Video surveillance has recently become a subject of wide debate both in and out of academia. It has been evaluated in relation to crime control, citizens' privacy as well as in relation to the development trends of contemporary urban space. Within this discussion a number of problems caused by expanding surveillance have been identified. Concerns have been raised about invaded privacy, and the limits and regulations needed as surveillance technology becomes ever more effective, cheap, small, and accessible. The public has become worried about potential misuse of surveillance cameras and videotapes. Surveillance is feared to have a negative "chilling effect" on urban life and culture. Further, it can be used as a tool for reinforcing the "purification" and "homogenization" processes of urban space (Davis, 1990; Mitchell, 1995). Finally, it has been questioned whether surveillance cameras are effective for the task they were to meet in the first place: to curb crime. Increasing number of studies show that surveillance only has a temporary effect on urban crime and that they produce crime displacement (Flusty, 1994; Fyfe and Bannister, 1996).

---

[1]Correspondence concerning this article should be addressed to Hille Koskela, Department of Geography, P.O. box 64, 00014 University of Helsinki, Helsinki, Finland; telephone: +358-9-19150778; fax: +358-9-19150760; e-mail: hille.koskela@helsinki.fi

What is at issue is not just whether a particular space is monitored or not. There are numerous other questions to be considered: who maintains surveillance, where, why, how, and with what kinds of consequences? What kinds of power-relationships are embedded within surveillance? Who has the right to look and who will be looked at? What behavior or appearance in a particular context is regarded as "deviant?" In this article my aim is to highlight one particular aspect of surveillance: I shall consider whether the practices and conceptual questions of surveillance are *gendered*, and, if so, how. This setting is not simple or straightforward. On one hand, since the purpose of surveillance is to increase urban safety and women are known to be the ones that are most often afraid, it might be especially beneficial for women. But on the other hand, the validity of this reasoning should not be taken for granted. Surveillance includes multiple power-relationships that do not remain without gender aspects. In public space, even the ostensibly innocent practices of seeing and being seen are gendered (Rose, 1993; Gardner, 1995). The field of vision is deeply gendered (Nast and Kobayashi, 1996). In this paper I aim to explore some of the complex relationships between security, surveillance technology and gender. Some empirical work is used to illustrate the points that are presented. It is derived from research conducted in two European cities: Edinburgh in Scotland and Helsinki in Finland (for more detail, see Koskela, 1999). However these local contexts are here as "supporting actors," and the task set is mainly to discuss this matter on a conceptual level.

I focus on surveillance as it is executed by surveillance cameras in urban space. Surveillance is examined *as an urban experience*. Speed control cameras on roads as well as various "nonvisual" forms of electronic surveillance—such as the ethical questions on geographical information systems, "data profiling," or the widespread "cyberspace surveillance" on the Internet (e.g., Curry, 1997; Lyon, 1998; Graham, 1998; Green, 1999)—are beyond the scope of this paper. Furthermore, my aim is to examine spaces, which are—at least in principal—*accessible* to everyone. This is not to deny that the public/private dichotomy needs critical evaluation and that many of the so-called public spaces are becoming increasingly exclusive and privatized (Mitchell, 1995; *Urban Geography*, 1996; Lees, 1998). Through the concept of public space has lately been much discussed a lot in the academia, there still is no consensus on what "public space" means in the first place. The boundaries between public and private space—if they ever existed—are blurring. In Nan Ellin's (1997, p. 36) words: "The contemporary built environment contains increasingly less meaningful public space, and existing public space is increasingly controlled by various forms of surveillance and increasingly invested with private meanings."

SURVEILLANCE IN URBAN PLANNING AGENDA

Planning safer cities is a matter of growing concern. In the Anglo-American countries the question on how to improve urban safety has been on political agendas for a long time. There are many views of how cities should be developed and who should be able to take part in this development. The theoretical as well as practical and political discussions on planning for safety are widespread. In her famous book *The Death and Life of Great American Cities* Jane Jacobs (1961) expressed her concern for safety and saw that natural surveillance was the key to increased safety. Oscar Newman developed the ideas of Jacobs further and attempted to operationalize them. In *Defensible Space* (1972) he outlined principles for improving safety by creating "defensible space." Newman is one of the first designers who mentioned the use of *surveillance cameras*. He suggested that security can be achieved through combining physical modifications and electronic technology. Visibility is considered as a prerequisite for safety. However, he saw electronic surveillance as subordinate to other means, and suggested its use in situations where it is "the only resource open" (Newman, 1972).

Lately, electronic means have more and more often be used to replace informal social control in an urban environment: *the eyes* of the people *on the street* are replaced by the eyes of surveillance cameras (Fyfe and Bannister, 1998). Video surveillance has become increasingly common and popular in cities all over the Western world. While Newman recommended it in exceptional circumstances, nowadays it has become the first and easiest option. More surveillance systems are being installed all the time. Arguably, it has become *the standard way* to restrain crime and guarantee security.

The obsession with security has been claimed to be the master narrative of contemporary urban design. The writings of Mike Davis and other scholars interpreting the design of "Los Angeles School" architects have enunciated polemic notions on "the urban fortress model" where safety is guaranteed by exclusionary design and technological surveillance (Davis, 1990; Flusty, 1994; Ellin, 1996; Soja, 1996; Dear and Flusty, 1998, among others). They show where the defence mentality in its extreme forms can lead: urban spaces have been divided and polarized. Some parts have been transformed into controlled, guarded fortresses, which are privately owned and maintained, whereas other places have become neglected and have been left to deteriorate. Social polarization, inequality and segregation are clearly legible in their urban form. According to this vision, increased fear has caused social groups to flee from each other into isolated homogenous enclaves (Davis, 1990; Flusty, 1994). The massive expansion of protection is claimed to lead to a vicious circle of defence: while increasing security might make some feel safer, it also creates increasing fear, racism and distrust among people (Ellin, 1996). Design and urban policy are characterized by paranoia, protectionism, and a lack of common interest. Various forms of surveillance are used to maintain the existing social and economic order.

Therefore, despite the goal for security, surveillance also has its dark sides. Territoriality includes exclusion and intolerance: "we wish to exclude but not to be excluded" (Marcuse, 1997, p. 112). Concurrently, urban space is increasingly becoming a means of exclusion rather than a way to support diversity and the positive notion of urbanity. Unwanted behavior is excluded, not tolerated. Video surveillance plays a crucial role in this process. The harder and harder solutions can make the city *less pleasant* to live in rather than more pleasant. It has accurately been pointed out, that "for those excluded, it would be hard to find anything positive in the exercise of surveillance" (Whitaker, 1999, p. 136). This development is crystallized in such American cities as Los Angeles, which has often been considered to be the archetype of exclusion and protective architecture (e.g., Soja, 1989, 1996; Davis, 1990, 1992; Jameson, 1991; Ellin, 1996, 1997).

Comparable developments are being implemented in Europe. Although the circumstances sometimes are not as "extreme," analogous development can be seen to be occurring. In the United States the trend has been to monitor both public space and private space: the police operate surveillance cameras in public space as well as well-off private housing areas to isolate criminal activities from outside the housing area. Cameras are used to protect high-class private premises—"gated communities" (e.g., Flusty, 1994;

Blakely and Snyder, 1997). In publicly accessible spaces surveillance not only aims to protect property but also tries to reduce violence and achieve better safety and inviolability for people. In European countries video surveillance has been most common in publicly accessible spaces. For example in Britain all major cities have a surveillance system monitoring city streets (Fyfe et al., 1998); likewise in Scandinavia. Public urban space is under constant scrutiny. An attentive walk around any Western city will make the point: surveillance cameras are everywhere—in shops and shopping malls, banks and autotellers, metro and train stations, cafeterias, libraries, hospitals, universities, schools, and even in churches.

It is claimed that the street environments have become "sadistic"; public space is ever more difficult to approach and stay in, "the streets are dead" and the natural social life in public space has ended: (Davis, 1990, pp. 230–232; also Mitchell, 1995; Soja, 1997). Whether the most pessimistic visions are accurate or not, it is clear that increased surveillance has effects on how urban space is experienced and, more importantly, *produced*. Surveillance is likely to change the nature of urban space (for more detailed arguments, see Koskela, 2000a). In contemporary geography, space is considered to be—and further conceptualized as—both the medium and the outcome of social practices (Gregory and Urry, 1985; Rose, 1993; Massey, 1994; Soja; 1996, among others). Space has an important role in exercising power (Foucault, 1977). It is constituted, (re)produced and changed by various social, political and cultural processes. Surveillance is among these.

LEGISLATIVE QUESTIONS AND CRITICS

It has been estimated that Britain and Finland have the most intensive surveillance systems among the member countries of the European Union (Takala, 1998). In both these countries of regulation of surveillance is very low. There is no licensing system. Increased surveillance is considered to be related to the increased power of the authorities, but in fact most surveillance cameras that monitor public urban space are privately owned, and the authorities have little control over how and where such surveillance is exercised. Video surveillance escapes the cover of law.

In Finland video surveillance is, especially considering its frequency and rapid expansion, one of the least regulated practices in urban space. On the streets of Helsinki permission is needed for public meetings, or selling handicraft but not for video surveillance (Koskela, 2000b). Anybody can install a surveillance camera. There are innumerable cameras operated by private institutions as well as by the police. Nevertheless, there is no legislation regulating video surveillance in particular. There is a bill, which regulates some aspects of surveillance by for example forbidding cameras in spaces of a personally intimate nature. (Takala, 1998; Turva-alan kehittäminen, 1998). Regulation is possible also by virtue of bills dealing with eavesdropping, indexes of persons, and domestic peace. At the moment few countries within the European Union have legislation especially designed for surveillance. Only Belgium, Sweden and Denmark demand that those who wish to install a surveillance camera should have permits (Takala, 1998). In most countries varying combination of laws considering privacy protection and data security are used to regulate surveillance. Legislation clearly has difficulties in keeping pace with evolving technology.

Since surveillance is, at the same time, underregulated and rapidly expanding, it is clear that critical voices have risen to question these development trends. Academics as well as the active members on civil liberty associations have voiced their concern:

> CCTV (closed circuit television) can be grossly abused by recording intimate and private conduct and marking innocent people for tracking solely on the basis of racial, gender or other characteristics. No other technique can record in such graphic detail personal and private behaviour (Steinhardt, 1999).

What are considered as requiring the most immediate regulation are computerized facial recognition systems, which have the capacity to automatically, compare faces captured on video with databases of facial images. Other types of sophisticated technology, such as miniature cameras designed for covert surveillance and high-sensitivity infrared cameras, which are able to record activities in darkness, create a risk to privacy (Whitaker, 1999; Lyon, 2001).

The details of how surveillance might (or might not) be gendered, has yet not been much discussed. The issue of gendered surveillance is not to be understood as an argument that gender-relations should be the only dimensions of power within the practice of surveillance. Rather, gender is seen as one example of the many forms of power and repression associated with surveillance. It is clear that age and race, for example, are as crucial as gender, and in many cases social class matters also. Indeed, surveillance is used to monitor and exclude "suspicious youths" (e.g., Judd, 1995; Lees, 1998), political activists, people of color, sexual minorities, or the ones that look like they cannot afford to "consume" (e.g., Davies, 1997; Steinhardt, 1999). The intolerant or racist attitudes of the ones responsible for surveillance is mediated and even reinforced by the cameras. An exciting example which shows that there is public debate on surveillance and race is the *Surveillance Camera Players*—a theater group from New York, NY who performs for surveillance cameras to pay attention to the racial exclusion that is practiced by monitoring (Surveillance Camera Players, 2000). Concern for misuse cuts across age, race, and gender. Thus, by focusing on gender relations negotiated under surveillance, we might also be able to understand more about other forms of power and exclusion.

THE GENDERED ASPECTS OF SURVEILLANCE

Gender Dimensions in Urban Planning

"What is at issue, therefore, is not whether public spaces were controlled, but rather whose norms would be used to define those controls" (Domosh, 1998, p. 211). There has been considerable discussion on planning "for women" and implementing policies, which take women's needs into account. It has often been argued that in the mainstream discussions of urban politics and planning the gender dimension is lacking or undervalued and that women have not gained equal recognition in urban design (e.g., Matrix, 1984; Little et al., 1988; Simonsen, 1990; Greed, 1994).

There are elements of urban life that simply cannot be understood without gender relations. Urban space is gendered in its essence: the existence of male violence, for example, modifies women's interpretations of space (Rose, 1993; Massey, 1994). The geography of fear is gendered (Valentine, 1989). According to surveys and qualitative data from all over the world, women are more worried about their personal safety in urban space than men. Although it is clear that the category of "women" should not be oversimplified or seen as a homogenous group (e.g., McDowell, 1993; Gilbert, 1997), fear-evoking experiences—such as sexual harassment, threat of violence, and actual violence—can be experienced by all women despite their differences. Often the highly gendered nature of the public realm, which for example sexual harassment (re)produces, is neglected (Gardner, 1995). The threat of (sexual) violence does, to some extent, touch all women. Arguably, the question of urban safety is an issue which very accurately illustrates the gendered nature of space.

Despite this, safety has not always been among the most significant aims of planning that takes better account of women's needs. This is apparent especially in the Scandinavian countries. Such planning has been considered to be about ecological housing, healthy building materials, more democratic planning process, lower housing costs, better transport facilities, etc. (Björk, 1991; Friberg, 1993; NordREFO, 1989). Until the late 1990s safety was hardly discussed. This is somewhat paradoxical since the Scandinavian countries do have a reputation for supporting gender equality. In the Anglo-American countries this issue has been debated much more. There has been both theoretical reasoning on the causes and structures of fear (e.g., Merry, 1981; Smith, 1987; Gordon and Riger, 1989; Valentine, 1989; Pain, 1991) and attempts to create "safe city initiatives" by applying this knowledge in urban policies and planning procedures (e.g., Trench et al., 1992; Wekerle and Whitzman, 1995). It has been stated that there is a need to "Ask for public funds to transform public spaces to make them safe and accessible to everyone at night as well as during the day" (Duncan, 1996, p. 132). Increased safety is commonly accepted as an important aim but there is much less consensus as to the means by which it could be achieved. I will now discuss whether video surveillance could be among these means.

Space is not just a macro-structure separate from human reality but it has an experienced dimension. Space is interpreted and confronted in the "micropolitics" of everyday life (Domosh, 1998). Meanings about gender and space are produced in social practices and "are not natural of fixed but continually contested and subverted" (Boys, 1999, p. 193). The ostensibly trivial gendered practices of the everyday (re)produce the power structures which restrict and confine women's space (Rose, 1993). In addition, as Doreen Massey argues "What is clear is that *spatial control*, whether enforced through the power of convention or symbolism, or through the straightforward threat of violence, can be a fundamental element in the constitution of gender in its (highly varied) forms." (1994, p. 180, emphasis added)

Gender, Security, and Surveillance Technology

Because of their levels of fear women have been alleged to be the ones that particularly enjoy the "pay-off" of surveillance (Honess and Charman, 1992, p. 11; also Koskela, 2000a). Is this conclusion valid? Is surveillance perceived by women as improving their personal safety? What kinds of gender relation and gendered practices does surveillance include?

First, I examine the gender relations of surveillance at the simplest level: who occupies the opposite sides of a surveillance camera? If we look at the places and spaces under surveillance, and the maintenance of surveillance, can we see practices which could be gendered? In public and semipublic space, the places where surveillance most often is practiced are the shopping malls and the shopping areas of city centers, and likewise public transport areas, such as metro stations, railway stations and busy bus stops. Who usually negotiates and decides about surveillance is the management: managers of shopping malls, leading politicians, and city mayors. Furthermore, people who maintain surveillance are the police and private guards. From this it is possible to draw conclusions about the gender structure of surveillance. Women spend more of their time shopping than men. Everyday purchases for the family are mostly bought by women. It is also known that a majority of the users of public transport are women. Thus women are often found in the typical places under surveillance. In contrast, the occupations in charge of deciding on surveillance are male dominated. Even more importantly, the professions that maintain surveillance, police and guards, are also male dominated. Thus, *at this simplest level*, surveillance is, indeed, gendered: most of the persons "behind" the camera are men and most of the persons "under" surveillance are women (Koskela, 2000a).

Disorder and Harassment

However, there are also other more complicated features of gender structures. Beyond the positions that women and men occupy are *gendered social practices*. Women are constantly reminded that an invisible observer is a threat. In crime prevention advice, for example, women are recommended to keep their curtains tightly closed whenever it might be possible for someone outside could see inside (Gardner, 1995). This potential observer is presented as male. In addition, video surveillance is sometimes interpreted as a part of "male policing in the broadest sense" (Brown, 1998, p. 217). The "masculine culture" of those who are "in control" is causing mistrust toward surveillance: women do not rely on those behind the camera because of the reproduction of patriarchal power by the guards and the police who are responsible for the daily routine of surveillance (e.g., Wajcman, 1991; Fyfe, 1995; Herbert, 1996).

Furthermore, surveillance in practice is insensitive to issues that would be of particular importance to women. Video is unable to identify situations where a sensitive interpretation of a social situation is needed. Namely, the overseers responsible for surveillance easily remark on clearly seen but otherwise minor offenses, such as someone smoking a cigarette in a metro station, while ignoring more serious situations which they regard as ambivalent—such as verbal sexual harassment (Koskela, 2000a). Most cameras are unable to interpret threatening situations, which are not visually recognizable, and cases of harassment are therefore left without notice. In some cases video surveillance is used as a replacement for personal policing. By using a surveillance camera sexual harassment is more difficult to identify and to interrupt than by the police or guards patrolling by foot. Alcohol related disturbances are also often not considered to be serious enough to be interrupted by the overseers. Hence, as Sheila Brown (1998, p. 218) writes, "CCTV cannot change the general intimidation, verbal harassment, staring, and drunken rowdiness amongst groups of men which constrains women's movement most strongly."

This insensitivity of the cameras—their restriction to the field of vision—is an urgent reason for doubt and disorientation. Again, this is not to argue that harassment only concerns women: class, race, sexual orientation, age, or other factors can also be "motives" for verbal harassment. Sexual harassment (of women) is one of a number of related problems.

Peeping Tom Goes High-Tech

The insensitivity of surveillance cameras is not all that there is in question. This insensitivity can be understood as a "passive" relation between surveillance and harassment. However, there is also a concept, which could be understood as an "active" relation between surveillance and harassment (Koskela, 2000a). It has been shown that there is public concern about the "potential 'Peeping Tom' element" of surveillance cameras (Honess and Charman, 1992), that women are worried about possible "voyeurism" (Trench, 1997; Brown, 1998), and that cameras placed in spaces of any intimate nature irritate women (Koskela, 1999).

Indeed, it is possible *to use surveillance cameras as an actual means of harassment.* Scrutiny is a common and effective form of harassment (Gardner, 1995). There is some voyeuristic fascination in looking, in being able to see. In urban space women are likely to be the ones who are looked at, the objects of the gaze (Massey, 1994). Moreover, voyeurism itself has been defined as a characteristic that is solely male. As Carol Brooks Gardner (1995) pointed out, in the United States until the sexual equality legislation voyeurism and peeping were legally defined as offenses that only men could commit. The offensive gaze belonged only to men.

Arguably, the female body is still an object of a gaze in different way than the male body. Women's appearance is public information addressed "to whom it may concern" (Gardner, 1995, p. 23). Women are placed to be constantly objects of a gaze. This also applies to their being viewed through a surveillance camera. An anecdote, which illustrates this well, is an advertisement of a major Finnish department store Stockmann that lately announced above some pictures of latest women's fashion: "You perform for the surveillance cameras every day. Are you dressed for it?"

The phrase was placed to sell classy women's dresses. It well described how women are the objects of the gaze. Women are used to constantly policing their appearances in public space and searching for an outfit which is suitable for each particular situation (Gardner, 1995). However, rhetoric such as the one presented above, indicates that women are not only gazed by people on the street but also by the hidden gazes behind the camera.

One of the very reasons for women's insecurity is their "exaggerated visibility" (Brown, 1998). Paradoxically, women are marginalized by being at the center (of the looks) (cf. Rose, 1993). Used by an abuser, a "look" can be a weapon. Surveillance can be a way of reproducing and reinforcing male power. It is "opening up new possibilities for harassment and stalking" (Ainley, 1998, p. 92). Since the gender structure of the persons positioned on each side of the camera is as described above, there is a temptation to (mis)use surveillance for voyeuristic purposes.

Little by little, incidents come up which reveal exactly the kind of abuse by the cameras that women are most worried about. Leisure centers with male control operators have been observed to have cameras placed in women's changing rooms. Operators have been caught in using surveillance cameras to spy on women and then making obscene phone calls to them from the control room. Police officers have been reprimanded for improper voyeuristic use of surveillance cameras. Real and manipulated images from the surveillance system—including sex acts and other intimate contacts—have been edited onto tapes for commercial purposes, as was the case in Britain in 1996. (Goulding, 1996; Davies, 1997; Steinhardt, 1999).

In 1997 a piece of news circulated around Scandinavia which shocked and irritated women (e.g., *Helsingin Sanomat*, 1997). It had been discovered that Swedish conscript solders had been "entertaining" themselves in summer 1997 by monitoring women on a beach near their navy base. They had videotaped topless women, printed pictures of them, and hung these pictures on the walls of their barracks. Since the cameras used were meant for military purposes, they were of extremely high quality and, therefore, the pictures were quite explicit. This case, now being investigated as a crime, showed a glaring example of gendered abuse of surveillance cameras.

A comparable but perhaps even more abusive incident has been documented in Australia. Jean Hillier (1996, p. 99) described the course of events in summer 1994 at Burswood Casino where security camera operators had misused their access to control equipment:

The gendered case of male operators monitoring cameras located in women's toilets and artistes' changing rooms, as well as in the car parks and main body of the Casino, had zoomed in on images of women's exposed breasts, genital areas and buttocks, together with couples fondling each other or having sex, generally "hidden" behind large indoor plants, and a woman urinating in the car park. Individual sequences from the four-year period had been edited onto one tape and shown locally at house parties by the operator(s) responsible.

The story went under a headline "rape by camera" in local newspapers, and, according to Hillier (1996, p. 100), "caused major public outrage in Perth." It was followed by a widespread debate on surveillance, its legal and moral aspects, as well as on the blurring boundaries between public and private space and activities. The setting was also clearly gendered. It showed that there is a possibility of gendering of surveillance and control, and that surveillance can be used as an active instrument for harassment. Because of this possible "active" role in harassment, surveillance reproduces the embodiment and sexualization of women, and contributes to the process of masculinization of space.

GENDERED PERCEPTIONS ON SURVEILLANCE

I shall now go on further to discuss the practice of surveillance in greater detail. Some interview quotations are presented verbatim to explain the points made by the examples. These empirical illustrations are based on stories of 35 women from two series of in-depth interviews conducted in Helsinki, Finland, in spring 1996, and in Edinburgh, Scotland, in spring 1997.[2] The interviews were conducted as part of a larger study on women's fear of violence and their perceptions of video surveillance (Koskela, 1999). The purpose of this study was to complement previous knowledge on women's fear of violence and their attitudes toward surveillance.

In Finland, the interview sessions included questions on experienced violence, frightening and threatening situations, and patterns of moving about. One part was devoted to video surveillance. Women described what they knew about surveillance practice, how they feel when being monitored, and evaluated surveillance as a crime prevention measure. In Edinburgh, the structure and form of the interviews were quite different from the interviews conducted in Helsinki. Since previous research on women's fear of violence, based on in-depth interviews, was available (Pain, 1994), there was no need to cover this subject. Rather, the motive was to have reference material on women's perceptions of video surveillance. The sessions included brief discussion on planning measures and on women's notions of what could be done to reduce crime and fear of crime. This included questions on video surveillance. This part was somewhat more detailed than in the interviews conducted in Helsinki, including questions on the location of surveillance cameras, the authorities in charge of surveillance, the location of the monitoring rooms, etc.

The differences in the forms of the materials mean that the two types of material are not directly comparable but, rather, complementary. In principal, in-depth interviews offer deeper information than street interviews. However, there was a cultural difference: in Britain, fear of violence and questions related to surveillance, and even the gendered nature of urban space, have long been issues of public debate. In contrast, in Finland these themes were just emerging. This meant that the interviewees in Edinburgh were more capable in evaluating the issue from different points of view and, thus, methodological differences were not as significant as they could have been in another context.

Placeless and Faceless Surveillance

Increased visibility is perhaps the most crucial factor in surveillance. However, it has been noted that the public is not necessarily aware that they are being watched (Hillier, 1996; Lyon, 1994). Sometimes the cameras are hidden; sometimes the public just does not notice them. However, even if the cameras are seen, the public may still not be aware of the location of the monitoring rooms. The watchers themselves remain hidden.

This is apparent in shopping malls, which are of particular interest in relation to surveillance. The "semipublic" spaces of the malls, where surveillance has become espe-

---

[2]The 18 women who took part in interviews in Helsinki were recruited with the help of the National Consumer Research Centre, which had collected "a panel," a group of citizens representing different ages and social classes willing to take part in research projects. Of the women interviewed, some were outgoing, spending time in the city center at night almost every weekend, whereas others had small children and lived much more privatized and spatially restricted lives. Thus their relationships to urban space varied a lot. The interview sessions lasted for between 1.5 and 2.5 hours. The interviews were not formal or strictly structured, the aim being to encourage informal discussion and to direct the situation to take the form of a conversation. The interviews were tape-recorded with the permission of the participants, and later transcribed. In the street interviews of 17 women conducted in Edinburgh, women who took part were recruited as a random sample "on the street" in a shopping mall in the city center. The interviews were semistructured, and were conducted anonymously. In contrast to the in-depth interviews, in these interviews the form and the order of the questions were more formal, and most women answered the questions asked quite precisely without indulging in a conversation. The sessions were relatively short, lasting for between 15 and 20 minutes. These interviews were also tape-recorded with the permission of the interviewees and transcribed.

cially common, have become an essentially contradictory space—"space suggesting an openness that is in fact carefully exclusive" (Marcuse, 1997, p. 107). Surveillance is easy to use to exclude groups, which are marginal in relation to the purpose of the mall (Crawford, 1992; Shields, 1989; Judd, 1995). The increasing monitoring of city streets reflects the development in semipublic spaces. In Britain one manifested reason for city authorities installing video surveillance systems in city centers has been an effort to *match* the level of safety which the shopping malls and out-of-town business parks have been able to offer (Fyfe and Bannister, 1998; also Brown, 1995; Fyfe et al., 1998). Shopping malls have in this sense become *icons* for urban space. Consequently, the purification and homogenization processes and the "erosion of public space" will increasingly spread from malls and shopping centers to open publicly owned urban space.

In Edinburgh my motive for conducting the interviews *in a shopping mall* was to analyze answers on where and how women perceived surveillance being conducted, while the interviews took place almost literally under a surveillance camera. Some women had noticed cameras in the mall or elsewhere in their daily environments while others had not. Also women's conceptions of the identity of the persons behind the camera and where they are located varied depending on each particular context. Even if they had seen the cameras they had no information on the identity or location of the persons behind the camera.

Interviewer: Would you know who is there watching behind the camera?

Jill: Do I know? No. I assume it would be authorities that would be watching. I hope so, anyway.

Lorraine: That's another question. No, not usually, but, maybe some independent body, or maybe the police are watching.

Fiona: I'm not sure who's watching, no.

Interviewer: Would you know where they are?

Fiona: Um, probably in an office somewhere, I don't know.

From the location of the camera it is impossible to infer the location of the persons behind the camera. There is hardly ever a direct contact between the security personnel and the public. Under a surveillance camera one does not know whether there is anybody looking, and if there is someone, who they are or how far away they are. Even the vertical perception is blurred: one does not know whether the overseers are above or below. Surveillance cameras have been conceptualized as being "literally above" (Fyfe and Bannister, 1998), they survey from "above the crowd," "up there." But quite often the case is actually not this simple. The camera is placed on a high position and seems to be looking at people from above but the monitoring room may be for example in the basement of a shopping mall where the premises are cheaper (Koskela, 1995).

Furthermore, not only can the monitoring room be on another floor of a building; it is possible to have monitoring conducted in a different country. In Finland, for example, there is a temptation to hire guards from Estonia where labor costs are much lower. In theory, the observation of the streets of Helsinki could very well take place in Tallinn. Hence, with contemporary technical abilities, video surveillance is *placeless*. This makes it difficult to ask for help through the agency of the camera when help is needed. Therefore, this kind of ostensibly innocent politics of locations is of great importance.

The context of the interviews in Helsinki was somewhat different from those in Edinburgh since there are commonly used metro stations where surveillance cameras are most visible and security guards also patrol by foot. Thus, most women knew that the guards also take care of the monitoring and commonly associated surveillance cameras with them. However, even when they knew who was watching they did not feel that they could contact them. In the metro stations the windows through which the guards look at the public are either dark or mirror-like. It is not self-evident that people know what is behind these nontransparent windows, and even if they do it is impossible to see whether there is someone inside or not.

> *Interviewer:* What do you think about surveillance cameras? There has been some discussion in the media lately, but what about you yourself? Have you paid attention to the cameras in your everyday life?

> *Kristiina:* I don't know. I wonder how do they work in practice. In the metro stations the situation is quite strange. There are the security rooms, where the guards are, and this glass-wall through which I can't see, and then there are the cameras. The guards could be looking at the monitors even if I was being mugged right there just one meter away on the platform.

To people under surveillance the forces of vigilance are the potential helpers who should intervene if they are attacked. In the contemporary urban architecture, forms are transparent from one side and opaque from the other and have became what Steven Flusty (1994) called "stealthy" and "jittery" space. Although the purpose of surveillance is supposed to be to increase safety, this design produces uncertainty instead, leaving the public passive and unable to be subjects of their own being.

It is clear that one's attitude toward surveillance depends on perceptions of the trustworthiness of the persons behind the camera. The women who knew who was watching often expressed suspicion toward security guards hired by private companies. In a discussion on how to ask for help through a surveillance camera, the interviewees pointed out that, not only the camera feels anonymous but, also, if there is a person behind it, it is not clear that this person is reliable.

> *Riikka:* I don't know but I don't really trust these private security services. I think they [the guards] are very arbitrary and I have somehow an awfully bad image of them.

Compared to social control created by the presence of other people, control accomplished with surveillance is not only placeless but also *faceless*. As much as ensuring security, the practices of surveillance are disrupting social control. One crucial problem in video surveillance is definitely its facelessness.

What supports the faceless image is "the politics of naming." In Finland the police—which is the only institution that legally has to inform the public about surveillance—uses the expression "technical surveillance" (tekninen valvonta) which does not reveal what the practice exactly is. The media has gradually started to use the term "safety camera" (turvakamera) instead of the term "surveillance camera" (valvontakamera) previously used. In Britain the abbreviation CCTV (closed circuit television) is commonly used. This expression echoes a technological jargon related to surveillance which is more naturally used by the experts behind a surveillance camera than the citizens walking under the camera.

There is also a great deal of variation in the degree of concealment of surveillance activities. The politics of veiling or unveiling surveillance varies from concealed "postage stamp sized spy cameras" to clear announcement signs and cameras placed on visible sites. The hidden agenda of surveillance seems to be that the public should know as little as possible about how and by whom they are monitored. For example, a managing direc-tor of one of the main malls in Helsinki city center recently gave an interview in which he clearly stated that "it is better that this matter [i.e., video surveillance] is known by as few as possible" (Koskela, 2000b). Another, just the opposite, attitude toward surveillance can be seen in the London underground or in shops where surveillance is clearly announced with such stickers as "For your security these premises are protected by a video surveil-lance system." The latter policies are more beneficial as they aim for an increased feeling of trust and safety.

Accountability is of great importance. Some countries, such as Britain, have *a code of practice* for surveillance (Simmons, 1996) while in other countries the discussion is yet to begin. Some cities have a policy of allowing public viewing or having specific visitors' hours to the control rooms in order to show the public that a system is not being abused. Also nongovernmental organizations, such as the Privacy International and the American Civil Liberties Union, spread knowledge and critical discussion on surveillance, urge sup-port for privacy laws to limit the use of surveillance, and take responsibility for "counter surveillance." A massive amount of discussion on surveillance takes place on the Internet. Surveillance cameras are seen as threatening privacy, as an infringement to urban citi-zens' right of anonymity and free mobility. Virtual space—as it has been argued—offers a space for more intensive and subtle surveillance than ever before (e.g., Curry, 1997; Lyon, 1998; 2001; Graham, 1998), but it also offers a place for resistance.

Unverifiability as an Emotional Experience

The emotional experience of being watched by a surveillance camera is different from that of being watched by a person directly. On an emotional level, the attitudes on surveil-lance are anything but straightforward. The variety of feelings surveillance evokes are enormous: the objects watched can feel guilty without reason, embarrassed or uneasy, irritated or angry, fearful; also safe (Koskela, 1999). On the one hand surveillance cam-eras increase security but on the other hand they produce mistrust. Surveillance is ambiv-alent: it appears to evoke simultaneous positive and negative feelings. After a discussion on fear of violence, the question of how to improve safety was pointed at surveillance cameras:

Interviewer: What do you think about surveillance cameras?

Petra (Helsinki): I think they are good and I don't find them as invading my privacy. But I also don't think they increase security. Even if there is a camera somewhere, I feel no safer at all.

Maria (Helsinki): Maybe they increase security. I wouldn't condemn them. But still I feel like "Big Brother" is watching if there's a camera.

Nadja (Helsinki): It is a two-edged sword. On one hand it is good that the cameras are there but on the other hand when something happens it doesn't help at all at the moment.

Unverifiability is a crucial dimension for maintaining power. Not all the cameras are placed so they can be seen and even if one sees the cameras it is impossible to infer whether there is somebody looking at that particular moment or not. Just as in the panoptic prison, "the inmate must never know whether he is being looked at at any moment; but he must be sure that he may always be so." (Foucault, 1977, p. 201). "While watching is only sporadic, the threat of being watched never ceases" (Hannah, 1997b, p. 347). The very notion that "you never know" is one of the most important reasons for mistrust:

Interviewer: How do you personally feel being surveilled?

Diane (Edinburgh): Probably safer. As long as someone is at the other end watching it (laugh). That's what you'd wanna know, wouldn't you?

Viivi (Helsinki): Somehow I feel safer if there's a camera. But on the other hand you can't always be sure that someone is looking, because there are lots of "dark" cameras. It would be nice if they had a red light on, or if they moved or something.

Surveillance is about "regulation of bodily and other visible activities" (Hannah, 1997a, p. 171). According to the conventional Foucauldian conceptualization of surveillance, the bodies under surveillance do not need to be regulated since they regulate themselves. They are "docile bodies" (Foucault, 1977). The camera works as a reminder of possible scrutiny, as a "deterrent" (Oc and Tiesdell, 1997). This perhaps ensures discipline but it simultaneously erodes confidence.

The Help That Comes Too Late

Despite all the policing with surveillance cameras, there is little agreement among researchers about whether surveillance cameras actually reduce crime (Flusty, 1994; Fyfe and Bannister, 1998; Takala, 1998). Studies on surveillance have produced contradictory results. There is evidence that surveillance causes "displacement" of crime, since whereas the areas under surveillance become safer, the areas not covered by cameras become more dangerous (Tilley, 1993; Fyfe and Bannister, 1996). Sometimes, however, cameras can "spread" their influence so that crime rates are reduced both in areas under surveillance and in the surrounding areas (Poyner, 1992; Brown, 1995). Studies suggest that the use of cameras has reduced property crime such as criminal damage, vehicle crime, theft, and burglary (Fyfe and Bannister, 1996; Brown, 1995). There is much less evidence showing that cameras can reduce violent crime, such as battery and sexual violence. Sexual offenses in particular are most common in places, which are rarely monitored, such as parks, suburban areas, and private space. Consequently, video surveillance is severely limited as a crime prevention measure since it is mainly effective in fighting the least serious crimes and not violent crimes or sexual offenses.

The strength of surveillance lies less in preventing offenses than in coordinating a response (Oc and Tiesdell, 1997). Perhaps the most severe restriction video surveillance has, as a means for increasing safety is that the help, which it is able to offer, is *backward*. In relation to property crime the gains of effective response are much more incontestable than in relation to violent crime. Sexual violence is of a different order in this respect: its effects are so serious that prevention is of much more value than any reaction after the violence has taken place. For a victim of violence the help mediated by a camera may come too late. Women clearly indicate this as a crucial reason for their mistrusting toward video surveillance:

Interviewer: Would video surveillance make you personally feel safer?

Jo (Edinburgh): The harm would be done then, you know. If somebody's watching it won't stop it happening.

Claire (Edinburgh): You know, you still can get mugged, if the video is there or not. And if they can catch the person who's done that to you, you know, it's like closing the door after the horse has bolted.

Petra (Helsinki): I think they [surveillance cameras] are good as long as there is always somebody watching and it isn't just like you afterwards notice that, oh, somebody was being mugged, what a shame.

In case of an attack it might be possible to use the videotape to catch the offender(s), and use it as evidence in court, but this would never erase the actual experience of violence.

"There Should be a Limit Somewhere"

It should be discussed in which cases surveillance justifies its place and where in goes "over the limit." It is not only the extreme cases of abuse of surveillance described above which should be questioned but also some legal practices. What was regarded as most worrying were the concealed cameras. Secrecy can encourage doubt and uncertainty. If you cannot see that you are being watched, you cannot act accordingly. For many women a (visible) camera made a difference on how they act and thus concealed cameras were considered insulting. Privacy is regarded to be invaded when the possibility of self-control is destroyed by hiding the cameras from the eye of the public. The question of privacy was discussed in both interviews, in Edinburgh as well as in Helsinki:

Interviewer: Does it make you feel safe yourself?

Lorraine (Edinburgh): That, yeah. Yes I think so. ... I think they could be used if they are used effectively enough, if they are placed in the places where they need to be put. In certain areas you don't need the cameras but in high risk areas, then probably yeah.

Jill (Edinburgh): I hope that if there was video surveillance it would be pointing at an area, and watching what's going on in that area, and not watching a specific person in that area. That's what I would hope that would be.

Veera (Helsinki): I think it's good to have them in places such as the railway station, where there are thefts and broken windows, and in shops of course, but what shocked me was that they are in some fitting rooms.... There should be a limit somewhere.

Indeed, the discussion on what kind of spaces should be legally allowed to be watched goes on in many countries. However, it seems to be that the "hype" surrounding new technologies often overruns critical discussions. We should ask is surveillance justified at any time in any spaces? Concerns for privacy rise—and, indeed, should rise—whenever surveillance is targeted toward activities regarded as intimate. This is especially important since the new advanced equipment makes it technically possible to see and tape at dusk and in the dark, and some images can even be caught from behind a wall (Privacy International, 1995). Questions on invasion of privacy are tied up with the experience of human dignity. Clearly, surveillance is more appropriate in some places than in others.

CONCLUSIONS

This article has examined some of the numerous problems related to the rapidly increasing surveillance. The urban experience of being watched through a surveillance camera is only one of the approaches to surveillance. Further, video surveillance is only one of the new forms of technological control. An important challenge for future research is to extend the perspective to cover surveillance in virtual space as well as in real urban space—and, within the field of urban geography, even more importantly, to examine the ever more complex ways these two are linked. At present, the marketing of computer integrated CCTV's is intense and the expansion of "webcams"—turned to both public and private space and distributing the real-time pictures to the audience on the Internet—is massive. The Internet is, indeed, more and more often connecting "local gazes" with the global community (Green, 1999). With computerization, surveillance is becoming more subtle and intense than ever before. When surveillance cameras are combined with visitors' registers and "people-finding tools," such as computerized face recognition systems, supervision and monitoring touches a wide range of issues around privacy and human rights. Even though the experience of being under surveillance usually deals with real time urban space, which has been the focus of this article, it can be argued that the contemporary "superpanopticon" exists in electronic environments (Lyon, 1994, 1998). There clearly is a need to understand more about the new forms of surveillance and the complex power relations that are produced by surveillance.

By discussing the issues of gender and surveillance I have endeavored to increase understanding of the interacting emotional and power-related processes that play a role in producing space. Space is produced, among other things, by the practice of surveillance, both "behind" and "in front of" a surveillance camera. Ever increasing surveillance will challenge us to reconstruct our notions of space. An interesting question related to surveillance is whether it will contribute in making space more or less public. The ostensible aim is to make space more public—in that sense that a safer space is more available for different groups, and it has been pointed out that one of the reasons why public space has perhaps never been truly public is that threat of violence has restricted women's use of space. However, if women's attitudes toward surveillance are controversial—as the interviews in this study suggest—and if surveillance is perceived as insulting privacy—surveillance can also be seen as making space less public. It is not "opening up public spaces" (Lyon, 2001, p. 135) but rather creating predetermined, calculated, and rigid urban space.

Nevertheless, surveillance is not just a technical solution but is connected with wider issues of criminal policy. Surveillance cameras do not deal with the reasons behind problems but only try to heal symptoms. Video surveillance is an easy solution for politicians and decision-makers. However, surveillance should be discussed in relation to more widespread social questions: crime and fear of crime should be regarded as problems that relate to inequality and polarization in societies. The use of technical surveillance is a solution that supports rather than criticizes the existing order. The questions of inequality are beyond the reach of technical surveillance. Fear and crime are definitely a part of a larger problem and the main focus of debate should be extended to cover more political issues than the technical ability of surveillance cameras.

> *Anne (Edinburgh):* I think it's just avoiding responsibility. Nobody has the responsibility, or the camera does. The responsibility has been given to the camera.... It's like avoiding the problem, not solving it, like sweeping the problem under the carpet.

What is comes to gender relations, it is clear that surveillance does not replace or erase other forms of embodiment: women still encounter sexual harassment and objectifying attitudes in face-to-face contacts in urban space. Surveillance can be understood as the "reembodiment" of women, as "an extension of male gaze." It has been declared that more information is needed about "how disciplinary power operates in connection with other tools of class and gender oppression" (Hannah, 1997a, p. 179). Arguably, in most cases the practice of surveillance contributes to perpetuating the existing imbalance in gender relations rather than challenging it.

This article has shown that the relationship between gender and surveillance is highly problematic. While surveillance might increase the safety of some women in some places, a more detailed examination shows that it also has many features which are problematic. What is of concern to women—and even more generally, if an increased feeling of safety is aimed at—is not only whether some places are monitored or not but rather the more widespread politics of surveillance. To meet the aim of increased safety and confidence, it is essential to eliminate any possibilities of abuse of the system. To avoid abuse, it is essential to have a clear regulation and an agreed code of practice for surveillance. This condition is yet to come.

What must not be forgotten, however, is that there is always an element of resistance. Control is never completely hegemonic. Surveillance can be turned to "countersurveil-lance," to a weapon for those who are oppressed. It is possible, for example, to use a surveillance camera to protect oneself as was recently done in Finland by a woman who had experienced violence. She had to prove that an offender had violated the restraining order given by the court, and installed a surveillance camera on her own front door to catch the offender on tape (Koskela, 2000b). Indeed, gender relations can be turned upside down.

Just as the new forms of control are widespread, so are the new forms of resistance creative. The ways to show disapproval are numerous. For example, the New York, NY Civil Liberties Union keeps up the debate about surveillance and, among other means, maintains a map on the Internet with all the surveillance cameras of New York, NY on it (New York City Surveillance Camera Project, 2000). Anyone who spots a camera, which is not on the map, can add it to this www-site. Further, the international Privacy International organization each year presents the "Big Brother" awards "to the government and private sector organizations which have done the most to threaten personal privacy in their countries" (Privacy International, 2000). The theater group Surveillance Camera Players, is another example of turning the pieces of this play upside down. An old play, presented to an audience placed behind a surveillance camera, and suddenly new meanings are revealed. The overseers who expect—and are expected—to watch the "real" world, at "real time," end up being the audience for a fictional play, suddenly, at any time, anywhere. As the theater group announces: "Meet the Surveillance Camera Players—coming to a video monitor near you." Don't miss it!

REFERENCES

Ainley, R.,1998, Watching the detectors: Control and the panopticon. In R. Ainley, editor, *New Frontiers of Space, Bodies and Gender.* London, UK: Routledge, 88–100.

Björk, M., 1991, Women as planners—a difference in visions: A conference on building and planning on women's terms. *Scandinavian Housing and Planning Research,* Vol. 8, 45–49.

Blakely, E. J. and Snyder, M. G., 1997, Divided we fall: Gated and walled communities in the United States. In N. Ellin, editor, *The Architecture of Fear.* New York, NY: Princeton Architectural Press, 85–99.

Boys, J., 1999, Positions in the landscape? Gender, space and the "nature" of virtual reality. In Cutting Edge, The Women's Research Group, editors, *Desire by Design. Body, Territories and New Technologies.* London, UK: I. B. Tauris, 183–202.

Brown, B., 1995, CCTV in town centres: Three case studies. *Crime Detection and Prevention Series,* Paper 68. London, UK: Home Office Police Research Group.

Brown, S., 1998, What's the problem, girls? CCTV and the gendering of public safety. In C. Norris, J. Moran and G. Armstrong, editors, *Surveillance, Closed Circuit Television and Social Control.* Aldershot, UK: Ashgate, 207–220.

Crawford, M., 1992, The world in a shopping mall. In M. Sorkin, editor, *Variations on a Theme Park. The New American City and the End of Public Space*. New York, NY: Noonday, 3–30.

Curry, M. R., 1997, The digital individual and the private realm. *Annals of the Association of American Geographers*, Vol. 87, 681–699.

Davies, S., 1997, KDIS Online. 10 reasons why public CCTV schemes are bad. *Privacy International*, April 28. Retrieved August 8, 1999 from http://merlin.legend.org.uk/~brs/cctv/tenrea sons.html

Davis, M., 1990, *The City of Quartz. Excavating the Future in Los Angeles*. New York, NY: Vintage.

Davis, M., 1992, Fortress Los Angeles: The militarization of urban space. In M. Sorkin, editor, *Variations on a Theme Park: The New American City and the End of Public Space*. New York, NY: Noonday, 154–180.

Dear, M. and Flusty, S., 1998, Postmodern urbanism. *Annals of the Association of American Geographers*, Vol. 88, 50–72.

Domosh, M., 1998, Those "Gorgeous incongruities": Polite politics and public space on the streets of nineteenth-century New York, NY City. *Annals of the Association of American Geographers*, Vol. 88, 209–226.

Duncan, N., 1996, Renegotiating gender and sexuality in public and private spaces. In N. Duncan, editor, *BodySpace: Destabilizing Geographies of Gender and Sexuality*. London, UK: Routledge, 127–145.

Ellin, N., 1996, *Postmodern Urbanism*. Oxford, UK: Blackwell.

Ellin, N., 1997, editor, *The Architecture of Fear*. New York, NY: Princeton Architectural Press.

Flusty, S., 1994, *Building Paranoia: The Proliferation of Interdictory Space and the Erosion of Spatial Justice*. Los Angeles, CA: Los Angeles Forum for Architecture and Urban Design.

Foucault, M., 1977, *Discipline and Punish: The Birth of a Prison*. London, UK: Penguin.

Friberg, T., 1993, Everyday Life: Women's Adaptive Strategies in Time and Space. *Lund Studies in Geography*, Series B, Human Geography. Lund, Sweden: Lund University Press.

Fyfe, N. R. and Bannister, J., 1996, City watching: Closed circuit television surveillance in public spaces. *Area*, Vol. 28, 37–46.

Fyfe, N. R. and Bannister, J., 1998, The "eyes upon the street": Closed circuit television surveillance and the city. In N. R. Fyfe, editor, *Images of the Street: Representation, Experience and Control in Public Space*. London, UK: Routledge, 254–267.

Fyfe, N. R., Bannister, J. and Kearns, A., 1998, Closed circuit television and the city. In C. Norris, J. Moran and G. Armstrong, editors, *Surveillance, Closed Circuit Television and Social Control*. Aldershot, UK: Ashgate, 21–39.

Fyfe, N. R., 1995, Policing the city. *Urban Studies*, Vol. 32, 759–778.

Gardner, C. B., 1995, *Passing By. Gender and Public Harassment*. Berkeley, CA: University of California Press.

Gilbert, M. R., 1997, Feminism and difference in urban geography. *Urban Geography*, Vol. 18, 166–179.

Gordon, M. T. and Riger, S., 1989, *The Female Fear: The Social Cost of Rape*. Urbana, IL: University of Illinois Press.

Goulding, B., 1996, *Caught in the act!* (videocassette). NTV Entertainment.

Graham, S., 1998, Spaces of surveillant simulation: New technologies, digital representations, and material geographies. *Environment and Planning D: Society and Space*, Vol. 16, 483–504.

Greed, C. H., 1994, *Women and Planning. Creating Gendered Realities*. London, UK: Routledge.

Green, S., 1999, A plague on the Panoptician: Surveillance and power in the global information economy. *Information, Communication & Society*, Vol. 2. Retrieved August 9, 2000 from wysiwyg://51/http://www.infosoc.co.uk/00105/ab2/htm

Gregory, D. and Urry, R., 1985, editors, *Social Relations and Spatial Structures*. Hampshire, UK: Macmillan.

Hannah, M., 1997a, Space and the structuring of disciplinary power: An interpretive review. *Geografiska Annaler*, Vol. 79B, 171–180.

Hannah, M., 1997b, Imperfect panopticism: Envisioning the construction of normal lives. In G. Benko and U. Stohmayer, editors, *Space and Social Theory. Interpreting Modernity and Postmodernity*. Oxford, UK: Blackwell, 344–359.

Helsingin Sanomat, 1997, "Ruotsin varusmiehet videoivat rannikolla sukellusveneiden sijasta nakutyttöjä" ["Swedish soldiers videotape naked girls instead of submarines"], December 17.

Herbert, S., 1996, The geopolitics of the police: Foucault, disciplinary power and the tactics of the Los Angeles Police Department. *Political Geography*, Vol. 15, 47–59.

Hillier, J., 1996, The gaze in the city: Video surveillance in Perth. *Australian Geographical Studies*, Vol. 34, 95v105.

Honess, T. and Charman E., 1992, Closed circuit television in public places. *Crime Prevention Unit Series*, Paper 35. London, UK: Home Office Police Research Group.

Jacobs, J., 1961, *The Death and Life of Great American Cities*. Harmondsworth, UK: Penguin.

Jameson, F., 1991, *Postmodernism, or the Cultural Logic of Late Capitalism*. London, UK: Verso.

Judd, D. R., 1995, The rise of the new walled cities. In H. Liggett and D. C. Perry, editors, *Spatial Practices. Critical Explorations in Social/Spatial Theory*. Thousand Oaks, CA: Sage, 144–166.

Koskela, H., 1995, Sähköinen silmä on ystäväsi? Elektronisen valvonnan kaupunkimaantiedettä. [The electronic eye is your friend? Urban geography of electronic surveillance] *Yhteiskuntasuunnittelu*, Vol. 33, 4–15.

Koskela, H., 1999, Fear, control and space. Geographies of gender, fear of violence and video surveillance. Helsinki, Finland: *Helsingin Yliopiston Maantieteen Laitoksen Julkaisuja* A137. [Publication A137 of the Department of Geography at the University of Helsinki].

Koskela, H., 2000a, The gaze without eyes: Video surveillance and the changing nature of urban space. *Progress in Human Geography,* Vol. 24, 243–265.

Koskela, H., 2000b, Turva-kamera-kontrolli: kadun näkymättömät katseet [Security-camera-control: the invisible eyes on the street], In Stadipiiri, editors, *URBS. Kirja Helsingin Kaupunkikulttuurista* [*URBS. A Book on Urban Culture in Helsinki*]. Helsinki, Finland: The City of Helsinki Information Management Centre, 167–181.

Lees, L., 1998, Urban renaissance and the street. Spaces of control and contestation. In N. R. Fyfe, editor, *Images of the Street: Representation, Experience and Control in Public Space*. London, UK: Routledge, 236–253.

Little, J., Peake, L. and Richardson P., 1988, editors, *Women in Cities. Gender and the Urban Environment*. Hampshire, UK: Macmillan.

Lyon, D., 1994, *The Electronic Eye. The Rise of Surveillance Society*. Cambridge, UK: Polity.

Lyon, D., 1998, The World Wide Web of surveillance. The Internet and off-world power-flows. *Information, Communication & Society*, Vol. 1. Retrieved August 20, 1999 from wysiwyg://36/http://www.infosoc.co.uk/00101/feature/htm

Lyon, D., 2001, *Surveillance Society. Monitoring Everyday Life*. Buckingham, UK: Open University Press.

Marcuse, P., 1997, Walls of fear and walls of support. In N. Ellin, editor, *The Architecture of Fear*. New York, NY: Princeton Architectural Press, 101–114.

Massey, D., 1994, *Space, Place and Gender*. Cambridge, UK: Polity.

Matrix, 1984, *Making Space. Women and the Man-Made Environment*. London, UK: Pluto.

McDowell, L., 1993, Space, place and gender relations: Part II. Identity, difference, feminist geometries and geographies. *Progress in Human Geography*, Vol. 17, 305–318.

Merry, S., 1981, *Urban Danger: Life in a Neighbourhood of Strangers*. Philadelphia, PA: Temple University Press.

Mitchell, D., 1995, The end of public space? People's Park, definitions of the public, and democracy. *Annals of the Association of American Geographers*, Vol. 85, 108–133.

Nast, H. J. and Kobayashi, A., 1996, Re-corporealizing vision. In N. Duncan, editor, *Body Space: Destabilizing Geographies of Gender and Sexuality*. London, UK: Routledge, 75–93.

Newman, O., 1972, *Defensible Space*. New York, NY: Macmillan.

New York City Surveillance Camera Project, 2000, *Surveillance Camera Project Summary*. Retrieved from http://www.mediaeater.com/cameras/summary.html

NordREFO, 1989, Kvinnor och regional utveckling. [Women and regional development], Vol. 19, No. 1.

Oc, T. and Tiesdell, S., 1997, Safer city centres: The role of closed circuit television. In T. Oc and S. Tiesdell, editors, *Safer City Centres. Reviving the Public Realm*. London, UK: Paul Chapman, 130–142.

Pain, R., 1991, Space, sexual violence and social control: Integrating geographical and feminist analyses of women's fear of crime. *Progress in Human Geography*, Vol. 15, 415–431.

Poyner, B., 1992, Situational crime prevention in two parking facilities. In R.V. Clarke, editor, *Situational Crime Prevention: Successful Case Studies*. New York, NY: Harrow and Heston, 174–184.

Privacy International, 1995, *Privacy International statement on closed circuit television (CCTV) surveillance devices*. Retrieved April 29, 2002 from http://www.privacy.org/pi/issues/cctv/statement.html

Privacy International, 2000, *The big brother awards*. Retrieved April 29, 2002 from http://www.privacy international.org/bigbrother

Rose, G., 1993, *Feminism and Geography. The Limits of Geographical Knowledge*. Minneapolis, MN: University of Minnesota Press.

Shields, R., 1989, Social spatialization and the built environment: The West Edmonton mall. *Environment and Planning D: Society and Space*, Vol. 7, 147–164.

Simmons, M., 1996, Who's watching the watchers? *The Guardian*, March 13.

Simonsen, K., 1990, Urban division of space: A gender category! The Danish case. *Scandinavian Housing and Planning Research*, Vol. 7, 143–153.

Smith, S. J., 1987, Fear of crime: Beyond a geography of deviance. *Progress in Human Geography*, Vol. 11, 1–23.

Soja, E. W., 1989, *Postmodern Geographies. The Reassertion of Space in Critical Social Theory*. London, UK: Verso.

Soja, E. W., 1996, *Thirdspace. Journeys to Los Angeles and Other Real-and-Imagined Places*. Cambridge, MA: Blackwell.

Soja, E. W., 1997, Six discourses on the postmetropolis. In S. Westwood and J. Williams, editors, *Imagining Cities. Scripts, Signs, Memory*. London, UK: Routledge, 19–30.

Steinhardt, B., 1999, *ACLU calls on law enforcement to support privacy laws for public video surveillance*. Retrieved April 29, 2002 from http://www.aclu.org/news/1999/n040899b.html

Surveillance Camera Players, 2000, *The Surveillance Camera Players: Completely distrustful of all government*. Retrieved April 29, 2002 from http://www.notbored.org/the-scp.html

Takala, H., 1998, Videovalvonta ja rikollisuuden ehkäisy. [Video surveillance and crime prevention]. Helsinki, Finland: *National Research Institute of Legal Policy, Research Communications*, Paper 41.

Tilley, N., 1993, Understanding car parks, crime and CCTV: Evaluation lessons from safer cities. *Crime Prevention Unit Series*, Paper 42. London, UK: Home Office Police Research Group.

Trench, S., 1997, Safer transport and parking. In T. Oc and S. Tiesdell, editors, *Safer City Centres. Reviving the Public Realm*. London, UK: Paul Chapman, 143–155.

Trench, S., Oc, T. and Tiesdell, S., 1992, Safer cities for women: Perceived risks and planning measures. *Town Planning Review*, Vol. 63, 279–296.

Turva-alan kehittäminen [Improving the security field], 1998. Helsinki, Finland: *Publications of the Ministry of Internal Affairs*, April.

Urban Geography, 1996, Vol. 17, No. 2, Special issue: Public space and the city.

Valentine, G., 1989, The geography of women's fear, *Area*, Vol. 21, 385–390.

Wajcman, J., 1991, *Feminism Confronts Technology*. Cambridge: Polity.

Whitaker, R., 1999, *The End of Privacy. How Total Surveillance Is Becoming a Reality*. New York, NY: The New Press.

Wekerle, G. R. and Whitzman, C., 1995, *Safe Cities: Guidelines for Planning, Design and Management*. New York, NY: Van Nostrand Reinhold.

Part III
Undercover Police Surveillance

[13]

Undercover policing in Canada: Wanting what is wrong

JEAN-PAUL BRODEUR
Centre International de Criminologie Comparée, Université de Montréal, Canada

Marx (1988) devotes three chapters to an examination of the intended and unintended consequences of undercover policing. The aim of this paper is to discuss the implications of the concepts of intended and unintended consequences of undercover policing and to identify some of these consequences within the Canadian context. In Marx (1988: 130), intended and unintended consequences of undercover policing coincide respectively with the desirable and undesirable consequences of this type of policing. I shall argue that a large number of the undesirable consequences of undercover policing can be viewed as intentional, in the legal sense of the word.

The paper is divided into three parts. First, I discuss specific features of the Canadian context of undercover policing and I briefly describe the Canadian policing apparatus. Second, I analyze the meaning of intended/unintended consequences in the field of undercover policing. Finally, I identify some of these consequences and classify them according to four categories, namely (i) consequences which are desirable, from a law enforcement perspective, and intended; (ii) consequences which are desirable and unintended; (iii) consequences which are undesirable and intended and (iv) consequences which are undesirable and unintended. In my conclusion I argue that the dichotomy between intended and unintended consequences is too narrow to account for the consequences of undercover policing.

1. Undercover operations in the Canadian context

In this paper, "undercover policing" is understood as policing operations which are covert and involve deception. This characterization is faithful to Gary Marx's concept of undercover policing (Marx, 1988: 12). There is a feature of Marx's account that deserves some discussion. Marx (1988: 12) characterizes undercover policing as *active* as opposed to passive surveillance. I believe that the line between active and passive undercover police operations is rather blurred and that the contrast between these two kinds of operations tends to be more salient depending on what model of undercover policing one is using.

106

I think that the model that Marx (1988) is using is that of police entrapment, a good example of which is a sting operation or a police controlled purchase of drugs ("buy and bust"). The following is a description of a true undercover operation as proposed by Marx (1988: 12).

> Unobtrusive surveillance does not directly intervene to shape the suspect's environment, perceptions, or behaviour. (...) Undercover work is both *covert* and *deceptive*. (...) Unlike conventional police work ..., the investigation may go on *before* and *during* the commission of the offence. It may start with the offender and only later document the offence. Discovery of the offender, the offence, and arrest may occur almost simultaneously. (emphasis in text)

Relying on this model involves a conception of undercover operations that I shall characterize as personalized and as dynamic. By personalized, I mean that undercover work is viewed as involving deceptive relationships between individual persons who hide their identities. By dynamic, I refer to the fact that deception is conceived to be more than artifice. It is artifice used to shape behaviour, in other words, it is manipulation. According to this conception, secret electronic surveillance is covert, but it is not deceptive and consequently does not qualify as undercover policing.

This conception of undercover policing is certainly defendable. Yet, it runs into difficulties. In Canada, the law which forbids electronic surveillance unless it is authorized by judicial warrant, defines a private communication as "any oral communication or any telecommunication made under circumstances in which it is reasonable for the originator thereof to expect that it will not be intercepted by any person other than the originator thereof to receive it." (*Canadian Criminal Code*, s. 178.1). If activists involved in the protection of the environment suddenly learned that their telephone lines were tapped, I believe they would feel that they were deceived in their reasonable expectation that their conversations were private. The deception in this case could be said to be systemic. It is performed on behalf of the State by anonymous agents. This does not make it any less deceptive.

A second difficulty is that the mere collection of intelligence can by itself involve a fair amount of active deception, even if its purpose is merely to learn something and not eventually to perform the arrest of an offender. Actually, the collection of intelligence may in itself involve a great deal of undercover work – surreptitious entry, covert search and seizure, mail opening, etc. In a very elaborate operation, the RCMP Security Service stole a computer disk storing a list of all members of the autonomist *Parti Québécois* (PQ) in order to copy it (the disk was returned unbeknownst to its owner during the same night that it was taken). This operation, whose sole purpose was the collection of information, would surely qualify as undercover work. It involved actively deceiving many people (a locksmith, the personnel of the computer company where the disk was stored, and eventually the police of Montreal if anything went wrong during the operation; nothing did). The *PQ* was never aware of the police break in until 5 years later. During this interval, the covert operation could not be said to have influenced the P.Q.'s behaviour. Hence it did not involve active deception with regard to its target and would probably not qualify as an undercover operation under Gary Marx's characterization, although it was certainly perceived as such in Canada.

I shall now provide some background on the Canadian context of undercover operations; first, a few general statements on the situation in Canada and afterwards a brief description of the Canadian policing apparatus.

The Canadian context

There is a series of points that need to be made in order to understand the Canadian situation in relation to undercover operations. Some of these points are very general, such as the unjustified reputation that Canada enjoys of being a liberal country. Together with the Soviet Union, the Eastern Bloc countries, Saudi Arabia and South Africa, Canada originally abstained from voting in favour of the United Nation's *Universal Charter of Rights* in 1948 (Brodeur, 1990: 263). In line with the rigid conservatism that permeates this country, police are granted a broad license by the law to exercise surveillance and investigative powers. In absolute numbers, the Canadian police intercepts private communications twice as frequently as the U.S. police (Law Reform Commission of Canada, 1986: 10). Taking into account that the U.S. is ten times as populated as Canada, the Canadian police resort to electronic surveillance twenty times more often than their U.S. colleagues. Many other examples could be cited, particularly in the field of the use of police informers.

This general point having been made, I will raise some issues that are more specific.

Political surveillance
In Canada, undercover policing is associated with political policing – particularly, counterterrorism – in both public and learned opinion. This situation is owed to the fact that almost everything that is publicly known about undercover policing in Canada was learned through the revelations of public commissions of inquiry that dealt exclusively with aspects of political policing.

Canada experienced a wave of terrorism from the early 1960s until 1973. In order to counter terrorism and French Canadian separatism, the police had to rely on an aggressive style of undercover operations, which occasionally resulted in a breach of human rights. Many of the commissions of inquiry on the police were appointed to investigate these violations of human rights, as in

108

the U.S. were the Church Committee, the Pike Committee and the Rockefeller Commission (see Johnson, 1985). From 1966 to 1981, there were no less than 6 major commissions that investigated the RCMP Security Service. These were: the Wells Commission (Canada, 1966a), the Spence Commission (Canada, 1966b), the Mackenzie Commission (Canada, 1969), the McDonald Commission (Canada, 1980 and 1981a and b), the Keable Commission (Québec, 1980) and the Krever Commission (Ontario, 1980). To the reports of these commissions must be added those of two Special Senate Committees appointed to investigate counterterrorism (Canada, Senate, 1987 and 1989) and, since 1985, the annual reports of the Security Intelligence Review Committee (SIRC). SIRC was created in 1984 to oversee the operations of the civilian Canadian Security Intelligence Service (CSIS), which was also formed in 1984, following the recommendations of the McDonald Commission. These reports have generated an extensive literature, which is mostly journalistic, on police deviance (Cléroux (1990) contains an extensive bibliography of this literature).

With the exception of the recent Marin report issued by the RCMP External Review Committee (RCMP, 1991) on allegations of entrapment by a Canadian member of the Senate, there is very little that is publicly known about undercover operations in fields other than political surveillance. The Marin report (RCMP, 1991: 92) actually recommends the establishment of a Central Registry for all coded informants used by the Force, which should put the RCMP in a position to assess the performance of its informers. This recommendation is an indication that the RCMP, which is the main police force in Canada, is not yet in a position to assess the impact of undercover policing, which is intrinsincally linked to the use of informants. The situation is no better with respect to other Canadian police forces.

The other main source of knowledge about undercover policing is the jurisprudence. In Canada, this is a rather limited source, since there are few cases where judges explicitly refer to undercover policing. This became evident when the jurisprudence was recently reviewed by Schiffer (1991) and Stober (1991). The LRCC will also shortly publish a report on the granting of immunity to criminals willing to testify against their accomplices.

To sum up: what is known in Canada about undercover policing deals almost exclusively with this kind of work in political surveillance, counterterrorism and anti-subversion. Although we know that such tactics play an important part in other fields, such as the enforcement of laws against drug trafficking, few specific cases of undercover policing have been documented.

Undercover police, informers and delators
Although they are frequently referred to, Marx (1988) does not devote many pages to informers (basically, pp. 152–158), the focus of the book being a

particular form of police surveillance rather than a particular group of surveil-
lants. Actually, if a group had to be singled out in Marx (1988), it would be the
police. Due to the fact that police informers were star witnesses in at least two
of the major Canadian public inquiries on policing (the McDonald and the
Keable) and that their role is discussed in the report of several others, they
were the object of much attention in this country. Some of these star witnesses
also published their story in a book (Deveault, 1980). Actually, the same
words – "police agent" and "undercover agent" – are used in official documents such as the McDonald report and others to refer both to police officers
working undercover and to police informers (see Canada, 1980 and 1981a and
b). Hence, it is virtually impossible to speak of undercover policing in Canada
without feeling the need to emphasize the part played by police informers in
these operations. One could say that informers and their handlers are seen in
Canada as the two pillars of any undercover operation.

Like Wool (1986), the Marin report defines a police informer as a person
who provides information to the police without being obliged to do so by law.
This definition is meant to counter W. and N. Kelly's claim that "anyone who
gives information to the police is a police informant" (Kelly and Kelly, 1976:
322). Many persons are required by statutes such as the *Motor Vehicles Act* to
report a great deal of information to the police. Referring to them as police
informants would be ludicrous. However, despite his intention to narrow
down the definition of a police informer, Wool's definition may still be too
broad.

In line with Wool's definition, a paid informer may be defined as any person
who provides information to the police without being obliged by the law, in
exchange for court and/or financial considerations. Not only is the middle part
of the definition superfluous (the police would not have to pay someone to
provide information, if that person was obliged to do so by law), but this
definition fails to make a distinction between what in Canada are considered
two very different kinds of police informants. We tend to distinguish between
the informer, in the traditional sense of the word, and the delator (in French,
délateur). As Kelly (1978: 233–234) rightly notes, an informer does not only
provide information to the police; he or she provides them with a fairly large
variety of services, such as making introductions in a police controlled narcotics "buy and bust" operation. More importantly, an informer is used proac-
tively and is not expected to testify in open court. Delators are Crown witnesses who are granted court and financial considerations to testify in open court
against their former accomplices in extremely serious crimes (usually murder).
However, contrary to ordinary Crown witnesses testifying against former
accomplices, delators also reveal to the police who committed crimes that are
yet unsolved. They are not proactive but reactive agents, since their intervention always occurs after one or several crimes have been committed and

110

are still unresolved by the police. In Canada, delators are not usually given full immunity from prosecution; rather, they are offered an advantageous plea bargain and a reduced sentence (e.g., manslaughter instead of first degree murder). The numerous members of the Italian Red Brigades who "repented" and testified against their former comrades would fit into the Canadian category of delators. The crucial difference between informers and delators is that only the former can be said to work undercover, since the latter agree to blow whatever cover they may have by accepting to testify in open court. In the U.S., Joseph Valachi was an example of what we call a delator, as opposed to an informer.

Although, as I just argued, delators are different from informers, there are also important similarities between the two categories. They both refer to persons involved in criminal activities, who are "flipped" or "turned" by the police in exchange for court and/or financial considerations; both kinds of persons provide the police with information on crimes and their authors (often associates) and both are also protected by the police (delators are physically protected, since they have no cover). Furthermore, there is a two-way circulation between the two categories. An informer may agree to reveal his identity and testify in open court, if the benefits that he or she may reap are substantial enough. Conversely, a "repentant" accused, willing to testify against former associates, may be offered complete immunity and returned to the criminal milieu, if the police (and, in certain cases, the prosecution) believe that there is more to gain in having this individual as an informer than as a witness for the prosecution.

Fields of undercover policing
Although I said previously that most publicly known cases of undercover policing fall within the range of political surveillance and counterterrorism, this kind of police tactic is used in other fields of law enforcement. The other type of crime that is most frequently cited in relation to the use of human and technical sources is consensual crime and, most particularly, drug offences. According to research cited in official reports on electronic surveillance, over 98% of the judicial authorizations granted to intercept private communications were for cases involving drug offences or offences against national security. There are other fields of criminal activities in which informers are used: illegal markets that parallel legal ones (e.g. cigarette smuggling), political corruption and corporate crime, tax evasion and low clearance rate crimes. With regard to the latter field of operation, special mention must be made of attempts to solve murders perpetrated in the context of organized crime ("hits" and "contracts") through the use of delators. A research project on delators conducted in Montreal by Sylvie Gravel has shown that 27 out of 46

court cases in which delators or self-interested Crown witnesses testified involved first-degree murder.

The diversity of these fields of undercover operations raises the important issue of the possibility of developing a unified theory of undercover policing, which can account for the differences between operations. This issue is particularly acute when we compare undercover operations in the field of political surveillance and criminal investigations (or instigations, to use the terminology of Wilson, 1978).

2. The Canadian police apparatus

Before 1984, the police were charged with protecting Canada's national security. In 1984, an independent civilian security service was created. I will first briefly describe the Canadian police forces. Afterwards, I shall present the organizations involved in political surveillance.

The Canadian police forces

In 1990, there were 56,034 peace officers (public police) in Canada; the police forces also employed 19,330 civilian personnel, thus putting the sum total of persons working for police forces at 75,364.

Canada is a federation of ten provinces and two northern territories. There are three kinds of police forces in Canada. First, there is a federal police force, which is the RCMP. There are also two provincial police forces, which are the Ontario Provincial Police (OPP), for the province of Ontario, and the Sûreté du Québec (SQ), for the province of Québec. These two forces number between 5,000 and 6,000 men (it varies slightly from year to year). Thirdly, there are municipal police forces in Canadian cities. In 1989, for example, there were 167 municipal police forces in the province of Québec; the figure is lower in Ontario, where there are now approximately 130 regional and municipal police forces. Except for the smaller ones (e.g., a force of 5 uniformed officers in a small rural town), all Canadian police forces have basically the same mandate. This mandate comprises order maintenance, which is basically upheld by uniformed police, criminal investigation and the provision of certain services (e.g., ambulance). Criminal investigators in Canada are not part of a separate force, as in certain European countries.

The largest police force in Canada is the RCMP, which today numbers 14,463 peace officers and 1,745 civilians. On top of the traditional police mandate described above, the RCMP performs several other important tasks.

112

First, it is charged with the enforcement of numerous federal statutes (e.g., customs, airport security, etc.). Second, it acts as a provincial police force for 8 of the 10 Canadian provinces and for the two territories. Third, it has specialized in the investigation of certain kinds of crime such as narcotics, political corruption and corporate crime. Fourth, it provides technical support and training assistance for all other Canadian forces (the Canadian Police Information Centre, which is the main centralized data bank on Canadian offenders, is managed by the RCMP, which collects and processes data from all other police forces and from Courts and Corrections). Lastly, the RCMP is making a strong comeback in political policing. I address this last issue in the next section.

The network of political surveillance

There exist a number of fairly recent and reliable descriptions of the Canadian intelligence and security community (Senate, 1987; SIRC, 1987 and Robertson, 1989). Although the private sector plays a large role in protecting individuals from terrorist attempts, I will limit my description to governmental security organizations.

There are several intelligence-gathering agencies in Canada. The Departments of External Affairs (DEA) and of National Defence (DND) each have their own intelligence units. The three major federal organizations are the CSIS, the RCMP and the Communication Security Establishment (CSE). Little is known of the intelligence units of the DEA and the DND, apart from the fact that they are small organizations. I will focus on the three main components of the political surveillance apparatus, that is, the CSIS, the RCMP and the CSE.

Previous to 1984, the Canadian security service was part of the RCMP, which like the F.B.I. in the U.S. investigated both politically-motivated and ordinary crime. Following a series of scandals that gave birth to the McDonald, the Krever and the Keable inquiries, the RCMP Security Service was abolished and the civilian CSIS was created. CSIS is not a police organization in the legal sense of the word. All Canadian police are peace officers who have the legal power to make arrests. The members of the CSIS do not have peace officer powers and must rely on the police to make arrests and, more generally speaking, enforce the law. The CSIS has approximately 3,000 employees and a budget of $213 millions.

Among the police organizations on which the CSIS must rely for its operations, there is one force which is given priority by section 61 of the *CSIS Act*. This section gives the RCMP the prime responsibility for enforcing the law in the field of offences against national security. In simple terms, the McDonald

Commission's concept of political policing rested on the assumption that the CSIS would be the brain and that the RCMP – and other police forces with which the RCMP was to have agreements – would be the arm. This concept was flawed from the start, because no police organization can agree to divorce intelligence from operations and vice-versa. Either the CSIS would grow its own arm or the RCMP would grow another brain. CSIS would have had to fight an uphill battle in order to develop its own arm, since its members lacked the legal power to use coercion and make arrests. The RCMP did not have any legal obstacles in its way, if it wanted to make a comeback into security intelligence. All it had to do was to wait long enough for its past sins to be forgotten. After 1988, the RCMP established its own directorate – the National Security Investigation Directorate – for its investigations into offences threatening the national security of Canada and, in particular, terrorism.

The third organization involved in security intelligence is the CSE, which falls under the governance of the DND. Except for a few articles in the Toronto *Globe and Mail* (Sallot, 1984 and a more recent series by Moon, 1991), this agency is a little known organization. The CSE collects signal intelligence (SIGINT). It operates within the framework of the 1947 UKUSA Agreement, to which the U.S., the U.K., Australia and to a lesser extent New Zealand are also parties. The CSE monitors and analyzes telephone, telex, facsimile, data-transmission, cables and radio messages going to and from Canada and other countries. It also listens to radar signals. As can be seen from this description, the CSE is the Canadian equivalent of the U.S. National Security Agency. It has approximately 850 civilian employees and the military assigns about 1,100 specialists to operate the agency's monitoring stations in Canada, Bermuda and Germany. Its budget is estimated at $250 million (Moon, 1991, May 27, p. A 4). The Canadian consumers of CSE intelligence include the military, the Privy Council Office, the federal departments of External Affairs, Transport and Employment and Immigration, the customs and excise branches, the RCMP and the CSIS.

3. Intention

The concept of intention plays a significant role in Gary Marx's work and particularly in Marx (1988), where one chapter is devoted to a description of the intended consequences of undercover policing and two others to its unintended consequences. In Marx (1988), the unintended consequences of undercover policing are seen as undesirable. The criterion used to determine whether a consequence is desirable is whether or not it benefits a formal law enforcement policy.

The concept of intention is notoriously fraught with difficulties and involves

114

logical, philosophical and legal notions. I cannot undertake a thorough examination of the concept of intention within the scope of this article. What I will
do is identify its main dimensions. I will be in part guided by legal doctrine,
although I want to make it clear that I am not undertaking a legal discussion.
After having identified the main components of intention, I will discuss four
cases to examine if it is conceivable to envisage effects of undercover policing
which are both intended and undesirable.

There are three main dimensions to intention: *cognizance, purposiveness*
and *premeditation*. The notion of premeditation – preparation of planning in
advance – is clear enough. Cognizance, on the other hand, raises an issue. A
distinction is generally made between knowledge of one's action and the
knowledge of its consequences. For example, the offence of manslaughter is a
kind of homicide where the offender wanted to cause serious harm to a person
but had not anticipated that the person would die as a result of his or her
injuries. Many factors intervene in assessing whether a person is justified in
claiming not to have anticipated the consequences of his or her action. The
most complex of these factors is the issue of common knowledge. A person
accused fifty years ago of polluting a river with mercury may have argued that
he or she was not aware that mercury contaminated fish, thus making their
consumption a serious health hazard. However, it would be very difficult to
present such a defence today, with all the knowledge that we have accumulated on water pollution by mercury. Hence, knowledge of the consequences
of one's acts tend to vary across time.

When it is divorced from the element of cognizance – a person knows that he
or she is committing an offence, but does it for a good purpose, like Robin
Hood who stole from the rich to give to the poor – purposiveness is almost
never admitted by the courts as a sound defence. There is, however, one noted
exception to this rule and it is when a policeman claims to have broken the law
– e.g., by committing an offence against privacy or by submitting a suspect to a
brutal interrogation – for reasons of efficiency in the struggle against crime
(Brodeur, 1981).

I will now review four cases of undesirable consequences from the point of
view of formal law enforcement policy to see whether any of these consequences could be said to be intended. Most examples will involve police
informants.

Violation of professional oath

The Krever commission of inquiry into the recruitment of doctors – particularly psychiatrists – as police informers giving confidential medical information
on some of their patients in spite of their medical oath issued its report in 1980

(Ontario, 1980). In trying to assess this case, we immediately run into trouble. It is not sure whether it is desirable or not from a formal law enforcement policy point of view to entice doctors to break their professional oath for the sake of acquiring medical information on known or potential offenders. It is one of the most serious violations of the right to privacy that one can imagine and it is in this sense highly undesirable. Yet, in a landmark ruling, the Supreme Court of Canada forbade the commission from trying to learn the identity of the doctors in order to submit them to disciplinary sanctions (*The Solicitor General of Canada v. The Royal Commission of Inquiry into the Confidentiality of Health Records in Ontario,* [1981]). In doing so, the Supreme Court gave legitimacy to the police practice of recruiting doctors as informers.

The police who recruited these doctors as informers were well aware of what they were doing; it was well-planned in advance. Hence the element of cognizance and premeditation are present. However, the element of purposiveness seems to be lacking. The police did not recruit these doctors for the sake of having them break their medical oath (although they might use this breach of oath to blackmail repenting doctors into remaining police informers). Rather they convinced them that breaking their oath served the higher purpose of helping the police. Nevertheless, it is doubtful that persons accused of having conspired to have doctors break their oath would have been acquitted by a judge by pleading that they did it for a good purpose. Hence, although this case is controversial, it could be considered as a consequence of undercover policing that is both undesirable and intended.

Laundering unresolved cases

One of the most notorious delators in the history of Québec courts, a fellow nicknamed "Apache" Trudeau, was offered to plead guilty to 42 counts of manslaughter, in return for testimony against accomplices who were accused of first-degree murder. Even though this man was a contract killer, it is unlikely that he was actually responsible for all 42 murders to which he pleaded guilty. The police used him to close some of their unresolved homicide files. This practice of laundering their files of unsuccessful investigations is frequent when the police make a deal with a delator.

In this instance, the element of cognizance is clearly present. Whether premeditation is also present is plausible. Purposiveness, however, is clearly a factor. There can be little doubt of the willingness of the police to launder their files, when they have an occasion to do so. Hence it would seem that the laundering of police files is an intended consequence of the use of delators.

Is this intended consequence undesirable from a law enforcement policy perspective? Since it means that the police will stop looking for the real culprits

116

of very serious crimes, such as homicide, this question can only be answered in the positive. However, from the point of view of a police organization's bureaucracy, such a consequence of the use of delators may appear desirable.

It would seem, then, that we have found a consequence that is clearly intentional and undesirable with respect to law enforcement policy. However, it must be said in all fairness that the recourse to delators is a practice that is not at the core of undercover policing, at least as it is defined by Gary Marx. Only that part of delation which precedes the trial is really covert. In some cases, it involves almost no deception, as when a criminal who fears he will be executed by associates surrenders voluntarily to the police and agrees to testify against them in exchange for police protection. In other cases, delators are used in the same way as informers to entrap former accomplices; these operations often take place among cellmates in prison.

Constructing national security threats

In the field of political surveillance, infiltration is conducted on a very long-term basis. In 1987, Mr. Marc Boivin was revealed to be an informer for several Canadian police agencies (the RCMP, the CSIS and the SQ). Mr. Boivin had been informing the police on a large labor union (the Confederation of National Trade Unions – CNTU) for more than ten years and acted on several occasions as an *agent provocateur*. SIRC, the civilian oversight committee for CSIS was asked to investigate this affair (SIRC, 1988).

There are groups and organizations which may lean toward violent action for a time – when the revolutionary myth's mobilizing power is at its height. Later, they may redefine themselves as non-violent dissidents. For example, many Marxist groups of yesteryear are now environmentalists. As reported by Québec (1981), the police are very reluctant to let go of groups that they have successfully infiltrated. Hence, an informer and his or her handlers will keep emphasizing – and, in most cases, reinventing – the potential of a group for violence, thus justifying its continued surveillance.

This reconstruction of a group's dangerousness is a frequent consequence of undercover surveillance. The informers and undercover police who are in the main responsible for this reconstruction are usually conscious of what they are doing, their action is often premeditated and they seek its result, which allows them to keep their job as the group's infiltrators. Hence this consequence is fully intended in every sense of the word.

Whether it is desirable or not depends on the degree of sensitivity of a law enforcement policy to civil liberties. For a purely utilitarian law enforcement policy, the only objection to surveilling groups which may pose a dubious threat is that it may unduly stretch the resources available to the police and

117

make them miss out on more potent risks for the State. If a law enforcement policy is sensitive to human rights, then the consequence that we have been describing is evidently undesirable.

Uninvolved parties

My last case is drawn from the recent report of the Marin commission (RCMP, 1991). The report describes "project Albus", which was a failed sting operation undertaken by the RCMP's Special Federal Inquiries Unit (SFIU). During August and September 1988, an RCMP member seconded to the Department of the Solicitor General received information concerning the transfer of illicit funds between Ottawa and Washington. The source of this information was ultimately revealed to be an ex-RCMP informer, whose use had been prohibited by the Commissioner, for a variety of reasons. This informer was reputed to be productive but difficult to handle. It was decided to reactivate him and the SFIU was to use him in an attempt to solve the problem of illicit transfers of money from Canada to other countries – Switzerland was also mentioned – through an undercover operation.

To facilitate his penetration of the Ottawa criminal milieu, it was decided to enhance his credibility by establishing his identity as a person with exploitable political connections (RCMP, 1991: 21). In order to achieve this, a meeting between the informer and a Canadian Senator was to be arranged by the handlers of the source, with the hope that this meeting would eventually be reported to the persons whose confidence the source was attempting to win. The Senator that was chosen for this purpose was under no suspicion whatsoever of peddling his unfluence nor was he connected with any criminal or illicit activities. He just happened to have been briefly spoken to by the informer at a previous cultural festival held in Ontario. The meeting was arranged and the Senator and the source talked for a few minutes.

Being addressed by the informer as "a man of some influence", the first Senator refused to take the bait and referred him to the official channels for whichever business he was trying to conclude. Subsequently, the informer telephoned the Senator to ask for his assistance and he was referred this time to another Senator (who happened to be under investigation by the RCMP for influence peddling). That was the end of the relationship between the informer and the Senator he tried to approach in order to acquire some status for the persons with whom he was attempting to ingratiate himself.

The Marin commission severely blamed the RCMP for allowing an informer to contact a senator who was under no suspicion of illicit activities merely for the purpose of enhancing that source's credibility as a man with political contacts. It may have led to the Senator's name being circulated in the criminal

118

milieu as a man who was willing to peddle his influence, with irretrievable damage to his reputation. This consequence was completely undesirable from a law enforcement perspective, which should be committed to preventing any harm done to innocent parties.

This action was premeditated and knowingly conducted. Its admitted purpose was neither to entrap the Senator nor to damage his reputation. Still, it may be asked whether there was any assessment of the risk that this operation might cause the Senator a serious prejudice and whether the informer's handlers were not careless to the point of neutralizing any claim they may have made of harbouring no intention of harming the Senator's reputation and career. As we have already seen, the Marin Commission finally judged that their action was blameworthy.

Tentative conclusions

The purpose of the above was to explore the concept of intended consequence and to prepare the ground for the classification that is going to be offered in the next part of this paper. In this section, I discussed the issue of whether consequences of undercover policing that were undesirable from a law enforcement perspective could also be said to be intended by persons actively involved in undercover operations.

I do not believe that any firm conclusion can be drawn from the analyses of cases that may exemplify consequences which are both undesirable and intended. On the one hand, I found that it was difficult to find a case to which both of these predicates could apply simultaneously without qualification. On the other, I believe I have shown that it cannot be asserted as a matter of principle that any consequences that were undesirable from a law enforcement perspective were also *bound to be unintended.* I shall elaborate on this statement in the following section of this paper.

4. Consequences of undercover policing

There are very few assessments in Canada of the collective impact of undercover policing. As seen before, the basic sources of information on undercover policing are government reports, jurisprudence, press clippings and a few unreliable autobiographies. There is very little field research on undercover policing and there is almost no quantitative research at all (what little field work we have was undertaken by commissions of inquiry and would not qualify as field work in the sociological sense of the word). Hence, any assessment of the consequences of undercover policing is based upon extrapolations made from a limited selection of cases. Hence, they involve a certain degree of speculation.

As previously announced, I generate four categories of consequences: desirable/intended, desirable/unintended, undesirable/intended and undesirable/unintended. This categorization is more exploratory than firm and is meant as an instrument to test the relevance of using such predicates to classify the consequences of undercover policing. This statement is particularly true with regard to the notion of intention, which is used here according to the criteria identified in the previous section. Cognizance and purposiveness will play a much larger role than premeditation in our discussion. Furthermore, we follow the legal tradition in giving to cognizance more weight than purposiveness. This means that *if it makes no sense to pretend that policing agencies are unaware of a given consequence, I will tend to classify it as being intended.* For reasons that will be apparent in the course of the discussion, this rule will not be consistently applied. Even if it is not consistently applied, it is bound to be controversial. I shall address the objections to this rule in the conclusion of the paper.

Consequences: desirable and intended

Justifiably or not, the use of informants is perceived to be at the core of law enforcement in the fields of consensual crime, corporate crime, political corruption and politically-motivated crime such as terrorism. Although Manning sees in the "agent/informant mode of targeting" only one of such targeting modes in the field of narcotics, most authors, and particularly those with a police background, see the use of informers within the context of undercover operations as the main tool for making cases in narcotics and other consensual crimes. Officers in the field of security intelligence would also agree that infiltration is the only effective way of countering terrorism and other politically-minded deviance.

Manning (1980: 13) is critical of undercover operations using informers in the field of narcotics. Manning's assessment receives weighty support from the 1991 report of the Inter-American Commission on Drug Policy (IACDP) – a private group of experts from Bolivia, Canada, Columbia, Mexico, Peru and the U.S. – which concluded that strategies aimed at the interception of drug shipments were extremely costly and did not produce the expected results (Campbell, 1991).

The intended desirable consequences of undercover policing can be classified in three categories.

120

Crime repression

Due to the complete lack of Canadian data on the impact of undercover tactics, it is impossible to provide any assessment which is not wholly speculative. Being perceived, as I just said, as the main tool of law enforcement in the field of consensual crime and related domains, undercover operations are automatically credited in part for any results achieved by the police in these fields. Hence, the RCMP provides us in its annual reports with the amount of drugs seized and gives no detail on how the seizures were achieved. We are left to speculate on the part played by undercover tactics.

The use of undercover tactics in drug law enforcement has two important consequences. It focuses law enforcement on the supply of drugs rather than on consumption and on the treatment of addicts, and it allows the police to target serious criminals, who are much less visible than their street hirelings. The first strategy is now coming under the fire of increasing criticism, as the above quoted report of the IACDP bears witness to. As for the second strategy, it rests in part on the assumption that illegal markets are managed by huge organizations shaped like pyramids, the top of the pyramid being what holds it together. Hence, the crucial interest in getting to the top of the pyramid. Reuter (1983a and 1985) has convincingly shown that this belief was mistaken and that organized crime is actually splintered into a variety of loosely organized feuding gangs.

The dearth of reliable data on undercover policing (RCMP, 1991) is indicated by the fact that the Marin report was compelled to devote a few pages to detailing the results of the Crime Stopper programs implemented in Toronto. These kinds of programs, where anonymous callers phone in information related to a crime reenacted on television, are very distantly related to undercover policing. They are merely enticements to mass delation.

The impact of the use of "professional delators" is being investigated in a research project undertaken at the Université de Montréal. The research is still in a preliminary stage and the data that was collected has not been processed in detail yet. Of a sum total of 23 cases involving delators, 6 resulted in the acquittal of the accused, 10 resulted in condemnations, 6 in pleas of guilty (in one case the accused died before being tried). These results are not very impressive. Not only can we see that more than a third of the suspects put on trial were acquitted, but the price paid to delators was often extremely high. For example, the delator "Apache" Trudeau, who pleaded guilty to 42 reduced charges of manslaughter, could be released on parole after 7 years in jail.

Crime prevention

By providing advanced knowledge of impending crimes, the use of informers is in theory one of the few policing strategies which can be said to be preventive in a precise sense. Preventive policing is crucial in the case of crimes of violence, such as terrorism.

Unfortunately, it is close to impossible to assess the preventive impact of undercover policing. Prevented crimes are non-events and difficult to calculate. Furthermore, it is the security services which are the most prone to claim success for foiling terrorist plots. The validity of these claims cannot be assessed, as any checking is made impossible by the confidential nature of the operations aimed at protecting national security.

Criminal and security intelligence
The accumulation of criminal and security intelligence is a clear outcome of undercover operations. With regard to such agencies as the CSIS, it is the only legitimate outcome.

Criminal intelligence should play a decisive part against crimes of very low visibility, such as political corruption and corporate crime. Security intelligence is vital to the prevention of politically motivated violence and other crimes shrouded in secrecy. Both kinds of intelligence, however, suffer from two limitations.

First, their influence on government decision-making is too often marginal; members of security services often complain that the government is very reluctant to act upon the intelligence provided. Second, it would also seem that the police intelligence units have inadequate analysis capacity, which results in severe shortcomings in the quality of their product. The Marin report (RCMP, 1991) found that Senator Cogger was targeted by the RCMP's SFIU only after "several news media alerted RCMP members of Senator Cogger's alleged involvement (in the acceptance of payment for political services) and the use of his office as Senator to influence government action" (RCMP, 1991: 61). It is the Montreal *Gazette* that initially broke the story of Senator Cogger's alleged involvement in influence peddling in 1988. One would expect investigative journalism to feed on the scraps from undercover policing rather than the police finding their targets in press clippings.

Consequences: desirable and unintended

The consequences that I am briefly going to describe are classified as unintended in the sense that they are usually not the specific purpose of undercover tactics. They are also largely unanticipated. However, in certain circumstances which I shall indicate, they may become the goal that is specifically intended. We have tentatively identified four consequences which are both desirable and unintended.

122

Deterrence

With regard to certain groups or individuals, the knowledge that they may possibly be the target of undercover operations spearheaded by informants can be enough to produce a deterrent effect. Generally speaking, however, this deterrent effect is stronger on persons who are not hardened criminals. The underside of deterrence is what is called the "chilling effect" that stifles the expression of legal dissent and which is undesirable. When a certain kind of criminal activity has not been a focus of police repression, undertaking an elaborate undercover operation – such as operation ABSCAM against corrupt politicians in the U.S. – may intentionally serve as a warning and help deter potential offenders. Due to their prohibitive costs, operations like ABSCAM could not be said to be worth the money, if it could be shown that they have no deterrent effect.

Disorganization

Hardened criminals may not be deterred by the knowledge that they are likely to be the targets of undercover operations. Nevertheless, this knowledge compels them to take elaborate precautions that can possibly become a true impediment to their activity. In other words, undercover policing can be a major hindrance to the smooth functioning of a criminal operation. Disorganization of criminal schemes is a general side-effect of the use of informers rather than a specific goal and it cannot be measured with any degree of accuracy.

Maintaining police morale

It is obvious that police organizations do not resort to undercover tactics spearheaded by informers in order to boost the morale of the troops. Nevertheless, undercover tactics may at least be viewed as an anti-depressant. Indeed, if we try to predict what would result from a complete ban on the use of informers and undercover tactics in such fields as drugs, the demoralization of narcotic squads is an entirely foreseeable effect. This raises an important issue. If it were shown that undercover tactics have only a marginal impact on drugs, would it be worth it to keep resorting to them just to prevent a collapse of police morale?

An alternative to escalation

In themselves, undercover operations and the use of informers are soft methods of social control, as compared to the militaristic mode of targeting referred to by Manning (1980). In some countries of Europe such as France, informers are irretrievably linked to the idea of policing and they have been systematically used since at least the 17th century (Brodeur, 1983). Yet civil liberties are still very much alive in countries like France. As compared to military repression, which is undiscriminating in its violence, the use of informants remains a police strategy that may threaten civil liberties, but which does not abrogate them.

Consequences: undesirable and intended

This category is admittedly the most problematic. How, it may be asked, can the criminal justice system, and particularly the police, intend to produce consequences that are undesirable with respect to formal law enforcement policy? Actually, if we use the criterion of cognizance, all of the consequences described in this section are intentional. Nevertheless, as we shall see, some are lacking true purposiveness and are not intended in themselves. I will justify my classification in the course of presenting it.

Licensing criminals

No consequence of undercover operations has generated as much discussion in Canada as licensing informers to commit crimes. This consequence of under-cover operations was particularly emphasized by Reuter (1983b). Reuter argues that the value of an informer depends upon the depth of his in-volvement in the crime milieu. In order to have their good informers maintain their position, police handlers have no other choice than to license them to commit crimes.

Described in this way, licensing criminals appears to be a pre-condition of undercover operations rather than a consequence of them. Actually, things are not as clear-cut in the field. All big police organizations have formal and informal guidelines on the handling of informers. They all proclaim that informers are not permitted to breach the law in the course of their assignment with the police (in certain police departments, this prohibition is set down in writing as part of a written agreement between the force and its informer; see Bozza, 1978). However, the application of these guidelines is often progressiv-ely suspended as handlers get more deeply involved with their informers in risky operations. In Canada, for instance, an officer from the RCMP is appealing his conviction for drug trafficking on the grounds that he only accepted a part of the benefits that his informer was making in selling drugs (the informer apparently found it unfair that his handler should not get his piece of the cake).

Hence it could be said that licensing criminals is as much an ongoing consequence of undercover policing as a pre-condition. Granting that this consequence is undesirable, is it intentional? The police are fully aware that most of their valuable informers are involved in crime (several informants in the field of narcotics are known drug addicts, to take a banal example). Hence

124

the element of cognizance is fully present. The case is different with regard to purposiveness. Unless the case officer is corrupted and wants a share of the profits, the purpose of licensing criminals is not to let them break the law with impunity; it is to develop valuable sources within the criminal milieu by licensing some criminals. However, since I decided to follow judicial practice and give more weight to cognizance than purposiveness (or lack of it), I classify this undesirable consequence as intended.

Statutory violations of confidentiality

These are cases that I already discussed. They involve recruiting persons, such as doctors, who have sworn an oath of confidentiality, as police informers. With regard to intention, these cases are similar to the licensing of criminals. The element of cognizance is obviously present. Yet the practice is more a means to achieve another goal, which falls under law enforcement, than an end in itself. The element of cognizance is even stronger than in the cases of licensing, since the police know that every time that a professional bound by an oath of confidentiality will give information about his clients/patients, he or she will be breaking the oath.

Crime facilitation

I borrow the expression of crime facilitation from Marx (1981; see also Marx, 1982) to designate all aspects of crime incitement that are intrinsically linked with undercover policing. These aspects were described by several authors under the name of instigation, entrapment, trickery and even framing. These practices are seen as undesirable – and even illegal – by the courts (for early descriptions, see Donnelly (1951) for the U.S. and Devlin (1971) for the U.K.; since the reality of entrapment was not fully acknowledged in Canada before the 1988 Supreme Court ruling *Mack v. the Queen,* there are no early descriptions in Canada).

There is no doubt that the police are fully aware that sting operations are instigative and that instigating the commission of a crime under controlled circumstances is the explicit purpose of such operations. Needless to say, sting operations do target some very unsavoury characters. However, the systematic implementation of an all-out crime facilitation strategy would have highly disturbing effects on any law abiding community. Crime facilitation is undesirable, but it is also an intentional practice that is at the core of undercover policing.

The subversion of the due process of law

I am referring here to all the violations of criminal law procedure, of the due process of law and of Charter guarantees that result from undercover operations. Some of these violations, such as perjury, are criminal offences.

Others, such as the use of an unreliable informer to trick a judge into granting his authorization for the installation of an electronic listening device, as in the *Atwal* case in British Columbia, involve deception of a non criminal nature. It would be naive to believe that the police are unaware of some of their informers' misconduct in court and that they do not condone it. Contingent fee arrangements with informers or delators are an open invitation to perjury. In other cases, it is the police themselves who trick a magistrate by presenting him with affidavits justifying the use of electronic surveillance, which they know to be false. Hence, we are once more correct in describing this consequence as undesirable and intentional.

The collection of intelligence damaging to personal reputation
While director of research for the Keable inquiry (Québec, 1981), I was asked to review all the informers' files of a large police force and to assess the value of the information provided by these sources. I concluded that a significant part of the information supplied by human sources could be described as malicious gossip, which devoted an inordinate importance to the sexual life of their targets. Such much-raking is unrelated to any actual or potential criminal prosecution. Yet it may be used as leverage to influence the behaviour of a perceived opponent and eventually to discredit that person (the FBI files on the extra-marital affairs of Dr. Martin Luther King is one of the better known instances of this practice). In Canada, ministers who wanted to keep the RCMP or the SQ on a tight leash were forced to resign amidst rumors of scandal (Mr. Francis Fox, who was Solicitor General of Canada, and M. Gérard Latulippe, who held the same post in the Province of Québec were two such casualties). When a police agency decides to keep hoarding this kind of information, its practice can be described as both intentional and undesirable.

Targeting non criminal opponents
This consequence if often described as political targeting. However, political targeting is just a particular instance of a wider practice that consists of targeting a person as the focus of a sting operation for reasons which are altogether extraneous to law enforcement or for the purpose of using persons who live highly visible unconventional life styles as scapegoats (e.g., artists or athletes). In Canada, the singer Claude Dubois, who was a heroin addict, was targeted by such an operation. Since sting operations rarely target a mere consumer of drugs, we may infer that M. Dubois was singled out more because of his popularity with the youth than for his addiction.

Unwitting informants can be manipulated into acting as a screen for such targeting, by making it appear that it is they who are actually doing the targeting. In some other cases, informers will deliberately seek revenge by depicting an enemy as a real or potential criminal or as a threat to Canada's

126

national security. From the viewpoint of their principal actors (informers or their handlers), these practices are deliberate. Needless to say, they are both unjustifiable and undesirable.

Consequences: undesirable and unintended

If we use the criterion of cognizance, most of the consequences that I characterize as unintended in this section might also be described as intended. There are, however, two main differences. The first one is the degree of purposiveness: the consequences that we will now describe are not even remotely produced for their own sake by police agencies. The second difference concerns cognizance. It can be argued that the police are *generally* aware of these consequences. However, they do not have specific and direct knowledge of the individuals involved in the undesirable situations potentially generated by undercover policing. An example will serve to make my point. It would not really be difficult for a police force to make a survey of all its informants who are drug addicts. The handler of an addicted informer usually knows of his or her addiction and decides not to interfere with it. However, a project to identify all the members of a police force who were corrupted by having too close a relationship with their informer(s) would be confronted with insurmountable difficulties. Hence, even if the leadership of a police force is aware that some corruption is bound to be the result of undercover work, it cannot be said to condone the corruption of any particular officer (unless, of course the corruption of an individual is revealed). I will now present what I believe to be the major unintended and undesirable consequences of the use of non-casual informers in the context of undercover policing.

Police corruption

Undercover operations using informers deeply involved in the criminal milieu tend to blur the differences between crime-fighters and hired criminals. They become partners widely sharing the same expectations and, not infrequently, the same risks. Hence, they develop the strong ties that usually bind together people facing the same risky situations. Such situations favour loss of police identity (either partial or complete) and is conducive to police corruption. Police corruption may also be fostered by the fact that the kinds of crime for which informers are used entail (i) a high degree of secrecy; (ii) very large sums of money (when dealing with drugs) and (iii) are likely to produce the feeling that law enforcement makes little difference (the sinking feeling that one works in vain is a strong enticement to becoming cynical and, eventually, corrupt – see Brodeur, 1981).

A shield for misconduct

This consequence of the use of informers in undercover operations is closely related to the preceding one, although it is different from outright corruption. I have been a member of a civilian police review committee for more than three years. I was struck by how often police officers whose behaviour was under review tried to justify the fact that they were at the wrong place (e.g., a strip joint), at the wrong time (being on duty) and doing the wrong thing (getting drunk) by alleging that they were "meeting with an informer". These claims being unverifiable, "working an informant" provides a shield for all kinds of misconduct unrelated to any undercover operation. Unintended by a police organization, this consequence may be fully willed by individual officers.

Innocent casualties

Gary Marx provides examples of cases where mistaken identities come to a tragic end, as when undercover operatives are killed by the police, unaware of their true identity. There are also numerous cases where persons suspected rightly or wrongly of being police informers are executed by the persons they are supposed to be informing on.

These are dramatic cases. There are others, less tragic, but involving dire consequences for innocent third parties. In the months that followed the 1970 October terrorist crisis, Mrs. Carole Deveault, a police informer working for the counterterrorist unit of the police of Montreal, drew a psychological profile of one of her professors, who exercised a charismatic influence on his students. In that psychological profile, the informer admitted that her professor was much too "brilliant" to ever join such a terrorist organization as the *Front de libération du Québec* (FLQ). That seemed to settle the matter and the professor was never interrogated nor arrested. He eventually became a Québec deputy minister in the early 1980s, when the *Parti Québécois* (PQ) was elected to head the government of the province of Québec.

Eight years later, the police of Montreal were investigated by a commission of inquiry on police wrongdoing, which had been appointed by the PQ government. Wanting to embarrass the government, the Montreal police lawyer cross-examined Mrs. Deveault on the profile that she had written many years before, during one of the public hearings of the commission. The press picked up the story and the career of the Deputy Minister, who had never been involved with terrorists, was ruined. In this case, the action taken by the police was fully intentional.

Police disorganization

The cases of mistaken identity which may result from a lack of police coor-

128

dination can foster disorganization. As is well known, all undercover operations are shrouded in a secrecy that can only be broken on a police "need to know" basis. Operating on the basis of the need to know is like handling actors scripts that are filled with blanks. The "need to know" basis is the weakest link in an operational chain of command.

Furthermore, the use of informers may strain the relationships between the police and the personnel of other components of the criminal justice system. Deals with delators are made without involving parole boards, which have later to reluctantly abide by them. Probation officers find themselves in a similar predicament.

Cost overruns

There is yet another unintended consequence of undercover policing that deserves its own heading, but that I cannot discuss in detail because of the limited scope of this paper. It is often pretended that informers are not expensive (e.g., Bouza, 1976), although trial disclosures reveal that they receive payments in excess of a hundred thousand Canadian dollars. Moreover, it is undisputed that some of the undercover operations that they trigger – such as ABSCAM – are enormously expensive, their cost running over several million U.S. dollars.

Whistle blowing

The Marin report (RCMP, 1991) describes two undercover policing projects of the RCMP, project Albus and the Sack operation, which was related to tenders for a communication system – code-named COSICS – for the Department of External Affairs. It was suspected that Senator Cogger had used his influence on behalf of a certain company. The RCMP tried to approach a Montreal businessman to assist in creating an opportunity for Senator Cogger to exercise his influence in a criminal manner (RCMP, 1991: 26–27). The Montreal businessman was not involved in crime in any manner; he was chosen precisely because he had complained of the unfairness of the procedure of tender in the COSICS contract. Not only did he refuse to cooperate, but he informed Senator Cogger that the RCMP was "trying to set (him) up". This information led the Senator to make his allegations on the floor of the Senate and to the Marin inquiry.

Informers or potential informers turning against their employers is more frequent than believed. Gary Marx described the shifting allegiances of informants and *agent provocateurs* in one of his earliest publications (Marx, 1974). As I previously said, one of the key witnesses of the Keable inquiry was an informer who turned against his Montreal police handler. Needless to say this consequence was both undesirable from a police perspective and unintended.

Delegitimization of the criminal law
One of the most damaging consequences of undertaking undercover operations that depend upon the use of paid informants is also the easiest to
describe. It generates scandals which shatter the image of law enforcement and
bring the whole criminal system into disrepute. In Canada, we have only to
recall the elaborate operation undertaken by the SQ against a Québec chapter
of the Hell's Angels (which turned into a circus), to realize how much the
image of the criminal law can be stained by scandals involving paid informants.
We should also remember that the Keable and McDonald inquiries, which led
to the downfall of the RCMP's Security Service were both triggered by an
undercover operation that misfired (a police break-in at the offices of a leftist
news agency – the *Agence de Presse Libre du Québec*).

Instigation of plot theories
There is a final issue which stems from the large variety of criminal fields in
which informers are used. There are individuals who are involved as informers
in one field (e.g., drugs) and in another as criminals (e.g., terrorism). Through
personal interviews with police, I learned that the handler of an informer
involved in his field of operation might himself inform on his colleagues
working in another field, in order to protect the informer. That would mean,
for example, that a narcotic agent could warn his drug informer that he was
being targeted by the security service because of his suspected involvement in
terrorism.

It can happen that such facts are brought to light by a commission of inquiry
or through investigative journalism. Hence, it may be disclosed that a known
terrorist worked as an informer in the field of drugs for a narcotic agent. It then
becomes very difficult to explain to anyone who is not familiar with undercover
work how the same individual can collaborate with the police in relation to
certain crimes and deceive them with regard to other (e.g., politically-motivated) crimes. Such facts usually bring grist to the mill of plot theorists, who
claim that the police could not have been ignorant of the politically-motivated
crimes, since they had an informer within the organization perpetrating these
crimes. Hence, the police are believed to have been facilitating these crimes
for perverse reasons. Plot theories are the media's cocaine and play an important part in undermining the credibility of law enforcement.

5. Conclusions

In this paper I have tried to build on Gary Marx's conception of undercover
policing. First, I provided background information on the Canadian police and
intelligence security apparatus and I discussed some of the features of under-

130

cover policing in Canada. Second, I analyzed the main consequences of undercover policing and tried to classify them according to four categories, established by the cross-tabulation of two pairs of predicates, namely desirable/undesirable and intended/unintended. These issues were approached within the framework of a dialogue of ideas, based on the work of Gary Marx.

In my discussion, I addressed two theoretical problems – whether undercover operations involve active deception, and whether undesirable consequences can also be considered as intended from a formal law enforcement policy perspective. I shall now sum up my conclusions with regard to these two issues. Finally, I will briefly add two additional considerations on the new surveillance.

Active deception and the new surveillance: the State as an undercover agent

According to Marx, undercover policing is characterized by active deception, which is the hallmark of the sting operations serving as models for Marx's conception of undercover policing. His position has two important implications. Since the purpose of a sting operation is to perform an arrest and to prosecute suspects, it would follow, first, that police operations which are limited to the collection of intelligence would not qualify as true undercover operations. Stopping short of an arrest, they would not be seen active enough to qualify. Secondly, this perspective also implies that the use of surveillance technology such as wiretaps and videotaping does not *per se* constitute undercover policing, since it does not involve active *interpersonal* deception.

I tried to show that both features of this account of undercover policing were problematic. When performed by agents of a security service, the collection of intelligence actually does involve a lot of active deception. Furthermore, the information collected serves eventually to perform mass arrests of political opponents in crisis situations. I also argued that electronic surveillance was perceived by the public as being deceptive. I would now like to show that this kind of surveillance also implies active deception in the sense proposed by Marx. I shall use as my example the most powerful Canadian organization engaged in electronic monitoring, that is, the CSE.

The very powerful technology that Canada's CSE and the U.S.' NSA use makes it possible for them to monitor "emanations" emitted not only at home but in the neighbouring country. Thus it becomes possible for these two countries to circumvent their respective legislation protecting private communications from interception. In theory, Canada monitors what is transmitted through the air waves in the U.S. and the U.S. does the same for Canada. Since these countries share the intelligence that they collect, both are given access to the private communications of their own citizens, albeit indirectly, while being allowed to claim that they respect their home privacy laws (Canada does not monitor Canadian personal messages nor does the U.S. for U.S. messages). This at least is the theory. Former employees of the CSE revealed that these agencies often do not go to the trouble of getting needed information on their own citizens through the co-operative system, and routinely break their own privacy laws. It would then seem that the distinction between passive surveillance and active undercover operations is largely irrelevant for agencies such as the CSE and the NSA. Whether the collection of SIGINT is a passive or an active undertaking is a rather spurious question. There can be no doubt that the way in which the CSE and the NSA circumvent the privacy laws of their country is strongly deceptive.

How deceptive it is can be assessed from the efforts of the government to keep the lid on any information about the CSE. The Canadian government is actively engaged in a campaign of disinformation about the true nature of the CSE's operations. When Mr. Ward Elcock, deputy clerk for security and intelligence and legal counsel to the Privy Council Office (the most powerful office in the Canadian government), was called to testify on the CSE by a parliamentary committee reviewing the first five years of operation of the *CSIS Act,* he infuriated the members of the Committee by refusing to provide anything else than the most general information on the CSE. He also testified to the effect that the CSE did not violate the Canadian privacy laws.

This governmental culture of vague and misleading statements and of half-truths concerning the real activities of the State apparatus for political and criminal surveillance extends far beyond the CSE. All policing agencies are to some extent under its protective cover. However, when the operations actually performed by these agencies come into full light, the extent of the deception actively resorted to by the State to disguise them is disclosed and comes as a shock to the general public.

Hence, if we stop being fascinated by particular operations, and focus on the relationship between the State, its surveillance agencies and the public, the State is shown to be actively engaged in systematic deception of the public on behalf of these agencies. The State's action can consequently be described as undercover policing, in the strict sense of the word. It shapes beliefs and behaviour through manipulation.

Consequences entailed in undercover policing

In my discussion of the consequences of undercover policing, I broke down the concept of intention into premeditation, cognizance and purposiveness. I also adopted an impartial quasi-judicial perspective. My impartiality consisted of adhering strictly to the legal tradition of giving more weight to cognizance than

132

to purposiveness in the assessment of intention. The critical stance adopted by the courts with respect to purposiveness manifests itself very clearly in the doctrine of "constructive malice", according to which an offender can be said to have intended all the consequences of the offence he originally planned to perpetrate, even if this offender did not will any of these consequences (e.g., if fleeing robbers accidentally kill a police officer by running into him with their getaway car, they can be prosecuted for murder, according to the doctrine of constructive malice). I would not go as far as to apply this doctrine to under-cover policing. However, I strongly object to the double standard applied by the courts in judging police wrongdoing. When police wrongdoing is judged, notions such as motive and purpose (or lack of criminal motive or purpose) come to play an exculpatory role that they never play in the case of an ordinary accused.

The results of my analyses are admittedly exploratory. However, they clearly imply that all consequences that are intended from a formal law enforcement policy perspective are not necessarily desirable or, conversely, that some undesirable consequences are intended. Moreover, we found that some important consequences of undercover policing, such as licensing crimi-nals, were particularly hard to classify with regard to intention. Actually, most concepts, including even the concept of consequence, proved to be fuzzy on the edges when applied to undercover policing.

The reason why I keep stressing the fact that some undesirable consequenc-es of undercover policing are intended is the following. The idea of an unin-tended negative consequence carries with it the false notion that this conse-quence is *accidental* and that it could eventually be avoided, if proper precau-tions were taken. Such an implication is not present in the work of Gary Marx, but it might be fostered by the use of the terminology of unintended negative consequences.

The general result of my analyses with regard to intention is that the dichotomy between intended and unintended consequences is far too rigid to accomodate all the consequences of undercover policing. I propose that the concept of *entailed consequence* be introduced into the analysis.

A consequence that is entailed by undercover policing is short of or beyond intention. It could be likened to the unavoidable price that has to be paid for a certain kind of police practice. For example, the fact that doctors are in breach of their medical oath is the price to be paid to recruit them as informers. Whether this consequence is intended or unintended is beside the point. This consequence is simply necessarily entailed by the recruitment of doctors and other professionals as informers, unless the medical and similar oaths are amended (any proposal to amend the medical oath to permit doctors to be police informers would stir up medical protest and generate public indigna-tion).

The benefits of viewing certain outcomes of undercover policing as entailed consequences is twofold. It first permits a lucid cost/benefit analysis, that may purport to assess whether we want to pay the price for a certain kind of policing. For example, granting that undercover operations entail the licensing of criminals and that their efficiency is limited in enforcing anti-drug legislation, do we want to pay the price of granting immunity to criminals just in order to make the police feel good in its losing war against drug traffickers? Second, it gives us the possibility to weigh political, social and ethical issues in undercover policing in the dispassionate and uncompromising perspective of *realpolitik*.

An Orwellian of a Kafkaesque new world?

In the last chapter of *Undercover,* Gary Marx says that "we are far from the distressing society that (George Orwell) described and (. . .) much current-trend data actually suggest increasing movement in the opposite direction" (Marx, 1988: 230). I entirely agree with Gary Marx, but for reasons which have no relation to political or social optimism. The inverted utopia imagined by Orwell bears little resemblance to our actual or potential world because it is based on a particularly simple brand of political rationalism, which views policing and the political world as permeated by mechanical constraints. In Orwell's *1984,* the State is in complete control of the social and political environment and it makes no mistake. From the State's point of view, Winston is actually guilty and his mind ought to be sanitized.

Kafka's perspective in works like *The trial* or in the opening tale to *The Castle* is much closer to our world and its bureaucratic contingency. The real threat is not that we will become entirely transparent to the State but that the accumulation of data in a dossier society overwhelmed by its powers of gathering information will infinitely increase the risks that we might be persecuted by mistake. In this regard the fate of Joseph K. is much more exemplary for us than George Orwell's Winston. Neither Joseph K. nor the system that eventually crushes him know what he is guilty of.

A choice of evils: a mistaken private identity or an accurate public vulnerability

In a provocative public lecture, in 1974, a Québec deputy minister for social affairs denied in 1974 the existence of a right to privacy. The only right that we have, said he, is to the accuracy of the data that is accumulated by the State on our quickly disappearing private life. This statement was perceived at the time as outrageous. Yet, in view of the capacity of the State and of private corpora-

134

tions to amass data on private citizens, and in view of the corresponding risks of making the wrong connections, it is to be wondered whether this deputy minister's stark wisdom was not preferable to the rear guard battles that we are still fighting and, sadly enough, losing.

References

Bouza, A.V., *Police Intelligence: The Operations of an Investigation Unit* (New York: AMS Press, 1976).

Bozza, C.M., *Criminal Investigation* (Chicago, Ill.: Nelson-Hall, 1978).

Brodeur, J.-P., "Legitimizing Police Deviance," in Cl. Shearing, ed., *Organizational Police Deviance* (Toronto: Butterworths, 1981).

—, "High Policing and Low Policing: Remarks About the Policing of Political Activities," *Social Problems,* 1983 (30:5), 507–520.

—, "Security Intelligence and Policing in Canada," in A.G. Gagnon and J.P. Bickerton (eds.), *Canadian Politics, an Introduction to the Discipline* (Peterborough: Broadview Press, 1990), 263–281.

Campbell, M., "Billions Wasted on Drug War, Report Charges," *The Globe and Mail,* June 12, 1991.

Canada (1966a), *Rapport de la Commission d'enquête quant aux plaintes formulées par George Victor Spencer* (Dalton Courtwright Wells, président). Ottawa. (available in English)

— (1966b). *Rapport de la Commission d'enquête sur certaines questions relatives à la dénommée Gerda Munsinger.* (Wishart Flett Spence, président). Ottawa: Imprimeur de la Reine. (available in English)

— (1969). *Rapport de la Commission d'enquête sur la sécurité.* (Maxwell Weir Mackenzie, président). Ottawa: Imprimeur de la Reine. (available in English)

— (1980). Commission d'enquête sur certaines activités de la Gendarmerie Royale du Canada. *Premier rapport: Sécurité et information.* (David C. McDonald, président). Ottawa: Approvisionnements et Services Canada. (available in English)

— (1981a) Commission d'enquête sur certaines activités de la Gendarmerie Royale du Canada. *Deuxième rapport: La liberté et la sécurité devant la loi.* (David C. McDonald, président). Ottawa: Approvisionnements et Services Canada. 2 volumes. (available in English under the title of "Freedom and Security under the Law". Commission of Inquiry Concerning Certain Activities of the Royal Canadian Mounted Police. Second report. Ottawa: Minister of Supply and Services.)

— (1981b). Commission d'enquête sur certaines activités de la Gendarmerie Royale du Canada. *Troisième rapport: Certaines activités de la GRC et la connaissance qu'en avait le gouvernement.* (David C. McDonald, président). Ottawa: Approvisionnements et Services Canada. (available in English)

Canada, Senate, *Terrorism. The Report of the Senate Special Committee on Terrorism and Public Safety* (Ottawa: Minister of Supply and Services, 1987).

—, *Terrorism. The Report of the Second Special Committee of the Senate on Terrorism and Public Safety* (Ottawa: Minister of Supply and Services, 1989).

Cléroux, R., *Official Secrets* (Scarborough: McGraw-Hill Ryerson, 1990).

Deveault, C., *Toute ma vérité* (Montréal: Stanké, [avec l'assistance de Monsieur William Johnson] 1980).

Devlin, K.L., "Informers, Spies, and Agents Provocateurs, *Chitty's Law Journal,* 1971 (19), 65–68.

Donnelly, R.C., "Judicial Control of Informants, Spies, Stool Pigeons, and Agents Provocateurs," *The Yale Law Journal,* 1951 (60), 1091–1131.

Johnson, L.K., *A Season of Inquiry: The Senate Intelligence Investigation* (Lexington, Ky.: The University Press of Kentucky, 1985).

Kelly, R.J., "Organized Crime: A Study in the Production of Knowledge by Law Enforcement Specialist." Ph.D. Dissertation, City University of New York, 1978.

Kelly, W. and Kelly, N., *Policing in Canada* (Toronto, Ontario: MacLean-Hunter, 1976).

Law Reform Commission of Canada, "Electronic Surveillance," Working Paper 47 (Ottawa: Law Reform Commission of Canada, 1986).

Manning, P.K., *The Narc's Game: Organizational and Informational Constraints on Drug Law Enforcement* (Cambridge, Mass.: MIT Press, 1980).

Marx, G.T., "Thoughts on a Neglected Category of Social Movement Participants: Agents Provocateurs and Informants," *American Journal of Sociology,* 1974 (80:2), 402–442.

—, "Ironies of Social Control: Authorities as Contributors to Deviance Through Escalation, Non-enforcement, and Covert Facilitation," *Social Problems,* 1981 (28:3), 221–246.

—, "Who Really Gets Stung? Some Issues Raised by the New Police Undercover Work," *Crime and Delinquency,* 1982 (28:2), 165–193.

—, *Under Cover: Police Surveillance in America* (Los Angeles: University of California Press, 1988).

Moon, P., *The Globe and Mail:* Series of Articles from May 27 to 30, 1991.

Ontario, (1980). *Report of the Commission of Inquiry into the Confidentiality of Health Information* (Horace Krever, chairman). Toronto: J.C. Thatcher, Queen's Printer. 3 volumes.

Québec (1981). *Rapport de la Commission d'enquête sur des opérations policières en territoire québécois* (Jean F. Keable, président). Québec: Ministère de la Justice.

Reuter, P., *Disorganized Crime: The Economics of the Visible Hand* (Cambridge, Mass.: MIT Press, 1983a).

—, "Licensing Criminals: Police and Informants," in G.M. Caplan (ed.). *ABSCAM Ethics: Moral Issues and Deception in Law Enforcement* (Cambridge, Mass.: Ballinger, 1983b, 100–117.

—, *The Organization of Illegal Markets: An Economic Analysis* (Washington, D.C.: U.S. Department of Justice, National Institute of Justice, 1985).

Robertson, K.G. (1989). "Canadian Intelligence Policy," Unpublished manuscript. Graduate School of European and International Studies, University of Reading, U.K.

Royal Canadian Mounted Police (R.C.M.P.) (1991), *Board of Inquiry on the Activities of the R.C.M.P. Related to Allegations Made in the Senate of Canada: Report.* [The Honourable René S. Marin, Chairman] (Ottawa: R.C.M.P., 1991).

Sallot, J., "Secret Agency Keeps Data on Individual 'Security Risks'." *The Globe and Mail,* November 21, 1984.

Schiffer, M.E., "Police Use of Paid Informers," in R.C.M.P., *Board of Inquiry on the Activities of the R.C.M.P. Related to Allegations Made in the Senate of Canada: Research Studies 1991.* [The Honourable René J. Marin, Chairman] (Ottawa: R.C.M.P., 1991).

Security Intelligence Review Committee (SIRC), *Section 54 Report to the Solicitor General of Canada on CSIS' Use of its Investigative Powers with Respect to the Labour Movement* (Ottawa: SIRC, 1988).

Stober, M., "The Limits of Police Provocation in Canada," in R.C.M.P., *Board of Inquiry on the Activities of the R.C.M.P. Related to Allegations Made in the Senate of Canada: Research Studies 1991.* [The Honourable René J. Marin, Chairman] (Ottawa: R.C.M.P., 1991).

Wilson, J.Q., *The Investigators* (New York: Basic Books, 1978).

136

Wool, G.L., "Police Informants in Canada: The Law and Reality," *Saskatchewan Law Review,* 1986 (50:2), 249–270.

Cases cited

Mack v. The Queen, (1988) 44 C.C.C. (3d) 513–565 (S.C.C.)
The Solicitor General of Canada v. Royal Commission of Inquiry into Confidentiality of Health Records in Ontario, (1981) 62 C.C.C. (2d) 193 (S.C.C.)

Acknowledgement

We wish to express our warm thanks to Ms Sylvie Gravel for granting us access to the preliminary results of her research on Police Delators.

[14]

Towards a sociological model of the police informant

Steven Greer

ABSTRACT

Despite the extensive legal, psychological, historical, and police studies literatures on a range of issues raised by police informants there is, as yet, no adequate sociological model. Proposing a particularly wide framework of inquiry, this article both suggests how such a model might be constructed and considers some of the related public policy implications.

A. INTRODUCTION

Police informants come in many forms, the information they supply can be used by crime control systems in a variety of ways, and together these variables open up a range of opportunities and dilemmas, particularly for law enforcement professing commitment to due process and the rule of law. There are two main difficulties. The first concerns the extent to which informants genuinely assist in the prevention, detection and punishment of crime, and how this contribution can be measured. It should be stressed that this is not the same issue as the extent to which the police consider certain types helpful in their investigations. The second problem concerns the establishment of effective mechanisms of democratic and legal accountability especially since reliance upon certain kinds of inform-ant appears to require much secrecy and great faith in police discretion. Political or administrative accountability involves the establishment of effective, thorough, systematic, and regular reviews by the legislature into internal police supervision of the use of certain types of informant by officers on the ground, while legal account-ability involves finding answers to three questions in particular: (1) when, if ever, is it appropriate to permit the police to refuse to disclose to a court that an informant has been used in a criminal prosecution or that his or her identity should be kept secret? (2) how can the reliability of the information which informants supply be assessed, particularly when it takes the form of testimony in criminal trials ? (3) when, if ever, can police use of *agents provocateurs* be justified?

Virtually all the legal, sociological/police studies, and historical literatures are concerned with police *informers* rather than *informants*, and there is, as yet, no adequate general sociological model (Skolnick 1975; Marx 1974 and 1988; Wool 1985–86; Oscapella 1980; Navasky 1982; Schliefman 1988: Dorn *et al.* 1992). While the term *informer* has certain cloak and dagger connotations, police *informants* include everyone who provides the police with information about any matter whatsoever, however useful or useless this may be for crime prevention and detection. It follows that many participants in the criminal justice process more familiar in other guises, for example the eye witness, the suspect who confesses, the accused who turns Queen's evidence, and even victims of crime, can be regarded as 'police informants'. It may be thought that to recast these familiar figures in this manner obscures rather than clarifies universally acknowledged roles, and it would certainly be a mistake to suggest, for example, that the victim's role as informant is more important than his or her role as victim. But this is not what is intended. The purpose of this article is to consider the implications of an expanded conception of the police informant both for social science and public policy.

The few attempts which have been made to understand the police informer (as opposed to the informant) have tended to distinguish different types by reference to motivation, criminal background, level of secrecy, and frequency of information-flow. While it cannot be denied that these are all important factors they can best be considered within a broader structural framework where the key to classification lies in two main variables: the relationship between informants and the people upon whom they inform, and their relationship with the policing agencies to whom they supply this information. Apart from the 'confession informant', considered more fully at the end of this study, two distinctions emerge when the first variable is applied. These are between, on the one hand, Outsiders and Insiders and, on the other, between Single Event Informants and Multiple Event Informants. Together these yield a fourfold typology: the Outside Single Event Informant (the casual observer), the Outside Multiple Event Informant (the snoop), the Inside Single Event Informant (the one-off accomplice witness), and the Inside Multiple Event Informant (the informer, *agent provocateur* and supergrass). Victims of crime can also be inside or outside informants depending upon whether or not they were present when the offence in question was committed. More research is needed to determine if their information is likely to be systematically distorted, and if so whether such defects are offence or offender related or derive from the manner in which victims are processed by the criminal justice and other official systems. Whether an informant is on the 'inside' or the 'outside' of an activity, and whether they have knowledge of just one or a whole series of incidents, will critically affect the kind of information which they can supply and its accuracy, detail, and the correct identification of suspects. The events reported by insiders and outsiders may be either criminal or political or a hybrid of the two but this distinction assumes greatest significance within the Inside Multiple Event Informant category where the relationship between informant and policing agencies critically determines whether the informant remains a pure informer, or becomes an *agent provocateur* or supergrass.

B. OUTSIDERS

As the name suggests outsiders are not directly involved in the activities they report to the police but merely observe them from the 'outside'. Recent research reveals the centrality of such informants to routine modern police work in Britain with some 80–90 per cent of offences reputedly brought to the attention of the police by victims, by-standers or other members of the public (Runciman Report 1993: 10).

1. The Casual Observer

The typical casual observer will be a member of the public who, on an isolated occasion and usually by chance, happens to observe a crime or any activity which they think should be brought to the attention of the police. Their information, which may either be volunteered or elicited during the course of a police investigation, may prove crucial in the detection and prosecution of crime or it may be of no significance whatsoever. Although it may also be systematically unreliable this is unlikely to be due to deliberate distortion by the witness him or herself. Psychological studies have sought to identify systematic sources of unreliability in the evidence of casual observers, e.g. poor quality of light at the scene, the distance between the observer and the event, the duration of the observation, the observer's contemporaneous awareness of what precisely was being observed, and the distorting effect of leading questions by investigators afterwards (Loftus and Wells 1984; Farrington *et al.* 1979; Clifford 1978 and 1979). In the UK juries are permitted to convict on the evidence of such witnesses without corroborative or supporting evidence, but judges must caution them about its possible defects (*R v Turnbull* [1976] 3 All ER 549).

2. The Snoop

As the name suggests, this kind of informant supplies the police with information about a number of incidents which will usually follow a pattern, e.g. drug dealing or vice. Some snoops are merely nosey parkers who like to tell tales on their neighbours while others, whose occupations put them in a position to observe other people without drawing undue attention to themselves – e.g. shop keepers, bar and hotel staff, janitors, street sweepers, post office delivery workers and taxi drivers – can provide a kind of informal police surveillance service (Skolnick 1975).

Snoops' motives may be varied. Some may act out of a sense of civic responsibility, while others may seek revenge for having been victimized by their targets in, for example, a protection racket which may or may not be connected with the activities they report to the police. Petty criminal snoops will themselves be actively involved in petty criminal activity, usually divorced from the behaviour they observe, and their prime motive for informing will generally be to ingratiate themselves with the police in the hope that their own criminality will be overlooked.

Since it may be given under the explicit or implicit threat of prosecution, information supplied by snoops, particularly petty criminal snoops, may be systematically unreliable, and there are also considerable opportunities for police corruption, i.e. not only connivance at the snoop's own criminality but sharing in its profits. The police will generally be strongly opposed to the disclosure of the identity of a particularly valued snoop, especially as a trial witness, unless the squandering of the source of information which this would entail is deemed cost-effective, while the courts have attempted to strike a balance between permitting non-disclosure to protect vital police sources and compelling disclosure when the defence of the accused demands it (Tapper 1990: 473–4). The common law treats snoops as eye witnesses unless the court takes the view that their evidence is given from improper motives in which case the judge may warn the jury of the dangers inherent in accepting their evidence (*R v Beck* [1982] 1 WLR 461).

C. INSIDERS

1. The One Off Accomplice Witness

The accomplice witness who testifies on a one off basis for the prosecution against his alleged associates may emerge with respect to any offence which involves more than one offender, in any part of the jurisdiction, and under the influence of one or more of a variety of motives including genuine contrition, the hope of striking a bargain with the prosecuting authorities in the selection of charges and/or the courts in passing sentence, revenge against fellow accomplices, or a configuration of all three. However, the decision to cooperate with the police is generally only taken after arrest and may be influenced by police suggestions. Since the accomplice witness is an offender who is likely to become a defendant and then a witness in the trial of others, there will generally be no problem from the police point of view in the disclosure of identity nor any opportunity for their participation in surveillance, much less as *agents provocateurs*, and little risk of police corruption. The transformation from suspect to Crown witness is thus amenable to an unusually high degree of public disclosure and legal accountability, although informal understandings regarding charge and sentence may be reached 'off stage' (Sanders and Young 1994: ch 7). Hitherto judges in the UK were obliged to warn juries about the dangers of convicting on the evidence of an uncorroborated accomplice testifying for the prosecution. However, s. 32 of the Criminal Justice and Public Order Act 1994 has made such warnings discretionary.

2. *Informers and Agents Provocateurs*

Inside Multiple Event Informants, the classic police informers, are notorious under a host of nicknames in the English language alone, for example, tout, rat, singer, finger, mule mouth, squealer, fink, snout, mut (apparently short for 'mutter'), snitch, stool pigeon, stoolie, and nark (probably derived from the French 'narquois', mocking or derisive). They have also been vilified in novels by, for example O'Flaherty (1925) and Seymour (1985), and despised by diverse cultures (Navasky 1982). The modern police informer will typically be closely involved in criminal organizations or political/ social associations which the police find suspicious. It should be observed, however, that these informants are likely to be merely cogs, albeit vital ones, in a complex intelligence-gathering system in which a variety of other methods, such as technological surveillance, are also likely to be employed. The pure informer merely supplies information to the police about the activities of any given political or criminal group and may do so with varying regularity. Some, generally described as police spies or agents, discharge what amounts to a professional informing role and may be either undercover police officers or private citizens, although in certain contexts the distinction may be difficult to draw. In Northern Ireland the British army distinguishes between

> an *agent*: . . . one who is authorized or instructed to obtain or to assist in obtaining information for intelligence or counter-intelligence purposes' and 'an *informant*: . . . any individual who gives information. The term is generally used to describe a casual or undirected source as distinct from an *informer*, who is normally

connected with criminal activities, can be directed, and receives payment for his services. (Dillon 1991: 309)

Informer information can be put to various uses by policing agencies; from merely keeping tabs on the activities of suspects, to the preparation of cases for court and even, in certain circumstances, selective assassination.

While also merely supplying information the *agent provocateur* will, by definition, also seek to encourage the activities of criminal or political organizations, whether or not authorized to do so by police handlers. Strangely, and in spite of strong evidence that their information is likely to be the most unreliable of all types of police informant, an *agent provocateur* or spy was not regarded by the common law as an accomplice with the result that the danger warning was not mandatory (Tapper 1990: 232). However, a warning could, and may still, be issued at the trial judge's discretion.

(i) In criminal organizations   Several studies have discussed the role of the informer in particular kinds of crime, e.g. official corruption (Grabosky 1991), conspiracy and related offences (Haglund 1990), narcotics, liquor law violations, larceny, vice, illegal gambling and prostitution (Lawler 1986; Manning and Redlinger 1977), auto theft and organized crime (Parker 1986), illegal gambling, prostitution, and pornography (Parliamentary Joint Committee on the National Crime Authority 1988), and insider dealing (Greer 1995: ch 10). Although the classic empirical study of the modern criminal informer was conducted in the USA by Skolnick in the 1960s (Skolnick 1975), more recent work suggests that little has changed in the processes described (Marx 1988; Dorn *et al.* 1992). Skolnick found that informers are particularly useful to the police in identifying those responsible for victimless offences with the police themselves typically playing the roles of complainant and witness. Policing which is heavily reliant upon informers, e.g. narcotics, tends to be highly proactive, providing the police with a challenging, high status, game-like job, and symbolizes efficient professionalism and thorough detective work (Baldwin and Kinsey 1982: 64–74). Attempts by the police to cultivate a relationship with the addict and build dependence upon particular police handlers hinge upon the bolstering of the informer's low sense of self-esteem, and the vital reinforcement of the undertaking that under no circumstances will his or her identity be disclosed to the underworld.

An informer's primary interest tends to be lenient treatment by the criminal justice system rather than financial reward (Harney and Cross 1960; Goodman and Will 1985). Skolnick also claims that the allegation that the police grant informers a licence to commit crime tends to be untrue although myths to this effect are often cultivated by informers themselves in order to ingratiate themselves with their quarry. However, officers in one police department, e.g. narcotics, tend to turn a blind eye to offences committed by their own informers which fall within the jurisdiction of another police department, e.g. burglary (Baldwin and Kinsey 1982: 72). Since secrecy is the key ingredient in the management of the informer system police records may even fail to record that an informer has been used in cases where, Skolnick claims, it is difficult to believe that this has not been the case. Even though informers are almost invariably used in crimes of vice, only 9 per cent of 508 narcotics cases on the files of the Westville police from December 1961 to March 1963 mentioned that an informer had been involved in the investigation.

Marx's study indicates that there have been two further important changes in the broader context since the mid-1970s. First, the technology available for covert policing in the USA has increased dramatically. Secondly, the scope of undercover police operations, including those in which informers are involved, has been greatly extended with these methods now increasingly being used by law enforcement agencies which never had recourse to them before, e.g. the Immigration and Naturalization Service and the Internal Revenue Service, and in respect of offences never before a target of this kind of policing, e.g. relatively unorganized street crime, burglary, and white-collar crime. A tendency has also developed for covert operations to be targeted upon individuals or groups to see what offences they may be committing, rather than upon offences to see who is committing them (Marx 1988).

(ii) In political movements   In spite of the rich historical literature on informers in various political movements, little systematic attempt has been made to study the phenomenon sociologically. In some ways this is surprising because, as the case-studies show, undercover agents can seriously affect the life of a movement by providing a means through which its activities are successfully repressed or contained. However, they can also, ironically, prolong a group's lifespan and even channel it in directions which are more dangerous to the status quo. As with the study of other brands of police informant, social scientists can find access to data difficult due to the inherent secrecy of the political informer's world. Researchers sympathetic to the groups under analysis may also be reluctant to admit that some of the movement's potency may have derived from planted agents rather than genuine devotees, while some observers may attribute participants' accounts of infiltration to paranoia and an exaggerated sense of their own importance. The source of much social research, the printed word, may also not give much indication of the informer's occult role.

In the nineteenth century police penetration of subversive organizations was widespread in Europe, especially in the Austro-Hungarian

empire during the Metternich period, in the France of Louis Phil-
ippe and Napoleon III, and in Prussia under Friedrich Wilhelm IV
(Schliefman 1988). Schliefman's study shows that those who informed on the Russian Socialist Revolutionary Party (hereafter referred to as SR) in the early twentieth century fell into three broad
categories: informers – non-party members who passed information
to the police which they had picked up casually; secret agents or
agents provocateurs – party members who reported regularly to the
police and were paid for their information; and external agents,
filers or *shpiki* – low-ranking police officers whose sole task was to tail
suspects, known only by a code-name, and to monitor where they
went and whom they met (Schliefman 1988). Although some were
volunteers, many secret agents were recruited after arrest and confession and, in order to dispel suspicion were released by way of a
staged 'escape'. Schliefman concludes that, although the number of
secret agents operating in the SR party was smaller than the party
itself believed, they eventually became the lynch-pin of political
police work hastening the party's organizational and ethical breakdown, deepening rifts within the leadership, and bringing grass roots
discontent to the surface. However, in spite of this, police preconceptions exaggerated the SR's importance and the inefficiency of
the police organizational structure resulted in poor intelligence co-
ordination which prevented its full potential from being realized.

Navasky (1982) and Marx (1974) offer some particularly valuable
insights into the role of informers in modern non-violent political
movements in the USA. In his study of informers in the McCarthy
anti-communist witch-hunts of the 1950s, Navasky distinguishes four
types according to motivation: the informer as patriot – who informed out of hostility to the group in question; the espionage informer – a police officer or other official who penetrated a given
movement; the conspiracy informer – a member of the movement
who regularly supplied official agencies with information; and the
liberal informer – the non-political individual who liked to be helpful
to the authorities when the opportunity arose. Navasky also identifies
numerous other kinds according to a variety of other variables: the
reluctant, enthusiastic, informed and philosophical, truth-telling,
combative, denigrating, noisey, comic, husband-and-wife, volunteer,
informer-by-dispensation, and resister-informer. The dubious information supplied by informers was not only instrumental in ruining
numerous careers, particularly in the glamorous Hollywood film industry, but also assisted in the conviction of many suspected subver-
sives in the late 1940s and early 1950s. The trial of eleven leaders of
the Communist Party in New York in 1949, for example, 'wrote the
script for a series of similar trials across the country' featuring a
'parade of FBI informants and ex-Communists many of them professional informers' (Navasky 1982: 4). Navasky concludes that apart

from the shattered lives of those denounced as communists or fellow-travellers,

> the informer's particular contribution was to pollute the public well, to poison social life in general, to destroy the very possibility of a community; for the informer operates on the principle of betrayal and the community survives on the principle of trust. (p 347)

In his study of informers in the radical US political and social movements of the 1960s Marx lists five principal motives – patriotism/ ideological opposition to the group in question; coercion from the police (principally the threat of arrest and prosecution followed by the prospect of offers of immunity from prosecution, leniency in the selection of charges, release from police custody or help with various official problems, e.g. those concerning naturalization); inducement; activist disaffection (e.g. a transformation in beliefs, personal vendettas, leadership contests, attempts to change the direction of the organization, and rivalry with other groups at the same end of the political spectrum); and the desire to become a double agent. While the line between the coercion and the inducement categories is blurred the distinction is none the less important, the latter referring to those informers who were motivated purely by the prospect of financial gain. The desire to become a double agent can also be complex. Marx found that some double agents deliberately gave the authorities false information and acted as the movement's spy deep in officialdom, others were opportunistic and cooperated with, or misled, either side as it suited their own interests, while others were ambivalent about their true allegiances and shifted their loyalties back and forth. The double agent can, therefore, present problems both for the police and the movement to which they belong.

Marx discovered that, in two-thirds of the 34 cases he examined, informers went beyond passive information gathering to active provocation and that certain kinds of agent may become *agents provocateurs* by 'going native', a particular risk with movements based upon distinct ethnic or socio-economic characteristics which the informer must share if he or she is to infiltrate effectively. The political *agent provocateur* may encourage both further legal and illegal activities but his or her classic function is to push political groups which have been acting legally into committing crimes in order to provide the police with a justification for making arrests and initiating prosecutions. The police may have other motives for using political *agents provocateurs*, e.g. to encourage divisions within a given group between those who favour and those who are opposed to illegality, or to damage the group's public image. Even with strong institutional supervision, however, bureaucratic pressures can militate against the careful and thorough assessment of the reliability of the information which a political informer or *agent provocateur* supplies. The efficiency of police checks on reliability is also likely to decrease the more the information confirms preconceptions of the nature of the group under surveillance.

Marx argues that since most of the information gathered by political informers never featured in court cases, the political informer in the USA in the 1960s may have merely enabled the police to take action 'consistent with their own sense of justice and morality, independent of the substantive and procedural requirements of the law' (Marx 1974: 436). Although police corruption, in the sense of bribery and profiteering, is not particularly likely in this context, there is a risk that distorted police perspectives will, in their turn, have a distorting impact upon the politics of the society in question, arguably a corruption of a potentially more serious kind. Civil libertarians have suggested various restrictions upon the deployment of undercover political agents, including making their use in a preventative capacity a violation of the First and Fourth amendments to the US Constitution; subjecting the use of informers to the same restrictions the authorities now face with respect to wire-tapping and search and seize operations; and the establishment of a domestic intelligence advisory council to monitor intelligence activities. As far as social science is concerned, the researcher interested in social movements would be well advised to be alert to the possible distorting effects that a police interloper may be exerting (Marx 1974: 439).

3. Supergrasses

The term 'supergrass' was first coined by journalists in the early 1970s – from the slang 'grass' for informer – to refer to members of the London underworld who were prepared to break the traditional code of silence and offer their testimony to the prosecution. While they can fulfill the functions of both pure informer and *agent provocateur* the supergrass's unique contribution is to allow the carefully cultivated results of sophisticated police intelligence-gathering systems to be presented in court for the purpose of convicting large numbers of suspected terrorists or organized criminals, typically in mass trials. For this reason they can have no role in legal political organizations. The four key factors conducive to the construction of supergrass systems are: the construction of mature informer and intelligence-gathering systems, the perceived failure of other methods to deal with a particularly serious problem of crime or political violence, a crisis of allegiance on the part of at least some members of the target organizations, and the attractiveness of the officially sanctioned rewards on offer – typically immunity from prosecution, reduced prison sentences, and new lives and new identities elsewhere (Greer 1995).

The dangers associated with accomplice evidence, discussed above, are particularly acute with respect to supergrasses. Each has been involved in serious, and mostly violent crime and will, therefore, be regarded by the legal system as of unusually bad character even compared with other possible accomplice witnesses. The pressure to tell a story sufficiently appealing to attract the various rewards on offer is also likely to be more intense than with most other accomplices turning State's evidence. There is, in addition, ample time and opportunity during the many months spent in police protective custody for false evidence to be rehearsed in preparation for a convincing courtroom performance. The risk of unreliability is greatly increased by the complexity of the issues which any case is likely to raise, even assuming incorrigible bona fides on the part of all concerned. As already noted, psychological studies illustrate how accuracy of recollection can be seriously, and unintentionally, distorted by the lapse of time between the event and the recording of statements and by intervening suggestions as to what, and who, the original event may have involved (Clifford 1979; Loftus and Wells 1984).

Employing the services of supergrasses is a high-risk strategy for the police and other agencies in the prosecution process since, if it succeeds, the punishment of tens, if not hundreds, of suspects is assured. But if it fails, a valuable source of intelligence plus considerable resources will have been squandered, exposing the police and criminal justice system to considerable public criticism. It follows that the decision to promote supergrass trials in any jurisdiction is likely to be taken at a high political level with resources made available in advance for its successful administration.

The police are the key agency in any supergrass process, since they will be most instrumental in deciding whom to recruit and whom to prosecute. Supergrass systems are based upon proactive policing and the deployment of what, in the context of criminal informers, Skolnick (1975) calls 'aggressive intelligence', with the management of the supergrasses themselves likely to be high-status police work. It is also clear that, like Skolnick's informers, what motivates supergrasses most is self-interest, particularly the prospect of leniency in, or the avoidance of, punishment. The rewards available are, characteristically, the most generous any criminal justice system is prepared to offer informants and can include immunity from prosecution, lenient prison sentences and comparative luxury while serving them, money, and new lives with fresh identities away from the original sphere of operations.

Supergrass systems create some risk of police profiteering, but only in relation to organized acquisitive crime. But the possibility of corruption of the rule of law is an inherent danger because without proper and effective supervision by legislature and courts, supergrass processes enable the police to by-pass more mundane and painstaking investigative methods effectively enabling them to determine who deserves punishment for which offence. Such systems also create the further risk that informer and supergrass-based policing may be extended into other areas of police work because of the amount of time and effort it can save.

(i) In criminal organizations Supergrass systems directed against organized crime appeared in England and the USA in the 1970s and in Italy in the 1980s. In spite of broad similarities each system has had its own unique characteristics with particularly significant differences having emerged in relation to institutionalization and formal inter-agency co-ordination. Both the US and English systems were successfully institutionalized, although co-ordination between relevant official agencies has been different in each jurisdiction, with more formal arrangements in the former than in the latter. The lack of effective inter-agency coordination in the Italian anti-mafia process has been a key factor inhibiting its successful institutionalization.

The English supergrass system was constructed in direct response to a dramatic rise in the incidence of serious organized crime, particularly bank robberies in the London area in the early 1970s and an official perception that existing methods of dealing with it were ineffective (Criminal Law Revision Committee 1972; Zander 1974; Seymour 1982; Goodman & Will 1985; Slipper 1981; O'Mahoney with Wooding 1978). It declined in the 1980s, however, for three main reasons. First, in order to facilitate the move from armed robbery to illegal drugs, professional criminals formed more close-knit organizations which were less open to penetration by informers. Secondly, the penalties for betrayal became much more severe – death or serious injury. Thirdly, juries became more distrustful of supergrass evidence (Campbell 1994).

The origins of the US Witness Protection (or Witness Security) Program lie in the US Task Force on Organized Crime which, in 1967, identified inadequate protection for vulnerable witnesses as a major law enforcement shortcoming in this context. From the decision of the Supreme Court in *Roviaro* v *United States* in 1957 (353 U.S. 53) both state and federal courts have upheld the principle that an informer's identity must be disclosed where it is relevant and helpful to the guilt or innocence of the accused, but not where it merely goes to the issue of probable cause in respect of an arrest or the issuing of a search warrant (Schlichter 1971). The Witness Protection Program, established by Title V of the Organized Crime Control Act 1970, authorized the Attorney General to provide short-term or permanent protection plus new identities, credit cards, indefinite subsistence payments, plus fictitious work histories, military service records and school reports, to vulnerable witnesses involved in organized crime trials – the majority of whom are criminals themselves – and to their families.

Towards a sociological model of the police informant   521

In 1984 the Witness Protection Program was overhauled by Congress to offer the public greater protection against recidivism by protected witnesses (Levin 1985). Title V of the 1970 Act was repealed and a new statutory foundation was provided by the Witness Security Reform Act 1984. The WPP was extended to include 'organized criminal activity or other serious offence' (Pub.L. No. 98–473, § 1208, 98 Stat. 2153) and the admission criteria were also more fully specified. Most of those involved in the WPP cooperate in return for one of three rewards: immunity from prosecution, a lenient sentence, or early release from prison. By law all inducements, including express or implicit promises of leniency must be disclosed to lawyers defending those implicated by a protected witness's testimony (*Giglio* v *United States*, 405 U.S. 150 (1972); *People* v *Westmoreland*, 58 CA3d 32 (1976); *United States* v *Oxman et al.*, 3d Cir. No. 83–1531, August 1, 1984; CNPDS 1987; 232). Requests for immunity from prosecution are reviewed by senior prosecutors but final approval needs to be obtained from the US Assistant Attorney General and the general rule is that immunity is to be given only as a last resort (CNPDS 1987: 159–160). It is also possible for accomplice witnesses to be offered 'post-conviction use-immunity', i.e. immunity from prosecution *after* they have given their testimony (CNPDS 1987: 255–259; *People* v *Stewart*, 1 CA3d 339 (1965); *People* v *Watson*, 89 CA3d 376 (1979); *People* v *Campbell*, 137 CA3d 867 (1982)) while those convicted can also be placed on probation on condition that they cooperate with the prosecution (*United States* v *Worcester*, 190 F. Supp. 548 (D. Mass. 1961)). Cooperative accomplices can also be convicted with sentence deferred until after they have testified in the trial of others (CNPDS 1987: 172; *United States* v *Dailey*, 759 F.2d 192 (1st Cir.) 1985).

An anti-mafia offensive in Italy, in which the evidence of *pentiti* (repentants) was of central importance, began with the arrest of the most celebrated supergrass of modern times, Tommaso Buscetta, in the USA in 1984 (Greer 1995: ch 10). However, as a result of political inerta stemming from collusion between the mafia and elements within the Italian political establishment, a formal witness protection scheme was not established until 1991, the success of which remains to be seen (Falcone with Padovani 1992: xvi and 46) Buscetta's information, plus other evidence including that of fellow *pentito* and US protected witness Salvatore Contorno, led to the first Italian mafia supergrass trial involving 475 defendants held in the specially constructed 'bunker' courtroom inside Palermo's ancient Ucciardone prison. On 16 December 1987, twenty two months after it had begun, the trial's 350th session ended with 338 convictions. These 'maxi-proceedings' were followed by a string of others involving both major and minor supergrasses. However, in February 1989, 80 allegedly prominent mafiosi were acquitted in Palermo's third bunker trial when the testimonies of the *pentiti* involved were rejected, and, on 22

February 1992, 40 defendants in the first bunker trial were set free under a new law prohibiting detention for longer than 12 months between conviction and appeal. In 1992 the mafia war in Italy entered a further deadly phase with the murders, in May and July respectively, of Italy's two most experienced anti-mafia investigating magistrates, Giovanni Falcone and Paolo Borsilino, amidst suspicions of security service involvement. In June that year legislation was passed which, amongst other things formalized the contribution of *pentiti* with guarantees of reduced sentences and protection. Some 700 alleged mafiosi were swiftly arrested and in the spring of 1993 Buscetta re-emerged from hiding confirming suspicions that, when in power, former Italian premier and senior statesman, Guilio Andreotti, had protected the clans from successful prosecution.

(ii) In violent political movements   In the 1980s counter-terrorist super-grass systems appeared in Northern Ireland and Italy. While the law in France and Spain was also changed in the 1980s to encourage members of violent political organizations to cooperate with the authorities in the arrest and prosecution of their confederates, this did not result in mass trials on informer evidence. Experiments with supergrass evidence also occurred in Germany in the mid-1970s but it was not until the 1990s that a supergrass process enabled the rump of the left-wing Red Army Faction to be successfully prosecuted. The supergrass processes in Italy and Germany have been regulated by temporary legislation and have been used to devastating effect particularly against both armed left and right. The Northern Irish process, on the other hand, uniquely failed to be successfully institutionalized, the result of an unusual judicial responsiveness to an effective public campaign against the lack of adherence to due process safeguards at its inception (Greer 1995).

The emergence of the supergrass system in Northern Ireland in the early 1980s stemmed from the maturing of the intelligence system throughout the 1970s, the difficulties which the police faced in obtaining confessions from key terrorist suspects following restrictions on police interrogation methods implemented in the wake of the Bennett report in 1979, and a crisis of allegiance amongst certain paramilitary activists especially the 'second-time rounders' who, by the early 1980s, had already served one period of imprisonment and, having been arrested again, could not face another. It began hesitantly with two comparatively modest trials in 1981, experienced a brief ascendancy in 1983 when three major trials resulted in the conviction of 56 of the 64 defendants, then experienced a prolonged decline and ultimate collapse as the courts reversed their original decisions that uncorroborated convictions could be justified. The only convictions to survive the appeal hearings, which ended in 1986, were those sustained almost entirely by confessions (Greer 1995).

The construction of a *pentiti* process against the armed left in Italy began with the re-organization of the intelligence-gathering system in the mid-1970s (Seaton-Watson 1988), followed by the enactment of a series of temporary laws designed to encourage terrorists to collaborate with the authorities (Vercher 1992). By the early 1980s the frequency of terrorist incidents has declined, *pentiti* had decimated the armed right (Seaton-Watson 1988), hundreds of left wing suspects had been arrested, and whole armed leftist organizations had been dismantled (Mosconi and Pisapia 1981). However, no attempt was made in Italy to protect the political *pentiti* in the manner of the Witness Protection Program of the USA, or even the less formal arrangements found in the supergrass system in Northern Ireland (Hallenstein 1984).

Although the trial, in May 1975 in Germany, of the four founding members of the Red Army Faction (or Baader-Meinhof gang), Andreas Baader, Ulrike Meinhof, Jan Karl Raspe and Gudrun Ensslin, hinged upon the testimony of Gerhard Müller – who had turned states evidence – it was not until the mid-1980s that a number of trials of leading neo-Nazi activists took place in which accomplice evidence was of some importance. In June 1989 a new temporary scheme which lapsed in 1992 was introduced by the legislature (*Nr. 26 Tag der Ausgabe: Bonn, 15 Juni 1989*) which enabled several former RAF activists, who had enjoyed the protection of the secret police in the former East Germany, to turn *staatzeuge* (state witness) in return for greatly reduced prison sentences.

D. THE CONFESSION INFORMANT

The term 'confession informant' is reserved here for those suspects who, unlike all the others considered so far, inform only against themselves. Although there are now substantial psychological and legal literatures on how and why confessions are made in police custody, the issues discussed have rarely, if ever, been considered part of the debate about police informants. Yet the process by which suspects confess is highly relevant to the informant debate for two reasons. In the first place confessions are prized by the police for their information content, for their potential use as evidence against those who have made them, and because they signify the point in police interrogations where the suspect has been 'broken' and where negotiation of charge and plea can begin in earnest. Secondly, the dynamics of the interrogation itself, together with certain psychological and sociological characteristics of the suspect, can be potent sources of distortion in this kind of information (McConville 1993).

The problem with confessions as a source of police information can be simply stated. True confessions voluntarily offered provide a

cast-iron legal basis for conviction. But confessions which may appear
to be true and apparently elicited without improper pressure may be
made by entirely innocent parties. The genuinely guilty may retract
true confessions falsely claiming they were improperly obtained, while
the innocent may offer no objection to what are in fact false
confessions. The Runciman report notes these difficulties and refers
to the substantial body of psychological research which has allowed
four types of false confession to be distinguished: what may be called
'fantasy confessions' made by people suffering from severe mental
problems which prevent them from distinguishing fact from reality;
what may be termed 'diversionary confessions' made in the attempt to
protect someone else from interrogation and prosecution; 'coerced-
complaint confessions' made by those who desperately want to escape
the stress created by police interviews; and 'coerced-internalized
confessions' made by the highly suggestible who, though entirely
innocent and sometimes even physically incapable of having done
what is alleged, none the less accept police accusations. (Runciman
Report 1993: 57; Gudjonsson 1992). The task for the criminal justice
system is to devise adequate procedures to enable true confessions to
be distinguished from false, and those obtained under undue pressure from those offered without it. There are broadly three, not
necessarily mutually exclusive, methods of attempting to achieve these
objectives: attempting to control the circumstances in which confessions are made, typically police custody, in order to reduce the risk
of unreliability; establishing appropriate tests for the admissibility of
this kind of evidence at trial linked to the manner in which the
confession was obtained or to the strength of other prosecution
evidence; and seeking to regulate reliance by courts upon confessions
which pass the admissibility test by, for example, discouraging or even
prohibiting, conviction on this basis alone. The majority of the Royal
Commission on Criminal Justice recommended that confessions
unsupported by other evidence should be capable of being put to the
jury subject to judicial warnings about unreliability (Runciman Report
1993: 54).

E. CONCLUSION

In spite of extensive literatures ranging across several disciplines the
problems posed by the police informant are still imperfectly understood. While the sources of systematic distortion in the information
provided by the casual observer are generally well appreciated and
recognized by the legal system, this is not so obviously true of that
provided by crime victims or snoops. The problem of the confession as
a source of information for the police has been hotly debated and the
proper approach which the criminal justice system should take

remains controversial. Although vital, the distinction between the accomplice witness and the supergrass has not always been fully accepted and while the justification for a mandatory accomplice evidence warning may be difficult to justify for all accomplices who testify for the Crown, the evidence of supergrasses clearly requires it. The failure of the legal system to treat the evidence of *agents provocateurs* as inherently unreliable and requiring a danger warning is also difficult to defend as is the use of police informants in legal political movements. Finally, the strong emphasis upon Congressional scrutiny in the US Witness Protection Program is, in this respect at least, a model worth following, and suggests that informer and supergrass systems in the UK should be much more closely monitored by parliament, perhaps through standing Informer Commissions.

It would be naive to think that modern democratic policing could dispense with the services of informants, but their role, and the effectiveness of existing and potential channels of public accountability, ought to be kept constantly under review in order to guard against the various problems identified above. The principal task for social scientists and policy analysts in this domain is to attempt to discover in more detail the role played in police investigations by information from various sources – informants, objects, documents, audio and video recording – together with the sources of systematic distortion and other problems to which it may give rise, and to suggest how the mechanisms of public accountability could be improved.

(Date accepted: January 1995)

Steven Greer
Department of Law
University of Bristol

BIBLIOGRAPHY

Baldwin, R. and R. Kinsey 1982 *Police Powers and Politics*, London: Quartet Books.

Bennett Report 1979 *Report of the Committee of Inquiry into Police Interrogation Procedures in Northern Ireland*, Cmnd. 7497, London: HMSO.

Campbell, D. 1994 *The Underworld*, London: BBC Books.

Clifford, B. 1978 *The Psychology of Person Identification*, London: Routledge and Kegan Paul.

Clifford, B. 1979 'Eye Witness Testimony: The Bridging of a Credibility Gap' in Farrington *et al.* (1979).

CNPDS 1987 *Convenzione per una recera su normative ed esperienza di maxiprocessi e sulla utilizzabilita e gestibilita probatoria dei c.d.testimoni della testimoni della corona e della relative tutela. Confronto con l' esperienza Italiane. Rapporto finale, 2 Allegati, II*, Milan: Centro Nazionale di Prevenzione e Difesa Sociale.

Criminal Law Revision Committee 1972 *Eleventh Report, Evidence General*, Cmnd 4991, London: HMSO.

Dillon, M. 1991 *The Dirty War*, London: Arrow Books.

Dorn, N., Murji, K. and South, N. 1992 *Traffickers: Drug Markets and Law Enforcement*, London: Routledge.

Falcone, G. with Padovani, M. 1992 *Men of Honour: The Truth About the Mafia*, London: Warner Books.

Farrington, D., Hawkins, K. and Lloyd-Bostock, S. 1979 *Psychology, Law and Legal Processes*, London: Macmillan Press.

Goodman, J. and Will, I. 1985 *Underworld*, London: Harrap.

Grabosky, P.N. 1991 'Prosecutors, Informants and the Integrity of the Criminal Justice System', Unpublished Report, Australian Institute of Criminology.

Greer, S. 1995 *Supergrasses: A Study in Anti-terrorist Law Enforcement in Northern Ireland*, Oxford: Clarendon Press.

Gudjonsson, G.H. 1992 *The Psychology of Interrogations, Confessions and Testimony*, Chichester: Wiley.

Haglund, E. 1990 'Impeaching the Underworld Informant', *Southern California Law Review* 63: 1407–47.

Hallenstein, D. 1984 'Walking Corpses', *The Sunday Times Colour Supplement* 4 September.

Harney, M.L. and Cross, J.C. 1960 *The Informer in Law Enforcement*, Springfield, Illinois, USA: Charles Thomas.

Lawler, L.E. 1986 'Police Informer Privilege: A Study for the Law Reform Commission of Canada', *Criminal Law Quarterly* 28: 91–128.

Levin, J.M. 1985 'Organized Crime and Insulated Violence: Federal Liability for Illegal Conduct in the Witness Protection Program', *Journal of Criminal Law and Criminology* 76: 208–50.

Loftus, E. and Wells, G. (eds) 1984 *Eyewitness Testimony: Psychological Perspectives*, Cambridge: Cambridge University Press.

Manning, P.K. and Redlinger, L.J. 1977 'Invitational Edges of Corruption: Some Consequences of Narcotic Law Enforcement' in P. Rock (ed.) *Drugs and Politics*, London: Transaction Books.

Marx, G.T. 1974 'Thoughts on a Neglected Category of Social Movement Participant: The *Agent Provocateur* and the Informant', *American Journal of Sociology* 80: 402–40.

Marx, G.T. 1988 *Undercover: Police Surveillance in America*, Berkeley: University of California Press.

McConville, M. 1993 *Corroboration and Confessions. The Impact of a Rule Requiring That No Conviction Can Be Sustained on the Basis of Confession Evidence Alone*, London: Royal Commission on Criminal Justice Research Study No. 13, HMSO.

Mosconi, G. and Pisapia, G. 1981 'The Stereotype of the Repentant Terrorist: His Nature and Functions', *European Group for the Study of Deviance and Social Control, Working Papers in Criminology* 3: 188–207.

Navasky, V. 1982 *Naming Names*, London: Calder.

O'Flaherty, L. 1925 *The Informer*, London: Jonathan Cape.

O'Mahoney, M. with Wooding, D. 1978 *King Squealer: The True Story of Maurice O'Mahoney*, London: W. H. Allen.

Oscapella, E. 1980 'A Study of Informers in England', *Criminal Law Review* 136–46.

Parker, R. 1986 Confidential Informants and the Truth Finding Function, *Cooley Law Review* 4: 565–73.

Parliamentary Joint Committee on the National Crime Authority 1988 *Witness Protection*, Canberra: Australian Government Publishing.

Runciman Report 1993 *Report of Royal Commission on Criminal Justice*, Cm.2263, London: HMSO.

Sanders, A. and Young, R. 1994 *Criminal Justice*, London: Butterworths.

Schliefman, N. 1988 *Undercover Agents in the Russian Revolutionary Movement: The SR Party, 1902–14*, London: Macmillan.

Schlichter, J. 1971 'The Outwardly Sufficient Search Warrant Affidavit: What If It's False?', *University of California Los Angeles Law Review* 96: 96–147.

Seaton-Watson, C. 1988 'Terrorism in Italy', in J. Lodge (ed) *The Threat of Terrorism*, Brighton: Wheatsheaf Books.

Seymour, D. 1982 'What good have supergrasses done for anyone but themselves?', *Legal Action Group Bulletin*, Dec. 7–9.

Seymour, G. 1985 *Field of Blood*, London: Collins.

Skolnick, J. H. 1975 *Justice Without Trial: Law Enforcement in Democratic Society* (2nd ed), New York: John Wiley and Sons.

Slipper, J. 1981 *Slipper of the Yard*, London: Sidgwick and Jackson.

Tapper, C. 1990 *Cross on Evidence* 7th edn, London: Butterworths.

Vercher, A. 1992 *Terrorism in Europe: An International Comparative Legal Analysis*, Oxford: Clarendon Press.

Wool, G.J. 1985–86 'Police Informants

in Canada: The Law and the Reality', *Saskatchewan Law Review* 50: 249–70.

Zander, M. 1974 'Are Too Many Professional Criminals Avoiding Conviction? – A Study in Britain's Two Busiest Courts', *Modern Law Review* 37: 28–61.

[15]

SUBTERRANEAN BLUES: CONFLICT AS AN UNINTENDED CONSEQUENCE OF THE POLICE USE OF INFORMERS

CLIVE NORRIS[a],* and COLIN DUNNIGHAN[b]

[a] *Centre for Criminology and Criminal Justice,
University of Hull, Hull HU6 7RX*
[b] *Police Training and Research Centre, University of Teesside*

(Received 23 September 1998; in final form 16 August 1999)

The paper begins by showing that pro-active policing methods, and in particular the use of paid informers, has become a *de facto* national policy for policing in the United Kingdom. It reviews some of the literature on this type of policing and suggests that a significant absence in the discussion about police use of informants has been the degree and nature of conflict consequent from such police methods. Drawing on data from an ESRC funded project, the paper then goes on to describe and delineate different forms of conflict that may emerge in the context of informant based policing and argues that such conflict operates at the heart of the symbolic imagery of the police organisation.

KEY WORDS: Pro-active policing; informants; surveillance; detectives; conflict; ethics; police deviance

INTRODUCTION

In a sobering review of police effectiveness across five countries, David Bayley, has written:

The police spend very little of their time in dealing with crime, and when they do, it is with crimes that have already been committed. Detectives know they are unlikely to be able to find the perpetrators of crimes unless they are identified by the victims of people at the scene. As a result most crime especially property crime, goes unsolved. (Bayley, 1996: 29)

The recognition of the limited potential for traditional detective work to solve crime has given official impetus in a number of countries to more proactive based methods of investigation (Marx, 1988). In England and Wales this impetus came in 1993 with the publication of the Audit Commission report *Helping with Enquiries: Tackling Crime Effectively* (Audit Commission, 1993). The report argued that in the wake of falling clear up rates and generally rising crime rates, the increased use of informers should become a key element in criminal investigation. This impetus has been given added authority from ACPO, Her Majesty's Inspectorate of Police and the Home Office's Police Research Group. In September 1995 ACPO launched its new 'National Guidelines on the Use and Management of Informants' (ACPO, 1995) aimed at facilitating the use of informers. Throughout the 1990s the Inspectorate has been paying special attention to the use of informers and its reports on individual forces and squads, are littered with exhortations as to the necessity and the desirability of informers. The following quotes from the inspection reports on Staffordshire Constabulary, and Number Seven Regional Crime Squads are typical:

A crucial element to the detection of crime is the ability of a force to concentrate its efforts on the active criminal. The development of a proactive informant base is essential to this. (HMIC, 1994a: 7)

   The regular and effective use of criminal informants is a cost effective means of detecting crime. (HMIC, 1994b: v)

The Home Office's Police Research Group which was formed in 1992 with a remit to 'identify and disseminate good policing practice', has also been instrumental in raising the issue of the police use of informers to the centre stage. Since 1993 it has published four studies into proactive policing and informant handling (Maguire and John, 1995; Hanvey, 1995; Balsdon, 1996; Police Research Group, 1995).

   With 52 police forces and the constitutionally enshrined independence of Chief Constables (Reiner, 1992) it is always difficult to talk about national police policy in the United Kingdom. However, when the key players in shaping police policy – identified by Weatheritt (1993) and Newburn and Jones (1996) as the Home Office, the Audit Commission, the Inspectorate and ACPO – appear to be simultaneously playing the same tune then, we have a de facto national policy to facilitate and encourage the use of informers.

It is perhaps a testimony to the weakness of the principle of account-ability surrounding the British police that such a major shift in policy has been achieved with almost no public debate or critical scrutiny. This is important because the increased use of informers has been presented as an unqualified good, and a particularly cost effective mechanism for detecting and clearing up crime (Audit Commission, 1993: 39; HMIC, 1993c: 14; ACPO, 1995: v).

What is missing from these appraisals is a systematic assessment of the consequences of informant based police strategies which balances the perceived cost effectiveness against the other less positive out-comes. As Marx has argued, under cover police work has various unin-tended and ironic outcomes, which include deviancy amplification, licensing criminals, and the covert facilitation of criminal activities (Marx, 1981; 1988; see also Reuter, 1983).

Brodeur (1991), following Marx, has argued that in relation to the Canadian use of informers, outcomes can be intended or unintended, desirable or undesirable – a four fold classification of consequences. The desirable and intended can include the repression and prevention of crime. The desirable but never-the-less unintended outcomes may include boosting police morale, particularly after a successful opera-tion, and the deterrence of criminal activity. Brodeur proposes that as knowledge of infiltration becomes more widespread, individuals will become reluctant to engage with others in criminal conspiracies. Weighed against these desirable consequences are those which are undesirable, and which may also be intended and unintended. Undesir-able but intended consequences include crime facilitation through the use of agent provocateurs, and the licensing of criminals. Finally, Bro-deur suggests outcomes which are both undersirable and unintended, such as police corruption, the delegitimisation of the criminal justice system as a result of inevitable scandals, and police disorganisation through the corrosive effects of secrecy (1991: 63–71).

We feel it appropriate to add another category to Brodeur's list of undesirable and unintended consequences: the use of informers gener-ates conflict. Indeed Brodeur touches on this when discussing police disorganisation, when he notes, 'the use of informers may strain the relationship between police and the personnel in other components in the criminal justice system'. However, we would go further and argue that not only can the use of informers create conflict with other agencies within the criminal justice system but creates major tensions and conflicts within the police organisation itself. In this paper we concentrate on the nature of these conflicts and examine how they are played out on the organisational stage. We start by examining the general ambivalence surrounding the use of informers within the police organisation and then consider the specific conflicts that arise in and between different segments of the organisation and other agencies within the criminal justice system.

Methodology

The research was primarily carried out in two English police force areas which, taken together, comprise four large urban conurbations and contain small and medium sized towns and villages with a combined population in excess of two million. Between 1993 and 1995 we carried out in-depth semi-structured interviews with a sample of sixty-two police officers and eleven professional informants; analysed a detailed questionnaire completed by two hundred and twenty-eight officers (a response rate of 79 per cent); scrutinised a sample of one hundred and fourteen cases involving the use of informants by detectives and examined police prosecution files and official records relating to such use. We also had formal and informal interviews with officers from a number of other police forces, Regional Crime Squads and Special Branch. A more detailed account of the methodological issues arising from this project can be found in Dunnighan (1995) and Norris (1996).

REPUGNANT RECIPROCITY: INFORMERS AS A GENERAL SOURCE OF CONFLICT

For informers to be useful on more than just a one off basis it is essential that reciprocity develops. This reciprocity, of course implies a mutuality of advantage and it is the recognition that informers are gaining as a result of their activities that lies at the heart of the tensions and conflicts surrounding the use of informers. For some detectives the idea that informers should gain from a morally repugnant activity is in itself repulsive. As one detective explained of his colleagues:

Tecs I know don't like informers, they can't really stand them and they think they are an evil ... they just don't like the thought of the evil little shits grassing up on their friends. (DS 22 years service)

As another explained in relation to his uniform colleagues:

I think they class them all as scum and depending on who the informer is, if he is a bad criminal they wouldn't do anything to help him, no matter what he's doing for us. (DC 12 years service)

It is not just those who avoid the use of informers who are uneasy about the morality of relying on information from a tainted source. As two experienced handlers remarked:

I do feel negatively about them . . . most are low life . . . I'm old fashioned. I believe in loyalty to family, friends, bosses. Informers are 180 degrees away from them. (DS 15 years service)
    . . . at the end of day these are the vermin, these are the low life and you've got to remember they are low life and you use them, then kick their back-sides out. (DC 12 years service)

For some officers, then, the idea that the police benefit from the duplicity and deceit of 'scum', 'low life' and 'vermin' is what makes them hostile to the use of informers. Others, however, take a more positive view. In the words of one detective sergeant:

It would be immoral if the police were told they couldn't use informers. In my view the public support the use of informers. I accept though that they would be horrified if they knew we turned a blind eye to informers committing crime in order for them to gain credibility [with other criminals]. The public would rather not know about the dark side of using informers. (DS 13 years service)

In the main, however, officers take a pragmatic and utilitarian approach which recognises the irony of allowing a criminal to benefit from police deals and the betrayal of family, friends, and associates. In the words of a number of officers, they see it as a 'necessary evil'.

The ambivalence that accompanies the irony is heightened when it comes to the specific operating practices of individual detectives, and in the absence of training, Force policy or official guidance in such matters, handlers either teach themselves or learn from each other in a clandestine pupilage (Dunnighan and Norris, 1995; 1996b; 1996c). In this situation it is difficult for generalised norms to emerge which would serve as a bench mark to guide conduct. Instead what emerges are individualised standards and a recognition that the limits on conduct are largely a matter of personal preference and conscience:

It is a very fine line and I think that once you get into more serious crimes and especially if the informants are so closely connected with criminal activities themselves then I think I have a problem with that. I appreciate that the only way that they are going to be able to become informers is to mix with the people who are committing the crimes but . . . I know what happens on occasions is that deals are done, then that's when I find it morally wrong or very difficult to come to terms with. If you've got somebody who is given money for it yes but when deals are starting to be done and well 'we'll turn a blind eye for that if you get information for this' then that's when I can't come to grips with it myself. (Uniform Inspector 15 years)

While this officer is ruling about the possibility of turning a blind eye to an informers offences in exchange for information, it is clear this is a personal decision for, as he went on to say, 'I can probably appreciate why they are done as well, but for myself I could never ever do that'. Other officers are happy to overlook offences as long as the 'price is right', and their criticisms are directed to the belief that some handlers are short changed:

I have a problem with the burglar giving us shoplifters. It should be the other way round. Why let informers off when all you are getting back is petty stuff? (DC 18 years service)

Other officers, while accepting the necessity of deals, believed that some serious offences should not be traded:

If it was a serious offence of burglaries and things like that, I wouldn't be bothered I would just let him go to court and get remanded. (DC 12 years)

Such views are not universally shared, however, and one officer reported, turning a blind eye to a major theft of £2500 by an informer, allowing the informer to keep half the proceeds in exchange for turning in his accomplice. Another DC explained that, although his informer was coming before the court charged with GBH for seriously assaulting a man with a cricket bat, 'he's been a good informer so I'll try and get him a reduced sentence with a letter (to the judge)'.

Different officers have different lines as to what is acceptable and what is not but as one DCI explained even his own line moved:

My line is in a different place as a DI than it was as a DS or a DC and it's changed since PACE. But to be honest my line is beginning to go back to where it was when I was a DC because I'm going no further in this job. I've failed five boards [promotion boards] and I'm turning back over and starting to do the job I enjoy, catching criminals. (DI 25 years service)

One consequence of this individualised line is that, in the absence of agreed norms, handlers are wise to keep details of the deals secret and thus avoiding stepping over somebody else's line:

I know some officers who wouldn't go through their supervision for anything to do with informers. But here the DI and the Super want results and are very flexible, so I would talk to them but other bosses have a different attitude about favours and letting people off. (DC 16 years service)

As we have seen both the type and quantum of exchange have, in the absence of shared norms, the potential to generate conflict. This is intensified by the realisation that the majority of officers see rule bending as an essential component of running informers. Indeed over 60% of those in our sample who ran informers, thought you could not run them in accordance with the Home Office guidelines. It is not possible for any organisation, especially the police charged with up-holding the rule of law, to have a formal policy which specifies what rule bending it will condone and sanction, so it is up to individual detectives to draw their own lines. And this indivualisation is explicitly condoned by some managers, since it also allows blame to be individualised when things go wrong. As one DCI responsible for overseeing his subordinates dealings with informants explained although he never pried, 'I've always told them not to put themselves or their informers at risk. As long as the officer is aware of the rules and is comfortable and is aware that if the wheel comes of its down to him then I'm happy'.

So far we have concentrated on the general areas of conflict that surround the use of informers. These provide the backcloth on which far more intense and localised conflicts can emerge. The nature of the conflicts is influenced by the organisational space in which they occur and are often at there most intense where the use of informers crosses the boundaries of organisational segments. We have identified three types of conflict which we define as, intra, inter and extra organisational. Intra-organisational conflict refers to conflicts arising between officers working in the same unit or squad, such as divisional detectives from the same office. Inter-organisational conflict occurs between different segments of the same organisation, for instance the detective branch and the uniform branch or divisional detectives with squad based detectives. Extra-organisational conflict occurs between officers in different forces or different agencies which use informers such as the police and customs.

INTRA ORGANISATIONAL CONFLICTS

The use of informers can be a considerable source of tension within a divisional or squad office. A significant minority of detectives, some for practical but many for personal and moral reasons, have no registered informers. This can cause friction as they resent the kudos which attaches to those who do run informers. This kudos itself becomes a source of conflict as officers compete for status through their informers. Also, the strategies that officers use to recruit and run informers may cross colleagues' personal lines as to what is acceptable practice. They may think the informer is getting the better part of the deal and the 'Tail is waging the dog'; or worse that a handler is actively shielding an informer from arrest by other officers. We shall deal with these themes in the following section. The ability to run informers is seen by many senior officers as an important, if not essential criterion for selection to the CID and to ensure a permanent posting. As one DI explained:

Well a personal opinion of mine is I don't think that a person should regard themselves as a detective unless he can handle and cultivate an informant. That's how highly I rate them. (DI 17 years service)

This view is echoed in the formal appraisal system in one force which used the number of registered informers as an indicator of a detective's effectiveness. Under these circumstances it is hardly surprising that status and kudos attach to officers running informers. As one senior officer told us:

They (HQ CID) have a particular perspective and part of that perspective is judging this subdivision and others by the number of informants it has. The efficiency, and in a sense the professionalism of the CID is judged to a large extent on the question of informants and certainly when I came here I received unsolicited feedback from HQ CID management that this subdivision was anti-informant and the DI was not keen, ethically, to get involved. (Uniform Superintendent 18 years)

Under these circumstances detectives are not just under abstract pressures to run informers but face day to day pressures from their senior officers who are also judged by the activities of their subordinates. As a detective sergeant explained:

When I first came here as Detective Sergeant I got a phone call from Detective Superintendent R saying welcome to the department. He said, as a friend, he wanted to suggest that I set myself, and the office, a development programme which would involve doubling the number of informers ran here. I think this is ridiculous. I could go out now and register six people as informers but there's no purpose in doing that is there, other than fiddling figures. I know that the number of informers you have affects your assessment and I know that this has been used against me in the past as an excuse for keeping me from rejoining the CID. (DS 13 years service)

This pressure can lead some detectives to lie about sources of information falsely attributing it to their informers. As a couple of detectives bemoaned:

A number of times police officers have told me that they have got information from an informer and the truth is they've got it from another police officer. The kudos makes people tell lies about where they get information. (DC 18 years service)

Some cops guild the lily when it comes to informers. They do it for the status, they come up with information and we sit around for hours watching a place and nothing happens. I don't know why they do it, because, although any job can go wrong, when they do it a few times they simply go down in your estimation. (DC 9 years service)

The quest for status can led to intense competition and outright conflict as an experienced detective reflected about his time on the Regional Crime Squad:

There was horrific problems in there. A lot of it was with informants. One DC used to make up information on jobs which he knew weren't going to happen, just to have this high profile all the time and people like DCI couldn't see through him, so there was horrendous problems in there. Lads from our force wanted to run a job and they were trying to be-little it all the time, so there was a lot of bloody problems in that office. It was horrendous. (DS 22 years service)

The kudos that attaches to handlers also tends to create conflict between those officers who run informers and those who do not:

It might be worth mentioning that I find there is sometimes a little bit of, I won't say back-biting, but sometimes a little bit of antagonism between the two different types of detectives, they'll take the piss saying, 'your snout has been on the phone'. I've never been able to understand it, can you, how they can take the piss out of that sort of thing (. . .) I think that is why they do take the piss out of you because they see (the kudos) other people attach it. (DC 15 years service)

At the most extreme the kudos and competition can lead to officers try-ing to steal their colleagues informers;

He tried to recruit her. She wanted none of this and rang me up and told me what had happened, about her getting hit and this cop ringing her up. I met the cop at a 'do' [a social function] and fronted him up about it. He denied it of course, so I went to my DCI and he was spoken to about it. Although I don't have any hard proof, I later found out that this cop had started to dip into my tray at work. He'd come into the office, look through the scraps of paper in my tray to see if there was anything about information that I was getting from her. As soon as I heard this, I started locking all my stuff away. (DC 20 years service)

Intra-organisational conflict is also heightened by the motivational and commitment building strategies used by handlers with their informers (see also Dunnighan and Norris, 1996a; 1996b; 1996c; 1999). The majority of informers are short term, often giving information on only one person in return for an immediate reward for instance getting bail or receiving a caution rather than being charged. The process of running a long term informer to give information on a number of offenders and offences over a period of time, particularly if they are going to be used as participating informers, creates special problems for handlers. To do so officers use a variety of motivational and trust-building strategies which include giving a variety of gifts. Children's clothes, toys, cigarettes and alcohol, and even a second hand cooker were all cited by our respondents. Paying in-formers out of their own pockets was also a common strategy and many would routinely give an informer five or ten pounds whenever they had contact, 'just to keep them sweet'. Occasionally these payments could be large. One officer gave an informer £90 out of his pocket to stop her electricity being cut off. Other officers spoke of providing a listening ear to a range of troubles such as bereavement or family illness and providing help with housing and benefit problems. While most of these favours are generally small, at times officers can put themselves out to a considerable extent to help as the following detective explained:

I've done him more than favours, for example his girlfriend was pregnant and in hospital. He gave the hospital my home phone number in case she was ill. At three in the morning they rang me. She was ill. I went round and took him through to the hospital. (DC 10 years service)

There is always the danger that strategic and instrumental displays of friendship, involving gifts, favours and unofficial rewards should they be known by others, will be read as indications of overfamiliarity and dubiously motivated intimacy. Officers who are seen getting too close to those others consider 'scum' and 'vermin' can be tainted by association. If personal favours and gifts are seen to be excessive this invites questions as to what is in it for the officer and are they personally gaining from the relationship. But more importantly it raises the spectre that if an officer is too close to an informant their motivation for deals and favours will not be 'for the good of the job' but borne out of the misplaced loyalty of friendship to an informer and then it is said that the 'tail is wagging the dog'.

The adage that the 'tail is wagging the dog' occupies a central place in the folk wisdom surrounding informers. It is the most oft cited fear mentioned by officers when taking about the problems of running informers. However, pinning the accusation on an individual handler and their informer is less easy as officers can keep many of their transactions hidden from colleagues and thus avoid the possibility of censure.

But there is a limit to secrecy. When informers have been arrested by other officers and are seeking to negotiate their way out of their predicament through the intervention of their handlers, the existence of such deals is less easy to conceal from others. This situation is not unusual since the most effective long term informers are likely to be active criminals themselves and liable to arrest by other officers. Handlers recognise this and many tell their snout they should be contacted if they are arrested and not to talk to other police officers. For many handlers these are not unreasonable strictures since the arrest of their informers provides both threat and opportunity. The threat is that their informer may be charged, remanded and eventually imprisoned, in which case, they may well lose a valuable resource they have spent a good deal of effort cultivating. On the other hand, it provides the opportunity to further reinforce commitment if they can arrange for charges to be dropped or lessened or other favours done. Even so, such strategies are viewed negatively by some officers. One Detective Sergeant complained that some 'tell their snout only to talk to them and not to talk to any other fucker. That's no system'. Others were concerned about the prospect of immunity they felt certain officers granted:

The ones I've come across are all active criminals and their first cry is 'I want to speak to so and so' expecting to get their charges dropped or lessened. They think that because they've been an informer for one officer that it grants them immunity from prosecution I sometimes get the feeling that the tail is wagging the dog. You hear stories about police men briefing their informers as to what to say when interviewed by other officers, about offences they're involved in and have been arrested for. It smacks of corruption. They (informers) should be run for the good of the job not the good of the policeman. (DC 18 years)

However, for most officers the issue is not about corruption but the sense that the informer is running the handler for their own advantage, which is disproportionate to the advantage gained by police, as the following officer explained:

There's an officer here who is being run by an informer. I don't want to go into it, I don't know enough about it, but I do know that he [the officer] is being contacted both at work and at home, sometimes at 5 or 6 in the morning, by this informer. Every time one of the informers' family is arrested, pressure is being brought to bear on this officer. I won't name him for you and I can't say much more. (Acting Inspector 22 years service).

In the main the accusations that 'the tail is wagging the dog' bubbles just under the surface and remains at the level of rumour and innuendo. Occasionally, however, supervisory officers do intervene as the following DI reported;

One detective, Bess, here let one informer have too much reign. She was becoming ridiculed by others in the department and, in fact, throughout the police station. The unfounded story in the office and around the station was that the informer was shagging her. This got back to her and it embarrassed her.

The problem with the informer was that when he first skipped Crown Court bail, his wife was pregnant and he told the detective that he wanted to be out for the birth of the child. When the child was born, the informer promised his handler that he could arrange for another person who the detective was interested in to be arrested in possession of stolen and forged vehicle documents. It didn't come off though and by now it was near Christmas and the snout wanted to be out for Christmas. It was New Years Eve when he was arrested.

Every tec in the office knew that Bess was running this man and gave a wide berth to any information they received about his activities. They were simply passing it on to Bess I had to arrange for that to stop, for them to deal with that information and not give it to Bess. The official protection that informer was receiving was withdrawn by me. I gave her strict orders that she was to deal with the informer strictly in accordance with guidelines and to give him no more free reign. Within three weeks of putting my foot down, he was arrested by his handler.' (DS 13 years service)

The strategy of arresting your own informer (or more often arranging for them to be arrested by other officers) and not intervening to mitigate the consequences is a useful way for many detectives of 'pulling them down a peg or two' and 'reminding who is the boss'. There is another consequence of this which is, perhaps, even more important. It serves to remind colleagues that there is a limit to the licence given, that the relationship between the handler and informer is for professional not personal advantage and, any display of friendship is an illusion fostered for the good of the job. In essence it allows the officer to symbolically reaffirm their commitment to organisational goals and lay to rest any doubt that they may be following their own personal and perhaps dubious, agenda.

However, for a number of handlers, the arrest of their informers is something they want to avoid at all costs. Handlers cannot officially grant immunity from arrest and subsequent prosecution. Where an informer is operating on their patch they may, by turning a blind eye, grant a personalised and limited immunity. If it is known a suspect is an informer, other local colleagues, may, in deference to the handler, give them a wide berth. But there is only so much licence to be given and frequently an informer becomes the target of other officers. One solution to this problem is that handlers occasionally supply their informer with a scanner to monitor police communications and thus enable them to be forewarned of any operation. If a handler knows their informer is entering the frame he or she can subtlely warn the informer to be careful. As one detective explained you need to tell them, 'just watch what you are doing at the minute, not tell him anything specific, but just don't get yourself involved in anything at the moment' Another officer reported being more direct and tipping off his informer, 'there were a number of raids planned on his house but I always managed to get word to him'.

Of course, conflict is inevitable whenever it is thought that an operation has been spoilt by a handler tipping off an informer. This is not just confined to intra – office conflict as the following example involving drug squad and divisional detectives illustrates:

Detectives start to protect their snouts and I've seen this cause problems in an office only recently. Five thirty in the morning we go to raid this house where an informer had told his Drug Squad handler that we would find amphetamines and cannabis. The Drug Squad had asked for our assistance to turn the place over. When we get there the punters are sitting looking out of the window. They were waiting for us, at five thirty in the morning! They'd been tipped off. The Drug Squad blamed us for leaking and it was said that one of our tecs had tipped off. The Drug Squad blamed us for leaking and it was said that one of our tecs had tipped the occupier off because he was snouting for him. There was a big enquiry. The full story never came out but it caused a big rift between us and the Squad.

In fact one of the Squad's DS's had been a personal friend of the tec who had allegedly tipped the punter off and because of this they've never spoken since. (DC 25 years service)

INTER-ORGANISATION CONFLICT

As the example above shows it is not just within organisational segments that informers generate conflict, but they also create tensions between segments. While most handlers will try and limit the involvement of others in their dealings with their informers there are some circumstances where this is not possible. Firstly, Headquarters CID has a formal ongoing role in monitoring registered informers and most importantly in authorising payments and agreeing their level of reward. Secondly, the uniform branch is involved through the formal role of the custody officer who is responsible for all persons in police custody, and in their role as providing back-up to CID in participating informer operations, where the aim is to catch the perpetrators on the job. We will deal with the conflicts with CID Headquarters and the Uniform branch in turn.

Headquarters CID

To try and rationalise payment practices to informers and to produce a degree of equity, HQ CID in one force had introduced a tariff which sets out the criteria for payment. Many handlers welcomed the explicit framework for deciding on the level of rewards that they applied for and attested that this measure had reduced uncertainty surrounding the amount of payment. In particular it had stopped what was perceived as the routine practice of HQ of 'knocking' back the original request and reducing the amount by some arbitrary figure such as twenty five percent. However, consistency and certainty have not served to dilute the almost universal belief that payments are ludicrously small:

The amount of rewards is derisory, pathetic – they'd be better off doing a house and selling the video. That's why I ask myself why do they do it. (DC 10 Years service)

He got £40. I wanted £100. The money is ridiculous. Often I pay out of my own pocket, but don't get it. I'm not bothered if we get good results because I get the overtime, or just the satisfaction. A couple of snouts have asked why they don't get as much as Crimestoppers. There's no encouragement money. I get knocked back nearly every occasion. It's at Detective Superintendent level nearly every time. (DC 15 years service)

Another common source of complaint is that payments are too slow and while HQ CID were aware of this problem and had taken steps to speed the process up these were not always successful. In particular, in cases involving the recovery of illicit drugs there was a reluctance to make payment until independent laboratory analysis confirmed the precise nature of the substances. Not unreasonably no senior officer wanted egg on their face having paid out a couple of hundred pounds for old tea leaves or caster sugar. However, for officers at the sharp end, delays caused friction with their informers, and in the following case, with senior supervisors:

We had to wait no less than, I think it was fifteen weeks prior to the payment coming down. When it did come (£150) down the informant turned round and stuck two fingers up and said 'you can piss off, I didn't get the money then, I have had some hassle since the job came off, I am not happy, you've haven't looked after me. I know you've been touch but I just don't want to do it any more'. So I put a report in, returning the money . . . I returned it with a report and myself and my partner at the time got nothing but trouble for putting the report in because I worded the report strongly, saying that due to the delay he had gone sour and it was definitely due to the delay and he could have been paid out sooner and maybe still had the informant running. I had nothing but trouble over it. (DC 8 years service)

This was not a one-off occurrence. A number of officers described their bitterness at losing a promising informer through the low levels of reward and delays in the system. The effect of such disaffection was to encourage the bypassing of official channels of payment, to bolster the need for other forms of non financial reward and to facilitate less accountable methods of payment. One officer stated that he knew officers on a Regional Crime Squad who were keeping a secret stash of drugs with which to pay their informers, and other handlers encouraged their informers to provide the information through Crime Stoppers and receive an anonymous, and higher, reward.

Conflicts with the Uniform Branch

The questionnaire data revealed striking contrasts in attitudes surrounding the use of informers between the two branches. Uniform officers were far more likely to see the need to maintain a strict line between the professional and the personal when dealing with informers. Three quarters of uniform officers, compared to about half of the detectives, believed it wrong for handlers to give informers their home phone numbers or to make out of pocket payments. Uniform officers were also twice as likely to believe informers might set up innocent people, with half of the uniform officers taking this line as opposed to a only a quarter of all detectives. Similarly, one half of uniform officers in contrast to one quarter of detectives preferred to keep their involvement with informers to a minimum.

These generalised differences in attitudes between the Uniform and CID were reinforced by conflicts over recruitment and operating practices of informant handlers in three specific areas. First the refusal of uniform officers to sanction deals with their prisoners, and second because uniform officers were often kept in the dark as to the true nature of events, and third because they were sometimes deceived as to a persons identity as an informer. As one detective sergeant lamented:

I'm constantly being disappointed by officers who go into a huff when they find out that we've let informers off. This is usually uniform officers. These officers need training, they need guidance about the reality of running informers. (DS 13 years service)

As with the problems of delay and dilution of payments, so the reluctance of some uniform officers to informally agree to deals can lead to a souring of relationships and terminate a useful source of intelligence – as the following divisional detective explained;

There was a lad who gave me some information that ended up being used in a large operation. He was giving me excellent information, I passed him on to two DC's on the operation and I said 'look I think you should use him'. Two days after I had introduced him to the two officers, he was suspected of driving while disqualified, suspected. He had been because he told me. I spoke to the officer in the case, they said they didn't have really any evidence but they had done a lot of digging and I said 'well look, sir, he's being very useful at the moment, I can't tell you what it's about but it is very, very useful. In fact I've passed him on, I can't deal with it'. The officer said, 'I'm not very happy about that. I've done a lot of digging on this and he'll have to go to court'. Fair enough, it's their decision. I didn't want to explain what I was talking about. It was quite sensitive at the time but I was disappointed in the fact I am sure that I made it clear that I was talking about something that I felt was very, very important. A good operation, a large operation and it was accurate quality information and I got that over to them and they still weren't prepared to help out. (DC 8 years service)

The general air of secrecy surrounding informers is heightened by a number of factors with the use of participating informers (see also Dunnighan and Norris, 1996a). Firstly, given that few are actually officially authorised, there is a need to ensure HQ CID does not become aware of the operation, and therefore, a desire to limit knowledge of the operation to as few people as possible; especially if they are in a position to ask awkward questions. As one experienced handler explained:

I've got this informer, Junior. He gave me this job at . . . They were going to break into an electrical store. It was about three in the morning and I was about to call it off when three stolen cars turn up. The lads get out, we go in and Junior gets away. The problem was that a traffic car chases Junior because we hadn't filled them in about him. There was a traffic Superintendent on that night and . . . [the DI] didn't want him involved. (DC 15 years service)

The classic modus operandi of participating informer operations requires that the offenders are caught red handed, preferably after they have broken into a premises at which time the informer is allowed to escape. This necessitates having sufficient officers available to ensure the perpetrators (apart from the informer) do not escape. Most detectives prefer to keep the 'strike' team limited to detectives from the same office or squads. However this is not always possible since the logistics constantly require more people than can be mustered so it then becomes necessary to call on the Uniform branch for assistance.

This leads to a dilemma which cannot easily be resolved. For if the uniform officers are told it is an operation involving a participating informer, there is a danger they may inadvertently let slip (for instance by not being careful about radio procedures) that an informer had been involved. It also may necessitate uniform officers being able to identify the informer (to allow him or her to escape). If this information is conveyed to uniform it is likely to be done without revealing the informers true identity but by identifying them by some article of clothing, a red scarf, for example. Even so, given that the informer is likely to be an active local criminal there is a strong likelihood of one of the uniform officers recognising him or her and being able to put a name to the face. Thus the worry is that if uniform are told of the existence of an informer this may lead to the identification of the informers by other officers or even the target criminals. Again if they are not made aware they may very well arrest the informer rather than allow him or her to escape. As one detective explained:

There's always somebody in the job who doesn't know who he is and might lock him up. I'm not decrying them, but if you use uniform personnel you don't always want everybody to know who the informer is. You don't mind the lads in the office knowing. I believe in that, I believe in keeping an open office on that. But you don't always want the lads in uniform because some of them have a different attitude towards informers than you do and nine times out of ten there's always a time when that informant will be running away and some keen uniformed lad will chase them and catch them and lock them up. (DC 12 years service)

It is the secretiveness that riles some uniform officers, as one explained:

There can be a elitist attitude such as 'we're better than you we don't deal with the dross, that's down to uniform to deal with'. A lot of it is a secretiveness where yes things are happening and we accept that there's got to be an air of secrecy but in the past there's things happened where uniform could have been put at risk for the fact that CID have not given any information out whatsoever and that tends to create barriers as well. Especially when uniformed officers find out that they have been put in the situation where they could have come across physical danger and CID knew. Such as armed robberies. I think they accept the fact there's got to be the secrecy but again there's got to be a give and take. (Uniform Inspector 13 years service)

It is not just 'participating informer' operations which can generate conflict. One protection strategy routinely used with participating and non-participating informers alike, is to arrest them. If an informer is arrested either after they have given information on a job or even at the scene of a participating informers operation this can help deflect attention away from them in the eyes of their criminal associates. However to be convincing and so as not to invite the censure of the custody officer it is commonplace to keep secret that the arrested suspect is in fact an informer.

He rang the next day and told that the fags from the job were in a car parked at the back of a public house. He said that two lads were coming through from Angeltown to buy them. We kept obs, caught the two from the town and one of the burglars who was doing the selling. For that job, I protected him by locking him up. He just no replies, goes through the system. The custody officer never knows what's going on with informers. (DC 15 years service)

Again such deceptive practices and secrecy can cause dissension between the two branches:

Despite what people may say, there is little change, there is still very little cooperation between the departments. Uniform still see the CID as a secret society, only being told what they need to know, when they need to know. I know of one WDC who was recently taken to one side by her DI and counselled about being too friendly with uniform officers. We're all policemen, although we wear different badges. I don't like being treated as a fool and that's the impression I get from the CID. (Uniform Sergeant 22 years service)

There is of course an irony here. One central strand to many of the conflicts surrounding informer is secrecy. Secrecy, however, is both a cause and effect of conflict. On the one hand secrecy is needed to protect the informer and to shield the officers actions from formal organisational scrutiny and from the informal censure of others whose line may be drawn in a different place. On the other, secrecy, invites speculation, antagonises the excluded, and engenders distrust. Secrecy is thus used by officers to limit the potential for overt conflict but simultaneously serves to promote the conditions that generate it.

EXTRA-ORGANISATIONAL CONFLICT

There are a variety of sources of extra organisational conflict and these can be broadly divided into two categories: those arising with other agencies in the criminal justice system, e.g. the Crown Prosecution Service and those with other investigative units such as customs and excise or even other police forces.

Others in the criminal justice system have a legitimate interest in police dealings with informers, for the police are not the sole agency in the discourse. Social workers attending a juvenile arrest as 'an appropriate adult' may become involved even as the officers are trying to recruit the youth. Then again the CPS (Crown Prosecution Service) should be notified of the role of an informer in order to properly prepare a case and fulfil their legal requirements of disclosure to the defence, or to seek the necessary judicial authority for non-disclosure (RCCJ, 1993: 91–97). Defence solicitors have a legitimate right to such information (unless this right has been limited through judicial order) so they can prepare the best possible defence. Finally, the judiciary in their role as criminal trial judges need to know the full details of a case and the manner in which evidence has been obtained, so they may exercise their discretionary duty under section 78 of PACE and exclude evidence which may adversely affect the fairness of the proceedings (Baxter, 1990: 134).

All these parties to the adversarial process of English Criminal Justice are in potential conflict with the police. For instance, if the full facts were known and it was revealed an informer was participating on a job, the defence might well contend that the police were using a fully fledged agent provocateur. They may then try and exercise their right to cross examine the informer under oath, as to the reality of their role. Not only may this confirm elements of entrapment but also make public the existence of an informer. Similarly, if the handler discloses to the CPS that the case involved a participating informer, the CPS will want to see documentary evidence that was properly authorised by a senior officer. If this is not forthcoming the CPS may well feel required to discontinue the prosecution since, if they disclose this information, the defence may have a field day with the fact that proper procedures were not followed and question the integrity of a handler who flouts organisational rules. Further, the judiciary have a duty to ensure the fairness and integrity of the court proceedings, and even if they grant the prosecution the right not to disclose information to the defence, this is not final. At any time during the proceedings the judge may order disclosure if he or she feels it is in the interest of justice, and given that this is likely to lead to the public identification of the informer, will probably result in the prosecution 'throwing in the towel' (RCCJ, 1993: 94; *Sunday Times*, 17/4/94: sec 1; 24).

Conflict is also at the heart of the adversarial process, and so its existence should not be surprising. What is surprising, however, is how rarely the judicial arena becomes a stage where these conflicts are contested. It is true, that recently in the UK there has been a flurry of high profile cases where the police, on being instructed by the judiciary to disclose the existence or identity of an informer, have offered no further evidence and thus abandoned the prosecution (*Sunday Times*, 17/10/93: 5). Our data would suggest, however, that a disclosure which leads to these overt conflicts is the exception rather than the rule. During the research we identified a total of 114 cases involving informers and examined 31 of the police prosecution case files. In not one of these, or in any of the confidential attachments, was the role of the informer indicated (see also Dunnighan and Norris, 1995; 1996a). And this is not just as a result of the wayward practices of individual handlers, as the following fieldnote transcript shows:

The DI reported that, in his department, he ensures that he, or a sergeant, examines each case file in which there has been a participating informer involved. He does this to ensure that the use of the informer is hidden – so that 'no problems arise' – either with the CPS or at court. He tries to ensure that his officers don't use phrases such as, 'as a result of information received' . . . which may well alert a solicitor to the existence of an informer. He only tells the CPS when it is obvious, by a reading of the case papers, that an informer has taken a part and there is no way of adequately disguising that fact. He justified this non-disclosure by saying that detectives (himself included) do not trust the solicitors employed by the CPS and was scathing in his remarks about their abilities and commitment to 'achieving justice'. He was in no doubt that solicitors employed by the CPS spoke to defence solicitors about the identities of informers.

Conflicts do not just occur with the agencies involved in presenting the prosecution and defence, but other investigatory units particularly other police forces. Our data suggests that there are three main types of conflict which relate to territoriality, deals, and implicit assumptions.

Four thirty one morning, I'm in bed and the snout phones me. He said that the burglar was planning to do a job and that he was going to the snouts house at six thirty. I quickly arranged obs on the snout's house and we see the burglar going into the house with property. The snout takes it to Anytown (in an adjoining force) and we follow. It's delivered to the shopkeeper, we wait a while and then go in, arrest the shopkeeper and get the gear. He named the burglar, who coughed the jobs and refused to name the middle man, the snout. This DCI at Anytown took exception to it all, took exception that we'd set somebody up on his patch. He accused me of using an agent provocateur. He got me in his office and I denied it. He lost his temper, got hold of me by the throat and put me up against a door. He had me by the lapels.

I think it was because it was one of his snouts that we'd nicked. That's a problem in Anytown, everybody's somebody's snout. We don't give them anything, especially the Drug Squad because you can guarantee that the information will leak.

I just wanted out of the whole situation. The shopkeeper was left for the Anytown tecs to deal with and by the time I got back to the office [his home station], my DCI was waiting for me. The Anytown DCI had been on the phone to him, saying I'd used an agent provocateur. We just had a laugh about it all and I was warned off dealing with Anytown. I never even enquired what happened to the handler. I think he never went to court. (DC 25 years service)

There are a number of features of this incident that are noteworthy. Implicitly by crossing force boundaries the officer was encroaching on somebody elses territory where his localised knowledge does not extend to knowing who may be protected by a handler, by turning a blind eye in exchange for information. The intrusion thus could be said to comprise local detectives ability to control their territory and undermines their credibility with informers. The Anytown DCI's ire is also caused by his recognition that his patch may be accruing the costs of utilising agent provocateurs without gaining the benefits. At a local level there may be unofficial toleration of agent provocateurs who set up jobs both to gain the confidence of their criminal associates and eventually to have them arrested 'on the job'. The cost of the increased crime is lessened by the perceived reduction that will occur in the local crime if those who are locked up are indeed prolific local criminals who are prevented from committing future crime. However, where the activities cross force boundaries there may be no such benefits to the second force.

A further source of conflict is that officers from other forces have no interest in the preservation of the relationship between a handler and detectives from another force. This is exacerbated because as we have seen detective in their own forces rely on personal contacts to arrange informal deals and the web of reciprocity between officers that this implies is absent with other forces. As the following officer lamented:

I'd arranged through a DC in Southshire that £275 would be paid to John from their informer fund, but the DC's DCI reneged on this. I was told that he'd said, 'He'll never be any fucking use to us again, fuck them'. To keep him sweet I applied to this force for the £275 and I got £160.

That conflicts only rarely surface in the public domain is a remarkable testimony to the ability of the police organisation avoid 'washing its dirty linen in public'. Even when the 'wheel does come off', it is often possible to 'keep the lid on' simply by evoking a construct of loyalty in the dichotomous vision of an inside/outside separation, so that the good image of policing is preserved by preventing the spillage of subterranean secrets, from defended boundaries, into the limelight of the public gaze. However, there are times when unacceptable activities do cross force boundaries, or result in public conflict local considerations then override the abstract loyalties of defending wider interests. This was most forcefully shown in the case of the Scotland Yard informer, Eaton Green.

Green, a professional Jamaican gunman, was recruited by the Metropolitan Police Intelligence Unit (SO11) to infiltrate the Jamaican Yardie gangs operating in London. At the same time as acting as an informer, however, he was involved in one of the largest armed robberies ever staged. One hundred and fifty people were gathered in an old warehouse in Nottingham for a blues party when, 'at about 3.30 am five men carrying guns suddenly turned off the music, fired several bullets into the ceiling and set about systematically robbing every single person in the club – credit cards, cash, mobile phones, jewellery right down to the rings on their fingers.' (*Guardian*: 6/11/95; Section II, page 4). Several of those present were beaten up and one was shot in the leg. Although DC Barker, the police handler, 'had known for five weeks that Green was a suspect for the robbery, and knew that Nottingham officers were actively trying to arrest him, he made no attempt to detain him. Instead he allowed Green to walk the streets of London' (*ibid*).

Green was eventually arrested by Nottinghamshire detectives and faced trail for the robbery and the truth eventually came out at the trial. As the Guardian reported; 'By this time detectives from the two forces were no longer on speaking terms. Judge Pollard listened to both sides and found that during the inquiry into the warehouse robbery by Nottingham detectives, Scotland Yard had failed to pass on key intelligence; that in the preparation for the trial, Scotland Yard had misled the Nottingham Detectives, the CPS and also himself. He rejected sworn evidence he had heard from Scotland Yard officers' (*ibid*: 5).

The aftermath saw the CPS lodge an official complaint against the Metropolitan Police with The Director of Public Prosecutions. She is reported to have personally asked, Commander John Grieve, the head of SO11, 'what on earth they were playing at'. The Guardian described how an internal inquiry had been launched by Scotland Yard and that a number of people previously convicted on evidence provided by, Green were said to be considering appeals (*Guardian*, 1/5/96). Commander Grieve was forced to publicly apologise to the Nottingham Police (*Police Review*, 22/9/95: 5).

DISCUSSION

As we argued in our introduction the 1990s have witnessed the emergence of a defacto national policy to facilitate and encourage the use of informers as a major strategy of crime control. The use of informers is presented as a cost effective means of solving crime, with few, if any, negative consequences. However, negative consequences abound: crime is facilitated as well as repressed; criminals are licensed to commit crime rather than apprehended for their violations; police rule bending is often organisationally condoned rather than condemned; police moral is sapped as well as boosted; relationships with colleagues are based on distrust and secrecy rather than honesty and openness; the courts are deceived, defendants misled, and in the end justice is as likely to be undermined rather than promoted.

The result of these negative consequences is conflict, real and potential, both within and outwith the police organisation. However, the conflicts we describe should not be seen as merely surface tensions caused by poor communication and inadequate training, supervision and leadership (although undoubtably these all contribute). Rather they operate at the heart of the symbolic imagery which constitutes the police organisation. (Manning, 1982: 130). As Young has argued the cultural identity of the police requires the 'manufacture of ranked social boundaries' and the 'tactical creation of the other' (Young, 1993: 10). In seeking to communally define who and what they are the police are drawn into a binary scheme of cultural categorisation which distinguishes the 'polises' from the 'prigs'. The category of prigs includes not only normal police property: the criminal and the disorderly, but also those who can symbolically challenge their world view, (Holdaway, 1983) such as social workers and academics. The category of 'polis' is also subject to a binary division into 'real polises' and nominal polis, this latter category containing the 'administrators, the hierarchy, the ESSO men [Every Saturday and Sunday Off], the academics, the NCOs (noncombatant officers) and "the men with no bottle".' (Young, 1991: 115). This occupational schema categorises 'real polis' as uniformed, straight, regulated, disciplined and us is contrasted with the 'prigs' who are disorderly, bent uncontrolled, sloppy and above all – other (1990: 113).

Such binary classification systems are never complete and there are always unruly elements which cannot be assigned unambiguously to one category or another. This ambiguous space is according to Young, 'the structural place of those insiders who pollute from within and turn the 'real world' into a complex disorder'. Informers fit precisely into this ambiguous space. They defy the conventional rules of classification. Are they good or bad, trustworthy or untrustworthy, loyal or disloyal, brave or stupid, pure or dangerous, noble or self serving? Or, even more confusingly are they simultaneously all of these?

The potential for these outsiders, who cross the boundary space between 'prigs' and 'polises' to create conflict within the organisation, is rooted within the deep structure of cultural classification. There existence calls into question the entire binary opposition of the classificatory system. Appearance is not what it seems Those on the outside may actually be on the inside. 'Real prigs' may not be 'real prigs' at all. The offender caught 'bang to rights' may be an informer as may be the latest 'suspect' in the custody office.

Further, this ambiguous space ebbs and flows in both directions: for not only may the informer have joined the world of the police but there is always the danger that an officer may have joined the world of the 'prigs'. The perennial adage the 'tail is wagging the dog' expresses the concern that the 'prigs' have managed to capture the police organisation, or at least some members of it, to serve there own interest. Police officers often stigmatise other agents in the criminal justice system such as lawyers (Mark, 1978) and social workers (Holdaway, 1983) as having been captured and, thus, in reality are prigs. However the idea that the police organisation itself has been captured creates extreme potential for conflict.

The injunction that 'the informer is the property of the police force and not the handler' is one way in which the organisation seeks to limit this conflict by exhorting its officers to ensure the relationship with informers is instrumental and not affective. This is why there is so much tension surrounding friendships and indications of intimacy. They disrupt the normal order of cultural expectations where villains are not friends of police, not done favours for, not let off, not given home phone numbers, not bought drinks and not the recipients of gifts. This classificatory disruption serves to shift the focus of attention away from what sort of person is the informer to what sort of person is the officer. As the Lundy case, illustrates. Once a detective is closely associated with successfully running informers their own moral integrity become the subject of intense speculation. As Lundy wrote:

I would seem to be the classic example that it does not pay to work hard and be successful as a CID officer because as a result, I have been subjected to years of pressure, with sinister overtones from within and without the police service. (cited in Short, 1992: 417)

The conflict engendered by the use of informers will be read by some, particularly police managers and reformers, as unhealthy, wholly negative and in need of eradication. As we have argued though some conflict is inevitable because informers defy the binary logic of cultural classification. Not only is there an inevitability about such conflicts but we would argue that they can be viewed positively. Fielding has recently suggested, how, in another contested organisational strategy, community policing – the role ambiguity engendered, 'should not be read as an entirely bad thing'. For the uncertainty, lack of clarity and conflict surrounding the construction of the community police role, tends to promote self reflexivity, a receptiveness to the position of others, and innovation, and can be used to inform the development of organisational policy (Fielding, 1994: 320).

Where the use of informants is granted a central place in detective work tensions between the formal rule system and operational practices abound. The ambivalence and subterranean conflict that emerge serve to highlight the boundaries of organisational tolerance. As we have seen, this provides a weak guarantee of police propriety. Ironically, in the absence of proper managerial and legal control, the parameters of organisational tolerance are defined by the subculture, which may prove to be the only limit on the licence that handlers grant to themselves and their informers in the quest for a result.

Acknowledgements

We gratefully acknowledge the support of the Economic and Social Research Council who funded the project entitled, 'The Role of Informants in the Criminal Justice System' (Grant no.: R000234202) on which this paper is based. We would also like to acknowledge the support of our colleagues at the Centre for Criminology and Criminal Justice at the University of Hull, especially Keith Bottomley, Clive Coleman and Norman Davidson. Finally we would like to thank various friends and colleagues who helped us along the way especially, Nigel Fielding, Barry Irving, Barry MacDonald, James Morton, Mike Maguire, Christopher Walker, Nigel Norris and Malcolm Young.

References

ACPO (Association of Chief Police Officers) (1995) *Guidelines on the Use and Management of Informants* (unpublished ACPO Crime Committee Document). London: ACPO.

Audit Commission (1993) *Helping with Enquiries: Tackling Crime Effectively*. London: HMSO.

Balsdon, S. (1996) *Improving the management of juvenile informants*. London: Home Office, Police Research Group.

Bayley, D. H. (1996) 'What do the police do?' in Saulsbury, W., Mott, J. and Newburn, T. (eds.) *Themes in Contemporary Policing*. London: Policy Studies Institute.

Baxter, J. D. (1990) *Protecting Privacy: State Security, Privacy and Information*. Brighton: Harvester Wheatsheaf.

Brodeur, J. P. (1991) *Police informants: A report presented to the Board of Inquiry on Activities of the RCMP Related to Allegations made in the Senate of Canada*. Ottawa: Senate of Canada.

CONFLICT AND THE POLICE USE OF INFORMERS 411

Dunnighan, C. (1995) 'Hello, hello, what's going on 'ere then? The dilemmas encountered in researching a sensitive topic', paper presented at the *British Criminology Conference*, University of Loughborough 18–21 July 1995.

Dunnighan, C. and Norris, C. (1995) *Practice, Problems and Policy: Management Issues in the Use of Informers*. Mimeograph, Hull: Centre for Criminology and Criminal Justice, University of Hull.

Dunnighan, C. and Norris, C. (1996a) 'A risky business: exchange, bargaining and risk in the recruitment and running of informers by English police officers', *Police Studies*, **19**(2).

Dunnighan, C. and Norris, C. (1996b) 'The nark's game', part 1, *New Law Journal*, **146**(6736) 22 March 1996, pp. 402–404.

Dunnighan, C. and Norris, C. (1996c) 'The nark's game', part 2, *New Law Journal*, **146**(6737) 22 March 1996, pp. 456–457.

Dunnighan, C. and Norris, C. (1999) 'The Detective, The Snout, and the Audit Commission: The Real Costs in Using Informants', *The Howard Journal*, **38**(1), February.

Fielding, N. (1994) The organizational and occupational troubles of community police, *Policing and Society*, **4**, pp. 305–322.

Hanvey, P. (1995) *Identification recruitment, targeting and handling informants*. London: Home Office Police Research Group.

HM Inspectorate of Constabulary (1994a) *A Report of HM Inspectorate of Constabulary: Staffordshire Constabulary 1993*. London: Home Office.

HM Inspectorate of Constabulary (1994b) *A Report of HM Inspectorate of Constabulary: Number 7 Regional Crime Squad, 1993*. London: Home Office.

HM Inspectorate of Constabulary (1994c) *A Report of HM Inspectorate of Constabulary: Northampton Constabulary 1993*. London: Home Office.

Holdaway, S. (1983) *Inside the British Police*. Oxford: Basil Blackwell.

Maguire, M. and John, T. (1995) *Intelligence, surveillance and informants: integrated approaches*, Crime Detection and Prevention Series Paper 64 Home Office Police Research Group, London, Home Office.

Manning, P. (1982) 'Organizational work: structuration of environments', *British Journal of Sociology*, **33**(1), March.

Mark, R. (1978) *In the Office of Constable*. London: Collins.

Marx, G. T. (1981) 'Ironies of social control: Authorities as contributors to deviance through escalation, nonenforcement and covert facilitation', *Social Problems*, **28**(3) February 1981, pp. 221–246.

Marx, G. T. (1988) *Undercover: police surveillance in America*. Berkeley: University of California Press.

Newburn, T. and Jones, T. (1996) 'Police Accountability' in Saulsbury, W., Mott, J. and Newburn, T. (eds.) *Themes in Contemporary Policing*. London: Policy Studies Institute.

Norris, C. (1996) *The role of the informant in the criminal justice system*, End of Award Report to the Economic and Social Research Council, Swindon, ESRC.

Police Research Group (1995) *Development and Evaluation of a National Crime Management Model: Progress to-date.*, Home Office Police Research Group Briefing Note. London: Home Office.

RCCJ (Royal Commission on Criminal Justice) (1993) Runiciman Report: Report of the Royal Commission on Criminal Justice, Cm. 2263. London: HMSO.

Reiner, R. (1992) *The Politcs of the Police*, Sussex: Harvester.

Reuter, P. (1983) 'Licensing Criminals: Police and Informants' in Caplan, G. (ed.) *Abscam Ethics*. Washington D.C.: The Police Foundation.

Short, M. (1992) *Lundy: The destruction of Scotland Yards finest detective*. London: Grafton.

Weatheritt, M. (1993) 'Measuring Police Performance: Accounting or Accountability?' in Reiner, R. and Spencer, S. (eds.) *Accountable Policing*. London: IPPR.

Young, M. (1991) *An Inside Job*. Oxford: Oxford University Press.

Young, M. (1993) *In the Sticks*. Oxford: Oxford University Press.

[16]

SNITCHING AND THE CODE OF THE STREET

RICHARD ROSENFELD, BRUCE A. JACOBS, and RICHARD WRIGHT*

Drawing from interviews with 20 active street offenders, we explore the social meaning and consequences of snitching (the exchange of incriminating information for reward or leniency). The snitch violates the code of the street and is universally despised by street criminals. Although few of our respondents reported that they had or would provide information to the police, the interviews indicate that snitching is rampant. We found that some forms of snitching are more acceptable than others, and that most offenders resist the identity of the snitch even when they perform the role. We also found evidence that police practices may contribute to the retaliatory violence associated with snitching. We conclude that expanded legal access for street criminals may reduce reliance on informers and help contain the spread of violence.

Street criminals are especially vulnerable to street crime. In part that is because they lead risky lives and associate with other criminals, but it is also because street criminals cannot rely on the police for protection and have great difficulty staking a legitimate claim to victim-status. The legal vulnerability of street criminals has two important consequences for the culture and structure of street crime. The first is the emergence of a 'code of the street' that substitutes for legal rules in the regulation of interpersonal disputes among criminal offenders (Anderson 1999). The second is 'snitching', the practice by which criminals give information to the police in exchange for material reward or reduced punishment.[1] If the code of the street is a functional substitute for the ends of formal law, snitching substitutes for the legitimate means by which law is accessed by offenders. Snitching is virtually the only form of legal mobilization available to outlaws.

The term 'legal mobilization' traditionally refers to the process by which people alert formal authorities to achieve a desired outcome. Because snitching often (though not always) occurs under duress, our use of the term is non-standard. Snitching, in effect, is legal mobilization in reverse. An institutionalized feature of the street landscape, the snitch permits access to worlds otherwise inaccessible to agents of formal social control (Marx 1988). Conventional wisdom in law enforcement holds that authorities would have no realistic hope of dismantling criminal enterprise without snitches. Despite the corruption and abuses of power that often accompany their use (see Laskey

* University of Missouri-St. Louis. The research on which this paper is based was funded by Grant No. 98–1SDRP from the National Consortium on Violence Research. Points of view or opinions expressed in this document are those of the authors and do not necessarily reflect the position of the funding agency. Please address correspondence to Bruce Jacobs, Department of Criminology and Criminal Justice, University of Missouri-St. Louis, 8001 Natural Bridge Road, St. Louis, MO 63121–4499.

[1] 'Snitch' is criminal slang dating to the eighteenth century. Its original reference was to petty theft. A rich variety of slang terms is used to characterize informers throughout the world. In contemporary England, informing is often called 'grassing on someone'. Other English expressions for the snitch include 'nark', 'copper's nark' and 'snout' (the latter apparently used by the police to describe informers). In France, an informer is called 'un indic', short for 'indicateur' (a guide), while in China terms for the snitch include goatuizi (literally dog's leg, but the translation is hired thug), zhaoya (talons and fangs), jingquan (police dog), changshe (long tongue), or taijian (eunuchs). The authors wish to thank an anonymous reviewer and Xun Zhou at the School of Oriental and Asian Studies in the University of London for bringing this information to our attention.

1997; Marx 1988), the role of the snitch in law enforcement is unlikely to diminish anytime soon.

Studies in the policing literature describe the development, recruitment, utilization, management, and protection of snitches, as well as the evolution of informer careers (see, e.g. Brown 1985; Marx 1988; Settle 1995). Studies of snitching based on self-reports from criminal offenders are more rare, but valuable. These studies suggest that snitching is driven by a variety of motives: fear, greed, revenge, altruism, the need for recognition, and, of course, a desire for reduced jail time (Akerstrom 1988; Heck 1992; Williams and Guess 1981). Informers also differ in the degree of their involvement in the criminal activities they report to the police and the scope of those activities. Some are on the 'inside' and others are on the 'outside' of an activity. Some report on a single activity while others have 'knowledge of... a whole series of incidents...' (Greer 1995: 510–11). Greer's model synthesizes how snitches operate in a variety of groups and settings, including street gangs (Laskey 1997), drug markets (Manning 1980; Williams and Guess 1981), prisons (Akerstrom 1988), organized crime (Marx 1988), street-level vice (Skolnick 1975), political movements (Marx 1974), and even police departments (i.e. police officers who snitch on other officers; see Heck 1992).

However, in spite of these significant inroads to the world of the snitch, several important research questions have not been adequately addressed, particularly concerning the snitch's role in the structure and culture of street crime. How do street criminals view the snitch? How is that view situated within their broader orientation to the code of the street and their conception of police behaviour? How prevalent is snitching? What are its primary costs and benefits for offenders? Can one adopt the *role* of the snitch while avoiding the *identity*? Does snitching contribute to the level and patterns of violence in communities where criminal offending is prevalent? How might offenders' access to law be broadened beyond snitching?

We address these questions on the basis of interviews conducted with 20 active street criminals. All of the offenders we spoke with reported that snitching is widespread on the street. Although none of them admitted to being a snitch, a few reported having played the snitching role in their relations with the police. The distinction between *being* and *playing* the snitch helps to make sense out of what otherwise is a basic contradiction that emerged from the interviews: Evidently, 'everybody' is a snitch, except for the offenders in our sample.

It is especially important, we believe, to pay close attention to the lip service our interviewees give to the code of the street and how they trumpet their non-cooperation with police requests for information, in light of their characterization of the streets as overrun with snitches. The code may be more talk than real, but that does not make it unimportant for understanding how street criminals regard one another, the police, and snitching. The reasons people give for their actions are not themselves without reasons (Mills 1940), and attending to them provides insight into the embedded meaning of their accounts.

We begin our assessment by placing snitching in the context of ongoing tensions between the police and street criminals. We then consider offenders' accounts of snitching in relation to the seeming incongruity between our interviewees' self-representations as upright defenders of the code of the street ('I'm no punk') and characterization of the motives and behaviour of others ('Everybody snitches'). Both claims, of course, could be true. We somehow may have drawn a sample of exceptionally honourable offenders. Or,

SNITCHING AND THE CODE OF THE STREET

one or both of the claims could be false. Our interviewees may have been lying to us about their own behaviour, or perhaps they exaggerated the prevalence of snitching by others. However, the interviews reveal a rather more complex story than suggested by such interpretations. Snitches, it turns out, may not simply be criminals who give the police information, but those who do so without good reason. So, our interviewees could tell us that they snitched, in the literal sense of exchanging information to avoid punishment or secure rewards, and at the same time claim that they are not, never were, and never will be a snitch.

Legal mobilization by criminals can lead to serious consequences for those who are suspected of engaging in it. We consider how specific police actions to induce or coerce information from offenders may contribute to the spread of violence, and conclude with some observations regarding how retaliatory violence might be limited by providing street criminals with alternatives to snitching as a means of legal access.

Data and Method

The data on which this article is based were obtained from interviews with 20 offenders actively involved in committing various forms of street crime, ranging from the relatively minor (e.g. shoplifting and personal drug use) to the very serious (e.g. aggravated assault and armed robbery). All of the individuals interviewed were black. Otherwise, the sample was quite heterogeneous, comprising 15 males and 5 females, aged from as young as 20 to as old as 52, with a mean age of 28. This comprehensiveness was crucial in the context of our research, which aimed to encompass the diversity of views found among the population of ordinary street criminals who bear the brunt of day-to-day police scrutiny.

The active criminals we interviewed were recruited from the streets of St Louis, Missouri, USA. They were located through the efforts of a street-based field recruiter, who himself is a member of the city's criminal underworld. This individual has worked with us on several previous projects, during which he has demonstrated his reliability and trustworthiness. He has extensive connections to networks of local street offenders and, within those networks, enjoys high status and a solid reputation for integrity.[2]

Trading on his reputation, the field recruiter approached relatives, friends, and acquaintances whom he knew to be currently involved in street crime and thus vulnerable to the daily pressures of police scrutiny. There were no formal eligibility criteria beyond this. The field recruiter explained our research objectives and told prospective interviewees that they would be paid fifty dollars for participation. As we have said on numerous occasions in the past, it is a cardinal rule of street life that you must never do anything for nothing (e.g. Wright and Decker 1994).

The interviews, which typically lasted between a half-hour and an hour, were semi-structured and conducted in an informal manner, thereby allowing offenders to speak freely using their own words. Initial questions centred on the offenders' experiences with the police: Had they ever called the police and, if so, why? When did they last speak to a

---

[2] The interesting question emerges as to whether our informant is viewed as a 'snitch' by other offenders, including those he recruited into our sample. Although this possibility cannot be discounted entirely, none of our respondents gave any indication that they mistrusted his motives or believed he was acting as anything other than as a broker for researchers interested in talking with street criminals.

police officer? In what context did this conversation occur? Questions such as these were followed with general inquiries into the prevalence of cooperation with the police in the offenders' neighbourhoods. For instance: Do people in their neighbourhood give information to the police? Why, and in what circumstances? The interviews then moved on to more sensitive topics concerning the offenders' own perceptions of, and experiences with, snitching and other forms of police cooperation. Had they ever gone to the police with information about a crime? Can they imagine a situation in which they would do so? Has the risk of being informed on affected the way they commit their crimes and, if so, how? The interviews typically ended with general questions concerning the offenders' views of the police. Are the police necessary? What should they do and not do to prevent crime?

We did not ask offenders for their names but rather for a nickname we could assign to their interview. This appeared to create a more relaxed atmosphere and to raise the confidence and level of cooperation of the interviewees. That said, there are few topics that provoke more anxiety among active street criminals than helping or receiving help from the police. Such activities are anathema on the street corner and, except in extraordinary circumstances, any admission that one has voluntarily cooperated with the police risks informal sanctions ranging from ridicule to serious injury or death. Although we took great pains to reassure interviewees that what they told us would be treated in strict confidence, their statements about police cooperation inevitably reflect this fact and must be interpreted in light of it. What follows, then, is best regarded as more an examination of the ways in which street offenders talk about and perceive various forms of police cooperation than a study of direct participation in these activities.

The Vulnerability of Street Criminals

For organizational and practical reasons, the bulk of enforcement attention falls on those engaged in regular, more visible forms of law breaking. Local law enforcement is not organized to go after white-collar and corporate offenders, and people who commit crime in public are more likely to be detected than those who do so in private. Street criminals spend a great deal of time on the corner, looking for action. They engage in activity that requires a street presence (e.g. dealing drugs, fencing stolen goods, robbery). The current constriction of crack markets, and substantial glut in available stolen goods, have made it harder to make 'fast' money, requiring more time on the street to net the same rewards (Jacobs 1999). To the degree this increased exposure increases offenders' vulnerability to arrest, it also may heighten the pressure to inform.

If the lure of opportunity pulls some offenders to the street, the lack of personal space pushes them there (see Maher 1997). Overcrowded and unstable households deny many young inner-city men a steady place to call home (Wilson 1987), and many 'decent' people do not want to live with street criminals (Anderson 1999). Active offenders tend to lead a nomadic existence. They 'stay' in many places (a girlfriend's, mother's, grand-mother's), but live nowhere. They roam from place to place as the mood strikes them (Wright and Decker 1997). The fear of retaliation often accelerates such movement. Offenders who are constantly 'on the go', particularly predatory criminals who have done a considerable amount of 'dirt' (serious crime) often believe they cannot be tracked down for past wrongs if they keep moving (Jacobs et al. 2000). However, constant

SNITCHING AND THE CODE OF THE STREET

mobility means more time spent on the street, promoting susceptibility to arrest, and greater opportunity and pressure to snitch.

Encounters with the Police

The form and content of snitching by street criminals is likely to vary according to their relations with authorities and perceptions of police behaviour. How offenders articulate those perceptions, and their role in mediating the nature of their cooperation with the police, are fundamental to the study of both policing and street criminals. At issue is not just the amount of enforcement attention directed at street criminals, but its quality, and most importantly, how it is perceived (Berger and Luckmann 1967).

In principle, offenders could perceive their treatment by the police, including requests for information, to be fair and even-handed. Or, they may perceive harshness and arbitrariness in how the police treat them, particularly in a climate of 'zero tolerance'. Whatever their perceptions, in so far as they accurately reflect the phenomenological foreground in which offenders operate, a greater understanding of the circumstances surrounding informing becomes possible.

In beginning this discussion, it is important to observe that offenders' day-to-day relations with the police are, for the most part, antagonistic. Harassment and unfair treatment are perceived to be common. Time and again, interviewees reported being stopped, detained, searched, and interrogated for no good reason:

[Most of my contact with the police is on] a false basis, you know, they want to screw around with somebody, want to fuck with people . . . The only fucking thing I had done [prior to being stopped was being in] a car with fucking people in it. [That's it . . .] that's what they do. Every day.[3] (PIE)

The interviews reveal an anxiety bordering on paranoia, a feeling of constantly being watched by the police such that one false move would bring immediate consequences. 'We only have to come outside,' Peaches complained, 'that's how bad they harass us . . .' Smoke Dog insisted that the police would 'stop him for anything . . . [walk] across a street and the light is red . . . [stop me] for that.' Cal labelled the police 'shady little busters' who 'ain't got nothing else better than to fuck with you. They get a hard-on fucking with another man . . .' Neck told us that he was 'scared' every time he saw the police because 'you don't know what they gonna do . . .' He recounted the following anecdote:

We was standing on the corner, police pulled up . . . told us all to get against the wall . . . We asked them, you know, what did we do, what we gotta get against the wall for? 'That ain't none of your motherfucking business! . . . Just turn your ass around and get against the wall.' . . . they searched us and shit, grabbed us, threw us against the wall . . . and all this stuff. Told us to sit down on the curb and . . . handcuffed us and made us sit down on the curb and told us that we weren't supposed to be on the corner . . . and we wasn't doing nothing but standing . . . They handcuffed us, made us sit out there in the rain for about 25 minutes while they ran a police check on us, and then after that when it came back clear they come back and threaten us if they catch us on the corner again, 'We gonna lock you up,' and this and that.

[3] Throughout the paper, words or phrases that appear in brackets indicate an attempt on our part to explain or amplify something a respondent has said.

Most of the offenders we interviewed do not dispute the authority of the police to patrol the streets, ask questions, conduct investigations, and make arrests (although some do). Many respondents asserted that life would be worse without the police, a Hobbesian free-for-all where chaos and anarchy reigned. But such assessments apply to policing in the abstract; the officers they actually encounter are portrayed as little better than criminals with badges who harass, taunt, intimidate, and abuse them. In this picture, the police spend most of their time engaging in unjustified intrusions on the civil liberties of our respondents and others like them—specifically, their right to be on the street.

From the offenders' perspective, they should be free to walk and drive the streets, stand on the corner, and engage in conversation without interference from the police, as long as they are not, at the moment, engaged in wrongdoing. Most of our respondents (again, not all) seem to recognize that if they were truly doing something wrong and were caught for it, then so be it. In this view, crime and crime control is a cat-and-mouse game. Competition is expected. But the competition has to be fair. What irks the offenders are attributions of guilt without, in their estimation, just cause. Overcharging, mischarging, and manipulating evidence to generate false charges figure prominently in respondents' complaints about police misbehaviour:

... polices ... frisk everybody down and [if they] ain't finding nothing [they] start getting petty ... lock us up for street demonstrations [loitering] or anything ... one time me and my friend we was standing out on my back porch ... but the police came back there, right, started frisking us, bringing the dogs back there, looking for dope, and then after they couldn't find none he wrote us a summons for demonstrating on the street—on my back porch! ('J')

Even when respondents admitted that they were involved in what they considered to be minor infractions, the police might well be accused of blowing them up into major incidents. During a street altercation with his girlfriend, Cora[4] reportedly ripped a necklace off her neck. The police, alerted by neighbours, arrived shortly thereafter, only to try to pin a *robbery* on him:

Once my girl and I were outside fighting so I guess the neighbours called them ... I took her chain off and broke it so what these motherfucking police was going to do me, they were gonna lock me up for stealing or trying to put a robbery on me or something ... The motherfuckers were gonna put a robbery on me, put something hectic on me ... [it was just a fight].

'Freecasing', however, was by far the most serious instance of alleged police malfeasance. It refers to the practice of planting contraband, usually guns or drugs, on someone the police believe is 'dirty'. Little Tony called it 'pencil-whipping'—like 'pistol-whipping' only the harm is wrought by paper, not force. 'Drop some boulders [crack] in your pocket. Send your ass in front of the judge. They gonna believe him before they believe you ...' Interviewees reported that freecasing is rampant. Many claimed to have been freecased at some point in the past, or to have friends or relatives who were:

... they can't catch me with no drugs so just keep fucking with me and keep fucking until they do catch me ... they freecase you ... They put some heroin in my car [during a traffic stop] but I ain't have no

---

[4] As noted earlier, we asked our respondents for a 'street name' to preserve anonymity in the interview process. A few took this request literally and, instead of giving us a nickname, offered the name of a familiar street. 'Cora' is the name of a city street and not, presumably, this male offender's nickname on the street.

SNITCHING AND THE CODE OF THE STREET

heroin, so they put it in my car . . . locked me up. (Block) I . . . seen the cops shoot a dude in his back and then . . . walk up and take a gun from his leg [holster] and put it in the dude's hand and tell the other police that he was shooting at him . . . you get . . . crooked ass cops that wanna . . . throw stuff on you . . . once they get that badge, [they think they can do anything and not] worry about going to jail for it. (Sleazy-E)

An ideal-typical view of good relations between street criminals and the police emerges from our interviews. The police behave appropriately, according to this view, when they carry out their official duties with due regard for your rights and liberties. They are permitted to ask questions, but not intrude unnecessarily into your personal life or private spaces, or to harass you, waste your time, try to catch you in a lie, cheat you, or move you off the street without reason. The police regularly violate this good-conduct standard, according to the offenders. They are power-hungry, could not care less about 'the facts', and have no regard for the particulars of your situation. All they want, it seems, is to keep you off the street.

It would be hazardous to truth to take our interviewees' depictions of their relations with the police at face value. Clearly, the police are neither so malevolent, nor the offenders so innocent, as portrayed here. But it would be equally erroneous to reject offenders' views of encounters with the police as without value for understanding the social context of snitching. Snitching occurs in the context of an ongoing struggle between offenders and the police for control over the streets. Street criminals do their business on the street. They need time on the street to plan, organize, and carry out crimes. Through routine patrols and surveillance, much less the constant round-ups, overcharging, and deception alleged by the offenders, the police cut off access to the staging area for criminal enterprise. It would not be surprising, particularly in the present era of zero-tolerance (see, e.g. Curtis and Wendel 2000; Wendel 2000), if the police pressed down hard on people they believe, based on their criminal histories, are about to commit another crime. Nor is it surprising that street criminals want freedom of action and dislike police attention, especially when, at that moment, they have done nothing wrong. Prevented from taking care of business, treated like 'criminals' even when they are not engaged in crime, and on occasion subjected to harassment or worse by the police, street criminals understandably take a dim view of the police and want to have as little to do with them as possible. Increased pressure on local law enforcement to bear down on minor offending and to improve arrest performance only worsens the ongoing antagonism that defines the day-to-day relationship between street criminals and the police.

The Ideology of Snitching

Against this backdrop, it is unremarkable that most of the offenders we interviewed claim to never or rarely enlist the police when they or others have a problem, or to help the police in any way. '[Mistreatment] deters you from . . . wanting to do any type of business with them,' K-ILL reported. Smoke Dog called the police 'dirt', insisting that 'if [he saw] somebody do something I just would never call [them] about it . . .' Big Mix couldn't 'stand the police' while J, who 'only had bad experiences with them', engaged in avoidance wherever possible. Cal declared that the police were 'outta [his] way' and that he didn't 'need them for nothing . . .'—even after being shot by another offender during a dispute. Rock told us that he could 'look into [our] eyes and honestly tell [us] I ain't never called the police . . .' Similarly, Jack-T was well into middle age but claimed to have never called the authorities. 'No. Never . . . I'm 52 and I ain't never called them.' Although PIE admitted to summoning the police on one occasion, it was as a young boy whose mother had suffered a stroke; reportedly, he did not know who else to call. Nowadays, he insists, 'I don't need [the police]. I don't really trust [them] around me.'

Other respondents did admit to calling the authorities, but only under very specific circumstances, such as when they or a close family member were in immediate and serious danger (e.g. getting shot at), or if the perpetrator in question had done something truly heinous (e.g. murder, child molestation, kidnapping). However, the general attitude among the interviewees is to avoid the police whenever possible.

Some feared that alerting the authorities would create the potential to transform them from complainants into suspects. 'You don't tell them nothing,' Rock insisted, '. . . what they trying to get you to do is talk yourself into a hole . . . say something to them and they'll just try to repeat shit and switch it around . . . snivel around and look at you too . . . so they can catch you lying . . .' Even if enlisting the authorities were a practical option, it may not be a realistic one for persons involved in crime. First, they risk drawing attention to their own misdeeds when they complain about those of others. Second, powerful street-based conduct norms work against reliance on formal authority to settle disputes or solve problems. Respect, security, and status come only to those with the proven ability to take care of their own business. As Jacobs (2000: 44, 130) notes, 'The streets are a stage. They are a place where dignity, honor, and respect are won and lost on a daily basis.' Because every encounter is loaded with reputational meaning, the image you project dominates your relations with others (see also Anderson 1999). Cooperation with the authorities, even if only to report being victimized, makes you look weak and ineffectual. And few monikers are more stigmatizing, or more enduring, than that of snitch. '[A] snitch is the worst thing you can be,' PIE proclaimed. 'Inside or outside of jail.'

Snitching is universally condemned by our interviewees. Smoke Dog reported that he was 'not the telling type', that he 'don't tell on nobody . . .' Cal declared he was 'no motherfucking rat. I ain't telling on nobody . . . lock me up but I'm not telling you shit . . . fuck that . . .' Beano pronounced snitching to be a 'cowardly' act and that 'you a real man [when] you stand on your own'. Jack-T reported that the police had tried to get him to snitch 'five or six times' but that he 'hadn't given them [any] information'. Sugar insisted that she 'ain't no snitch and . . . ain't gonna give out no names,' adding, intriguingly, that what the police should really do is 'start recording people and have surveillance cameras [all] around . . .'

Although most of our respondents reportedly did not cooperate with the police, *everyone else* apparently did. As Little Tony said, 'Everybody and their momma snitching, so [don't] let nobody ever tell you they [haven't] . . .' That is curious because, if the streets really are saturated with informers, it is hard to believe we would not capture more of them in our sample. (In one sense we did; our respondents, it might be said, were snitching on the snitches.[5]) However, many of our respondents appear to honour the code of the street in the breach. The code dictates that no one should ever snitch on

---

[5] As one of our respondents said: 'If criminals didn't exchange information for money, I wouldn't be talking to you now.'

SNITCHING AND THE CODE OF THE STREET

anyone else. But, as we shall see, some of the interviewees acknowledged that they had given information, including names, to the police. Perhaps that means that the code of the street is not as strong as we and other criminologists have assumed. Or, for some reason, the code may not exist in the St Louis neighbourhoods from which our respondents were recruited. Consistent with this interpretation is the response by Jack-T when asked about the code of the street: '[the code is] bullshit, that's bullshit . . . there ain't no code . . . '

But Jack-T's outright rejection of the code is a minority view in our sample of street offenders. Most of the interviewees accept both its reality and desirability. If they did not, why would we have heard so many and such insistent, sometimes angry, proclamations that snitching is cowardly and despicable behaviour? The code of the street matters for our interviewees. They cannot ignore it. It shapes world-views and provides a compelling vocabulary of motives for social action on the street. But, like all normative systems, it is not an infallible guide to behaviour. We believe that most of our respondents would abide by the code of the street if they could. But the pressures to deviate from the code's prohibition on snitching are enormous.

The Reality of Snitching

The practice of using offenders to get incriminating information about other offenders is as old as policing itself. It is used with particular tenacity in urban contexts like the one we studied, owing to the virulence of street crime and the practical importance of controlling it by any available means. Typically, the authorities offer a deal: reduced charges—or outright freedom—in exchange for information. The offer is appealing. Nearly all of our interviewees had done some time in jail, and a few had served lengthy prison sentences. All want to avoid incarceration, which ends the street lifestyle so many are accustomed to, with its fast pace, freedoms and hedonistic allure. We asked our respondents if they had ever wanted to spend a little time in jail, to 'cool out', escape a debt or enemy or just rest. Hardly any said they did. Foregone liberty is a high price to pay and, faced with prolonged deprivation, many will not pay it. But the motivation goes beyond hedonism. On the streets, the ability to 'keep the party going' is a direct measure of one's social worth. Those who fail are rapidly marginalized as losers and 'scum bums' (Anderson 1999; Wright and Decker 1994). So, what the police have to offer in exchange for information is very valuable indeed, and for many offenders, the offer is irresistible.

The decision to inform is made easier by a process of risk minimization that is common among active street criminals (Walters 1990). Just as offenders tend to underestimate their chances of getting caught, informers may believe they can keep their identity secret from others. But many of the offenders we spoke with claimed that snitches could be identified with ease (see also Akerstrom 1988). Prodding from authorities further simplifies the decision, often by convincing offenders that they really have no choice at all. The police routinely use a variety of subtle and not-so-subtle tactics to ratchet up the pressure. One is to play two or more offenders off on one another, getting one to believe that the other sold him or her out, and vice-versa (the classic Prisoner's Dilemma). The logic is that if a suspect believes that s/he is going to take the fall for somebody else, then snitching is the only realistic option. 'They played that . . . with me,' recalled Jack-T, 'told me that 'such-and-such told me you did [a crime], somebody gave me a name.' J recounted similarly: '[H]e'll [police officer] tell me he done told me he done this, then he'd go back to him [an associate] and say I told them he done it. They just trying to get something going . . . get us against each other.'

Several respondents claimed that such tactics did not work on them. Being well-schooled in the arts of police pressure evidently enables some offenders to remain cool under fire and, at least according to them, tight-lipped:

. . . I don't believe this what the police said, you know, I don't believe that stuff. I figure they're planning for us to catch each other. (Jack-T)

They pull you over . . . handcuff you and . . . [always talk to you separately] . . . 'I know he selling dope, I know he's doing this and that, ain't he?' 'I don't know what that man doing, you know, I'm just walking down the street. I don't know what that man doing.' 'Now you lying.' And then I been in a situation where they had locked us up for something and they turned to me . . . separated us and they came back and told me that he said that you said this and he said that . . . and stuff like that . . . I just told them I don't know nothing . . . after that he punched me in the face . . . 'you trying to be a smart ass.' (Neck)

Most of the offenders with whom we spoke had been arrested numerous times, were aware of the tactics geared to pressure and badger them, and said they knew how to respond. Detained for drug possession, Block concluded that the threat of jail time was not as real as the arresting officer wanted him to believe. In essence, he saw no compelling reason to cooperate:

'We'll let you go by eight tonight' [if you tell us what we want to know, said the police], and I'm like, the warrant got to get issued . . . if the warrant don't get issued, you gonna get out anyway by 8 o'clock tonight. They don't think I know that, but I've been locked up so much I know all that shit . . . got out that night . . .

Cora used his knowledge of the inner workings of the system to allege that the police were in no position to offer any deals, despite their claims to the contrary. '[T]he police ain't got no fucking control over what time you gonna get,' he remarked confidently. 'That's up to the prosecutor and all the others in the ball of shit . . .' The belief that the police routinely give out misinformation is for some offenders a powerful motivator to remain close-mouthed. A number of interviewees implied or declared outright that the authorities would promise one thing and do another, going back on their word and leaving them, as 'tattletales', in the lurch. Informing, in this sense, was pointless. 'Why [don't I snitch?]' Sleazy-E asked. 'What it gonna get me? If I tell them about this person they gonna lock me up for knowing too much . . .'

In such cases, offenders choose not to snitch because they see little to gain from it. Based on their experience in the system and knowledge of police practices, they make a rational assessment of the benefits and costs of cooperating. These are not, we should note, the thoughts and actions of righteous conformists to the code, who will never snitch, no matter what the consequences. The true believer does not ask 'what's in it for me?' when deciding to uphold a code of conduct. For the true believer, there is no decision.

Our respondents, however, including some of those who claimed never to have snitched, are more calculating in their conformity to the code of the street. They avoid snitching when they can, or snitch only when they are convinced they have no other option. Even then, it appears that they do not reject the code but rather claim legitimate exceptions to otherwise valid rules. When it comes to snitching, offenders seem to be skilled in the use of neutralization techniques.

Denial of injury

A technique commonly used by the few offenders who admitted cooperating with the police to justify that cooperation is *denial of injury*, a tactic first identified by Sykes and Matza (1957) in their classic study of juvenile delinquency. No one is hurt if the information given to the police is disingenuous. Sleazy-E reported that when he had no choice but to provide a lead, he might offer 'any old information' to make sure he got himself off the hook. It was information, but not 'real' information:

you gotta give them something so . . . they will let you go. Or they gonna keep biting and biting you so you give them something so they leave you alone.

Cora, similarly detained and threatened, told the police 'what they wanted to hear . . . I took them around and showed them some houses, but I ain't showed them *the* [drug] houses,' which we interpreted to mean houses where the bulk of illicit activity was going on. Arrested on a third weapons charge and about to face serious time, Little Tony provided information but not the kind, in his estimation, that could really hurt him or others later:

[Officer] took me outside the police station, in front of the police station—I ain't never told nobody that . . . 'Come on tell me who got the dope' and all that shit . . . and I'm like 'Lousy Bouser got that shit!' Whoopee woo . . . I'm smoking my cigarette and . . . every time I hit my cigarette I was just faking the shit. 'Hey he round the corner, he got all the dope, he got a red jacket . . .' blah blah blah . . . I made it up off the top of my head.

Actually, part of Tony's story was true; he *knew of* the person he was describing, but he really didn't 'know' him or exactly what contraband he possessed.

Arrests may still result from such 'fabricated' information, but not as many, not as many good ones, or most importantly, not the kind that can get the teller into serious trouble later. Just as it is unwise to rob someone with whom you are well-acquainted, it is equally unwise to inform on them. The shorter the social distance between informer and target, the greater the risk of retaliation. Information about distant or nondescript others ('one of those guys who hangs on that corner, that's him') even if broadly true, may not be sufficiently precise or incriminating to seal a violent fate later. Conversely, inside information about close associates most likely would.

Offenders like Little Tony, Sleazy-E, and Cora can give the police information and yet remain convinced that they did not *really* cooperate. They certainly do not regard themselves as snitches. In their minds, their actions fail to qualify, especially when they give the police false, misleading, or imprecise information, because no one is likely to get into much trouble. Because such information doesn't *really* help the police, and may even set back an investigation, it might be seen as the antithesis of snitching, a way of 'getting over' on the police, as when Little Tony takes a hit off his cigarette and tells the police another half-truth. And if we take these subjects at their word, they are not snitching. They are assuming the pose of the snitch to escape punishment. Perhaps this is why so many of our respondents could confidently and, in their minds, truthfully claim never to have snitched.

ROSENFELD, JACOBS, AND WRIGHT

Denial of a victim

A second technique used to neutralize transgression of the code of the street and avoid the identity of snitch is *denial of a victim* (Sykes and Matza 1957). In contrast to denial of injury, this neutralization technique justifies snitching as a means of punishing people who need to be brought down a peg or two, or of eliminating competitive rivals. People who deserve to be punished cannot claim to be a 'victim'. Snitching of this sort is not to help the police or to escape jail time, although those outcomes may be part of the bargain, but to maintain, solidify, or improve your competitive position relative to others. Relative deprivation is a persistent theme in street culture. Those who have 'more', be it drugs, money, clothes, cars, or anything else of value, are often despised by those who have less (see Anderson 1999). Success breeds envy, and envy breeds behaviour to equalize the playing field (Jacobs 2000).

Enlisting the authorities to 'take others down' is reportedly a popular equalization device, although the offenders in our sample rarely admitted doing it themselves. Our respondents call it 'player hating', or just 'hating' for short. As Big Mix described the practice, 'somebody else making a little more money than them they'll tell on them just to get them from out there . . . Mad cause you got this . . . and they don't . . . I've seen it happen, I can't even count . . .' Little Tony, Smoke Dog, and Sleazy-E were reportedly victimized in this fashion:

When I was selling dope, a motherfucker started talking. I was popping, I was making more money than [he] was . . . [had] more dope than [he did] . . . They didn't like that. They told . . . (Little Tony) . . . you got jewelry, you're dressing good, you're looking good . . . so they're like, 'Where did this nigger get that money from?' . . . 'I got to put the man on him' . . . all of a sudden you're driving around when [the] man flags you . . .' (Smoke Dog)

. . . if I got more money than he got . . . that makes him mad cause [I] got more, then he wants to take what I got, and . . . he'd tell [the police] 'he's selling drugs or stealing cars, he's jacking people and all kinds of that shit just to get me caught up, and when I get caught up he can step in and take my place for what I was doing. So he's making the money that I was making. (Sleazy-E)

Peaches fessed up to 'hating on' rival drug dealers in retaliation for them hating on her previously. But the motivation was apparently the same in both cases: to eliminate the competition (see also Akerstrom 1988: 162). 'I wanted them to get off our street,' Peaches explained, 'because if they are making the money we're making then we ain't making enough money, so either they gotta go or we gotta go . . . so, as you know, we the ones that are left.'

Motives to 'hate' do not appear to be limited to status envy or competitive rivalries. For Sugar, plain-old dislike was enough. She admitted to telling on her 'little partner' for a credit card scam because he was a 'buster', 'a little punk you know. A little bitch . . .' She boldly added that 'if it was another motherfucker I don't like then I'd do it again.'[6] When hating in particular, or snitching in general, is materially rewarded by authorities (see Williams and Guess 1981), the motivation to do it is greater still:

---

[6] We found out later that she avoided jail time by snitching, but she did not like her associate and wasn't about to take a fall for him, which would have allowed him to come out 'ahead'.

SNITCHING AND THE CODE OF THE STREET

. . . somebody's out there messing with heroin . . . they [the police] give you, for instance, say a half gram of boy [heroin], 'you tell me about what's happening with this situation over here with these people' . . . it's about the money. You got snitches . . . that snort heroin . . . you got some out there that just don't give a fuck about whatever it takes to get some money . . . (Smoke Dog)

Once the prospect of payment enters into the equation, the pretence that the offender is only 'acting' like a snitch, or that no one is really hurt or the victim deserves punishment, begins to break down, and unabashed, full-blown tit-for-tat snitching emerges. Cora confessed to an arrangement with a police officer who allegedly told him he'd 'pay me whatever I want . . . drugs . . . weed . . . cocaine . . .' Apparently, no exchange had yet been made. He went on to talk broadly of others who snitch for rewards, in an attempt, perhaps, to justify his own behaviour:

[Informers say], 'I want these new shoes, I want this or I want drugs to sell,' or something like that . . . 'and the police asked me for information.' I'm just gonna give it to them to get what I want, even if they gonna give me some drugs or give me some money, or whatever, whatever they gonna give me I'm still gaining . . . I'm gaining to get something in my pocket . . . And in another way, I could fucking well get caught with a gang of cocaine and I know the man they want, they'll tell me 'I'm gonna let you stay on the street a little bit longer if you tell me where he is.' Sure I'm gonna tell him, he's right over there.

Active vs passive snitching

The image of the snitch who *enlists* the authorities or cooperates with eager willingness to secure positively valued benefits rather than to avoid punishment is prominent in fictional crime drama, but is not found very often in the criminological literature (but see Heck 1992; Marx 1988; Williams and Guess 1981). Few of our respondents embrace the role of the *active snitch*; the few who admitted to cooperating with the police said they did so because they had little or no choice or, less frequently, to punish someone who had it coming. They are, at worst, *passive snitches*. Passive snitching can extend from cooperating with the police to bring down a rival or enemy to informing when refusal would almost certainly lead to long-term confinement. Offenders who inform in these ways attempt to neutralize the reputational consequences of their conduct by suggesting that snitching is not snitching if helping the police is tangential to other motives (for a comparison, see Akerstrom 1989: 23).

But the boundary between the passive and active snitch is difficult to maintain. First of all, despite claims to have given the police 'bullshit', others can never know what actually transpired in the patrol car or station house. Successful use of denial of injury as a neutralization technique for snitching ultimately depends on whether others believe you when you claim to have lied to the police, but not to them.[7] In addition, there is a difference between informing to 'save your ass' and informing to improve your strategic position. On the streets, it is the same difference between being a coward and being a predator. Predators will use any means necessary to advance their interests. Although the coward may appeal to the same logic, the coward deals from a position of weakness,

[7] Hoping to avoid the need to defend himself, Little Tony stayed out of sight for several days after giving information to the police. A quick appearance after his arrest for a third weapons charge, he reasoned, almost certainly would indicate that he had snitched in exchange for his freedom.

the predator from a position of strength. This subtle but all-important moral distinction cannot simply be proclaimed, it must be sustained through actions.

Predators who cooperate with the police do so on their own terms, snitching only when it suits their interests; the coward is a tool of the authorities. What makes this distinction so difficult to sustain is the widespread belief among street criminals that 'once a snitch, always a snitch'. Once you give information to the police, you will have to keep providing it, 'or else.' The shelf life of an informer is only as long as the leads s/he provides are worthwhile. This is understandable given the fundamentally asymmetrical relationship between informers and their police contacts. Snitches who no longer fulfil their end of the bargain reportedly are given cases or exposed as payback for a 'break' that is no longer justified. 'You got to [keep giving them information.],' Jack-T explained, 'if you stop, you gone . . . you ain't no good to them man . . . put you in the penitentiary . . .' Smoke Dog put it this way:

I mean you can tell them you don't want to be a snitch no more. They'd say OK . . . but . . . they gonna give you a case . . . send them to the penitentiary, get them off the streets . . . They gonna tell you you got to be a snitch until the day you die.

Snitching and Street Violence

If such claims are correct and apply to the predator-snitch, the role will be inherently short-lived, because most are in jail—or worse. Exposure seems more worrisome to street criminals than jail time, and for good reason. As Settle (1995: 200) notes, 'An informer is always in jeopardy of retaliation from other offenders for collaboration and that danger does not disappear when s/he has ceased to provide information to police—indeed, it may increase.' Street justice tends to be far more swift, certain, and severe than formal sanctions like arrest and prosecution. The police are evidently keyed into this retaliatory potential, and yet reportedly act in ways that create more, rather than less, instability on the streets:

. . . you start informing then you got to keep informing cause if you stop they . . . gonna talk to the person that you told on and then they gonna wind up killing you . . . (Neck)

. . . they have you riding in the car . . . then let [others] know you're the snitch . . . The police gonna make it be known that you're the snitch . . . Get my head blown off! (Block)

. . . the police come and get you . . . and drop you off in the middle of the fucking neighbourhood where everybody's at. 'Thank you!' They ride the fuck off and throw $50 out the window. That sort of shit, you know what I mean? (PIE)

. . . put you in the back of the car and you riding around in the back of the car with them and they ride through your hood and everybody see you . . . and then . . . they let you out . . . you got to walk all the way back through the hood . . . to where your homies are at, and then everybody's looking at you like, 'what you doing in the back of the car, was you talking?' . . . (Sleazy-E)

Whether such tactics are intended to threaten or extort or punish, they contribute to the violence in already dangerous communities. In such areas, the streets are ruled by a dog-eat-dog mentality where every action is supposed to, and often does, incite an equal and opposite reaction (Anderson 1999). Freedom taken away by someone else trying to maintain their own is a cost too high to bear, so violent reprisal is expected. Retaliation often spawns counter-retaliation, and progressively larger numbers of persons get sucked into retributive cycles (see Lawler 1986; Loftin 1986).

Discussion

Our interviews with 20 active street criminals produce a complex picture of snitching. On the one hand, very few offenders admit to giving information to the police. On the other, we heard frequently that snitching is rampant. This apparent contradiction in accounts is resolved, uneasily, by drawing distinctions between types of cooperation with the police that are considered acceptable under the terms of the code of the street, and others that violate the ban on ratting out other offenders. Genuine snitching is defined as volunteering damaging information in exchange for a reward or reduced punishment. Cooperation under pressure that does not harm others does not seem to qualify as snitching. Providing information to deliver just punishment to others is not *really* snitching, because only those who deserve it are hurt (see also Akerstrom 1988: 165). However, the credibility of these defences against snitching, particularly the latter, is difficult to sustain, especially when the tables are turned and you become the target of an informer. Behaviour that, to the informer, seems to be acceptable cooperation or unavoidable compliance, to the target seems like snitching. Often it seems the line between acceptable and unacceptable cooperation is drawn on the basis of the dominant street conceptions of predator and prey. Predators rule the streets, prey are used by others, including the police. Predators give information to the police when it suits their interests and refuse to cooperate when it does not. Prey become 'snitches for life'. But, again, in objective terms, there is little difference between the two. The differences are almost entirely subjective and perceptual. Those who would adopt the role of predator-snitch, or passive snitch, have daily to convince others on the street to accept these self-presentations.

Such subtle but important distinctions are necessitated by the code of the street. In the absence of the code, it would not be necessary to worry over whether this or that kind of cooperation with the police qualified as 'real' snitching. And so, in one sense, the significance of the code for street offenders is confirmed by their efforts to present convincing accounts of their actions within its terms. But our findings also reveal the weakness of the code as a prescription for behaviour. The code must contend with powerful pressures to cooperate with the police. Although it is difficult to know with precision from our interviews, a reasonable supposition is that most street criminals give information to the police. The police control access to the streets and can make life miserable and unprofitable for offenders they want to put out of business. At some point, offenders who want to remain free and active will have to come to terms with these pressures. Simple defiance risks continued harassment, at best, and long-term confinement at worst. Active cooperation, however, carries its own risks. To be widely known as a snitch invites reputational loss, diminished access to criminal opportunities, and retaliatory violence. The result, we believe, is widespread 'passive snitching' and strenuous efforts to avoid the identity of the snitch.

This interpretation of our findings is situated within a large and important literature on *accounts*, the linguistic devices people employ whenever their behaviour is subject to evaluative inquiry (Scott and Lyman 1968; for a very good example of a recent study in the accounts tradition, see Pogrebin et al. 1992). Accounts range in form and content, from excuses and justifications to disclaimers, apologies and offers of compensation. Each, however, is geared to separate act from identity so that deviant behaviour does not come to define a person's master status and basic character. The sincerity of any particular account is not as important as its viability. What matters is whether it succeeds in absolving actors of responsibility for the behaviour in question.

Few offenders will admit to being stool pigeons, so the denials we heard are hardly surprising. To be identified as a snitch is to sacrifice all hope of respect, and in the volatile world of the streets, respect is everything. In the communities from which our interviewees were drawn, the traditional means of securing respect have been eroded by high rates of joblessness, poverty and family disruption (Wilson 1987). When respect cannot be earned through traditional occupational and familial roles, it must be sought elsewhere. For a sizable segment of the inner-city population, and all of our respondents, respect is established and defended on the street. Among impoverished and isolated inner-city residents generally, the ability to handle your own affairs and to defend your honour and possessions, with violence if necessary, are the key attributes of respect (Anderson 1990, 1999). For street criminals, these imperatives carry very specific implications: Don't cooperate with the police, and strike back at those who do. Cooperating with the authorities is tantamount to treason, and in the era of zero-tolerance policing, the enemy may be regarded as especially villainous. No wonder so many of our respondents talked up allegations of mistreatment at the hands of police. Such experiences provide the discursive ammunition they needed to make their accounts more convincing, to themselves and to us.

One thing is clear: snitching is a pervasive element of inner-city street life that poses dangers for street criminals and law-abiding residents alike. As Miller (1996: 102) writes, 'No single tactic of law enforcement has contributed more to violence in the inner city than the practice of seeding the streets with informers and offering deals to [them].' The practice undermines trust and breaks apart communities. It erodes faith in official authorities. It foments retaliation, which ignites the street-level microstructure in potentially deadly conflict spirals. The threat of betrayal may change offender behaviour in ways that promote instability. For example, in some circles of serious criminals, solitary offending has become preferred over team approaches (see Jacobs 2000). Where trust cannot be taken-for-granted, relying on co-offenders is both foolhardy and dangerous. As a result, dependence on firearms is likely to rise; without accomplices, guns become the back-up.

A criminal justice system based on ever-tougher punishment exacerbates this instability. With mandatory minimums, sentence-enhancements, and three-strikes laws comes a heightened premium on freedom, and an enhanced impetus to inform when that freedom is threatened. Faced with life in prison for a third felony conviction, many offenders will trade 'honour' for freedom. On the enforcement end of the war on crime, excessive use of force, discretionary lapses, and racial profiling threaten to undermine the entire system's perceived legitimacy. Perceptions of inequity breed defiance for authority, and defiance for authority generates more crime (Sherman 1993).

By heightening instability and reducing the legitimacy of formal social control, snitching reinforces the reliance on self-help by street criminals. The code of the street is thereby strengthened and passive snitching becomes even more prevalent as the only

SNITCHING AND THE CODE OF THE STREET

means of legal mobilization realistically available to those who live largely beyond the law. The inevitable result is a downward spiral into yet more instability fuelled by cycles of violent retaliation and counter-retaliation. There are two ironies here. The first is that such instability results from informal attempts by criminal disputants to restore stability through various forms of street justice. The second is that the police may play a major role in intensifying reliance on informal (and illegal) mechanisms of dispute resolution by using snitches to achieve the ends of formal social control. In both cases, the pursuit of order serves to generate greater disorder.

Although those who break the law may appear undeserving of the benefits of formal justice, the cost of denying them those benefits is that many will resort to informal methods of dispute resolution. The resulting crime and violence are not easily contained, threatening populations at far remove from the original disputants. Altering the relationship between police and street criminals could help contain the spread of retaliatory violence. The police must begin to treat the victimization of criminals by fellow law breakers as the serious problem that it is, and not as something to be tolerated or even encouraged by pitting offenders against one another. As a corollary, they should make every effort to protect offenders who pass information to them from being identified as 'snitches' by other criminals. To do otherwise plays directly into the code of the street, with all of its attendant retaliatory violence.

The police need information from offenders to do their jobs effectively. As it stands now, however, the information they receive too often appears to be coerced by the threat of exposure. In turn, this convinces offenders that everybody, including the police, really lives by the code of the street, thereby setting the stage for yet more crime and violence. Offenders will be suspicious of purported changes in police behaviour; certainly any improvement in the relationship between police and criminals will happen slowly and piecemeal. But we know that change is possible because it has begun to occur, albeit incrementally, in the relationship between the police and one category of offenders: sex workers (Jenness 1993).

Public health concerns about the spread of HIV-AIDS and pressures from the women's movement have made the police more responsive to sex workers' reports of criminal victimization. The police are more likely than in the past to treat prostitutes as genuine victims and credible complainants when they report a crime. Nothing prevents police from granting other street offenders the same opportunities for legitimate access to the law. But, as of yet, nothing impels the police to do so either. No social movement has taken up the cause of legal access for street criminals, but the prisoners' rights movement conceivably could move in that direction, especially as prison-to-community 're-entry' programmes gain momentum (Travis et al. 2000). Several analysts have proposed that firearm violence be treated as a public health problem, and snitching, we have suggested, contributes to the epidemic-like cycles of violence in inner-city communities.

It is not farfetched, then, to propose that the kinds of political pressures and social conditions that altered relations between the police and sex workers could lead to expanded legal access for street criminals. Criminals, virtually by definition, will never have the legal rights and opportunities of non-criminals, and the police are unlikely to grant victim status and expanded legal access to the most violent street criminals. But the bulk of street crime consists of property offences, simple assaults and low-level drug dealing. Persons who engage in these illegal activities on a regular basis make up a disproportionate share of crime victims. Widening their access to legal resources could reduce their reliance on informal means of dispute resolution, and help contain the spread of contagious violence.

REFERENCES

AKERSTROM, M. (1988), 'The Social Construction of Snitches', *Deviant Behavior*, 9: 155–67.

——(1989), 'Snitches on Snitching', *Society*, January/February: 22–6.

ANDERSON, E. (1999), *Code of the Street*. New York: Norton.

——(1990), *Streetwise*. Chicago: University of Chicago Press.

BERGER, P. and LUCKMANN, T. (1967), *The Social Construction of Reality*. Garden City, New York: Anchor.

BLACK, D. (1973), 'The Mobilization of Law', *Journal of Legal Studies*.

BROWN, M. F. (1985), 'Criminal Informants: Some Observations on Use, Abuse, and Control', *Journal of Police Science and Administration*, 13: 251–6.

CURTIS, R. and TRAVIS, W. (2000), '"Lockin' Niggas up Like it's Goin' Out of Style": The Differing Consequences of Police Interventions in Three Brooklyn, New York Drug Markets', paper presented at the American Society of Criminology's Annual Meeting in San Francisco, CA.

GREER, S. (1995), 'Towards a Sociological Model of the Police Informant', *British Journal of Sociology*, 46: 509–27.

HECK, W. P. (1992), 'Police Who Snitch: Deviant Actors in a Secret Society', *Deviant Behaviour*, 13: 253–70.

JACOBS, B. A. (1999), *Dealing Crack: The Social World of Streetcorner Selling*. Boston, MA: Northeastern University Press.

——(2000), *Robbing Drug Dealers: Violence beyond the Law*. New York: Aldine de Gruyter.

JACOBS, B. A., TOPALLI, V. and WRIGHT, R. (2000), 'Managing Retaliation: Drug Robbery and Informal Sanction Threats', *Criminology*, 38: 171–98.

JENNESS, V. (1993), *Making It Work: The Prostitutes' Rights Movement in Perspective*. New York: Aldine de Gruyter.

LASKEY, J. A. (1997), 'The Gang Snitch Profile', *Journal of Gang Research*, 4: 1–16.

LAWLER, E. J. (1986), 'Bilateral Deterrence and Conflict Spiral: A Theoretical Analysis', in E. J. Lawler, ed., *Advances in Group Processes*, 3: 107–30. Greenwich, CT: JAI Press.

LOFTIN, C. (1985), 'Assaultive Violence as a Contagious Social Process', *Bulletin of the New York Academy of Medicine*, 62: 550–5.

MAHER, L. (1997), *Sexed Work*. New York: Clarendon Press.

MANNING, P. K. (1980), *The Narcs' Game*. Cambridge: MIT Press.

MARX, G. T. (1988), *Undercover: Police Surveillance in America*. Berkeley: University of California Press.

——(1974), 'Thoughts on a Neglected Category of Social Movement Participant: The Agent Provocateur and the Informant', *American Journal of Sociology*, 80: 402–40.

MILLER, J. G. (1996), *Search and Destroy: African-American Males in the Criminal Justice System*. Cambridge: Cambridge University Press.

MILLS, C. WRIGHT (1940), 'Situated Actions and the Vocabulary of Motive, *American Sociological Review*, 6: 904–13.

POGREBIN, M. R., POOLE, E. D. and MARTINEZ, A. (1992), 'Accounts of Professional Misdeeds: The Sexual Exploitation of Clients by Psychotherapists', *Deviant Behavior*, 13: 229–52.

SCOTT, M. B. and LYMAN, S. M. (1968), 'Accounts', *American Sociological Review*, 33: 46–62.

SETTLE, R. (1995), *Police Informers: Negotiation and Power*. Sydney: Federation Press.

SNITCHING AND THE CODE OF THE STREET

SHERMAN, L. (1993), 'Defiance, Deterrence, and Irrelevance: A Theory of the Criminal Sanction', *Journal of Research in Crime and Delinquency*, 30: 445–73.

SKOLNICK, J. (1975), *Justice Without Trial: Law Enforcement in Democratic Society*, 2nd edn. New York: John Wiley and Sons.

SYKES, G. and MATZA, D. (1957), 'Techniques of Neutralization: A Theory of Delinquency', *American Sociological Review*, 22: 667–70.

TRAVIS, J., SOLOMON, A. and WAUL, M. (2001), *From Prison to Home: The Dimensions and Consequences of Prisoner Re-entry*. Washington, DC: Urban Institute.

WALTERS, G. B. (1990), *The Criminal Lifestyle*. Newbury Park: Sage.

WENDEL, T. (2000), 'Zero Tolerance: Misleading Results', *Drug Link*, November/December: 3–6.

WILLIAMS, J. R. and GUESS, L. L. (1981), 'The Informant: A Narcotics Enforcement Dilemma', *Journal of Psychoactive Drugs*, July–September: 235–45.

WILSON, W. J. (1987), *The Truly Disadvantaged*. Chicago: University of Chicago Press.

WRIGHT, R. and DECKER, SCOTT, H. (1997), *Armed Robbers in Action*. Boston: Northeastern University Press.

——(1994), *Burglars on the Job*. Boston: Northeastern University Press.

Part IV
Bodies, Databases and Technologies

[17]

The Body and the Archive[*]

ALLAN SEKULA

> . . . there must be arranged a comprehensive
> system of exchanges, so that there might grow
> up something like a universal currency of these
> banknotes, or promises to pay in solid sub-
> stance, which the sun has engraved for the
> great Bank of Nature.
>
> —Oliver Wendell Holmes, 1859

> On the one side we approach more closely to
> what is good and beautiful; on the other, vice
> and suffering are shut up within narrower
> limits; and we have to dread less the mon-
> strosities, physical and moral, which have the
> power to throw perturbation into the social
> framework.
>
> —Adolphe Quetelet, 1842

I.

The sheer range and volume of photographic practice offers ample evidence of the paradoxical status of photography within bourgeois culture. The
simultaneous threat and promise of the new medium was recognized at a very
early date, even before the daguerreotype process had proliferated. For exam-

[*]   Earlier versions of this essay were presented at the National Gallery of Canada, Ottawa,
October 2, 1982, and at the College Art Association Annual Meeting, New York, February 13,
1986. This version was completed with the assistance of a Visiting Senior Fellowship at the Center
for Advanced Studies in the Visual Arts, The National Gallery of Art, Washington, D.C., summer
1986.

ple, following the French government announcement of the daguerreotype in
August 1839, a song circulated in London which began with the following
verse:

> O Mister Daguerre! Sure you're not aware
> Of half the impressions you're making,
> By the sun's potent rays you'll set Thames in a blaze,
> While the National Gallery's breaking.

Initially, photography threatens to overwhelm the citadels of high culture.
The somewhat mocking humor of this verse is more pronounced if we consider
that the National Gallery had only moved to its new, classical building on
Trafalgar Square in 1838, the collection having grown rapidly since the
gallery's founding in 1824. I stress this point because this song does not pit
photography against a static traditional culture, but rather plays on the possibility of a technological outpacing of *already* expanding cultural institutions. In
this context, photography is not the harbinger of modernity, for the world is
already modernizing. Rather, photography is modernity run riot. But danger
resides not only in the numerical proliferation of images. This is also a premature fantasy of the triumph of a *mass* culture, a fantasy which reverberates with
political foreboding. Photography promises an enhanced mastery of nature,
but photography also threatens conflagration and anarchy, an incendiary leveling of the existing cultural order.

By the third verse of this song, however, a new *social* order is predicted:

> The new Police Act will *take down* each fact
> That occurs in its wide jurisdiction
> And each beggar and thief in the boldest relief
> Will be *giving a color* to fiction.[1]

Again, the last line of the verse yields a surplus wit, playing on the figurative
ambiguity of "giving a color," which could suggest both the elaboration and un-
masking of an untruth, playing further on the obvious monochromatic limitations of the new medium, and on the approximate homophony of *color* and *collar*.
But this velvet wit plays about an iron cage which was then in the process of being constructed. Although no "Police Act" had yet embraced photography, the
1820s and '30s had engendered a spate of governmental inquiries and legislation designed to professionalize and standardize police and penal procedures in
Britain, the most important of which were the Gaols Act of 1823 and the Metropolitan Police Acts of 1829 and 1839. (The prime instigator of these modernization efforts, Sir Robert Peel, happened to be a major collector of seven-

---

1.   Quoted in Helmut and Alison Gernshiem, *L. J. M. Daguerre*, New York, Dover, 1968,
p. 105 (italics in original).

William Henry Fox Talbot. Articles of China, *plate III from* The Pencil of Nature, *1844.*

teenth-century Dutch paintings, and a trustee of the National Gallery.) Directly to the point of the song, however, was a provision in the 1839 act for taking into custody vagrants, the homeless, and other offenders "whose name and residence [could] not be ascertained."[2]

Although photographic documentation of prisoners was not at all common until the 1860s, the potential for a new juridical photographic realism was widely recognized in the 1840s, in the general context of these systematic efforts to regulate the growing urban presence of the "dangerous classes," of a chronically unemployed sub-proletariat. The anonymous lyricist voiced sentiments that were also heard in the higher chambers of the new culture of photography.

Consider that incunabulum in the history of photography, Henry Fox Talbot's *The Pencil of Nature*. Talbot, the English gentleman-amateur scientist who paralleled Daguerre's metallic invention with his own paper process, produced a lavish book that was not only the first to be illustrated with photographic prints, but also a compendium of wide-ranging and prescient meditations on the promise of photography. These meditations took the form of brief commentaries on each of the book's calotype prints. Talbot's aesthetic ambition was clear: for one austere image of a broom leaning beside an (allegori-

---

2. The Metropolitan Police Act, 1839, in *Halsbury's Statutes of England*, vol. 25, London, Butterworth, 1970, p. 250. For a useful summary of parliamentary debates on crime and punishment in the nineteenth century, see *Catalogue of British Parliamentary Papers*, Dublin, Irish University Press, 1977, pp. 58–73. On the history of the National Gallery, see Michael Wilson, *The National Gallery: London*, London, Philip Wilson Publishers.

cally) open door, he claimed the "authority of the Dutch school of art, for taking as subjects of representation scenes of daily and familiar occurrence."[3] But an entirely different order of naturalism emerges in his notes on another quite beautiful calotype depicting several shelves bearing "articles of china." Here Talbot speculates that "should a thief afterwards purloin the treasures—if the mute testimony of the picture were to be produced against him in court—it would certainly be evidence of a novel kind."[4] Talbot lays claim to a new legalistic truth, the truth of an indexical rather than textual inventory. Although this frontal arrangement of objects had its precedents in scientific and technical illustration, a claim is being made here that would not have been made for a drawing or a descriptive list. Only the photograph could begin to claim the legal status of a *visual* document of ownership. Although the calotype was too insensitive to light to record any but the most willing and patient sitters, its evidentiary promise could be explored in this property-conscious variant of the still life.

Both Talbot and the author of the comic homage to Daguerre recognized a new *instrumental* potential in photography: a silence that silences. The protean oral "texts" of the criminal and pauper yield to a "mute testimony" that "takes down" (that diminishes in credibility, that transcribes) and unmasks the disguises, the alibis, the excuses and multiple biographies of those who find or place themselves on the wrong side of the law. This battle between the presumed denotative univocality of the legal image and the multiplicity and presumed duplicity of the criminal voice is played out during the remainder of the nineteenth century. In the course of this battle a new object is defined—the criminal body—and, as a result, a more extensive "social body" is invented.

We are confronting, then, a double system: a system of representation capable of functioning both *honorifically* and *repressively*. This double operation is most evident in the workings of photographic portraiture. On the one hand, the photographic portrait extends, accelerates, popularizes, and degrades a traditional function. This function, which can be said to have taken its early modern form in the seventeenth century, is that of providing for the ceremonial presentation of the bourgeois *self*. Photography subverted the privileges inherent in portraiture, but without any more extensive leveling of social relationships, these privileges could be reconstructed on a new basis. That is, photography could be assigned a proper role within a new hierarchy of taste. Honorific conventions were thus able to proliferate downward.[5] At the same time,

3.   William Henry Fox Talbot, *The Pencil of Nature*, 1844, facsimile edition, New York, Da Capo, 1968, pl. 6, n.p.
4.   *Ibid.*, pl. 3.
5.   The clearest of the early, optimistic understandings of photography's role within a new hierarchy of taste, necessitating a restructuring of the portrait labor market along industrial lines, can be found in an unsigned review by Elizabeth Eastlake, "Photography," *Quarterly Review*, vol. 101, no. 202 (April 1857), pp. 442–468.

photographic portraiture began to perform a role no painted portrait could have performed in the same thorough and rigorous fashion. This role derived, not from any honorific portrait tradition, but from the imperatives of medical and anatomical illustration. Thus photography came to establish and delimit the terrain of the *other*, to define both the *generalized look* — the typology — and the *contingent instance* of deviance and social pathology.

Michel Foucault has argued, quite crucially, that it is a mistake to describe the new regulatory sciences directed at the body in the early nineteenth century as exercises in a wholly negative, repressive power. Rather, social power operates by virtue of a positive therapeutic or reformative channeling of the body.[6] Still, we need to understand those modes of instrumental realism that do in fact operate according to a very explicit deterrent or repressive logic. These modes constitute the lower limit or "zero degree" of socially instrumental realism. Criminal identification photographs are a case in point, since they are designed quite literally to facilitate the *arrest* of their referent.[7] I will argue in the second part of this essay that the semantic refinement and rationalization of precisely this sort of realism was central to the process of defining and regulating the criminal.

But first, what general connections can be charted between the honorific and repressive poles of portrait practice? To the extent that bourgeois order depends upon the systematic defense of social relations based on private property, to the extent that the legal basis of the self lies in the model of property rights, in what has been termed "possessive individualism," every proper portrait has its lurking, objectifying inverse in the files of the police. In other words, a covert Hobbesian logic links the terrain of the "National Gallery" with that of the "Police Act."[8]

---

6. See Michel Foucault, *Discipline and Punish: The Birth of the Prison*, trans. Alan Sheridan, New York, Pantheon, 1977, and, *The History of Sexuality, Volume I: An Introduction*, trans. Robert Hurley, New York, Pantheon, 1978.

7. Any photographs that seek to identify a *target*, such as military reconnaissance photographs, operate according to the same general logic. See my 1975 essay "The Instrumental Image: Steichen at War," in *Photography against the Grain: Essays and Photo Works, 1973–1983*, Halifax, The Press of the Nova Scotia College of Art and Design, 1984.

8. The theoretical ground for the construction of a specifically *bourgeois* subject can be found in Hobbes's *Leviathan* (1651). C. B. Macpherson has argued that Hobbes's axiomatic positing of an essentially competitive individual human "nature" was in fact quite specific to a developing market society, moreover, to a market society in which human labor power increasingly took the form of an alienable commodity. As Hobbes put it, "The *Value* or WORTH of a man, is as of all things, his Price; that is to say, so much as would be given for the use of his Power: and therefore is not absolute; but a thing dependent on the need and judgement of another" (Thomas Hobbes, *Leviathan*, Harmondsworth, Penguin, 1968, Chap. 10, pp. 151–152. See Macpherson's introduction to this edition and his *Political Theory of Possessive Individualism: Hobbes to Locke*, London, Oxford University Press, 1962).

While it would be farfetched to present Hobbes as a theorist of the "bourgeois portrait," it is interesting to note how he defined individual autonomy and its relinquishment through contractual obligation in terms of dramaturgical metaphors, thus distinguishing between two categories of the

In the mid-nineteenth century, the terms of this linkage between the sphere of culture and that of social regulation were specifically utilitarian.[9] Many of the early promoters of photography struck up a Benthamite chorus, stressing the medium's promise for a social calculus of pleasure and discipline. Here was a machine for providing small doses of happiness on a mass scale, for contributing to Jeremy Bentham's famous goal: "the greatest happiness of the greatest number."[10] Thus the photographic portrait in particular was welcomed as a socially ameliorative as well as a socially repressive instrument. Jane Welsh Carlyle voiced characteristic hopes in 1859, when she described inexpensive portrait photography as a social palliative:

> Blessed be the inventor of photography. I set him even above the inventor of chloroform! It has given more positive pleasure to poor suffering humanity than anything that has been "cast up" in my time . . .—this art, by which even the poor can possess themselves of tolerable likenesses of their absent dear ones.[11]

In the United States, similar but more extensive utilitarian claims were made by the portrait photographer Marcus Aurelius Root, who was able to articulate the connection between pleasure and discipline, to argue explicitly for a moral economy of the image. Like Carlyle, he stressed the salutory effects of photography on working-class family life. Not only was photography to serve as a means of cultural enlightenment for the working classes, but family photographs sustained sentimental ties in a nation of migrants. This "primal household affection" served a socially cohesive function, Root argued—articulating a nineteenth-century familialism that would survive and become an essential ideo-

---

person, the "Author" and the "Actor" (*Leviathan*, Chap. 16, pp. 217-218). The analogy between symbolic representation and political-legal representation is central to his thought. (An amusing history of portrait photography could be written on the vicissitudes of the Hobbesian struggle between photographer and sitter, both in the actual portrait encounter and in the subsequent reception of portrait photographs.)

Furthermore, the frontispiece to *Leviathan* took the form of an allegorical portrait. The commonwealth, or state, is literally embodied in the figure of a sovereign, an "artificial man," whose body is itself composed of a multitude of bodies, all of whom have ceded a portion of their individual power to the commonwealth in order to prevent the civil war that would inevitably result from their unchecked pursuit of "natural" appetites. Thus the "body" of the Leviathan is a kind of pressure vessel, containing explosive natural forces. This image is perhaps the first attempt to diagram the social field visually. As such, it has a definite, if usually indirect, resonance in nineteenth-century attempts to construct visual metaphors for the conceptual models of the new social sciences.

9.   "The utilitarian doctrine . . . is at bottom only a restatement of the individualist principles which were worked out in the seventeenth century: Bentham built on Hobbes" (C. B. Macpherson, *Political Theory of Possessive Individualism*, p. 2).

10.   Jeremy Bentham, "A Fragment on Government" (1776), in Mary P. Mack, ed., *A Bentham Reader*, New York, Pegasus, 1969, p. 45.

11.   Quoted in Helmut Gernsheim, *The History of Photography: From the Camera Obscura to the Beginning of the Modern Era*, New York, McGraw-Hill, 1969, p. 239.

logical feature of American mass culture. Furthermore, widely distributed portraits of the great would subject everyday experience to a regular parade of moral exemplars. Root's concern for respectability and order led him to applaud the adoption of photography by the police, arguing that convicted offenders would "not find it easy to resume their criminal careers, while their faces and general aspects are familiar to so many, especially to the keen-sighted detective police."[12] The "so many" is significant here, since it implicitly enlists a wider citizenry in the vigilant work of detection. Thus Root's utilitarianism comes full circle. Beginning with cheaply affordable aesthetic pleasures and moral lessons, he ends up with the photographic extension of that exemplary utilitarian social machine, the Panopticon.[13]

12.   Marcus Aurelius Root, *The Camera and the Pencil*, 1864, reprint, Pawlett, Vermont, Helios, 1971, pp. 420-421.
13.   The Panopticon, or Inspection House, was Jeremy Bentham's proposal, written in 1787, for an architectural system of social discipline, applicable to prison, factory, workhouse, asylum, and school. The operative principles of the Panopticon were isolation and perpetual surveillance. Inmates were to be held in a ring of individual cells. Unable to see into a central observation tower, they would be forced to assume that they were watched continually. (As Hobbes remarked over a century earlier, "the reputation of Power is Power.") The beneficial effects of this program were trumpeted by Bentham in the famous opening remarks of his proposal: "Morals reformed — health preserved — industry invigorated — instruction diffused — public burdens lightened — Economy seated, as it were, upon a rock — all by a simple idea of architecture" (John Bowring, ed., *The Works of Jeremy Bentham*, vol. 4, London, Simpkin, Marshall, 1843, p. 49). With Bentham the principle of supervision takes on an explicit industrial capitalist character: his prisons were to function as profit-making establishments, based on the private contracting-out of convict labor. Bentham was a prototypical efficiency expert. (On these last two points see, respectively, Gertrude Himmelfarb, "The Haunted House of Jeremy Bentham," in *Victorian Minds*, New York, Knopf, 1968, pp. 32-81; and Daniel Bell, "Work and Its Discontents," in *The End of Ideology: On the Exhaustion of Political Ideas in the Fifties*, Glencoe, Illinois, Free Press, 1960, pp. 227-274.)
   For Foucault, "Panopticism" provides the central metaphor for modern disciplinary power based on isolation, individuation, and supervision (*Discipline and Punish*, pp. 195-228). Foucault traces the "birth of the prison" only to the 1840s, just when photography appears with all of its instrumental promise. Given the central optical metaphor in Foucault's work, a reading of the subsequent development of disciplinary systems would need logically to take photography into account. John Tagg has written a Foucauldian account of the "panoptic" character of early police and psychiatric photography in Britain. While I am in frequent agreement with his argument, I disagree with his claim that the "cumbersome architecture" of the Panopticon became redundant with the development of photography ("Power and Photography: Part 1, A Means of Surveillance: The Photograph as Evidence in Law," *Screen Education*, no. 36 [Winter 1980], p. 45). This seems to accord too much power to photography, and to imply that domination operates entirely by the force of visual representation. To suggest that cameras replaced prisons is more than a little hyperbolic. The fact that Bentham's plan was never realized in the form he proposed has perhaps contributed to the confusion; models are more easily transformed into metaphors than are realized projects. Once discourse turns on metaphor, it becomes a simple matter to substitute a photographic metaphor for an architectural one. My main point here is that any history of disciplinary institutions must recognize the multiplicity of material devices involved — some literally concrete — in tracing not only the importance of surveillance, but also the continued importance of confinement. After all, Bentham's proposal *was* partially realized in the cellular and separate systems of confinement that emerged in the nineteenth century. At least one "genuine" panopticon prison was constructed: the Stateville Penitentiary in Illinois, built between 1916 and 1924. (For works on early prison history, see D. Melossi and M. Pavarini, *The Prison and the Factory:*

Notwithstanding the standard liberal accounts of the history of photography, the new medium did not simply inherit and "democratize" the honorific functions of bourgeois portraiture. Nor did police photography simply function repressively, although it is foolish to argue that the immediate function of police photographs was somehow more ideological or positively instrumental than negatively instrumental. But in a more general, dispersed fashion, in serving to introduce the panoptic principle into daily life, photography welded the honorific and repressive functions together. Every portrait implicitly took its place within a social and moral hierarchy. The *private* moment of sentimental individuation, the look at the frozen gaze-of-the-loved-one, was shadowed by two other more *public* looks: a look up, at one's "betters," and a look down, at one's "inferiors." Especially in the United States, photography could sustain an imaginary mobility on this vertical scale, thus provoking both ambition and fear, and interpellating, in class terms, a characteristically "petit-bourgeois" subject.

We can speak then of a generalized, inclusive *archive*, a *shadow archive* that encompasses an entire social terrain while positioning individuals within that terrain.[14] This archive contains subordinate, territorialized archives: archives whose semantic interdependence is normally obscured by the "coherence" and "mutual exclusivity" of the social groups registered within each. The general, all-inclusive archive necessarily contains both the traces of the visible bodies of heroes, leaders, moral exemplars, celebrities, and those of the poor, the diseased, the insane, the criminal, the nonwhite, the female, and all other embodiments of the unworthy. The clearest indication of the essential unity of this archive of images of the body lies in the fact that by the mid-nineteenth century a single hermeneutic paradigm had gained widespread prestige. This paradigm had

Origins of the Penitentiary System, trans. Glynis Cousin, London, Macmillan, 1981; David Rothman, *The Discovery of the Asylum: Social Order and Disorder in the New Republic*, Boston, Little, Brown, 1971; and Michael Ignatieff, *A Just Measure of Pain: The Penitentiary in the Industrial Revolution, 1750–1850*, London, Macmillan, 1978.)

Certainly prison architecture and the spatial positioning of prisons in the larger environment remain matters of crucial importance. Especially in the United States, where economic crisis and Reaganite judicial tough-mindedness have lead to record prison populations, these are paramount issues of what is euphemistically called "public policy." In fact, the current wave of ambitious prison building has led to at least one instance of (postmodern?) return to the model of the Panopticon. The new Montgomery County Detention Center in Virginia was designed by prison architect James Kessler according to a "new" principle of "podular/direct supervision." In this scaled-down, rumpus-room version of the Panopticon, inmates can see into the central control room from which they are continually observed (see Benjamin Forgey, "Answering the Jail Question," *The Washington Post*, August 2, 1986, pp. G1–G2).

14. For earlier arguments on the archival paradigm in photography, see Rosalind Krauss, "Photography's Discursive Spaces: Landscape/View," *The Art Journal*, vol. 42, no. 4 (Winter 1982), pp. 311–319; and Allan Sekula, "Photography between Labour and Capital," in B. Buchloh and R. Wilkie, eds., *Mining Photographs and Other Pictures: Photographs by Leslie Shedden*, Halifax, The Press of the Nova Scotia College of Art and Design, 1983, pp. 193–268.

two tightly entwined branches, physiognomy and phrenology. Both shared the belief that the surface of the body, and especially the face and head, bore the outward signs of inner character.

Accordingly, in reviving and to some extent systematizing physiognomy in the late 1770s, Johann Caspar Lavater argued that the "original language of Nature, written on the face of Man" could be deciphered by a rigorous physiognomic *science*.[15] Physiognomy analytically isolated the profile of the head and the various anatomic features of the head and face, assigning a characterological significance to each element: forehead, eyes, ears, nose, chin, etc. Individual character was judged through the loose concatenation of these readings. In both its analytic and synthetic stages, this interpretive process required that distinctive individual features be read in conformity to type. Phrenology, which emerged in the first decade of the nineteenth century in the researches of the Viennese physician Franz Josef Gall, sought to discern correspondences between the topography of the skull and what were thought to be specific localized mental faculties seated within the brain. This was a crude forerunner of more modern neurological attempts to map out localized cerebral functions.

In general, physiognomy, and more specifically phrenology, linked an everyday nonspecialist empiricism with increasingly authoritative attempts to medicalize the study of the mind. The ambitious effort to construct a materialist science of the self led to the dissection of brains, including those of prominent phrenologists, and to the accumulation of vast collections of skulls. Eventually this effort would lead to a volumetrics of the skull, termed craniometry. But presumably any observant reader of one of the numerous handbooks and manuals of phrenology could master the interpretive codes. The humble origins of phrenological research were described by Gall in these terms:

> I assembled a large number of persons at my house, drawn from the lowest classes and engaged in various occupations, such as fiacre driver, street porter and so on. I gained their confidence and induced them to speak frankly by giving them money and having wine and beer distributed to them. When I saw that they were favorably disposed, I urged them to tell me everything they knew about one another, both their good and bad qualities, and I carefully examined their heads. This was the origin of the craniological chart that was seized upon so avidly by the public; even artists took it over and distributed a large number among the public in the form of masks of all kinds.[16]

15.   John [*sic*] Caspar Lavater, Preface to *Essays on Physiognomy Designed to Promote the Knowledge and the Love of Mankind*, vol. 1, trans. Henry Hunter, London, J. Murray, 1792, n.p.
16.   Quoted in Louis Chevalier, *Labouring Classes and Dangerous Classes in Paris during the First Half of the Nineteenth Century*, trans. Frank Jellineck, London, Routledge, 1973, p. 411.

The broad appeal and influence of these practices on literary and artistic realism, and on the general culture of the mid-nineteenth-century city is well known.[17] And we understand the culture of the photographic portrait only dimly if we fail to recognize the enormous prestige and popularity of a general physiognomic paradigm in the 1840s and 1850s. Especially in the United States, the proliferation of photography and that of phrenology were quite coincident.

Since physiognomy and phrenology were comparative, taxonomic disciplines, they sought to encompass an entire range of human diversity. In this respect, these disciplines were instrumental in constructing the very archive they claimed to interpret. Virtually every manual deployed an array of individual cases and types along a loose set of "moral, intellectual, and animal" continua.[18] Thus zones of genius, virtue, and strength were charted only in relation to zones of idiocy, vice, and weakness. The boundaries between these zones were vaguely demarcated; thus it was possible to speak, for example, of "moral idiocy." Generally, in this pre-evolutionary system of difference, the lower zones shaded off into varieties of animality and pathology.

In the almost exclusive emphasis on the head and face we can discover the idealist secret lurking at the heart of these putatively materialist sciences. These were discourses *of* the head *for* the head. Whatever the tendency of physiognomic or phrenologic thought — whether fatalistic or therapeutic in relation to the inexorable logic of the body's signs, whether uncompromisingly materialist in tone or vaguely spiritualist in relation to certain zones of the organic, whether republican or elitist in pedagogical stance — these disciplines would serve to legitimate on organic grounds the dominion of intellectual over manual labor. Thus physiognomy and phrenology contributed to the ideological hegemony of a capitalism that increasingly relied upon a hierarchical division of labor, a capitalism that applauded its own progress as the outcome of individual cleverness and cunning.

In claiming to provide a means for distinguishing the stigmata of vice from the shining marks of virtue, physiognomy and phrenology offered an essential hermeneutic service to a world of fleeting and often anonymous market transactions. Here was a method for quickly assessing the character of strangers in the dangerous and congested spaces of the nineteenth-century city. Here was a gauge of the intentions and capabilities of the other. In the United States in the 1840s, newspaper advertisements for jobs frequently requested

17.   In addition to Chevalier's book just cited, see Walter Benjamin's 1938 essay, "The Paris of the Second Empire in Baudelaire," in *Charles Baudelaire: A Lyric Poet in the Era of High Capitalism*, trans. Harry Zohn, London, New Left Books, 1973, pp. 35–66. See also Judith Wechsler, *A Human Comedy: Physiognomy and Caricature in Nineteenth Century Paris*, Chicago, University of Chicago Press, 1982. For specific histories of phrenology, see David de Guistino, *Conquest of Mind: Phrenology and Victorian Social Thought*, London, Croom Helm, 1975; and John Davies, *Phrenology: Fad and Science*, New Haven, Yale University Press, 1955.
18.   Lavater, vol. 1, p. 13.

that applicants submit a phrenological analysis.[19] Thus phrenology delivered the moral and intellectual "facts" that are today delivered in more "refined" and abstract form by psychometricians and polygraph experts.

Perhaps it is no surprise, then, that photography and phrenology should have met formally in 1846 in a book on "criminal jurisprudence." Here was an opportunity to lend a new organic facticity to the already established medical and psychiatric genre of the case study.[20] A phrenologically inclined American penal reformer and matron of the women's prison at Sing Sing, Eliza Farnham commissioned Mathew Brady to make a series of portraits of inmates at two New York prisons. Engravings based on these photographs were appended to Farnham's new edition, entitled *Rationale of Crime*, of a previously unillustrated English work by Marmaduke Sampson. Sampson regarded criminal behavior as a form of "moral insanity." Both he and Farnham subscribed to a variant of phrenology that argued for the possibility of therapeutic modification or enhancement of organically predetermined characteristics. Presumably, good organs could be made to triumph over bad. Farnham's contribution is distinctive for its unabashed nonspecialist appeal. She sought to speak to "the popular mind of Republican America," in presenting an argument for the abolition of the death penalty and the establishment of a therapeutic system of treatment.[21] Her contribution to the book consisted of a polemical introduction, extensive notes, and several appendices, including the illustrated case studies. Farnham was assisted in her selection of case-study subjects by the prominent New York publisher-entrepreneur of phrenology, Lorenzo Fowler, who clearly lent further authority to the sample.

Ten adult prisoners are pictured, evenly divided between men and women. Three are identified as Negro, one as Irish, one as German; one woman is identified as a "Jewess of German birth," another as a "half-breed Indian and negro." The remaining three inmates are presumably Anglo-Saxon, but are not identified as such. A series of eight pictures of child inmates is not annotated in racial or ethnic terms, although one child is presumably black. Although Farnham professed a variant of phrenology that was not overtly racist— unlike other pre-Darwinian head analysts who sought conclusive proof of the "separate creation" of the non-Caucasian races—this differential marking of race and ethnicity according to age is significant in other ways. After all, Farnham's work appeared in an American context—characterized by slavery and the massive immigration of Irish peasants—that was profoundly stratified

19. Davies, p. 38.
20. On the history of the illustrated psychiatric case study, see Sander Gilman, *Seeing the Insane*, New York, J. Wiley, 1982.
21. Eliza Farnham, "Introductory Preface" to Marmaduke Sampson, *Rationale of Crime and its Appropriate Treatment, Being a Treatise on Criminal Jurisprudence Considered in Relation to Cerebral Organization*, New York, Appleton, 1846, p. xiii.

along these lines. By marking children less in racial and ethnic terms, Farnham avoided stigmatizing them. Thus children in general were presented as more malleable figures than adults. Children were also presented as less weighted down by criminal biographies or by the habitual exercise of their worst faculties. Despite the fact that some of these boys were explicitly described as incorrigibles, children provided Farnham with a general figure of moral renewal. Because their potential for "respectability" was greater than that of the adult offenders, they were presented as miniature versions of their potential adult-male-respectable-Anglo-Saxon-proletarian selves. Farnham, Fowler, and Brady can be seen as significant inventors of that privileged figure of social reform discourse: the figure of the child rescued by a paternalistic medicosocial science.[22]

Farnham's concerns touch on two of the central issues of nineteenth-century penal discourse: the practical drawing of distinctions between incorrigible and pliant criminals, and the disciplined conversion of the reformable into "useful" proletarians (or at least into useful informers). Thus even though she credited several inmates with "well developed" intellects, and despite the fact that her detractors accused her of Fourierism, her reformist vision had a definite ceiling. This limit was defined quite explicitly by the conclusion of her study. There she underscored the baseness shared by all her criminal subjects by illustrating three "heads of persons possessing superior intellect" (two of which, both male, were treated as classical busts). Her readers were asked to note the "striking contrast."[23]

I emphasize this point because it is emblematic of the manner in which the criminal archive came into existence. That is, it was only on the basis of mutual comparison, on the basis of the tentative construction of a larger, "universal" archive, that zones of deviance and respectability could be clearly demarcated. In this instance of the first sustained application of photography to the task of phrenological analysis, it seems clear that the comparative description of the criminal body came first. The book ends with a self-congratulatory mirror held up to the middle-class reader. It is striking that the pictorial labor behind Farnham's criminal sample was that of Brady, who devoted virtually his entire antebellum career to the construction of a massive honorific archive of photographs of "illustrious," celebrated, and would-be celebrated American figures.[24]

22.   For a reading of the emergence of this system in France, see Jacques Donzelot, *The Policing of Families*, trans. Robert Hurley, New York, Pantheon, 1979. Donzelot seems to place inordinate blame on women for the emergence of a "tutelary" mode of social regulation. For a Marxist-feminist critique of Donzelot, see Michelle Barrett and Mary McIntosh, *The Anti-Social Family*, London, New Left Books, 1982.
23.   Sampson, p. 175.
24.   See Madeline Stern, "Mathew B. Brady and the *Rationale of Crime,*" *The Quarterly Journal of the Library of Congress*, vol. 31, no. 3 (July 1974), pp. 128–135; and Alan Trachtenberg, "Brady's Portraits," *The Yale Review*, vol. 73, no. 2 (Winter 1984), pp. 230–253.

Thus far I have described a number of early attempts, by turns comic, speculative, and practical, to bring the camera to bear upon the body of the criminal. I have also argued, following the general line of investigation charted in the later works of Foucault, that the position assigned the criminal body was a relative one, that the invention of the modern criminal cannot be dissociated from the construction of a law-abiding body—a body that was either bourgeois or subject to the dominion of the bourgeoisie. The law-abiding body recognized its threatening other in the criminal body, recognized its own acquisitive and aggressive impulses unchecked, and sought to reassure itself in two contradictory ways. The first was the invention of an exceptional criminal who was indistinguishable from the bourgeois, save for a conspicuous lack of moral inhibition: herein lay the figure of the criminal genius.[25] The second was the in-

25.   On this point see Michel Foucault, "Prison Talk," in *Power/Knowledge: Selected Interviews and Other Writings, 1972-1977,* ed. Colin Gordon, New York, Pantheon, 1980, p. 46.

174   RATIONALE OF CRIME.   APPENDIX   175

HEADS OF PERSONS POSSESSING SUPERIOR
INTELLECT.

The following drawings are introduced for the purpose of showing the striking contrast between the cerebral development of such persons as we have been describing and those who are endowed with superior powers of intellect and sentiment

B. F. is one of the inmates of the Long Island Farms. He is partially idiotic, and the very imperfect development of the superior portion of the brain, with the small size of the whole, clearly indicates the character of his mental capacities. It affords a striking contrast to the last drawing, R. A., and is in harmony with the actual difference between the minds of the two individuals. B. F. is vicious, cruel, and apparently incapable of any elevated or humane sentiments

From Eliza Farnham, *Appendix to Marmaduke Sampson,*
Rationale of Crime, *1846.*

From Alphonse Bertillon, Service d'identification.
Exposition universelle de Chicago, *1893. (Album
collection National Gallery of Canada, Ottawa.)*

vention of a criminal who was organically distinct from the bourgeois: a *biotype*.
The science of criminology emerged from this latter operation.

A physiognomic code of visual interpretation of the body's signs — specifically the signs of the head — and a technique of mechanized visual representation intersected in the 1840s. This unified system of representation and interpretation promised a vast taxonomic ordering of images of the body. This was
an archival promise. Its realization would seem to be grounded primarily in the
technical refinement of strictly optical means. This turns out not to be the case.

I am especially concerned that exaggerated claims not be made for the
powers of optical realism, whether in a celebratory or critical vein. One danger
lies in constructing an overly monolithic or unitary model of nineteenth-
century realist discourse. Within the rather limited and usually ignored field of
instrumental scientific and technical realism, we discover a house divided. Nowhere was this division more pronounced than in the pursuit of the criminal
body. If we examine the manner in which photography was made useful by the
late-nineteenth-century police, we find plentiful evidence of a crisis of faith in
optical empiricism. In short, we need to describe the emergence of a truth-
apparatus that cannot be adequately reduced to the optical model provided by
the camera. The camera is integrated into a larger ensemble: a bureaucratic-
clerical-statistical system of "intelligence." This system can be described as a
sophisticated form of the archive. The central artifact of this system is not the
camera but the filing cabinet.

II.

The institution of the photographic archive received its most thorough early articulation in precise conjunction with an increasingly professionalized and technological mode of police work and an emerging social science of criminology. This occurred in the 1880s and 1890s. Why was the model of the archive of such import for these linked disciplines?

In structural terms, the archive is both an abstract paradigmatic entity and a concrete institution. In both senses, the archive is a vast substitution set, providing for a relation of general equivalence between images. This image of the archive as an encyclopedic repository of exchangeable images was articulated most profoundly in the late 1850s by the American physician and essayist Oliver Wendell Holmes when he compared photographs to paper currency.[26] The capacity of the archive to reduce all possible sights to a single code of equivalence was grounded in the metrical accuracy of the camera. Here was a medium from which exact mathematical data could be extracted, or as the physicist François Arago put it in 1839, a medium "in which objects preserve mathematically their forms."[27] For nineteenth-century positivists, photography doubly fulfilled the Enlightenment dream of a universal language: the universal mimetic language of the camera yielded up a higher, more cerebral truth, a truth that could be uttered in the universal abstract language of mathematics. For this reason, photography could be accommodated to a Galilean vision of the world as a book "written in the language of mathematics." Photography promised more than a wealth of detail; it promised to reduce nature to its geometrical essence. Presumably then, the archive could provide a standard physiognomic gauge of the criminal, could assign each criminal body a relative and quantitative position within a larger ensemble.

This archival promise was frustrated, however, both by the messy contingency of the photograph and by the sheer quantity of images. The photographic archive's components are not conventional lexical units, but rather are subject to the circumstantial character of all that is photographable. Thus it is absurd to imagine a dictionary of photographs, unless one is willing to disregard the specificity of individual images in favor of some model of typicality, such as that underlying the iconography of Vesalian anatomy or of most of the plates accompanying the *Encyclopédie* of Diderot and d'Alembert. Clearly, one way of "taming" photography is by means of this transformation of the circumstantial and idiosyncratic into the typical and emblematic. This is usually achieved by stylistic or interpretive fiat, or by a sampling of the archive's offerings for a

26. Oliver Wendell Holmes, "The Stereoscope and the Stereograph," *Atlantic Monthly*, vol. 3, no. 20 (June 1859), p. 748. For a more extensive treatment of this issue, see my 1981 essay, "The Traffic in Photographs," in *Photography against the Grain*, pp. 96–101.
27. François Arago, letter to Duchâtel, in Gernsheim, *Daguerre*, p. 91.

"representative" instance. Another way is to invent a machine, or rather a clerical apparatus, a filing system, which allows the operator/researcher/editor to retrieve the individual instance from the huge quantity of images contained within the archive. Here the photograph is not regarded as necessarily typical or emblematic of anything, but only as a particular image which has been isolated for purposes of inspection. These two semantic paths are so fundamental to the culture of photographic realism that their very existence is usually ignored.

The difference between these two models of photographic meaning are played out in two different approaches to the photographic representation of the criminal body: the "realist" approach, and by realism here I mean that venerable (medieval) philosophical realism that insists upon the truth of general propositions, on the reality of species and types, and the equally venerable "nominalist" approach, which denies the reality of generic categories as anything other than mental constructs. The first approach can be seen as overtly theoretical and "scientific" in its aims, if more covertly practical. The other can be seen as overtly practical and "technical" in its aims, if only covertly theoretical. Thus the would-be scientists of crime sought a knowledge and mastery of an elusive "criminal type." And the "technicians" of crime sought knowledge and mastery of individual criminals. Herein lies a terminological distinction, and a division of labor, between "criminology" and "criminalistics." Criminology hunted "the" criminal body. Criminalistics hunted "this" or "that" criminal body.

Contrary to the commonplace understanding of the "mug shot" as the very exemplar of a powerful, artless, and wholly denotative visual empiricism, these early instrumental uses of photographic realism were systematized on the basis of an acute recognition of the *inadequacies* and limitations of ordinary visual empiricism. Thus two systems of description of the criminal body were deployed in the 1880s; both sought to ground photographic evidence in more abstract *statistical* methods. This merger of optics and statistics was fundamental to a broader integration of the discourses of visual representation and those of the social sciences in the nineteenth century. Despite a common theoretical source, the intersection of photography and statistics led to strikingly different results in the work of two different men: Alphonse Bertillon and Francis Galton.

The Paris police official Alphonse Bertillon invented the first effective modern system of *criminal identification*. His was a bipartite system, positioning a "microscopic" individual record within a "macroscopic" aggregate. First, he combined photographic portraiture, anthropometric description, and highly standardized and abbreviated written notes on a single *fiche*, or card. Second, he organized these cards within a comprehensive, statistically based filing system.

The English statistician and founder of eugenics, Francis Galton, invented a method of composite portraiture. Galton operated on the periphery of criminology. Nonetheless, his interest in heredity and racial "betterment" led him to join in the search for a biologically determined "criminal type." Through one of his several applications of composite portraiture, Galton attempted to construct a *purely optical* apparition of the criminal type. This photographic impression of an abstract, statistically defined, and empirically nonexistent criminal face was both the most bizarre and the most sophisticated of many concurrent attempts to marshall photographic evidence in the search for the essence of crime.

The projects of Bertillon and Galton constitute two methodological poles of the positivist attempts to define and regulate social deviance. Bertillon sought to individuate. His aims were practical and operational, a response to the demands of urban police work and the politics of fragmented class struggle during the Third Republic. Galton sought to visualize the generic evidence of hereditarian laws. His aims were theoretical, the result of eclectic but ultimately single-minded curiosities of one of the last Victorian gentleman-amateur scientists. Nonetheless, Bertillon's work had its own theoretical context and implications, just as Galton's grimly playful research realized its practical implications in the ideological and political program of the international eugenics movement. Both men were committed to technologies of demographic regulation. Bertillon's system of criminal identification was integral to the efforts to quarantine permanently a class of habitual or professional criminals. Galton sought to intervene in human reproduction by means of public policy, encouraging the propagation of the "fit," and discouraging or preventing outright that of the "unfit."

The idealist proclivities, territorialism, and status consciousness of intellectual history have prevented us from recognizing Bertillon and Galton's shared ground. While Galton has been considered a proper, if somewhat eccentric, object of the history of science, Bertillon remains an ignored mechanic and clerk, commemorated mostly by anecdotal historians of the police.

In order to explore this terrain shared by a police clerk and gentleman statistician, I need to introduce a third figure. Both Bertillon's and Galton's projects were grounded in the emergence and codification of *social statistics* in the 1830s and 1840s. Both relied upon the central conceptual category of social statistics: the notion of the "average man" (*l'homme moyen*). This concept was invented (I will argue shortly that it was actually reinvented) by the Belgian astronomer and statistician Adolphe Quetelet. Although less well remembered than Auguste Comte, Quetelet is the most significant other early architect of sociology. Certainly he laid the foundations of the quantitative paradigm in the social sciences. By seeking statistical regularities in rates of birth, death, and crime, Quetelet hoped to realize the Enlightenment philosopher Condorcet's proposal for a "social mathematics," a mathematically exact science that would discover the fundamental laws of social phenomena. Quetelet helped to establish some of the first actuarial tables used in Belgium, and to found in 1853 an international society for the promotion of statistical methods. As the philosopher of science Ian Hacking has suggested, the rise of social statistics in the mid-nineteenth century was crucial to the replacement of strictly mechanistic theories of causality by a more probabilistic paradigm. Quetelet was a determinist, but he invented a determinism based on iron laws of chance. This emergent paradigm would lead eventually to indeterminism.[28]

Who, or what, was the average man? A less flippant query would be, *how* was the average man? Quetelet introduced this composite character in his 1835 treatise *Sur l'homme*. Quetelet argued that large aggregates of social data revealed a regularity of occurrence that could only be taken as evidence of determinate social laws. This regularity had political and moral as well as epistemological implications:

> The greater the number of individuals observed, the more do individual peculiarities, whether physical or moral, become effaced, and leave in a prominent point of view the general facts, by virtue of which society exists and is preserved.[29]

Quetelet sought to move from the mathematicization of individual bodies to that of society in general. In *Sur l'homme* he charted various quantitative biographies of the productive and reproductive powers of the average man and woman. For example, he calculated the fluctuation of fecundity with respect to female age. Using data from dynamometer studies, he charted the average muscular power of men and women of different ages. At the level of the social aggregate, life history read as a graphic curve. (Here was prefiguration, in extreme form, of Zola's naturalism: a subliterary, quantitative narrative of the generalized social organism.)

Just as Quetelet's early statistical contributions to the life insurance industry can be seen as crucial to the regularization of that organized form of gambling known as finance capital, so also his charting of the waxing and waning of human energies can be seen as an attempt to conceptualize that Hercules of industrial capitalism, termed by Marx the "average worker," the abstract embodiment of labor power in the aggregate.[30] And outside the sphere of waged work, Quetelet invented but did not name the figure of the average mother, crucial to the new demographic sciences which sought nervously to chart the relative numeric strengths of class against class and nation against nation.

For Quetelet the most emphatic demonstration of the regularity of social

28.　See Ian Hacking, "How Should We Do the History of Statistics?" *Ideology and Consciousness*, no. 8 (Spring 1981), pp. 15–26; and "Biopower and the Avalanche of Printed Numbers," *Humanities and Society*, vol. 5, nos. 3–4 (Summer and Fall 1982), pp. 279–295.

29.　Adolphe Quetelet, *A Treatise on Man and the Development of His Faculties*, trans. R. Knox, Edinburgh, Chambers, 1842, p. 6.

30.　Karl Marx, *Capital: A Critique of Political Economy*, trans. Ben Fowkes, London, New Left Books, vol. 1, 1976, pp. 440–441.

phenomena was given by crime statistics. "Moral statistics" provided the linch-pin for his construction of a "social physics" that would demolish the prestige of moral paradigms grounded in free will. The criminal was no more than an agent of determining social forces. Furthermore, crime statistics provided the synec-dochic basis for a broader description of the social field. As Louis Chevalier has argued, Quetelet inaugurated a "quantitative description which took criminal statistics as the starting point for a description of urban living as a whole."[31] Chevalier has argued further that criminal statistics contributed thus to a per-vasive bourgeois conception of the essentially *pathological* character of metropol-itan life, especially in the Paris of the July Monarchy. Quetelet's terminological

Tailles des Belges de 18 à 20 ans.

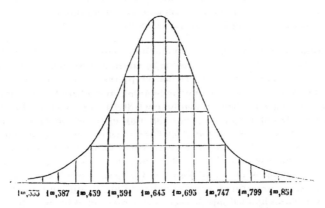

1ᵐ,555 1ᵐ,587 1ᵐ,439 1ᵐ,591 1ᵐ,643 1ᵐ,695 1ᵐ,747 1ᵐ,799 1ᵐ,851

From Adolphe Quetelet, Physique sociale, ou Essai sur le développement des facultés de l'homme, *1869.*

contribution to this medicalization of the social field is evident in his reference to the statistical study of crime as a form of "moral anatomy."

Quetelet refined his notion of the "average man" with conceptual tools borrowed from astronomy and probability theory. He observed that large ag-gregates of social data—notably anthropometric data—fell into a pattern cor-responding to the bell-shaped curve derived by Gauss in 1809 in an attempt to determine accurate astronomical measurements from the distribution of random errors around a central mean. Quetelet came to regard this symmetrical bino-

31.   Chevalier, p. 10.

mial curve as the mathematical expression of fundamental social law. While he admitted that the average man was a statistical fiction, this fiction lived within the abstract configuration of the binomial distribution. In an extraordinary metaphoric conflation of individual difference with mathematical error, Quetelet defined the central portion of the curve, that large number of measurements clustered around the mean, as a zone of normality. Divergent measurements tended toward darker regions of monstrosity and biosocial pathology.[32]

Thus conceived, the "average man" constituted an ideal, not only of social health, but of social stability and of beauty. In interesting metaphors, revealing both the astronomical sources and aesthetico-political ambitions inherent in Quetelet's "social physics," he defined the social norm as a "center of gravity," and the average man as "the type of all which is beautiful — of all which is good."[33] Crime constituted a "perturbing force," acting to throw the delicate balance of this implicitly republican social mechanism into disarray. Although Quetelet was constructing a quantitative model of civil society and only indirectly describing the contours of an ideal commonwealth, his model of a gravitational social order bears striking similarity to Hobbes's Leviathan.[34]

Like Hobbes, Quetelet began with atomized individual bodies and returned to the image of the body in describing the social aggregate. Quetelet worked, however, in a climate of physiognomic and phrenologic enthusiasm, and indeed early social statistics can be regarded as a variant of physiognomy writ large. For example, Quetelet accepted, despite his republicanism, the late-eighteenth-century notion of the *cranial angle*, which, as George Mosse has argued, emerges from the appropriation by preevolutionary Enlightenment anthropology of the classicist idealism of Wincklemann.[35] Based in part on the art-historical evidence of noble Grecian foreheads, this racist geometrical fiction defined a descending hierarchy of head types, with presumably upright Caucasian brows approaching this lost ideal more closely than did the presumably apelike brows of Africans. For his part, Quetelet was less interested in a broadly racist physical anthropology than in detecting within European society patterns of bodily evidence of deviation from "normality." It is understandable that he would be drawn to those variants of physiognomic thought which sought to systematize the body's signs in terms of a quantifying geometrical

32.   Adolphe Quetelet, *Lettres sur la théorie des probabilités*, Brussels, Académie Royale, 1846. (*Letters on the Theory of Probability*, trans. O. G. Downes, London, Layton, 1849). See also Georges Canguilhem, *On the Normal and the Pathological*, trans. Carolyn Fawcett, Boston, Reidel, 1978, pp. 86–104.
33.   Quetelet, *Treatise on Man*, p. 100.
34.   See note 8. Of course, Quetelet's extreme determinist view of the social field was diametrically opposed to the contractual model of human relations advanced by Hobbes.
35.   See George Mosse, *Toward the Final Solution: A History of European Racism*, New York, Fertig, 1978, pp. 17–34.

schema. From Quetelet on, biosocial statisticians became increasingly absorbed with *anthropometrical* researches, focusing both on the skeletal proportions of the body and upon the volume and configuration of the head.[36] The inherited idealist fascination with the upright forehead can be detected even in Quetelet's model of an ideal society: he argued that social progress would lead to a diminished number of defective and inferior cases, thus increasing the zone of normality. If we consider what this utopian projection meant in terms of the binomial curve, we have to imagine an increasingly peaked, erect configuration: a classical ideal to a fault.

Certainly physiognomy provided a discursive terrain upon which art and the emerging bio-social sciences met during the middle of the nineteenth century. Quetelet's explicitly stated enthusiasm for the model of artistic practice is understandable in this context, but the matter is more complicated. Despite the abstract character of his procedures, Quetelet possessed the aesthetic ambition to compare his project to Dürer's studies of human bodily proportion. The statistician argued that his "aim had been, not only to go once more through the task of Albert [*sic*] Dürer, but to execute it also on an extended scale."[37] Thus visual empiricism retained its prestige in the face of a new object — society — which could in no way be effectively or comprehensively visualized.[38]

36.   See Adolphe Quetelet, *Anthropométrie, ou mesure des différents facultés de l'homme*, Brussels, Muquardt, 1871. Quetelet suffered from aphasia after 1855, and his later works tend to be repetitious and incoherent (see Frank H. Hankins, *Adolphe Quetelet as Statistician*, New York, Columbia University Press, 1908, pp. 31–32). On the intersection of anthropometry and race science, see Stephen Jay Gould, *The Mismeasure of Man*, New York, Norton, 1981.
37.   Quetelet, *Treatise on Man*, p. v.
38.   Here are some ways in which Quetelet's position in relation to idealist aesthetic theory become very curious. The "average man" can be regarded as a bastard child of Kant. In the "Critique of Aesthetical Judgement" Kant describes the psychological basis of the construction of the empirically based "normal Idea" of human beauty, arguing that "the Imagination can, in all probability, actually though unconsciously let one image glide into another, and thus by the concurrence of several of the same kind come by an average, which serves as the common measure of all. Every one has seen a thousand full-grown men. Now if you wish to judge of the normal size, estimating it by means of comparison, the Imagination (as I think) allows a great number of images (perhaps the whole thousand) to fall on one another. If I am allowed here the analogy of optical presentation, it is the space where most of them are combined and inside the contour, where the place is illuminated with the most vivid colors, that the *average size* is cognizable; which, both in height and breadth, is equally far removed from the extreme bounds of the greatest and smallest stature. And this is the stature of a beautiful man" (Immanuel Kant, *Critique of Judgement*, trans. J. H. Bernard, London, Macmillan, 1914, pp. 87–88). This passage prefigures not only Quetelet but also — as we shall see — Galton. However, Kant was careful to respect differences between normal Ideas of beauty appropriate to different races. On an empirical level, he constructed no hierarchy. Furthermore, he distinguished between the empirically based normal Idea, and the "Ideal of beauty," which is constructed in conformity with a concept of morality. Quetelet can be accused of unwittingly collapsing Kant's distinction between the normal Idea and the Ideal, and thus fusing aesthetics and morality on a purely quantitative basis, preparing thus the ground for Galton's plan for the engineering of human reproduction.
     Although Kant's more general proposal for a science of the human species based on the model of the natural sciences was known to Comte, Quetelet, "a stranger to all philosophical

By the end of the nineteenth century, this essentially *organismic* model of a *visible* social field was in crisis. The terms of Quetelet's honorific linkage of an emergent statistics to a venerable optical paradigm were explicitly reversed. The French sociologist Gabriel Tarde argued in 1883 that "a statistical bureau might be compared to an eye or ear," claiming further that "each of our senses gives us, in its own way and from its special point of view, the statistics of the external world. Their characteristic sensations are in a certain way their special graphical tables. Every sensation . . . is only a number."[39] Here the transition is made from the prestige of the visual and the organic to the prestige of institutionalized, bureaucratic abstraction.

Tarde was a central figure, not only in the demise of organismic models of society, but also in the development of a French school of criminological thought during the 1880s. Tarde was a magistrate during his early career, and by 1894 became the head of the Bureau of Statistics within the Department of Justice in Paris, which made him the abstract overseer of the quantitative ebbs and flows of a regulated criminality. His background in legal theory and practice led him to attempt a criticism and modification of Quetelet's extreme determinism, which had absolved the criminal of all responsibility. After all, classical legal theory was not about to abandon its ideological capacity to uphold the state's right to punish criminals for their deeds. In 1890, Tarde advanced a notion of "criminal responsibility" based upon the continuity of individual identity within a shared social milieu, a milieu of "social similarity." Tarde's psychological model of individuality assumed an essential internal nar-

---

speculation," seems never to have read Kant (Joseph Lottin, *Quetelet, statisticien et sociologue*, Louvain, Institut supérieur de philosophie, 1912, p. 367).

    Quetelet's persistent likening of his project to the work of the visual artist can certainly be taken as emblematic of the fusion of idealist aesthetics with Enlightenment theories of social perfection. More specifically, however, Quetelet's evocations of art history — which extended to the measurement of classical sculpture and to long chronological tables of artists who had dealt with problems of bodily proportion — can be seen as a legitimating maneuver to ward off accusations that his strict determinism obliterated the possibility of a human creativity based on the exercise of free will. (It was also an attempt to compare the average bodily types of "ancients" and "moderns.") Thus Quetelet colors his gray determinism with a self-justifying hint of romanticism. But this maneuver also converts the visual artist into a protoscientist, linking Quetelet to the emerging discourse of artistic realism. (See his *Anthropométrie*, pp. 61–169. In this work Quetelet constructed a visual diagram of the biographical course of an average body type from infancy to old age, based on anthropometrical data.)

39.   Gabriel Tarde, "Archaeology and Statistics," in *The Laws of Imitation*, trans. Elsie Parsons, New York, Henry Holt, 1903, pp. 134–135 (this essay first appeared in the *Revue philosophique*, October 1883). In an extraordinary passage of the same essay Tarde compares the graphical curve for criminal recidivism with the "curve traced on [the] retina by the flight of [a] swallow," metaphorically linking within the same epistemological paradigm the work of Bertillon with that of the physiologist Etienne Jules Marey, chronophotographer of human and animal locomotion (*ibid.*, p. 133).

rative coherence of the self: "Identity is the permanence of the person, it is the personality looked at from the point of view of its duration."[40]

Tarde's rather nominalist approach to the philosophy of crime and punishment paralleled a more practical formulation by Alphonse Bertillon, director of the Identification Bureau of the Paris Prefecture of Police. In 1893, Bertillon offered the following introduction to his system, then in use for ten years, known variously as "Bertillonage" and the "signaletic notice":

> In prison practice the signaletic notice accompanies every reception and every delivery of a human individuality; this register guards the trace of the real, actual presence of the person sought by the administrative or judicial document. . . . [The] task is always the same: to preserve a sufficient record of a personality to be able to *identify* the present description with one which may be presented at some future time. From this point of view signalment is the best instrument for the *proof of recidivation*, which necessarily implies the *proof of identity*.[41]

In effect, then, Bertillon's police archive functioned as a complex biographical machine which produced presumably simple and unambiguous results. He sought to identify repeat offenders, that is, criminals who were liable to be considered "habitual" or "professional" in their deviant behavior. The concern with recidivism was of profound social importance in the 1880s. Bertillon, however, professed no theory of a criminal type, nor of the psychic continuities or discontinuities that might differentiate "responsible" criminals from "irresponsible" criminals. He was sensitive to the status hierarchy between his Identification Bureau and the more "theoretical" mission of the Bureau of Statistics. (Bertillon was the son of a prominent anthropometrician, Louis Adolphe Bertillon, and seems to have labored mightily to vindicate himself after an inauspicious start as a mere police clerk.) He was more a social engineer, an inventive clerk-technician, than a criminologist. He sought to ground police work in scientific principles, while recognizing that most police operatives were unfamiliar with consistent and rigorous empirical procedures. Part of his ambition was to accelerate the work of processing criminals and to employ effectively the labors of unskilled clerks. He resembles in many respects his American contemporary, Frederick Winslow Taylor, the inventor of scientific management, the first system of modern factory discipline. Bertillon can be seen, like Taylor, as a prophet of rationalization. Here is Bertillon describing the rapidity of his process: "Four pairs of police officers suffice, at Paris, for the measurement, every

40.   Gabriel Tarde, *Penal Philosophy*, trans. Rapelje Howell, Boston, Little, Brown, 1912, p. 116.
41.   Alphonse Bertillon, *Identification anthropométrique; instructions signalétiques*, Paris, Melun, 1893, p. xiii. I have modified the translation given in the American edition, *Signaletic Instructions*, trans. R. W. Mclaughry, Chicago, Werner, 1896.

From *Alphonse Bertillon,* Service d'identification.   *Classification cabinets, Paris Prefecture of Police.*
Exposition universelle de Chicago, *1893.*

morning between nine o'clock and noon, of from 100 to 150 men who were arrested the day before."[42] Ultimately, this was not fast enough, and therein lay a principal reason for the demise, some thirty years later, of the Bertillon system.

How did the Bertillon system work? The problems with prior attempts at criminal identification were many. The early promise of photography had faded in the face of a massive and chaotic archive of images. The problem of *classification* was paramount:

> The collection of criminal portraits has already attained a size so considerable that it has become physically impossible to discover among them the likeness of an individual who has assumed a false name. It goes for nothing that in the past ten years the Paris police have collected more than 100,000 photographs. Does the reader believe it practicable to compare successively each of these with each one of the 100 individuals who are arrested daily in Paris? When this was attempted in the case of a criminal particularly easy to identify, the search demanded more than a week of application, not to speak of the errors and oversights which a task so fatiguing to the eye could

42.   Alphonse Bertillon, "The Bertillon System of Identification," *Forum,* vol. 11, no. 3 (May 1891), p. 335.

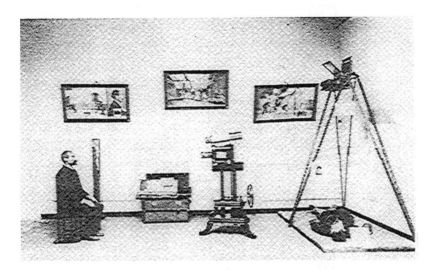

Display of apparatus, Chicago Exposition.

> not fail to occasion. There was a need for a method of elimination
> analogous to that in use in botany and zoology; that is to say, one
> based on the characteristic elements of individuality.[43]

Despite the last part of this remark, Bertillon sought not to relate individual to
species, but to extract the individual from the species. Thus he invented a classifying scheme that was based less upon a taxonomic categorization of types
than upon an ordering of individual cases within a segmented aggregate. He
had failed miserably in an earlier attempt to classify police photographs according to the genre of offense, for obvious reasons.[44] Criminals may have constituted a "professional type," as Tarde argued, but they did not necessarily
observe a narrow specialization in their work.

Bertillon sought to break the professional criminal's mastery of disguises,
false identities, multiple biographies, and alibis. He did this by yoking anthro-
pometrics, the optical precision of the camera, a refined physiognomic vocabulary, and statistics.

First Bertillon calculated, without a very sophisticated grasp of the
calculus of probabilities, that the chance that two individuals might share the
same series of eleven bodily measurements ran on the order of one in four

43.   *Ibid.*, p. 331.
44.   Alphonse Bertillon, *L'identité des récidivistes et la loi de relégation*, Paris, Masson, 1883, p. 11.

RELEVÉ
DU
SIGNALEMENT ANTHROPOMÉTRIQUE

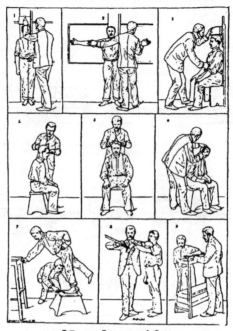

1. Taille. — 2. Envergure. — 3. Buste. --
4. Longueur de la tête. — 5. Largeur de la tête. — 6. Oreille droite. —
7. Pied gauche. — 8. Médius gauche. — 9. Coudée gauche.

*Frontispiece (left) and figures (right) from Alphonse
Bertillon,* Identification anthropométrique, *1893.*

million.[45] He regarded these eleven measurements as constant in any adult body. His signaletic notice linked this "anthropometrical signalment," recorded as a numerical series, with a shorthand verbal description of distinguishing marks, and a pair of photographic portraits, both frontal and profile views.

Bertillon's second problem was the organization of individual cards in a comprehensive system from which records could be retrieved in short order. To this end, Bertillon enlisted the prodigious rationalizing energies of Quetelet's "average man." By organizing his measurements into successive subdivisions, each based on a tripartite separation of below-average, average, and above-average figures, Bertillon was able to file 100,000 records into a grid of file drawers, with the smallest subset within any one drawer consisting of approximately a dozen identification cards. Having thus separately processed 100,000

45.   Bertillon, *Identification anthropométrique*, pp. xvii–xviii.

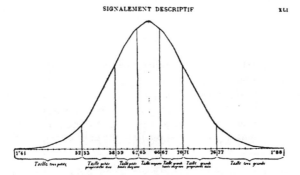

Fig. 4. — Courbe binomiale de la taille sur laquelle on a séparé par des verticales l'emplacement des sept catégories de taille.

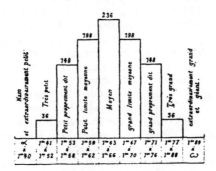

Fig. 5. — Diagramme de la taille indiquant par la hauteur proportionnelle des colonnes le nombre des sujets ressortissant à chacune des sept catégories de taille indiquées sur la courbe binomiale (Fig. 4).

male and 20,000 female prisoners over the decade between 1883 and 1893, Bertillon felt confident in boasting that his system was "infallible." He had in the process "infallibly" identified 4,564 recidivists.[46]

Bertillon can be said to have realized the binomial curve as office furniture. He is one of the first users of photographic documents to comprehend fully the fundamental problem of the archive, the problem of volume. Given his recourse to statistical method, what semantic value did he find in photographs? He clearly saw the photograph as the final conclusive sign in the process of identification. Ultimately, it was the photographed face pulled from the file that had to match the rephotographed face of the suspect, even if this final "photographic" proof was dependent upon a series of more abstract steps.

Bertillon was critical of the inconsistent photography practiced by earlier

46. *Ibid.*, pp. xxi–xxiii, lxxiv.

police technicians and jobbers. He argued at length for an aesthetically neutral standard of representation:

> In commercial and artistic portraits, questions of fashion and taste are all important. Judicial photography, liberated from these considerations, allows us to look at the problem from a more simple point of view: which pose is theoretically the best for such and such a case?[47]

Bertillon insisted on a standard focal length, even and consistent lighting, and a fixed distance between the camera and the unwilling sitter. The profile view served to cancel the contingency of expression; the contour of the head remained consistent with time. The frontal view provided a face that was more likely to be recognizable within the other, less systematized departments of police work. These latter photographs served better in the search for suspects who had not yet been arrested, whose faces were to be recognized by detectives on the street.

Just as Bertillon sought to classify the photograph by means of the Vitruvian register of the anthropometrical signalment and the binomial curve, so also he sought to translate the signs offered by the photograph itself into another, verbal register. Thus he was engaged in a two-sided, internal and external, taming of the contingency of the photograph. His invention of the *portrait-parlé*—the "speaking likeness" or verbal portrait—was an attempt to overcome the inadequacies of a purely visual empiricism. He organized voluminous taxonomic grids of the features of the male human head, using sectional photographs. He devoted particular attention to the morphology of the ear, repeating a physiognomic fascination with that organ that extended back to Lavater.[48] But on the basis of this comparative anatomy, Bertillon sought to reinvent physiognomy in precise nonmetaphysical, ethnographic terms. Through the construction of a strictly denotative signaletic vocabulary, this project aimed for the precise and unambiguous translation of appearance into words.

For Bertillon, the criminal body expressed nothing. No characterological secrets were hidden beneath the surface of this body. Rather, the surface and the skeleton were indices of a more strictly material sort. The anthropometrical signalment was the register of the morphological constancy of the adult

---

47.   Alphonse Bertillon, *La photographie judiciare*, Paris, Gauthier-Villars, 1890, p. 2 (my translation).
48.   In 1872, O. G. Rejlander suggested that photographs of ears be used to identify criminals ("Hints Concerning the Photographing of Criminals," *British Journal Photographic Almanac*, 1872, pp. 116–117). Carlo Ginzburg has noted the coincidence of Bertillon's attention to the "individuality" of the ear and Giovanni Morelli's attempt to construct a model of art-historical authentication based on the careful examination of the rendering of the ear by different painters ("Morelli, Freud, and Sherlock Holmes: Clues and Scientific Method," *History Workshop*, no. 9 [Spring 1980], pp. 5–29).

Plate 41 from Alphonse Bertillon, Identification anthropométrique, *1893.*

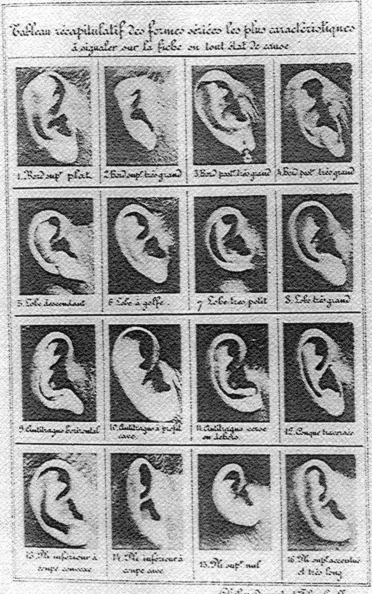

Plate 56 from Alphonse Bertillon, Identification anthropométrique, *1893.*

skeleton, thus the key to biographical identity. Likewise, scars and other deformations of the flesh were clues, not to any innate propensity for crime, but to
the body's physical history: its trades, occupations, calamities.

For Bertillon, the mastery of the criminal body necessitated a massive
campaign of *inscription*, a transformation of the body's signs into a *text*, a text
that pared verbal description down to a denotative shorthand, which was then
linked to a numerical series. Thus Bertillon arrested the criminal body, determined its identity as a body that had *already* been defined as criminal, by means
that subordinated the image — which remained necessary but insufficient — to
verbal text and numerical series. This was not merely a self-contained archival
project. We can understand another, more global, imperative if we remember
that one problem for the late-nineteenth-century police was the telegraphic
transmission of information regarding suspects. The police were competing
with opponents who availed themselves of the devices of modernity as well, including the railroad.

Why was the issue of recidivism so important in France during the 1880s?
Robert Nye has argued recently that the issue emerged on the political agenda
of Gambettist Republicans during the Third Republic, leading to the passage
of the Relegation Law of 1885, which established a Draconian policy of colonial transport for repeat offenders. The bill worked out a variable quota of
misdemeanors and felonies, including vagabondage, that could lead to permanent exile in Guyana or New Caledonia. The French agricultural crisis had led
to a renewed massive urban influx of displaced peasants during the 1880s. The
recidivism debate focused on the social danger posed by the vagrant, while
also seeing the milieu of the chronically unemployed urban poor as a source of
increased criminality. Not least in provoking the fears of the defenders of order
was the evidence of renewed working-class militancy in the strike wave of 1881,
after a decade of peace purchased by the slaughter of the Communards. At its
most extreme, the debate on recidivism combined the vagabond, the anarchist,
and recidivist into a single composite figure of social menace.[49]

Bertillon himself promoted his system within the context of this debate.
Having only succeeded in identifying his first recidivist in February of 1883, he
quickly argued that his binomial classification system would be essential to the
application of any law of relegation. He described a Parisian working-class
milieu that was undergoing what might facetiously be called a "crisis of identity." During the Commune, all city records prior to 1859 had been burned;
any Parisian over twenty-two years old was at liberty to invent and reinvent an

49.   See Robert Nye, *Crime, Madness, and Politics in Modern France: The Medical Concept of National
Decline*, Princeton, Princeton University Press, 1984, pp. 49–96. Although Nye mentions
Bertillon's project only in passing, I have relied upon his social history for an understanding of
the politics of French criminology during the late nineteenth century. A more directly relevant
study of Bertillon, Christian Pheline's *L'image accusatrice* (Paris, Cahiers de la Photographie,
1985), unfortunately came to my attention only after this essay was going to press.

entirely bogus nativity. Furthermore, Bertillon claimed that there was an extraordinary traffic in false documents, citing the testimony of foremen at the more "insalubrious" industrial establishment—white lead and fertilizer factories, for example—that job applicants frequently reappeared two weeks after being rejected with entirely new papers and different names.[50] In effect, Bertillon sought to reregister a social field that had exploded into multiplicity.

One curious aspect of Bertillon's reputation lies in the way in which his method, which runs counter to any metaphysical or essentialist doctrine of the self, could be regarded as a triumph of humanism. One biographer put it this way: "A man of his type inevitably found a kind of romance in a technique the aim of which was to individualize human beings."[51] Bertillon himself contributed to this "humane" reading of his project: "Is it not at bottom a problem of this sort that forms the basis of the everlasting popular melodrama about lost, exchanged, and recovered children?"[52] But in more technical and theoretical contexts, the degree to which Bertillonage actually eroded the "uniqueness" of the self became clear. Writing with a coauthor in 1909, Bertillon noted that according to the logic of the binomial curve, "each observation or each group of observations is to be defined, not by its absolute value, but by its deviation from the arithmetic mean."[53] Thus even the nominalist Bertillon was forced to recognize the higher reality of the "average man." The individual could only be identified by invoking the powers of this genie. And the individual only existed *as an individual* by being identified. Individuality as such had no meaning. Viewed "objectively," the self occupied a position that was wholly relative.

The Bertillon system proliferated widely, receiving an enthusiastic reception especially in the United States and contributing to the internationalization and standardization of police methods. The anthropometric system faced competition from the fingerprint system, a more radically synecdochic procedure, invented in part by Francis Galton, who had interests in identification as well as typology. With the advent of fingerprinting, it became evident that the body did not have to be "circumscribed" in order to be identified. Rather, the key to identity could be found in the merest trace of the body's tactile presence in the world. Furthermore, fingerprinting was more promising in a Taylorist sense, since it could be properly executed by less-skilled clerks. By the late nineteen-tens, the Bertillon system had begun to yield to this more efficient and less cumbersome method, although hybrid systems operated for some years.[54]

50.   Bertillon, *L'identité des récidivistes*, pp. 2, 5.
51.   Henry Rhodes, *Alphonse Bertillon: Father of Scientific Detection*, London, Abelard-Schuman, 1956, p. 83.
52.   Bertillon, "The Bertillon System of Identification," p. 330.
53.   A. Bertillon and A. Chervin, *Anthropologie métrique*, Paris, Imprimerie Nationale, 1909, p. 51 (my translation). The same text drolly likens the shape of the binomial curve to that of a "gendarme's hat."
54.   Bertillon noted that his system was adopted by 1893 in the United States, Belgium,

Bertillon card, 1913.

Switzerland, Russia, much of South America, Tunisia, the British West Indies, and Rumania (*Identification anthropométrique*, p. lxxxi). Translations of Bertillon's manuals of signaletic instructions appeared in Germany, Switzerland, England, and Peru, as well as the United States. On the enthusiastic American reception of the Bertillon system, see Donald Dilworth, ed., *Identification Wanted: Development of the American Criminal Identification System, 1893-1943*, Gaithersburg, Maryland, International Association of Chiefs of Police, 1977. The IACP promoted the general adoption of Bertillonage by the geographically dispersed and municipally autonomous police forces of the United States and Canada, and the establishment of a National Identification Bureau in Washington, D.C. This office was absorbed into the Federal Bureau of Investigation in 1924. (Canada adopted Bertillonage with the Criminal Identification Act of 1898.) Starting in 1898, a quasi-official monthly publication of the IACP, called *The Detective*, carried Bertillon measurements and photographs of wanted criminals. This publication provides a reasonable gauge of the ratio of reliance by American police on the Bertillon and fingerprint systems over the next twenty-five years. The British resisted Bertillon's method, largely because the fingerprint system

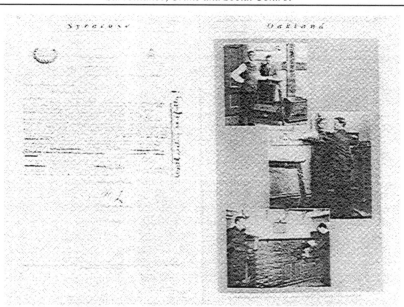

From Yawman and Erbe Mfg. Co., Criminal
Identification by "Y and E": Bertillon and Finger
Print Systems, *1913*.

---

was of British origin. Nonetheless, regulations were established in 1896 under the Penal Servitude Act of 1891 for the photographing, fingerprinting, *and* Bertillon measurement of criminal prisoners (Great Britain, *Statutory Rules and Orders*, London, H. M. Stationary Office, 1896, no. 762, pp. 364-365). By 1901, however, the anthropometric signalment was abandoned.

The Bertillon and Galton traded jibes at their respective systems. Bertillon faulted Galton for the difficulties encountered in classifying fingerprints ("The Bertillon System of Identification," p. 331). Galton faulted Bertillon for his failure to recognize that bodily measurements were correlated and not independent variables, thus grossly underestimating the probability of duplicate measurements (Francis Galton, *Memories of My Life*, London, Methuen, 1908, p. 251; see also his "Personal Identification and Description," *Journal of the Anthropological Institute*, vol. 18 [May 29, 1888], pp. 177-191).

The two men's obsession with authorship may have been a bit misplaced, however. In "Morelli, Freud, and Sherlock Holmes" (cited in note 48, above), Carlo Ginzburg has suggested that the whole enterprise of rationalized criminal identification rested on the *theft* of a more popular, conjectural form of empiricism, grounded in hunting and divining. Sir William Herschel had appropriated fingerprinting in 1860 from a usage customary among Bengali peasants under his colonial administration. The source of police methods in what Ginzburg describes as "low intuition" was obliquely acknowledged by Bertillon in a passage in which he argues for a rigorously *scientific* policing, while invoking at the same time the distinctly *premodern* image of the hunter: "Anthropology, by definition, is nothing but the natural history of man. Have not hunters in all times been interested in natural history? And, on the other hand, have not naturalists something of the hunter in them? No doubt the police of the future will apply to their particular form of the chase the rules of anthropology and psychology, just as the engineers of our locomotives are putting in practice the laws of mechanics and thermodynamics" ("The Bertillon System of Identification," p. 341). Ginzburg has proposed a model of observation and description that is more open to multiplicity and resistance than that advanced by John Tagg, who subsumes all documentary within the paradigm of the Panopticon (Tagg, "Power and Photography," p. 55).

For Bertillon, the type existed only as a means for refining the description of individuality. Detectives could not afford not to be nominalists. Bertillon was not alone in this understanding of the peculiarities of the policeman's search for the specificity of crime. For example, the New York City detective chief Thomas Byrnes published in 1886 a lavish "rogues' gallery" entitled *Professional Criminals of America*. Although Byrnes practiced a less systematic mode of photography than did Bertillon, he clearly articulated the position that classical physiognomic typing was of no value whatsoever in the hunt for the "higher and more dangerous order" of criminals, who "carried no suggestion of their calling about them."[55] In Bertillon's case, the resistance to the theory of a *biologically given* criminal type was also in keeping with the general drift of late-nineteenth-century French criminological theory, which stressed the importance of environmental factors in determining criminal behavior. Thus the "French school," notably Gabriel Tarde and Alexandre Lacassagne, opposed the biological determinism of the "Italian school" of criminal anthropology, which centered on the anatomist-craniometrician Cesare Lombroso's quasi-Darwinian theory of the criminal as an "atavistic being who reproduces in his person the ferocious instincts of primitive humanity and the inferior animals."[56] Against this line of reasoning, Lacassagne argued that "the social milieu is the mother culture of criminality; the microbe is the criminal."[57] (In this context, it is worth noting the mutual admiration that passed between Pasteur, the microbe-hunter, and Bertillon, the hunter of recidivists.[58]) The French were able to medicalize crime while simultaneously pointing to environmental factors. A range of positions emerged, some more medical, some more sociological in emphasis. Tarde insisted that crime was a profession that proliferated through channels of imitative behavior. Others argued that the criminal was a "degenerate type," suffering more than noncriminals from the bad environmental effects of urbanism.[59]

Despite the acute differences between the warring factions of the emerging criminological profession, a common enthusiasm for photographic illustration of the criminal type was shared by almost all of the practitioners, with the notable exception of Tarde, who shunned the lowly empiricism of the case study for more lofty, even if nominalist, meditations on the problem of crime. Before looking at Francis Galton's peculiar contribution to the search for a criminal type, I will note that during the 1890s in particular, a profusion of texts ap-

55.   Thomas Byrnes, "Why Thieves are Photographed," in *Professional Criminals of America*, New York, Cassell, 1886, p. 53.
56.   Cesare Lombroso, "Introduction," to Gina Lombroso-Ferrero, *Criminal Man*, New York, Putnam, 1911, p. xxv.
57.   Quoted by Nye, p. 104.
58.   Rhodes, p. 190.
59.   See Nye, pp. 97–131.

From Thomas Byrnes, **Professional Criminals of**
America, *1886.*

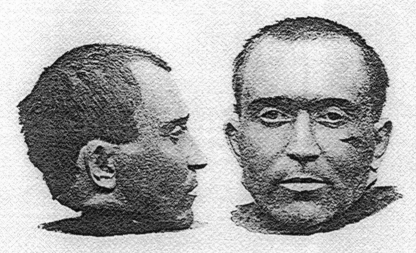

LA PHYSIONOMIE DU CRIMINEL   275

Fig. 110. — *Clayes*.   Fig. 111. — *Clayes*.

(Photographies prises 1 ½ d'heure après la décapitation).

Fig. 112. — *Beyssade*.   Fig. 113. — *Beyssade*.

From Charles Marie Debierre, Le crâne des criminels, *1895.*

peared in France and Italy offering photographic evidence of basic criminal
types. Although the authors were frequently at odds with one another over the
"atavistic" or "degenerate" nature of the criminal, on a more fundamental level
they shared a common battle. This was a war of representations. The photograph operated as the *image* of scientific truth, even in the face of Bertillon's
demonstration of the inadequacies of the medium. Photographs and technical
illustrations were deployed, not only against the body of the representative
criminal, but also against that body as a bearer and producer of its own, inferior representations. These texts can be seen as a battle between the camera
and the tattoo, the erotic drawing, and the graffiti of a prison subculture. For
Lombroso, tattooing was a particular mark of atavism, since criminals shared
the practice with presumably less evolved tribal peoples. But even works which
sought to demolish Lombroso's dogmatic biologism established a similar hierarchy. Scientific rationalism *looked down* at the visual products of a *primitive*
criminality. This was a quasi-ethnologic discourse. Consider, for example, a
work which argued against atavism and for degeneracy, Charles Marie
Debierre's typologically titled *Le crâne des criminels*. This book contained an illustrated chapter treating "les beaux-arts dans les prisons" as subject matter for
the psychological study of the criminal. A subsequent chapter offered a set of
photographs of the severed heads of convicts, "taken one quarter of an hour
after decapitation." Faced with these specimens of degeneracy, this physiog-
nomist of the guillotine remarked: "Degroote and Clayes . . . their dull faces
and wild eyes reveal that beneath their skulls there is no place for pity." Works
of this sort depended upon an extreme form of statistical inference: basing
physiognomic generalizations on very limited samples.[60]

This brings us finally to Francis Galton, who attempted to overcome the
limitations of this sort of inferential reading of individual case studies.

Where Bertillon was a compulsive systematizer, Galton was a compulsive
quantifier. While Bertillon was concerned primarily with the triumph of social
order over social disorder, Galton was concerned primarily with the triumph of
established rank over the forces of social leveling and decline. Certainly these
were not incompatible projects. On a theoretical plane, however, Galton can
be linked more closely to the concerns of the Italian school of criminal anthropology and to biological determinism in general. Composite images based on
Galton's procedure, first proposed in 1877, proliferated widely over the following three decades. A composite of criminal skulls appears in the albums of the

---

60.   Charles Marie Debierre, *Le crâne des criminels*, Lyon and Paris, Storck and Masson, 1895,
p. 274. The other important illustrated works are by members of the Italian school: Lombroso's
revised French and Italian editions of his 1876 *L'uomo delinquente* included separate albums of illustrations (Paris, Alcan, 1895 and Turin, Fratelli Bocca, 1896–97). The plates of criminal types
in these albums were taken from materials prepared for Enrico Ferri, *Atlante antropologico-statistico
dell'omicidio*, Turin, Fratelli Bocca, 1895.

> *Plate XXXIX from Cesare Lombroso,* L'homme
> criminel, *1895.*

C. Lombroso — *L'homme criminel.* Pl. XXXIX.

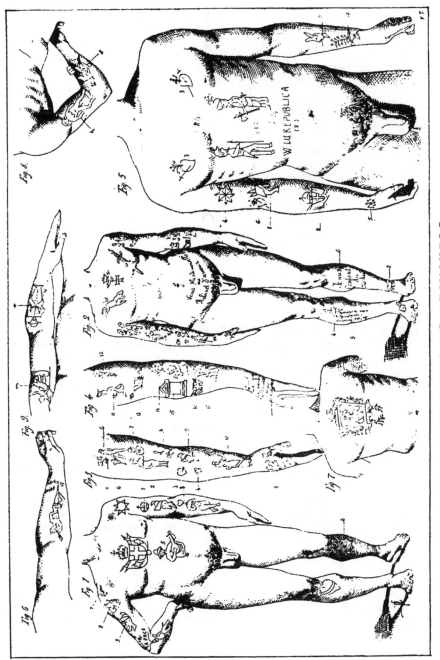

TATOUAGES DE CRIMINELS.

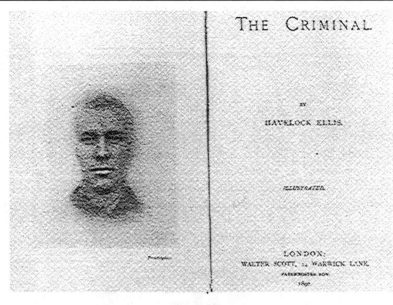

Galtonian composite.

1895 French edition and the 1896–97 Italian edition of Lombroso's *Criminal Man*. Likewise, Havelock Ellis's *The Criminal*, which adhered to the positions of the Italian school and marked the high tide of Lombrosoism in England, bore a Galtonian frontispiece in its first, 1890 edition.[61]

Both Galton and his quasi-official biographer, the statistician Karl Pearson, regarded the composite photograph as one of the central intellectual inventions of Galton's career. More recent studies of Galton have tended to neglect the importance attached to what now seems like an optical curiosity.[62]

Galton is significant in the history of science for developing the first statistical methods for studying heredity.[63] His career was suspended between the triumph of his cousin Charles Darwin's evolutionary paradigm in the late 1860s and the belated discovery in 1899 of Gregor Mendel's work on the genetic ratio underlying inheritance. Politically, Galton sought to construct a program of social betterment through breeding. This program pivoted on a profoundly ideological *biologization* of existing class relations in England. Eugenicists justified their program in utilitarian terms: by seeking to reduce the numbers of the

61.   Havelock Ellis, *The Criminal*, London, Walter Scott, 1890.
62.   The exception is David Green, "Veins of Resemblance: Photography and Eugenics," *The Oxford Art Journal*, vol. 7, no. 2 (1984), pp. 3–16.
63.   See Ruth Schwartz Cowan, *Sir Francis Galton and the Study of Heredity in the Nineteenth Century*, New York, Garland, 1985.

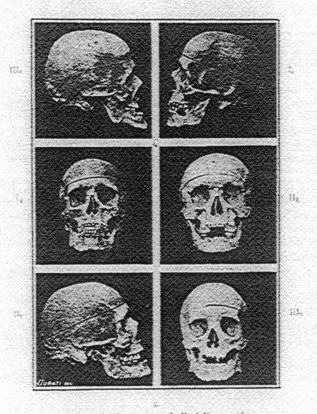

Plate XXVII from Cesare Lombroso, L'uomo delinquente, *1896–97.*

"unfit" they claimed to be reducing the numbers of those predestined to unhappiness. But the eugenics movement Galton founded flourished in a historical context — similar in this respect to Third Republic France — of declining middle-class birthrates coupled with middle-class fears of a burgeoning residuum of degenerate urban poor.[64]

Galton's early, 1869 work *Hereditary Genius* was an attempt to demonstrate the priority, in his words, of "nature" over "nurture" in determining the quality of human intelligence. In a rather tautological fashion, Galton set out to demonstrate that a reputation for intelligence amounted to intelligence, and that men with (reputations for) intelligence begat offspring with (reputations for) intelligence. He appropriated Quetelet's binomial distribution, observing that the entrance examination scores of military cadets at Sandhurst fell into a bell-shaped pattern around a central mean. On the basis of this "naturalizing" evidence, he proposed a general quantitative hierarchy of intelligence, and applied it to racial groups. This hierarchy was characterized by a distinct classicist longing: "The average ability of the Athenian race is, on the lowest possible estimate, very nearly two grades higher than our own — that is, about as much as our race is above that of the African negro."[65] Eugenics can be seen as an attempt to push the English social average toward an imaginary, lost Athens, and away from an equally imaginary, threatening Africa.

Galton's passion for quantification and numerical ranking coexisted with a qualified faith in physiognomic description. His writings demonstrate a remarkable parallelism and tension between the desire to measure and the desire to look. His composites emerged from the attempt to merge optical and statistical procedures within a single "organic" operation. Galton's *Inquiries into Human Faculty* of 1883 began by suggesting some of the limitations of prior — and subsequent — attempts at physiognomic typing:

> The physiognomical difference between different men being so numerous and small, it is impossible to measure and compare them each to each, and to discover by ordinary statistical methods the true physiognomy of a race. The usual way is to select individuals who are judged to be representative of the prevalent type, and to photograph them; but this method is not trustworthy, because the judgment itself is fallacious. It is swayed by exceptional and grotesque features more than by ordinary ones, and the portraits supposed to be typical are likely to be caricatures.[66]

64. See Gareth Stedman Jones, *Outcast London: A Study in the Relationship between Classes in Victorian Society*, Oxford, Clarendon, 1971.
65. Francis Galton, *Hereditary Genius*, London, Friedman, 1978, p. 342.
66. Francis Galton, *Inquiries into Human Faculty and Its Development*, London, Macmillan, 1883, pp. 5-6.

Frontispiece from Francis Galton, Inquiries into Human Faculty, *1883.*

SPECIMENS OF COMPOSITE PORTRAITURE

PERSONAL AND FAMILY.

Alexander the Great From 6 Different Medals

Two Sisters.

From 6 Members of same Family Male & Female

HEALTH. | DISEASE. | CRIMINALITY.

23 Cases Royal Engineers *12 Officers* *11 Privates*

6 Cases

9 Cases

Tubercular Disease

8 Cases

4 Cases

2 Of the many Criminal Types

CONSUMPTION AND OTHER MALADIES

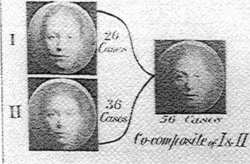

I *26 Cases*

II *36 Cases*

56 Cases Co-composite of I & II

Consumptive Cases.

100 Cases

50 Cases

Not Consumptive

DIAGRAM SHOWING THE ESSENTIAL PARTS.

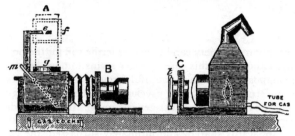

Side View.

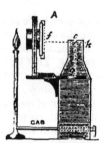

End View.

A The body of the camera, which is fixed.

B Lens on a carriage, which can be moved to and fro.

C Frame for the transparency, on a carriage that also supports the lantern; the whole can be moved to and fro.

r The reflector inside the camera.

m The arm outside the camera attached to the axis of the reflector; by moving it, the reflector can be moved up or down.

g A ground-glass screen on the roof, which receives the image when the reflector is turned down, as in the diagram.

e The eye-hole through which the image is viewed on *g*; a thin piece of glass immediately below *e*, reflects the illuminated fiducial lines in the transparency at *f*, and gives them the appearance of lying upon *g*,—the distances *f e* and *g e* being made equal, the angle *f e g* being made a right angle, and the plane of the thin piece of glass being made to bisect *f e g*.

f Framework, adjustable, holding the transparency with the fiducial lines on it.

t Framework, adjustable, holding the transparency of the portrait.

This book was a summary of Galton's researches over the preceding fifteen years. From this initial criticism of a more naive physiognomic stance, Galton moved directly to an outline of his composite method. The composite frontispiece and the recurrent references in various contexts throughout the book to lessons to be learned from the composites suggest that Galton believed that he had invented a prodigious epistemological tool. Accordingly, his interest in composite imagery should not be regarded as a transparent ideological stunt, but as an overdetermined instance of biopositivism.

How did Galton produce his blurred, fictitious apparitions? How did he understand them? He acknowledged at the outset of his experiments Herbert Spencer's prior proposal for a similar process of superimposition. Spencer's or-

The composite apparatus, from Francis Galton, Inquiries into Human Faculty, *1883.*

ganismic conception of society can be seen as fertile soil for the notion of a generalized body, although in this case Spencer seems to have been drawn to the notion of a composite through a youthful fascination with phrenology.[67] But Galton was concerned also with the psychology of the visual imagination, with the capacity of the mind to construct generic images from sense data. Here he found his inspiration in Thomas Huxley. He claimed in fact that the composite photographic apparatus shared, and ultimately surpassed, the capacity of artistic intelligence to generalize. Here, as with Quetelet, one witnesses the statistician as artist manqué.

Galton fabricated his composites by a process of successive registration and exposure of portraits in front of a copy camera holding a single plate. Each successive image was given a fractional exposure based on the inverse of the total number of images in the sample. That is, if a composite were to be made from a dozen originals, each would receive one-twelfth of the required total exposure. Thus, individual distinctive features, features that were unshared and idiosyncratic, faded away into the night of underexposure. What remained was the blurred, nervous configuration of those features that were held in common throughout the sample. Galton claimed that these images constituted legitimate averages, and he claimed further that one could infer larger generalities from the small sample that made up the composites. He proposed that "statistical constancy" was attained after "thirty haphazard pictures of the same class [had] been combined."[68]

Galton made more expansive claims for his process, which he has described as a form of "pictorial statistics":

> Composite pictures are . . . much more than averages; they are rather the equivalents of those large statistical tables whose totals, divided by the number of cases and entered on the bottom line, are the averages. They are real generalizations, because they include the whole of the material under consideration. The blur of their outlines, which is never great in truly generic composites, except in unimpor-

67.   Galton acknowledged Spencer in an 1878 paper read before the Anthropological Institute, extracted in *ibid.*, p. 340. Spencer's previously unpublished 1846 proposal for producing and superimposing phrenological diagrams of the head, "On a Proposed Cephalograph," can be found as an appendix to his *An Autobiography*, vol. 1, New York, Appleton, 1904, pp. 634–638. Like Quetelet, Spencer appears not to have read Kant on the notion of an average type, or on any other topic for that matter (see David Wiltshire, *The Social and Political Thought of Herbert Spencer*, Oxford, Oxford University Press, 1978, p. 67). Spencer's organismic defense of a hierarchical social division of labor is articulated in a review of the collected works of Plato and Hobbes: "The Social Organism," *The Westminster Review*, New Series, vol. 17, no. 1 (January 1860), pp. 90–121. This extended metaphor goes so far as to compare the circulation of blood with that of money (p. 111). On the connections between Spencerian social Darwinism and eugenics, see Greta Jones, *Social Darwinism and English Thought*, Sussex, Harvester, 1980.
68.   Galton, *Inquiries*, p. 17.

tant details, measures the tendency of individuals to deviate from the
central type.[69]

In this passage the tension between claims for empirical specificity and claims
for generality reaches the point of logical rupture: what are we to make of this
glib slide from "they include the whole" to "except unimportant details"? In his
search for a type, Galton did not believe that anything *significant* was lost in underexposure. This required an unacknowledged presupposition: only the gross
features of the head mattered. Ears, for example, which were highly marked as
signs in other physiognomic systems, both as individuating *and* as typical
features, were not registered at all by the composite process. (Later Galton
sought to "recapture" small differences or "unimportant details" by means of a
technique he called "analytical photography," which superimposed positive and
negative images, thereby isolating their unshared elements.[70])

Just as he had acknowledged Quetelet as a source for his earlier ranking of
intelligence, so Galton claimed that the composite photograph produced an improved impression of *l'homme moyen*:

> The process . . . of pictorial statistics [is] suitable to give us generic
> pictures of man, such as Quetelet obtained in outline by the ordi-
> nary numerical methods of statistics, as described in his work on *An-
> thropométrie* . . . . By the process of composites we obtain a picture
> and not a mere outline.[71]

In effect Galton believed that he had translated the Gaussian error curve into
pictorial form. The symmetrical bell curve now wore a human face. This was
an extraordinary hypostatization. Consider the way in which Galton conveniently exiled blurring to the *edges* of the composite, when in fact blurring
would occur over the entire surface of the image, although less perceptibly.
Only an imagination that wanted to *see* a visual analogue of the binomial curve
would make this mistake, finding the type at the center and the idiosyncratic
and individual at the outer periphery.

The frontispiece to *Inquiries into Human Faculty* consists of eight sets of composites. Galton describes these images as an integrated ensemble in his text, in
what amounts to an illustrated lecture on eugenics. The first, upper left com-

69.   Francis Galton, "On Generic Images," *Proceedings of the Royal Institution*, vol. 9 (1879), p. 166.
70.   Francis Galton, "Analytical Photography," *Nature*, vol. 18 (August 2, 1890), p. 383.
71.   Francis Galton, "Generic Images," *Nineteenth Century*, vol. 6, no. 29 (July 1879), p. 162. In
the related, previously cited paper "On Generic Images," Galton stated that Quetelet was the first
to give "the idea of type" a "rigorous interpretation" (p. 162). Ruth Schwartz Cowan has argued,
following Karl Pearson, that Quetelet was of no particular import in Galton's development as a
statistician; but Cowan is interested in Galton's position as a statistician in the lineage of hereditarian thought, and not in his attempt to negotiate the merger of optical and statistical methods.
That is, Cowan prefers to define biostatistics as a science which began with Galton, a science having no prehereditarian precursor in Quetelet (see *Sir Francis Galton*, pp. 145–200).

Francis Galton. Criminal Composites. c. 1878.
Plate XXVII from Karl Pearson, The Life, Letters
and Labours of Francis Galton, *vol. 2, 1924.*

posite of six portrait medallions of Alexander the Great serves Galton as an introductory, epistemological benchmark, not only to the series, but to the entire book. Oblivious to issues of style or artistic convention, Galton assumed that individual engravers had erred in various ways in their representations. The composite, according to a Gaussian logic of averaged measurements, would contain a "truer likeness." An unspoken desire, however, lurks, behind this construction. Galton made many composites of Greek and Roman portrait coins and medallions, seeking in the blurred "likenesses" the vanished physiognomy of a higher race.

Galton's next two sets of composites were made from members of the same family. With these he charged into the active terrain of eugenic research and manipulation. By exhibiting the blending of individual characteristics in a single composite image, Galton seems to have been searching for a ratio of hereditary influence. He extended these experiments to composites tracing the lineage of race horses.

The next composite was probably the most democratic construction of Galton's entire career: a combination of portraits of twelve officers and eleven enlisted men of the Royal Engineers. This was offered as a "clue to the direction in which the stock of the English race might most easily be improved."[72] This utopian image was paired with its dystopian counterparts, generic images of disease and criminality.

While tuberculosis seemed to produce a vaguely wan physiognomy, crime was less easy to type. Galton had obtained identification photographs of convicts from the Director of Prisons, Edmund Du Cane, and these were the source of his first composites in 1878. Despite this early start in the search for the biological criminal type, Galton came to a position that was less enthusiastic than that of Lombroso: "The individual faces are villainous enough, but they are villainous in different ways, and when they are combined, the individual peculiarities disappear, and the common humanity of a low type is all that is left."[73] Thus Galton seems to have dissolved the boundary between the criminal and the working-class poor, the residuum that so haunted the political imagination of the late-Victorian bourgeoisie. Given Galton's eugenic stance, this meant that he merely included the criminal in the general pool of the "unfit."

Later, following Charles Booth's sociological stratification of the London population, Galton classified "criminals, semi-criminals, and loafers" as the worst of the eugenically unfit: the bottom one percent of the urban hierarchy. On this basis, he supported long sentences for "habitual criminals," in hopes of "restricting their opportunities for producing low-class offspring."[74]

Galton concluded the introductory sample of composite portraits in his *In-*

72. Galton, *Inquiries*, p. 14.
73. *Ibid.*, p. 15.
74. Francis Galton, *Essays in Eugenics*, London, Eugenics Education Society, 1909, pp. 8–9, 62.

quiries with contrasted sets of composites made from very large samples: representing "consumptive" and "not consumptive" cases. With these he underlined both the *statistical* and the *social hygenic* ambitions behind his optical process and his political program.

Galton harbored other *psychological* and *philosophical* ambitions. In his earlier essays on "generic images" he examined "analogies" between mental images, which he claimed consisted of "blended memories," and the genera produced by his optical process. Citing the Weber-Fechner Law of psychophysics, which demonstrated that relative perceptual sensitivity decreased as the level of stimulus increased, Galton concluded that "the human mind is therefore a most imperfect apparatus for the elaboration of general ideas," when compared with the relentless and untiring quantitative consistency of "pictorial statistics."[75] In *Inquiries*, he returned to this theme: "The ideal faces obtained by the method of composite portraiture appear to have a great deal in common with . . . so-called abstract ideas." He wondered whether abstract ideas might not be more correctly termed "cumulative ideas."[76] Galton's rather reified notions of what constituted thought is perhaps most clearly, if unwittingly, expressed in his offhand definition of introspection: "taking stock of my own mental furniture."[77]

The composite apparatus provided Galton with a model of scientific intelligence, a mechanical model of intellectual labor. Furthermore, this intelligence answered to the logic of philosophical realism. Galton argued that his composites refuted nominalist approaches to the human sciences, demonstrating with certainty the reality of distinct racial types. This amounted to an essentialist physical anthropology of race.[78]

It is not surprising, then, that Galton would come to regard his most successful composite as that depicting "the Jewish type." In a historical context in which there was no clear anthropological consensus on the racial or ethnic character of modern Jews, Galton produced an image that was, according to Karl Pearson, "a landmark in composite photography": "We all know the Jewish boy, and Galton's portraiture brings him before us in a way that only a great work of art could equal—scarcely excel, for the artist would only idealise from *one* model."[79] This applause, ominous enough as it is, takes on an even more sinister tone in retrospect when one considers the line of influence which led from Anglo-American eugenics to National Socialist *Rassentheorie.*[80]

75.   Galton, "Generic Images," p. 169.
76.   Galton, *Inquiries,* p. 183.
77.   *Ibid.*, p. 182.
78.   Galton, "Generic Images," pp. 163–164.
79.   Karl Pearson, *The Life, Letters and Labours of Francis Galton,* vol. 2, Cambridge, Cambridge University Press, 1924, p. 293.
80.   On the role played by eugenics in Nazi racial policy, see Allan Chase, *The Legacy of Malthus: The Social Costs of the New Scientific Racism,* Urbana, University of Illinois Press, 1980, pp. 342–360.
      Galton was asked to make the composites in 1883 by Joseph Jacobs, who was attempting to

Francis Galton. The Jewish Type. *1883. Plate XXXV from Pearson.*

Galton's composite process enjoyed a wide prestige until about 1915. Despite its origins in a discourse of racial essentialism, the composite was used to make a variety of points, some of which favored "nurture" over "nature." For

demonstrate the existence of a relatively pure racial type of modern Jew, intact despite the Diaspora. For the portraits, Jacobs recruited boy students from the Jews' Free School and from the Jewish Working Men's Club in London. Galton and Jacobs both agreed that a racial type had been produced, but they disagreed profoundly on the *moral essence* of that type. Galton, the great quantifier, met his imaginary Other: "The feature that struck me most, as I drove through the . . . Jewish quarter, was the cold scanning gaze of man, woman, and child. . . . I felt, rightly or wrongly, that every one of them was cooly appraising me at market value, without the slightest interest of any other kind" ("Photographic Composites," *The Photographic News*, vol. 29, no. 1389 [April 17, 1885]). Jacobs responded to Galton's anti-Semitism with a more honorific reading of the composites, suggesting that "here we have something . . . more spiritual than a spirit. . . . The composite face must represent this Jewish forefather. In these Jewish composites we have the nearest representation we can hope to possess of the lad Samuel as he ministered before the Ark, or the youthful David when he tended his father's sheep" ("The Jewish Type, and Galton's Composite Photographs," *The Photographic News*, vol. 29, no. 1390 [April 24, 1885]). Thus Jacobs counters Galton's myth of the Jew as the embodiment of capital with a proto-Zionist myth of origins. (On the medical and racial stereotyping of Jews in the late nineteenth century, and the Jewish reaction, see Sander Gilman, "The Madness of the Jews," in *Difference and Pathology: Stereotypes of Sexuality, Race, and Madness*, Ithaca, Cornell University Press, 1985, pp. 150–162.)

Lewis Hine. Composite photograph of child laborers employed in cotton mill. 1913. (National Gallery of Canada, Ottawa.)

example, Lewis Hine made a number of crude composite prints of girl mill-workers in 1913, in what was evidently an attempt to trace the general effects of factory working conditions on young bodies. And, in a curious twist, the book which provided the conclusive refutation from within criminology of Lombroso's theory of the innate criminal with the telltale skull, Henry Goring's *The English Convict*, opened its attack with a comparison between composites of free-hand drawings and composites of tracings from photographs of criminal heads. The former had been used by Havelock Ellis to make his physiognomic case in *The Criminal*. The discrepancy between these and the tracings revealed a great degree of caricature in Ellis's pictures.[81] With both Hine and Goring, a faith in the objectivity of the camera persisted. However, with the general demise of an optical model of empiricism, Galton's hybridization of the camera and the statistical table approached extinction. Photography continued to serve the sci-

81.   Henry Goring, *The English Convict: A Statistical Study*, London, H. M. Stationery Office, 1913. Lombroso's theoretical fixation with convict head size had already been undercut within physical anthropology by Franz Boas. See his 1910–1913 essay, "Changes in Bodily Form of Descendants of Immigrants," in *Race, Language and Culture*, New York, Macmillan, 1949, pp. 60–75.

ences, but in a less grandiose and exalted fashion, and consequently with more modest — and frequently more casual — truth claims, especially on the periphery of the social sciences.

In retrospect, the Galtonian composite can be seen as the collapsed version of the archive. In this blurred configuration, the archive attempts to exist as a potent single image, and the single image attempts to achieve the authority of the archive, of the general, abstract proposition. Galton was certainly a vociferous ideologue for the extension and elaboration of archival methods. He actively promoted familial self-surveillance for hereditarian purposes, calling for his readers to "obtain photographs and ordinary measurements periodically of themselves and their children, making it a family custom to do so."[82] His model here was the British Admiralty's voluminous registry of sailors. Here again, eugenics modeled itself on the military. Galton founded an Anthropometrical Laboratory in 1884, situated first at the International Health Exposition, then moving to the Science Museum in South Kensington. Nine thousand visitors were measured, paying three or four pence each for the privilege of contributing to Galton's eugenic research.[83]

Although married for many years, Galton left no children. Instead, he left behind an immense archive of documents. One curious aspect of Karl Pearson's massive pharaonic biography of Galton is its profusion of photographic illustrations, including not only Galton's many photographic experiments, but also a kind of intermittent family album of more personal pictures.

Eugenics was a utopian ideology, but it was a utopianism inspired and haunted by a sense of social decline and exhaustion. Where Quetelet had approached the question of the average with optimism, finding in averages both a moral and an aesthetic ideal, Galton's eugenicist hope for an improved racial stock was always limited by his early discovery that successive generations of eugenically bred stock tended to regress back toward the mean, and "mediocrity."[84] Thus the fantasy of absolute racial betterment was haunted by what must have seemed a kind of biological entropy.[85] Later, in the twentieth century, eugenics would only operate with brutal certainty in its negative mode, through the sterilization and extermination of the Other.

What can we conclude, finally, about the photographic problems encountered and "solved" by Bertillon, the nominalist detective, and Galton, the essentialist biometrician? The American philosopher and semiotician Charles

82.   Galton, *Inquiries*, p. 43.
83.   Pearson, *Life, Letters and Labours*, vol. 2, p. 357.
84.   Galton, *Hereditary Genius*, pp. xvii–xviii.
85.   On the cultural resonance of the concept of entropy in the nineteenth century, see Anson Rabinbach, "The Body without Fatigue: A Nineteenth Century Utopia," in Seymour Drescher et al., eds., *Political Symbolism in Modern Europe: Essays in Honor of George Mosse*, New Brunswick, Transaction Books, 1982, pp. 42–62.

Sanders Peirce, their contemporary, made a useful distinction between signs that referred to their objects indexically, and those that operated symbolically. To the extent that photographs are "effects of the radiations from the object," they are indexical signs, as are all signs which register a physical trace. Symbols, on the other hand, signify by virtue of conventions or rules. Verbal language in general, and all conceptual thought, is symbolic in Peirce's system.[86] Paradoxically, Bertillon, in taming the photograph by subordinating it to the verbal text of the *portrait parlé*, remained wedded to an *indexical* order of meaning. The photograph was nothing more than the physical *trace* of its contingent instance. Galton, in seeking the apotheosis of the optical, attempted to elevate the indexical photographic composite to the level of the *symbolic*, thus expressing a *general law* through the accretion of contingent instances. In so doing, Galton produced an unwitting caricature of inductive reason. The composites signified, not by embodying the law of error, but by being rhetorically annexed to that law. Galton's ambition, although scientistic, was not unlike that of those other elevators of photography, the neosymbolists of the Photo Secession. Both Galton and Stieglitz wanted something more than a mere trace, something that would match or surpass the abstract capabilities of the imaginative or generalizing intellect. In both cases, meaning that was fervently believed to emerge from the "organic" character of the sign was in fact certified by a hidden framing convention. Bertillon, on the other hand, kept his (or at least his underlings') eye and nose to the ground. This made him, in the prejudiced and probably inconsequential opinion of one of his biographers, Henry Rhodes, "the most advanced photographer in Europe."[87] Despite their differences, both Bertillon and Galton were caught up in the attempt to preserve the value of an older, optical model of truth in a historical context in which abstract, statistical procedures seemed to offer the high road to social truth and social control.

III.

The first rigorous system of archival cataloguing and retrieval of photographs was that invented by Bertillon. Bertillon's nominalist system of identification and Galton's essentialist system of typology constitute not only the two poles of positivist attempts to regulate social deviance by means of photography, but also the two poles of these attempts to regulate the semantic traffic in photographs. Bertillon sought to embed the photograph in the archive. Galton sought to embed the archive in the photograph. While their projects were specialized and idiosyncratic, these pioneers of scientific policing and

---

86.   Charles Sanders Peirce, *The Philosophical Writings of Peirce*, ed. Justus Buchler, New York, Dover, 1955, pp. 99–119.
87.   Rhodes, p. 191.

eugenics mapped out general parameters for the bureaucratic handling of visual documents. It is quite extraordinary that histories of photography have been written thus far with little more than passing reference to their work. I suspect that this has something to do with a certain bourgeois scholarly discretion concerning the dirty work of modernization, especially when the status of photography as a fine art is at stake.[88] It is even more extraordinary that histories of social documentary photography have been written without taking the police into account. Here the issue is the maintenance of a certain liberal humanist myth of the wholly benign origins of socially concerned photography.[89]

Roughly between 1880 and 1910, the archive became the dominant institutional basis for photographic meaning. Increasingly, photographic archives were seen as central to a bewildering range of empirical disciplines, ranging from art history to military intelligence.[90] Bertillon had demonstrated the usefulness of his model for police purposes, but other disciplines faced significantly different problems of image cataloguing. An emergent *bibliographic science* provided the utopian model of classification for these expansive and unruly collections of photographs. Here again Bertillon was prescient in his effort to reduce the multiple signs of the criminal body to a textual shorthand and numerical series. At a variety of separate but related congresses on the internationalization and standardization of photographic and bibliographic methods, held between 1895 and 1910, it was recommended that photographs be catalogued topically according to the decimal system invented by the American librarian Melvil Dewey in 1876. The lingering prestige of optical empiricism was sufficiently strong to ensure that the terrain of the photographable was still regarded as roughly congruent with that of knowledge in general. The Institute for International Bibliography built on the universalist logic of the eighteenth-century encyclopedists. But appropriate to the triumphal years of an epoch of scientific

88.   Compare Josef Maria Eder, *History of Photography*, trans. Edward Epstean, New York, Columbia University Press, 1945, with Beaumont Newhall, *Photography: A Short Critical History*, New York, Museum of Modern Art, 1938. Eder, very much part of the movement to rationalize photography during the first decade of this century, is quite willing to treat police photography as a proper object of his narrative. Eder in fact wrote an introduction to a German edition of Bertillon's manual (*Die gerichtliche Photographie*, Halle a. S., Knapp, 1895). Newhall, on the other hand, wrote a modernist history in 1938 that privileged technical photography, including First World War aerial reconnaissance work, without once mentioning the use of photography by the police. Clearly, Newhall found it easier to speak of the more glamorous, abstract, and chivalrous state violence of early air power than to dwell on the everyday state violence of the police.
89.   An exception would be Sally Stein's revisionist account of Jacob Riis, "Making Connections with the Camera: Photography and Social Mobility in the Career of Jacob Riis," *Afterimage*, vol. 10, no. 10 (May 1983), pp. 9–16.
90.   Compare Bernard Berenson, "Isochromatic Photography and Venetian Pictures," *The Nation*, vol. 57, no. 1480 (November 9, 1893), pp. 346–347, with Fred Jane, "Preface," *Fighting Ships*, London, Marsten, 1905–1906, p. 2. However different their objects, these texts share an enthusiasm for large quantities of well-defined photographs.

positivism and the early years of bureaucratic rationalization, a grandiose clerical mentality had now taken hold.[91]

The new scientific bibliographers articulated an operationalist model of knowledge, based on the "general equivalence" established by the numerical shorthand code. This was a system for regulating and accelerating the flow of texts, profoundly linked to the logic of Taylorism. Is it surprising that the main reading room of that American Beaux-Arts temple of democratic and imperial knowledge, the Library of Congress, built during this period of bibliographic rationalization, should so closely resemble the Panopticon, or that the outer perimeter of the building should bear thirty-three "ethnological heads" of various racial types?[92] Or is it any more surprising that the same American manufacturing company produced Bertillon cabinets, business files, and library card catalogue cabinets?[93]

Photography was to be both an *object* and *means* of bibliographic rationalization. The latter possibility emerged from the development of microfilm reproduction of documents. Just as photographs were to be incorporated into the realm of the text, so also the text could be incorporated into the realm of the photograph. If photography retained its prestige as a universal language, it increasingly did so in conjunction with a textual paradigm that was housed within the library.[94]

The grand ambitions of the new encyclopedists of photography were eventually realized but not in the grand encyclopedic fashion one might have expected. With the increasing specialization of intellectual disciplines, archives tended to remain segregated. Nonetheless, the dominant culture of photography did rely heavily on the archival model for its legitimacy. The shadowy presence of the archive authenticated the truth claims made for individual pho-

---

91.   The Institut International de Bibliographie, founded in 1895 with headquarters in Brussels, campaigned for the establishment of a *bibliographia universalis* registered on standardized filing cards. Following Dewey, the Institute recommended that literature on photography be assigned the seventh position within the graphic arts, which were in turn assigned the seventh position within the categories of human knowledge. The last subcategory within the classification of photography was to hold photographic prints. See the Institute's following publications: *Manuel pour l'usage du répertoire bibliographique de la photographie établi d'après la classification décimale*, Brussels (copublished with the Société Française de la Photographie), 1900; *Code pour l'organisation de la documentation photographique*, Brussels, 1910.

92.   I am grateful to Daniel Bluestone for pointing out this latter architectural detail. For a contemporary description of the heads, see Herbert Small, *Handbook of the New Library of Congress*, Boston, Curtis and Cameron, 1901, pp. 13–16.

93.   See the following catalogues published by the Yawman and Erbe Mfg. Co.: *Card Ledger System and Cabinets*, Rochester, N.Y., 1904; *Criminal Identification by "Y and E": Bertillon and Finger Print Systems*, Rochester, 1913; and *"Y and E" Library Equipment*, Rochester, 192-?.

94.   On early microfilm, see *Livre microphotographique: le bibliophoto ou livre à projection*, Brussels, Institut International de Bibliographie, 1911. On the more recent conversion of the photograph from library-document to museum-object, see Douglas Crimp, "The Museum's Old/The Library's New Subject," *Parachute*, no. 22 (Spring 1981), pp. 32–37.

tographs, especially within the emerging mass media. The authority of any particular syntagmatic configuration was underwritten by the encyclopedic authority of the archive. One example will suffice. Companies like Keystone Views or Underwood and Underwood serially published short pictorial groupings of stereograph cards. Although individual sequences of pictures were often organized according to a narrative logic, one sees clearly that the overall structure was informed not by a narrative paradigm, but by the paradigm of the archive. After all, the sequence could be rearranged; its temporality was indeterminate, its narrativity relatively weak. The pleasures of this discourse were grounded not in narrative necessarily, but in archival play, in substitution, and in a voracious optical encyclopedism. There were always more images to be acquired, obtainable at a price, from a relentlessly expanding, globally dispersed picture-gathering agency.[95]

Archival rationalization was most imperative for those modes of photographic realism that were instrumental, that were designed to contribute directly or indirectly to the practical transformation or manipulation of their referent. Can any connections be traced between the archival mode of photography and the emergence of photographic modernism? To what degree did self-conscious modernist practice accommodate itself to the model of the archive? To what degree did modernists consciously or unconsciously resist or subvert the model of the archive, which tended to relegate the individual photographer to the status of a detail worker, providing fragmentary images for an apparatus beyond his or her control? Detailed answers to this question are clearly beyond the scope of this essay. But a few provisional lines of investigation can be charted.

The protomodernism of the Photo Secession and its affiliated movements, extending roughly to 1916, can be seen as an attempt to resist the achival mode through a strategy of avoidance and denial based on craft production. The elegant *few* were opposed to the mechanized *many*, in terms both of images and authors. This strategy required the ostentatious display of the "honorific marks of hand labor," to borrow the phrase coined by the American sociologist Thorstein Veblen in 1899.[96] After 1916, however, aesthetically ambitious photographers abandoned the painterly and embraced pictorial rhetorics much closer to those already operative within the instrumental realist and archival paradigms. Understandably, a variety of contradictory attitudes to the archive emerge within photographic discourse in the 1920s. Some modernists em-

95.   This suggests that the historiography of photography will have to approach the question of an "institutional mode" in different terms than those already developed for the historiography of cinema. See, for example, Noël Burch, "Film's Institutional Mode of Representation and the Soviet Response," *October*, no. 11 (Winter 1979), pp. 77–96.
96.   Thorstein Veblen, *The Theory of the Leisure Class: An Economic Study of Institutions*, New York, Modern Library, 1934, pp. 163–164.

braced the archival paradigm: August Sander is a case in point. Others resisted through modernist reworkings of the antipositivism and antirationalism of the Photo Secession: the later Stieglitz and Edward Weston are obvious examples.

In many respects the most complicated and intellectually sophisticated response to the model of the archive was that of Walker Evans. Evans's book sequences, especially in his 1938 *American Photographs*, can be read as attempts to counterpose the "poetic" structure of the sequence to the model of the archive. Evans began the book with a prefatory note *reclaiming* his photographs from the various archival repositories which held copyright to or authority over his pictures.[97] Furthermore, the first photograph in the book describes a site of the archival and instrumental mode's proliferation into the spaces of metropolitan daily life in the 1930s: *License-Photo Studio, New York, 1943*. We now know that Evans was fascinated with police photographs during the period in which he made the photographs in this book. A terse topical list on "New York society in the 1930s" contains a central, telegraphic, underlined inscription: "*This project get police cards.*"[98] Certainly Evans's subway photographs of the late 1930s and early 1940s are evidence of a sophisticated dialogue with the empirical methods of the detective police. Evans styled himself as a flaneur, and late in life likened his sensibility to that of Baudelaire. Though Walter Benjamin had proposed that "no matter what trail the *flâneur* may follow, every one will lead him to a crime,"[99] Evans avoided his final rendezvous. This final detour was explicitly described in a 1971 interview in which he took care to distinguish between his own "documentary style" and a "literal document" such as "a police photograph of a murder scene."[100] He stressed the necessary element of poetic transcendence in any art photograph of consequence. The elderly Evans, transformed into the senior figure of modernist genius by a curatorial apparatus with its own archival imperative, could no longer recognize the combative and antiarchival stance of his earlier sequential work. Evans was forced to fall back on an organicist notion of style, searching for that refined surplus of stylistic meaning which would guarantee his authorship, and which in general served to distinguish the art photographer from a flunky in a hierarchy of flunkies.

With the advent of postmodernism, many photographers have abandoned any serious commitment to stylistic transcendence, but they fail to recognize the degree to which they share Evans's social fatalism, his sense of the immutability of the existing social order. Modernism offers other models, however, in-

97.   Walker Evans, *American Photographs*, New York, Museum of Modern Art, 1938.
98.   Reproduced in Jerry Thompson, ed., *Walker Evans at Work*, New York, Harper and Row, 1982, p. 107.
99.   Walter Benjamin, "The Paris of the Second Empire in Baudelaire," in *Charles Baudelaire*, p. 41.
100. Leslie Katz, "Interview with Walker Evans," *Art in America*, vol. 59, no. 2 (March–April 1971), p. 87.

Walker Evans. License-Photo Studio, New York, 1934. *Plate 1 from* American Photographs, *1938.*

cluding more militant and equally intelligent models of photographic practice. Consider Camille Recht's reading of the photographs of Eugène Atget, a photographer of acknowledged import in Evans's own development. Recht comments on interior views "which remind us of a police photograph of a crime scene" and then on "the photograph of a worker's dwelling which testifies to the housing problem." For Recht, the proximity of a "nuptial bed and an unavoidable chimney flue," provided grimly comic testimony of everyday life in an exploitative social formation.[101] This emphasis on the telling detail, the metonymic fragment that points to the systemic crimes of the powerful, would be repeated and refined in the writings of Walter Benjamin.[102] Our tendency to associate Benjamin with the theory and practice of montage tends to obscure the degree to which he built his modernism from an empiricist model, from a model of careful, idiosyncratic observation of detail. This model could argue both for the photographer as *monteur*, and for the photographer as revolutionary spy or detective, or, more "respectably," as critical journalist of the working class.

101. Camille Recht, introduction to Eugène Atget, *Lichtbilder*, Paris and Leipzig, Henri Jonquières, 1930, pp. 18–19 (my translation).
102. See Benjamin's 1931 essay "A Short History of Photography," trans. Stanley Mitchell, *Screen*, vol. 13, no. 1 (Spring 1972), p. 25.

Eugène Atget. Plate 12 from Lichtbilder, *1930.*

Metrical photograph and planimetric sketch. From
A. Bertillon and A. Chervin, Anthropologie métrique,
1909.

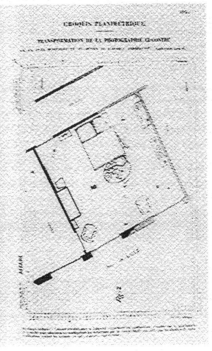

This essay could end with this sketch of modernist responses to the prior institutionalization of the instrumental realist archive. Social history would lead to art history, and we would arrive at a safe archival closure. Unfortunately, Bertillon and Galton are still with us. "Bertillon" survives in the operations of the national security state, in the condition of intensive and extensive surveillance that characterizes both everyday life and the geopolitical sphere. "Galton" lives in the renewed authority of biological determinism, founded in the increased hegemony of the political Right in the Western democracies. That is, Galton lives quite specifically in the neo-Spencerian pronouncements of Reaganism, Thatcherism, and the French National Front.[103] Galton's spirit also survives in the neoeugenicist implications of some of the new biotechnologies.

These are political issues. As such, their resonance can be heard in the aesthetic sphere. In the United States in the 1970s, a number of works, primarily in film and video, took an aggressive stance toward both biological determinism and the prerogatives of the police. Martha Rosler's video "opera" *The Vital Statistics of a Citizen, Simply Obtained* (1976) retains its force as an allegorical feminist attack on the normalizing legacy of Quetelet and Galton. Other, more nominalist works, took on the police at the level of counter-testimony and counter-surveillance. I am thinking here of a number of documentary films: Howard Gray's and Michael Alk's *The Murder of Fred Hampton* (1971), Cinda Firestone's *Attica* (1973), and the Pacific Street Film Collective's *Red Squad* (1972). These examples tend to be forgotten or overlooked in a contemporary art scene rife with a variety of what can be termed "neophysiognomic" concerns. The body has returned with a vengeance. The heavily expressionist character of this return makes the scientistic and racialist underpinnings of physiognomy seem rather remote. In photography, however, this lineage is harder to repress. In one particularly troubling instance, this returned body is specifically Galtonian in its configuration. I refer here to the computer generated composites of Nancy Burson, enveloped in a promotional discourse so appallingly stupid in its fetishistic belief in cybernetic truth and its desperate desire to remain grounded in the optical and organic that it would be dismissable were it not for its smug scientism. For an artist or critic to resurrect the methods of biosocial typology without once acknowledging the historical context and consequences of these procedures is naive at best and cynical at worst.[104]

In the interests of a certain internationalism, however, I want to end with a story that takes us outside the contemporary art scene and away from the simultaneously inflated and deflated figure of the postmodernist author. This anecdote might suggest something of the hardships and dilemmas of a photo-

103. For an example of the high regard for Galton among contemporary hereditarians, see H. J. Eysenck's introduction to the 1978 edition of *Hereditary Genius* previously cited.
104. See Nancy Burson et al., *Composites: Computer Generated Portraits*, New York, William Morrow, 1986.

graphic practice engaged in from below, a photographic practice on ground
patrolled by the police. In 1967, a young Black South African photographer
named Ernest Cole published a book in the United States called *House of Bondage*. Cole's book and his story are remarkable. In order to photograph a broad
range of South African society, Cole had first to change his racial classification
from black to colored, no mean feat in a world of multiple bureaus of identity,
staffed by officials who have mastered a subtle bureaucratic taxonomy of even
the offhand gestures of the different racial and ethnic groups. He countered this
apparatus, probably the last *physiognomic* system of domination in the world,
with a descriptive strategy of his own, mapping out the various checkpoints in
the multiple channels of apartheid.

Cole photographed during a period of relative political "calm" in South
Africa, midway between the Sharpeville massacre of 1960 and the Soweto students' revolt of 1976. At a time when black resistance was fragmented and subterranean in the wake of the banning of the main opposition groups, he discovered a limited, and by his own account problematic, figure of resistance in
young black toughs, or *tsotsis*, who lived lives of petty criminality. Cole photo-

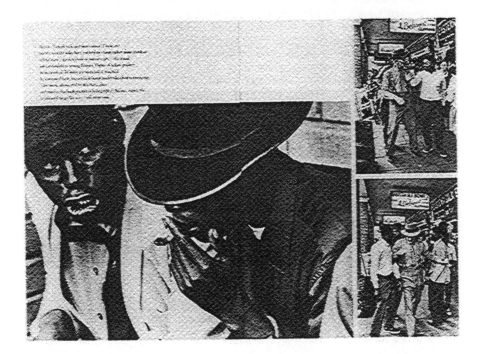

From Ernest Cole, House of Bondage, *1967.*

graphed *tsotsis* mugging a white worker for his pay envelope, as well as a scene of a white man slapping a black beggar child. And he regularly photographed the routine passbook arrests of blacks who were caught outside the zones in which they were permitted to travel. As might be expected, Cole's documentation of the everyday flows of power, survival, and criminal resistance got him into trouble with the law. He was questioned repeatedly by police, who assumed he was carrying stolen camera equipment. Finally he was stopped after photographing passbook arrests. Asked to explain himself, he claimed to be making a documentary on juvenile delinquency. Sensing his criminological promise, the police, who then as now operated through a pervasive system of informers, invited him to join the ranks. At that point, Cole decided to leave the country while he still could. *House of Bondage* was assembled from the negatives he smuggled out of South Africa. Since publishing his book in exile, Cole has disappeared from the world of professional photojournalism.[105]

The example of Cole's work suggests that we would be wise to avoid an overly monolithic conception of realism. Not all realisms necessarily play into the hands of the police, despite Theodor Adorno's remark, designed to lampoon a Leninist epistemology once and for all, that "knowledge has not, like the state police, a rogues' gallery of its objects."[106] If we are to listen to, and act in solidarity with, the polyphonic testimony of the oppressed and exploited, we should recognize that some of this testimony, like Cole's, will take the ambiguous form of visual documents, documents of the "microphysics" of barbarism. These documents can easily fall into the hands of the police or their intellectual apologists. Our problem, as artists and intellectuals living near but not at the center of a global system of power, will be to help prevent the cancellation of that testimony by more authoritative and official texts.

105. Ernest Cole (with Thomas Flaherty), *House of Bondage*, New York, Random House, 1967. For the account of Cole's own struggle to produce the pictures in the book, I have relied upon Joseph Lelyveld's introduction, "One of the Least-Known Countries in the World," pp. 7–24.
106. Theodor Adorno, *Negative Dialectics*, trans. E. B. Ashton, New York, Seabury, 1973, p. 206.

[18]

The Electronic Panopticon:
A Case Study of the Development of the
National Criminal Records System

DIANA R. GORDON

THE military is not the only expanding government activity in the United States. Even though most nondefense programs have been shrinking, criminal justice continues to grow. One of its most rapidly expanding but least noticed activities is the collection, combination, and dissemination of computerized criminal justice records at all levels of government. The past fifteen years have seen the creation, through electronic storage and linkage, of a national system of "hot files"—outstanding warrants for arrest or current identifying information on stolen items like vehicles or securities—and "criminal histories"—identifying information and chronological accounts of an individual's transactions with the police, courts, and corrections agencies.

Routine management of the emerging system is shared by local, state, and federal law enforcement agencies. Data collection and local dissemination of records are state matters; the federal government oversees national dissemination. The FBI, the dynamic center of the system, takes the initiative in major system expansion and innovation.

Although the national criminal records system is a far-reaching expansion of government power, it has received little analytic attention from the scholarly community. This case study is intended to contribute to an understanding of one dimension of expanding state activity in the United States.

INTRODUCTION TO THE SYSTEM

Computerized criminal justice record keeping has grown to immense proportions in the United States since the early 1970s. In 1971 the FBI's computerized clearinghouse of criminal justice information, the National Crime Information Center (NCIC), contained almost 2.5 million records; today it stores or indexes more than 17 million and is expected to handle a million transactions each day by 1989.[1] The other FBI source of computerized criminal records, the Automated Identification Division System (AIDS), launched in 1973, now contains over 9 million criminal history records and is increasing by 15,000 records per week. [2] In the past fifteen years, central repositories of criminal history information in all 50 states "have been the focus of a data-gathering effort more massive and more coordinated than any other in criminal justice."[3] Forty-four states that responded to a recent survey reported holding an estimated 35 million records (manual and automated) in their central repositories. Thirty-five of the responding states have at least partially automated their records system, and three others plan to do so.[4]

The majority of these records are used for criminal justice purposes—arrests, bail setting, sentencing. But the fastest-growing area of use is employment and licensing.[5] In eight states, including New York, at least one-third of criminal history record requests are for non-criminal justice uses.[6] In some states, criminal histories are more widely available—to landlords and financial institutions, for example.

Although individual states and cities—and the police, courts, and corrections agencies within them—have their own records systems subject to local policy, that decentralization does not preclude a significant federal role. Local and state systems are routinely linked to each other and to the FBI, either through an electronic switchboard called the National Law Enforcement Telecommunications System (NLETS) or through FBI computers. The Comprehensive Data Systems program of the now-defunct Law Enforcement Assistance Administration (LEAA) provided the bulk of funding for starting state systems. Federal standards—or the lack of them—define both users and uses of the data.

The national system of warrants and criminal histories (and perhaps, eventually, investigative files) is not yet complete. But even at this stage, it constitutes law enforcement data surveillance on an unprecedented scale.[7] By the turn of the century, most of the estimated 36 million Americans with arrest records will be included in what is, in effect, a national data base constructed from networks of local and federal data bases.[8]

It is possible to visualize circumstances in which computerized criminal records systems would be efficient, effective, and broadly accountable. Such systems might include a national data base, linked to state and local law enforcement agencies, containing complete and accurate criminal history records on a relatively small number (probably about a million) of serious, multistate offenders—as proposed, for example, by Kenneth Laudon. [9] This file would be subject to continuous public oversight, available only for criminal justice uses and for limited high-security job checks, and subject to dissemination restrictions in accordance with state laws. Supplementing the national criminal history system would be separate state systems covering a wider range of offenders and tightly regulated as to file content, data quality, and access to records. State and federal warrant systems would regularly be audited for timeliness and accuracy, and national dissemination of warrant information would be limited to felonies. Penalties for violating system regulatory standards would be enforced.

The emerging system does not remotely resemble that tidy picture. Its deficiencies are myriad and complex. This article focuses on two characteristics of the system's political and organizational structure that, taken together, have potentially grave consequences for individual liberties and social justice.

1. State recordkeeping, the source of all data in the system except for those on federal crimes, is essentially unregulated, resulting in inaccurate and incomplete criminal histories, "wrong warrants," and widespread use of records outside the criminal justice system.

2. Central coordination and expansion of the system perpetuates the defects of state systems through national dissemination, permits overinclusiveness of files and undiscriminating access to records, and seeks to increase the use of system data for purposes only tenuously related to crime control.

One of the difficulties of anticipating and responding to the problems of the criminal records system is the complexity of its structure. On the one hand, criminal justice falls outside the centralized federalism characteristic of the U.S. state in the post-World War II period. Law enforcement is still relatively free of national control. On the other hand, federal initiatives have increased since the late 1960s—research and evaluation grants, new federal crimes, federal participation in drug and organized crime investigations. Modern criminal justice recordkeeping reflects both the traditional local character of law enforcement and the burgeoning national presence in crime control.

We are accustomed to thinking that there are characteristic advantages and disadvantages of the U.S. state structure of multiple centers of power. Local responsibility for some functions maximizes participation and accountability, but local interests may promote inequality or repress fundamental rights. National power can impose uniform standards for distributing rights or benefits but may prove unresponsive or tyrannical.

This paper argues that the emerging national criminal records system manifests many of the disadvantages of both local and national control while providing few of the advantages of either. The combination of disadvantages heightens the importance of controlling and restructuring the system, but the complexity of the allocation of powers among various sites renders control extremely difficult. [10]

These problems have not gone completely unnoticed. Initial concerns about criminal justice recordkeeping flowed from traditional civil libertarian perspectives. In the early 1970s, senators, scholars, journalists, and a few law enforcement officials worried about the consequences for due process and the right to privacy of an essentially unregulated computerized criminal records system that could reach into any police precinct and would be accessible to employers and the military, as well as to law enforcement officials. They pointed out that such a system would, in the words of U.S. District Court Judge Gerard A. Gesell, "inhibit freedom to speak, to work, and to move about in this land."[11] Robert Gallati, then director of the New York State Identification and Intelligence System, testified at Senator Sam Ervin's 1971 hearings on federal data banks that "there is an absence in American law of institutional procedures to protect against improper collection of information, storage of inadequate or false data, and intragovernmental use of information for farreaching decisions about individuals outside or inside the organization."[12]

The protestations of the early 1970s now seem merely ritualistic. Nothing more than a general, one-paragraph legislative exhortation to keep criminal histories private and secure resulted from them, and that was intended to be temporary.[13] As the scope and intrusiveness of data surveillance in criminal justice mushroomed, resistance to it dwindled. The Privacy Act of 1974 (5 U.S.C. 552a), which establishes standards for records on individuals maintained by federal agencies and some federal contractors, excluded specific provision for law enforcement files "until such time as more comprehensive criminal justice legislation is passed."[14]

That time never came. Although hearings were held on several criminal justice privacy bills, none ever passed.[15] Finally, in 1975, LEAA issued administrative regulations requiring that state and local systems receiving federal funding establish procedures to ensure the accuracy and completeness of records. Revised a year later to meet the objections of law enforcement officials, the regulations are virtually toothless.[16] They acknowledge, for example, that maintaining complete criminal history records is "administratively impractical . . . at the local level." They do not even attempt to limit dissemination of records to law enforcement personnel, and states are not prohibited from sharing their criminal justice computers with non-law enforcement agencies. It is no wonder that a consultant study in 1977 found little compliance with the regulations. [17]

State policies as a whole are no more protective. Few states have laws requiring timely reporting of data on a person's contacts with the criminal justice system; only eleven states require annual audits of their records.[18] Most states now authorize access to criminal history records for non-criminal justice uses, some—the "open record" states—to anyone willing to pay a modest fee. Litigation over the use of criminal records has generally been limited to the consequences of mistakes, and a privacy theory that would limit state power to disseminate records has been explicitly rejected by the U.S. Supreme Court.[19]

The problems of regulation and control are serious in their impact on the due process rights of individuals. But the effects of the national criminal records system may go even farther. The second critical danger is that the centralization of control over the system will render it a tool of discipline more generalized than the democratic ideal of targeted, publicly accountable administration of justice. Michel Foucault's use of Jeremy Bentham's model prison as an image of the "machinery of power" is apt in this case.[20] Bentham's Panopticon was a circular prison with individual cells around a central tower so that a single warden could observe the movements of all inmates at all times. With the national computerized system, the entire function of crime control, not just the prison, becomes a "panoptic schema," with the record a surrogate for the inmate and all of law enforcement as warden. Such an image has no boundaries; the warden becomes boss and landlord and banker, too. And then we are all enclosed in an electronic Panopticon.

It is too early to assess systematically the full range of effects that the developing national criminal records system will have on individuals, on the social structure, and on future developments in criminal justice. But anecdotal revelations of system operatives and public interest lawyers around the country are telling. Later in this paper, after discussing the structure of the system, I review some evidence of the Panopticon's dangers.

Identification of the absence of regulation and the centralization of control as key issues in the system's development suggests two groups of questions for analytic investigation:

1.   What are the principal forces that have acted to keep the system free of meaningful regulation and to maintain centralized control? How have those

forces prevailed, even as the negative effects of the system have become increasingly apparent?

2. Why was initial opposition to the system's expansion and centralization so ineffective? Why did it fade? Why is there now so little attention to this area of actual and potential social control?

Most of the scant literature on computerized criminal records does not address these kinds of questions. The major sources all focus on the growth and effects of criminal history systems, primarily federal, and do not include the hot files as part of the totality. For example, David Burnham, in *The Rise of the Computer State,* describes the FBI criminal history repositories to illustrate the reach of linked data bases, and Gordon Karl Zenk, in *Project SEARCH,* traces the history of the bureaucratic battle between LEAA (and its subcontractor, Project SEARCH) and the FBI over control of the national computerized criminal history system.[21] There has been some government research on data quality in criminal history records, most notably a 1982 Office of Technology Assessment (OTA) study that emphasized omissions in criminal history records.[22]

The most important analytical work in this area is Laudon's recent book, *The Dossier Society,* which examines the social impacts of the national criminal history system and compares state systems.[23] Laudon concludes that institutional factors (a strong executive, other computer projects in the government) are as significant as environmental needs (high crime, population growth) in explaining state variations in adoption and use of computerized criminal history systems. He also examines the relationship between a number of variables (crime rate, income, federal funding) and non-criminal justice use of criminal history records systems.

Even Laudon does not explore the political and bureaucratic forces behind the development of the system as a whole—state and local files and warrant records as well as criminal history data bases. This article defines the system as including linked records from all sources and of whatever kind and updates the descriptive picture of earlier literature with current (1984-85) examples of proposed and actual expansions of the system. It also goes beyond existing critiques, which focus primarily on the system's civil liberties consequences for individuals, to raise questions about its implications for social and political structure and methods of social control.

The next two sections of this article develop the raw material of the case study, describing the system's current scope and reviewing its unregulated character and central policy control. The following section analyzes the forces that contributed to its development and examines the lack of an effective force for system control.

Along one dimension, the relatively unchecked expansion of the national records sytem can be understood as the product of pluralist political influence and bureaucratic imperatives. At the same time, along another axis, I argue that one must understand the uneven contest between system proponents and opponents as a battle of political symbols. The symbolic images at the disposal of criminal justice officials helped embed and legitimate the criminal records system. The ideological modes of discourse available to system skeptics, by contrast, were relatively indeterminate and readily turned against themselves. The unevenness of this symbolic contest suggests some conclusion about the dynamics of expanding social control policy in the 1980s.

SOME DIMENSIONS OF THE SYSTEM

To understand the reach of the national criminal records system and the distribution of government authority over it, one must look beyond information on its volume, reported above, to the linkages of the system and their implications. Consider, for instance, one way in which the FBI's two theoretically separate computerized criminal history files are combined. The FBI's Identification Division includes a partially automated criminal file, in existence for 50 years, which holds fingerprint cards and criminal histories on 23 million people, sent to it from the states. And NCIC, the FBI's computerized criminal justice information clearinghouse, now contains the Interstate Identification Index (usually called Triple-I), the locator for about 10 million criminal histories stored in 20 states and available by computer to 64,000 law enforcement agencies around the country. The Identification Division file is directly available to law enforcement agencies and authorized employers and licensing agencies only by mail, and Triple-I records are supposed to be exchanged between states only through NLETS to maintain local control. But NCIC now accesses the automated records of the Identification Division in order to respond electronically to NCIC users when they request criminal histories from the 30 states that do not yet participate in the Triple-I. So some information that state and local law enforcement could not get quickly from the Identification Division, they can now get almost instantly through Triple-I. And the FBI is running state records through its computer, doing indirectly what it was prohibited from doing directly by Congress and the attorney general a decade ago.

Other connections of FBI files are being made. An inquirer to Triple-I is now notified not only about what state has a complete criminal history on the record subject but also about any outstanding warrant information that the FBI may hold.[24] Just as this article was going to print, the *New York Times* reported that NCIC's advisory board had recommended that federal, state, and local law enforcement agencies be permitted to exchange information on the whereabouts of anyone under investigation, whether or not charged with a crime; the board also proposed that NCIC users be given access to the files of the Securities and Exchange Commission, the Internal Revenue Service, the Immigration and Naturalization Service, the Social Security Administration, and the Passport Office of the State Department. The developing technology of electronic fingerprint image comparison will soon enable California, New York, and the FBI to match a job applicant's fingerprint or a "cold print" found at the scene of a crime with computerized fingerprint files in the Identification Division.

The likelihood of political abuse of FBI files and the bureau's access to the files of others seems greatly reduced since the days of J. Edgar Hoover. But the age of computers has extended the operational opportunities for abuse in a political "emergency." The automated files of NCIC and the Identification Division could be sorted by Hispanic or Arabic surname, for example, or for drug convictions or arrests for participating in demonstrations. Matching other data bases like taxpayer or welfare records with criminal history files is also made easier by central access.

As the reach of information collection broadens, so does authorization of access to records. Virtually everywhere, law enforcement agencies have access to the national system without reservation. And the range of employers or licensing agencies authorized for access to both state and federal criminal records is growing rapidly. An examination of state experience reveals that, although some states are making an effort to improve data quality—requiring audits, for example—record systems are becoming more and more open.[25]

New York, for instance, allows or requires government agencies, schools, day care programs, museums, hospitals, banks, and law enforcement agencies, among others, to screen criminal records for employment purposes. Those who seek licenses for such enterprises as games of chance, guns, check-cashing operations, securities firms, and funeral homes as well as insurance adjustors, are screened. In all of these cases, nonconviction data may be disseminated—that is, information about arrests that are pending or charges that were dismissed or for which the defendant was acquitted.

Requests for record checks for non-criminal justice purposes jumped from about 100,000 in 1979 to an estimated 209,000 in 1984.

California makes even greater use of record checks for employment and licensing. Screening is authorized for the following occupations, among others: auto mechanic, barber, cosmetologist, optometrist, liquor store owner, shorthand reporter, pest control employee, TV repair person, real estate broker, and notary public.[26] If a "compelling need" is demonstrated, records may also be released to out-of-state district attorneys; to the inspectors general of most federal agencies with any regulatory powers; to the Postal Service and the Veterans Administration; to state hospital officers; to security officers for a number of state and local agencies; and to many more. As of 1983, more than 3.7 million state records had been reviewed for employment purposes. Fred Wynbrandt, head of the NCIC Advisory Policy Board, says of the expansionist tendency in California—where access has gone from public agencies to youth-service organizations to banks—"It just crept and crept."

Employer use of federal records is more restricted. The FBI is limited by federal legislation to the dissemination of criminal history records "for the official use of authorized officials of the Federal Government, the states, cities and penal and other institutions."[27] Although this excludes private employers, it means that many public jobs, and most at the federal level, are subject to careful and extensive screening, particularly where a sensitive position is involved.[28]

Federal law may override state privacy standards to authorize the screening by federal agencies of state and local records for employment purposes. There, too, authorization is widening, with a growing tendency to cover menial as well as skilled occupations. Perhaps as a reaction to the threat of terrorism, the U.S. Customs Service has now issued emergency regulations allowing record checks for airport employees, including baggage handlers and members of the ground crews; and the secretary of transportation has submitted legislation that would make that procedure permanent. [29] The proposed Intelligence Authorization Act of 1987 would allow the Department of Defense, the CIA, and the Office of Personnel Management access to local records for security clearances, which now cover 4 million people.[30]

PROBLEMS OF THE SYSTEM

Defenders of the national criminal records system usually justify its reach (defined both in terms of the inclusiveness of its subjects and the data included in it) by alleging that it provides significant benefits in the war against crime.

This section argues that those benefits are slight and are outweighed by serious deficiencies, some of which may actually give rise to crime. The section then examines some consequences of inadequate regulation—errors and omissions in records, possibilities for abuse, and the access to records of many outside the criminal justice system. It concludes with a more speculative discussion of some of the implications of national, centralized control of the system.

The System's Ineffectiveness as Crime Control

For the criminal records system to reflect a proper balance between the state's legitimate interest in criminal law enforcement and the individual rights of record subjects, it must be shown to improve the quality of information that decisionmakers need to control crime. For assisting an arrest decision or aiding a police investigation, the availability of warrant information from other states is theoretically very useful. But that usefulness is limited by several problems. Many of the warrants in the national system contain erroneous identifying information, reflecting local mistakes. They may have been discharged locally but not removed from NCIC. The lack of fingerprint identification for most warrants results in cases of mistaken identity. Finally, the file is not comprehensive since the contribution of warrants to the NCIC Wanted Persons file is totally voluntary and NCIC charges a fee for each warrant entered into the system. As a result of these problems police tend to use NCIC warrants only when they are investigating a very serious crime or need an excuse to pick up someone they suspect of a current crime but have no evidence on which to base prosecution. The availability of the information neither improves the reliability of decisions that would be made anyway nor provides a sound basis for making new ones; instead, it broadens the range of situations in which policy discretion can be exercised, an outcome outside the declared objectives of the system.

With criminal histories the problem goes deeper, to the basic justification for making the data available. The traditionally local quality of criminal justice is deemed appropriate for tailoring decisions about the use of society's most coercive power over individuals to local needs and culture. To introduce into the criminal process of one jurisdiction data reflecting the activities and standards of another subverts that value. And records obtained through Triple-I may be meaningless for most common needs. A judge's determination of what to take into account in sentencing, for instance, becomes merely more complicated when the record from another jurisdiction is considered. Police standards vary greatly from state to state, even from city to city. "In Oakland [California], for a black male to have five or six arrests is unremarkable," Laudon says. "Busting them is part of controlling the streets."[31] And police, except in "stop-car" situations, do not usually need another state's files, at least not instantly, to conduct investigations; 70 percent of offenders commit crimes in only one state.

Law enforcement officials, justifying large system expenditures, publicly cite dramatic examples of the one that didn't get away because of the computers' fancy footwork.[32] But privately they most often justify computerized criminal history records in terms of internal office efficiency, not as investigative tools for police or management information for judges. Laudon has concluded that any assertion that the billion dollars invested in reporting systems thus far is cost-effective in crime control terms is based only on "a wing and a prayer." "The empirical relationships are unproven, maybe irrelevant," he says.

Crime prevention, not capture or containment, is the issue when employers or licensing agencies use criminal records. Recent experience induces skepticism as to the cost-effectiveness of records searches for ferreting out dangerous criminals. The results of criminal records checks on current or prospective New York City child care workers may be indicative. At last count, record checks had been run on 21,778 people.[33] Of these, 152 (0.7 percent) were found to have records for such offenses as assault, robbery, drug offenses, or possession of a weapon; 14 (0.06 percent) were for sexual offenses (rape, sodomy, sexual abuse), and 4 (0.02 percent) were for endangering the welfare of a child. Almost half of those with records were custodial staff; many of the records were very old. The seven people in the Bronx day care centers who actually committed the crimes that led to the screening requirement would not have been found if the system had gone into effect before the incidents of abuse; none of the seven had a record.

The Effects of Absence of Regulation

Criminal records are full of mistakes. Although there are probably, in fact, fewer errors in computerized records than there were in manual files, mistakes have more impact now because they travel farther, are seen by more people, are copied and recopied, and have more uses. The national system is only as accurate as the local and state law enforcement records that constitute it.

One common problem is the incomplete criminal history record. What a particular record means is unclear unless it indicates how an arrest was disposed of—by acquittal, dismissal, or conviction. In fact, convictions are the exception. A 1983 report by the U.S. Bureau of Justice Statistics looked at data from several states concerning arrests for serious crimes and found a variation from 39 percent resulting in conviction in Pennsylvania to 56 percent in New York.[34] Employers seeing an arrest without a disposition, however, are unlikely to take the risk that the job applicant is among the group not convicted.[35]

Both state and federal criminal history files (computerized and manual) contain many arrests without dispositions. The OTA study found, for example, that only about two-thirds of a state's records, on the average, contained timely accounts of how the case was disposed of. Eight states reported that less than a quarter of their records were complete.[36]

No systematic review has been done of how many or what kinds of people have lost or been denied jobs as a result of records that failed to report a dismissal or acquittal. Anecdotal evidence suggests that the impact is felt by professionals and workers in a wide range of occupations. Two California teachers successfully sued the state for disseminating to the education licensing agency records that failed to show that criminal charges brought against them had been dismissed. Their injury included not only many months' delay in granting their teachers' licenses but dismissal by their local school boards from the temporary jobs they had held.[37] Presumably most people injured by incomplete records do not go to court; two students denied jobs because of inaccurate traffic offense reports told me that they no longer applied for jobs where record checks were likely. People with records in rural areas are probably most vulnerable; rural courts are said to be slowest to record their dispositions. Blacks may be more vulnerable than whites. Some research has found that blacks are more likely to be released after arrest; so the probability that an incomplete record conceals a dismissal may be higher than for whites.[38]

Error is not limited to criminal histories; it extends to other types of files. Cases of mistaken identification of warrant subjects are springing up all over the country. Plaintiffs in Louisiana, California, New York, Michigan, and Massachusetts, to name a few, have sued police for wrongful detention of up to four months.[39] Typically, the victim is black or Hispanic (in nineteen of the twenty cases I have examined), has a relatively common name, and is picked up in a traffic offense or border check on the warrant of someone charged with a serious offense. Sometimes the problem is the failure to remove a warrant that was in error in the first place; a Boston plaintiff was jailed because the police had not corrected the report of a stolen car that had, in fact, been borrowed by a relative. Recent FBI audits have revealed that at least 12,000 inaccurate or invalid reports on wanted persons alone are sent each day by state and local law enforcemnet agencies to the NCIC. [40]

Once made, these errors are hard to correct—as law enforcement officials are the first to admit. Once a victim of mistaken identity has been arrested on a "wrong warrant," his or her name goes into the FBI's Triple-I (assuming that the crime charged is a felony and that the arresting state participates in the program) and the arrest record into the state repository, from which it may be sent to requesting law enforcement agencies in other states even if the mistake in the original warrant file was corrected. A court order—and, therefore, the time and expense of consultation with a lawyer—is usually required to alter the record, and even that does not correct the mistake in the other locations to which it has traveled. If a criminal history is released to an employer or licensing agency, there is no guarantee that it will not get into other hands and become untraceable.

Data quality is not the only operational problem of the system; abuse of record dissemination is another. Sometimes the prevention of crime becomes the justification for an illegal use of the system, such as getting access to Triple-I or state records for unauthorized employment checks. In Louisiana, for example, despite state legislation calling for "the privacy and security of information" contained in the state repository, it became common practice in New Orleans for employers needing an unauthorized record check to obtain it through personal contacts with people who had access to records in a law enforcement agency.

The abuse may also stem from efforts to track possible political dissent. Revelations of police spying at all levels of government have continued into the 1980s. [41] Personal financial gain is sometimes the motive for abuse of the files; criminal history system officials in both California and New York recount anecdotes of information sold by police to political campaigns, disgruntled spouses, and landlords.

Potential Effects of Central Control of the System

Significant regulation of state data collection and dissemination seems unlikely in the near future. State administrators say they cannot afford it, and both they and FBI officials maintain that the Constitution precludes a larger federal role. Even if the system were more tightly regulated, its centralized control would retain the potential for contributing to the Foucaultian "machinery of power." Two tendencies that flow from the system's centralized character are suggestive of some of its actual or potential effects:

In an age when information is power and more is almost always better, the dynamic of system expansion is very powerful.

At times when the state is predisposed to using its power to regulate personal behavior, the system will reflect concerns going beyond crime control to larger political priorities.

Spreading access to records suggests the system's dynamic tendency to expand. In 1984 the FBI made at least six significant proposals for either expanded access to or additional information for its NCIC files. [42] It has also proposed a cross-search (where an inquiry of one file automatically triggers a review of others) of three of the NCIC files, which would effectively combine records. As the number and variety of records grows, along with the amount and kind of data contained in them, judgments about what persons and behaviors are appropriate subjects for data surveillance become less and less discriminating. Similarly, there is less and less resistance to expanding the range of authorized users of the system. When access to records cuts across many jurisdictions, different standards—some mandated by law—for the interpretation of data and judgment as to their significance apply.[43] Lines of political accountability become blurred, and constitutional concepts like the separation of powers and federalism are so diluted as to be meaningless.

Recent proposals for new files to be added to NCIC also illustrate the system's expansionary tendency. In 1983 the NCIC's Advisory Policy Board considered setting up several new files of investigative data, including a file on people not wanted for or suspected of a specific crime but thought by NCIC users to be involved with terrorism, organized crime, or narcotics.[44] That file was to include investigative information—not matters of public record like arrests or convictions—on people "known to be, believed to be, likely or may be" associated with a drug dealer, whether or not they were suspected of participating in or knowing of the dealer's illegal activities. [45]

Although the FBI tabled that idea in response to congressional concern and press attention, a year later the NCIC's Advisory Policy Board approved the testing of an inclusive new investigative file, the Economic Crime Index (ECI). It would include such information as name, physical description, address, phone numbers, Social Security and license plate numbers, bank account numbers, and names of associates of people suspected of white-collar crimes, particularly large-scale bank and securities frauds. The ECI would eventually allow the Justice Department, other federal agencies with investigatory authority, and all 60,000 NCIC users to exchange information about white-collar crime suspects.[46] The FBI has not said what crimes it would be investigating or defined the term "associates" or indicated what standard would be used for index entries. Presumably anyone who worked with a suspect could be included in the index, and surely all family members and close friends would be. (Although former Deputy Attorney General D. Lowell Jensen stated in early 1985 that the index is being set up, then-FBI Director William H. Webster responded to the privacy concerns of the House Subcommittee on Civil and Constitutional Rights by saying that "the FBI is considering several alternatives." The test has apparently been delayed.)

The ECI proposal is related to another innovation in federal law enforcement that illustrates the proposition that centralized, federal control may supplement the law enforcement justification for the system with more general political imperatives. In April 1984, the four federal bank regulatory agencies and the Justice Department entered into an agreement to record suspicions of bank fraud in an FBI computer (not part of NCIC) to enable, among other things, the earliest possible Justice Department "assessment and evaluation."[47] This expansion of authority for bank fraud investigations will give federal law enforcement personnel access to bank records before the depositors are even reasonably suspected of a crime. No evidentiary standard need be applied by the regulatory agencies when they make a referral, and the new system applies equally to suspicions of individual teller theft and massive frauds that may lead to a bank's collapse.[48] (In fact, the overwhelming majority of suspected frauds reported to the Justice Department in a test of its referral form were for what the Attorney General's Bank Fraud Working Group considered the "smaller" crimes of suspected losses not involving bank insiders and worth less than $10,000.)

Fishing expeditions of screening child care workers and bank depositors will surely yield a catch of some sort. But record checks are probably less effective at reducing crime than careful non-criminal background assessments of job applicants and training that alerts day care administrators to spot abusive tendencies in employees. And greater regulatory vigilance in financial institutions would probably prevent more crime than would giving the FBI access to bank records on the basis of the examiner's first hunch. The House Subcommittee on Commerce, Consumer, and Monetary Affairs, after studying four major bank failures caused by insider fraud, concluded in 1984 that "in each of these failures, the appropriate Federal bank regulatory agency had ample advance warning of unsafe and unsound banking practices—particularly insider misconduct—prior to insolvency, but failed to take prompt and effective remedial action."[49]

But the Reagan administration is not concerned that law enforcement may be driving out good program management. Screening has latent but powerful aims beyond the reduction of crime, as illustrated by the dragnet of child care workers and the expansion of federal law enforcement authority over financial institutions. The Reagan administration is willing to bear the social cost of subjecting millions of bank depositors and their friends to the perpetual risk of criminal investigation in order to convey the message that surveillance and punishment are government activities preferable to business regulation.

EXPLAINING THE PANOPTICON

The coercive power of the criminal law can enforce and shape the political system. Its application and influence are therefore important subjects of inquiry for social scientists. The developing criminal records system contributes to a trend, begun in the Jacksonian period in the United States and 50 years earlier in Europe, of rationalizing punishments and reducing their harshness and visibility while making them more pervasive.[50] Having eliminated public hangings and legal torture, the United States now maintains an estimated 3 million adults under some form of correctional custody—prison or jail, probation, or parole.[51] To respond to the latest developments in this trend, we must understand their sources. This section explores the reasons for the criminal records system's lack of regulation in a regulatory era and its central control in a policy area where localism has been a guiding imperative.

Several perspectives are necessary to explore the centralizing dynamic and the failure to regulate, on the one side, and the lack of effective resistance to those tendencies, on the other side. Pluralist political influence expressed through public concern about street crime provided a general license for developing more efficient law enforcement measures, but it does not explain the development of uncontrolled national data surveillance. Similarly, bureaucratic imperatives such as the "vigor to expand" and interagency competition contributed to the generous funding of the system and expansion of its uses, but they did not determine its lack of regulation.

Neither of these perspectives tells us much about how government actors have used public concern and bureaucratic imperatives to bring us the electronic Panopticon. To understand policy strategy in the development of the criminal records system, we must look to symbolic politics. Criminal justice officials have been able to manipulate traditional law enforcement symbols of public protection, modern visions of the unmitigated good of unlimited information, and broader images of the U.S. political system to support an unregulated crime information system controlled by the national law enforcement agencies. By contrast, system opponents—generally civil libertarians—have been able to rely only on largely indeterminate legal rules and symbols that could often be invoked with equal effect by proponents of the system. I suggest in what follows that the competition of symbols has played a critical role in policy development in this area.

Before beginning, I wish to address one potential criticism of the analytic task of this section. I analyze the dynamics of the development of the electronic Panopticon as if it were explicable by internal and external systemic forces. Some of those who work closely with the national criminal records system deny that it is either a system or a national policy and maintain that it therefore poses no coherent or determinate threats to civil liberties or social justice.[52] Many researchers in this area complain, in fact, of insufficient data collection on the local level and see the principal policy issue as the need for greater comparability among local and state criminal history systems. Local law enforcement officials and legislators often see their state's crime control agenda as technically and politically discrete and self-determined.

It is true that geographic and jurisdictional decentralization of parts of the system make its growth and structure difficult to explain simply or with a single policy model. State criminal justice information policies vary in both nature and source and therefore do not uniformly shape the basic materials or activities of the national system.[53] Even a major part of central coordination—the NCIC's management of the Triple-I and the automated hot files—is subject to the diverse policy influences of the different states since the FBI must accommodate itself to some degree to the wishes of the NCIC Advisory Policy Board, which is made up of state law enforcement officials. In addition, the system affects all branches of government and operates at every level, from the police precinct to the U.S. attorney general's office.

To call the system diffuse and inchoate is not, however, to mitigate its effects or to deny its evolution. The forces suggested earlier in this paper (with state variations, of course) determine the development of a national course of action even without explicit or comprehensive license. By all but the most static and formal definitions, that constitutes the creation of policy.[54]

Forces for Central Control

Viewed from a long historical perspective, a records system whose expansion and political direction is centrally controlled is perhaps to be expected, given the forces for standardization and comprehensiveness in modern states. But in the short run, it is quite surprising, given the vogue of the New Federalism among conservatives and the traditional bias toward local control of law enforcement. What influences have prevailed over the latter imperatives to provide central control of criminal records?

Mainstream, instrumental policy models would be most likely to find explanations in policymakers' rational, causal response to serious crime.[55] Corollary propositions would be that centralization improves the efficiency of criminal justice recordkeeping and responds to public doubts about law enforcement efficiency and effectiveness.

There is some support for the "crime problem" hypothesis in the initial creation of computerized files at federal and state levels. NCIC came into being in 1967 when serious property and personal crime as reported by the FBI had been increasing for several years and had become an issue in local and national political campaigns. [56] Laudon confirms the empirical hypothesis that high crime rates (along with population and incarceration rate) are statistically associated with the early adoption of computerized criminal history systems at the state level.[57] But the continuing development of the dynamic central core of the system cannot be explained by rising crime. System development at state and federal levels continued throughout the 1970s and into the 1980s despite the drop in reported crime at the turn of the decade. In fact, the big push to automate name and fingerprint searching in the FBI's Identification Division occurred as rates of reported crime declined in the 1980s.[58]

If public support for central control over records exists, I have not been able to identify any direct link between general concern over crime and the development of the computerized criminal records system. None of the criminal justice officials interviewed for this article attempted to maintain that there was a traceable, articulated link between public fear of crime and proposals for a national information system; a few did mention pressures from interest groups that either represent criminal justice or monitor it for "good data" on "career criminals."

What V. O. Key would call a "permissive consensus" certainly exists for taking strong measures to reduce traditional crimes like murder, rape, and robbery. [59] National polls taken during the 1970s and 1980s consistently show that most Americans think too little is spent on crime control, and a majority of respondents often think courts are too easy on offenders.[60] But these views do not necessarily indicate support for either the inclusiveness of a national system or the control of information by state and federal authorities.[61] Furthermore, the traditional American antagonism to concentrations of power appears to have intensified since the late 1960s, with polls consistently showing a loss of faith in the major institutions of American society, including government.[62]   Revelations in the 1970s of FBI spying have surely contributed to this crisis of authority.

A more useful perspective on the pressures for central control of the system can be found in the interacting forces of federalization and elite influence in the administration of justice. Although criminal justice is still primarily a local function, national involvement has grown steadily during the twentieth century. In the first decade, the FBI (then called the Identification Bureau) was created, and the U.S. Children's Bureau developed the first juvenile justice standards; national campaigns against the scourges of drugs and organized crime began in the 1920s and reappeared in the 1950s; and starting with the "Lindbergh law" against kidnapping, federal jurisdiction over criminal activity has expanded continually, most recently through the Comprehensive Crime Control Act of 1984. [63] Elite influence has shaped crime control policy through such developments as Supreme Court definition of the rights of defendants and Progressive reform of police practices.

The two tendencies have often overlapped. Of particular significance is President's Commission on Law Enforcement and Administration of Justice. Chaired by a former U.S. attorney general and including the president of Yale and a future U.S. Supreme Court justice, among others, the group issued a report in 1967 that provided the initial push for a national criminal history system and lent authority to the legislative proposal that created LEAA.[64] That agency set up state repositories, funded the electronic pathways between local law enforcement and the FBI, and challenged J. Edgar Hoover's 50-year dream of a comprehensive national crime information system, giving rise to a decade-long struggle between the two agencies over resources and control of the computerized criminal history system. [65]

The continuing development of the criminal records system no longer commands the attention of blue-ribbon commissions or senators. But elite influence continues in the federal courts' support of FBI authorization of wide dissemination of criminal records. And it can be seen in the aura of the system's technology and its application in organizational settings. The recent literature analyzing the social and political implications of computer use in government is helpful in understanding this dynamic. This initial view of computers as apolitical tools for rationally improving services to people has been supplemented by the conclusion that computer applications in government constitute a kind of "reinforcement politics" that serves the values and status of those in charge.[66] The development of the criminal records system bears out this perspective. Early endorsements of central control of recordkeeping are reinforced by the technological superiority of the FBI, the new class of information managers in the FBI and the state record repositories, and the increased capacity of criminal justice officials to provide technical support to other government agencies and to mayors and governors. This patina of technical expertise seems to exercise a persistent, relatively persuasive pressure for central expansion of and innovation in the system.

Opposing.Regulation

The mainstream rationalist perspective helps to explain the lack of regulation at the state and federal levels of file size, data quality, and access to the system. To monitor data collection and dissemination in many thousands of jurisdictions is a monumental administrative and fiscal burden. To impose a comprehensive federal regulatory scheme also challenges legislative initiatives already taken in most states and therefore raises political issues. From the criminal justice official's point of view, these concrete costs of regulation weigh heavily against the intangible benefits of protecting the privacy and social justice interests of an undetermined number of present and past criminal defendants, the majority of whom are poor and powerless.

Predictable bureaucratic imperatives have also determined the lack of regulation. The pressure for continuous and impersonal rationalization of program activities and the Weberian "vigor to expand" help explain the seemingly limitless discovery of new uses for the criminal records system—for finding missing children, for example, or for reinforcing bank regulatory activities—and the unwillingness to set limits on that process. Agency competition is relevant, too; LEAA abandoned its early support for comprehensive regulation of the criminal history system as soon as the battle with the FBI heated up. As for passivity about regulating state systems, the "budgetary feast" of LEAA grants for criminal justice information systems development simply overwhelmed most initiatives for developing a regulatory scheme.[67]

Perhaps most important in this context is the relative power of the symbols manipulated by proponents and opponents of regulation in both their organizational relationships and their representations to Congress and the public. Murray Edelman's analysis of politics as a symbolic form is useful here.[68] He asserts that most controversial or important political acts serve as "condensation symbols," that is, evoking through an act or position memories and emotions that affect the observer more than the objective consequences of what has just occurred. The Constitution is therefore seen as important more for its condensation of human dreams and fears than for the rational appeal of its provisions.[69] Administrative agencies commonly rely on symbolic politics to rally support for their programs, sometimes creating or inflating an intangible political threat to legitimize their own aggrandizement; Edelman cites the FBI's traditional posture on the communist "conspiracy" in the United States.[70]

The conflict of system managers who opposed regulation and civil libertarians who sought it may thus be seen as a competition of symbols. Unable to demonstrate the crime control effectiveness of an inclusive criminal records system controlled by the FBI, criminal justice officials now rely on various images of the police role to protect their autonomy. Police serve as mediators between the community and the law, empowered with broad discretion for the protection of the community in an emergency. [71] To monitor information for police use is to challenge the protective discretion that is the essence of the law enforcement role. To impose management checks is just as threatening. When legislation was proposed that would have shared policy control of the system at the federal level with private citizens and officials outside the Department of Justice, former FBI Director Clarence Kelley responded by defending the autonomy and professionalism of law enforcement, rather than by addressing the objective consequences of the proposal.[72]

One of the most powerful symbols law enforcement has at its command is that of federalism, the sharing of political power between national and local governments. Defying the evolution since World War II of centralized federalism, where most domestic policy problems have been seen as calling for national remedies, criminal law enforcement has continued to be largely a local function guided by state law (except where federal crimes are at issue). The imposition of detailed, comprehensive privacy and security regulations would surely be a complex administrative task and would alter local political culture to some degree in every state. But law enforcement officials at both state and federal levels cast the issue in constitutional terms, describing the prospect of audits, logs, and expungements as violations of state sovereignty and the Tenth Amendment. (That federalism is not seen as a barrier to the central control of the system is a contradiction that reflects the relative power of those who bear the costs of the system. Regulation would burden law enforcement personnel, whereas the deleterious effects of central control affect only individual record subjects, many of whom are criminals.)

Law enforcement officials also have recourse to the ideal of comprehensiveness in crime control. Here, as in the push for central control, "computer madness" plays a part. Criminal justice is perpetually under the gun for its inability to capture and contain all wrongdoers. Although reality inevitably falls far short of the desired end of nabbing every wrongdoer, stakes are also high in pursuing the ideal since the alternative is crime without punishment and regulation without sanction. The computer's ability to store infinite amounts of information and to transfer it instantly symbolizes the quest for perfect efficiency. For the criminal justice official, regulating the collection and dissemination of data means depleting the raw material of a level of law enforcement effectiveness that has previously been only theoretical.

(The analogy of the "panoptic schema," which oppresses its subjects with the potential for surveillance as well as its actuality, is relevant here. The managers of the modern Panopticon have at least the option of using every bit of available information. The option of going beyond the symbolic to the operational level, however, is not exercised. Laudon found that two-fifths of the states do not use their criminal history systems much, suggesting that for many communities computerization may not be perceived as a practical way to fight everyday crime.)[73]

Those who fought for regulation—civil libertarians in Congress, scholars, ACLU lawyers—also used symbolic weapons. At first glance, their arsenal might appear to be even more compelling than that of system supporters, resting as it does on prevailing legal ideology in general and legal rules derived from widely accepted constitutional ideals in particular. But these concepts have limited value when competing with the symbols of security, efficiency, and state sovereignty that can be invoked today to support government coercion of individuals. Furthermore, proponents of the system can also have recourse to powerful legal symbols.

Consider the constitutional ideal of equal protection. Although it has been a powerful force for the preservation of human dignity in the face of state action, its application to the administration of justice has been limited to outlawing overt discrimination—making it difficult for prosecutors to exclude black jurors in trials of blacks, for instance—or to developing the right to participate in the criminal justice process—like ensuring adequate appellate review and the right to counsel.[74] Equal protection has not gone very far in compensating for inequalities of condition among those who run afoul of the criminal law; it has been held not to require equal access to bail or consideration of a defendant's financial circumstances in sentencing, for example.[75] Even though it is clear that an overinclusive, inaccurate criminal records system is more likely to entrap low-income citizens, the constitutional concept of equal protection is unlikely to mitigate its effects.

Due process is not a very useful concept for the system's critics either. Lurking within it, in fact, is a justification for the breadth of access to criminal records. Fundamental procedural fairness requires that the state's power of compulsion be exercised within certain limits to protect people against governmental arbitrariness and excess. One limitation on official sanctions, which finds constitutional expression most directly in the right to trial guaranteed by the Sixth Amendment, is that they be imposed and recorded publicly.[76] With respect to warrants and criminal histories, this presumed requirement of publicity serves as powerful justification for unbridled data collection and for dissemination to employers and landlords, as well as to law enforcement agencies. Middle-level administrators in the state record repositories of California and New York interviewed on the application of state crime information policies repeatedly cited the public nature of the original records as justification for their collection and combination, even while they acknowledged that the totality of the picture of a subject's contracts with police, courts, and corrections systems has a qualitatively different impact from that of a contemporaneous record of arrest, charge, or conviction. Both a federal agency head and a Harvard professor stated in conversation with me that they did not see what the fuss was about since the data on individuals were all matters of public record.

Judicial interpretations of the right to privacy are generally consistent with this perspective. Although a few state and federal cases have prohibited the dissemination of incomplete records beyond criminal justice agencies, *Paul* v. *Davis*, the only Supreme Court case dealing with the use of arrest records, summarily rejected the record subject's allegations of a right to privacy.[77] After holding that a person's reputation is not a "liberty" or "property" interest sufficient to invoke the due process protections of the Fourteenth Amendment, then-Associate Justice William Rehnquist, writing for the majority, found that "none of our substantive privacy decisions" support the "claim that the State may not publicize a record of an official act such as an arrest."[78]

Another federal case illustrates the tendency of courts to favor law enforcement's efforts to be comprehensive over due process and privacy rights of individuals. *Menard* v. *Mitchell*, decided in 1971, found that the 50-year-old statute authorizing the U.S. attorney general to collect and disseminate criminal records could not be stretched to permit the FBI to disseminate arrest records without convictions to employers outside the federal government. The court was nonetheless willing to allow criminal justice agencies to receive those records on the basis of the "compelling necessity" of data exchange in law enforcement and the administrative rulings that provide general FBI authorization for the collection and exchange of identification records.[79] With this case, as with the national criminal records system in general, a strong cultural value with respect to information (more is better) came together with a broad legal rule (the guilty must pay) to override the fundamental fairness concern that supplies the content of formal protections of individual rights. The FBI record would not be expunged, although it reflected a burglary charge that had been dropped because it could not be connected with "any felony or misdemeanor." [80] And it would continue to be available to law enforcement agencies nationwide and to federal employers.[81]

The arguments that provide legal justification for an inclusive, open records system—that it merely records public information and that it advances comprehensiveness in uncovering criminal conduct—have answers, of course. As Justice William J. Brennan said in his dissent in *Paul* v. *Davis*, it is basic constitutional doctrine that the government not "single an individual out for punishment outside the judicial process"; yet the criminal records system does just that.[82] The requirement of publicity for criminal records has been stood on its head to justify the Panopticon. Intended as a defense against state power, the rule is invoked to endorse its encroachment.

Perhaps that contradiction is the clue to the system's most fundamental significance, its place in a retreat from many welfare state initiatives of the past 50 years. Reconciling systems of automated recordkeeping for criminal justice with systematic protection of personal rights is not inconceivable; legal doctrine could easily accommodate both objectives. Although there is a way, however, it is not obvious that there is a will in the political climate of the 1980s.

Because the effects on individuals of the Panopticon are as yet either potential or unmeasured in any systematic way, it is easy to dismiss it as a minor civil liberties issue unrelated to structural problems. But the continuing extension of record checks goes beyond the right to be let alone or the right to speak up. Those who have records in the system—disproportionately poor and darker-skinned—run the risk of more or less permanent unemployability. As more employers, landlords, and insurers gain access to the system on a national basis, and as more investigative files are included within it, the system

DIANA R. GORDON　　　　　507

may become a hidden stratifier of social and economic power, channeling many millions of Americans away from jobs and services because they have been arrested at some time for something other than a traffic offense. It is not so fanciful to worry about the emergence of a sophisticated computer quarantine that has profound implications for social structure.

To marshall sufficient political force to limit state power in this area, critics need to develop a much more precise and widely shared perception of the potential risks of emerging patterns of governmental coercion of individual behavior. What are the linkages between expanding systems of observation and control in the criminal justice system and in other dimensions of the state-citizen relationship, such as education and public assistance? What are the implications of computerized recordkeeping by the government beyond the relatively tangible risks for individual liberties? What barriers to a progressive crime information policy are posed by the character of the U.S. state, with its many centers of power? We are used to joking that "Big Brother is watching," but we have not yet adequately understood the mechanisms and potential impact of modern forms of state monitoring of individuals' lives. That work lies ahead.

NOTES

1. The 1971 figure comes from a statement by J. Edgar Hoover submitted to the Senate Committee on the Judiciary, Subcommittee on Constitutional Rights, *Hearings on Federal Data Banks, Computers and the Bill of Rights* (92d Cong., Mar. 15, 1971). Current data on NCIC files are from a draft paper prepared in Oct. 1985 by the Subcommittee on Civil and Constitutional Rights of the House Judiciary Committee for the American Bar Association Section on Individual Rights and Responsibilities. The estimate of 1989 transactions is from "Testimony of David F. Nemecek at Hearing on Proposed Contract to Study and Redesign the National Crime Information Center Before the Subcommittee on Civil and Constitutional Rights of the House Committee on the Judiciary" (98th Cong., Aug. 1, 1984), 5.

2. "Statement of FBI Assistant Director Lawrence K. York Before the House Subcommittee on Civil and Constitutional Rights" (Mar. 24, 1986), 2. There is considerable overlap between records included in AIDS and those held or indexed in NCIC.

3. Bureau of Justice Statistics, "State Criminal Records Repositories" (U.S. Department of Justice, 1985), 1.

4. Ibid., 2. All ten of the most populous states, as determined by the 1980 census, have automated a portion of their records. All the states that have no plans for automating records, except Massachusetts and Indiana, are among the twenty least populous states. U.S. Bureau of the Census, *Statistical Abstract of the United States: 1986*, 106th ed. (Washington, D.C.: Superintendent of Documents, 1985).

5. I am greatly indebted to Kenneth C. Laudon's study of the dimensions and problems of the developing national criminal history system, *The Dossier Society: Value Choices in the Design of National Information Systems* (New York: Columbia

University Press, 1986).   His discussion of non-criminal justice uses of criminal history data is in chaps. 5 and 9.

    6.   Ibid., 123.

    7.   Criminal records are of several types. In this article, examples of how the national criminal records system works are taken from experience with the hot files and criminal histories.   In addition to individual records of official acts, law enforcement agencies maintain investigative files, which include data on people suspected of planning or committing crimes—identifiers, personal information on associations and activities, etc. As of mid-1986, it appeared that most investigative files either had not been automated or were not linked to computerized criminal histories or warrant files. (The principal exception is the NCIC's Secret Service Protective File, which contains leads on about a hundred people deemed to be a threat to the president and others whom the Secret Service is assigned to protect.)   The significance of automating these files and connecting them to records of official acts should not, however, be overlooked. If requests for information in criminal history files flag investigative records, they, too, become part of the national system.

    8.   Neal Miller, *A Study of the Number of Persons with Records of Arrest or Conviction in the Labor Force* (U.S. Department of Labor, Technical Analysis Paper no. 63, 1979).

    9.   Laudon, *Dossier Society,* 309-13.

    10.   Although other Western democracies have some of the same problems with automated police files, many (Sweden, Great Britain, Canada, Germany) have agencies charged with oversight of computerized data systems, a proposal that has been rejected in the United States as antithetical to the federal system. See David Flaherty, "Protecting Privacy in Policy Information Systems," *University of Toronto Law Journal* 36 (Spring 1986): 116-48.

    11.   *Menard* v. *Mitchell,* 328 F. Supp. 718, 726 (1971).

    12.   Senate Committee on the Judiciary, Subcommittee on Constitutional Rights, *Hearings on Federal Data Banks, Computers and the Bill of Rights* (92d Cong., Mar. 10, 1971), 649.

    13.   Section 812(b), Justice Assistance Act of 1984, P.L. 98-473.

    14.   Senate Committee on Government Operations, *Protecting Individual Privacy in Federal Gathering, Use and Disclosure of Information: Report to Accompany S.3418* (93d Cong., Sept. 26, 1974), 23.

    15.   See, e.g., House Subcommittee No. 4 of the Committee on the Judiciary, *Hearings on H.R. 13315* (92d Cong., Mar. 16, 22, and 23, Apr. 13 and 26, 1972); House Subcommittee on Civil and Constitutional Rights of the Committee on the Judiciary, *Hearings on H.R. 188, H.R. 9783, H.R. 12574 and H.R. 12575* (93d Cong., July 26, Aug. 2, Sept. 26, Oct. 11, 1973; Feb. 26 and 28, Mar. 5 and 28, and Apr. 3, 1974); House Subcommittee on Civil and Constitutional Rights of the Committee on the Judiciary, *Hearings on H.R. 8227* (94th Cong., July 14 and 17 and Sept. 5, 1975).

    16.   28 Code of Federal Regulations, Section 20.

    17.   MITRE Corporation, "Implementing the Federal Privacy and Security Regulations" (McLean, Va., 1977).

    18.   SEARCH Group, Inc., *Compendium of State Privacy and Security Legislation* (U.S. Department of Justice, Bureau of Justice Statistics, 1985).

    19.   *Paul* v. *Davis,* 424 U.S. 693 (1976).

20. Michel Foucault, *Discipline and Punish: The Birth of the Prison* (New York: Pantheon, 1977).

21. David Burnham, *The Rise of the Computer State* (New York: Random House, 1983); Gordon Karl Zenk, *Project SEARCH: The Struggle for Control of Criminal Information in America* (Westport, Conn.; Greenwood Press, 1979).

22. Office of Technology Assessment, *An Assessment of Alternatives for a National Computerized Criminal History System* (Washington, D.C.: GPO, 1982).

23. See note 5.

24. Exchange between David Nemecek, NCIC section chief, and James Dempsey, assistant counsel, *FBI Authorization Hearings for FY 1986 Before the Subcommittee on Civil and Constitutional Rights of the House Judiciary Committee* (99th Cong., Apr. 25, 1985), 165-66.

25. Unless otherwise noted, material on state records systems comes from interviews conducted by the author (and internal documents collected at those interviews) with officials of record repositories in New York, California, and Massachusetts during the latter half of 1984.

26. "Agencies Authorized to Receive Criminal History Information," photocopied report of the Criminal Records Security Unit, California Department of Justice (1983).

27. 28 U.S.C., Section 534(a)(2).

28. SEARCH Group, Inc., *Criminal Justice Information Policy: Privacy and the Public Employer* (Washington, D.C.: Bureau of Justice Statistics, 1981), 48-49.

29. *Washington Post*, Feb. 15, 1986; U.S. Department of Transportation news release, Feb. 19, 1986.

30. H.R. 4759, S. 2477.

31. Interview with author, Nov. 1984.

32. See, e.g., anecdotes in the NCIC booklet, "The Investigative Tool: A Guide to the Use and Benefits of NCIC" (Washington, D.C.: Federal Bureau of Investigation, n.d.). Recent achievements are most often traceable to the new computers that compare fingerprint images found at the scene of a crime to prints on file.

33. "HRA/ACD Day Care/Head Start Program Fingerprinting and Criminal Record Review Report for the Month of October, 1985," photocopied (Human Resources Administration, City of New York), unpaginated.

34. Bureau of Justice Statistics, *Report to the Nation on Crime and Justice* (U.S. Department of Justice, Bureau of Justice Statistics, 1983.)

35. Several studies have found, not surprisingly, that an arrest record has a negative effect on employment opportunity. For the conclusion that arrest without conviction is an obstacle to employment, see Herbert S. Miller, "The Closed Door: The Effect of a Criminal Record on Employment with State and Local Public Agencies" (U.S. Department of Labor, Manpower Administration Office of Research and Development, Report No. 81-09-70-02, 1972).

36. OTA, *Assessment of Alternatives*, 91-102.

37. *Central Valley* v. *Younger*, Sup. Ct. California, Co. of Alameda, Case Nos. 497394-6 and 524298-6 (1984).

38. Joan Petersilia, *Racial Disparities in the Criminal Justice System* (Santa Monica, Calif.: Rand Corporation, 1983).

39. See, e.g., *Jones* v. *New Orleans*, U.S. District Court, Eastern District of Louisiana, Civil Action No. 83-703 (1985); *Smith* v. *Gates*, Sup. Ct. California, Co.

of Los Angeles, Case No. CA 000619 (1984); *Emma v. Boston,* U.S. District Ct., Civil Action No. 85-3232-Y (1985).

40. *New York Times,* Aug. 25, 1985.

41. See, e.g., "California Agencies Got Spy Dossiers on Non-Criminal Groups from Chicago Police," *Los Angeles Times,* Dec. 6, 1984, pt. 1, p. 6.

42. Letter from FBI Director William H. Webster to Representative Don Edwards (D., Calif.), chairman, Subcommittee on Civil and Constitutional Rights, Committee on the Judiciary, Apr. 12, 1985.

43. Report of the Secretary's Advisory Committee on Automated Personal Data Systems, *Records, Computers and the Rights of Citizens* (Washington, D.C.: GPO, 1973), 19.

44. "Minutes, National Crime Information Center Advisory Policy Board, October 5-6, 1983" (unpublished FBI document).

45. *New York Times,* Jan. 1, 1984.

46. Testimony of D. Lowell Jensen, *Hearing on FBI Authorization Request for FY 1986 Before the Subcommittee on Civil and Constitutional Rights, House Committee on the Judiciary* (99th Cong., Apr. 25, 1985), 104.

47. "Agreements and Recommendations of the Attorney General's Bank Fraud Working Group," U.S. Department of Justice photocopied report (Apr. 2, 1985).

48. "Summary of the Rationale for Certain of the Matters Set Forth in the Attached Agreements and Recommendations of the Justice Department-Supervisory Agencies Working Group," U.S. Department of Justice photocopied report (Apr. 2, 1985), 3.

49. House Committee on Government Operations, *Federal Response to Criminal Misconduct and Insider Abuse in the Nation's Financial Associations* (98th Cong., 1984, H. Rept. 1137), 2.

50. Historical sources for this trend include Foucault, *Discipline and Punish;* and David J. Rothman, *The Discovery of the Asylum: Social Order and Disorder in the New Republic* (Boston: Little, Brown & Co., 1971.) A discussion of how modern "diversion" programs fit into the picture can be found in Norval Morris, *The Future of Imprisonment* (Chicago: University of Chicago Press, 1974), 9-12.

51. See Bureau of Justice Statistics, "Prisoners in 1985" (U.S. Department of Justice, Bureau of Justice Statistics, 1986); idem, "Probation and Parole, 1985" (U.S. Department of Justice, Bureau of Justice Statistics, 1986); idem, "Jail Inmates, 1984" (U.S. Department of Justice, Bureau of Justice Statistics, 1985).

52. James Q. Wilson, "Problems in the Creation of Adequate Criminal Justice Information Systems," in SEARCH Group, Inc., *Information Policy and Crime Control Strategies* (U.S. Department of Justice, Bureau of Justice Statistics, 1984), 8.

53. SEARCH Group, *Compendium.*

54. For a discussion of policy as "a course of action or inaction rather than specific decisions or actions," see H. Hugh Heclo, "Review Article: Policy Analysis," *British Journal of Political Science* 2 (Jan. 1972): 85.

55. Yehezkel Dror, *Public Policymaking Reexamined* (San Francisco: Chandler Publishing Co., 1968), chap. 2.

56. FBI Uniform Crime Reports, *Crime in the United States, 1970* (Washington, D.C.: Superintendent of Documents, 1970), 65.

57. Laudon, *Dossier Society,* 105.

58. FBI Uniform Crime Reports, *Crime in the United States, 1985* (Washington, D.C.: Superintendent of Documents, 1985), 41.

59. V. O. Key, *Public Opinion and American Democracy* (New York: Alfred A. Knopf, 1961), 32.

60. Edmund F. McGarrell and Timothy J. Flanagan, eds., *Sourcebook of Criminal Justice Statistics, 1984*, for U.S. Department of Justice, Bureau of Justice Statistics (Washington, D.C.: GPO, 1985), 187 (fig. 2.4), 188 (table 2.19), and 192 (table 2.23); Timothy J. Flanagan and Maureen McLeod, eds., *Sourcebook of Criminal Justice Statistics, 1982*, for U.S. Department of Justice, Bureau of Justice Statistics (Washington D.C.: GPO, 1983), 248 (table 2.40).

61. See Alan F. Westin, "Public and Group Attitudes Toward Information Policies and Boundaries for Criminal Justice," in SEARCH Group, *Information Policy*, 37.

62. Seymour Martin Lipset and William Schneider, *The Confidence Gap: Business, Labor and Government in the Public Mind* (New York: Free Press, 1983).

63. Samuel Walker, *Popular Justice: A History of American Criminal Justice* (New York: Oxford University Press, 1980), 127-238.

64. President's Commission on Law Enforcement and the Administration of Justice, *The Challenge of Crime in a Free Society* (Washington, D.C.: GPO, 1967).

65. The best account of agency competition for control of the computerized criminal history system is an unpublished history of LEAA by Mae Churchill and Harold Brackman, "The Hidden Agenda: LEAA and the Tools of Repression" (1980). See also Zenk, *Project SEARCH*.

66. James N. Danziger, William H. Dutton, Rob Kling, and Kenneth L. Kraemer, *Computers and Politics* (New York: Columbia University Press, 1982), 19, 163-68, 188-93.

67. Graham T. Allison, *The Essence of Decision* (Boston: Little, Brown & Co., 1971), 85.

68. Murray Edelman, *The Symbolic Uses of Politics* (Urbana: University of Illinois Press, 1964).

69. Ibid., 19.

70. Ibid., 69-71.

71. Albert J. Reiss, Jr., *The Police and the Public* (New Haven: Yale University Press, 1971).

72. Laudon, *Dossier Society*, 233.

73. Ibid., 97.

74. *Batson* v. *Kentucky*, U.S. Supreme Court, No. 84-6263, decided Apr. 30, 1986.

75. *Burns* v. *Ohio*, 360 U.S. 258 (1959); *Douglas* v. *California*, 372 U.S. 353 (1963); *Gideon* v. *Wainwright*, 372 U.S. 335 (1963).

76. In re *Oliver*, 333 U.S. 257 (1948).

77. 424 U.S. 694 (1976).

78. Ibid., at 713.

79. *Menard* v. *Mitchell*, 328 F. Supp. 718 (1971). The restriction on dissemination was later nullified by federal legislation.

80. Ibid., at 720.

81. In 1974 the record subject sued to have his record expunged, on the basis that the arrest had been downgraded to a detention, and won. *Menard* v. *Saxbe*, 498 F. 2d 1017 (1974). The other outcome of the 1971 case was that Congress immediately authorized the FBI to release arrest information for employment purposes where authorized by state law.

82. *Paul* v. *Davis*, at 735, n. 18 (J. Brennan, dissenting).

Politics & Society 15, no. 4 (1986-87): 483-511.

[19]

CRITIQUE: NO SOUL IN THE NEW MACHINE: TECHNOFALLACIES IN THE ELECTRONIC MONITORING MOVEMENT*

RONALD CORBETT
Massachusetts Department of Probation

GARY T. MARX
Massachusetts Institute of Technology

"It's a remarkable piece of apparatus."
      Opening line, *The Penal Colony*, by Franz Kafka

Since its legendary inception in the mind of a New Mexico judge inspired by *Spiderman* comics, the use of electronic monitoring as a correctional tool has grown in a manner most often described as "explosive" (U.S. Dept. of Justice 1990). From very isolated use in 1984, the use of electronic monitoring (hereafter EM) has expanded to at least 33 states (ACA 1989), with a threefold increase during 1988 alone (Schmidt 1989).

Although hardly a mature industry, EM has attracted a growing number of manufacturers now totaling at least 14 (Tonry and Will 1989). For the last several years, exhibition areas at the annual conference of the American Probation and Parole Association have been occupied almost entirely by vendors of new technology, most of it EM equipment.

Clearly, EM has arrived on the correctional scene and has drawn much attention. Significant research findings regarding its impact recently have begun to come in. These studies have intensified the debate about the proper place of EM in criminal justice. In this paper we locate EM in the context of broader societal developments regarding surveillance, and we argue that unfortunately it has fallen prey to a series of technofallacies which undermine practice. Viewing the current electronic monitoring frenzy from the perspective of several decades of observing and participating in the correctional process, we have Yogi Berra's sense that "it's deja vu all over again," as yet another panacea is

* An earlier version of this paper was presented at the Annual Meeting of the American Society of Criminology, Baltimore, 1990.

400   ELECTRONIC MONITORING

offered to criminal justice without adequate thought or preparation.

We address both academic and practitioner audiences. The former will recognize the sociological perspectives of unintended consequences, irony, and paradox (e.g., Marx 1981; Merton 1967; Seiber 1982) as applied to a new area. We hope that the latter— those who develop and administer policy—will gain from this presentation by seeing that innovations never stand alone and that avoidance of the fallacies identified here can mean improved practice.

THE NEW SURVEILLANCE

The development of EM in the 1980s not only is a response to specific factors (to be discussed below), but also reflects broader changes in surveillance. It must be viewed along with drug testing, video and audio surveillance, computer monitoring and dossiers, night vision technology, and a rich variety of other means that are changing the nature of watching.

Although these extractive technologies have unique elements, they also tend to share certain characteristics that set them apart from many traditional means. Some of the ethos and the information-gathering techniques found in the maximum-security prison are diffusing into the broader society. We appear to be moving toward, rather than away from, becoming a "maximum-security society."[1]

Such a society is transparent and porous. Information leakage is rampant. Barriers and boundaries—distance, darkness, time, walls, windows, and even skin, which have been fundamental to our conceptions of privacy, liberty, and individuality—give way.

Actions, as well as feelings, thoughts, pasts, and even futures, are increasingly visible. The line between the public and the private is weakened; observations seem constant; more and more information goes on a permanent record, whether we will this or not, and even whether we know about it or not. Data in many different forms, from widely separated geographical areas, organizations, and time periods, can easily be merged and analyzed.

Surveillance becomes capital- rather than labor-intensive. Technical developments drastically alter the economics of surveillance such that it becomes much less expensive per unit watched. Aided by technology, a few persons can monitor many people and factors. The situation contrasts with the traditional gumshoe or

---

[1] This section draws from G. Marx, 1988, Undercover: Police Surveillance in America (Berkeley: University of California Press); chps. 1 and 10.

guard watching a few persons and the almost exclusive reliance on firsthand information from the unenhanced senses.

One aspect of this efficiency, and the ultimate in decentralized control, is self or participatory monitoring. Persons watched become active "partners" in their own monitoring. Surveillance systems may be triggered directly when a person walks, talks on the telephone, turns on a TV set, takes a magnetically marked item through a checkpoint, or enters or leaves a controlled area.

There is an emphasis on the engineering of control, whether by weakening the object of surveillance (as in the case of EM) or by hardening potential victims (as with access codes or better locks). Themes of prevention, soft control, and the replacement of people with machines are present. Where it is not possible to prevent violations physically, or when that process is too expensive, the system may be engineered so that profit from a violation cannot be enjoyed, or so that the violator is identified immediately.

As the technology becomes ever more penetrating and more intrusive, it becomes possible to gather information with laserlike specificity and spongelike absorbency. If we consider the information-gathering net as analogous to a fishing net, then, as Stanley Cohen (1985) suggests, the mesh of the net has become finer and the net wider.

Like the discovery of the atom or the unconscious, new techniques bring to the surface bits of reality that previously were hidden or did not contain informational clues. People, in a sense, are turned inside out; what was previously invisible or meaningless is made visible and meaningful. Electronic monitoring and the forms that increasingly accompany it, such as video identification and drug/alcohol testing, are part of this qualitative change in monitoring. The home is opened up as never before. In focusing on the details, we must not forget that they are part of a much broader group of changes.

TEN TECHNOFALLACIES OF ELECTRONIC SALVATION

New public policies are based partly on politics and interests, partly on empirical assessment, and partly on values. Unfortunately, wisdom too often plays only a modest role.

EM must be approached cautiously, or the stampeding herd may fall off the cliff. Before technical solutions such as monitoring are implemented, it is important to examine the broader cultural climate, the rationales for action, and the empirical and value assumptions on which they are based. Policy analysts must offer not only theories, concepts, methods, and data, but also—one

hopes—wisdom. Part of this wisdom consists of being able to identify and question the structure of tacit assumptions that undergird
action.

In the analysis of new surveillance technologies, Marx (1990,
forthcoming) identifies a number of "tarnished silver bullet
techno-fallacies" that characterize many recent efforts to use technology to deal with social issues. Some of these apply to the case
at hand. In critiquing the EM movement, the following discussion
draws on and expands this more general framework. We discuss
ten such fallacies:

    1) The fallacy of explicit agendas;
    2) The fallacy of novelty;
    3) The fallacy of intuitive appeal or surface plausibility;
    4) The fallacy of the free lunch or painless dentistry;
    5) The fallacy of quantification;
    6) The fallacy of ignoring the recent past;
    7) The fallacy of technical neutrality;
    8) The fallacy of the 100% accurate or fail-safe system;
    9) The fallacy of the sure shot;
    10) The fallacy of assuming that if a critic questions the
means, he or she must be opposed to the ends.

1. The fallacy of explicit agendas. This entails assuming that
new programs are developed for their declared purpose and/or
that there *is* a clearly developed purpose. It also assumes that the
ostensible reasons for policy decisions are the real reasons rather
than a mask for a decision based on other considerations (e.g., fiscal or political). In the case of EM the goals are varied, contradictory, and shifting, and sometimes hide other goals.

An important theme in contemporary corrections (Petersilla,
1990; Tonry and Morris 1990) is the emphasis placed on proportionality or symmetry in sentencing. It is argued that traditionally, little in the way of penal sanctions "between probation and prison"
has been available. No appropriate sanction exists for offenders
who occupy the middle ground on a scale of severity of deserts.
Liberals and conservatives alike have found appeal in this argument. A major rationale for EM is that it is an intermediate sanction which promises simultaneously to lighten onerous penalties
and to increase lenient ones.

Nevertheless, EM has a number of other goals, sometimes acknowledged informally but rarely stated officially or in public.
Policy disasters are more likely to occur when the declared purposes of a program are supplemented privately or eclipsed by additional, even contrary, objectives. With regard to EM, the foremost
of these objectives is a powerful financial imperative.

In the late 1970s and early 1980s a "get tough" approach to sentencing offenders emerged from the presumed demise of the rehabilitative ideal. This was reflected first in the rhetoric of public officials and then in a spate of sentencing reform schemes, all pointing toward stricter and more certain punishment. Predictably enough, this approach put a tremendous strain on existing prison stock, and is an important cause of the decade-long prison overcrowding crisis.

Although building more prisons seemed the obvious solution, here again the agenda was by no means clear or uncomplicated. Prisons are very expensive institutions, averaging (in 1987 dollars) between $50,000 and $75,000 per new cell for construction and $14,000 for imprisoning one offender for a year (Petersilia 1987). "Get tough" suddenly meant "Go broke!" The goal of sentencing severity gave way fairly quickly to the goal of fiscal stability. As Petersilia reported, this financial concern became "the bottom line in deciding what to do with lawbreakers" (1987:xi).

Compounding the financial crisis was a nascent legal crisis of constitutional dimensions, brought on by overcrowded conditions in prisons. So serious was this situation that by 1987, 37 states were subject to judicial orders to address illegal conditions in their institutions (Petersilia 1987).

The conservative trend in sentencing philosophy potentially was jeopardized by an emerging legal/fiscal crisis. If these multiple and conflicting goals were to be served, clearly it would be necessary to develop a program that would sound tough while also reducing and relieving overcrowding. Thus were born "sentencing alternatives," which in time would be renamed "intermediate sanctions" and, most recently, "intermediate punishments," of which EM is perhaps the leading example. Pressure was put on probation to remake itself. State correctional administrators looked to the lower-cost option to bail them out. Offenders who might be incarcerated under the prevailing philosophy would now, of necessity, face technologically enhanced home imprisonment, which was believed to cost only one-third as much as prison.

Another equally powerful (if less noted) agenda item—a desire to enhance the public image of probation—was also present. Internally, the probation profession was feeling pressure to make itself more palatable in conservative times. Consequently the field adopted rhetoric that was, in Clear and Hardyman's view, "unabashedly fierce," emphasizing qualities of toughness, strictness, and harshness (1990: 46). In the face of a public relations crisis, wherein probation was depicted as pathetically soft, it became politically wise to put on a meaner face and develop a more punitive approach. Probation would seek to pack the same punch as prison, minus the expensive bricks and mortar, by launching programs involving intensive supervision, boot camps, shock incarceration, and home confinement with electronic monitoring.

If EM has not worked in an empirical sense to date, as the incoming evidence suggests, that failure might be traced, at least in part, to this melange of shifting and conflicting goals.

2. *The fallacy of novelty.* This fallacy entails the assumption that new means are invariably better than the old. Decisions are often based on newness rather than on data suggesting that the new will work or that the old has failed. The symbolism of wanting to appear up-to-date is important.

The fallacy of novelty is related to a "vanguard" fallacy: "If the big guys are doing it, it must be good." Smaller organizations copy the actions of the larger or more prestigious organizations in an effort to appear modern.

The field of corrections often has been accused of being in constant thrall to fads and panaceas (Finckenauer 1982). Technofix attitudes unfortunately have become the knee-jerk response of our society to complex issues whose causes are social, not technical. In a theme with solid roots in American history, newness is equated too quickly with goodness. New technology is inherently attractive to an industrial society. It's risky to be against new technology, however mysterious its operations or recondite its underlying engineering. Technical innovation becomes synonymous with progress. To be opposed to new technology is to be a heretic, to be old-fashioned, backwards, resistant to change, regressive, out of step. Reinecke observes sardonically, "To fall behind in the great technorace is to demonstrate a pathetic unwillingness to change with the times, to invite universal ridicule, and to write a recipe for economic disaster" (1982: 13).

Agency administrators become fond of the new and the original as a matter of careerism and survival. Fast-track reputations are more likely to be built on introducing new programs than on maintaining the old; few professionals want to be regarded as caretakers. Invitations to speak at conferences, media coverage, job offers, and, most significantly, the availability of grant money depend on the implementation of novel approaches. Questions about the fit of the innovation with the agency's mission and goals or about the existence of empirical support for the innovation will be considered mere details in the face of these forces. This point leads directly to our next fallacy.

3. The fallacy of intuitive appeal or surface plausibility. This entails the adoption of a policy because "it sure seems as if it would work." The emphasis is on commonsense "real-world" experience and a dash of wish fulfillment in approaching new programs. In this ahistorical and anti-empirical world, evaluative research has little currency.

The models for rational policy development taught in schools of public administration advance the notion that in the domain of social policy, research and evaluation determine policy. Unfortunately, these models usually bear little resemblance to actual occurrences in corrections practice. Finckenauer (1982) refers to a tendency for agencies to ignore evidence of program failure if the ideological "spin" is right. Clear and Hardyman (1990) speak of a rush to embrace intensive probation supervision when the evidence supporting such adoption is "weak." Tonry and Will cite administrators who proliferate programs and believe in their efficacy, even in the absence of careful evaluations. They note that "in a field (community corrections) . . . in which few rigorous evaluations have been conducted, the persuasive force of conventional but untested wisdom is great" (1990: 29).

Enthusiasm for EM programs runs high, even when data that call them into question are available. Petersilia's three-county random-assignment experiment involving EM in California found the following: "The highest technical violation and arrest rate occurred in the Electronic Monitoring Program in Los Angeles. About 35% of participants in the program had a technical violation, and 35% an arrest, after six months" (1990: 105). Probation with EM was found to result in rearrest rates identical to those of offenders under regular supervision.

An Indianapolis study released in 1990 compared the effectiveness of EM with that of human monitoring. No significant differences were found between the two methods. The study revealed, however, that nearly 44 percent of all participants "sneaked out" on the monitoring (Baumer and Mendelsohn 1990).

In Irwin's (1990) report on the use of EM in the Georgia IPS program, she concludes that it was a failure and that it seemed to exacerbate recidivism rates. Palumbo, Clifford, and Snyder-Joy (190) report that in an Arizona EM study concentrating on cost-effectiveness, the evidence suggests that EM did not reduce and might very well increase overall correctional costs due to net widening.

Just as innovations are promoted without regard to supporting data, so can traditional approaches be abandoned casually with a lack of evidence. In the late 1970s and early 1980s it became the

conventional wisdom that rehabilitation was a failure and that programs aimed at reforming offenders were bankrupt. EM and other
"get tough" approaches to community corrections flourished in
this environment, as the emphasis shifted toward punishment and
deterrence.

Again, it is remarkable how little this conventional wisdom
was supported by the available research. Byrne (1990), in an overview of intensive supervision programming, inveighs against systems that blindly negate or minimize the importance of treatment
interventions and overestimate the impact of control-oriented interventions such as EM. Petersilia's methodologically rigorous
study reports, as its only *positive* finding, that lower recidivism
rates were found "among those ISP offenders who were fortunate
enough to receive some rehabilitative programming" (1990: 3). In
a major study of the effects of a sanctioning approach versus a
treatment approach in reducing recidivism, Andrews and his colleagues (1990) found that across 80 different studies, criminal sanctioning without the provision of rehabilitative services did not
work and that only programs incorporating principles of rehabilitation reduced recidivism significantly. They conclude, "There is a
reasonably solid clinical and research basis for the political reaffir-
mation of rehabilitation" (384).

4.   The fallacy of the free lunch or painless dentistry.   This fallacy involves the belief that there are programs which will return
only good results without any offsetting losses. It ignores the
existence of low-visibility or longer-range collateral costs, and fails
to recognize that any format or structure both channels and
excludes.

In the making of public policy, new ideas all too often drive
out old ideas, irrespective of their merit. New programs draw attention and resources away from the traditional efforts. This situation can entail significant opportunity costs. Personnel and other
resources will be allocated to the innovation, often starving (or un-
dernourishing) existing programs. Over time, the conventional
ways of doing business may suffer from choked-off budgets and
the retention of less competent staff members who have been excluded from the new, high-priority program. Such persons also
may be angry about not being included in the new programs.

Eventually this "Gresham"-style effect may develop a self-fulfilling quality. Whatever the merit of conventional programs, they
become defenseless against the drain of resources into the innovation. Conversely, the innovation, whatever its merits, is provided

with an introduction under the most favorable circumstances (ample start-up funds, generous publicity, an elite, hand-picked staff). This makes for an unrealistic test of its potential under normal non-"hallo" conditions.

The EM movement illustrates these dynamics nicely. Clear and his colleagues (1987), in their review of three intensive supervision projects, discuss the "secondary place" taken by treatment efforts when control is emphasized. Irwin, in discussing the use of EM in Georgia, observes that although the technology makes the control function easier, "at the same time [it] may make more difficult the part of the job that involves the motivation of offenders and gaining their cooperation" (1990: 73). Palumbo and colleagues conclude that because the program is sold on the basis of its capacity to control offenders, treatment becomes at best an "add-on": "Under these conditions, there is likely to be little if any real treatment provided" (1990: 16).

5. *The fallacy of quantification.* When this fallacy is operating, costs and benefits and the value of goods and services are defined in a manner that gives priority to those things which can be measured easily. In a related fallacy, seemingly attractive means can serve to determine the end, rather than the reverse.

One potentially attractive feature of EM systems for administrators and line officers alike is its seeming operational simplicity. EM is a comparatively straightforward process, easy to learn, implement, and monitor. In this respect it stands in sharp contrast to the traditional "casework" approach to probation.

Traditional probation supervision might be characterized as counseling with an edge. It resembles social work plus the complications of coercion and involuntariness. Although offenders clearly prefer probation to prison, they could hardly be said to embrace the experience in the same way, for instance, as mental health "clients" may embrace therapy. Probation officers work in the shadow of the prison cell and can arrange for the imprisonment of intractable offenders. Simultaneously they are expected to remediate a range of profound personal difficulties (e.g., drug abuse, illiteracy, mental illness, joblessness) that are pushing the offender toward crime. Therefore, they are charged with hating the sin and loving the sinner. They have a dual role—cop and counselor—which is often misunderstood, if not resented, by offenders, who correctly sense the mixed message.

The complexity and the contradictory nature of the job are compounded by the "technical uncertainty" (Thompson 1967) inherent in the role. Traditional casework is assumed to be an imprecise science at best, even though a line of research by Andrews and colleagues (1980, 1986, 1990) has established a strong empirical foundation for effective supervision. Clear and Gallagher suggest that in the face of this technical uncertainty, "officers will tend to select conservative practices in offender management" (1985: 426)

The EM movement reconceptualizes the task before the probation officer as more mechanical and more concrete: install equipment, test, monitor, record, and respond. Redefining the goal as offender surveillance through technology eliminates the professional anxiety and guesswork endemic to the casework approach. EM minimizes, if it does not eliminate, the discretionary judgment and complex analysis required of the treatment model and replaces it with responsibilities akin to those of a clerk/technician.

EM also makes the manager's job less taxing. The traditional approach requires considerable investment in staff training in a variety of higher-order skills (interpersonal communications, personality assessment, diagnostic protocols, crisis intervention, substance abuse assessment and referral). Supervising staff members with these responsibilities is difficult, as is the related task of setting performance criteria and organizational goals.

Small wonder, then, that organizations will find the relatively uncomplicated world of EM attractive. What had been nebulous and "soft" in casework systems becomes quantifiable and concrete with EM. If only it worked! A major change in the probation officer's job is being introduced without broad discussion, simply as an artifact of a seemingly simple technology.

6. *The fallacy of ignoring the recent past.* For the case at hand, this fallacy involves denying the possibility that EM might be just another corrections fad. Of course this characterizes nontechnical reforms as well. Yet whether from genuine enthusiasm or as a political strategy, those caught up in the excitement and the high stakes of promoting a reform often wear historical blinders. They do so at their peril.

The intense interest in EM has all the earmarks of a fad— broad media attention, quick, widespread adoption, rapid expansion and diversification of the product. Even a superficial familiarity with the recent history of community corrections should encourage a skeptical, or at least a go-slow, approach.

The history of the last 20 years of community corrections is punctuated at about five-year intervals by the appearance of new "panaceas," typically arriving suddenly and attracting enormous attention. The bad news is that they tend to disappear just as quickly. Examples include pretrial diversion in the late 1960s, mandatory sentencing in the mid-1970s, and intensive probation supervision (IPS) in the early 1980s. Their trajectory has been roughly similar: great early enthusiasm, widespread adoption, less-than-positive evaluations followed by disillusionment, and finally downscaling or elimination and receptiveness to the next panacea.

7. *The fallacy of technical neutrality.* This involves the assumption that technology per se is morally and ethically neutral; that any piece of machinery can have both good and bad implications, *depending on how it is used.* This fallacy can stop critical thought. It ignores the fact that the technology is always developed and applied in a social context which is never neutral.

EM technology is morally distinguishable from a microchip, for example. It is meant as a form of human restraint and tracking; with few exceptions, it has been used to incarcerate people in their own homes. Thus the moral rub.

In a democracy, the concept of "home" is a near-national icon; home represents a refuge, a sanctuary, the last bastion of privacy. The walls of a home have been thought to serve as an impermeable barrier, inviolate in defining the line between public and private domains. The Fourth Amendment incorporates this understanding into law: it admonishes the state that in a free society, it is to have little dominion over and very limited intrusion into the activities within a home.

With EM the home becomes deprivatized. The intrusion is telemetric and nearly invisible, and, as such, perhaps more insidious (Marx 1989). We have progressed from first-generation equipment that simply monitored physical presence, through emissions transmitted over telephone lines, to more recently manufactured equipment that allows for visual inspection and telemetric alcohol tests. Tonry and Will (1989) report that two-way video transmission soon will be cost-effective for use in home confinement programs.

The use of EM typifies trends toward decentralization of social control. Figuratively, prisons have been dismantled, and each individual cell has been reassembled in private homes. Once homes start to serve as modular prisons and bedrooms as cells, what will become of our cherished notion of "home"? If privacy is obliterated *legally* in prison and if EM provides the functional equivalent of prison at home, privacy rights for home confinees and family members are potentially jeopardized.

What price intermediate sanctions? In finding feasible alternatives to traditional incarceration, we might wish to preserve rather than dilute or corrode the time-honored distinctions between private and public realms. In Robert Frost's poem "The Hired Hand," we read:

> Home is the place that when you have to go there, they
> have to take you in.

The proliferation of EM programs may require that we update the poet as follows:

> In the late twentieth century, home is the place that when
> you want to leave there, they have to keep you in.

8. *The fallacy of the 100% accurate or fail-safe system.* The glamour surrounding sophisticated electronic technology may lead the uncritical to assume that its results are invariably reliable. In their enthusiasm vendors and program entrepreneurs may fail to acknowledge the technology's weaknesses. As an assessment of EM in Florida put it "the technology has proven both reliable and unreliable" (Papy and Nimer) 191. It may break or fail to work under certain conditions. The technology is also applied and interpreted by humans, with the possibility for errors and corruption.

There are many examples of technical failures: transmissions can be blocked or distorted by environmental conditions such as lightning, proximity to an FM radio station, the metal in mylar wallpaper and trailer walls, some house construction materials, and water in a waterbed or bathtub (with some early versions participants even got electrical shocks while bathing). Poor telephone lines, wiring and equipment may transmit signals that cannot be accurately read. Power, telephone and computer failures may make it appear that a violation has occurred when it hasn't, or the reverse. The quality of telephone service required for confidence in the voice verification system is not available in many places. Those monitoring the system to report violations can be compromised and with private contractors there may be less accountability than in the public sector. Of course in the adversarial context many participants will seek ways to neutralize the system and to exploit its ambiguities (at least four in ten do so according to research by Bauman and Mendelsohn 1990).

9. *The fallacy of the sure shot.* This fallacy assumes that technically based social interventions will reach their intended target with laser-like precision—the public policy equivalent of a surgical strike. There will be no impact on adjacent or unintended targets. Key participants are seen to be cooperative and of good will and to

agree on the goal—rather than passively resisting or adhering to established customs and business-as-usual.

This fallacy encompasses "net widening" in the sense that programs may reach their intended target group and beyond. But it also includes the many criminal justice programs in which displacement occurs instead. Research on intermediate sanctions has frequently found that the intended target group is bypassed.

Highly independent judges may apply intermediate sanctions to an offender pool not envisioned by program planners. Judges may reduce their vulnerability by sentencing less risky clients to EM, even when the program is intended as an alternative to incarceration for more serious offenders. Morris and Tonry (1990) in a study of intermediate sanctions report, "when an intermediate choice is offered, it will tend to be filled more by those previously treated more leniently than by those previously treated more severely."

It is possible that the announced target is not the intended target. Intensive supervision programs such as EM are anxious to present themselves as directed at high-risk, prison bound offenders, since the expected savings of prison bed space and related expenses would otherwise not ensue. Hence, the publicized target group is variously described as "serious", "dangerous", and "recidivist".

However, the fine-print of selection criteria for program participants often incorporates exceptions and exclusions which minimize the possibility that truly serious offenders will participate. This lessens the stakes for administrators who naturally wish to decrease their exposure. Clear and Hardyman (1990) offer examples of the recruitment of comparatively low risk offenders for what was promoted as an intensive program aimed at high-risk offenders.

Implementing the program with the original target group may come to be seen as practically or politically too difficult. Palumo et. al. (1990) report that in Arizona, where the legislature set definite criteria for participation in the EM program, the board of Pardons and Parole (BPP) was reluctant to utilize them, waiting five months to place the first inmate in the program. The BPP eventually came to substitute their own criteria—applying EM only to low-risk offenders who would ordinarily have received regular supervision, thereby undermining the intended cost-savings. Clear and Hardyman (1990) report on sites that had to repeatedly alter their eligibility requirements when insufficient referrals threatened the visibility of the programs.

Rather than the ready-aim-fire model of the traditional bureaucracy some of the initial experience with EM suggests that Peter Drucker's ready-fire-aim model may be more appropriate. One fires first and whatever is hit becomes the target.

10. The fallacy of assuming that if a critic questions the means, he or she must be opposed to the ends. This fallacy involves an attempt by technology's cheerleaders to meet any criticism of their means with the claim that the critics are really soft on, or opposed to, the end—in this case, alternatives to incarceration or enhanced forms of probation. This insinuation of bad faith is often a cheap shot. Nevertheless, critics have an obligation to acknowledge the decent intentions and real problems often associated with attempts at innovation.

And we do. To understand that policy experiments are often riddled with hidden, contradictory, ironic, and sometimes perverse consequences is not to suggest that they are inevitably doomed or necessarily directed toward the wrong goals. Awareness of technofallacies can sensitize policy makers to potential pitfalls, but it need not paralyze them. That which we distort through our eagerness to innovate and our infatuation with technical progress, we can correct in part through a growing policy "wisdom," sound program design, and sensitive and intelligent management.

We approach this topic not as Luddites who want to ban new technology, but in a spirit of responsible conservatism, which asks us to pause in the face of any proposed change and to consider its fit within the agency, the appropriateness of its possible latent agenda, alternative development scenarios, the costs of doing nothing, and its likely short- and long-range unintended consequences.

In Kafka's short story *The Penal Colony*, a correctional officer and his superior develop a complicated new machine capable of inflicting horrible mortal punishment on inmates. In the end, the officer who argued so proudly for the new technology is horrifically consumed by it. We don't suggest that anything like this will necessarily happen in corrections, but it is clear that innovations which are not thought out carefully and offered honestly and modestly run the risk of doing great damage. So far we have seen little theoretical or empirical support to justify the rush to EM.

REFERENCES

Andrews, D.A. and J.J. Kiessling (1980) "Program Structure and Effective Correctional Practice: A Summary of the CaVIC Research." In R.R. Ross and P.

Gendreau (eds.), *Effective Correctional Treatment*. Toronto: Butterworth, pp. 441-63.

Andrews, D.A., J.J. Kiessling, D. Robinson, and S. Mickus (1986) "The Risk Principle of Case Classification: An Outcome Evaluation with Adult Probationers." *Canadian Journal of Criminology*. 28:377-96.

Andrews, D.A., Ivan Zinger, Robert D. Hoge, James Bonta, Paul Gendreau, and Francis T. Cullen (1990) "A Clinically Relevant and Psychologically Informed Meta-analysis." *Criminology* 28:369-97.

American Correctional Association (ACA) (1989) *Emerging Technologies and Community Corrections*. Laurel, MD.

Baumer, Terry L. and Robert I. Mendelsohn (1990) *The Electronic Monitoring of Non-Violent Convicting Felons: An Experiment in Home Detention*. Washington, DC: National Institute of Justice.

Bryne, James M. (1990) "The Future of Probation Supervision and New Intermediate Sanctions." *Crime and Delinquency* 36:6-41.

Clear, Todd R., Suzanne Flynn, and Carol Shapiro (1987) "Intensive Supervision in Probation: A Comparison of Three Projects." In B. McCarthy (ed.), *Intermediate Punishments: Intensive Supervision, Home Confinement, and Electronic Surveillance*. Monsey, NY: Willow Tree Press, pp. 31-50.

Clear, Todd R. and Kenneth W. Gallagher (1985). "Probation and Parole Supervision: A Review of Current Classification Practices." *Crime and Delinquency* 31:423-44.

Clear, Todd R. and Patricia Hardyman (1990) "The New Intensive Supervision Movement." *Crime and Delinquency* 36:42-60.

Cohen, Stanley (1985) *Visions of Social Control*. Cambridge Engl: Polity.

Finckenauer, James O. (1982) *Sacred Straight and the Panacea Phenomenon*. Englewood Cliffs, NJ: Prentice-Hall.

Irwin, Billie (1990) "Old and New Tools for the Modern Probation Officer." *Crime and Delinquency* 36:61-74.

Lempert, Richard D. and Christy A. Visher, eds. (1987) "Randomized Field Experiments in Criminal Justice Agencies: A Summary of Workshop Proceedings." Washington, DC: National Research Council, Commission on Research on Law Enforcement and the Administration of Justice.

Marx, Gary T. (1981) "Ironies of Social Control: Authorities as Contributors to Deviance through Escalation, Nonenforcement and Covert Facilitation." *Social Problems* 28:222-46.

_____ (1988) *Undercover: Police Surveillance in America*. Berkeley: University of California Press.

_____ (1989) "Privacy and the Home: The King Doesn't Have to Enter Your Cottage to Invade Your Privacy." *Impact Assessment Bulletin* 7(1):31-59.

_____ (1990) "Privacy and Technology." *World & I* 3:523-541 (Sept.).

_____ (forthcoming) *Windows into the Soul: Surveillance and Society in an Age of High Technology*. Book based on the Jensen Lecture delivered to the American Sociological Association meetings, Cincinnati, 1991.

Merton, R. (1957) *Social Theory and Social Structure*. Glencoe, IL: Free Pres.

Palumbo, Dennis J., Mary Clifford, and Zoann Snyder-Joy (1990) "From Net Widening to Intermediate Sanctions: The Transformation of Alternatives to Incarceration from Malevolence to Benevolence." Prepared for delivery at the meetings of the American Criminological Association, Baltimore.

Papy, Joseph and Richard Nimer (1991) "Electronic Monitoring in Florida." *Federal Probation* 31-33.

Petersilia, Joan M. (1987) *Expanding Options for Criminal Sentencing*. Santa Monica: RAND.

_____ (1990) "Officials Aim to Fill the Gap between Probation and Parole." *Criminal Justice Newsletter*, Sept. 17, pp. 2-3.

Petersilia, Joan M. and Susan Turner (1990) "Comparing Intensive and Regular Supervision for High-Risk Probationer: Early Results from an Experiment in California." *Crime and Delinquency* 36:87-111.

Reinecke, Ian (1982) *Electronic Illusions*. New York: Penguin.

Schmidt, Annesley K. (1989) "Electronic Monitoring of Offenders Increases." *NIJ Reports* no. 212 (Jan/Feb).

Seiber, S. (1982) *Fatal Remedies*. New York: Plenum.

Thompson, J.D. (1967) *Organizations in Action*. New York: McGraw-Hill.

414   ELECTRONIC MONITORING

Tonry, Michael and Norval Morris (1990) *Between Prison and Probation*. New
    York: Oxford University Press.
Tonry, Michael and Richard Will (1990) *Intermediate Sanctions*. Washington, DC:
    Report to National Institute of Justice.
U.S. Department of Justice (1990) *Survey of Intermediate Sanctions*. Washington,
    DC: Dept. of Justice.

[20]

News Media, Popular Culture and the Electronic Monitoring of Offenders in England and Wales

MIKE NELLIS

Senior Lecturer in Criminal Justice Studies, University of Birmingham

Abstract: On 10 January 2002, I was asked to provide a little expert comment on electronic monitoring (EM) on BBC Radio Birmingham's 'Late Show', the pretext being a newspaper report earlier that day indicating that Scotland was soon to roll out a national EM programme. It was clear when I met her that the show's host had no idea that electronic monitoring had already been underway in England and Wales for several years. Her immediate reaction to the idea of it was hostile: being sentenced to serve time in one's own living room hardly seemed like punishment. Several callers to the show were invited to comment on it in these terms, and most were adamant that it was obviously no substitute for imprisonment. The experience was, for me, indicative (in microcosm) of the generally poor quality of media debate about EM in England and Wales, and suggested that EM has simply not registered with the public as the tough punishment that its supporters hoped and its opponents feared it would be. This article is a preliminary attempt to map the nature and level of awareness that has been shown about EM in various manifestations of popular culture – the press, TV, cinema and literature – and to tentatively suggest why it has taken the forms that it has. The article understands popular culture primarily as a resource for interpreting and bestowing meaning upon EM but also, more cursorily, considers it as an aspect of the milieu in which creative technological developments are conceived.

England and Wales first experimented with the electronic monitoring of offenders (EM) in 1989/90, renewed interest in it the mid-1990s, developed it country-wide in the late-1990s and now uses it on a larger proportion of its offenders than any other country – (whilst also having one of the highest prison populations in Europe). Thus far, it has been used to enforce home confinement. The present technology consists of a small transmitter fitted to the offender's ankle which, so long as the offender remains close to a signalling device installed in his home, can be monitored by a computer which may be hundreds of miles away. Voice recognition technology has also been experimented with in England, and in the USA experiments have been conducted to track the movements of convicted offenders using orbiting satellites; this latter technology is not yet commercially viable, although it is anticipated that it will become so (Renzema 1998). The capacity to track, rather than the possibly 'interim' measure of home confinement, has long been the ideal of Tom Stacey's Offender Tag Association (OTA), the body which first promoted the technology in Britain, and which has survived to see its once derided ideas become significant realities in criminal justice (Nellis 2001).

EM in England is used in four ways. Firstly, as a community penalty – curfew orders, which were introduced experimentally in three areas in 1996, and rolled out nationally in December 1999. These were little used by sentencers – 4,693 had been made by November 2000. Secondly, as a means of early release from prison – Home Detention Curfew (HDC), introduced in January 1999. It is the extensive use of HDC – 34,900 offenders have been released on it (*NAPO News,* June 2001, p. 2) – that has made England such a proportionately high user of tagging. Both curfew orders and HDC can be used on their own, or in conjunction with support from probation officers. Thirdly, EM was made integral to the Intensive Supervision and Surveillance Programmes, a new initiative for young offenders launched in February 2001. Fourthly, young offenders who would otherwise be remanded in custody were tagged from April 2002. Other uses have been foreshadowed in the Criminal Justice and Court Services Act 2000, and may develop in future. A growing body of technical data and criminological analysis is available to those who are professionally, politically and commercially interested in these developments (see Whitfield 2001 for a valuable summary).

But how well informed is the English public – or, more accurately, publics – about this new development in crime control and on what cultural resources are they drawing to make sense of it? One should not assume that, if they know about EM at all, they acquire knowledge only from official sources, as mediated by the press, and radio and TV news programmes – and certainly not from academic criminology. Some professional commentators have expressed fears that EM is an unwelcome Orwellian development in criminal justice (Ball and Lilly 1988; McCulloch 1997), others that it is a gimmicky and trivial technology of limited utility (Fletcher 1997), but does it register with the various publics in either of these ways – or as something different? What moods might be stimulated by popular representations of EM – enthusiasm, reassurance, scepticism, indifference, paranoia? – and for what reasons?[1]

In an important article on surveillance, Gary Marx (1995) mapped the ways in which CCTV, bugging and tagging devices, and databanks generally have been represented in a variety of cultural forms, popular songs, cartoons, comic books, jokes, advertisements and visual art. He is not particularly concerned with EM, although he reminds us in passing that modern developments in this field were inspired by a Spiderman comic in 1981. He concludes that there are images and tropes of both a protective and a threatening nature, guardian angels as well as Big Brothers, and a range of associated emotional tones: of enthusiasm, complacency, despondency and alarm. Overall, he offers 'thick description' of the cultural resources which citizens might use, intermittently and haphazardly (unless they had studied the subject as exhaustively as he has) to learn about, and to develop and bestow meaning on actual developments in surveillance. His view that representations of surveillance in the journalistic, literary and artistic fields serve both to legitimate and delegitimate it simultaneously, is wholly persuasive, and is of relevance to the policy makers and commercial organisations who are seeking support to install EM in the criminal justice systems of contemporary societies.

This article has more limited ambitions than Marx, although it is written in a similar spirit. It is more narrowly focused, on EM rather than surveillance generally, and whilst recognising the range of popular cultural forms which could be drawn on, it concentrates only on representation in newspapers, on television (in various formats), in cinema and in popular literature. It accepts (without elaboration, for reasons of space) Bourdieu's (1998, p. 74) broad premise that 'the journalistic field exercises [some] power over other fields of cultural production' (defining realities, shaping agendas, mediating reception) and Wykes's (2001, p. 6) narrower premise that, in Britain at least, 'the press dictates what is to be news' in other 'news media' (TV and radio[2]). It modestly heeds Braithwaite's (2000, p. 63) advice to 'sweep across the disciplines to become an educated scholar of the new regulation', in which EM is of growing significance. It makes a sharper distinction between actual and imaginary developments than does Marx, concentrating mostly, but not completely, on the former. Coverage is restricted to England and Wales, whilst drawing inevitably on the American films and novels which are available here. It tentatively goes beyond Marx by drawing on Bender's (1987) analysis of the literary and artistic roots of 'the penitentiary idea', to raise preliminary questions about the role of popular culture in *generating* the mentalities from which new forms of punishment (such as tagging) can emerge, rather than simply *interpreting* them.

Public Knowledge of Electronic Monitoring

A survey of public awareness of and attitudes towards electronically monitored curfew orders (not HDC), based on interviews with a nationally representative sample of 1,850 people in England and Wales, was commissioned by On Guard Plus and undertaken in November 1999 (Taylor *et al.* 1999). This showed that spontaneous awareness of tagging stood at 19%, although when the phenomenon was explained to them, this increased to 89%. It was still one of the least known community penalties, community service orders being by far the best known. There were age differences in awareness but no gender differences; people in the 25 to 34 years age bracket were the most likely to know of it (24%), those aged over 65 years least likely (13%). Owner occupiers were marginally more likely to have heard of it than tenants. People living in two of the areas where the trials took place – East Anglia and the North West, but also in the South East, were all more likely to be aware of it (above 93%) than people in Greater London, (73%) where no trials had taken place since 1989/90.

Once the nature of curfew tagging had been explained, the respondents were asked to score (on a 1 to 10 scale ranging from strongly disagree, through agree, to strongly agree) the suitability of electronic tagging for certain types of offender and certain types of offence. In essence, the majority of respondents were 'reasonably well disposed' (scores of 6 and 7) towards tagging for unemployed or full- time education offenders, offenders aged

3

under 16 years, persistent offenders and female offenders with children. There was more scepticism about using it with mentally ill offenders, although there was a strong belief that it could (and presumably should?) be used in conjunction with other measures. Scores of between 5 and 7 were given for its use with the following crimes: burglary, harassment, shoplifting, sex offences, drug dealing, violence and assault, public order, drunk driving and deception and theft. Small percentages from a minority of respondents (n = 284) also volunteered the view that it could also be used in certain cases of homicide (7%) and rape (6%), and on child abusers (16%), car thieves (13%) and perpetrators of criminal damage (7%). While there is room for doubt about the adequacy of the methodology used in the survey – were respondents really able to imagine how tagging might punish or control particular types of offender when its duration could not exceed six months? – it seems clear that respondents did accept that the tag had the potential to exert effective control; it was expressly not dismissed out of hand.

The sample appear not to have been asked to identify reservations or problems with tagging, nor to have volunteered any. Nor were they asked to indicate what the source of their information was, other than the pollster themselves. Spontaneous awareness of only 19%, at the end of a year in which there had been considerable development of tagging, suggest that it had not registered all that strongly in public consciousness. It might reasonably be assumed, given the higher levels of awareness in two of the areas where tagging took place, that local media coverage – or national media coverage of local issues – was an important, if not unique, source of information. Specific studies might validate this, but in their absence the next section offers a preliminary mapping of the themes and issues surrounding EM that appeared in the English press between 1995 and early 2002.

Press Coverage of Electronic Monitoring

News analysis can be a methodologically complex matter (Wykes 2001). What follows does not claim any sophistication, or to be the final word. It distinguishes between broadsheet and tabloid papers (broadly middle class and working class oriented respectively), and identifies recurrent themes and issues in the reporting of electronic monitoring. Both types of paper seem to have relied on Home Office press releases; the same stories tend to be covered in several papers simultaneously, citing the same facts and statistics (or slight variations), quoting the same sources, but sometimes in a tone that reflects the distinctive ethos of each paper. Attentive readers of the broadsheets could, over time have compiled a fairly accurate if superficial account of how tagging policy has evolved, the basic operating procedure, and the costs of the various schemes and the numbers involved. Richard Ford in *The Times*, Alan Travis in *The Guardian* and Jason Bennetto in *The Independent* have shown a consistent and mostly fair-minded interest in it, and their views have sometimes been augmented by feature articles commissioned (or placed) to advance a particular position.

The English press have contributed to the public awareness of EM from the outset; Aldridge (1994, p. 127) notes a 'bifurcation in [its] press treatment' in

4

1989, within the context of very limited interest at that time. Nonetheless, via the press, the very terms 'the tag' and 'tagging' became the commonest colloquial descriptions of both the overall sentence and the technology, before any schemes were implemented. This reflects the preferred terminology of the Offender Tag Association (OTA), established in 1982 and responsible for the earliest publicity about EM in England, and whose founder, Tom Stacey, was himself a former *Sunday Times* journalist (and novelist). (The terms 'tag' and 'tagging' are not ubiquitous internationally. In the USA the innovation has been referred to more formally, by both press and practitioners, as house arrest, home detention, home confinement, home incarceration, Electronically Monitored Home Confinement (EMHC) and Electronic Monitoring Programme (EMP), though it is known colloquially as 'tethering' in the state of Michigan (Mark Renzema, personal communication, 23 March 2002) and to some American offenders as being 'on the box'.)

The American origins of EM has been a significant theme in the English press, indeed more reference has been made to Judge Jack Love's inspiration by a Spiderman comic, (for example, in *The Guardian*, 13 November 1997) (Fox 1987) than to the lobbying role of the OTA. *The Independent* (15 May 1994) had earlier published two frames from the particular comic in an article critical of tagging both because of its comic book origins and because it was perceived as an alien American development. Hostility to it as an American practice was also evident in an article headlined 'Tagging delay as US equipment fails' (*The Independent*, 1 June 1995). *The Guardian* (7 December 1995) commented disparagingly that 'only 17 US-style tagging orders have been made during the first five months of the nine month trials, three of which have broken down'. Later, when the Home Office first announced the use of curfew orders for fine defaulters it referred to 'the further extension of American-style tagging experiments' (*The Guardian*, 1 August 1996).

In 1995, from whence the present expansion of EM in England has occurred, the press were acutely conscious that it had been tried once before, and found wanting. Their stance was sceptical. *The Times* (7 March 1995) referred to Michael Howard 'reviving' tagging and reminded readers that in the original experiment in 1989/90 'the equipment broke down regularly and 29 (out of 50) offenders violated their curfew, or were charged with a new offence'. *The Daily Telegraph* (7 March 1995) noted that it had been 'dropped by Mr. Kenneth Clarke when he was Home Secretary, only to be resurrected by Mr. Howard'. *The Independent* (1 June 1995) referred to tagging as 'a technique that ended in disaster when it was last used in Britain'. *The Daily Mail* (7 March 1995) headlined an article 'Whitehall rethink on technology branded a failure'. Only *The Daily Express*, a very strong supporter of the Conservative government, was upbeat about the prospect of its reintroduction:

The electronic tagging of young thugs was first tried five years ago, and failed. But the failure was in the technology not in the idea. Now with improved technology, the idea is back, bringing with it a real prospect of effectively combating crime. . . . electronic tagging was always too good an idea to cast aside just because the know-how was lacking. And Home Secretary Michael Howard was applauded for his determination to see it kept alive and kicking. (*The Daily Express*, 30 December 1994)

5

Looked at overall, there has been a tendency in the press to make premature estimates of the likely scale of its development, and some of what has appeared has been mistaken or misleading. Journalists must bear some responsibility for this, but certainly not all, for they have been reliant on official press releases and leaked internal Home Office documents which may themselves have been inconsistent over time. One such document, circulating in the period immediately before reintroduction in 1995, was summarised thus by Alan Travis in *The Guardian*:

For the first time in the history of British criminal justice, private security companies are to be given powers to prosecute offenders as well as to organise and supervise their sentences. The departure is part of the Government's plans for the electronic tagging of offenders, which the Home Office believes will eventually become the principal community sentence with up to 20,000 orders imposed a year. (22 September 1994)

These powers never were invested in the private security companies, and the Home Office has never *explicitly and publicly* said that it envisaged electronic monitoring as the 'principal community sentence'. It is nonetheless interesting to know (unless there is an element of journalistic licence here) that these possibilities were once being entertained in the Home Office. Some estimates of the likely scale of its use have certainly been ridiculously high. 'At its peak', wrote *The Daily Telegraph* of curfew orders (7 March 1995) 'ministers believe the technology will be able to monitor up to 250,000 people', without indicating when the peak was expected to occur, and without explaining that the figure 250,000 exceeds the total of all offenders on community supervision in any given year. Other forms of misrepresentation include a *Daily Express* editorial (30 December 1994) which stated that the monitoring centres for tagging would be located 'at local police stations'. This creates a subtle symbolic link between tagging and policing (as opposed to probation), and quite possibly trades on the public knowledge that CCTV is sometimes monitored from police stations, but it is factually inaccurate; monitoring stations are invariably located in the service providers or monitoring companies' offices. Even *The Guardian* (18 August 1996) is not immune. A definitively headlined article – 'sex offenders face tagging' – made clear in the small print that the government's proposal was *a possibility* not an actuality. Ambiguous references to 'tracking' in this same article meant placement on the sex offenders' register, rather than tracking in the electronic sense – monitoring the movement, rather than simply the fixed location, of the offender.

Some reporting of EM has been openly hostile. Nick Cohen, an investigative journalist with a regular *Observer* column, has been the most hostile. He exposed the failings of the first trial in great detail, and also (a rarity in England) some of the sharp practices associated with its development in America (*The Independent*, 15 September 1994). Soon after the second English trial began he dismissed tagging as an 'expensive fiasco', noting that in the first two weeks of its availability magistrates made not a single curfew order (*The Independent*, 16 July 1995). Later, he used the case of a group of three Manchester women, with children, who were tagged rather than imprisoned for violent offences, but with curfew restrictions (8am to 1pm) which deliberately prevented them from maintaining their employment as nightclub dancers (*The Independent*, 7 April 1996). This was one of the few tagging stories about women offenders, of whom far fewer have been tagged compared to men, and it showed how EM could be destructive of employment, rather than supportive of it. The women appeared to have good grounds for an appeal against sentence, but that story was not followed up: the negative impression of tagging therefore lingers.

Many press reports draw, in brief, on expert opinion. Harry Fletcher, of the National Association of Probation Officers (NAPO), remains by far the most commonly quoted opponent of EM *in all press reports* (and some of Nick Cohen's stories appear to have originated with him). His pithy faultfinding with tagging – he acknowledges no advantages – have undoubtedly irritated the Home Office and the monitoring companies.[3] His tone has rarely altered over the years, whereas that of other expert voices, notably Paul Cavadino of the Penal Affairs Consortium (see letters, *The Guardian*, 7 March 1995) and Mary Honeyball of the Association of Chief Officers of Probation (ACOP), who were once as hostile, has become more muted. Honeyball initially gave expression to ACOP's scepticism, dampening government enthusiasm for a 1995 retrial with the claim that 'tagging has a rather inglorious history, and this may be the start of another chapter. We know that it is being scaled down in the United States because of the unreliability of the equipment' (quoted in *The Guardian*, 1 June 1995). Two years later she was conceding that 'tagging cannot be uninvented. Now the technology is proved to work, the task now is to find the best way of using it for public protection' (quoted in *The Guardian*, 31 January 1997).

Most of the hostile press comment on EM has come from left-leaning individuals and newspapers. Ironically, however, the single worst-case publicity that it received came, in a short-lived burst, from the right. Under devastating headlines 'Tagging puts public at risk', '"Public endangered" by tagging scheme' and 'Lag tag shock', *The Yorkshire Post*, *The Daily Telegraph* and *The Daily Star* respectively (all on 4 March 2000), reported the then Shadow Home Secretary, Anne Widdecombe's, discovery that of the 17,871 prisoners released so far on HDC, 185 had 'been charged with offences committed while wearing tags, including two rapes' (*The Daily Telegraph*)[4]. Rather than emphasise the 95% success rate of the HDC scheme, Widdecombe highlighted its failings, and whilst giving enough information to let readers make independent judgments, *The Daily Telegraph* gave her a platform. Widdecombe's real target was the principle of early release, which she deployed to portray New Labour, in time honoured Conservative fashion, as soft on crime, but a clear impression was nonetheless given that tagged offenders were offending with impunity. Other newspapers picked up the story, including *The Daily Mail* (4 March 2000 under the headline 'Tagged Crimewave') and *The Times* (4 March 2000), although there were interesting variations in the statistical detail. The story was quickly seen as cynical opportunism on Widdecombe's part and petered out within a few days. In a letter to *The Daily Telegraph* (30 March 2000) Tom Stacey warned that Widdecombe 'was rubbishing an essentially Conservative political initiative'.

7

There has been a mix of human interest and issue-based stories about tagging in both the tabloids and the broadsheets, and to the average, casual reader the more personalised stories probably convey the most vivid and memorable understanding of tagging's strengths and weaknesses. The first person to be given a curfew order, Clive Barratt, age 29, from Kings Lynn, Norfolk was arrested on suspicion of theft after only a fortnight. Under the ambiguous headline 'Alarm bells ring as first "tagged" offender is arrested again' *The Guardian* (19 August 1995) described how the Home Office undertook damage limitation in this case: 'officials admitted disappointment at Mr. Barratt's behaviour, [but] said the fact his breach was spotted was a sign that the scheme worked'. Not all human interest stories are negative. *The Kettering Evening Standard* (30 March 2000) ran a story (without distinguishing curfew order or HDC) under the headline 'Man had perfect alibi: electronic tag proved he was innocent' describing how a suspected car vandal was incriminated by a mendacious witness, but exonerated when his presence at home at the alleged time of the offence was verified by the monitoring company. Positive accounts about HDC also appeared in *Time Out* (24 October 1999) and *The Big Issue* (8–14 March 1999), based on interviews with offenders who were clearly appreciative of early release, and happy to see the irksome restrictions of the tag as a lesser evil than prison. Steve Taylor (2000) and Jim Allen (2000) appear to have written the first 'first person' accounts of tagging, both in *The Guardian*, one satirical, the other serious. The most humorous of tagging stories – and embarrassing for the monitoring company involved, although it attracted no coverage in major newspapers – concerned a released prisoner whose easily unscrewed artificial leg was unknowingly tagged, allowing him to leave home at will (*Birmingham Metro*, 4 July 2000).

Occasionally, the human interest stories have focused on celebrities and, arguably, gossip about these particular cases contributes disproportionately, if unevenly, to public awareness. It is at least conceivable that the relatively widespread name recognition of community service (attested to in the On Guard Plus survey mentioned earlier), owes something to the publicity given in recent years to footballers Eric Cantona and Vinnie Jones, and boxer Chris Eubank who received CSOs for offences of violence. Thus far only very minor celebrities have been tagged. Gary Croft, a professional footballer (Ipswich Town) imprisoned for driving while disqualified and perverting the course of justice, was released on HDC, although the team manager vainly tried to persuade the authorities to remove the tag during matches (*The Times*, 8 January 2000; *The Daily Mail*, 11 January 2000). John Alford, a TV actor, jailed for supplying drugs, received some publicity, but not in all major newspapers. Press coverage of the release of a once high-profile politician, Jonathan Aitken, in January 2000, made repeated reference to the fact that he was tagged. Rather than emphasising the 'privilege' of early release, it implicitly depicted tagging as a gratuitously punitive measure – as perhaps it is for many offenders, who, like Aitken, are not realistically at risk of immediate post-release offending. In his case, the tagging had a shaming element, which added to his ignominy (see *The Guardian*, 8 January 2002).

8

It is perhaps ironic that the most concerted attempt to date, (in February/March 2002) by the Home Office to portray tagging as a tough and controlling 'penalty' occurred in relation to its proposed introduction as an adjunct to a remand on bail for young offenders, which was intended to reduce repeat offending by bailees. This coincided with an expected announcement on the expansion of the HDC scheme, in respect of which the Home Secretary, David Blunkett, was determined to face down critics who claimed that it had jeopardised public safety. Both initiatives were connected to steep rises in custodial populations, and were clearly seen by the press, sometimes cynically, sometimes neutrally, as attempts to ameliorate this. Rather unfortunately, they also coincided with a short and intense media campaign in the more right-wing newspapers, (partly orchestrated by the police to pressure the Home Office for more resources and to resist unwelcome reorganisation) to heighten awareness of rising violent crime throughout Britain. Against this background, tagging for juveniles was easily made to look gimmicky and ineffectual, and its credibility was further damaged by police doubts about its likely effectiveness with recalcitrant bailees. Typical headlines were 'Teenage thugs will ignore tag plan, say police' (*The Yorkshire Post*); 'Police attack Blunkett scheme to tag muggers' (*The Independent*), both on 27 February 2002. The extension of HDC fared little better, with both a *Sunday Times* columnist (Marrin 2002) and *The Sunday Telegraph* (10 March 2002) portraying it as an unacceptable risk to the public. Lumping together both issues, a columnist (and former Conservative MP) (Mellor 2002) in one of the more notorious tabloids, argued along with other papers, including *The Daily Express* (27 April 2002), that tagging would only be viable if backed up by the threat of prison for the slightest infraction. This negative coverage did appear to have an effect in respect of the youth bail tagging; within a month, seemingly to appease critics in the police, the Home Secretary announced increased use of custodial remands, with tagging barely mentioned. The extension of the HDC scheme proved more robust, and survived the press onslaught.

Electronic Tagging and American Movies

Electronic monitoring has been shown in at least three American movies, which have also been released in Britain (as films and home videos). All three portray the tagging of ethnic minority men – two African-Americans, one Hispanic – and are centrally concerned with questions of crime and race. Two of the films 'One Eight Seven' (1994, d. Kevin Reynolds) and 'He Got Game' (1998, d. Spike Lee) fall midway between mainstream and independent cinema, but both had major Black stars (Samuel Jackson and Denzel Washington respectively, without whose presence they may never have achieved widespread distribution, or even been made). Because of Spike Lee's standing as a significant Black intellectual, 'He Got Game' must be regarded as a film of some cultural importance, which among other things, directs its youthful Black audience towards the view that EM is to be understood as yet another facet of racial oppression. The third film 'First Time Felon' (1998, d. Charles S. Dutton) was made for American television

9

and only released on video in Britain; it is part of a long tradition of 'contemporary-issue' TV movies, inspired in varying degrees by true stories, with which its production company, HBO, is particularly associated. Its view of race in America – and of electronic monitoring – is rather different from Spike Lee's.

EM is neither a central feature nor a major theme in any of these movies; either it is part of the backdrop, or it is simply an episode in the story. Nonetheless, for many people, particularly the young people who comprise contemporary cinema audiences and who rent videos, these images will have been their first sight of EM (unless they have actually been tagged). These cinema images are more realistically contextualised, and probably more vivid, than anything else they might have seen or read about EM, and it would be difficult to believe that they play no part in shaping the perception and understanding of the technology. I will deal with each of the films in turn.

'One Eight Seven' is a sombre account of the failings of the American public education system, dedicated, in a concluding on-screen text, to the one-in-nine teachers who have been assaulted by their pupils. It focuses on a creative and dedicated African-American science teacher, Trevor Garfield (Samuel Jackson), already the victim of an attempted murder by an aggrieved pupil in a New York school, who resumes his chosen career in a poor neighbourhood school in Los Angeles. Most of the teachers are cynical timeservers who struggle, in dilapidated buildings, with an unsupportive Principal, to maintain reasonable order among the mostly insolent and indifferent Hispanic teenagers. Garfield soon encounters 16-year-old Benny Chacon, who, after refusing a simple request, slams his foot on a desktop and proudly displays the electronic signalling device fastened to his ankle. 'I'm already on house arrest', he sneers, ' there's nothing more you can do to me'. Some of Benny's associates – members of the Tagging Crew (graffiti sprayers) – cheer approvingly. Garfield learns that in addition to being subject to EM, Benny is also on probation for violence, and that despite threatening a woman teacher (whom he is probably stalking), attending school had been made a condition of the probation. Neither measure is an adequate curb on his behaviour. This pessimism is affirmed in a later scene when, one evening, Benny and two friends kill a lone youngster who has despoiled some of their graffiti. Even as Benny's anklet bleeps – warning him that his curfew begins in 15 minutes, he explains to his friends – he shoots the fleeing youngster in the back, then stands over him to finish him off. A more telling image of EM's ineffectualness would be hard to imagine. Shortly afterwards, we learn that Benny has breached his probation and gone on the run. To underline the film's dismissive view of EM the discarded anklet is briefly shown being picked up off the street and thrown into a scrap collector's barrow.

'One Eight Seven' – the police code for the offence of murder – is clearly of the view that feral, emotionally disturbed, violent young men are being dealt with too leniently by the criminal justice system and that public schools are wrongly being expected to contain and control them, to the detriment of the education of the few pupils who do want to learn. Prison sentences

10

themselves are deemed too short: we learn in an aside that the New York pupil who had stabbed Garfield only got a couple of years. The absence of moral and practical support for good teachers ultimately breaks Garfield, who, despite his religious faith, turns first to vigilante violence and then, in self-disgust and despair, to suicide. EM, for him, was part of the problem, certainly not the solution to youth crime or to overcrowded prisons.

'He Got Game' is also hostile to EM, but in a quite different way. Jake Shuttlesworth (Denzell Washington), a poor black from Coney Island, New York, is serving the sixth year of a one-to-fifteen sentence in the Attica Correctional Facility for the manslaughter of his wife during a row over the pressure he was putting on their 12-year-old son, Jesus, to practice his baseball – the route, in Jake's view, out of the ghetto. Jesus, now 18, has become a star junior baseball player. Self-interestedly, the state governor wants Jesus to sign up for his old university – and bring in lucrative sponsorship deals. The Attica governor is pressured to release Jake for one week to persuade Jesus to choose the 'right' university, the deal being sweetened by the promise of reduced prison time. Jake is released into the company of two watchful parole officers who, the moment he arrives in his hotel room, remove his handcuffs and fit an electronic device to his ankle, simultaneously plugging a slim black box into his telephone. Nothing is said about how the device functions, except that it is to discourage him from absconding – ' in case you get any smart ideas', his parole officer says, 'we will track you down and when we find you we will shoot you'. Ostensibly, the equipment is that used in home confinement, but the impression is vaguely given that it can track his movements rather than just monitor his presence in the hotel. Jake is also expected to keep in pager contact with his parole officers, although beyond the initial mention this is never alluded to again.

Jake is embarrassed when the anklet is seen by a black shop assistant from whom he buys trainers; he passes it off as a treatment for arthritis, but the black youngster smiles knowingly, explaining that his brother also wears one. At one point, Jesus disparages the device on his father's ankle as a 'Lo-Jack' (the brand name of a car tracking device), and it is this which provides the key to the symbolic role which tagging has in the film. In essence, 'He Got Game' is about the control and commodification of black men by schools, universities, media organisations, corporate sponsors, sports agents and, not least, prisons – 'you are not a free man', the parole officer reminds him, 'your ass is ours . . . you understand that ? . . . do you?'. Although the tag has little direct bearing on the plot it here signifies the full extent of the power which white society, in this instance via the penal system, has over Jake, a hi-tech synthesis of the shackles, brands and bells once used on slaves[5]. Allowing the vague impression that Jake's tag actually tracks his movements (although technically inaccurate) was a form of artistic licence on Lee's part, adding to its potency as a symbol of racial domination[6].

'First Time Felon', also focused on an African-American offender, is more sympathetic to electronic tagging. Set in Chicago, based loosely on the true story of Greg Yance (Omar Epps), a 20-ish street dealer in heroin (albeit one from a respectable if fatherless family), the film largely showcases the Illinois Impact Incarceration Programme. Yance chooses four

11

months in this intensive military-style 'boot camp' (a measure that has replaced probation for first time offenders) over five years without parole in the penitentiary, where he doubts his capacity to survive the lethal gang rivalries. The rigours of boot camp – which are as much rehabilitative as punitive – force Yance to re-consider his future. He resolves to go straight, and returns home, subject to electronic monitoring for four months. To the chagrin of his mother, his drug dealing friends soon call round to recruit him back to the streets. He shows them the anklet:

'Can't go nowhere, can't go 100 feet with that' he explains
'Bust that shit', says his friend, 'by the time they come to fix it it'll be next month'.
'No, dog, I'm going to play it straight'.

Despite its evident effectiveness as a constraint on Yance, the tag is not portrayed as an unmitigated good. His mother argues with the parole officer that four months permanent house arrest is unfair and counterproductive, preventing Yance from attending job interviews and visiting the library. She secures some two hour breaks for him, but it is within those breaks, when he is repeatedly refused work because of his record, as well as being tempted to resume lucrative drug dealing, that his problems intensify. The tag is shown being removed – 'feels lighter', Yance says, shaking his leg – but his continual rejection by prospective employers, the derision of his former girlfriend (who mocks his lack of money), and the assassination of an old associate by a rival gang push him to consider suicide. He resists, and a concluding onscreen note informs us that after five months the real Yance did find work and eventually became a youth worker. The film as a whole, however, avoids cheap triumphalism, tempering its initial view of boot camps and electronic monitoring as effective punishments, by questioning whether their impact on young black people can reasonably be sustained after release unless entrenched racism is also addressed, and unless ex-inmates are helped to find satisfying work.

Electronic Tagging on English Television

The various types of television programme – drama, light entertainment, news bulletins, documentaries and films – are also potential sources of information about EM, the meaning of which may vary according to the type of programme it appears in, and the type of story being told. Although claims must be tentative, because a comprehensive knowledge of everything on TV, and of who watches what and when, even in one country, is increasingly impossible, EM appears to have figured very little, thus far. Key developments, such as the start of the trials in 1995, have been covered briefly in prime time news bulletins, and references have been made to it in documentaries concerned with broader penal issues. No single TV documentary has been devoted to it. Drama seems barely to have touched on tagging – and comedy, perhaps surprisingly, given the ubiquity of living-room based sit-coms – has, as yet, seen no potential in it. It is difficult to ascertain film scheduling on the multiplicity of cable and satellite channels, but 'One Eight Seven' is the only one of the American movies mentioned above to have been shown prime time on a major terrestrial channel in Britain. In this section, the contribution of five programmes to public awareness and understanding of EM will be appraised.

Appropriately enough for something deemed futuristic, a device called 'the Sobrietor', which is used to enforce a prohibition on alcohol consumption by home-confined offenders in Denver, Colorado, was featured on 'Tomorrows World' (BBC 1, 25 April 2001), an authoritative, early evening 'magazine' series highlighting developments in science and technology. The eight-minute item was introduced as follows by the two presenters:

Crime and punishment. Thanks to electronic monitoring it may not be the slam of a cell door that marks the start of a sentence, it could be your own front door closing. It might sound a lot more comfortable that way, but electronic jailers are getting tougher every day. . . . The next generation of devices will be able to monitor not only where you are but what you do.

The existing form of EM, using a close-up of an anklet being fitted, was briefly outlined, followed by an explanation of the way in which the Sobrietor augmented this, using breathalyser and voice recognition technology – the latter guaranteeing that someone else does not substitute for the offender before the test. An American probation officer extolled the virtues of EM in general – 'it creates a jail setting in their home' – and the Sobrietor in particular for drink-driving offenders, for whom imprisonment would mean loss of employment. An anonymous offender, monitored by the Sobrietor, likened the experience of being phoned three to five times daily by a computer demanding a breath test to the intrusiveness of 'Big Brother. . . . When the system was first set up in my home it never felt like I was alone'. Nonetheless, he preferred it to six months in prison, and welcomed retaining his job, despite also having to pay for the device's installation in his home. The presenters concluded cheerily:

This could be the future of doing time. . . . There are obviously huge financial benefits to an electronic monitoring system like this. The one in Denver has already paid for itself.

Among British TV drama series, only 'Bad Girls', first televised in May 1999, has made use of EM. Set in a women's prison, the rather comically-named HMP Larkhall, the series does occasionally address serious and realistic issues (Reynolds and McCallum 2001). By the time it had reached its third series in 2001, it had acquired a weekly audience of 8.6 million, and EM figured in the third episode of that series, (3 April 2001). One of the regular characters, Julie, was released on the tag to a halfway house, in order to spend some time with her teenage son. She had been advised to apply for it by a helpful older inmate, but nothing was shown of the application and assessment process; at the start of episode three the governor simply tells Julie that her application has been successful (while her best friend's, who was also hoping for it, has been refused). The impression given was that monitoring was being used to facilitate home leave, rather than early release, and the tag, in fact, was only incidental to the story – an excuse for setting some action outside the prison. The monitoring officer was shown

13

leaving the halfway house after fitting the tag, and Julie, after a close up of her ankle, then briefly explained to the warden how the device worked (as much for the benefit of the TV audience). After this, the tag is never mentioned. There is no sense of Julie's freedom being constrained. The episode ends when she starts to miss her best friend, and kicks up a fuss outside the prison until she is let back in.

Strictly speaking, 'Cyclops' (d. Bharat Nalluri, Channel 4, 28 May 2001) does not belong in this section, because it concerns an imaginary rather than an actual form of electronic tagging. I include it because of the oblique light it seeks to casts on actual developments, of which it is clearly cognisant. A one-off, late night, hour-long play, 'Cyclops' postulated that in the near future high-risk sex offenders would be released on parole, not with external cameras watching their every move, but with a miniature camera and transmitter implanted behind their right eye, relaying everything they see to a supervising probation officer's laptop screen. 'A ball and chain for the 21st century', the probation officer calls it, although the device still relies on trust and personal restraint by the offender [7]. In the play, Carl Gatiss, a camera-fitted rapist who has served six years of a twelve-year sentence, turns his bemused female probation officer into a voyeur, taunting her with his eye-view of sexual encounters, a murder (after which he absconds), and finally the outside of her house, letting her know that he is stalking her, before breaking in. In the ensuing fight, she kills him by stabbing him in the camera-eye with a rather more prosaic item of technology – a handy pair of scissors. The apparent message of this interesting but ultimately unedifying story concerned the naivete of probation officers, the futility of gimmicky technology in dealing with criminals and the ease with which evil men can outwit it. It may also have been suggesting that if the state invades the privacy of offenders with devices like this, offenders may well, in revenge, invade the privacy of their supervisers. Either way, 'Cyclops' was hostile-by-innuendo to the actual forms of EM currently operating, implying, as an alternative response, that atavistic violence – people acting out of instinctive self-preservation – is what works best with rapists.

Unlike the other TV programmes mentioned here, party political broadcasts are specifically intended to influence viewer attitudes in a certain way. The Conservative Party's first such broadcast in the June 2001 election campaign (backed up on radio and by linked billboard posters) sought to damage the Labour government's credibility on law and order. Although not focused on a real individual it palely imitated the infamous advertisement about Willie Horton – a Massachusetts prisoner who committed rape while on home leave – used very effectively by Republicans to discredit a Democratic presidential candidate in 1988. It seemingly derived from Anne Widdecombe's earlier press attack on the HDC/early release scheme. Using actors, it showed a series of uncouth, mean-looking young men leaving prison, patently unreformed, some of whom then rob and assault unsuspecting members of the public, often women (Butler and Kavanagh 2002, p. 151). There was no explicit mention or showing of tagging – it was the *principle and reality* of early release that was targeted – but insofar as there was an intimate connection between the two in this particular policy, this was

14

clearly an indirect criticism of tagging's potential to reduce the use of custody.

'Soaps' – long running drama serials, showing several nights a week, at peak viewing times – are routinely used as vehicles for exploring topical social issues in Britain – sometimes realistically, sometimes not – and ITV's rural-set 'Emmerdale' was the first to feature tagging, shortly after the expansion of HDC had been announced in early 2002. Several months before, a series regular, decent teenager Marc Reynolds, had been given twelve months' custody for his reluctant participation in a car theft that resulted in a fatality. Prison scenes were periodically included in the series, his eligibility for HDC raised appropriately, and in April 2002, he returned home. The fitting of the tag to his ankle was briefly shown, and the nature of the technology and the rules of his curfew explained to him and his mother (10 April 2002). The white, middle-aged, monitoring officer was portrayed as firm-but-fair, redolent of the better prison officers in the custodial scenes. Securicor had in fact asked for the aggressiveness of the officer to be toned down in this scene when they were originally asked to advise on the script (personal communication, Clare Sims, Securicor, 18 March 2002). Mark is accepting of the tag, happy to be out of prison, and determined to go straight, and, because he is basically a good kid 'Emmerdale's' ten million audience were encouraged to see electronic monitoring as a beneficial measure *in his case*, removing him from undoubted bad influences in prison. The question of whether it would be an effective measure with bad kids did not arise.

Electronic Monitoring in a Crime Novel

Writers of crime fiction are, on the whole, a conservative bunch when it comes to new technology. Even now, a lot of the books seem ignorant of the existence of mobile phones and are only just recognising the ubiquity of computers and the Internet. (Marcel Berlins (legal journalist and crime novel reviewer) 2001)

This section is concerned with the literary representation of tagging as an actual development in criminal justice, not with the imaginary forms of tagging envisaged in science fiction, which I will deal with later. To the best of my knowledge, the only crime novel in which electronic monitoring is mentioned is Elmore Leonard's (1992) *Maximum Bob*, the nickname of a tough Florida judge. Leonard is one of the world's best-selling, most prestigious and most respected crime novelists and one critic (Taylor 1997) has discerned 'a great deal of surveillance' in his novels generally `(for example, stake-outs and undercover operations), *which tends, however, to be easily disrupted and evaded*. In *Maximum Bob*, Tommy Vasco, a wealthy, drunken doctor on probation for writing fake prescriptions for drug addicts, is already under house arrest when the story opens. He is only a minor character, and the fact of his being tagged is of no great relevance to the plot, except that the rather affluent home to which he is confined is the venue in which the story's lead villain, Elvin Crowe, newly released from prison, plans revenge on 'Maximum Bob'. The following dialogue between Crowe and

15

Vasco is probably the first reference to electronic monitoring in contemporary crime writing:

Elvin said: 'What's that thing on your ankle, looks like a little radio?'
'It's how they keep track of me'. Dr Tommy was at the counter now, putting more rum in his drink. 'You never saw an anklet?. You wear it, and you can't go no more than a hundred and fifty feet from your telephone. There's a receiver in this thing and a box hooked up to the telephone line, like you have with your cable TV'.
Elvin didn't have cable TV or know what he was talking about, but said 'Yeah?'
'A computer calls my number every now and then and if I am not in the house or close by the computer doesn't get a signal back and it lets them know'.
Elvin had heard of that. 'You're on probation? Shit, so am I. . . . Why don't you take the goddam thing off and set it by the phone?'
'You'd have to break it'. Dr Tommy struck his leg straight out. 'You can, all it has is the strap holding it on. But there's some kind of sensor in there, tells them if it is not on your leg'
'You mean you can't ever leave the house?'
'Only to go to Alcoholics Anonymous, twice a week'. (Leonard 1992, pp. 165–6; see also pp. 250–1)

Tommy Vasco is a minor middle class offender who abides by the conditions of his house arrest, and in that very limited sense (the conspiracy hatched in his house notwithstanding) EM is portrayed in *Maximum Bob* in a positive light. But, didactic as this exchange is, it conveys little or nothing about the implications and significance of EM, nor what it feels like to be subjected to it. The monitoring personnel themselves – and their relationship to other players in criminal justice – never figure. *Maximum Bob* works perfectly well as a story without this – and it is culturally useful that the innovation of EM has at least been acknowledged by a major crime writer – but the fact remains that its depiction here is superficial, and that in the genre as a whole, its presence in the world has been overlooked. How long will this continue? Some elements of the crime writing genre are self-consciously backward looking, some are responsive to actual developments and seek verisimilitude; but on balance, as the use of EM becomes more widespread, it seems likely that it will gradually figure in other crime novels. The form it takes remains to be seen[8].

Crime *genre* writing, of course, segues into modern mainstream literature (P.D. James, John le Carre, J. G. Ballard), and crime and punishment themes have always figured in the Western canon (Dostoevsky, Dickens, Hugo). Writers as diverse as John Cheever (1977) and Irving Welsh (1999) have, respectively, conveyed impressions of imprisonment and policing without ever being categorised specifically as 'crime writers', and all such work becomes a cultural resource for understanding, interpreting, and perhaps even *constituting* the emergent realities of criminal justice. Without losing sight of my main theme – the interpretive role of popular culture – I will here draw on John Bender's (1987) work to consider this latter issue[9]. Bender demonstrates the subtle, shaping influence of 18th century novels and paintings on the structures of feeling that gave rise to 'the penitentiary idea'. If we accept his view that 'fabrications *in narrative* of the power of confinement to shape personality contributed to the process of cultural

16

representation whereby prisons were themselves reconceived and ultimately reinvented' (Bender 1987, p. 1, italics added) we can also reasonably ask what narratives, what processes of cultural representation have been shaping more recent developments in criminal justice (such as tagging), and what may have a bearing on the future. Bender was not specifically concerned with art and literature that self-consciously addressed the future but, as future-consciousness became, throughout the 20th century, ever more deeply embedded in Western time horizons, it seems reasonable in this context to examine the genre – science fiction – that has been most directly concerned with such consciousness.

Imaginary Forms of Electronic Monitoring

I consider that there is a certain particular sense in which the novel enabled the penitentiary by formulating, and thereby giving conscious access to, a real texture of attitudes, a structure of feeling that I call 'the penitentiary idea'. (Bender 1987, p. 5)

Science fiction (sf) has often sought to anticipate the future, or to stimulate insight into the present through future-set stories, and, in the midst of countless works which have explored 'the deliberate use of technology to promote an unworthy quiescence' (Amis 1960, p. 196) criminal justice themes have been commonplace. Quite specifically, 'numerous sf stories have anticipated the use of "electronic tagging", although usually the tags were capable of administering on-the-spot punishment' (Clute and Nichols 1992, p. 276) – and, it should be added, have been of the tracking rather than the home confinement variety. *The Reefs of Space* (Pohl and Williamson 1964), and *The Ring* (Anthony and Margroff 1968) both explore the idea of controlling offenders by attaching devices to them. Pohl and Williamson envisaged a potentially explosive, tamper-proof neck collar fitted to dissidents – presciently called 'Risks' – in a future totalitarian society. Anthony and Margroff, whose book was re-issued in 1986, after EM had emerged in the USA, envisaged a surgically implanted ring on a finger or (particularly for women) toe, fitted in court at the point of sentence for between five and ten years, which monitors mental, spoken and enacted infringements of an artificially heightened (computer-imprinted) conscience – 'law by machine', as one character puts it. To avoid agonising pain, ringed offenders condition themselves into becoming good citizens, establishing habits which outlast the eventual removal of the ring; in that sense it is both cure and punishment. [10]

In science fiction films, pain-inflicting tracking tags are almost always intended to be lethal, not merely uncomfortable, and have not been linked to the idea of an imprinted conscience. In director John Carpenter's (1981) 'Escape from New York', for example, the American government order the release of a war veteran/prisoner to undertake a particularly risky rescue mission for them, over a set 24-hour period. To ensure he returns to base as planned a miniature transmitter is implanted in his neck, attached to a small explosive device which can only be deactivated if he returns on time. [11] 'The Running Man' (1990, d. Paul Michael Glaser), 'Wedlock' (1990, d. Lewis

17

Teague) and 'Fortress' (1998, d, Stuart Gordon), prisons-of-the-near-future movies, all borrowed Pohl and Williamson's basic idea: prisoners are fitted with explosive tags (a collar in the first two, an intestinator in the latter) to prevent escape and to ensure that they keep to prescribed areas within the prison. (In 'Fortress' this form of control is augmented by electronic brain scans of sleeping/dreaming prisoners, which enable the Mentel Corporation who run the prison to anticipate trouble). In a neglected American film, 'Virtuosity' (1995, d. Brett Leonard) an imprisoned policeman (inside for killing the terrorists who murdered his family) is released to help find a serial killer; to ensure his co-operation with the authorities he is fitted with a 'microlocater implant', tracked by satellites, 'which can trigger the release of toxins if he needs to be stopped'.[12]

In contemporary 'technothrillers' – a prevalent and popular genre which combines actual or imaginary science (or both) with the conventions of crime, spy and political fiction – the use of technology to track particular individuals has often been linked to the broader issues of surveillance, the secret state and the (mal)distribution of power (rather than to the more mundane issue of controlling low- and medium-risk criminals). In the ironically entitled 'The End of Violence' (1996, d. Wim Wenders) the possibility is raised that mass surveillance systems, ostensibly designed to deter and prevent crime, are themselves forms of structural violence. In 'Enemy of the State' (1999, d. Tony Scott), a wholly innocent man, unaware that a tiny signalling device has been mistakenly clipped to him is tracked remorselessly throughout Washington DC by rogue agents from the National Security Agency, via satellite and high resolution CCTV. The story unfolds against a backcloth of media debate about the legitimacy of such technology – it is the murder of one of its high-profile opponents that precipitates the chase. Thoughtful viewers of this film, which is set in the present day not the future, might reasonably ask whether the technology shown here is actual or imaginary, and, if actual, whether it could it be used in this way? Although developed for military purposes it clearly has implications for the policing of cities.

As popular cinema, 'Enemy of the State' plays on liberal Western anxieties about the growth of 'surveillance societies' (Lyon 2000) and concomitant fears about loss of privacy (Rosen 2000). George Orwell's (1948) *Nineteen Eighty Four* remains a touchstone of debate about such issues, although as Lyon (2000, p. 35) points out there now exists a technological capacity for surveillance 'undreamed of in the worst Orwellian nightmare'. The capacity includes the deployment of CCTV in public and private places, monitoring of telephone and internet communications, satellite photography and, above all, dataveillance, the computerised aggregating of the trails and traces left by consumers in the course of electronic commercial transactions. Much surveillance, though significantly not all, has been legitimated in terms of its assumed contribution to crime prevention and public safety, although its roots lie in much deeper shifts in the structures and cultures of contemporary societies. Numerous writers see these developments as fundamental, defining characteristics of the postmodern Western world, which have by no means reached their limit. Lyon (2000), in particular, discerns in those who champion and support them 'an idolatrous dream of omniperception' (p. 147), a desire for God-like knowledge – and power.

Such is the cultural and political milieu in which actual forms of EM have been growing, although insufficient attention has been paid to this, even by criminologists. Lilly (1990) rightly argued, more than a decade ago, that EM should be analysed more broadly as an aspect of surveillance, rather than simply as an innovation in community penalties – but much debate on EM is still framed in terms of the latter. Later, Lilly and Ball (1993) – not entirely consistently – also questioned whether EM was just a passing fashion in criminal justice, and, of course, the *present forms* of technology may well be just that. But if Lyon is right about the hunger for omniperception, and maybe omniscience, on the part of powerful political and commercial interests, a desire to pinpoint and track individual people in the interests of control, consumerism and convenience, which is already deeply embedded in contemporary society, then the pursuit of progressively more viable technologies of omniperception is unlikely to be abandoned. Biometric surveillance, of which fingerprinting was the precursor, and of which voice and iris recognition are simply the latest practical applications, is likely to become more prevalent.

McCormick (1994) and Mair (2001) have both reflected on the burgeoning application of pre-given forms of 'new ' technology to crime control, but neither address the processes by which technology is itself shaped. In what cultural milieu does new thinking about technology emerge, and where might signposts to the future be found? There is a complex inter-relationship, a matrix of mutual stimulation, between technology, imagination and desire to which 21st century criminologists may need to pay more attention, starting perhaps with the field of science fiction. Hitherto, with rare exception (see Pease 1978), criminologists have shared in the prevailing highbrow disdain for sf, and the utopian and dystopian literature which has largely been its seedbed, despite the academic attention it now receives (for example, Fekete 2001) and despite its own many forays into criminal justice. Yet Thomas Disch (1998), one of the strongest intellectual commentators on science fiction, whilst acknowledging the crassness, inaccuracy and irrelevance of much the genre has convincingly argued that a great deal of it has impacted on social reality, has supplied 'the dreams our stuff is made of'. Throughout the 20th century there has undeniably been a symbiosis between scientists and technologists and the best of sf writers, each inspiring and intriguing the other. There have been, and are, scientists and engineers who have written sf themselves, extrapolating possible futures from present trends, and sometimes devising devices and scenarios – and narratives of legitimation – that may not even have been imaginable without the stimulus of science fiction. Traditions of speculation, fabulation and prediction can function both as the milieu in which new technologies are conceived and generated, as well as the interpretive lens through which new technologies are initially received and filtered.[13]

All fictitious worlds, even those in mainstream literature, are *alternative* worlds to some degree, counterfactual accounts which create a sense of verisimilitude. By *amplifying* the element of 'cognitive estrangement' which exists in all literature, science fiction simply expands the parameters of the imaginable, some aspects of which are, or become, feasible. The fact that in England EM was first envisaged by a novelist, (albeit not of science fiction)[14], and that in the USA a Spiderman comic helped trigger its initial development are events whose significance for penal reform has not been properly appreciated – the locus of innovation in penal reform, broadly conceived, may be shifting. The cultural resources on which Tom Stacey and Jack Love drew were outside the frame of conventional penal analysis. It seems increasingly likely – even the Department of Trade and Industry (2000) Foresight panel implies it – that new responses to crime might henceforth emerge as much from interaction between government and innovators in the telecommunication, biotechnology, nanotechnology and security industries, as from established penal policy networks. Criminology's past neglect of the socio-technical sphere, and of the mentalities found in science fiction and 'technothrillers', despite many of modernity's deepest fears having been addressed in these declassé genres, may need to change. Even if, with Disch (1998), after Freud, we accept that dystopian entertainments help primarily to make our nightmares manageable, rather than actually to predict the future, we should still be attentive to those stories about pain-inflicting tags, and keep track of those latter-day Judge Loves who might well want them to come true.[15]

Conclusion

What has, and has not, been accomplished here? The main accomplishment has been a partial sketch of how news media, various TV formats, novels and films have addressed the issue of EM in the latter part of the decade during which England and Wales became the world leader in the application of this technology. A rough and by no means exhaustive guide has been drawn of the cultural milieu in which policy makers, penal reformers and commercial organisations are vying to position EM as a new criminal justice tool. It must be emphasised that no easy inference can be drawn as to what people actually think about EM – it is better simply to ask them, as Taylor *et al.* (1999) did – but some indication has been given here of the kind of cultural resources on which they *might* conceivably be drawing to form a judgment, which Taylor *et al.* did not do.

The first thing that can be said about representations of EM in the press and popular culture is that they have confounded both the hopes of its supporters and the fears of its detractors – they have neither consistently proclaimed its potential nor consistently warned of its dangers in any clear and compelling way. The tilt has been towards the negative, and includes instances of dramatic hostility, but the overall picture is mixed, and strikingly muted – EM is not seen to raise 'big issues'. Thus, by no stretch of the imagination can tagging be said to have been seriously debated or explored in the journalistic, literary or cinematic fields in England and Wales. Whilst one could not reasonably expect media coverage (in the broadest sense) to be as comprehensive as the specialised EM literature used by professionals and policy makers, it is still worth remarking that this country has become a world leader in the use of tagging without any significant public delibera-tion. There are some parallels to be drawn with the expansion of CCTV in public spaces, in whose use Britain is also a world leader, although in respect of CCTV public debate has been deeper and more sustained. Significant changes can occur in society without much general awareness of them, and that seems to be true of both these contributions to surveillance. One might tentatively conclude from this that the media, broadly conceived, have not significantly affected EM's development in England and Wales; its relative inattention to EM – despite the sceptical tone of much coverage – may actu-ally have eased its birth. It remains to be seen, however, if the more overtly derisive coverage in early 2002, which damaged the credibility of Home Office plans to tag youthful bailees, (an ostensibly plausible target group) was a turning point.

For now, only a single qualification about press influence needs to be introduced here, in respect of curfew orders. Far fewer have been made than the government wished or anticipated, and magistrates' reluctance to make them may well owe something to the negative portrayal of tagging in the press. According to a *Guardian* (7 December 1995) article, drawing on a the leaked minutes of a seminar, the Home Office themselves believed that 'bad publicity' was one cause of the low take up of curfew orders (the other two being probation service hostility and magistrates' confusions as to whether EM was a punishment in its own right).[16] Because the vast majority of them had no *direct experience* of tagging between 1995 and 1999 – there were only three, later six, trial areas – magistrates nationally may well have taken cues from the press (or other media) on this matter. Government circulars, house journals, knowledgeable colleagues and the lobbying of the monitoring companies may all have shaped their perception of EM, but given their role requirement of responsiveness to the public mood, it seems implausible that press coverage never impinged on them.

Different segments of the public draw information from different media, and it is a mistake – especially for those professionally and politically involved in positioning EM – to regard mainstream news reports alone (in the press and TV) as definitive and direct influences on public attitudes. Diverse influences are in play, and while audiences rarely react passively to media representations, the fact remains that, all told, few portrayals of tagging in popular culture have sought to inspire confidence in it as a penal measure, and those which have, have been the more transient. Sympathetic appreciations of HDC in *Time Out* and *The Big Issue*, sophisticated rebuttals of premature criticism (Stacey 1995), and a tentative expression of hope that EM might help to reduce the prison population (Collett 1999), backed up by an episode of 'Emmerdale', will not necessarily outweigh in influence the vivid and relatively more durable (and recyclable, on video) disparage-ment of EM in 'He Got Game' and 'One Eight Seven', or in 'Maximum Bob', or counter regular, sustained, press scepticism. 'First Time Felon' certainly portrayed tagging positively, but made-for-TV or straight-to-video movies are generally less prestigious and authoritative than cinema-releases. If one adds in a range of media not covered in this article – advertising,

21

comic books and computer games – the latter two drawing heavily on science fiction, and likely at some point to deploy imaginary forms of tagging – it seems highly unlikely that positive messages and meanings will have been received by the younger generation who mostly use these media.

Let us now turn to two key issues, the efficacy of EM as a form of crime control, and its alleged threat to civil liberties. Firstly, this analysis yields little evidence to suggest that EM is taken seriously as a means of dealing with crime, despite the claims of its supporters that it is a tough punishment capable of restraining offenders who would otherwise be sent to prison, and that it could therefore contribute to a revived strategy of penal reductionism. This argument has quite simply not been won in the press or in popular culture, despite some convincing research evidence that a combination of tagging and rehabilitative measures are effective means of community control (see Whitfield 2001). In this sense the reporting and representation of EM has been the opposite of the reporting and representation of CCTV, which the press (if not popular culture) tends to assume is highly effective, despite continuing doubts in the research community. Quite why the press has been so sceptical about EM is harder to explain. It may reflect a general press scepticism about all community penalties, about any punishment which is 'less than' prison; community service and probation, overall, have not had particularly positive coverage (Aldridge 1994). It may simply be a deflationary reaction to the ostensibly exaggerated claims that have sometimes been made by the boosters of EM. Notwithstanding the fact that EM has expanded considerably in England and Wales *despite media scepticism (and possible indifference)* if it is to stand a chance of contributing to a revitalised penal reduction strategy, as Lilly and Nellis (2001) argue it could, its supporters are in dire need, at the very least, of better public relations. It may even be the case that unless positive media coverage, and public support, can be secured for EM – a controlling measure by definition – it cannot be got for any community penalty at a time of 'popular punitiveness'.

Secondly, in respect of offenders' civil liberties, there is no prevailing sense in the press or popular culture that EM constitutes a threat to them (or, by implication, to us); it is simply not rigorous or invasive enough. EM's supporters can hardly take heart from this ethical judgment, as it is merely the corollary of EM not being perceived as efficacious. There are, of course, particular exceptions. In the context of racial politics in the United States, Spike Lee does see EM as at least a *symbol* of oppression (he does not explore how controlling it actually is) but other films about ethnic minority youth have either simply disparaged it, or even welcomed it as helpful to rehabilitation. Human interest stories in the Anglo-Welsh press have either welcomed EM when it has worked, or derided it when it has not – an ethico-political dimension, a larger strategic possibility such as reducing prison numbers has never entered the frame. This may reflect a journalistic assumption that the civil-rights-of-offenders issue is so obviously settled that it needs no airing – that is, EM is patently less of an infringement of civil liberties than prison, and the inroad into the hitherto private zone of the home is therefore a small price to pay. There is nonetheless, a nagging sense of under-deliberation here. The Anglo-Welsh press debate on CCTV, which affects citizens more generally, not just offenders, has arguably been more perceptive, more sustained, more rounded and more mindful of civil rights, although the extent to which the fullness of this debate has actually constrained and shaped its expansion remains questionable.[17]

How might these findings be interpreted? Is there a deeper reason, beyond the internal dynamics of the journalistic, literary, and cinematic fields why EM has signally failed to register as a significant penal innovation in the press and in popular culture? A possible and plausible explanation emerges if the distinguishing features of EM (whether in its actual confining forms or its envisaged tracking forms) are conceptualised as *pinpointing* and *locatability*,[18] and if these are set in the context of contemporary developments in punishment and workplace surveillance. Consider: over the same period in which EM has been deployed, and been hailed and represented by its supporters as a thoroughly *distinctive* innovation in community penalties, the technical capacity for, and cultural desirability of locating individuals (and goods) in general has grown enormously (Bloomfield 2001; Sussex Technology Group 2001). To a very great extent, personal locatability has come to be seen, at least in part, as a useful convenience rather than a wholly unwarranted invasion of privacy. The electronic trails left by consumers, and the traces left by pager and cellphone users, have all made it easier to pinpoint and track people, and increasing numbers of employers expect their workers, outsourced or otherwise, to be accessible and 'on call' in this way. Seen in this light, the mechanism of EM is hardly distinctive, it is only a variant (for convicted offenders) of an experience that, in more muted and diffuse forms, is increasingly widespread in contemporary society, whether as workplace surveillance (Lyon and Zureik 1996) or as a lifestyle preference. In the contemporary context, the type of control which EM imposes signally lacks the aura – the taint – of less eligibility with which serious, publicly credible punishments are commonly associated, (and which may, in some respects, be intensifying (Vaughn 2000)). Contrary to those who, with Stacey (1996), believe that tracking tagging constitutes an even more intrusive and regulatory measure than home confinement, it may all too easily be *perceived* as being only a little further along a continuum shared with ordinary, mobile, law abiding, *locatable* citizens – and therefore hardly much of a punishment.

Clearly, there are still significant differences between being an offender subject to EM and an ordinary person accessible via a mobile phone to employers, customers, friends and relatives – although the technology which makes both events possible has common roots, and innovations in one sphere have the potential to affect the other. Ordinary citizens nonetheless still have choices about how locatable they make themselves, and to whom. But the choice is by no means absolute or unconstrained, for there is a growing expectation of real-time locatability by employer, employees and among families and friendship networks. Communications technology is expanding the possibilities of *remote intimacy* and as with so many aspects of contemporary surveillance we seem to be experiencing it more as convenience than – as Orwell hoped – as threat. In the absence of deep deliberation on the matter there is no reason to think that this sensibility will do other than

23

intensify: locatability will increasingly be normalised and desired as a source of personal security, and as a sign, to others, that one lives a certain sort of cosmopolitan, 'just-in-time lifestyle, [that one is] a person-in-demand' (Sussex Technology Group 2001, p. 210). Public scepticism about these developments is negligible, although in one of the few press comments on mobile phones and the emergent culture of locatability, a *Times* leader (7 March 2000) issued an uncharacteristically shrill warning:

Electronic tagging will no longer be confined merely to criminals. That which renders you more mobile (sic) does not necessarily make you more free.

This is crudely put. 'Mobile' is the wrong word. 'Locatable' would be better. But it is perhaps symptomatic of the state of public understanding of the socio-technical changes that are developing around us, that even *The Times*, a journal of record, is still groping for a vocabulary adequate to the new realities of surveillance, of which the electronic monitoring of offenders is indisputably a part.

Notes

1 To the extent that EM has been framed largely as a new community penalty, and not as something different in kind from all that has gone before, it may simply have suffered from limited media interest in community penalties generally (Aldridge 1994). The modern probation service, for example, has rarely been represented in popular culture, compared, say, to other law enforcement professionals – and recent portrayals of it might be read as expressions of cultural scepticism about its role. In a recent British film comedy 'The Parole Officer' (d. John Guinan 2001) (actually a probation officer) was portrayed as bumbling and inept but decent and well-meaning, a worm who turns on a corrupt police officer and recruits a group of his old clients to break into a bank where incriminating evidence is being stored. Interestingly, he resigns from his job in the course of the story, as do the far better drawn (American) probation officer protagonists in Pete Blauner's (1991) *Slow Motion Riot* and Elmore Leonard's (1991) *Maximum Bob* (to become lawyer and police officer respectively). Whether these portrayals signify or presage the growing untenability of traditional probation practice, comparable, say, to Bender's (1987) view that the imminent obsolescence of antiquated, pre-penitential punishments are discernible in the work of Daniel Defoe, is at least worth contemplating.
2 The medium of radio has undoubtedly been neglected among those who study media images of crime and criminal justice; I know of not one single study. Marx (1995) did not cover radio in his analysis of surveillance, although he did cover popular music. I am grateful to an anonymous reviewer of this article for pointing out that radio should be regarded as a source of understanding EM alongside the sources I have mentioned. S/he indicates that the ethics, practice and potential of electronic monitoring has been covered on the whole spectrum of radio in Britain – Radio 1, Radio 2 (The Jimmy Young Show – twice), Radio 4 in both news and specialist programmes, Radio 5 Live, 'which, in the early days of the pilot projects, gave it serious and sustained attention', as well as local radio stations. My own (limited) experience of tagging coverage on the radio (see abstract) bears out Wykes's general point that radio derives its agenda from the press, but even if radio has not framed the issue of EM in ways distinctively different from any other medium, the vivid immediacy of radio talk, even with very short items, may indeed make a powerful impression on listeners.

3 In conversation with me, in the mid-1990s, an exasperated senior person in the monitoring industry once credited 'the luddite' Harry Fletcher with single-handedly holding back the development of tagging in England. NAPO had launched its Anti-Electronic Monitoring Campaign in June 1989. The campaign has consisted of data-gathering about the operation of tagging, exhortations to its membership, and the placing of critical accounts in the press. In the aftermath of the first trial, which it believed to have been disastrous, NAPO believed that tagging had been vanquished ('Tagging dumped – official' was a small wishful headline in *NAPO News* in February 1993, above a parliamentary item *which did not in fact imply this*). It has noted more recently that tagging 'returned in 1994 with limited success and then with a vengeance after the 1997 election' (*NAPO News*, July/August 2001, p. 7).

4 All prisoners eligible for HDC are subject to risk assessment and prison governors responsible for this are known to have been cautious in their judgments. Neither of the two taggees charged with rape had previous convictions for this, or for other sex offences. Further monitoring of HDC by HM Inspectorates of Prisons and Probation (2001) convinced the Home Office of its efficacy, and its further use was encouraged. (see also Lilly and Nellis 2001).

5 At least in terms of operational principle, 'belled slave collars' have a real claim to being one precursor of electronic tags. These were collars, with small bells hooped above them, locked around the necks of slaves who persistently sought to escape from their master's plantations (Everett 1978, p. 121). The jangling of the bells made it easy for them to be tracked if they attempted escape again. In the late-1980s, at the time of the first trials of EM, I heard a representative of the Association of Black Probation Officers solemnly oppose it on the grounds that 'Black people have been tagged before'.

6 'He Got Game' is one of several recent hip-hop movies which explore the opportunities offered by basketball to African-Americans, all nodding respectfully to the influential 'epic documentary "Hoop Dreams"' (1994, d. Steve James), which highlighted 'the artistic impulses and mercenary business practices that both elevate (a few) and destroy (many) gifted young black athletes' (George 1998, p. 108). Written and directed by Spike Lee, 'He Got Game' is a richly textured depiction of the way in which both seduction and coercion entwine to oppress African-American men. The use of electronic tagging is shown simply as a new permutation of coercion and Lee makes it emblematic of racial oppression more generally. As in his other films, Lee is particularly harsh towards African-American men (or women) who collude with or get seduced by the system, exemplified here by Spivey, the hardline parole officer (Jim Brown) who throughout treats Jake with contempt. There is no sense of 'Black' solidarity between the two men. The closing scenes of the film, where Jake practices basketball in the prison yard at Attica, and deliberately steps into an area marked 'out of bounds', risking being shot from the guntower above him, symbolises the exclusion zones of white America – the restricted opportunities – experienced by African-American men.

7 The same technology was used to control prisoners on the orbiting penal colony in the film 'Fortress 2: Re-entry' (2000, d. Geoff Murphy), although it is not until an escape attempt is underway that the prisoners realise that cameras have been implanted behind their eyes, (whilst unconscious, on the journey out from Earth) and that this is how the private prison authorities (the Mentel Corporation) know their every move.

8 Romanticised and improbable 'private eye' stories have steadily been displaced by 'police procedural' crime stories, although common elements remain, 'maverick personalities' particularly. New types of 'official investigator' have already

25

emerged as protagonists in crime fiction because scientific and technological advances have changed the division of detective labour in the real world (Messent 1997). This diversification has also arisen, it must be said, because publishers and producers continually want novel angles *within established and profitable genres*, rather than wholly new – and perhaps commercially risky – ideas. Patricia Cornwell's 'quasi-police procedurals' about a forensic pathologist – not the first fictions of this kind, and distantly connected to the deductive scientific approach taken by Sherlock Holmes – have steadily generated derivative books and TV series – Kathy Reich's books, the BBC's 'Silent Witness' in Britain and CBS's 'CSI – Crime Scene investigators' from the USA. A background character, perhaps even a protagonist, in the electronic monitoring field is by no means an impossibility in crime fiction.

9 I may be bowdlerising Bender here, for I recognise that his claim relates as much to the form of the 18th century novel *per se* – the novel as a new artistic institution, with its characteristically refined representation of the interior lives of individuals – rather than to the content of particular texts and stories. But, as his analysis of paintings shows, content as well as form is relevant to the shaping of thoughts and feelings, and to the stimulation of imagination. I recognise too the historical specificity of his claim that 'the institutions of eighteenth century culture were arranged to allow for literary discourse to have causative force' (Bender 1987, p. 6). In the 20th and 21st centuries it needs to be acknowledged that cultural institutions, not least because of their own immense diversity, have 'causative force' in much more complex ways, but Bender's general insight remains and informs certain aspects of this article:

I consider literature and the visual arts as advanced forms of knowledge, as cognitive instruments that anticipate and contribute to institutional formation. Novels as I describe them are primarily historical and ideological documents; the vehicles not the reflections of social change. (Bender 1987, p. 1)

10 Science fiction, like much genre writing, is inveterately self-referential, and Anthony and Margroff may have been doing no more than developing a permutation of a pre-existing idea. *The Ring*, badly written, badly characterised, set in a poorly imagined mid-21st century (at most), with a ridiculous ending, is not a great sf novel – far from Piers Anthony's best. It was nonetheless prescient in respect of tagging, and several aspects of the 1960s milieu in which it was conceived may have contributed to its depiction of the device. Firstly, prominent debates were taking place on the social and political implications of psychologist B. F. Skinner's behaviourism, some with reference to crime control. Skinner had famously anticipated utopian consequences for his theories in a novel of his own (Skinner 1948), and the more didactic elements of *The Ring* may well have been Anthony's critical rejoinder to that debate. Secondly, the Schwitzgebel (1963) experiments using radio telephony to track delinquents – 'pioneers of what has become known as the "house arrest concept"' (Victorian 1999, p. 150; see also Fox 1987) – took place in this period (and were themselves influenced by behaviourism). Thirdly, there are recognisable similarities between *The Ring* and Anthony Burgess's (1962) far richer and more philosophical near-future novel, *A Clockwork Orange*. In the latter a violent young thug is conditioned into harmlessness by a one-off programme of aversion therapy rather than the wearing of a pain-inflicting tag. (See *The Analogues* (Knight 1952) for a pioneering story in this vein.) Because of the conditioning the central characters in both *A Clockwork Orange* and *The Ring* are both rendered incapable of defending themselves against attack, or using force to rescue someone else from attack. But whereas Burgess decides that it is better to

allow evil in order to permit courage, Anthony's protagonist finally accepts that if the computer-imprinted conscience were moderated, the ring is a viable means of shaping good citizens. Quite why such a forgettable novel was republished in 1986 is unclear, unless it was to capitalise on the advent of real EM (as the cover of the paperback implies). Piers Anthony lives in Florida, the state which used tagging the most in the early 1980s, and presumably knew of the development.

11 'Escape from LA' (d. John Carpenter 1998) – recycled the same plot, only this time the prisoner/rescuer is injected with poison, and must return, mission accomplished, for the antidote within 24 hours. But he is tricked – the poison turns out to have been a placebo, a simulated form of control, although no less effective for all that. (See Bogard (1996) on 'simulated surveillance'.)

12 In 1992 – note the date – I presented a critical paper on 'Electronic tagging : grounds for resistance?' (Nellis 1993) at a conference organised and funded by various monitoring companies at Leicester Polytechnic. Noting the tendency for all previous alternatives to custody to be toughened-up over time, as early versions are perceived to fail, and as expectations change, I speculated that an electric shock tag may one day be thought desirable, and become feasible. At the end of my talk, a man from Marconi, one of the companies involved in the 1989/90 trials, approached me and said: 'We could do that now'. Precedents for administering electric shocks to offenders already exist in the shape of 'a stun gun used by 850 United States police forces, and currently on trial in the metropolitan police force' (*The Guardian*, 6 August 2001), electrified body belts and 'electronic stun shields, growing and crackling with electric currents', to extract recalcitrant inmates from cells (Wynn 2001, p. 25).

13 The interplay of literary and technical elements in the construction of scientific narratives is beginning to be addressed in social constructivist accounts of science, and there is an interesting history of EM yet to be written from this perspective. Writing about the discovery of the fission of uranium atoms in 1938, Robert Pool (1997) writes that 'scientists [then] didn't have to stop and think what this might mean. *Decades of speculation and prediction had already created an image of a world with nuclear power*' (p. 67, italics added). He quotes a famous physicist, Leo Szilard, as saying of this discovery: '"all the things which H G Wells had predicted appeared suddenly real to me"' (Pool 1997, p. 67). In a 1914 novel, H. G. Wells had depicted a utopian society which had harnessed atomic power, which was in turn partly inspired by the innovative work of British radiochemist, Frederick Soddy, which had appeared several years earlier. More recently, sf novelist William Gibson famously invented 'cyberspace' in *Neuromancer* in 1984 and contributed to the narrative by which the internet has come to be publicly understood. Something like the internet itself had been envisaged in a science fiction novella, *True Names*, in 1981, by a reputable computer scientist at San Diego State University, Vernor Vinge (see Frenkel 2001). Vinge, age 56, typifies those scientists of his generation who claim that reading and, in his case, writing science fiction in his youth influenced his world view and choice of career, and 'he is [now] one of several science fiction writers who have worked with Global Business Network in anticipating future situations and plotting strategies for several major companies' (*New York Times*, 2 August 2001). Criminologists need to understand this milieu – it impinges on 'the commercial corrections complex' (Lilly and Knepper 1992).

14 Tom Stacey (b.1930) is a creative thinker, a polymath, politically Conservative, well outside the network of those conventionally regarded as innovators in criminal justice. An ex-journalist, who dropped out of Oxford without completing his degree, he is now a successful publisher. A brief period of imprisonment whilst working abroad, plus many years as a prison visitor in London convinced him that

prison was a destructive experience for many offenders. He had little faith in welfare professions like probation, and believed that stronger forms of control were needed if offenders were to be dealt with in the community. The tag was a product of his imagination, and of a general knowledge about what might have been becoming technically possible, which he decided to check with more scientifically-inclined acquaintances. He has written seven well-received novels – of which *Decline* (Stacey 1991) deals well with the experience of imprisonment – one collection of short stories and three works of non-fiction (see Kendall 1991; Nellis 2001).

15 *The Sum of All Fears* by Tom Clancy (1991), a leading technothriller writer, had anticipated a September 11th-style attack but in its audacity and horror the actual event apparently exceeded anything that such writers had believed *would* happen, even if they had imagined worse things that *could* happen (Cowley 2001). Of the New York attacks, Clancy himself is reported to have said, 'what happened today was not credible' (in Amis 2001). *The Guardian* (12 September 2001) noted (as many other papers, worldwide, also did) that the first news reports of the airborne attack on the World Trade Towers were distinctly redolent of 'some far-fetched Hollywood disaster movie'. For example, in Warner Brothers' film 'Executive Decision' (1996, d. Stuart Baird) Kurt Russell thwarted an attempt by a Muslim suicide bomber to crash a hijacked Boeing 747 into Washington DC, and unleash nerve gas into the city. The weekly TV documentary *Panorama* (24 March 2002) revealed that in the aftermath of September 11th Pentagon officials had sought to tap the imaginative capacities of Hollywood scriptwriters in order to help anticipate future terrorist targets and techniques (Billen 2002).

16 It is perhaps inevitable that innovators, seemingly pushing against an 'establishment', will exaggerate the extent of media hostility, real though the core of it may be. Senderson (1996, pp. 240/243) a strong believer in the potential of EM to reduce the use of custody, albeit via 'free market capitalism', lists bureaucratic inertia, government underfunding and media hostility for the continuing underusage of EM 13 years after its inception in America:

> EMHC has received more than its fair share of negative publicity. A single major crime committed by someone in such a programme will receive much publicity while hundreds of successes will be ignored. This tendency of the American media colours public perceptions of many innovations in an undeservedly negative way. ... it is the media's task to point out problems and failures but we should not let the publicity accorded to the misapplications of a new technology discourage its further development and usage.

17 This claim is necessarily subjective and tentative, and research on the media coverage of CCTV is overdue. But in respect of CCTV significant social commentators such as Germaine Greer (1994) have engaged in debate, and the most significant academic research on the subject (Norris and Armstrong 2000) has been the subject of a broadsheet feature article (Arnot 1999). No public intellectual of Greer's stature has ever commented on EM in Britain, and while the Home Office research on it is well known in the relevant professional and policy-making circles, it has received no serious attention in the mainstream press.

18 The implications of new technology for the locatability of individuals are debated in other contexts apart from criminal justice. Mountaineers are apparently divided by the use of mobile phones and satellite navigation systems which may well make the sport safer, reducing risk and saving lives, but which also, by definition, reduce the need for courage and self-reliance in the wilderness. In a paper on 'Modern technology and mountaineering', the Mountaineering Council of

28

Scotland argued that mobile phones conflicted with the core values of mountaineering. Mountain rescue services, needless to say, prefer and encourage their use (*The Daily Telegraph*, 28 October 1995).

References

Aldridge, M. (1994) *Making Social Work News*, London: Routledge.

Allen, J. (2000) 'A strange kind of freedom', *The Guardian, 22 November*.

Amis, K. (1960) *New Maps of Hell*, London: Victor Gollancz. (New English Library Edition 1969).

Amis, M. (2001) 'The first circle of hell', *The Guardian Review, 18 September*.

Anthony, P. and Margroff, R. E. (1968, 1986 ed)) *The Ring*, New York: Tom Doherty Associates.

Arnot, C. (1999) 'We've all been framed', *The Guardian Society, 9 December*.

Ball, R. A. and Lilly, J. R. (1988) 'Home incarceration with electronic monitoring', in: J.E. Scott and T. Hirschi (Eds.), *Controversial Issues in Crime and Justice*, London: Sage.

Bender, J. (1987) *Imagining the Penitentiary: Fiction and the Architecture of Mind in Eighteenth Century England*, Chicago: University of Chicago Press.

Berlins, M. (2001) 'Oldies still the goodies: review of crime novels in 2001', *The Times, 5 December*.

Billen, A. (2002) 'The Sibyls of Los Angeles', *New Statesman, 1 April*.

Blauner, P. (1991) *Slow Motion Riot*, Harmondsworth: Penguin.

Bloomfield, B. (2001) 'In the right place at the right time: electronic tagging and problems of social order/disorder', *The Sociological Review, 49*(2), 174–201.

Bogard, W. (1996) *The Simulation of Surveillance: Hyper Control in Telematic Societies*, Cambridge: Cambridge University Press.

Bourdieu, P. (1998) *On Television and Journalism*, London: Pluto Press.

Braithwaite, J. (2000) 'The new regulatory state and the transformation of criminology', in: D. Garland and R. Sparks (Eds.), *Criminology and Social Theory*, Oxford: Oxford University Press.

Burgess, A. (1962) *A Clockwork Orange*, Harmondsworth: Penguin.

Butler, D. and Kavanagh, D. (2002) *The British General Election of 2001*, London: Palgrave.

Cheever, J. (1977) *Falconer*, London: Jonathan Cape.

Clancy, T. (1991) *The Sum of All Fears*, London: Harper Collins.

Clute, J. and Nichols, P. (1992) *The Encyclopaedia of Science Fiction*, London. Orbit.

Collett, S. (1999) 'Checking out', *The Guardian, 27 January*.

Cowley, J. (2001) 'Profile on Tom Clancy', *New Statesman, 24 September*, 28–9.

Department of Trade and Industry Foresight Crime Prevention Panel (2000) *Just Around the Corner : A Consultation Document*, London: DTI.

Disch, T. M. (1998) *The Dreams our Stuff is Made of : How Science Fiction Conquered the World*, New York: Simon and Schuster.

Everett, S. (1978) *The Slaves: An Illustrated History of a Monstrous Evil*, New York: G. P. Putnam's Sons.

Fekete, J. (2001) 'Doing the time warp again: science fiction as adversarial culture', *Science Fiction Studies, 28*(1), 77–96.

Fletcher, H. (1997) 'Electronic tagging : purpose, reliability and implications for penal policy', *NAPO News, May*, 89.

Fox, R. G. (1987) 'Dr Schwitzgebel's machine revisited: electronic monitoring of offenders', *Australian and New Zealand Journal of Criminology, 20*, 131–47.

Frenkel, J. (Ed.) (2001) *True Names and The Opening of the Cyberspace Frontier*, South Yarra: Tor Books.

George, N. (1998) *Hip Hop America*, Harmondsworth: Penguin.

Gibson, W. (1984) *Neuromancer*, London: Vintage.

Greer, G. (1994) 'Liberty is the loser in the scanned society', *The Guardian, 5 September.*

HM Inspectorates of Prisons and Probation (2001) *Through the Prison Gates: A Joint Review*, London: Home Office.

Kendall, E. (1991) 'Interview with Tom Stacey', *The Observer Magazine, 12 March,* 64.

Knight, D. (1952/1976) *The Analogues*, in: *The Best of Damon Knight*, New York: Nelson Doubleday.

Leonard, E. (1992) *Maximum Bob*, Harmondsworth: Penguin.

Lilly, J. R. (1990) 'Tagging reviewed', *Howard Journal, 29,* 229–45.

Lilly, J. R. and Ball, R. A. (1993) 'Selling justice: will electronic monitoring last?', *Northern Kentucky Law Review, 20*(2), 505–30.

Lilly, J. R. and Knepper, P. (1992) 'An international perspective on the privatisation of corrections', *Howard Journal, 31,* 174–91.

Lilly, J. R. and Nellis, M. (2001) 'Home detention curfew and the future of electronic monitoring', *Prison Service Journal, 135,* 59–69.

Lyon, D. (2000) *Surveillance Society: Monitoring Everyday Life*, London: Sage.

Lyon, D. and Zureik, E. (1996) 'Surveillance, privacy and the new technology', in: D. Lyon and E. Zureik (Eds.), *Computers, Surveillance and Privacy*, London: University of Minnesota Press.

Mair, G. (2001) 'Technology and the future of community penalties', in: A. E. Bottoms, L. Gelsthorpe and S. Rex (Eds.), *Community Penalties: Change and Challenges*, Cullompton, Devon: Willan.

Marrin, M. (2002) 'Releasing prisoners early is a crime waiting to happen', *The Sunday Times, 24 March.*

Marx, G. (1995) 'Electric eye in the sky: some reflections on the new surveillance and popular culture', in: J. Ferrel and C. R. Saunders (Eds.), *Cultural Criminology*, Boston: Northern University Press. (reprinted in: D. Lyon and E. Zureik (Eds.), *Computers, Surveillance and Privacy*, London: University of Minnesota Press.)

McCormick, K. R. E. (1994) 'Prisoners of their own device: computer applications in the Canadian correctional system', in: K. R. E. McCormick (Ed.), *Carceral Contexts: Readings in Control*, Toronto: Canadian Scholars' Press Inc.

McCulloch, C. (1997) 'Electronic monitoring: a task for probation officers?', *Vista, May,* 12–19.

Mellor, D. (2002) 'Stop conning us with crime crackdowns', *The People, 27 February.*

Messent, P. (1997) 'Introduction: from private eye to police procedural – the logic of contemporary crime fiction', in: P. Messent (Ed.), *Criminal Proceedings: The Contemporary American Crime Novel*, London: Pluto Press.

Nellis, M. (1993) 'Electronic tagging: grounds for resistance?', in: J.R. Lilly and J. Hyman (Eds.), *The Electronic Monitoring of Offenders* (Law School Monograph), Leicester: Leicester Polytechnic.

Nellis, M. (2001) 'Interview with Tom Stacey', *Prison Service Journal, 135,* 76–9.

Norris, C. and Armstrong, G. (2000) *The Maximum Surveillance Society*, Oxford: Berg Publishers.

Orwell, G. (1948) *Nineteen Eighty Four*, London: Secker and Warburg.

Pease, K. (1978) 'Prediction', British Psychological Society Division of Criminological and Legal Psychology *Newsletter, August,* 11–14.

Pohl, F. and Williamson, J. (1984) *The Reefs of Space*, Harmondsworth: Penguin.

Pool, R. (1997) *Beyond Engineering: How Society Shapes Technology*, Oxford: Oxford University Press.

Reynolds, J. and McCallum, J. (2001) *Bad Girls: The Inside Story*, London: Harper Collins.

Renzema, M. (1998) 'GPS: is now the time to adopt?', *Journal of Offender Monitoring, Spring*, 5.

Rosen, J. (2000) *The Unwanted Gaze: The Destruction of Privacy in America*, New York: Vintage Books.

Schwitzgebel, R. R. (1963) 'Delinquents with tape recorders', *New Society, 18, 31 January*, 11–13.

Senderson, J. (1996) 'Electronic supervision technology and community corrections', in: K. Schultz (Ed.), *Electronic Monitoring and Corrections: The Policy, the Operation, the Research*, Vancouver: Simon Fraser University.

Skinner, B. F. (1948) *Walden Two*, New York: Macmillan.

Stacey, T. (1991) *Decline*, London: Heinemann.

Stacey, T. (1995) 'A tag they want to stop', *The Daily Telegraph, 22 August*.

Stacey, T. (1996) 'Innovations in technology', in: K. Schultz (Ed.), *Electronic Monitoring and Corrections: The Policy, the Operation, the Research*, Vancouver: Simon Fraser University.

Sussex Technology Group (2001) 'In the company of strangers: mobile phones and the conception of space', in: S. R. Munt (Ed.), *Technospaces: Inside the New Media*, London: Continuum.

Taylor, B. (1997) 'Criminal suits: style and surveillance, strategy and tactics in Elmore Leonard', in: P. Messent (Ed.), *Criminal Proceedings: The Contemporary American Crime Novel*, London: Pluto Press.

Taylor, S. (2000) 'Diary of a tagged prisoner: chain reaction', *The Guardian (Society), 12 January*.

Taylor, Nelson, Sofres and Harris (1999) *Electronic Tagging of Offenders – A Survey of Public Awareness and Attitudes: Executive Summary*, Manchester: Harris Research.

Vaughn, B. (2000) 'Punishment and conditional citizenship', *Punishment and Society*, 2(1), 23–39.

Victorian, A. (1999) *Mind Controllers*, London: Satin Publications.

Welsh, I. (1999) *Filth*, London: Vintage.

Whitfield, D. (2001) *The Magic Bracelet: Technology and Offender Supervision*, Winchester: Waterside Press.

Wykes, M. (2001) *News, Crime and Culture*, London: Pluto Press.

Wynn, J. (2001) *Inside Rikers: Stories from the World's Largest Penal Colony*, New York: St Martin's Press.

Date submitted: January 2002
Date accepted: May 2002

[21]

Written on the Body: Biometrics and Identity[1]

Irma van der Ploeg
Erasmus University of Rotterdam, The Netherlands
Email: Y.H.vanderPloeg@fwb.eur.nl and/or I.vdPloeg@gw.unimaas.nl

In may 1996, the Department of Public Aid of Illinois launched a project called I-SCAN. After buying software and equipment from a company named EyeDentify, the department invited all eligible welfare clients for interviews, at the end of which they were asked to look into an eyepiece, and to focus on a lighted target. A camera scanning the retina registered the highly individual pattern of blood vessels, and the image thus obtained was stored in the central computer system. The clients were told that compliance was conditional for receiving further benefits, and people who refused or did not show up for the interview were disqualified, or subjected to other forms of administrative sanctions.[2]

In december 1997, a New Jersey company demonstrated a new client identification system for ATM's (automatic teller machines) to an audience at the Banking Administration Institute's Conference in New Orleans. Instead of checking and matching pin numbers or passwords, the ATM would be equiped with a stereo camera. On introduction of an ATM card, this camera would be able to locate the face, find the eye, and take a digital picture of the iris at a distance of up to three feet. This image would then be compared with the one the customer supplied initially. To operationalize the system for existing ATM clients, the bank could take pictures during eight to ten ATM transactions, the best of which would then be used for the record copy.[3]

At the same occasion, an other ATM security system was demonstrated displaying a completely "hands off" authentication method, based on face recognition and voice verification. The software, 'FaceIT', detects, locates, tracks and identifies the face, after which the user is to speak his or her password into a microphone. The system then matches the voice against a previously recorded 'voiceprint', and, if all goes well, the user is granted access to their account[4]

In the autumn of 1997, the face recognition system of the Sentri automated inspection commuter lane for low-risk vehicular traffic on the Otay Mesa crossing of the US/Mexican border was turned on. Dr. Atick, CEO of Visionics, Inc, indicated that the system uses FaceIt technology to automatically capture faces of drivers as they drive through the border, and performs facial verification against the enrollment record of the authorized driver. "Sentri has provided biometrics with one of the most difficult scenarios to date - it requires acquisition in an outdoors environment (while

enrollment is indoors). It also involves totally uncontrolled conditions, lighting variability, uncontrolled pose and distance, car height, and all that has to be done in real time with moving subjects."[5]

Biometrics is often described as 'the next big thing in information technology'. Since the revolution in IT, with all its new forms of communication, surveillance, transaction, data generating, gathering and commodification, has changed so many aspects of social and economic life in western countries, the new levels of complexity call forth a need for new ways of maintaining order and providing security. Although some feel that biometrics are much overhyped, all major IT developers and many smaller companies are rushing to put their biometric products, with names like UareU, FaceIT, TrueFace, SpeakEZ Voice Print, HourTrack, Veincheck, I-Scan, Viisage Gallery, Cybertouch, or NRIdentity, on the market.

Generally speaking, biometric technology involves the collection with a sensoring device of digital representations of physiological features unique to an individual, like a fingerprint, pattern of the iris, the retina, the veins of e.g. the hand, physiognomic features, shape of the hand, or voicepatterns; it may also include typical behavioral patterns like typing or writing a signature. This digital representation of biometric data is then usually transformed via some algorithm to produce a socalled 'template'. This algorithmic transformation is said to be irreversible, meaning that from the template one cannot deduce the biometric data themselves. These templates are stored in a centralized database that is accessed when on following occasions the finger, hand, face, eye or voice is presented to the system. After a similar algorithmic transformation of this second biometric image, a comparison can be executed. If a matching template is found, the person presenting themselves is 'recognized' and counts as 'known' to the system. It may also be the case that templates are not stored centrally, but on a chipcard instead. The user then has to present both chipcard and requested body part to 'prove' they are the legitimate user of the card, quite like pincodes now - the difference being, obviously, that pins can be forgotten or told to friend in order to authorize them to use the card. In this form, biometric data in principle need not be stored by the organization, but given the opacity of information systems to common users, it may be worthwhile to observe that the biometric signal will always be available for a moment during each interaction of the user with the system.

At first glance, biometrics appears not so different from older and existing forms of establishing and verifying personal identity in the deliverance of all kinds of social services and securing economic exchanges. The practices of requesting birth certificates, passports, identity cards or drivers licences, providing signatures, pictures, and data like place of birth, current address, have been around for a long time, and similarly serve the purpose of proving that one is who one claims to be - that is, a person entitled to the services, benefits or privileges applied for. Such identification practices are based on certified documents issued by certifying agencies and institutions, and subsequent chains of such documents that serve their purpose by virtue of their referring to each other[6]. For example, a birth certificate is needed to get a passport; a passport, in turn, is requested when applying for a university student card, which then must be presented to get the university library card, and so on. Thus, the right to walk into the library, to make use of its computers, catalogues, attendants' time and expertise, and to take valuable books home, is premised on a set of identity markers that together, and by internal reference, establish that one is student so and so, who payed their university tuition, paid previous fines on late returns, and thus is a deserving member of the population the library is there to serve. Such chains or webs of referencing documents are perceived as cumbersome and have often been proven sensitive to fraud and forgery. The issue of 'seed documents' is usually not accompanied by extensive checking of the identity of the requesting person; once issued, a false seed document can be used to obtain several other identity-documents that, in accumulation, are supposed to present reliable evidence of a person's identity. This is what Roger Clarke (1994) calls 'the entry-point paradox': the problem of low integrity being propagated from seed documents onwards to derivative documents, or, phrased differently, the perception of high integrity identity produced by accumulating a collection of low integrity evidence.[7]

This general problem of socalled 'token-based' identification schemes, that is, identification based on possession of a 'thing', usually a document - alternative schemes are name, code, or knowledge based schemes, which each suffer from particular weaknesses with regard to security and efficiency - is hoped to be solved by the much more reliable and efficient ways of establishing identity that biometrics can provide: a mere glance in a camera or a touch of some special table pad might do away with all the bureaucratic paperwork and the carrying around of endlessly multiplying identity papers, smart cards, and pins that always seem to get lost or forgotten when one needs them. Instead the inalienable features of ones own body will suffice to establish 'real', or 'positive' identification, so it is promised. "Biometrics are

turning the human body into the universal ID card of the future."[8]

Major buyers of biometric technology can be found in the private sector, particularly among corporations with high security interests and/or limited access areas like banks and nuclear plants, but an important impetus comes from governments and government related departments and services catering to client populations of thousands, often millions of people. Public institutions concerned with, e.g., the distribution of welfare and child benefits, immigration and applications for political asylum, or the issue of passports and car licenses are increasingly looking towards biometrics in order to improve what are perceived as system threatening levels of fraud. Also, employers interested in keeping track of the whereabouts and activities of their employees; hospitals, and insurance companies in the process of introducing electronic patient records are among the many interested parties. Finally, access to PCs and information systems themselves, instead of being controlled by passwords, codes and loginnames, can be regulated by biometrics.

In april 1998, a couple of major IT corporations, among which IBM, Microsoft, Novell and Compaq, took the initiative to found "The BioApI (tm) Consortium", dedicated to the development of a socalled 'generic application programming interface', or 'API'. This involves the development of a specification for a global standard for existing and new biometric systems that will allow for their easy implementation in operating systems and application software already in use. To enhance its chances for succes, The Consortium invites as many other actors from industry and (US) government involved in biometrics and security technology as possible to participate in shaping the API. Recently, Siemens, Unisys, IriScan, Recognition Systems, The National Registry, The National Security Agency, and the Information Technology Laboratory of the National Institute of Standards and Technology have joined in.[9]

Although as of yet biometrics still represents a small portion of the total activity in IT, it is expected to grow significantly in years to come. Moreover, with so many forces joining in a coordinated effort to *make* it succeed, biometrics can be expected to become one of the dominant ways for bodies and information systems to connect. In the process, the very notion of identity is being reconstructed in ways that are highly relevant for the contemporary philosophical debate on the relations between the body, identity and information technology.

This paper tries to contribute to this debate by exploring the type of questions that can be raised in relation to biometrics as a new type of technology affecting how we perceive of identity. It seeks to articulate the significance of the fact that biometrics puts the body center stage in matters of identification and information technology. To this task, it reviews some of the literature about IT and identity as it has developed during roughly the past decade, and asks whether this literature can help to make sense of biometrics, or whether this new technology perhaps poses genuinely new challenges. I argue, first, that biometrics requires a theory of identity that, unlike much of the available literature, takes the body and the embodied nature of subjectivity fully into account; and, second, that we need to investigate what *kind* of body the biometric body is, by researching the practices and informational configurations of which the 'readable' biometric body becomes part.

Identifying biometric identity

The main question arising is in what sense 'identity' is at stake in biometric identification techniques. There are some indications that these techniques actually involve a very narrow concept of identity, that may not be very significant from a social theoretical or philosophical perspective.

In one of the few significant Dutch studies on legal aspects of biometrics, for instance, Van Kralingen et al. (1997) make a distinction between *determination* of identity and *verification* of identity. Whereas determination of identity, or 'real' identification, refers to a process involving investigation into a range of personal data, a right reserved to just a few agencies like the police and public services, verification is said to involve merely the comparison of two data, in order to determine whether they belong to the same person. Technically, the difference can be expressed as follows: identification refers to a search for a 'one to many' match, whereas verification refers to a search for a 'one to one' match. According to Van Kralingen et al., it is mainly the latter that is involved in biometric identification. Generally, the authors claim, verification can never provide certainty about the 'true identity' of a person.[10]

In the philosophical literature, some efforts can be discerned to make a comparable distinction. Schechtman (1990) for instance, claims that most of the analytical philosophical literature on identity is concerned with answering the question of *reidentification* as opposed to the question of *self-knowledge*. According to her, in a formulation typical of analytical philosophy, the question of reidentification involves spelling out "the necessary and sufficient conditions for saying that a person at t1 is the same person as a person at t2", resulting in criteria of personal identity over time. The question of identity as selfknowledge is said to involve something quite different, for it refers to the beliefs, values and desires that are "expressive of who one really is."[11] Thus, whereas the first concept is said to refer to an answer to the question 'what makes a person the same as herself through time and space', the second answers 'what makes a person unique and different from others'.

Although Schechtman is not in any way concerned with biometrics, one can see how her concept of 'reidentification' and that of 'verification' of Van Kralingen et al. both serve to distinguish a more narrow concept of identification from a broader one. Only the former may be at stake in biometrics, while the latter is taken to refer to something like both authors perceive as "true" identity. The 'sameness of body' as mentioned by Schechtman as a primary criterion of sameness of the person - next to sameness of mind, or psychological identity, which traditionally has received far more philosophical attention - is obviously the one that biometric verfication is concerned with.

In view of comments and distinctions like these, the question must be raised in what sense, then, biometrics is about identity. Is it really just about verification of identity, as Van Kralingen et al. claim? If not, is it then perhaps merely about reidentification in the sense of Schechtman's continuity of the person, having nothing to do with one's personal identity understood as that which makes a person unique and different from others?

With respect to the first question it should be made clear that there is indeed more at stake in biometrics than Van Kralingen's 'verification' practices. A quick look at available biometric products soon reveals that there are many systems being introduced, for example by government social services interested in combatting fraud, that do not just involve the search for a 'one to one' match, but indeed a 'one to many', as Van Kralingen defined the difference between the two technically. Whereas the first suffices for, say, biometrically secured ATM's where the client simultaneously presents the requested body part and a smart card on which biometric data are stored for comparison, it will not do for systems that are used for detection of "double dippers". Many biometric systems in social services are introduced precisely to prevent or catch people using fake identities in order to receive more benefit or welfare payments. These systems are designed to check an applicant's identity against an already enrolled client population, which necessitates the identity check of the 'one to many' kind. The crucial difference is whether the biometric feature is compared to a database containing a collection of centrally stored biometric data or not. In the case of personalized smart cards it is indeed possible to have the biometric data, once processed and stored on the card, destroyed. But even for ATM's and comparable applications, the technology tends toward replacement of token-based identification altogether, and promises to do away with not just the pincodes but the smart cards themselves. This means that the biometric data will have to be stored in the system - and, one might add, it also means that control over the data shifts from the card holder to the system controller. But apart from the promises of the imminent advent of the "completely hands-off ATM" (see introduction), it should be noted, as George Tomko (1998) explains, that at the basis of every verification procedure - he calls it 'authentication', as many others do - lies an identification procedure, so that even 'just' verification always implies that an identification procedure has taken place at some time.[12] Verification of identity as sufficient for establishing whether or not the requesting person is entitled to the service or benefit applied for, *only* makes sense if eligibility has been established before. In order to establish eligibility, identity (and usually many other personal data as well) is checked. Verification then serves to confirm that the requesting person is indeed the person whose eligibility was demonstrated before. Moreover, if biometrically personalized tokens are to become as ubiquitous in the future as is being planned for today, Tomko quite plausibly conjectures, then 'efficiency' and 'cost reduction' of replacement of lost, stolen or damaged cards will probably become the justification to have biometric data stored centrally by many organizations.

Thus, biometrics is not just about as narrow an identity check as some authors maintain. It does involve the generation and storage of digital representations of unique fysical features for the purpose of identifying that person within an information system. And although it may differ from system to system to whom or what exactly (which authority, which social servant, which machine, or database) the system "reports back" its findings and to what effect; or whether this effect requires other people to intervene or triggers automated action ("no you have not been recognized, you may not enter this building"; "yes, you have been recognized, you will be prosecuted for "double dipping"), the general potential of biometric representation and recognition schemes is exactly that they differentiate between one human individual and another. They recognize *both* sameness and difference.

This latter point is pertinent to Schechtman's philosophical distinction between different kinds of identification, or better, different concepts of identity, too. It may appear quite plausible to argue - as it is often done - that biometrics is merely about establishing *sameness* of the person rather than affecting the issue of what makes this person unique and different from others. At first glance there seems to be a fundamental difference here that renders biometrics an innocent technological practice that only in a rather trivial sense is concerned with personal identity. However, here too, several reasons exist not to accept such an account too readily.

First, the traditional stress in philosophical accounts of identity (in both senses) on psychology (character, beliefs, desires) rather than the body, is unwarranted, and reflects the longstanding denial of the relevance of embodiment to subjectivity within western philosophy. Whereas in accounts like Schechtman's the body is recognized when talking about criteria for identity as sameness of the person - albeit short and as a mere aside to the extensive treatment of the psychological criterion - in the matter of identity as unicity of the person the body has dissappeared completely, and only a disembodied kind of self-reflexivity and subjectivity remains. However, if we would consider the body for just one moment in the matter of what makes a person unique and different from others, it would become immediately clear that it is, of course, highly relevant. There are obviously no two bodies the same, and it is actually quite a tour de force to

ignore the body in how we differentiate one person from another (a fact of which biometricists, unlike some philosophers, are obviously quite aware). It seems almost too banal, but it appears quite plausible that the mind-body split in modern Western discourses is accountible for the fact that it is apparently still hard to acknowledge that, even in talking individual psychology, the kind of body one has, the fact of embodiment, is quite relevant. Perhaps the Cartesian relegation of the body to the domain of objects and matter has made philosophers equate the body too much with the standardized, normalized, generalized medical textbook version of the body to remain sensitive to the unicity of each body. And while the 'mind' has been associated with immateriality and subjectivity, psychology as a discipline itself is the most obvious example of treating 'the mind' as an object of study amenable to lawlike generalizations and normalization.

A second indication that relativizes the philosophical distinction between the two concepts of identity can be found in the way Schechtman characterizes the difference between the concept of identity as sameness of the person, and identity as the object of self-knowledge about ones "true values, beliefs and desires".[13] Another way to express this difference would be to characterize the former as involving a third person perspective, and the latter as requiring a first person perspective. Schechtman speaks of 'objectification' and 'subjectification' here. There are, however, several problems with absolutizing the distinction between third person and first person perspectives in matters of identity, and hence with the assumption that biometrics is only concerned with third person establishment of sameness of the person.

First, absolutizing the difference implies the assumption that there is something like an authentic, true self to which the subject has an exclusive, epistemologically privileged access. This ignores the social and cultural dimension in identity formation of even the most 'private' self. For a long time now, theories on the constitution of the subject from many different hues, ranging from psychoanalysis, symbolic interactionism, to poststructuralism, feminist theory, and communitarian ethics, have converged towards a consensus on the fact that the notion of a centered, authentic core self existing prior to the social and cultural is a fiction - however valuable and "real in its consequences" this fiction may be. Rather, this centered self is a contingent achievement, that is constantly, and often only partly, or temporarily succesfully, *performed.*

Second, this performance, which involves the simultaneous co-construction of 'the other', 'the object' etc., occurs in a cultural, social and material world of which technology forms an increasingly significant, constitutive element. In view of this as well, the assumption that biometrics merely involves establishing identity in the sense of sameness of the person becomes questionable. Rather than assuming that technology expresses or registers a pregiven identity, we may want to look into the possibility and the ways in which technology is *actively involved* in practices defining of who we are. The growing contemporary interest in theorizing the issue of identity in relation to rapidly developing and changing technological practices - among which medical and information technologies in particular attract much attention - signalls the importance of this issue.[14]

For instance, on the issue of identity in relation to information technology, a growing literature is developing that doubtless *is* concerned with identity in the "broader" sense: it deals with personal identity as self-conception that is performed in computer mediated social interaction and informed by cultural narratives. This mostly interdisciplinary literature builds upon the theoretical traditions mentioned and often involves empirical research. It seeks to answer the question *how* information technology is involved in shaping and changing our identities. The next section reviews some exemplary work on this question, in order to evaluate its usefulness in making sense of biometrics.

Virtual identities

One of the first examples that springs to mind in this context is, of course, the seminal work of Sherry Turkle. A relatively early, and by now almost classical work on the question of identity in relation to information technology is her 1984 *The Second Self. Computers and the Human Spirit,* followed in 1995 by *Life on the Screen. Identity in the Age of Internet.* Turkle observed and interviewed a large number of different computer users, varying from school children to members of the early 'hacker culture' at MIT. Extending her research into the developments surrounding the internet during the early 1990s, she consistently finds people redefining themselves through their interactions with computers.[15]

A perspective combining psychoanalysis and critical theory is represented by Raymond Barglow's *The Crisis of the Self in the Age of Information* (1994). Barglow bases his analysis of human-computer interaction and the constitution of subjectivity and identity on empirical data in the form of dreams of (professional) computer users and their own interpretations of these. He finds that while mechanical technologies such as the car support the modernist conception of the autonomous, well defined, separate subject, information technology undermines it, or rather, engenders a form of 'hyperindividualism' and isolation, while simultaneously endorsing experiences of fragmented, decentered selves, and dissolution of the boundary between self and machine.[16]

Rooted in a more monodisciplinary philosophical tradition is the work of Robyn Brothers, who, in *Cyborg Identities and the Relational Web* (1997), argues that IT and virtual reality give us cause to rethink our ethical concepts of personhood and identity more thoroughly, since computer mediated communication and interaction give rise to forms of agency and social interaction that challenge traditional notions of community. Arguing from a conception of iden-

tity as found in the hermeneutics of Ricoeur, or in the work of communitarians and narrativists like Macintyre, Nussbaum, Rorty and Taylor, Brothers finds their accounts of narrative identity based on too restricted a form of narrative to accommodate the effects of new forms of fictional interaction on personal identity formation that information technology engenders. She argues that what is needed, is a reinterpretation of both individualism and the underlying assumptions of communitarianism, since the electronic revolution is changing the very ontological underpinnings of these accounts of self and identity.[17]

From a different perspective, Mark Poster (1990, 1995) presents arguments amounting to a position comparable to that of Brothers. He too sees the new information and communication technologies as entailing a fundamental change in culture, that encourages a different type of subject, and changes the very way identities are structured.[18] "Discussions of these [ICT] technologies tend often to miss precisely this level of analysis," he claims, "treating them as enhancements for already formed individuals to deploy to their advantage or disadvantage."[19]

This selection, although inevitably somewhat idiosyncratic, can nevertheless be viewed as representative of the kind of positions taken on the issue of IT and identity. In this literature, IT is seen as a fundamental challenge to traditional concepts of the self and personal identity. Usually, the concepts of subjectivity and identity at stake are described as the paradigmatic modernist, autonomous, centered self as the one being either threatened, falsified, or merely historically overtaken, whereas the kind of subjectivity fostered by IT is described as the paradigmatic postmodernist view on the subject: decentered, with uncertain boundaries, fragmented and multiple.

However, what most of this literature has in common - and the four authors discussed are no exception - is that the most distinguishing characteristic of IT mediated interaction, and the identities it affords, is the *absence of bodies.* Relying much on the metaphor of cyberspace as a virtual space in which identities are performed or narratives are being developed, it is above all the disembodied nature of subjectivity in relation to IT that takes on significance in these accounts. It is perhaps no coincidence that the primary example of IT use in the context of debates on identity concerns that of cyberspace and virtual reality, or specifically, the electronic 'spaces' exemplified by discussion lists, MUDs, MOOs, and other games. What captures the imagination of many authors is the way such games afford opportunities for role-playing with multiple invented or fictional characters referred to as 'virtual selves' or 'avatars'. Thus it is claimed that IT allows for the extension and multiplication of personal identities, which, in many cases, is likened to the postmodernist idea of the fragmented or multiple self. Characterized by the absence of bodies and other identity clues, these 'playgrounds' are perceived as a realm of social freedom, where the restraints of ordinary life are left behind and the imagination is set free.

There are obvious questions to be raised against such views - for instance, about the significance of the fact that most of these accounts tend to overemphasize the importance of interactive games, to the utter neglect of, e.g., administrative uses of IT, or the overoptimistic views on what setting peoples' fantasies free will accomplish in terms of social freedom. But it is, first, the assumption that the body / embodiment *could* be irrelevant to identity, and, second, the assumption that in electronic interaction the body is 'left behind', that are most problematic.

With regard to the first assumption, it appears that these very contemporary and even 'postmodernist' accounts of identity are still haunted by a 'modernist' mind-body dualism, despite the fact that situatedness, embodiment, 'difference', are highly thematized within postmodernist theories on subjectivity and identity. Indeed, concepts like these were at the core of the deconstruction of modern, universalist accounts of the rational subject in the first place. Whereas the literature discussed does subscribe, in general, to the insight that identity is performative, intersubjectively and socially constituted within culturally defined parameters, it manages to ignore the material and physical dimensions implied in this process. In this respect, ironically enough, it risks ending up in the corner of those believing that 'consciousness' is so independent of materiality and embodiment that they actually phantasize about 'downloading' consciousness into an electronic network, leaving the cumbersome physical body, the "wet platform", behind forgood.[20]

The second assumption is also dubious, especially in the context of biometrics. Today already, one is repeatedly warned about the ease with which one's name, location and movements on the Internet can be traced by anyone so interested. An abundant privacy literature, accompanied by actual activism, legislation efforts and policy regulations, testifies to the identifying and tracking potential of many IT practices. The concept of the 'digital persona', coined by Clarke (1994) to capture how the enormous amount of personal data existing dispersed through databases and electronic networks, amounts to a kind of shadow identity of which the subject in question may be unaware, but which can be assembled into an extensive biography.[21] While Clarke remained somewhat vague about the relationship between the 'digital persona' and the subject whose identity is concerned, it may be that biometrics will become the 'missing link', unequivocally tying the digital biography to one particular body.

Moreover, one of the fastest growing applications of biometrics is in access control and security of PC's and electronic networks themselves. As Oscar Pieper, president of Identicator Technology, a large company specializing in fingerprint recognition, and supplier to the US Ministry of Defense, put it: "The world is wired. The world is online. And so one of the greatest applications for biometric technology is access to that wired PC world. Biometrics is a method of being sure that the person who is gaining access, who is a faceless person, to whatever it is, a financial transaction, a data access type of transaction, a brokerage account or something like that, is who he really claims to be."[22] Thus, rather than IT rendering the body irrelevant to identity - a mistaken idea to begin with - the coupling of biometrics with IT unequivocally puts the body center stage.

Questioning the biometric body

The question to be raised about biometrics is what the ramifications are of the fact, that, quite contrary to what has been written on the subject of IT and identity thus far, bodies *will* become important to identity. One ist tempted to add "once again", for despite philosophical theories to the contrary, it is not particularly new for bodies to be taken as a crucial clue to identity. Far from it: for the larger part of history, and often to extreme extents, the kind of body one has, has been perceived as determining of one's identity. Though the attributed importance and significance may have varied over time, and the particular characteristics deemed significant (skin, eye, and hair color, size and shape of various body parts, age, gender, sexual inclination, language use etc.) as well, *who* one is perceived to be, what one essentially is like, capable of, or allowed to do, has, at one time or an other, depended largely on whether one had blond hair and blue eyes, a small skull and thick, connecting eyebrows, or a high pitched voice and an elegant gait - and it still often does. Challenged as 'biological determinism', these ways of tying identity to the body took the biomedical body as signifyer of identity. Historical research has shown how the modern, biomedical body was not the result of objective scientific method, as the standard view on the developments of the18th and 19th century science would have it, but was in fact demonstrably shaped in relation and response to political challenges of the time. Claims to equality from women and people of color from the colonies during the period in which the 'universal rights of man' were proclaimed made anatomical and physiological scientists focus on sexual and racial bodily traits that could justify exclusion of certain groups from citizenship.[23] The contemporary emphasis on historical specificity, situatedness and embodiment is in large part a reaction to double tongued discourses that on the one hand proclaimed the universal equality of man, while simultaneously taking only one small category of humans as exemplary, defining everyone else as deviant by nature. The abstractions that proclaimed one form of human subjectivity to be generic have been brought back down to earth to show their hidden specificity and rootedness in particular forms of human embodiment. So, paradoxically, fighting the spectre of biological determinism necessitates taking issue with views on (rational) subjectivity and identity that disregard embodiment and situatedness.

How does the biometric body and its determination of identity relate to all this? What is the significance of the fact that it is the *body* that is used as an identifier? Is the identifying biometric body somehow biological determinism in a new guise? To attempt answering these questions, we will need theories of identity that take the body and the embodied nature of subjectivity fully into account. And, first of all, we need to investigate what *kind* of body the biometric body is.

To approach this latter question, let me first quote once more from the congressional hearing on biometrics, held by the Committee on Banking and Financial Services in May 1998. One of the representatives present tried to express what he found disturbing about biometrics, saying: "what we are gathering is medical information. It is not just biometrics and fascinating technology, which it absolutely is; biometrics: bio, as in having to study biology; biometrics, this is specific fingerprinting of each human individual."[24] Despite the somewhat clumsy formulation, we can clearly sense that the biometric body is likened here to the biomedical body; comparable to it with regard to its personal nature and its close 'belonging' to the individual. Biometric data are therefore perceived as very sensitive information. In contrast, J.L. Wayman, director of the National Biometric Test Centre at San Jose State University, argued: "We must note that with almost all biometric devices, there is virtual no personal information contained therein. From my fingerprint, you cannot tell my gender; you cannot tell my height; my age, or my weight. There is far less personal information exposed by giving you my fingerprint than by showing you my driver's license."[25]

At first glance, the representative seems to be mistaken, and Wayman getting it right; it is of course not *medical* information that is gathered and stored through biometric technology; it is not about the functioning of the body, nor about its history of pathologies and diseases. Biometrics is not a branch of medicine, but instead a special form of mathematical and statistical science. But if the body that biometrics is concerned with is not a biomedical body, what kind of body is it? Mr. Wayman seems to have a point in saying that from a fingerprint, or any other biometric alone, we, in general, will not be able to tell anything about another person. Nevertheless, the recently proposed Californian 'Consumer Biometric Privacy Act' includes the provision that "collection of a biometric identifyer must not conflict with race, gender or other anti-discrimination laws", which suggest that there are at least some people perceiving dangers in this respect.[26]

So we are stuck with a riddle: how can a biometric identifyer be both identifying and not say anything particular about you? I think the key to this riddle may be found in the idea that meaning is not something intrinsic, but, following Wittgenstein, determined by *use*. Following this kind of reasoning, we should perhaps not expect to be able to determine any intrinsic meaning of biometric data, or the biometric body in general, but investigate quite specifically what uses and practices biometrics will become part of. That way, we can see how the biometric body might differ from the biological body of biological determinism: the whole idea of biological determinism derived its force (and its threat) from the concept of the biological body as existing and being knowable independently from culture, history and society (even though this has repeatedly been shown to be a myth). This body functioned in political arguments by virtue of the proclaimed objectivity and ahistoricity of the qualities and characteristics attributed to it.

Unlike the body of biological determinism, the biometric body is quite clearly and undeniably a body that does not exist apart from technology and its concomitant cultural practices, but is inseparable from the technology that produces it. Unlike the body rendered *knowable* in the biomedical sciences, biometrics generates a *readible* body: it transforms the body's surfaces into digital codes and ciphers to be read by a machine. "Your iris is read, in the same way that your voice can be printed, and your fingerprint can be read",[27] by computers that, in turn, have become "touch-sensitive", and endowed with seeing and hearing capacities. Thus transformed into readible "text", the meaning and significance of the biometric body will be contingent upon "context", and the relations established with other "texts". Building on these metaphors, we might say that the contexts giving meaning to biometrics are constituted by the practices it is part of, while its meaning in an intertextual sense will be brought about by the data to which it is going to be linked electronically.

This opens up ways to investigate the different meanings that will become attached to the biometric body and the ways in which it will be tied to identity. Anticipating the empirical work this will require, we may hypothesize some plausible outcomes. Judging from the uses to which biometrics are being put today, and the forces motivating its rapid development, testing, and implementation, biometrics seem to be about maintaining social order by regulating in- and exclusion from socio-economic goods, geographic spaces and liberties. The groups targeted for (obligatory) biometric identification disproportionately include criminals, recipients of welfare, medicaid or other benefits, workers, asylants, and immigrants. There are indications that most of the applications involving "one to many" searches will be found in social services, where fears of "double dipping" are the motivation behind implementing the new systems. Conversely, biometric identification may exemplify privilege as well, as for example in airports and border control, where "members of the club", after being assessed as 'low-risk travelers' (who will be seen as high risk travelers?), are given the privilege to jump the queue and avoid thorough controls. Other examples of privilege regulated by biometrics might include granting access to secured geographical spaces, particular parts of IT systems and types of information, or authorizations for executing remote financial transactions.

If these intuitions would be confirmed we could conclude that it is not a form of biological determinism we are encountering in biometrics. Instead, biometrics would become one of the clearest examples of the way technology renders the nature-culture distinction and the nature-nurture debate obsolete altogether, since the difference between natural bodies and social structures has become meaningless. Just like our culture of biotechnology transforms innate bodily characteristics, rendering 'nature' more and more an object of design, through biometrics bodies may become inscribed with identities shaped by longstanding social and political inequalities. ◆

References

[1]. The research for this paper has been made possible by a grant from the Dutch Organization for Scientific Research (NWO). I wish to thank Jeroen van den Hoven, Jos de Mul and Deborah Johnson for their encouragements and useful suggestions

[2]. *Biometrics in Human Services*, Vol.1, No.4, 1997, p 3.

[3]. *Biometrics in Human Services*, Vol.2, No1, 1998, p.10.

[4]. Ibidem, p.12.

[5]. *Biometrics in Human Services*, Vol.1, No.6, p.2

[6]. Roger Clarke (1994) Human Identification in Information Systems: Management Challenges and Public Policy Issues. *Information Technology and People*, Vol.7, No.4, pp.6-37.

[7]. Ibidem, p.16.

[8]. ABC News, jan 15, 1998, quoted in *Biometrics in Human Services*, Vol.2, No.1, p.14.

[9]. *Biometrics in Human Services* Vol.2, No.5, p.15.

[10]. Robert Van Kralingen, Corien Prins, Jan Grijpink (1997) *Het lichaam als sleutel. Juridische beschouwingen over biometrie* [The body as key. Legal aspects of biometrics],

Samsom Bedrijfsinformatie, Alphen aan den Rijn/Diegem. pp.3-66, specifically p.9 (see for a version in English http:\\ www.consortium.org)

[11]. Marya Schechtman (1990) Personhood and Personal Identity. *The Journal of Philosophy*, Vol 87, No.2, pp.71-92.

[12]. George Tomko (1998) *Biometrics as a Privacy-Enhancing Technology: Friend or Foe of Privacy?* Paper presented at the Privacy Laws & Business 9th Privacy Commissioners' / Data Protection Authorities Workshop, Santiago de Compostela, Spain.

[13]. Schechtman (1990) p.71.

[14]. Important work in this area, though not discussed in this paper, is done by Donna Haraway and by Katherine Hayles.

[15]. Sherry Turkle (1984) *The Second Self. Computers and the Human Spirit* Simon and Schuster, New York; (1995) *Life on the Screen. Identity in the Age of Internet*. Simon and Schuster, New York.

[16]. Raymond Barglow (1994) *The Crisis of the Self in the Age of Information. Computers, Dolphins and Dreams*. Routledge, London / New York, p73-4.

[17]. Robyn Brothers (1997) Cyborg Identities and the Relational Web: Recasting 'Narrative Identity' in Moral and Political Theory. *Metaphilosophy* Vol.28, No.3, pp.249-258; specifically p.255-6.

[18]. Mark Poster (1990) *The Mode of Information. Poststructuralism and Social Context* Polity Press, Cambridge, UK.; (1995) *Postmodern Virtualities*. In: Mike Featherstone and Roger Burrows (eds.) Cyberspace, Cyberbodies, Cyberpunk. Cultures of Technological Embodiment. Sage, London, pp.79-95, specifically p.79.

[19]. Ibidem, p.80.

[20]. This refers to the ideas of "transhumanists" like Marvin Minsky, Hans Moravec and their followers.

[21]. Roger Clarke (1994) The Digital Persona and Its Application to Data Surveillance. *The Information Society*, Vol.10, pp. 77-92.

[22]. Michael N. Castle (Chair) (1998), *Hearing on Biometrics and the Future of Money*, Committee on Banking and Financial Services, Washington, May 20, p.104.

[23]. Two excellent studies on this subject are: Londa Schiebinger (1993) *Nature's Body. Gender in the Making of Modern Science*. Beacon Press, Boston and Thomas Lacqueur (1990) *Making Sex. Body and Gender from the Greeks to Freud*. Harvard U.P., Cambridge Mass./ London.

[24]. Michael N. Castle (Chair) (1998), *Hearing on Biometrics and the Future of Money*, Committee on Banking and Financial Services, Washington, May 20, p.47.

[25]. Ibidem, p.49.

[26]. *Biometrics in Human Services*, Vol.2, No.2, May 1998, p.11.

[27]. Michael N. Castle (Chair) (1998), *Hearing on Biometrics and the Future of Money*, Committee on Banking and Financial Services, Washington, May 20, p.80.

[22]

GOVERNANCE, SECURITY AND TECHNOLOGY: THE CASE OF BIOMETRICS

Elia Zureik with Contribution from Karen Hindle

Introduction: Governance, Government, and Governmentality Several writers have advanced "governance" as an alternative framework to the traditional notion of "government." At the state level, governance emphasizes cooperation between the civil and political spheres of society, whereas government is usually thought of in terms of the formal political structure of the nation-state—its executive and legislative branches. Governance is intended to "bring the citizen back in" by stressing participation, accountability, transparency, and human rights as basic elements in the management of society. Because of its ability to connect individuals and groups to the centres of power, information technology is being singled out as a requisite for good governance.[1] It is also being seen, however, as a double-edged sword with the potential of facilitating wider control of information and centralization in formal state structures to the detriment of good governance; state surveillance is advanced by the critics as a case in point.[2]

Governance is more encompassing in its reach because it allows us to locate power outside the formal boundaries of government. Foucault's notion of governmentality is useful in furthering our understanding of governing beyond the formal conception of the citizen and her relationship to the state. Governmentality focuses on the constitution of the self in the power nexus of society's institutions, political or otherwise. It acknowledges power in its productive aspects i.e., it reconfigures the subject but, at the same time, creates resistance. Through governmentality, the citizen is viewed as an active subject, though labouring under "complex chains of constraints, calculations of interests, patterns and habits, and obligations and fears."[3] For us, governance involves not only understanding "relations of ruling" (to quote

Studies in Political Economy

Dorothy Smith)[4] in their political, economic, and formal sense, but also the nature of the discursive practices used to administer and manage people through what Michel Foucault calls "bio-politics."[5] In its totality, governance involves the use of knowledge (technical, social, administrative) to manage population groups through identification, categorization (inclusion and exclusion), and a monitoring process the purpose of which is to create a disciplinary, hegemonic regime based on self-normalization.[6]

Security and Technology Security is usually defined in military terms to refer to national security. Security thus defined aims at protecting the nation-state from external threats. With an increase in religious, ethnic, and racial conflicts within states, the United Nations agencies and some countries—Canada in particular—began to view human security as a complementary concept that concerns itself with human rights, protection of the environment, and guaranteeing of basic needs related to health, education, and personal security.[7] Human security and good governance dovetailed as requisites for a stable international order. Yet, national-cum-military security remains the defining feature of security as articulated in state policies. The events of 11 September 2001 have further dashed any hope that human security will establish a lasting foothold in the security discourse and pose serious challenge to the military and technological conception of national security.

But security in its various dimensions has a longer history. High modernity, Peter Manning claims, has transformed personal security from its internal and immediate context based on communal life and interpersonal relationships to one that depends upon external factors such as technology.[8] Technology is being touted as the main tool of risk assessment and the guarantor of security. This substitution has created an illusory sense of security which, in turn, has given rise to "corrupting" influences manifest in appeals to "technological conceit:"

> Agents of control, governmental experts in security and private corporations that carry out risk management and risk estimates for business, those who promote and sell high tech devices - machines to read retinas, explosive detectors, "smart" cards that contain personal information in a chip in a card,

and the mirage of electronic protections in and around airports and computer-based data, promotes the [corrupting] illusion. The anxious public is willing to pay for them directly and indirectly and promote the illusion. The public, eager for reassurance, accepts the efficacy of such innovations.[9]

Manning goes on to suggest that at times of crisis, such as in the aftermath of 11 September, something akin to a panic campaign is orchestrated by state agents of social control, supported by a media-simulated depiction of the enemy as a shadowy, external "other." Terrorism is no longer associated with understanding the context of action, but with singling out certain groups who are profiled on the basis of national origin, race, and religion. Surveillance becomes part of a "tautological" universe in which, to quote Gary Marx, "everything that moves" and is captured on a video camera becomes part of a deviant world.[10] To put it another way, "The claim is that what is seen can and must be controlled, rather than seeing what is seen as a limited, specialized, rather flawed narrow window into the violent complexity of humanity."[11]

Mariana Valverde makes a related point that security is an abstract concept, not something to be measured and quantified: "The impossibility of guaranteeing security is rooted in the fact that like justice, and like democracy, 'security' is not so much an empirical state of affairs but an ideal—an ideal in the name of which a vast number of procedures, gadgets, social relations, and political institutions are designed and deployed."[12] In the context of post-11 September events security, according to her, meant "state security" and not necessarily "citizen security." State security has been defined in a Hobbesian, zero-sum fashion and is monopolized by experts and professionals who by-pass public participation and design "top down" security solutions. In noting that American and Canadian antiterrorism legislations extend beyond immediate, temporary concerns to deal with immigration and other issues of personal and public nature, we end up with "governance through security."[13]

This paper addresses the nature of biometric as "body technology," with claims to authenticate identity and enhance security and trust. Both in Canada and the United States, the campaign to introduce the technology has triggered national debates. The discussion surrounding these debates will be situated in the context of American and Canadian antiterrorism legislations introduced after 11 September 2001. Because of their claims to authenticate and verify personal identity on the basis of behavioural and physiological features, biometrics are presented as desirable key elements in the categorization and processing of people such as immigrants, travellers, welfare recipients and eventually citizens through the introduction of a biometric national identity card. As shown in the final part of the paper, this raises fears of using the technology for social profiling purposes.

Body Technology: Dimensions of Biometrics DNA "fingerprinting" and biometrics are two monitoring technologies that focus exclusively on the body as a unique identifier of individuals. While DNA analysis uses blood, body fluids, hair, and human tissues for unique identification purposes, biometrics use human physiology and certain types of behaviour such as voice recognition, gait, and signature analysis. Those who write about identity authentication and security are fond of making a distinction between something one knows (such as a password or personal identification number (PIN)), something that one has (such as a card key or smart card), and something that one is i.e., a biometric. The assumption here is that it is possible to forget, lose, or fall victim to fraud because of what one has or knows, but one will always be what one is—at least in terms of body parts.[14]

The International Biometrics Industry Association (IBIA), an advocacy organization that represents major biometric companies in the United States, defines biometrics as follows:

> Biometric technology involves the automatic identification or verification of an individual based on physiological or behavioral characteristics. Such authentication is accomplished by using computer technology in non-invasive way to match patterns of live individuals in real time against enrolled records that use face, iris, hand, fingerprint, signature, and voice measurements in applications such as border control, information security, physical access control, financial privacy safeguards, time and attendance management, law enforcement, and other civil and government uses.[15]

Biometric technology uses two main methods for identity checks: verification (sometimes called authentication) and identification. Verification confirms that people are who they say they are, while identification determines who the person is. Regardless of the biometrics measured, the technology relies on pattern recognition, which converts images into a binary code by means of an algorithm. To use the verification system, individuals must enroll first, which involves submitting an identifier such as an identity card, and then linking the information obtained from the document to biometric (hand, eye, fingertips, etc.) images. A reference template is created and stored to link information on the document to unique biometric data. This reference template must be updated to incorporate any physiological changes of the enrollee. Verification is accomplished when an individual presents an identifier with which he enrolled, and the system compares the trial template with the reference one. Verification is referred to as one-to-one matching. Identification, on the other hand, is one-to-many matching. The idea here is not to confirm that people are who they say they are, but to check if the temporary template is present in the stored files of reference templates. In other words, one's biometrics are compared against the many that are stored in the system. An example here would be a passenger whose scanned image (trial template) is compared to many existing reference templates, such as those who are on an FBI "watch list." Another example provided by the US General Accounting Office (GAO) is to check on a welfare recipient for negative matching. Here the system attempts to verify that the recipient is not "double dipping," i.e., using fraudulent documentation with multiple identities to qualify for welfare.

Biometrics as Trust Enhancing Technologies Writers on surveillance concur that underlying the need for surveillance is a lack, or potential lack, of trust by those in positions of power vis-à-vis those who are below them. This is true whether the surveilled is classified as a deviant or normal person. For our purpose, however, surveillance is examined in so-called normal situations, in everyday life, particularly in organizational settings such as airports, workplaces, and public arenas. Of the various factors mentioned in the discussion of monitoring and surveillance, risk and trust rank paramount.

117

Under this conception, surveillance technology is construed as a trust-enhancing tool. And the more capable the technology is of capturing people's unique biological identifiers, the more reliable and trustworthy it is perceived to be – particularly by its promoters. For this reason, genetic profiling and biometrics occupy a special place in the range of available surveillance technologies. According to David Knights, et al.:

> One response to pressures to find means of manufacturing trust has been to collect and check details of users' physical characteristics through the use of retina scans, hand geometry, fingerprints, voice recognition, digitized photographs, and DNA.[16]

Knights and his colleagues question if this technology, even when used in combination with smart cards that carry a user's biometric information, will contribute to greater (manufactured) trust and lower the risk levels among users, as its promoters claim. It is difficult to say, they conclude, because of the dialectical relationship between control (power) and agency. If trust in institutions depends on the type of technology in use, trust in technology is also a function of level of trust in institutions that use the technology to begin with. Thus, "the consuming public may express mistrust in the data collection activities of business in general, and financial institutions in particular. Yet, at the same time, it shows a willingness to 'entrust' ever increasing amounts of personal data to those same businesses and institutions in exchange for various benefits."[17] And "such methods of personal authentication constitute an uneasy mixture of strategies and activities which elude allocation along the trust/control opposition."[18] Clearly, biology as a signifier of persona is back in use, and is in the process of displacing impersonal technologies that rely on PINs and passwords. In a telling manner, the body (eyes, hand, and face) returns as the absent Other, this time encased in biometric technology. Thus, instead of the eye being the source of the surveillance gaze, now the eye becomes the object of the gaze.

A view of surveillance from the point of view of the surveilled argues that, under certain conditions, surveillance can create a criminogenic environment that encourages distrust, stigmatizes innocent people, and may victimize those affected by it.[19] In contrast to objective crime wherein the effect of

118

criminal behaviour is immediate and visible, surveillance-type victimization falls under the subjective crime category that is associated with psychological and emotional stress, which in certain cases can outweigh objective, material loss. McCahill and Norris cite examples of army personnel who
were punished for refusing to give DNA evidence to their superiors. Other
cases of surveillance victimization involve insurance companies and employers[20] who share information about their employees and clients with third parties, and in the process jeopardize a terminated employee's prospects of securing employment elsewhere.[21]

To cite another example borrowed from biometric technology, face recognition has received extensive press and media coverage as a promising and
reliable surveillance tool in security-conscious environments. Yet, the reliability of face recognition technology has been questioned, and some even
describe it as impractical. David Birch demonstrates the point by using the
example of London Heathrow Airport, which processes in excess of one million passengers weekly.[22] For the sake of example, he assumes that 10 individuals who are the real targets of security checks pass through the screening system and are accurately identified by the cameras. With a success rate
of 99.90 percent, face recognition cameras will end up registering around
990 cases of false positives (.001 of 1 million), in addition to the 10 target-
ted individuals. To verify and reject close to one thousand false positives
per week—averaging more than one hundred cases per day—is impractical. It would surely be costly and overload the surveillance system. Birch concludes by pointing out that face recognition technology, similar to closed circuit television (CCTV), may make us "feel" safe; in reality, however, we are
not any safer.

The effectiveness of face-recognition technology depends on the quality
of the captured images, camera angle, and lighting. Effectiveness is also constrained by changes in the physiological features of the target. It is difficult
to capture accurate images of people in motion or far away from the cameras. Changes in appearance, such as one's hairstyle, a new beard, or glass-
es, will also cause problems in matching captured images with information
stored in databases. Face recognition is more reliable in static situations, such
as in workplaces and other organizational settings where individuals are

required to submit to routine checks and provide up-to-date information on their appearance.

A recent report prepared by the US National Institute for Standards and Technology recommends the combined application of face recognition and fingerprint scanning technologies on all foreign visitors to the United States. Based on test data provided by the State Department, the study discovered 90 percent accuracy in one-to-one face recognition (the person scanned is actually the same one to whom the document was issued), and one percent false positive rate. In the case of pictures with low quality, the accuracy rate declines to 47 percent. In the case of one-to-many searches (matching a single face against a database), identification had a success rate of 77 percent. Although finger scanning accuracy rate exceeded face recognition, "fingerprint recognition had its problems as well, especially with individuals whose fingertips had worn down, like farm workers, house cleaners, and the elderly."[23]

The Electronic Privacy Information Center (EPIC), a privacy advocacy group in Washington, DC, lists six areas of concern in the use of biometrics: 1) method of data storage and whether it will be centralized or decentralized; 2) data vulnerability to theft and abuse; 3) confidence level in carrying out authentication, and the implications of errors such as false positives or false negatives; 4) knowing how to judge whether the information is authentic; 5) being clear on who decides about possible linkages of biometric information to other types of information such as police records, consumer habits, etc., and 6) any unintended consequences at the societal level of having citizens being constantly under the gaze of cameras and other video surveillance equipment.[24]

These are not exactly reassuring results from the point of view of good governance. While the state may persist in deploying the technology in the name of governmentality and the administration of people—seen for example in the current government drive in Canada and other western countries to introduce national identification cards that use biometrics—privacy violations and other social costs resulting from such an undertaking may outweigh claims of efficiency and indeed security. In particular, as shown in this paper, such technological measures may end up stigmatizing marginal groups and visible minorities.

Promoting Biometrics: The United States In spite of expressed doubts about the efficacy of the technology, the biometrics industry persisted in promoting its role in guaranteeing security at the personal, institutional, and national levels. This became most apparent in the marketing strategy of the biometrics industry in the wake of 11 September. The economic payoff for the biometrics industry in the United States has been substantial. With a budget of $38 billion for Homeland Security Administration, major defense manufacturers are adapting their technologies for domestic use. In the words of one commentator, "11 September, created a long-waited moment for the biometric industry."[25] The 11 September attack came at a time when the high-tech and dot-com industries were in a severe economic slump, following the boom period of the 1990s. One report estimates that the size of the biometric market would exceed $4 billion in the United States in 2007, which would reflect an 80 percent growth in the market.[26]

A panic campaign that went into effect after the terrorist attacks on the twin towers of the World Trade Center in New York was seized upon by the biometrics industry to market its wares. In the words of George Radwanski, former Canadian Privacy Commissioner:

> In the days and weeks following the attacks, the general public got a good look at what privacy advocates have been worrying about. They saw that there is a huge industry eager to manufacture and sell the technology of surveillance: video cameras, facial recognition systems, fingerprint readers, e-mail and web-monitoring, "smart" identification cards, location tracking. And they saw how many people are eager to argue that if you don't have anything to hide, you shouldn't mind revealing everything.[27]

Within a fortnight of the 11 September attack, the IBIA issued a press release highlighting the role of biometrics in the fight against terrorism.[28] While the statement advised against the overly optimistic view that biometrics alone could provide the "panacea" for combating and halting terrorism, the advocacy group never doubted the scientific and technological competency of its member companies. Any shortcomings had to do with insufficient government backing. What the industry needs is government support so that biometrics will occupy "mainstream applications for improved security."[29] In the press release, the mission statement of the IBIA stressed its role in assisting government agencies through "unobtrusive" methods to detect criminals and illegal travellers at airports and international borders, protect the national communications infrastructure, prevent unauthorized physical access to security-sensitive locations, and unauthorized virtual access to "sensitive information systems and data."

Probably the boldest statement promoting biometrics as an essential tool in the fight against terrorism comes from a white paper put out by Visionics, an American manufacturer of face recognition technology, which was recently acquired by Identix, a large manufacturer of fingerprinting technology. In *Protecting Civilization from the Faces of Terror*, the company reminded its readers that airport security, which is the responsibility of the federal government, "demands substantial financial resources" so as to develop a "technology that can be implemented to immediately spot terrorists and prevent their actions." Boarding a plane should no longer be considered "a right granted to all, but as a privilege accorded to those who can be cleared as having no terrorist or dangerous affiliation."[30] A headline in the *New York Times* described this two-tiered approach as "reverse profiling" in which, for an annual fee, travellers can enroll in the system, have their biometrics stored on a pass card for speedy processing at airports, and exercise their "class consciousness."[31] What follows from this is clear: there is a need to verify the identities of millions of people who board planes daily and "biometrics are the only means available to achieve this."[32] Biometric deployment would not be limited to national borders; it would also be used to secure "a more effective international security framework."[33] Facial recognition and finger scanning technology, which are at the heart of airport and border security, will have to work in tandem with intelligence agencies which are asked "to build databases of terrorists' faces and identities. These can be used to track them through computerized facial recognition."[34] As a matter of fact, the whole system hinges on intelligence agencies developing and maintaining "terrorist watch lists." This task has begun in earnest in the United States.

A "master terrorist watch list" containing 100,000 names has been developed by the FBI, the CIA, the Justice Department, the Department of Homeland Security, and the State Department, about which civil rights and privacy advocates have expressed serious concerns. They fear that the list will give the government wide power to store and collect information on people who have no connection with terrorism.[35]

What makes facial recognition "most suited," according to Visionics, is its ability to "function from a distance, in a crowd and in real time without subject participation."[36] Authentication, the white paper advocates, should be equally applied to airport and other transportation employees.

The same message is provided in a white paper issued by the California office of Bioscrypt, a Canadian biometric company based in Toronto. Advantages of fingerprint biometrics were outlined for both employers and employees, but they were mainly aimed at employers. For employers, biometrics are used to screen employees, access control and keep track of attendance, while for employees biometrics make it possible that "instead of having to carry around the office keys, you simply bring your finger with you."[37]

Nuance, another California biometric company that manufactures speech recognition technology used mainly in call centres, describes its product as an essential money-saving tool for business, since it costs as little as $1/12^{th}$ the cost compared to using live agents to answer telephone calls.[38]

In their testimonies before the US Senate Subcommittee on Technology, Terrorism, and Government Information, the executive directors of the IBIA and the Biometrics Foundation (BF), a two-year old organization dedicated to researching and raising public awareness of biometrics, reiterated many of the above points, and stressed others such as the need to protect security of national infrastructure, individual privacy, and mount programs to educate the public about the technology.[39]

Paul Collier of the BF told the Senate Subcommittee on 12 October 2001 that the United States is ahead of other countries in developing the technology, but lags behind in implementing it. Biometrics provide increased security while, at the same time, protecting privacy. Since other countries use the technology, Collier called for "encoding biometric data in passports, visas, identification cards, and other travel documents."[40] Echoing the words of his colleague, Richard Norton from IBIA, Collier proceeded to tell the Subcommittee on 17 October 2001 that biometric technology will act as a "digital lock and key on personal information."[41] He sounded a word of caution that the success of the technology depends on the trust of travellers and on it being used responsibly.

By late October 2001, members of the IBIA were "deluged with requests for testimony at hearings and for direct advice and counsel from staff and Members of the Congress and from senior officials of the executive Branch."[42] During the same short period of a few weeks after the attacks on New York and Washington, no fewer than nine bills were introduced in the House of Representatives and another eight in the Senate. These bills called for the implementation of biometric technology in one form or another (with special focus on fingerprint technology) in order to tighten immigration, visa, and naturalization procedures, allow tax benefits to companies that use biometrics, and check employee background at border and maritime check points. The House bills culminated in the Uniting and Strengthening America by Providing Appropriate Tools Required to Intercept and Obstruct Terrorism Act (USA Patriot Act), which was signed into law on 26 October 2001. The Bill requires consular offices of the US government to obtain fingerprints from visa applicants in their home countries.[43]

Canada On the Canadian side, the issue of biometrics is equally salient, but the size of the sector is naturally smaller. In early January 2002, a biometric advocacy group was established within the Canadian Advanced Technology Alliance (CATA). The mandate of the CATA Biometrics Group (CBG) includes "a comprehensive public education strategy that compels industry and government to recognize the value of biometrics technologies," "protection of privacy and the integrity of personal data," "the creation of secure environments that protect both people and information," and to "empower people to choose biometrics to enable their applications … with peace of mind."[44] The executive director of CBG, Howard Stanley, spelled out in greater detail the role of biometrics in society using "computer technology in noninvasive ways [to] help us attain the security levels our society requires, while streamlining commerce, avoiding fraud and abuse and reducing waste."[45] He went on to say that "biometrics will increase privacy, not decrease it," and that "civil rights [is] an area where policies must be advocated to ensure that freedoms are respected."[46] To demonstrate its concern for privacy, the CBG promised to coordinate with the Canadian Privacy Commissioner and Justice Canada.

While there is promise of future cooperation between the American and Canadian biometric advocacy groups, at the governmental level a close coordination is already in place. Following the 11 September 2001 attacks, Tom Ridge, Director of the US Homeland Security Administration, met on 12 December 2001 with Canada's Deputy Prime Minister John Manley to discuss means to strengthen border security between the two countries. The Standing Committee on Citizenship and Immigration issued its report *Hands Across the Border*, which included recommendations dealing with increased coordination between the United States and Canadian authorities and the use of new technologies. In response to one of the recommendations, the government of Canada agreed that "The implementation of new technological tools is essential to successful intelligence gathering activities. This includes increased use of biometric tools, electronic finger print systems, linked databases and proximity card technology."[47]

These efforts resulted in "The Smart Border Declaration" and "The 30-Point Action Plan." The latter was released on 9 September 2002 during a meeting between George W. Bush and Jean Chrétien. Included in the 30-point plan is the need to develop common standards for biometric use for iris scanning and fingerprinting which would incorporate "interoperable and compatible technology to read these biometrics" along border points between the United States and Canada.[48] As a starter, Canada undertook to introduce a new Canadian Permanent Resident card that is "biometric-ready" and to implement the NEXUS-Air pilot program for air travellers. This will be in addition to exchanging information about airline passengers between the two countries in advance of travel. Thus, Canada and the United States have agreed to share Advanced Passenger Information and Passenger Name records on high-risk travellers destined to either country. As well, the two countries will work towards developing "compatible immigration databases."[49]

Although it does not spell out what constitutes "high-risk travellers," it is becoming clear that the designation refers to people of colour, minorities, immigrants, and refugees. Gentleman argues that the introduction of biometric ID cards in Europe does not bode well for "migrant workers," and "is associated with police abuses and repression of minority groups." She continues to say that "there is evidence in continental Europe that members of ethnic minorities are asked to provide ID [cards] more often than other citizens."[50]

This particular program, called the Advance Passenger Information/ Passenger Name Record (API/PNR), which will be administered on the Canadian side by the Canadian Customs and Revenue Agency, drew sharp criticism from Canada's Privacy Commissioner, who dubbed it the "Big Brother" database. In a letter dated 26 September 2002 to Elinor Caplan, the minister responsible for the program, Commissioner Radwanski stated:

> Very frankly, the government of Canada has no business systematically recording and tracking where all law-abiding Canadians travel, with whom we travel, or how often we travel. And the government of Canada has no business compiling databases of personal information about Canadians solely for having this information available to use against us if and when it becomes expedient to do so. Such behavior violates the key principles of respect for privacy rights and fair information practices, and has no place in a free society.[51]

The criticism was repeated in a letter sent to Caplan on 12 November 2002 and endorsed by six provincial Privacy Commissioners.[52] On 9 January 2003, the federal Commissioner released another letter sent to Caplan in which he cited endorsements of his position from other legal experts, such as a former Justice of the Supreme Court and a former Justice Minister of Canada.[53] Finally, on 9 April 2003, the Privacy Commissioner of Canada released a statement and an appended letter from Caplan in which she acknowledged the privacy concerns of the Commissioner, and outlined steps taken by her Ministry to insure that data collected on air travellers will be limited in scope and access to safeguard privacy.[54]

Bill C-36, 2001, the Anti-Terrorism Bill, is Canada's main response to the 11 September events. In commenting on the Bill in its draft stage, David

Zureik and Hindle / BIOMETRICS

Schneiderman saw it as a response to living in a "risk" society.[55] Such a response, according to him, can be understood in terms of three factors: first, that the risk society is a global society in which risk transcends national borders; second, that the risk society tends to over-rely on "expert and professional knowledges," and third, that there is a tendency to "overreach" by adopting legislations which profess to cope with risk, without paying sufficient attention to rights and freedoms.[56] Lisa Austin was more emphatic in pointing out that privacy will be the biggest casualty of Bill C-36, because "[t]he anti-terrorism legislation, and other impending reforms, increases the level of surveillance in our society."[57] In its brief to the House of Commons Justice Committee, the Ottawa-based Canadian Centre for Policy Alternatives (CCPA) expanded on the list of concerns regarding Bill C-36, and pointed out that the Bill does not contain a sunset clause.[58]

The final version of the Act responded to some of the concerns voiced by the critics. For example, a sunset clause extending over five years is now included in Bill C-36, except that the clause does not cover the entire Bill, as some would prefer, but is limited to provisions dealing with preventive arrest and investigative hearings.[59] Similarly, amending the Access to Information Act, giving government the right to withhold public access to information for as long as fifteen years, provides "little comfort to those facing criminal and immigration proceedings where access to vital information has been denied on the grounds of national security."[60]

Debate in Canada over the introduction of a national ID that uses biometric data is in its infancy,[61] although it is gathering momentum. Immigration Minister Denis Coderre appeared before the House of Commons Immigration Committee to explore the need to adopt such a biometric ID in order to expedite entry-exit control to and from the United States. Coderre suggested the adoption of an offline system wherein biometric information stored on the card will not be linked at a central database, but will be checked against card holders.[62] By invoking privacy concerns, the *The Globe and Mail* editorialized against the proposal whose intention is "to satisfy the Americans."[63] Canada seems to be inching closer to adopting national ID cards, as evident in Coderre's statements when he hosted a Citizenship and Immigration Consultation Forum in Ottawa in

October 2003 to discuss the adoption of biometrics in national ID cards.[64]
If the panellists are any indication, the forum was heavily weighted in favour
of a national ID card. Among those featured at the forum were industry
spokesmen, biometrics advocacy groups, and officials from other countries
that either have adopted or are on the verge of adopting biometrics, such
as the European Union and the United Kingdom. Quebec's Privacy
Commissioner was the only provincial privacy representative to address the
conference. Alan Dershowitz, a Harvard law professor and keynote speaker
at the forum, who is also known for condoning preemptive assassinations
and "mild torture" as means of self-defense by governments, provided a rationale for adopting biometrics technology. He argued that the technology does
away with subjective evaluations by officials in charge of administering travel and immigration procedures.[65]

What is significant about the Canadian data is the willingness of the public to endorse the use of biometrics and ID national cards in order to check
against fraud and abuse of government services. For example, 78 percent of
those who condoned the introduction of biometrics ID national cards, did
so in order to "reduce the abuse of government programmes," thus giving
credence to the argument that the technology is on the way to becoming a
surveillance tool in the arsenal of a declining welfare state.[66]

Social Profiling and Reaction to Biometrics The purpose of this section
is to analyze public attitudes to biometrics and privacy in the wake of 11
September. There is a deeply ingrained attitude in western societies that
equates technology with progress; anyone who is skeptical about the use of
technology is liable to be portrayed as standing against progress. In the post-
11 September era, to object to technology is tantamount to compromising
state security. As argued by Mike Davis, "the globalization of fear became a
self-fulfilling prophecy" after 11 September.[67] When portrayed as a safeguard
against terrorism, identity theft, and general personal insecurity, several
surveys that will be dealt with here confirm wide public acceptance of invasive biometric technology. It should be pointed out, however, that this acceptance is tempered with high levels of concern about privacy issues. This is
true in the United States, Canada, and Britain.

Biometrics technology is being introduced primarily in passports and at locations such as airports and border crossings. As we have shown above, concerted efforts are being made in Canada and other Western European countries under the auspices of the European Community to introduce biometrics as a means of administering immigrant entry. A spokeswoman for the European Commission, in charge of the biometrics project, spoke at the Ottawa forum and made it explicit that the thrust of the Commission's adoption of biometrics is to check the movement of illegal immigrants and seekers of refugee asylum. The Electronic Frontier Foundation (EFF) points out immigrant and refugee groups are unlikely to object to the use of biometrics for identity checks since they lack any power to speak of and do not have an advocacy group to lobby on their behalf. The EFF also warns that the same technology could become part of creeping surveillance apparati whose uses will extend beyond borders and airports, and immigrant and foreigners. This is probably more true for the United States than it is for Canada where the impact of immigration on Canadian life is more pronounced through the presence of numerous community-based ethnic associations and lobby groups, and where multiculturalism is more entrenched in legislation and public consciousness. Clearly the use of biometric technology in the fight against terrorism has direct bearing on racial and other types of profiling—welfare recipients, for example—and indeed on governance as a whole.[68] Bill C-36 in Canada is a clear example of this. This was also the case in several post-11 September legislations in the United States. For example, in addition to the USA-Patriot Act (2001), the Enhanced Border Security and Visa Entry Reform Act (2002), the Aviation and Transportation Security Act (2001) and, previous to this, the Illegal Immigration Reform and Immigrant Responsibility Act (1996) —all of which specifically mention biometric technology. There are two other Acts which do not mention biometrics as such, but the language of the Acts lends itself to the deployment of biometrics. These are the Personal Responsibility and Work Opportunity Act (1995), aimed at welfare recipients, and the Immigration Control and Financial Responsibility Act (1996), intended to verify immigration status and eligibility for public assistance.

By using biology and physical appearance as means of identification, biometrics are likely to legitimize group differentiation and racialization in society in the name of security. The surreptitious nature of the technology and the ease with which it can be used leave little room for escaping the gaze of the authorities.

Following 11 September, several surveys were carried out in the United States concerning the use of technology for establishing identity.[69] One of the most detailed national opinion surveys focusing exclusively on biometrics was carried out in the United States in September 2001, a week after the attack, and repeated in August 2002.[70] The proportion of those exposed to biometrics is fairly small, hovering around five percent in the 2002 study and four percent a year earlier, which, when prorated for the United States population, amounts to 10 million people. Within the five percent who reported experience with the technology, a large majority (from 72 percent to 85 percent depending on the type of biometric) reported "general comfort" in using the technology. Yet close to 90 percent expressed concern about possible misuse of personal information collected through biometrics, and more than one in four (28 percent) reported personal privacy victimization. ID-based fraud was ranked by 95 percent of the sample as a serious problem, with around 20 percent saying that they have been victims of ID fraud. Biometrics is perceived by the majority of respondents as a safeguard for passport identity verification (88 percent), access to secure government buildings (84 percent), airport check-ins (82 percent), identity for driver's license (77 percent), and car rental (60 percent). Overall, around two-thirds stated that the technology should "not be misused in ways that would threaten legitimate privacy." Those with low income and education, women, and conservatives all expressed high-level confidence that biometric technology would not be used for purposes other than to detect terrorists. Between 85 to 95 percent endorsed the use of biometrics by government authorities to screen entry in high-security government facilities and schools, licensing special occupations, facilitated entry at passport control, and for people receiving welfare cheques.

What is significant about the rest of the findings is the sheer magnitude of endorsement by the public of Fair Information Practices i.e., that people should be informed in advance about the use of the technology (95 percent), that information should not be collected secretly (95 percent), should not be used for purposes other than what it was originally collected for (95 percent), should be coded and not shared (94 percent), should not be combined with other personal identifiers (86 percent), that citizens should have the right to check if the information stored on them is accurate, and that biometrics data not be used to track people's movements. With less than 50 percent of the sample having heard of, or read about, biometrics, and one in four having experienced biometrics, the public is nevertheless enthusiastic that its use will be widespread within a decade.

Publicly available results of Canadian surveys are not as extensive as American ones but the major issues are touched upon, nevertheless. An Ipsos-Reid poll of 1000 Canadians during the first week of October 2001 showed that 80 percent would be willing to provide fingerprints for a national ID, 59 percent would allow the police to randomly stop and search people, 52 percent are ready to give up some of their liberties to fight terrorism, and 61 percent approve of monitoring personal credit purchases. More than 70 percent opposed giving the police and intelligence officials the power to intercept and read e-mail, regular mail, and listen to private phone conversations. While 58 percent felt that terrorism threats outweigh the protection of individual rights and freedoms, 38 percent believed that even with the threat of terrorism the Charter of Rights and Freedoms should be respected and enforced.[71]

In September 2001, EKOS polling in Canada showed similar results, with one additional finding. Whereas 40 percent of all Canadians disapprove of airport check-in times increasing by one to two hours, among visible minorities it is 58 percent, and for non-visible minority Canadians the proportion is 38 percent. Undoubtedly, this is a statistically significant difference, and it underscores suspicion among visible minorities that profiling is primarily directed against them.[72]

Two years later, Pollara discovered that 73 percent of Canadians were in favour of a biometrics ID card, and in excess of 80 percent supported the use of biometrics in passports, airports, government programs, and border crossings, even though the public knew very little about the details of the technology.[73] However, more than one-third of Canadians thought that the use of ID cards "goes against Canadian values of freedom and fairness," and more than 50 percent said it would reduce privacy. The EKOS poll of the same year was more substantial in its scope, although the overall picture that emerges is the same.[74] Only 15 percent knew what the term biometrics meant. There was greater support for voluntary, as opposed to mandatory government introduction of the ID card. The survey did offer some contradictory interpretations. For example, although a minority of Canadians (around 12 percent) thought that Canada would be exposed to a terrorist attack, and fewer (2.5 percent) thought they personally would be affected, around 45 percent agreed with the statement that "there is a serious problem with groups supporting terrorist activity in Canada," and 61 percent agreed with the statement that "given the potential of terrorism, the Government of Canada should be given special (extraordinary) powers to deal with possible terrorism-related offences."

As evident in the order of the questions, the EKOS survey tapped an implicit association between immigrants and terrorism in the minds of the public, even though national data in Canada show that immigrants have substantially lower crime rates than native-born Canadians. For example, the lead question asked if respondents thought there were "too many immigrants" in Canada, to which one third answered in the affirmative. From there on, the survey proceeded to ask a battery of questions on terrorism. The Standing Committee on Citizenship and Immigration spotted a similar, though more severe, problem in another survey that was carried out in October 2003 by COMPASS/National Post. The survey asked "do you see the terrorist threat from Islamic extremists as more serious than most threats," and "should people in Canada who are accused of being terrorists have the same rights as accused terrorists?" To its credit, the Committee saw the contaminating effect and dismissed the survey because these questions "raised doubt about the usefulness of the response."[75]

Conclusion Fascination with biometric technology is but one recent example in a long history of modernity's eager embrace of technology generally. What makes the technology intriguing is its cyborg nature; the line between humans and machines is being further eroded. The technology is being used to authenticate one's identity on the basis of digitized biological and behavioural identifiers as if the technology has become an extension of us and we of it, with an algorithm standing in for our biology.

At the governance level, biometric technologies are being promoted with vigour and some notable success as a result of 11 September. They are being marketed as essential tools to be used in conjunction with other surveillance technologies, to reduce risk and enhance security. The combination of public fear, lobbying efforts of the industry, and linkages between political and economic interests, have catapulted the industry to centre stage in the fight against terrorism —an industry that until 11 September was a marginal player in the security field. This development conjures up President Eisenhower's warning of nearly half a century ago concerning the rise of the military-industrial complex and its influence on politics. An addendum to Eisenhower's observation is the emergence in the twenty-first century of a security-industrial complex in which, in the name of security, the state embarks upon population management and control.

If unchecked through proper oversight, far from being a friend of governance and enhancer of privacy, future developments in the application of technology are likely to exacerbate social division. It is clear that the primary targets of biometric technology are people on the move in pursuit of better life chances elsewhere, preferably in the developed world. Policies of exclusion and categorization of national groups do not bode well for multicultural societies, among which Canada occupies a special place.

What emerges from the above analysis is the public's willingness to accept a tradeoff between privacy concerns and promises of security through technology. Little attention is being paid to unsubstantiated claims of the technology and its unintended consequences. All of this is being made possible through three main convergent forces: first, there is little willingness to question the reliability of the technology lest one is accused of being a Luddite and against progress; second, the formidable lobbying campaign, mounted by corporate stakeholders since 11 September, to adopt biometric technology has found more than willing partners in the corridors of power, and third, the use of biometrics for surveillance purposes will contribute to

133

widening the surveillance net and gathering of personal information that goes beyond security concerns to include aspects of day-to-day governance and administration. Gradually, biometric technology will emerge as a centrepiece in the design and adoption of ID cards, and the administration of so-called high-risk individuals not only at airports and in security places, but in society generally, including the poor, marginal, and vulnerable people.

The 11 September crisis has demonstrated the nature of extreme risk in high modernity, and how risk and insecurity drive political agendas such as the enacting of various antiterrorism legislations after 11 September. Technological dominance and political dominance go hand in hand. The role of the United States as the dominant technological and military power has had significant spillover effects on the way other countries react to terrorism. Because of its proximity to the United States, Canada's increasing use of biometrics, and the enacting of legislation to counter terrorism, will undoubtedly place Canada more firmly within the techno-administrative orbit of the United States. This is becoming clearly evident in the sharing of information and harmonization of administrative and technological measures across entry points between the United States and Canada.

Notes

The research for this study was funded by a strategic grant from the Social Science and Humanities Research Council. The authors are grateful for the helpful comments made on an earlier draft by Fiona Kay, David Lyon, André Mazawi, Norman Macintosh, Vincent Mosco, Abbe Mowshowitz, Reg Whitaker, and an anonymous reviewer.

1. L. Juillett and G. Paquet, *Information Policy and Governance* (Ottawa: University of Ottawa, 2001), http://www.governance.uottawa.ca/background-e.asp#what.
2. C. Parenti, *The Soft Cage: Surveillance in America from Slave Passes to the War on Terror* (New York: Basic Books, 2003).
3. J. Morison, "Democracy, Government and Governmentality: Civic Public Space and Constitutional Renewal in Northern Ireland," *Oxford Journal of Legal Studies* 21/2, (2001), pp. 287-310, p. 289.
4. D. Smith, "From Women's Standpoint to a Sociology for People," in J. Abu-Lughod, (ed.), *Sociology for the Twenty-First Century: Continuities and Cutting Edges* (Chicago: University of Chicago Press, 1999).
5. M. Foucault, *Discipline and Punish: The Birth of the Prison* (New York: Random House, 1979).
6. A. Hunt and G. Wickham, *Foucault and the Law: Towards a Sociology of Law as Governance* (London: Pluto Press, 1994).
7. L. Axworthy, "Canada and Human Security: The Need for Leadership," *International Journal* 11/2, (1997), pp. 183-196.
8. P.K. Manning, *Security in High Modernity: Corrupting Illusions* (Boston: Northeastern University, 2002).

Zureik and Hindle / BIOMETRICS

9. *Ibid.*, pp. 2-3.
10. G. Marx, "Measuring Everything that Moves," *Research in the Sociology of Work* 8 (1999), pp. 165-189.
11. Manning, *Security in High Modernity*, p. 11.
12. M. Valverde, "Governing Security, Governing through Security," in R.J. Daniels, P. Macklem, and K. Roach, (eds.), *The Security of Freedom: Essays on Canada's Anti-Terrorism Bill* (Toronto: University of Toronto Press, 2002), pp. 83-92, especially p. 85.
13. *Ibid.*, p. 89.
14. US General Accounting Office (GAO), *Technology Assessment Report: Using Biometrics for Border Security* (Washington, DC: 2002).
15. International Biometrics Industry Association (IBIA), *Interest in Biometric Industry Continues to Soar: 120,000 Visit IBIA Website in July 2000* (Washington, DC: 8 August 2000), available at http://www.ibia.org.
16. D. Knights, F. Noble, T. Vurdubakis, and H. Willmott, "Chasing Shadows: Control, Virtuality and the Production of Trust," *Organization Studies* 22/2 (2001), pp. 311-340, p. 325.
17. *Ibid.*, p. 329.
18. *Ibid.*, p. 330.
19. M. McCahill and C. Norris, "Victims of Surveillance," in P. Francis, V. Jupp, and P. Davies, (eds.), *Understanding Victimization*, Forthcoming.
20. M. McTeer, "Privacy Comes First," *The Globe and Mail* (28 June 2001).
21. D. Nelkin and L. Andrews, "Surveillance Creep in the Electronic Age," in D. Lyon, (ed.), *Privacy, Risk and Digital Discrimination* (London: Routledge, 2002), pp. 94-110; E. Zureik, "Theorizing Surveillance: The Case of the Workplace," in D. Lyon, (ed.), *Privacy, Risk and Digital Discrimination* (London: Routledge, 2002), pp. 31-56.
22. D. Birch, "A World Away from the Reality," *The Guardian* (24 January 2002), http://www.guardian.co.uk.
23. J. Lee, "Report Suggests Use of Facial and Fingerprint Scanning on Foreigners," *New York Times* (12 February 2003), http://www.nytimes.com/2003/02/12/technology.
24. Electronic Privacy Information Center (EPIC), *Biometrics Identifiers* (7 January 2003), http://www.epic.org/privacy/biometrics/.
25. B. J. Feder, "Technology and Media: A Surge in Demand to Use Biometrics," *New York Times* (17 December 2001).
26. M. Ciarracca, "Post-9/11 Economic Windfalls for Arms Manufacturers," *Foreign Policy In Focus* 7/10 (2002), http://www.fpil.org.
27. Privacy Commissioner of Canada, *Annual Report 2000-2001* (Ottawa: Government of Canada, 2001).
28. International Biometrics Industry Association (IBIA), *Biometrics and Counter-Terrorism, A Statement by the Board of Directors of the International Biometrics Industry Association* (Washington, DC: 21 September 2001), http://www.ibia@ibia.org.
29. *Ibid.*
30. Visionics, *Protecting Civilization from the Faces of Terror: A Primer on the Role Facial Recognition Technology Can Play in Enhancing Airport Security* (24 September 2001), http://www.vision-ics.com.
31. J. Sharkey, "The Nation: Class Consciousness Comes to Airport Security," *New York Times* (6 January 2002), http://www.nytimes.com.
32. Visionics, *Protecting Civilization*.
33. *Ibid.*
34. *Ibid.*
35. E. Lichtblau, "Administration Creates Center for Master Terror 'Watch List,'" *New York Times* (17 September 2003), http://www.nytimes.com.
36. Visionics, *Protecting Civilization*.
37. Robert Gailing. "Biometrics in the Workplace," (White Pape, Bioscrypt Inc., Van Nuys, California), p. 2.
38. Nuance, *The Business Case for Speech Recognition. White Paper* (Menlo Park, California: 2000), http://www.nuance.com.

39. Biometric Foundation (BF), "Mission Statement (2002)," available at http://www.biometric-foundation.org/tbfmission.htm.
40. P. Collier, "Executive Director of the Biometric Foundation Testifies on October 12 Before the Senate Subcommittee on Technology, Terrorism, and Government Information," *Biometrics Advocacy Report* III/17 (19 October 2001).
41. *Ibid.*
42. IBIA, *Biometrics Advocacy Report* III/18 (2 November 2001).
43. *Ibid.*
44. CATA Biometrics Group, *Mission and Mandate Statement* (2002), http://www.cata.ca/biometrics.
45. CATA Biometrics Group, *CATA News* (17 January 2002), http://www.cata.ca/biometrics.
46. *Ibid.*
47. Canada, *Government Response to the Report of the Standing Committee on Citizenship and Immigration "Across the Border: Working Together at our Shared Border and Abroad to Ensure Safety, Security and Efficiency"* (2002), http://www.cic.gc.ca/english/pub/hab.html.
48. *Ibid.*
49. *Ibid.*
50. A. Gentleman, "ID Cards May Cut Queues but Learn Lesson of History, Warn Europeans," *The Guardian* (15 November, 2003).
51. Privacy Commissioner of Canada, *News Release. Privacy Commissioner of Canada criticizes CCRA's Plans for "Big Brother" Database* (26 September 2002), http://www.privcom.gc.ca/media/nr-c/02_05_b_020926_2_e.asp?V=Print.
52. Privacy Commissioner of Canada, *Statement of Support from Provincial and Territorial Information and Privacy Commissioners* (12 November 2002) available at http://www.privcom.gc.ca/media/le_021113_e.asp?V=Print.
53. Privacy Commissioner of Canada, *News Release* (9 January 2003), http://www.privcom.gc.ca/media/nr-c/02_05_b_030109_e.asp?V=Print.
54. Privacy Commissioner of Canada, *News Release – Breakthrough for Privacy Rights* (9 April 2003) available at http://www.privcom.gc.ca/media/.
55. D. Schneiderman, "Terrorism and the Risk Society," in R.J. Daniels, P. Macklem, and K. Roach, (eds.), *The Security of Freedom: Essays on Canada's Anti-terrorism Bill* (Toronto: University of Toronto Press, 2002), pp. 64-72.
56. *Ibid.*
57. L. Austin, "Is Privacy a Casualty of the War on Terrorism?," in R.J. Daniels, P. Macklem, and K. Roach, (eds.), *The Security of Freedom: Essays on Canada's Anti-terrorism Bill* (Toronto: University of Toronto Press, 2002), pp. 251-267, especially p. 260.
58. Canadian Centre for Policy Alternatives, *CCPA Analysis of Bill C-36: An Act to Combat Terrorism* (Ottawa: CCPA, 2001).
59. S. Armstrong, "Does Bill C-36 Need a Sunset Clause?" *University of Toronto Faculty of Law Review* 60/1 (2002), pp. 73-78.
60. P. McMahon, "Amending the *Access to Information Act*: Does National Security Require the Proposed Amendments of Bill C-36?" *University of Toronto Faculty of Law Review* 60/1 (2002), pp. 89-101.
61. F. Stalder and D. Lyon, "Electronic Identity Cards and Social Classification," in David Lyon, (ed.), *Surveillance as Social Sorting* (London: Routledge, 2001), pp. 77-93.
62. C. Clark, "Coderre Pushes Ottawa to Adopt National ID Cards," *The Globe and Mail* (9 February 2003).
63. "Why the Proposal for a National Identity Card (editorial)," *The Globe and Mail* (11 February 2003).
64. Citizenship and Immigration Canada Forum, *Biometrics: Implications and Applications for Citizenship and Immigration*, Ottawa (7-8 October 2003); "National ID Card Puts Rights at Risk (editorial)," *Toronto Star* (17 August 2003).
65. Alan Dershowitz, "Should this Man be Assassinated?" *The Globe and Mail* (16 September, 2003).

66. J. Gilliom, *Overseers of the Poor: Surveillance, Resistance, and the Limits of Privacy* (Chicago: University of Chicago Press, 2001); D. Lyon, *Surveillance After September 11* (Cambridge, England: Polity Press, 2003).

67. M. Davis, "The Flames of New York," *New Left Review* (November/December 2001), pp. 34-50, especially p. 50.

68. Electronic Frontier Foundation (EFF), "Biometrics: Who's Watching You?" (2002), http://www.eff.org/Privacy/Surveillance/biometrics.html.

69. Accenture, *Majority Travelers Continue with Holiday Flight Plans, According to New Accenture Research* (7 November 2001), http://www.accenture.com; Harris Poll, *The Harris Poll #49* (3 October 2001), http:www.harrisinteractive.com/harris_poll/ lates.asp; Los Angeles *Times*, "Los Angeles *Times* Poll Alert (6 September 2001).

70. A.F. Westin, *The American Public and Biometrics*, presented at a conference organized by the National Consortium of Justice and Information Statistics, New York City (5 November 2002), http://www.search.org/policy/bio_conf/Westin%20Final.ppt. See the full findings of the survey at http://www.search.org/policy/bio_conf/Biometricsurveyfindings.pdf.

71. D. Leblanc, "80 percent Would Back National ID Cards," *The Globe and Mail* (6 October 2001).

72. EKOS Research Associates Inc., *Security, Sovereignty and Continentalism: Canadian Perspectives on September 11* (27 September 2001), http://www.ekos.ca/admin/ press_releases/27-sept-2001e.pdf.

73. Public Policy Forum, *Biometrics: Implications and Applications for Citizenship and Immigration.* Background paper prepared for the Citizenship and Immigration Canada Forum, Ottawa (7-8 October 2003).

74. EKOS, *Canadian Attitudes Towards Biometrics and Document Integrity.* Paper presented at the Citizenship and Immigration Canada Forum, Ottawa (7-8 October 2003).

75. Canada, *A National Identity Card in Canada.* Report of the Standing Committee on Citizenship and Immigration (Joe Fontana, Chair: 2003), http://www.parl.gov.ca.

Part V
Surveillance Futures

[23]

Algorithmic surveillance: the future of automated visual surveillance

Clive Norris, Jade Moran & Gary Armstrong

Algorithm: procedure or series of steps that can be used to solve a problem. In computer science, it describes the logical sequence of operations to be performed by a program. (Hutchinson, 1994: 14)

The algorithm is still in development but can already track vechicles in a standard video picture. (Bogeart, 1996: 150)

Introduction: cameras, cameras and more cameras[1]

As many commentators have noted, the rise of video surveillance in public spaces in Britain has been dramatic. All the major cities with a population over 500,000 boast city centre schemes, and there are in excess of 200 police and local authority schemes operating in high streets and smaller towns.[2] But it is not just city centre streets which have seen a proliferation of systems. In the retail sector CCTV monitoring of customers to deter theft is now almost ubiquitous. The major out of town shopping parks, such as the Gateshead Metro Centre and Sheffield's Meadow Hall development, which attract millions of shoppers annually, have invested heavily in visual surveillance. The Metro Centre's system, for example, cost £500,000 to install, consists of 73 cameras and its security budget runs to £1 million pounds each year (Graham *et al.* 1996). Most of the major petrol distributors have introduced forecourt cameras to deter drive away thefts of petrol and to provide added security for their staff. High street banks and building societies continuously record their customers on entry to the premises and many display prominent notices insisting that crash helmets be removed on entry, to ensure that each person's face is adequately filmed. More recently, a number of High Street banks have taken to (covertly) photographing customers as they make withdrawals from 'hole-in-the-wall' automated cash machines in an effort to provide evidence in cases of disputed withdrawals (*Guardian*, 17 July, 1994).

What has been happening in our city centres has also been mirrored on our roads and railways. There are now some 450 surveillance and enforcement cameras operating on the roads in London. Each of the 30 junctions of the M25 London orbital motorway has cameras for monitoring and enforcement purposes (Hook, 1995). The city of Oxford has installed 16 speed cameras, as have forty other local authorities. Schemes are also in operation on all the major motorways and are being extended each year. Phillips, a leading CCTV company, has recently announced the award of a £400,000 contract from the Highway Agency to extend the camera system on the M1. The Railways have also seen a dramatic increase in the number of cameras. On the London Underground, for example, what started out as a small scheme in 1975 covering four South London stations has, in twenty years risen, to a system encompassing 5,000 cameras. In the wake of the Fennell Report, British Rail has been introducing cameras on all its major stations. Neither has the public sector escaped: increasingly schools (Home Office, 1996), housing estates (Anon, 1993) and hospitals (Brahams, 1993 & *Guardian*, 12 February, 1995) are coming under the camera's gaze.

Technological trends: the drive for automated surveillance

This exponential increase in visual surveillance creates a massive and costly problem of information processing and handling. If we imagine a typical town centre CCTV system, consisting of twenty cameras filming twenty four hours each day, this produces the equivalent of 480 hours of video footage. To be fully effective, many schemes have recognised the necessity of providing 24 hour monitoring of the screens; this, however, is a very expensive resource. To adequately monitor any large scale system 24 hours a day requires a minimum of ten full time personnel. This allows for two operatives to be on duty on each shift, three shifts per day, one shift on rest days and two people to cover for sickness and holidays. Even at the low rates of pay found in the security industry (Jones & Newburn, 1996) it is unlikely that the total cost of employing an operative is less than £8,000 a year, and thus the minimum cost to properly monitor a system is £80,000 per annum. As a result, some systems are not monitored at all, and many only part-time.

From our own data base of 150 sites, we have details of the running costs of 45 of them. The average annual costs for these sites is £72,000. The highest, £250,000 and the lowest, £2,000. We would estimate that about 80% of any budget is for staff costs associated with monitoring the system, so the average cost of monitoring a scheme is £58,000. With 200 town centre and street schemes now in operation and at least another 200 to be funded in 1996, a conservative estimate of the total cost of monitoring would be £23 million per year. This merely represents the cost of town centre systems; if one adds to this the retail sector, the transport sector and work place surveillance, it may not be unreasonable to 'guesstimate' that by the year 2000 the total annual cost of monitoring CCTV systems will be nearing the £100 million mark.

It is clear that the financial cost associated with the human monitoring of CCTV systems is already considerable and continuing to grow. Because of this, human monitoring is still very limited. The inherent boredom of watching dozens of screens and the resulting inattentiveness is another such limitation, as is information overload. The Glasgow system, for example, has 12 screens displaying images from 32 cameras watched by only two operatives. These 32 cameras produce 768 hours of tape per day. The enormity of the information processing task can be illustrated by asking a simple hypothetical question. How many frames would have to be processed if it were necessary to try and confirm the presence of a terrorist suspect in the city on any given day? The answer is quite staggering. A standard three hour video tape records 25 frames per second, equivalent to 90,000 pictures per hour. With thirty two cameras the number of individual pictures that would have to reviewed for a twenty four hour period is 69 million.

If our example seems far fetched consider the events in the aftermath of the IRA bombing in Manchester city centre in June 1996 when an unattended van was detonated and injured over 200 people. The police, in an effort to trace the movements of the van and establish the identity of its occupants, appealed for any video footage from private or public CCTV systems which might contain images of the van or the bombers. Within days they were inundated with some 2,000 hours of footage. As a consequence, the viewing team was increased from two to six officers. Even so, if they were to view the footage in real time (without pressing the fast forward button) and each working a twelve hour day, it would take them one month to view all the tapes. Between them they will have viewed 180 million pictures.

The growth in visual surveillance systems creates a vast pool of previously unavailable information. The CCTV industry has not been slow to realise that the problem is how to exploit this and develop marketable applications for crime control, traffic management and work place security. Given the physical and cost limitations of anything but limited human monitoring of such systems, the industry is increasingly developing and marketing automated systems for incident detection, personal identification and licence plate recognition.

The growth of automated surveillance has been made possible by the intersection of three traditionally separate industries: telecommunications, photography and computing. The telecommunications industry has provided the infrastructure through which images can be transmitted. The development of fibre optic technology has made possible the cheap and rapid transmission of huge amounts of data over long distances. A single fibre optic cable, for example, is able to transmit several hundred television channels simultaneously: the equivalent of 8,000 pictures per second. The photographic industry has, with the development of camera and lens technology, provided durable, all weather cameras capable of three hundred and sixty degree monitoring. Pan, tilt and zoom facilities enable large areas to be monitored and, for example, a car number plate to be accurately read at distances of up to a mile. The problems associated with poor lighting conditions have been addressed by the introduction of additional infra-red facilities and highlight compression functions which reduce glare. Finally, the developments in photography which allows for images to be captured digitally (numerically rather than chemically), is perhaps most significant, for this greatly enhances the capacity of images to be transmitted through a variety of media, such as telephone lines and computer networks. This also means that as soon as a picture is taken it can be viewed, stored and processed using a personal computer.

If the developments in telecommunications and photography provide the technology whereby high quality images can increasingly be transmitted in digital form, to centralised control rooms, the advancements in computing technology allow for images to be stored, retrieved and analysed speedily and cheaply. It is the developments in storage and processing that have been most important. Put simply, since the mid 1970s every two years the size of processing power and storage capacity has doubled while the cost has halved. Thus, in 1976 1 megabyte of hard drive (storage) and a quarter of megabyte of RAM (processing) would cost £1,000. In 1996 it was possible to purchase 32 megabytes of RAM and 1,000 megabytes of hard disk for the same price. This is important because computerised images are memory hungry. A reasonably sized and good quality facial image may well take 200 kilobytes of memory. To store a database of 5,000 faces requires 1,000 megabytes of memory. However, advances in storage techniques mean that these images can be compressed to a fraction of their original size allowing the size of the database to be considerably increased. The analysis and comparison of images also requires a vast amounts of processing power and the availability of cheap and extensive RAM makes this increasingly possible. Now, with compression techniques which also increase the speed of processing, it is possible to compare two computer held pictures in a fraction of a second (Geake, 1993).

Cameras in context: social and economic trends

To understand the rise of visual surveillance it is necessary to avoid falling into the trap of technological determinism. Technological developments have indeed, as we have argued, facilitated the introduction of CCTV technology; however, such use needs to be seen in the context of broader social and economic trends.

Nock (1993), in his book *The Costs of Privacy*, asks the deceptively simple question of how, in a society of strangers, is trust possible? The twentieth century, he goes on to argue, has undergone a major transformation, and though increasing personal autonomy, has broken down traditional community ties and natural forms of surveillance. Increases in social and geographical mobility, urbanisation, the rapid rise of mass transportation systems and the changing family and household structure have given rise to a society of strangers. However, as individuals are freed from the constraints of familial obligations and surveillance and disembedded from traditional community networks, it becomes increasingly difficult to know what kind of person they really are; or even if they really are who they say they are! In this context, it is hardly coincidental that many of the applications of the new surveillance technology are aimed at personal identity verification.

For Nock, the cost of autonomy and privacy lies not so much in the growth of surveillance but in its changing form: from the local and intimate, based on personal knowledge and mutuality of associations, towards the impersonal, the standardised and the bureaucratic. When the famous charge card company declared 'American Express says more about you than cash ever can', they were epitomising this trend; for to know whether you should do business with someone is based on an abstract token which symbolises their creditworthiness. In order to ascertain whether they have reliable employees, many American (and some British) firms are now demanding job applicants submit to drug testing, and insist their permanent employees agree to ongoing, random testing (Gilliom, 1994).

Underlying these broad sociological shifts has been a series of major economic transformations. Capital, like people, is increasingly mobile, moving through global markets in search of the most conducive locations for investment and production. This has also driven the development of a global communications infrastructure to service an increasingly geographically dispersed production process enabling the rapid movement of investment capital from one international market place to another. It is not just the site of production that has changed but the process of production itself. The dynamics of international competition has driven the need to constantly increase worker productivity, to decrease the need for expensive stock holding, and to produce a greater variety within product lines. This has led corporations to rapidly embrace the new management techniques of 'Just in Time Management' and 'Total Quality Management'. Both of these are information hungry and require vast amounts of data to be recorded, stored and analysed in an effort to constantly monitor work performance and the production process. Thus, word processing operatives' performance is automatically monitored by the number of key strokes they make in an hour; service personnel, such as check-out assistants and cashiers, are watched by constant video recording of their performance to ensure 'correct' demeanour; and production lines are monitored by CCTV cameras so that any disruptions can be attended to immediately. (Davies, 1996; Sewell and Wilkinson, 1992).

There has also been an intensification of surveillance at the point of consumption. The spending and purchasing patterns of customers and potential customers are now easily monitored and analysed with the aid of computerised databases and information from new forms of cashless transactions and in-store loyalty cards. For large retailers this can provide a significant competitive advantage as they can engage in sophisticated niche marketing, only targeting those statistically most likely to purchase their products and services. It also enables accurate, on the spot credit decisions to be made which both facilitate consumer spending and allow businesses to reduce loss through risky credit decisions (Lyon, 1994: 153).

We have briefly outlined how the developments and convergence in a range of industries have laid the foundations for the technological possibility of automated surveillance and have also outlined some broad social and economic trends which have have given impetus to the rise of what some have called a 'surveillance society'. There are two features of this we wish to highlight. First, that the rise of CCTV surveillance systems in general, and automated systems in particular, should not be seen primarily as a distinctively criminological phenomenon. The expansion of these systems owes as much to the need to manage increasingly congested traffic flows, to provide management information on staff behaviour, and to enhance the 'feel good factor' in recession-hit high streets and town centres. Seondly, we do not claim that the technological developments have been fuelled by the concerns of crime control. The rapid advancement of automated licence plate recognition, for example, has been spurred on by the prospect of 'toll' roads which can be built by the private sector and operated commercially for private profit. Similarly, advances in the image handling capacities of computers have been primarily driven by the broadcasting and telecommunications industries who, in an increasingly deregulated and international market, are seeking to diversify and increase their market share.

Automated surveillance

Anyone who has a domestic burglar alarm is probably familiar with the principle of automated surveillance. Most alarms now include remote movement sensors in which a small microchip measures changes in air pressure or air flow so that if the changes are above a specific intensity the alarm is triggered. Commercial, rather than domestic systems utilise far more sophisticated automation techniques which rely on the integration of three elements: remote sensors, cameras and microcomputers. When the remote sensors are triggered, the information is relayed to the computer which automatically directs the camera to the site of the intrusion, from then on images are automatically recorded and displayed on the system monitor. Security personnel can then evaluate the cause of the alarm and decide on appropriate action. The president of one company, aptly named 'Big Brother Surveillance and Security', explained the advantages of this new combination:

> In the past, intruder intimidation was limited to a sticker on the door and a siren ringing. Now someone comes in and our central station remotely turns on the lights and cameras. And we can issue a barrage of verbal commands over a loud speaker, to let them know they're being observed by a live system. (Bouley, 1994: 49)

Although such systems may appear technologically advanced they are relatively primitive, relying as they do on remote sensors and fail to exploit the capacity of image handling, software to record, monitor and evaluate the images supplied by the camera. The most significant advances in this field have been in the areas of traffic management and licence plate recognition, and though law enforcement agencies have not been slow to recognise the potential of automated licence plate recognition, the main thrust has come from the commercial sector, as described above in relation to toll road implementation. Traditionally the problem has been the physical nature of toll booths which disrupt the free flow of traffic, leading to long queues and limiting the number of access and egress points in any network. The managerial preference is for completely open access to private roads where any vehicle can enter and leave without passing through a physical barrier. But this of course presents the dual problem of how to collect tolls from legitimate users, and how to prevent free riders.

The solution has come through the development of a variety of new technologies. These include camera and lens technology to capture the licence plates of fast moving vehicles in all weather and light conditions; computer technology which can store the images from the cameras; optical character recognition software to process the images and accurately extract the licence number to match it against a database of account holders; and billing technology which automatically records and charges account holders. This process is increasingly achieved by vehicles being fitted with a 'smart-card' which contains account holders' details. Utilising information from the cameras, the centralised computer software, records entry and exit from the system, calculates the distance travelled and records this on the smart card.

There are now a number of major electronics and photographic corporations actively involved in developing and marketing these technologies: Kodak, Philips, Sony and Westinghouse to name but a few. Perceptics, for example, part of the Westinghouse corporation, declares: 'With our licence plate reader every highway is an open book.' The Perceptics system has now been installed at over 175 locations worldwide. (Perceptics, nd) and includes a licence plate reader which:

> ... captures an image of the vehicle's front and rear at highway speeds. The licence plate is located, read, and identified in milliseconds.' The 'unique geometric shape analyser' guarantees recognition of characters despite variations in font, syntax, size, perspective, and tilt. Upon identification, the licence plate number...can be stored locally for future

261

queries or immediately searched against specified databases to determine whether the vehicle belongs to a target group. (Perceptics, n.d.)

For tolling purposes this means bona fide account holders can be verified and, with access to a central licensing database, 'free riders' can be identified traced and billed.

Once such technology has been developed its applications reach far beyond the needs of tolling systems. As Perceptics notes, one major application is border security as the system can 'quickly and easily identify high risk traffic and frequent travellers' and automatically monitor unmanned crossings. It is this same technology which has recently been deployed in the Square Mile of the City of London. The so called 'Ring of Steel' was set up in the wake of the Bishopsgate bombing in 1993 (*Guardian*, 4 August, 1993) to protect the financial heart of Europe from further terrorist attack. The system consists of ninety CCTV cameras recording the movement of all traffic in and out of the square mile of the city. Twenty eight of these security cameras have been installed at the eight official entry points. The camera lenses are capable of preventing wide screen glare and reflection, and clearly identify the occupants of the car and the vehicle registration plate (*Guardian*, 24 November, 1993). Technology perfected during the Gulf War in 1991 has been utilised to track vehicles coming in to the City of London and will trigger an alarm when a car travels in the wrong direction on the one-way system (Potter, 1995). In May 1996, however, the capacity of the system was significantly enhanced with the addition of automated licence plate recognition. The system creates a database of the licence plates of all cars entering and exiting the area. Any vehicle which does not exit the system after a specified time automatically triggers an alarm and alerts the operators to the presence of a suspect vehicle. Additionally once all the licence plates are held on a computerised database they can be automatically run against any number of other databases; for instance, an index of stolen cars or the vehicles associated with known suspects.

While the prevention of terrorist activities provides the main justification for the adoption of CCTV in the City of London, these system have tremendous potential for more conventional traffic policing. The same technology which allows the automatic reading of licence plates can also be used to evaluate the speed of a vehicle passing between two points and identify traffic light, weight or emission violations. Since 1993, when automated speed-trap camera evidence saw the first driver in England prosecuted for speeding, these camera based enforcement systems have mushroomed, as have prosecutions. In 1994 some 20,000 were prosecuted and this number doubled in the following year to 40,000 (*Guardian*, 29 January, 1996, *Independent*, 1 January, 1996). As yet these cameras are not digitised. Nor does filming take place continuously, but occurs when the cameras are triggered by roadside speed sensors. In essence the pictures provide the evidential base for prosecution, rather than the data for continuous computer monitoring. More importantly, the systems are cumbersome and labour intensive. Each camera still has to be traditionally loaded with film, and this has to be unloaded and replaced when it runs out. The film then has to be processed and individually scrutinised by human operatives to extract the licence plate details which are then manually submitted to the DVLA central computer to provide the identification details for prosecution. Given this laborious and costly process, it is perhaps not surprising that under-enforcement is the norm. When speed cameras were first introduced to a stretch of road in West London with a 40 MPH limit in 'three weeks the Twickenham camera caught 22,000 motorists doing 60 MPH or more. Yet after 4 months, only 1,100 cases were being processed - from all the camera installations in London' (Geake, 1993: 23).

The limitations of these semi-automated systems ensures that the next generation of traffic cameras will certainly be digitised and exploit computerised image recognition software (Gibson, 1995). As Lemarie (1994) pointed out, the use of computerised vision-based traffic detection technologies allows for multiple data to be produced and analysed from one image or set of images to reveal speed, location, type of vehicle, licence plate, and occupancy data. Trafficon's CCIDS (Camera and Computer aided Incident Detection Sensor) system needs only ten video frames (less than half of a second) to detect a stationary vehicle on a free flowing highway and can simultaneously count the number of cars, the gap times and queue lengths. Thus a single camera can replace a host of other sensors and dramatically increase the range of applications available, while digitised cameras without film are cheaper to install and maintain, with processing times and costs significantly reduced through automation (Lemaire, 1994).

The implications for policing, not only in the fields of traffic enforcement but also for traditional detective work and intelligence gathering are enormous. Literally at the flick of a switch, enforcement of speed limits could become exponentially increased and the chances of escaping detection made much more unlikely. With computerised processing of offenders and linkage to existing databases held at the DVLC, there is no technical reason why fixed penalty notices could not automatically be produced and dispatched within hours or even minutes of a violation occurring. However, this same technology also enables the automatic tracking of any vehicle on a monitored road space, which will soon encompass the entire motorway network (Jenkins, 1992). This represents a massive increase in the surveillance capacity of the police and security services; meanwhile the legal, civil liberty and regulatory implications of this capacity have hardly been given any attention.

The emerging technology of motorway management and tolling is now rapidly finding its way into the the more traditional concerns of the private security industry. EDS, a leading security company specialising in 'intelligent scene monitoring', sees the problem as being one of an inability of companies to process and evaluate the incoming information as CCTV systems expand to enhance security. As their advertising literature states:

> ... the camera is only a remote electronic eye. Video images have to be monitored and interpreted. A major problem with such security installations is that operators faced with a large number of monitors, will miss events occurring ...(and monitors)...may not be displaying a scene when an event happens. The problem is compounded by human error due to tiredness, boredom, or distraction. (EDS, 1995)

One solution to this problem is to combine the use of digitised cameras, microcomputers and neural network technology which allows the computer system to learn the features of a scene and to detect changes to it. Rather than relying on remote sensors, these intelligent image processing systems can detect up to six events in any one scene, merely by analysing the information provided by the incoming pictures. Through the use of algorithms to interpret the images, a system can react to motion or non-motion; to object size, speed and direction; to duration in an area; and to recognise the direction of exit and entry. What this means in practice is that such systems can automatically monitor complex scenes and trigger alarms and other security mechanisms when unsanctioned events occur. For instance, a stationary vehicle can trigger an alarm as can a person heading in the 'wrong' direction (EDS, 1995).

The intelligent image recognition ability of these systems enables them to be, 'highly discriminatory and to raise alarms only when objects that satisfy all of the rules are detected on the scene.' Whereas light or pressure sensors are triggered when anything breaks the circuit, such as a rabbit or bird, intelligent systems will ignore these on the basis of a size discriminator algorithm. Similarly, the presence of a person loitering in a specific location, even in a busy street, can be identified through tracking and dwell time algorithms which will successfully discriminate between loiterers and passers-by (Signal, July 1995).

The implications of such technology are manifold, but two are especially worthy of note. First, as software engineers start to exploit its potential, they will develop more and more sophisticated algorithms which allow for the evaluation of more complex scenes. The kinds of applications that are currently under review include the development of an algorithm which will monitor bank queues in an effort to predict which behaviours are indicative of an imminent hold up and others trying to produce algorithms responsive to crowd behaviour which will warn of potential disorder. Second, this new technology gives substance to the claim of permanent and continuous surveillance '24 hours a day, 7 days a week and 52 weeks a year'; which, moreover, can be achieved with limited labour input. The EDS system installed at Dolland's Moor, the Channel tunnel rail freight marshalling yard, currently monitors inputs from 48 cameras. Without a physical responsibility for monitoring the screens there is only a need for one operative to be on duty at any one time to respond to system triggered alarms. As Brock predicted in 1987 when writing about the security industry in the year 2000, 'Guards will be reduced in number in many organisations because their spiralling cost cannot be justified in the face of technologies which can accomplish the same functions' (Brock, 1987). In Britain, the private security industry is now worth over 2 billion pounds each year (Jones and Newburn, 1995). This is reflected in the steady rise in numbers employed in the industry over the last two decades, with recent estimates putting the total at between 160,000 and 250,000 people. It is no surprise then that the reduction in labour costs offered by intelligent image processing has major appeal.

Naming names and naming faces

As Virilio (1994, 44) points out, human visual capability has difficulty competing with the high resolution surveillance capabilities of a digital camera. Unlike security footage, the human visual surveillance system cannot be rewound or replayed in a court of law. The evidential value of CCTV is perhaps best demonstrated by a high level of guilty pleas when suspects are faced with the prospect of having their wrongdoings replayed in the court. This assumes, of course, the suspects have been caught. However, if the identity and whereabouts of the suspect is unknown, the police are still reliant on public cooperation to put a name to a face. In the 1990s, the release of 'Wanted' posters, sometimes with a bounty of £500 being offered for information, may seem a retrogressive technique of criminal identification and tracking. However, the publication of 'mugshots' in local newspapers reminds us of their age-old reliance on the public to accurately identify wanted suspects or witnesses (*Hull Daily Mail*,14 December, 1995; *Newcastle Evening Chronicle*, 29 May, 1996). Of course, the world has progressed a little since the days of Dick Turpin and scenes from security camera footage are now regularly broadcast on prime-time television shows such as 'Crimewatch UK' and 'Crimestoppers'.

While the new technologies surrounding CCTV have dramatically increased the information available to law enforcement agencies, as yet they do not allow for the automatic identification of suspects, although this is increasingly a prize sought by private security agencies and police alike. Research funded by the Home Office, the Police Foundation, and Marks and Spencer's, is currently being directed at solving the problem of facial image matching. The 1990s has simultaneously seen a proliferation of academic conferences and articles on the problem of facial recognition, though the question remains as to what prospects the technique holds in the context of law enforcement?

The major technical problem of automatic facial recognition is essentially one of pattern matching. The uniqueness of each face needs to be mathematically described in order to enable statistical comparison with other faces to be made. There are various mathematical and statistical

265

approaches to this problem and these rely on different methodologies for segmenting, classifying and measuring facial features and different statistical techniques for analysing the results.[3] All these techniques have various strengths. For example, Kamel *et al.* (1994) utilised a Cross Ratio Configuration technique. This technique, unlike many others, allows for pictures taken from different perspectives and different distances from the subject to be compared. This mirrors the problem for automatic facial recognition in town centre CCTV systems since there would almost certainly be perspective and distance differences between the data base image and the CCTV system image. Kamel *et al.* state that their results produced a 'very good retrieval rate', yet even on a limited database containing 84 pictures (some of the same person) they only achieved a correct match in 66% of cases. As they note, even though this technique represents the brightest hope for practical automatic facial recognition outside of highly controlled situations, 'Much more work is required in order to provide the system with a fully automated features capture mechanism'(Kamel *et al.* 1994).

Similar sorts of results in experimental situations are described in a growing number of studies, with test results often reported in the 90% to 100% range.[4] Despite these impressive sounding results, caution is necessary before predicting that CCTV systems coupled to image processing software will be able to name us as we walk down our high streets. In the real world the artificial and controlled settings of the laboratory are unlikely to be reproduced and the experimental results show that the more realistic the settings are made, the lower the success rate.

Nearly all the experimental studies compared pictures of pre-defined faces. However, in security camera footage, faces are not dismembered from bodies or isolated from the backgrounds in which they occur. Burel and Carel (1994: 963) note the following experimental problems for merely locating a face in a frame: the diversity and non-rigidity of the human face; the distance between the camera and the face is often unknown in a real setting; the lighting conditions are only partly controlled; facial orientation and rotation are not held constant and neither are backgrounds or shadows; faces may be partially occluded, for example by a hand or a piece of clothing.

These difficulties mean that the prospect of being able to match a face from a city centre surveillance scene with one held on a computerised data base is advancing but still a long way off. However, as Robertson *et al.* (1994) have argued in their evaluation of facial recognition systems, automatic detection has been shown to work with, 'restricted types of data and data that has been carefully structured'. This suggests that, for law enforcement purpose, advances will be piecemeal and incremental. Applications will first be developed which exploit the storage and retrieval capacities of digitised databases. As the technology advances, these databases will be subject to limited automatic matching. Rather than producing a definitive single match, the system will identify, for example, the four most likely faces and the human operative will make the final judgment. Increasingly, as the technology advances, in more or less controlled conditions, reliable automatic recognition systems will be introduced.

This process has already begun, for the 'Football Intelligence System' has been developed by the Greater Manchester Police Football Intelligence Unit and consists of a lap top computer running a 'windows database'. The system collates information and photographic records of suspects and offenders associated with football violence and is used at Manchester City's Maine Road ground. From a set of personal descriptors entered by the operator the system will display the pictures of the 12 most likely suspects from a database of 150 'known' offenders. Details can be cross referenced with details relating to previous convictions, intelligence information, 'hooligan' associates, and gang membership. This system mirrors the National Criminal Intelligence Service's database which holds details and pictures of 6,000 suspected football hooligans. In the run up to the 1996 European football championship, the NCIS database was made available to all the participating football grounds through the use of 'photophones' enabling digitised photographs to be transmitted from one central location to a remote terminal in each stadium (*Guardian*, 10 February, 1996).

Then again, the Public Order Unit of the Metropolitan Police, drawing on experience gained from the detection and identification of football hooligans, is now deploying Kodak Digital cameras at demonstrations. As Hook reported, 'The camera allows images to be processed on a lap top computer within seconds, thus allowing, for example, the identification of persons leaving premises under observation' (1994: 11). And as the head of the Unit stated, the main purpose of the system is to identify and bring before the courts a 'hard core of people who travel from one demonstration to another and who are responsible for much of the violence'. The Metropolitan Police were also said to working on another system 'designed to compare human features and to reduce the time spent identifying a person from a database' (Hook, 1994: 11). In 1993 it was reported that:

> ... in Australia, a team at the University of Wollongong is developing an automatic face recognition system for Sydney's International Airport to be installed within four years. Like an electronic Identikit, it picks out peoples facial characteristics - their eyes, nose, mouth, chin and hair. For each characteristic it recognises about 14 variations in size and shape, giving more than half a million different 'faces'. Using a picture of a face from a standard security camera, the system uses a neural network to compare it with a database of up 2,000 suspects' faces. On finding a 'close' match - a measure yet to be defined - it will alert immigration officials. (Geake, 1993)

We do not know whether this system is still on target to be delivered in 1997. However, if the environment in which the pictures are taken can be sufficiently controlled (so there is only limited variation in head orientation, lighting conditions and so forth) with currently available technology the system may provide a reasonably reliable, although only semi automated identification system.   Again in a partially controlled environment such as a football ground, the possibility of identifying one face in the crowd as belonging to a known hooligan is drawing nearer. With existing technology and extrapolating from the work of Kamel *et al* (1994), it would seem that if an individual face were matched against a small database of around two hundred suspects there would be a 95% chance that the target face would be in the best ten matches.

The consistent feature of all these systems is the existence of a computer held photographic database of suspects or potential suspects.   One consequence of this is that in the short-term we will see a proliferation of separate pictorial databases created for various subgroups. Following in the footsteps of the hooligan database, others will be compiled on animal rights activists, environmental campaigners, suspect terrorists and their sympathisers and political groups on the extremes of both left and right, and so on. However, the potential for creating a near national database of all citizens is moving closer with the proposed introduction of the new photo Drivers Licence which Davies argues will almost certainly be stored in digital form by the DVLA (1996: 196). It is therefore now technologically feasible to imagine that, in some not too distant future, as we walk down the city streets we will not only be photographed, but automatically identified as well.

Discussion and implications

The growth of automated surveillance systems simultaneously increases the size, scope and intensity of the formal control system with all the developments expanding the gaze to reach the parts that previous systems could not reach. This will no doubt be coupled to a growing reliance on formal systems of intervention. If being observed is not a significant deterrence to manifestations of deviant behaviour, then physical intervention by police or private security personnel will result, for intervention is maximised by the ease of identifying the otherwise anonymous rule breakers and the 'incontrovertibility' of the evidence. To use Cohen's analogy, the size and reach of the social control nets are widened and the mesh strengthened and thinned (Cohen, 1985). In practice, this widening and thinning will mean that more and more people will be drawn into the net of the formal system.   We can already see this happening in traffic and public order policing. In traffic enforcement, as digitalisation and automation becomes standard, more and more offenders can be detected and processed and, because the system is more efficient, there will be no need to concentrate efforts only on the most serious violations. In public order policing, the priority has traditionally been the preservation of public tranquility rather than the detection and prosecution of offenders. However, the potential of the new technologies is increasingly being exploited with the use of surveillance and intelligence gathering squads and footage from CCTV systems being retrospectively examined and analysed to provide evidence for prosecution. Not only, therefore, is the net widened, but the potential for deviancy amplification in public order situations is increased. And as previously marginal demonstrators are caught up in the melee and subsequently identified, arrested and prosecuted, their fledging deviant identities may well become entrenched.

Discrimination and discretion

The use of automated surveillance systems has fundamental implications for the use of police discretion. In traffic enforcement systems, as we have already noted, the prospect of near full enforcement becomes a reality. Research on routine police work has shown that the manner in which such incidents are dealt with and the outcome cannot merely be reduced to a strict application of the law. Other factors come into play: the officer's assessment of the moral worthiness of the offender and the victim, the demeanour of the offender to the officer, whether there are more important incidents to be dealt with, the status of any victims, and so forth.

Discretion is fundamental to policing and the smooth workings of the criminal justice system. If near full enforcement were pursued, an already overstretched criminal justice system could crumble under the pressure of processing ever increasing numbers. Discretion allows that many minor violations are dealt with informally and kept out of a cumbersome and costly criminal justice system.

Discretion fosters legitimacy: it allows officers to use their conceptions of justice and fairness to temper the over-reach of law. Is it really desirable to prosecute a surgeon on her way to a life saving operation for breaking the speed limit by 12 miles an hour? Moreover, most people like the idea of the police until their attention is focussed upon them. By under-enforcing the law, the police can build up legitimacy with an ambivalent citizenry. Such credit is fundamental to the rhetoric of policing by consent, as without the consent of the population the information flow dries up and policing becomes oppressive and inefficient. Information is the life blood of policing and the majority of crime is solved not by some latter day Sherlock Holmes sifting meticulously through the evidence, but by a victim or witness directly naming the suspect. The prospect of automated detection and identification might radically shift this balance. If the police become less dependent on the public for information, the pragmatic impetus for consent is simultaneously lessened and the symbiotic relationships between police and public may be transformed to one of subordination.

Discretion also allows for local norms to be given weight, and in a pluralist society with many different cultures, subcultures and communities what is acceptable in one community is not in another. These subcultural norms and variations are significant in another way as the majority of police work originates from requests from the public for assistance. Such requests have already been filtered through local community norms; for example, youths hanging around on the street are considered normal in some communities, while in others they are considered threatening.

A citizen's decision to call the police is therefore contextual and influenced by complex and personalised knowledge of locales. Automated systems are unlikely to be able to process such sophisticated evaluative capacities, for they will trigger alarms on the basis of only two or three simple rules, such as size of group, location, and duration of stay. There is, of course, the danger that as the response to such scenarios becomes automated and targets of algorithmic suspicion feel increasingly singled out and harassed, then conflict will expand rather than reduce.

However, as Marx has pointed there are also more optimistic visions of this new technology:

> Fixed physical responses that eliminate discretion also eliminate the potential for corruption and discrimination. The video surveillance camera and heat sensing devices do not differentiate between social classes. Data are gathered democratically from all within their purview. Accountability is thus increased and the prior ability of those with power to shield their behaviour is lessened by electronic trails and tails. (Marx, 1995: 238)

Whether such optimism is warranted depends not on the technology but on the social and political contexts in which it is implemented and regulated. The equalisation of detection rates, for instance depends on systems being introduced uniformly across communities. Already, however, we can see that, rather than focussing on town centres, (arguably democratic) particular residential trouble spots are being singled out for special attention: the Meadowell Estate in North Shields and Chapeltown in Leeds to name two examples. Rather than equalising the rates of detection of middle class and working class delinquency, the effect is to intensify an already unequal pattern of policing.

It is true that automatic heat or light sensors cannot discriminate on the basis of social class, race, or gender, however intelligent image processing systems suffer from no such limitations. The same algorithmic techniques that can differentiate faces can also be used to differentiate between black and white and, with time, may also be able to distinguish between young and old and male and female. Again, rather than removing discrimination, the new automated technologies may intensify it. It is here that the regulatory context becomes crucial. As yet there are no laws banning, or even regulating the use of discriminatory algorithms.

Exclusion

The new automated detection and identification technologies may not have been developed for explicitly exclusionary purposes but the exclusionary potential remains just the same. Those who cannot pay will be excluded from motorways; known and suspected trouble makers from football grounds; the unsightly casualties of 'care in the community' removed from the decorous order of city streets and shopping malls; known shoplifters and fare dodgers excluded from shops and transport systems. It can be argued the threat of such exclusion will encourage conformity. However, if the growing divide between those who have and have not and those who are included and excluded is intensified through the use of new technology, there is a real danger that our cities will come to resemble the dystopian vision so beloved by futuristic film-makers. Fortified, armed and electronically protected pockets of privilege will be surrounded by the ever increasing presence of poverty, resentment and hostility and as Mike Davis has so ably informed us, the future is here and now in the shape of Los Angeles (Davis, 1990 & 1992).

More pragmatically, exclusionary social and criminal justice does not induce conformity. The problem with automated systems is that they aim to facilitate exclusionary rather than inclusionary goals. Not unreasonably, high street stores faced with high losses from shoplifting and fraud seek to exclude those who are responsible. Once a person is convicted of an offence, automated systems can be deployed to monitor all those entering a store and alert for the presence of known shoplifters. Security personnel can then be swiftly deployed to remove them from the premises. This exclusionary policy can be extended within a high street chain, and, as systems become widespread, can encompass all city centre stores. It will then not be possible to simply be a 'customer buying groceries' on certain days in some venues, and to become a 'shoplifter intent on stealing' on other days and in other stores. The status of 'shoplifter' is likely to prevail, and the designation 'once a shoplifter always a shoplifter' will predominate. The digitised persona of 'data subjects' (Lyon, 1994) thus has the potential to become a truly powerful 'master status' through which exclusionary social control can be achieved However, as Braithwaite has argued (1988), the weight of criminological evidence suggests that those societies which seek to reintegrate rather than exclude their deviant members have the lowest crime rates. On the basis of this evidence algorithmic justice may not, after all, provide a quick technological fix to the crime problem. Rather, it may actually make it worse.

Notes

1. We would like to thank Jim Sheptycki, Nigel Fielding, Clive Coleman and especially Malcolm Young for comments on an earlier draft of this paper.
2. For instance, Aberdeen, Birmingham, Bradford, Brighton, Cardiff Coventry, City of London, Doncaster, Glasgow, Liverpool, Manchester, Newcastle, Scarborough, Sheffield all have city centre schemes.
3. For further information on the techniques see - Samaria *et al.* (1994) on Hidden Markov Models; Samaria *et al.* (1994) on Eigenface Methods; Li *et al.* (1993), and Burel *et al.* (1994) on Neural Networks and Kamel *et al*, (1994) on Cross Ratio Configuration.
4. Goldstein et al (1991) achieved 50% recognition with 250 target subjects. Akamatsu *et al.* (1992) had 94% recognition with about 400 trials and 12 targets. Nakamura *et al.* (1991) managed a 100% recognition rate of 10 cue images, matched against 10 targets. Sutherland *et al.* (1992) achieved 89% recognition from a set of 600 pool images consisting of 30 people and 300 cue images containing the same 30 people. Robertson *et al* (1994) obtained 100% recognition, with a pool of 45 images containing pictures of 3 different people matched against another 60 test images of the same three people. Turk and Pentland (1991) achieved 96% recognition for constrained images and 85% recognition for unconstrained head orientations.

References

Agre, P.E. (1994), 'The Digital Individual', *The Information Society*, Vol.10, No.2, April-June, Special Issue, pp. 73-138.

Akamatsu, S., T. Sasaki, H. Fukamachi, N. Masui, & Y. Suenaga (1992), An Accurate and Robust Face Identification Scheme', *International Conference on Pattern Recognition*, The Hague, Netherlands.

Anonymous (1995), 'Met Uses Lap-top Technology to try to catch Muggers', *Police Review*, Vol 103, Number 5336, 22 September, p. 4 .

Anonymous.(1994), 'Scare Tactics: See, Hear, Speak to Intruders at Remote Sites', *Security*, January, p. 49.

Anonymous. (1993), 'Crackdown on Tower Block Crime', *Security Gazette*, January, pp. 35-6.

Beats, N. (1995), 'Neural Network Licence Plate Recognition' *Traffic Technology International*, Summer, pp. 72-4.

Beatt, A. (1992), 'The Eyes Have It', *Policing Review*, Vol. 100, 11 Dec, pp. 2300-1.

Blumenthal, H.J. (1988), 'CCTV: The Big Picture', *Security Management*, Vol.32, Iss. 11, pp.7A-10A, November.

Bogaert, M. (1996), 'Video-based solutions for data collection and incident detection' in *Traffic Technology International '96*, pp. 150-56. Traffic Technology International, UK and International Press: Dorking, Surrey.

Bouley, J. (1994), 'No More Tapes? Digital Tech may Erase VHS Storage', *Security*, January, p. 23.

Bouley, J. (1994), 'Night Vision Technology Cuts Through Darkness', *Security* Vol. 31, Iss. 2, February, p. 23.

Brahams, D. (1993), 'Video Surveillance and Child Abuse', *The Lancet*, Vol. 342, No. 8877, p. 994, October.

Braithwaite, J. (1989), *Crime, Shame and Reintegration*, Cambridge University Press, Cambridge.

Brock, R. (1987), 'The Guard in the Year 2000', in *Security in the Year 2000 and Beyond*, L. Tyska & L. Fennelly (eds) ETC Publications: California.

Burel, G.& D. Carel (1994), 'Detection and Localisation of Faces on Digital Images',*Pattern Recognition Letters.*Vol. 15, pp. 963-67.

Cohen S. (1985),*Visions of Social Control*, Polity Press: Cambridge.

Davies, S. (1996),*Big Brother: Britain's Web of Surveillance and the New Technological Order*, Pan Books: London.

Davis, M. (1992), 'Beyond Blade Runner: Urban Control',*Open Magazine Pamphlet Series.* Pamphlet 23, December, pp. 1-20.

Davis, M. (1990),*City of Quartz* , Vintage: London.

Dawson, T. (1994), 'Framing the Villains', *New Statesman and Society* , 23 January, pp. 12-13.

De Lia, R. (1993), 'Seeing in to the World of Fibre Optics for Security' *Security Management*, Vol. 37, No. 3, March, pp. 7a-11a.

Durham, P. (1995), 'Villains in the Frame' *Police Review* , 20 January, pp. 20- 21.

EDS (1995),*Sentinel: Intelligent Scene Monitoring*, (product information), Senintel, EDS Defence Group: Surrey.

Flaherty, D.H. (1988), 'The Emergence of Surveillance Societies in the Western World: Toward the Year 2000', *Government Information Quarterly*, Vol.5, No.4, pp. 377-87.

Fyfe, N.R. & J. Bannister (1994), 'The Eyes On The Street: Closed Circuit Television Surveillance in Public Spaces', paper presented at the *Association of American Geographers Conference*, Chicago, March, pp. 1-13.

Gandy, O. (1989), 'The Surveillance Society: Information Technology and Bureaucratic Social Control', *Journal of Communication*, Vol. 39, No.3, Summer, pp. 61-76.

Geake, E. (1993), 'Tiny Brother is Watching You'. *New Scientist*. 8 May, pp. 21-3.

Gibbons, S. (1995), 'Faces that Fit', *Police Review*, 14 April, pp. 28-29

Gibson, T. (1995), 'Recognition for the Law', *Traffic Technology International*, Summer, pp. 28-31.

Gilliom, J. (1994), *Surveillance, Privacy and the Law: Employee Drug Testing and the Politics of Social Control*, University of Michigan Press: Michigan.

Goldstein, A. J., Harmon, L. D. & Lesk, A. B. (1991) 'Identification of human faces', *Proceedings of the Institute of Electrical Engineers* , Vol. 59, No. 5, May, pp. 748-60.

Graham, S., J. Brooks & D. Heery (1996), 'Towns on television: Closed Circuit TV in British Towns and Cities', *Local Government Studies*, 22(3) pp. 3-27.

Graham, V. (1995), 'Caught on Film', *Police Review* , 31 March, pp. 18-19.

Harris, J. & Sands, M. (1995), 'Life-saving Speed Camera Technology', *Traffic Technology International*, Spring, pp. 63-4.

Hook, P. (1994), 'Faces in the Crowd', *Police Review,* 22 July, pp. 22-23.

Hook, P. (1995), 'Speed Cameras to Target M25 Snarl-ups', *Police Review* , 20 January, p. 11.

Home Office (1996), *Closed Circuit Television Challenge Competition 1996/7 Successful Bids*, Home Office: London.

Hutchinson (1994), *The Huchinson Dictionary of Ideas.* Helicon: Oxford.

Jenkins, J. (1992), 'Eye Can See You', *New Statesman and Society*, 2 1 February, pp. 14-15.

Jones, T. & T. Newburn (1995), 'How Big is the Private Security Sector', *Policing and Society*, Vol 5, pp. 221-32.

Jones, T. & T. Newburn, (1996), 'The Regulation and Control of the Private Security Industry' in Saulsbury, W., Mott, J., and Newburn,.T., (eds),*Themes in Contemporary Policing*, Policy Studies Institute: London.

Kamel M.S. & H.C. Shen (1994), 'Face Recognition using Perspective Invariant Features', *Pattern Recognition Letters.*Vol.15, pp. 877-83.

Lemarie, F. (1994),*Video-and Image Processing for Traffic Data Analysis and Automatic Incident Detection*, Traficon Company Product Information: Belgium.

Li, H. & D. Psaltis (1993), 'Optical Networks for Real-time Recognition', *Applied Optics.* Vol. 32, No. 26, pp. 5026-35.

Local Government Information Unit. (1994), *Candid Cameras: A Report On Closed Circuit Television*, June, LGIU: London.

Lyon, D. (1994),*The Electronic Eye: The Rise of Surveillance Society*, Polity Press: Cambridge.

Marx, G. (1995), 'The Engineering of Social Control:The Search for the Silver Bullet' in Hagan, J. & Peterson, R. (eds),*Crime and Inequality*, Stanford University Press: California.

Nakamura, O., S. Mathur & T. Minami (1991),'Identification of Human Faces Based on Isodensity Maps', *Pattern Recognition*, Vol. 24 , No 3, pp. 263-72

Nock, S. (1993), *The Costs of Privacy*, Aldine De Gruyter: New York.

Norris, C. (1995), 'Algorithmic Surveillance' *Criminal Justice Matters*, No. 20, Summer, pp.7-8.

Perceptics (nd), Licence Plate Reader, Advertising Brochure.

Potter, K. (1995), 'Lens Support' *Police Review*, 8 September, pp. 18-20 .

Robertson,G. & I. Craw (1994), 'Testing Face Recognition Systems.' *Image and Vision Computing*, Vol. 12, No. 9, pp. 609-14.

Samaria, F. & S. Young. (1994) 'HMM-Based Architecture for Face Identification', *Image and Vision Computing.* Vol.12, No.8, pp. 537-43.

Sewell, G. & B. Wilkinson, (1992), 'Someone to Watch Over Me: Surveillance, Discipline, and the Just-In-Time Labour Process', *Sociology* Vol.26, May, pp. 271-89.

Sutherland, K., D. Rensham, & P. Denyer (1992), 'A Novel Automatic Face Recognition Algorithm Employing Vector Quantization', *Colloquium on Machine Storage and Recognition of Faces,* Institute of Electrical Engineers Digest 017.

Thomas, T. (1994), 'Covert Video Surveillance', *New Law Journal,* 15 July, pp. 966-67.

Turk, M. & A. Pentland. (1991), 'Eigenfaces for Recognition', *Journal of Cognitive Neuroscience* Vol. 3, No. 1, pp. 71 - 86.

Virilio, P. (1994), *The Vision Machine,* B.F.I Publishing, Indiana University Press: Indiana.

Wilcox, R. (1996), *Facial Feature Database. Standardised Input Information,* Home Office, London.

Wright, T. (1995), 'Eyes On The Road: Privacy and ITS'. *Traffic Technology International,* Autumn, pp. 88-92.

[24]

Digital rule

Punishment, control and technology

RICHARD JONES
University of Edinburgh, UK

Abstract

This article develops a theoretical model of 'digital rule'. This is a form of at-a-distance monitoring which becomes possible with the advent of certain electronic technologies. It is argued that this form of monitoring gives rise to a related form of decision-making, and to particular forms of punishment, both directly and indirectly. The article begins with a review of Foucault's work on 'discipline'. It is argued that while his general approach remains useful, his 'technology of power' model requires updating, because of certain moves within many criminal justice systems away from reliance on the disciplinary techniques Foucault associates with modernity. I argue that comments by Deleuze suggest a way of developing a theoretical adjunct to Foucault's model, and this new control form I characterize as one of 'digital rule'. Various emerging electronic technologies are examined, and it is shown how they operate specifically through restrictions specified in terms of time and space. The relationship between formal control, exclusion and punishment measures is considered, and it is concluded that in this emerging form of rule, these aspects continue to have a very close relationship, manifest here in a particular new way.

Key Words

control systems · exclusion · monitoring · sociology of punishment · technology

INTRODUCTION

In this article, I develop a theoretical model of 'digital rule'. This is a form of at-a-distance monitoring which becomes possible with the advent of certain electronic technology. I argue that this form of monitoring gives rise to a related form of decision-making, and to particular forms of punishment, both directly and indirectly. I begin by reviewing the Foucauldian argument that there is no essence to 'punishment', and that punitive sanctions should be considered as one part of a wider continuum of punishing and controlling measures. I then argue that we should retain this anti-essentialist and sociological aspect of Foucault's work, together with his specific theoretical model of 'technologies of power', despite its historical flaws. However, I argue that while the general approach remains useful, the model requires updating, because of certain moves within many criminal justice systems away from reliance on the disciplinary techniques Foucault associates with modernity. I argue that comments by Deleuze suggest a way of developing a theoretical adjunct to Foucault's model, which from a penological and social control perspective I term 'digital rule'. I examine various emerging electronic technologies, and show how they operate specifically through restrictions specified in terms of time and space. The relationship between formal control, exclusion and punishment measures is examined, and it is concluded that in this emerging modality of rule, these aspects continue to have a very close relationship, here in a specific new way.

Foucault's legacy: punishment and control

It has been recognized for some time that while the term 'punishment' is readily understood colloquially, as a sociological concept it has certain limitations. Garland and Young argued that the sociological study of this area should not have 'punishment' but rather the '"field of penal practices" or "penality"' as its primary research object (1983b: 14). Their reasoning was that the term 'punishment' was essentialist (that it presupposed a nature or essence to its practice) and that a sociological approach instead should, among other things, seek to establish how punishment operated in different places at different points in time. The term 'punishment' was also criticized as one of the reasons why study of punishment had often overly been restricted to study of the prison.

The broader term 'penality' suggests that 'the penal realm' is 'a complex', a network of different institutions and practices (1983b: 15). The term itself, along with the title of Garland and Young's (1983a) collection is taken from Foucault's *Discipline and punish* (1979: 11ff., 23ff.). The project suggested by Garland and Young thus shows a Foucauldian orientation, even if their (and their contributors') work is by no means limited to Foucauldian analyses.

In a later work, Garland defines 'penality' as referring to:

> the whole of the penal complex, including its sanctions, institutions, discourses and represen-
> tations. It is useful in so far as it avoids the connotations of the terms 'penal system' (which
> tends to stress institutional practices, not their representation, and to imply a systematicity
> which is often absent); and 'punishment' (which seriously begs the question of the nature of the
> phenomenon). (1985: x, n.1)

The attraction of the term for Garland was that it more easily permitted discussion of penal-welfare elements (such as probation orders), than did such terms as 'penal system' and 'punishment', while recognizing that these elements are still sanctions.

Foucault's (1979) own understanding of 'penality' is perhaps somewhat different from either Garland's (1985) or Garland and Young's (1983a). Foucault suggests that 'penality' (loosely) describes a mode of 'punishing', but that there are different, historically specific, modes of penality (1979: 11, 16). The content of his book is an analysis of the abstract qualities of three such modes of penality (monarchical, classical and modern), with a particular focus on the historical emergence of the third of these modes. For Foucault penality, in the modern age, does not merely describe legal sanctions or welfare measures themselves, but also the overall system within which they operate –

specifically a wider system which 'administers' 'illegalities'. There is a whole integrated system of social regulation, of which formal punishment and policing are just one part:

> Penality would then appear to be a way of handling illegalities, of laying down the limits of tolerance, of giving free reign to some, of putting pressure on others, of excluding a particular section, of making another useful, of neutralizing certain individuals and of profiting from others . . . Legal punishments are to be resituated in an overall strategy of illegalities. (1979: 272)

For Foucault then, penality includes systems of punishments, but is not reducible to them. It is a system of administering the social through a 'continuous gradation' of competent authorities, the whole being anchored, as it were, by the 'serious' punishments of the prison system. He describes this entirety as a 'carceral network' (1979: 299–301). This definition of 'penality' would therefore appear somewhat wider than that of Garland (1985), or of Garland and Young (1983b). The advantage of Foucault's definition is that it sees both 'punishing' and 'policing' (in broad terms) as elements of a single system of dealing with illegalities.

To date, Foucault's work on penality has been developed in criminology in two main ways. The sociology of punishment continued for a short time with a focus on penality, but aside from a few exceptions (see, for example, Howe, 1994) little research has been done since. More work seems to have been done on the disciplinary social control side, perhaps fanned during the 1980s by fears of the emergence of a 'Big Brother' state utilizing new, powerful, electronic surveillance technologies. Foucauldian-inspired approaches were used to supplement Marxist approaches in the repressive 'social control' perspective. However, as early as 1985, Stan Cohen noted that 'social control' (in the Marxist/repressive sense) had 'lately become something of a Mickey Mouse concept' (1985: 2). The concept having somewhat fallen into disrepute in recent years, we are now at the point of witnessing almost nostalgic calls for its revival. Scheerer and Hess, in particular, have argued that the concept should be salvaged and reformulated. They propose that the concept be understood as referring to:

> all social (and technical) arrangements, mechanisms, norms, belief systems, positive and negative sanctions that either aim and/or result in the prevention of undesired behaviour or, if this has already occurred, respond to the undesired act in a way that tries to prevent its occurrence in the future. (1997: 103–4)

While they admit that such a reformulation has a certain 'vastness', such admission does little to lessen the resulting theoretical problem. As Sumner notes (following Chunn and Gavigan, 1988), 'any . . . action . . . can be seen as an agency of social control [giving this term] a certain monumental vagueness as a concept'. As he also implies, even if it is reformulated, the concept could still 'refer to either a liberal welfare-state interventionism in the hands of a social democratic sociology or, in the hands of radical sociology, a totalizing, almost totalitarian form of state repressiveness permeating all nooks and crannies of society' (Sumner, 1997: 142).

Scheerer and Hess argue that nevertheless there is an empirical need for a reformed social control concept, in order to understand such recent phenomena as the emergence of 'techno-prevention' measures including situational crime prevention measures such

7

PUNISHMENT AND SOCIETY 2(1)

as landscaping, interior architecture and environmental design (1997: 107–8, 122ff.). They point too to the apparent rise in deployment in many western city centres of Disneyland-type human control systems (landscaping and norm-policing) (see Shearing and Stenning, 1986); the 'bum-proof' street furniture described by Davis (1992); and the carefully designed and policed spaces of shopping malls and entertainment facilities.

But we should remember that these techniques have been quite deliberately designed and refined, with the deliberate aim of controlling social groups. This is a quite deliberate form of 'social control'. If Scheerer and Hess's concept of social control seemingly has a renewed relevance today, it is probably because of the emergence of specific techniques, practices and knowledges explicitly designed to 'control' social interaction in certain specific spaces. But this is a subtly different type of 'social control' to the one they earlier suggested, being neither entirely state-formal nor social-informal, but instead private-formal or state-sponsored-formal. This social control is, as Scheerer and Hess themselves recognize, a proactive rather than reactive form of control. It is a preventative control type, and is particularly characteristic of the 'artificial environ- ments' of the (private) retail and entertainment sectors (1997: 122–6). But to refer to this as 'social control' is to gloss the inadequacies of the earlier uses of the concept, and to overlook how the new anticipatory form of 'control' is control in a very different sense.

TOWARDS A THEORETICAL MODEL OF ELECTRONIC CONTROL AND PUNISHMENT

Deleuze's development of *Discipline and punish*: 'Postscript on the societies of control'

Over the last two or three decades, a range of new technologies has come to be used in policing and in criminal justice, bringing with them ways of working which many have seen as in some respects 'new', or at the very least as antagonistic towards existing practices. Some commentators have suggested that Michel Foucault's theory of 'disci- plinary' power, as described in great detail in *Discipline and punish*, offers a way of understanding these new technologies. It has, for example, been argued that CCTV could be a part of a societally dispersed 'electronic Panopticon' (Fyfe and Bannister, 1996). Certain sections of Foucault's description of discipline can indeed be found to support such a claim. However, in other respects, technologies such as CCTV seem not to fit so well with Foucault's notion of discipline. For example, CCTV provides a (literally) *superficial*[1] image of an individual and their outward behaviour, in contrast to the depth and personality sought by traditional disciplinary observation. As I have argued elsewhere, the same is true of other 'new technologies', both electronic and organizational.

Gilles Deleuze, the late French philosopher, and friend of Foucault, provides a schematic outline of a new model for conceptualizing these various new technologies. Best known for his philosophical and social-theoretical work, especially with Félix Guattari, Deleuze is also the author of an elegantly written, though highly abstract, interpretative exposition of Foucault's oeuvre (Deleuze, 1988). Later, Deleuze went on to write two brief pieces offering a further creative reinterpretation of parts of Foucault's work, and which also suggest a new research direction.

In one of these short pieces, written in 1990, Deleuze offers a thumbnail sketch updating of Foucault's (1979) theory of historical 'technologies of power' (Deleuze, 1997).[2] Deleuze's 'Postscript on the societies of control' develops Foucault's thesis in *Discipline and punish* that historical change is epochal, prone only to occasional but relatively rapid change, and that in each historical epoch different social techniques for exercising power are dominant. For Foucault, the 'modern' period (c.1800–1970s) sees the emergence of 'disciplinary' social power techniques. Foucault's account works rather better as an abstract theoretical model than as a historical account (for a summary of historical criticisms see Garland, 1991: 157–62).

Foucault's *Discipline and punish* was written in 1975. His account of disciplinary power provides, alongside Weber's (1978) account of rationality, a model for understanding certain aspects of bureaucratic-administrative institutions and practices. But written as it was before the widespread availability and use of electronic and computer technologies, its applicability to such technologies is questionable.

Deleuze accepts Foucault's tripartite historical model of 'technologies of power' (monarchical, juridical and disciplinary), but argues that the 1990s are witnessing a process of transition to a fourth technology or mode of power, namely one of 'control'. In other words, he argues that Foucault's theoretical model is basically correct, but now needs to be updated. For Deleuze, the transition from 'discipline' to 'control' is to be understood as one part of a wide range of social and economic changes happening over the last few decades, which amount to a 'mutation' in capitalism.

Deleuze contends that 'discipline' as a power-form is today in crisis in such key modern institutions as the prison, hospital, factory, school and family. Within these institutions, he argues, the last few decades have seen a series of announcements of reforms, restructurings, new policies and programmes. But, he suggests,

> everyone knows that these institutions are finished, whatever the length of their expiration periods. It's only a matter of administering their last rites and of keeping people employed until the installation of the new forces knocking at the door. These are the *societies of control*, which are in the process of replacing the disciplinary societies. (1997: 309, emphasis in original)

Traditional institutional forms such as 'prisons, schools, hospitals ... are breaking down ... because they're fighting a losing battle. New kinds of punishment, education, health care are being stealthily introduced' (1995b: 174–5).

In order to highlight the characteristics of the new, emerging form of power, Deleuze compares and contrasts it with disciplinary power. He argues that a key feature of disciplinary 'spaces of enclosure' such as the prison, school and factory is that they are architecturally and hence operationally separate from one another (1997: 310). In societies of control, on the other hand, the various control mechanisms are 'inseparable variations, forming a system' (1997: 310). The social system is unified, (in a certain sense) through its shared language of numbers, a language which is *'digital'*, '(which doesn't necessarily mean binary)' (1995a: 178, 1997: 310, emphasis in original).

One could say that whereas in disciplinary societies, one was 'always starting all over again', in societies of control, 'one is never finished with anything' (1995a: 179, 1997: 310). For example, where formerly a person might move from a school to a factory, finishing as a pupil and beginning anew as a worker (perhaps as an apprentice engineer), now there is a much closer and much less distinct relationship between the corporation

9

and education. Not only is 'work experience' encouraged by schools and colleges, but within the commercial sector we now have such concepts as 'life-long learning', and many face the possibility that they will have to retrain completely at least once during their working lives.

Deleuze's hypothesis is that not only is there an overlap developing between the fields of education and commerce, but that all social fields are now becoming determined by a single deep, organizing logic. (In Deleuze's somewhat unintelligible phrase, each field is now a 'coexisting metastable state of a single modulation' [1995a: 179].) If this happens, it is likely to contribute to the decline in centrality of the old institutional sites that had separated out the different social fields – indeed, for this reason it will become anomalous to refer to the old 'institutions' as such.

Deleuze argues that such a change in institutional form brings with it a fundamentally new way in which we understand ourselves and others (subjectivity). (Remember too that for Foucault discipline was always as much a mode of subjectivity as it was a mode of objectivity [see Dreyfus and Rabinow, 1982].) Disciplinary society was based upon conceiving people in terms of their individuality, which was also to see them as individuals within a mass. A file or files would be kept on each prisoner, for example; on their history, criminal record, personal statements supporting application for parole, disciplinary record, and so on. In this system the prisoner is also just one prisoner among many. Certain administrative–bureaucratic practices rely on this duality, such as the birth certificate, signature or prisoner number (unique to each individual, but of a generic form). Some of these are seen as a 'natural' reflection of an individual's individuality (for example, the hand-written signature) whereas others seem an attempt to 'dehumanize' and deny this selfsame individuality (for example, the prisoner number).

In control societies, however, a different type of understanding of people emerges, one which could broadly be described as anti-humanist. It conceives neither of people as unique individuals, nor of institutional groups as discrete entities. A series of changes in societal practices encourage us to see ourselves differently (indeed to be different), and encourage organizations to understand us differently. For example, instead of the modern hand-written or typed file, we now have electronic databases. Instead of the signature, we have the PIN number. This language of numbers is also one of codes. The 'numerical language of control is made of codes that mark access to information, or reject it' (Deleuze, 1997: 311). Codes are 'passwords'.

Deleuze argues that in control societies, '[w]e no longer find ourselves dealing with the mass/individual pair. Individuals have become "dividuals", and masses have become samples, data, markets or "banks"' (1997: 311). For the moderns, the 'individual' was the smallest possible socio-political unit, that which could not be subdivided any further, the social 'atom'. Deleuze's suggestion that further division is possible and indeed presently in some sense happening, in part echoes his earlier works (with Guattari) on capitalism and schizophrenia (1984, 1987), and in part highlights the managerial and marketing conception of a person as no more than a bundle of traits.

Disciplinary institutions worked with long-term schemes, but these were nevertheless discontinuous, as people moved within and between institutions. Control, on the other hand, is 'short-term and of rapid rates of turnover' (1997: 312), but is continuous. People are no longer enclosed by institutions but instead are indebted to systems and their systemic goodwill. For example,

Félix Guattari has imagined a city where one would be able to leave one's apartment, one's street, one's neighbourhood, thanks to one's (dividual) electronic card that raises a given barrier; but the card could just as easily be rejected on a given day or between certain hours; what counts is not the barrier but the computer that tracks each person's position – licit or illicit – and effects a universal modulation. (1997: 312)

'Digital rule'

Within the areas of crime control and punishment, the operation of 'control' in Deleuze's sense can usefully be broadened out into what I term 'digital rule' (avoiding the word 'control' which already has certain other meanings within criminology). 'Digital rule' describes a new form of at-a-distance monitoring which becomes possible with the advent of certain electronic technology. This form of monitoring gives rise to a related form of decision-making, based upon prima facie evidence provided by the electronic system that a rule either has been followed or has been violated (for example, when an electronic signal has been received indicating that a valid PIN code has been entered in a door access keypad, or that an electronically monitored offender has violated their curfew conditions). Typically, a decision is made automatically by the system, based on certain rules (algorithms), either to allow/continue access or to instigate proceedings of some kind. The decision is decided algorithmically, and hence a PIN or electronic bracelet can be made to work differently to a key (which always works in a certain lock): instead, the electronically policed rule may, for example, allow or deny access at certain times of day. Furthermore, the initial proceedings instigated for a rule breach typically involve a measure which is in some sense 'internal' to the control system, usually the removal of certain system 'access privileges' (misuse of a card or PIN will lead to some or all of that card or number's former properties being curtailed, or breach of a curfew order may lead to a more restrictive curfew order being imposed, or to the offender being denied the 'privilege' of participation in the monitoring programme altogether and instead being sent to prison, for example). Such measures are quasi-crime preventive, quasi-punitive. Lastly, the system allows not only for the rapid, indeed almost instantaneous, determining of infraction and sanctioning, but also for similarly rapid changes to the rules themselves.

Actuarial justice, the new penology, managerialism theories, and risk-based theories, all describe some of the techniques used in the calculation or assessments beginning to be made in deciding who should be stopped and searched, released, admitted to a programme, arrested and in deciding which resources to deploy and where (see, for example, Peters, 1988; Feeley and Simon, 1992, 1994; O'Malley, 1992; Bottoms, 1995; O'Malley and Palmer, 1996; Scheerer and Hess, 1997). Situational crime prevention has described many of the physical barriers and ploys used to enforce or coax certain desired behaviours from people in different social spaces (for example, Clarke, 1995; Clarke and Homel, 1997; see also Scheerer and Hess, 1997). By linking these two areas together the new form of control becomes visible. Digital rule describes how system managers run systems. It can describe a managerial function, but can also refer to more direct electronically controlled punishment and crime control systems. These new systems can in theory be managed by a very small number of people ('system administrators').

PUNISHMENT AND SOCIETY 2(1)

PUNISHMENT, CONTROL AND DIGITAL RULE

In the previous section I introduced Deleuze's article on control societies, arguing that it could be used to suggest a concept of 'digital rule' within criminology. In this section, I shall develop the digital rule concept by exploring the relationship between four different areas, namely managerialism, electronic control and access technologies, formal (social) exclusion and punishment.

Managerialism

Managerialism, in its descriptive sense (I shall not discuss here its pejorative connotation) is the incursion of practices and ideologies of business management into the public sector. 'Management' has, of course, long been seen as normal in the private sector where it is usually simply thought of as 'management'. The introduction of such an approach in the public sector in the 1980s was, however, sufficiently novel and at odds with traditional public sector values to have earned the tag 'managerialism'. Managerialism has become prevalent in criminal justice and crime control over the last 20 or 30 years in many western countries (Peters, 1986; Feeley and Simon, 1992, 1994; Bottoms, 1995; Bottoms and Wiles, 1996; Jones, 1997). It should be noted that managerialism has developed throughout the entire public sector over this same time period (Pollitt, 1993; Pollitt and Bouckaert, 1995). Bottoms identifies three distinct aspects within managerialism, namely its 'systemic', 'consumerist' and 'actuarial' dimensions. It is worth expanding on these dimensions for the purposes of the ensuing discussion.

An emphasis on the 'systemic' character of criminal justice is relatively new, seeming to emerge only in the 1960s (as, for example, in the 'funnel of justice' diagram in the President's Commission Report, 1967; see also Wilkins, 1964). Bottoms notes that this emphasis usually involves such features as inter-agency co-operation, strategic planning, key performance indicators and/or the active monitoring of aggregate information about the system (1995: 25). The second of the three dimensions, consumerism, relates to the idea of efficient and effective 'service delivery'. Consumerism becomes a goal of the system (that it should serve one or more 'consumers' of its services), but also a means of obtaining information on its present standard of service (through direct or indirect feedback). The third aspect, actuarialism, refers to the emphasis on 'an actuarial language of probabilistic calculations' (Feeley and Simon, 1992: 452): a language of statistics, risk and probability. It is associated with a shift of focus away from the individual and towards groups and traits. It is future-oriented, and is geared towards prevention and risk minimization (Feeley and Simon, 1994: 177–8).

Managerialism is not only a useful way of studying aims and methods within an organization, but is also a feature of digital rule. In fact, there are several aspects to this relationship: an organization must be flexible, efficient and managerial successfully to operate at-a-distance control systems (it must be 'post-bureaucratic' public sector, or a private company); managerialism is dependent upon (indeed intimately associated with) information technology; and at a deeper level still, both are information gathering, decision-making and control systems. Moreover, and more figuratively, managerialism could actually be reinterpreted within the model of digital rule, rather than the other way around. In other words, instead of seeing electronic control systems, for example, as a technology employed by managerialism, we could see managerialism as the variant of 'control-at-a-distance' in the specific realm of businesses, institutions and organizations.

Electronic monitoring of offenders

The past two decades have seen the emergence in the UK and the US of sanctions involving the 'electronic monitoring' (tagging) of offenders. The history of electronic tagging has now been reasonably well documented (Ball and Lilly, 1986a, 1986b; Petersilia, 1986; Ball et al., 1988; Mair et al., 1990; Renzema, 1992; Clowes, 1993; Mair and Mortimer, 1996; Jones, 1997: Ch. 8). In the UK, legislation now allows for use of tagging as a means of enforcing a home confinement curfew order, during certain hours of certain days of the week (for example, 7pm–7am from Monday to Friday). The principal legislation is in the Criminal Justice Act 1991, whose provisions relating to electronic monitoring came into force in 1995. Section 43 of the Crime (Sentences) Act 1997 extends curfew orders enforced by electronic tagging to offenders under the age of 16 (Cavadino, 1997: 4).

At present, the technology used is a simple radio receiver–transmitter circuit, where a receiver is connected to a specially installed telephone in the offender's home, and a transmitter is incorporated in the tag attached to the offender's body. Moving the tag out of range of the receiver, typically by leaving the house, causes the circuit to be broken. The receiver unit checks to see if this is an authorized breach, depending on the day and time, and if it is unauthorized, the unit alerts a remote monitoring centre by phone. Further UK trials and research is presently being conducted.

In another application of the same technology, the Government has recently announced that certain prisoners are to become eligible for release under an electronically monitored 'Home Detention Curfew' programme. It is estimated that 60,000 prisoners will be eligible for consideration, and up to 35,000 prisoners could be released on curfew in any one year, with about 4000 on the HDC programme at any one time. The scheme is to be run by private contractors, and failures to comply with the scheme are to be reported immediately to the police (Prison Reform Trust, 1999: 22–3).

Electronic monitoring in the UK is not at present based on geographic tracking technology, but may become so within a few years. Trials apparently have begun in the United States using 'Global Positioning System' technology, a mobile geographic location determining system, which triangulates signals sent from a network of geostationary satellites.[3] However, at present, GPS-based tags remain prohibitively cumbersome.

To date, criticism of the sanction of electronically monitored home confinement has focused on its alleged inhumanity, its cost (fixed costs remain fairly high at present, so with low numbers of offenders on a scheme, average cost per offender is high), or on its 'failure' rates (order breaches) (see, for example, Nellis, 1991; Cavadino, 1997).

As a sanction it seems to have at least two punitive elements: first, that one's freedom of movement is somewhat curtailed; and second, that one is required to have an electronic device semi-permanently attached to one's body – an indicator of lack of trust or of opprobrium (in certain circumstances, tags may be 'stigmatic', though if this were the general intent, they could be made much more visible still). The key feature of electronic tagging, however, is its automation of the sanction into a largely automatic electronic system. Home confinement enforced by peripatetic probation officers pre-dates its electronically monitored counterpart. One of the problems with this earlier form was its inefficiency. To probation officers' obvious horror, electronic tags replace their policing function. (In the UK, Conservative government administrations of the late 1980s and early 1990s also saw it as an opportunity to undermine probation work more generally, but there seems no reason why probation work could not be used alongside an electronic monitoring programme.)

This sanction, then, involves the electronic systematization of a penal measure (the partial loss of liberty). In fact, the physical attachment of the tag to the body goes some way to integrating the biological body into an electronic system. The sanction's operation involves all the key definitions of digital rule set out above. The scheme involves a system whose parameters (day, time, place) are rapidly modifiable; in which a large number of subjects can be monitored by a small number of system administrators; prima facie rule breaches are detected immediately. Furthermore, it signals a shift from bureaucratic-punitive to system-punitive measures. By this, I mean that whereas prison involves not only loss of liberty but also various other 'pains' of imprisonment (Sykes, 1958; Mathiesen, 1965; Goffman, 1991), the new punishment appears more of a 'pure' punishment of liberty deprivation. Potentially at least, it 'empties' a former probation-oriented sanction of its welfare-punitive element.

Electronic access, exclusion and control

In the next section I will explore how exclusion and punishment are related. First, however, I will discuss three forms of electronic access in particular – namely, door-opening card access systems, biological indicator entry access systems and keyboard/keypad access to computer systems. Though based on various different technologies, such systems can be seen as conceptually similar approaches to the governing of access to places, whether these be real or 'virtual'. Each of the electronic access systems discussed relies on the existence of a secure perimeter, requiring potential users to obtain 'entry' via an automated gateway or checkpoint – each allows for a form of control-at-a-distance. I shall argue that to the extent that sanctioning for misuse of electronic access systems involves withdrawal of privileges previously enjoyed by a user within the system itself, this potentially introduces a form of (exclusionary) punishment.

At the outset of this article, I argued for the study of formal regulatory systems as a whole, rather than the attempt to study distinct punitive or social control systems. By so doing, we can reapproach the study of punishment from a different perspective. In this section, I shall show how card entry/access systems are in certain ways related to systems designed to electronically monitor offenders, and I shall argue that such systems bring with them a potentially punitive moment by virtue of their ability to passively or actively exclude. A number of different technologies have been used in electronic access systems, including systems based on plastic 'swipe' cards and/or personal code numbers, systems based on 'unique' personal biological indicators, and password/log-in access to computer systems (which may be thought of as virtual spaces). I shall briefly discuss these various systems in turn.

Card entry/access systems offer several advantages over key-based door systems: they can be programmed with a time-expiry date; each card is unique, meaning that selected cards can be disabled without requiring the 'lock' to be changed; individual cards can be assigned additional tasks, for example as a store of 'electronic cash'; card systems can record each card's usage if required; and the ability of a card or cards to open specific doors or perform other functions can be reassigned centrally. As is well known, most card-entry systems require a short, private numerical code (personal identification number, or PIN) to be entered each time the card is used, thus guarding against simple theft of cards. Card entry systems thus have similarities with 'cashpoint' (ATM) bank systems. They have been seen as a situational crime prevention measure (Clarke and Homel, 1997), and require other technologies such as electromagnetic locks and indeed sturdy doors and perimeter barriers to work. But, in addition, they usually require each door control to be networked, thus creating a single entry/exit *system*. An example of a smart card scheme with a card capable of multiple functions is the 'Mondex' scheme presently in use at six British universities. Mondex cards act as a combined matriculation card, library card, door 'swipe' card and electronic purse (the card can be used to make low-value purchases around campus and elsewhere).[4] It remains to be seen whether this particular brand of smart card will succeed in the long run, but the convenience offered by combination cards seems likely to assure a future to the technology in general.

Biological indicator access systems are similar to card access systems, but instead of identifying individual system users by their smart card and PIN code combination, they rely on identifying known 'unique' biological features of each person. One such system, already being tested by a British bank in trials, involves an iris-recognition system (a camera scans a potential user's iris, and a computer tries to make a match from its database of pre-scanned irises). Other systems use fingerprint, handprint or facial recognition systems. The advantage of such systems is that they do not require a card to be carried around or a PIN code to be remembered: the disadvantage is that matches are inherently probabilistic, and as with drug-testing technologies require system operators to choose whether the system should be weighted towards accepting false positives or false negatives (Jones, 1997).

Computer access systems also operate on a coded gateway principle. A criminological literature has already emerged on 'Internet crime' and its policing (including Loader, 1997; Barrett, 1998; Grabosky et al., 1998; Mann and Sutton, 1998). Computer 'hacking' is now a widely known if somewhat vague term, and suggests a certain level of activity, even damage. In fact, usage of computer systems is now frequently oriented around the concepts of authorized and non-authorized access. From a regulatory point of view, this has the advantage that it does not rely on having to prove that any 'damage' was done, and also accepts that entry to a computer system may be achieved, but that whether by active 'hacking', looking over a colleague's shoulder, luck or accident, such access is 'unauthorized' and can be dealt with accordingly if detected. This regulatory approach goes hand-in-hand with the now familiar practice of policing computer usage through requiring users to pre-register with a systems administrator and then to enter a user identification code and a password when accessing certain computers or files.

Access, (zonal) exclusion and punishment

Electronic access codes, swipe cards or computer-recognition of biological features (irises, fingerprints) in certain respects operate as a contemporary form of the mechanical key, but in other ways are fundamentally distinct. Their integration within an electronic system allows for such features as time-expiry access cards, single cards

PUNISHMENT AND SOCIETY 2(1)

accessing numerous but specific doors and instantaneous recalibration in the event of a security breach. Much of these systems' operation could be seen as a new form of what previously was known as social control (the new form is, however, clearly deliberate, intentional and formal). In addition to these *control* functions, however, the concept of digital rule also describes certain *penal* measures (both state and corporate sanctioned).

Exclusion has long been a form of punishment, the most dramatic form being state-sanctioned banishment (as in an English banishment sanction of 1597, cited in Rusche and Kirchheimer, 1968: 59). In the UK 'exclusion' has more recently come to be associated with 'social exclusion', a term associated with social democratic politics. The term has been used in numerous different contexts, including education (the exclusion of troublesome pupils from schools); welfare (the 'underclass' as a group falling through the welfare net and hence 'excluded' from social welfare and indeed society); and citizenship (the homeless and/or immigrants). Social exclusion may also describe an aspect of the lawful ejecting of individuals from quasi-public or private property by the owners or their representatives. Ejection or 'barring' from such places as shops, bars, entertainment complexes or shopping malls may be used not only as a form of crime control, but also as a form of discrimination or of punishment.

Theoretically, one might say that (social) exclusion more generally is a form of social censure. To censure is to mark off (negatively) and to set apart (Sumner, 1990). Censuring typically involves some sort of excluding, though censure cannot be reduced to exclusion alone. However, the social-democratic usage of the term 'social exclusion' brings with it the connotation that exclusion is from 'the social', as a single more-or-less unifying entity. As Baudrillard (1983, 1993) argues, such concern may be symptomatic of a nostalgic desire to recover that which is already lost ('the social', as an entirety), or rather that which we now realize never really to have existed. Instead, we can see social life as consisting of a number of discrete, specialized areas. It is exclusion from one or more of these specific areas to which exclusion in this article refers, rather than to a more wholesale loss of citizenship.

Electronic systems also rely on modes of exclusion, at present most usually for security purposes (to prevent hacking [computers] or break-ins [electronically controlled door-entry systems]. But electronic exclusion could, and in some limited areas, already is, being used as a sanction – a potential punishment. Indeed, in my hypothesis, this form of punishment will become increasingly common, as it seems to fit well with the emerging digitally reliant society. Such sanctioning may also be related to the idea of civil disqualifications attending conviction, as examined by von Hirsch and Wasik (1997), though instead as principal rather than additional penalties.

Within the sphere of computer systems, exclusion can be worded as the 'withdrawing of access privileges'. Maybe this is a new euphemistic language of punishment in a post-bureaucratic age. 'Privileges' which had previously been 'granted' can be 'removed' if they are 'abused'.

A university, for example, may use this sanction against students believed to have been involved in hacking, downloading prohibited materials or using computer resources for (unauthorized) commercial activities (see, for example, University of Cambridge, 1999). Such activities may also be criminal acts, but at present unless they are deemed unusually serious and/or on a huge scale, they may well be dealt with internally by the university (see also Wasik, 1990). Rather than prosecute, it is likely to be quicker, cheaper and easier for a university to discipline the miscreant internally, with part of the sanction being the 'removal' of 'access privileges' to computers, information and networks, as, for example, in the following procedural system:

> There is an approved disciplinary procedure for dealing with users who may be in breach of the [University Information Technology Syndicate's] Rules. Minor cases are dealt with summarily by the Director and more serious ones by a Disciplinary Panel of the Information Technology Syndicate. If found guilty, users face a fine of up to 150 pounds and/or the suspension of authorisation to use computing and network facilities. (University of Cambridge, 1999: section on 'Discipline')

'Suspension of authorization' may not sound much but is potentially quite serious. It is most serious for students taking courses in computer science (it could seriously threaten the viability of their studies), but is also potentially punitive for what might be expected to be an increasing number of others as well. Removal of university e-mail, web and word-processing facilities may still at present be considered a relatively minor sanction, possibly with more symbolic than practical significance. But as course materials, library catalogues, journal reference databases and student discussion forums become distributed electronically, it could become increasingly punitive to remove access to them. Britain's Open University, at the forefront of distance learning in this country, already conducts much of its teaching and administration through dial-in networks for its students, and for all universities information technology is set to increase in importance in research and teaching for the foreseeable future. While we could also predict that counter-measures to such electronic exclusion will be developed by students and certain enterprising individuals, this simply attests further to the importance of continued access to electronic information.

Localized physical exclusion

The policing of (physical) spaces can be assisted using additional technologies. A key technology for so doing is closed-circuit television (CCTV), whose operation can be seen as consistent with the digital rule model. I shall argue that CCTV is a technological means which has become used as a way of checking that 'users' of social space are doing so in an 'authorized' manner, and that 'unauthorized' use may be met with the sanction of 'withdrawal of access privileges'.

Discussion of CCTV use is often in terms of 'discipline' or 'surveillance', but in practice, whether in shops, shopping malls, shopping centres or prisons, CCTV's main application may in fact be as a real-time resource co-ordination and management system (see Jones, 1997: Ch. 6). A person monitoring and operating a CCTV camera system can alert security staff to where the problem is, and can immediately suggest the nature and scale of the incident. Depending on the person's behaviour, criminal or disciplinary charges may be brought. But in each case it is likely that enforcement personnel will check whether the person in question is 'authorized' to be doing what they are doing (which may just be being there), and if they are not authorized, will escort (remove) that person from that area.

Even future generations of CCTV systems, featuring integrated computerized facial recognition systems (so-called 'algorithmic surveillance': see Norris et al., 1998) are

17

likely to be used for this purpose: such systems are not designed to recognize 'theft', for example, but rather a known shop-lifter. The system might be used to prompt shop security staff to focus their surveillance on that individual in the hope of catching the individual 'in action', but a managerially more prudent (if from a civil liberties point of view, more disturbing) response would be simply to escort that individual from the premises and to inform them they were not welcome to return.

Punishment through exclusion ('withdrawal of access privileges' in society)

Exclusion from entertainment facilities is in certain respects an analogous measure. A person can be prohibited from attending designated football matches in England and Wales by an exclusion order under the Public Order Act 1986 (ss. 30–7), and can be prevented from attending designated football matches outside England and Wales by a restriction order under the Football Spectators Act 1989. Formally, such orders are crime prevention measures (future hooliganism) rather than sanctions (punishment) (though failure to comply with an order is punishable). Yet the restriction on social activities, travel, through restrictions specified in terms of times and places, is reminiscent of home confinement orders, which are a sanction. Despite attempts in the Crime and Disorder Act 1998 to tighten up the law relating to football match restriction orders, their efficacy has been questioned. Their use is at present very limited, with only 71 people subject to restriction orders in June 1998 (the month of the World Cup football finals in nearby France) (Card and Ward, 1998: 326–7). Restriction and exclusion orders relating to football matches may seem trivial, not least to non-football fans. Nevertheless, in questioning the present policing utility of such measures we should avoid complacency, for both political and sociological reasons.

In other spheres of social life, exclusion is more evidently serious. For example, exclusion from the world of driving, as a consequence of accumulating endorsement 'points' on a UK driving licence, could lead to dismissal from work. Even a substantial fine may be preferred by the traffic offender over the loss of their licence.

The sanction of *withdrawal of system access authorization* can also be seen elsewhere in western criminal justice. Electronic monitoring of curfew order compliance can be understood as an attempt to withdraw the societal 'privilege' of doing certain activities, through restrictions in time and/or space, such as spending the evening drinking in a pub or bar. Indeed the sanction of an electronically monitored curfew is itself often presented by the criminal justice system as a 'privilege' to offenders, in the sense that such offenders might instead have faced a custodial sentence, and that failure to comply with the curfew order could lead them to prison.

The privilege concept is also implicit in the recently announced Home Detention Curfew programme for the early release of prisoners in England and Wales onto electronically monitored curfew programmes as mentioned earlier. Failure by a prisoner to comply with the scheme will not necessarily lead to their immediate reincarceration, but will lead to their automatic disqualification of participating in the scheme on any future prison sentence they receive.

Another instance of usage of 'privilege' terminology can be found in prisoner 'incentives schemes' as now found in the Prison Service for England and Wales. Prisoners typically start off on the middle of three tiers of amenity provision, and can have 'privileges' added or removed by the prison depending on their behaviour and/or compliance with other schemes such as drug use testing programmes (Prison Service, 1995a, 1995b).

CONCLUSION

In this article, I have argued that the sociological study of punishment ought to proceed within a wider notion of social regulation. Punishment and control often overlap, in the sense that frequently penal measures involve preventative controls and preventative measures involve penal elements. In the new forms that I term digital rule, these two aspects of regulation are especially pronounced and co-present. I developed a theoretical model of digital rule, this being the name I gave to a particular form of social regulation reliant on certain electronic and other technologies. By examining various instances of the use of electronic monitoring and control systems, both in sanctioning and in situational crime prevention, I showed that punishment and control issues re-emerge in each case. Moreover, novel forms of punishment and control, especially based on inclusion and exclusion, become apparent in the digital rule model. I have not claimed that we are now living in an era of 'digital rule', nor that all sanctions or policing methods or electronic crime control systems are now based on post-disciplinary techniques. Rather I have developed what I hope is a coherent theoretical account of a new modality of rule and used this to show significant connections between a number of emerging, if still relatively marginal, areas of penality.

ACKNOWLEDGEMENTS

I would like to thank David Garland for his extremely helpful and constructive comments on this article at various stages of its preparation. I would also like to thank two anonymous reviewers for their comments on an earlier draft of this article.

NOTES

1 'Superficial' from the Late Latin *superficialis*, meaning 'of the surface'.
2 Quotes given are referenced throughout to the appropriate page of the 'standard' 1995 translation (Deleuze, 1995a). However, I have in several places used parts of an alternative translation (Deleuze, 1997). Use of the alternative translation is indicated with square brackets.
3 GPS technology was originally developed by the United States as a part of the guidance system for its 'Cruise' missiles. Its signals are now available for private and commercial use, although at a reduced accuracy level, and many electronics manufacturers already sell small hand-held GPS navigation devices, intended for users such as small boat owners and hikers. At time of writing, an electronics manufacturer has just begun selling a wristwatch GPS unit (see Internet site: www.casio.com).
4 Mondex is a subsidiary of MasterCard International (for further details of their system see Internet site: www.mondex.com).

REFERENCES

Ball, R.A. and Lilly, J.R. (1986a) 'A theoretical examination of home incarceration', *Federal Probation* 50(1): 17–24.

PUNISHMENT AND SOCIETY 2(1)

Ball, R.A. and Lilly, J.R. (1986b) 'The potential use of home incarceration for drunken drivers', *Crime & Delinquency* 32(2): 224–47.

Ball, R.A., Lilly, J.R. and Huff, R.C. (1988) *House arrest and correctional policy: doing time at home*. London: Sage.

Barrett, N. (1998) *Digital crime: policing the cybernation*. London: Kogan Page.

Baudrillard, J. (1983) *In the shadow of the silent majorities, or, the end of the social and other essays*. New York: Semiotext(e).

Baudrillard, J. (1993) *Symbolic exchange and death*. London: Sage.

Bottoms, A.E. (1995) 'The philosophy and politics of punishment and sentencing', in C. Clarkson and R. Morgan (eds) *The politics of sentencing reform*. Oxford: Clarendon Press.

Bottoms, A.E. and Wiles, P. (1996) 'Understanding crime prevention in late modern societies', in T. Bennett (ed.) *Preventing crime and disorder: targeting strategies and responsibilities (Cropwood Series)*. Cambridge: Institute of Criminology, University of Cambridge.

Card and Ward (1998) *The Crime and Disorder Act 1998*. Bristol: Jordans.

Cavadino, P. (1997) 'Electronic tagging: the evidence so far', *Criminal Justice* 15(2): 4–5.

Chunn, D. and Gavigan, S. (1988) 'Social control: analytic tool or analytic quagmire?', *Contemporary Crises* 12: 107–24.

Clarke, R.V. (1995) 'Situational crime prevention', in M. Tonry and D. Farrington (eds) *Building a safer society: crime and justice: a review of research, vol. 19*. Chicago, IL: University of Chicago Press.

Clarke, R.V. and Homel, R. (1997) 'A revised classification of situational crime prevention techniques', in S.P. Lab (ed.) *Crime prevention at the crossroads*. Cincinnati, OH: Anderson.

Clowes, N. (1993) 'Electronic monitoring: the Home Office trials', in J.R. Lilly and J. Himan (eds) *The electronic monitoring of offenders: symposium papers, second series*. Leicester: De Montfort University Law School Monographs.

Cohen, S. (1985) *Visions of social control: crime, punishment and classification*. Cambridge: Polity.

Davis, M. (1992) *City of quartz: excavating the future in Los Angeles*. London: Verso.

Deleuze, G. (1988) *Foucault*. London: The Athlone Press.

Deleuze, G. (1995a) 'Postscript on control societies', in G. Deleuze *Negotiations: 1972–1990*. New York: Columbia University Press.

Deleuze, G. (1995b) 'Control and becoming', in G. Deleuze *Negotiations: 1972–1990*. New York: Columbia University Press.

Deleuze, G. (1997) 'Postscript on the societies of control' [alternative translation of Deleuze, 1995a], in N. Leach (ed.) *Rethinking architecture: a reader in cultural theory*. London: Routledge.

Deleuze, G. and Guattari, F. (1984) *Anti-Oedipus: capitalism and schizophrenia*. London: The Athlone Press.

Deleuze, G. and Guattari, F. (1987) *A thousand plateaus: capitalism and schizophrenia*. Minneapolis, MN: University of Minnesota Press.

Dreyfus, H. and Rabinow, P. (1982) *Michel Foucault: Beyond Structuralism and Hermeneutics*. Hemel Hempstead: Harvester Wheatsheaf.

Feeley, M. and Simon, J. (1992) 'The new penology: notes on the emerging strategy of corrections and its implications', *Criminology* 30: 449–74.

Feeley, M. and Simon, J. (1994) 'Actuarial justice: the emerging new criminal law', in D. Nelken (ed.) *The futures of criminology*. London: Sage.

Foucault, M. (1979) *Discipline and punish: the birth of the prison*. London: Penguin.

Fyfe, N. and Bannister, J. (1996) 'City watching: closed circuit television in public spaces', *Area* 28(1): 37–46.

Garland, D. (1985) *Punishment and Welfare: A History of Penal Strategies*. Aldershot: Gower.

Garland, D. (1991) *Punishment and modern society: a study in social theory*. Oxford: Clarendon Press.

Garland, D. and Young, P., eds (1983a) *The power to punish*. Aldershot: Gower.

Garland, D. and Young, P. (1983b) 'Towards a social analysis of penality', in Garland and Young (eds) *The power to punish*. Aldershot: Gower.

Goffman, E. (1991) *Asylums: essays on the social situation of mental patients and other inmates*. London: Penguin.

Grabosky, P., Smith, R., with Wright, P. (1998) *Crime in the digital age: controlling telecommunications and cyberspace illegalities*. Leichhardt, NSW: The Federation Press.

Howe, A. (1994) *Punish and critique: towards a feminist analysis of penality*. London: Routledge.

Jones, R. (1997) 'Modern penality and social theory', unpublished doctoral thesis, Cambridge: Institute of Criminology, University of Cambridge.

Loader, B., ed. (1997) *The governance of cyberspace: politics, technology and global restructuring*. London: Routledge.

Mair, G. and Mortimer, E. (1996) *Curfew orders with electronic monitoring: an evaluation of the first twelve months of trials in Greater Manchester, Norfolk and Berkshire (Home Office Research Study 163)*. London: Home Office.

Mair, G. and Nec, C., with the assistance of Barclay, G. and Wickham, K. (1990) *Electronic monitoring: the trials and their results (Home Office Research & Planning Unit Report, No.120)*. London: HMSO.

Mann, D. and Sutton, M. (1998) 'Netcrime: more change in the organization of thieving', *British Journal of Criminology* 38(2): 201–29.

Mathiesen, T. (1965) *The defences of the weak: a sociological study of a Norwegian correctional institution*. London: Tavistock.

Nellis, M. (1991) 'The electronic monitoring of offenders in England and Wales: recent developments and future prospects', *British Journal of Criminology* 31(2): 165–85.

Norris, C., Moran, J. and Armstrong, G. (1998) 'Algorithmic surveillance: the future of automated visual surveillance', in C. Norris, J. Moran and G. Armstrong (eds) *Surveillance, closed circuit television and social control*. Aldershot: Ashgate.

O'Malley, P. (1992) 'Risk, power and crime prevention', *Economy and Society* 21(3): 252–75.

O'Malley, P. and Palmer, D. (1996) 'Post-Keynesian policing', *Economy and Society* 25(2): 137–55.

Peters, A. (1988) 'Main currents in criminal law theory', in J.J.M. van Dijk et al. (eds) *Criminal law in action*. Deventer: Kluwer.

PUNISHMENT AND SOCIETY 2(1)

Petersilia, J. (1986) 'Exploring the option of house arrest', *Federal Probation* 50(2): 50–4.

Pollitt, C. (1993) *Managerialism and the public services: cuts or cultural change in the 1990s?*, 2nd edn. Oxford: Basil Blackwell.

Pollitt, C. and Bouckaert, G., eds (1995) *Quality improvement in European public services: concepts, cases and commentary.* London: Sage.

President's Commission on Law Enforcement and Administration of Justice (1967) *Task force report: science and technology.* Washington, DC: US Government Printing Office.

Prison Reform Trust (1999) 'Home detention curfew: your questions answered', in *Prison Report*, Issue No. 46 (February 1999), London: Prison Reform Trust.

Prison Service (1995a) '*Briefing': incentives and privileges: new national framework*, no. 83 (27 June 1995), London: Prison Service.

Prison Service (1995b) *Instruction to governors: incentives and earned privileges for prisoners: national framework*, IG74/1995 (6 July 1995), London: Prison Service.

Renzema, M. (1992) 'Home confinement programs: development, implementation, and impact', in J.M. Byrne, A.J. Lurigio and J. Petersilia (eds) *Smart sentencing: the emergence of intermediate sanctions.* London: Sage.

Rusche, G. and Kirchheimer, O. (1968) *Punishment and social structure.* New York: Russell & Russell.

Scheerer, S. and Hess, H. (1997) 'Social control: a defence and reformulation', in R. Bergalli and C. Sumner (eds) *Social control and political order: European perspectives at the end of the century.* London: Sage.

Shearing, C. and Stenning, P. (1986) 'Say "Cheese!": The Disney order that is not so Mickey Mouse', in C. Shearing and P. Stenning (eds) *Private Policing.* Beverley Hills: Sage.

Sumner, C., ed. (1990) *Censure, politics and criminal justice.* Buckingham: Open University Press.

Sumner, C. (1997) 'The Decline of Social Control and the Rise of Vocabularies of Struggle', in R. Bergalli and C. Sumner (eds) *Social Control and Political Order.* London: Sage.

Sykes, G. (1958) *The society of captives.* Princeton, NJ: Princeton University Press.

University of Cambridge (1999) 'Use and misuse of computer facilities'. Internet URL (at time of writing) http: //www.cam.ac.uk/CS//ITSyndicate/guidelines.html

von Hirsch, A. and Wasik, M. (1997) 'Civil disqualifications attending conviction: a suggested conceptual framework', *Cambridge Law Journal* 56(3): 599–626.

Wasik, M. (1990) *Crime and the computer.* Oxford: Clarendon Press.

Weber, M. (1978) *Economy and society: an outline of interpretive sociology, volume 2.* Berkeley, CA: University of California Press.

Wilkins, L. (1964) *Social deviance: social policy, action and research.* London: Tavistock.

DR RICHARD JONES is a Lecturer in Criminology at the Centre for Law and Society, School of Law, University of Edinburgh. His research areas include theoretical criminology, sociology of law and contemporary social theory.

[25]

Digitizing surveillance: categorization, space, inequality

❑ STEPHEN GRAHAM & DAVID WOOD

University of Newcastle-upon-Tyne

Abstract

In this article, we seek to add to current debates about surveillance and society by critically exploring the social implications of a new and emerging raft of surveillance practices: those that specifically surround digital techniques and technologies. The article has four parts. In the first, we outline the nature of digital surveillance and consider how it differs from other forms of surveillance. The second part of the article explores the interconnections between digital techniques and the changing political economies of cities and urban societies. Here we explore the essential ambivalence of digital surveillance within the context of wider trends towards privatization, liberalization and social polarization. The third part provides some insights into particular aspects of digital surveillance through three examples: algorithmic video surveillance (in which closed circuit television systems are linked to software for the recognition of movement or identity); the increasingly prevalent practices of digital prioritization in transport and communications; and the medical surveillance of populations, wherein databases are created for increasingly mixed state and commercial medical purposes. Following this, in part four, we reflect on the policy and research implications raised by the spread of digital surveillance.

Key words: automation, biometrics, cities, ICTs, social exclusion

Introduction

Wherever there has been the creation and enforcement of categories, there has been surveillance. Historically, this was reinforced through religious and cultural norms. With capitalism and the modern state, such practices were systematized through rational organization: bureaucracy, management and policing. Now a further shift is taking place away from those direct supervisory techniques famously analysed by Foucault (1975). Advances in the technologies of sensing and recording have enabled a massive growth in the monitoring of individuals and groups without the need for constant direct observation or containment of those monitored within particular spaces (Deleuze, 1992; Gandy, 1993; Lianos, 2001; Lyon, 1994, 2001; Poster, 1990). For Gary Marx (1988), this 'new surveillance' is characterized by 'the use of technical means to extract or create personal data . . . taken from individuals or contexts' (Marx, 2002: 12).

Our aim in this article is to critically explore the social implications of the *digital* within the 'new surveillance'. Bureaucratic and electromechanical surveillance systems (a foundation for the modern nation state, public health and welfare) are being supplemented and increasingly replaced by digital technologies and techniques, enabling what Jones (2001) calls 'digital rule'. Digitization is significant for two reasons: first, it enables monitoring, prioritization and judgement to occur across widening geographical distances and with little time delay (Lyon, 1994); second, it allows the active sorting, identification, prioritization and tracking of bodies, behaviours and characteristics of subject populations on a continuous, real-time basis. Thus, digitization encourages a tendency towards automation. Crucially, the work of human operators shifts from direct mediation and discretion to the design, programming, supervision and maintenance of automated or semi-automatic surveillance systems (Lianos and Douglas, 2000).

Digitization facilitates a step change in the power, intensity and scope of surveillance. Surveillance is everywhere. Computers are everywhere. Their combination already has that air of inevitability that can attach itself to the history of technology. Computer technology certainly is, as Henman (1997) argues, a player in social policy processes, but it is crucial not to read social and policy implications and effects of digital surveillance deterministically from the intrinsic capabilities of the technologies involved. As McCahill (2002) and Thrift and French (2002) demonstrate, such techniques are mediated, at all levels, by social practices that interact with all aspects of the making and functioning of the technological system. Even apparently automated systems, far from being inhuman domains, involve continuous complex social practices and decisions that do much to shape digital surveillance in practice.

This is important because a characteristic of digital surveillance technologies is their extreme flexibility and ambivalence. On the one hand, systems can be designed to socially exclude, based on automated judgements of social or economic worth; on the other hand, the same systems can be programmed to help overcome social barriers and processes of marginalization. The broad social effects and policy implications of digital surveillance are thus contingent and, while flexible, are likely to be strongly biased by the political, economic and social conditions that shape the principles embedded in their design and implementation.

Currently, these conditions are marked by the widespread liberalization and privatization of public services and spaces. This reflects a movement from free, universal public services and spaces, based on notions of citizenship, to markets and quasi-markets based on consumerism. These markets continually differentiate between users based on ability to pay, risk or eligibility of access. While there is clearly much variation and detail in particular cases, this broad political-economic bias means that digital surveillance is likely to be geared overwhelmingly towards supporting the processes of individualization, commodification and consumerization that are necessary to support broader political-economic shifts towards markets, quasi-markets and prioritized public services and spaces (see Graham and Marvin, 2001).

This article seeks, in four parts, to explore the nature, scope and implications of the growth of digital surveillance techniques and technologies. In the first, we outline the nature of digital surveillance and consider how it differs from earlier forms. We argue that, while the changes may be considered merely quantitative (size, coverage, speed, and so on), important new forms of social practice are facilitated by these changes. The second part develops an exploratory analysis of the interconnections between digitization and the changing political economies of cities and urban societies. Here we examine the essential ambivalence of digital surveillance within the context of wider trends towards privatization, liberalization and social polarization. We argue that the techniques may facilitate better services for mobile, affluent citizens, but that this is often paralleled by a relative worsening of the position of more marginalized groups

who are physically or electronically excluded or bypassed by automated surveillance. The third part illustrates these points through
three examples: algorithmic video surveillance; digital prioritization
in transport and communications; and, finally, electronic patient
records and genetic research. Finally, in part four, we reflect on the
policy challenges raised by the spread of digital surveillance.

Digital surveillance: making a difference?

Digital encoding works by reducing information to the minimum
necessary for accurate reconstruction: the binary code of 1s and 0s. In
contrast, analogue forms aim at perfect reproduction of the original.
Digital surveillance thus makes the information more amenable to
storage, transmission and computation. But is it sufficiently different
from analogue forms to merit rethinking and retheorization?

Michel Foucault's (1975) concept of 'panopticism'[1] (the tendency
towards a disciplinary state based on direct surveillance) is still a
dominant metaphor. However, Poster claims that digitization requires
a re-evaluation of this concept because Foucault failed to notice that
late 20th-century technological and infrastructural developments were
qualitatively different from the earlier examples he studied:

> Today's circuits of communication and the databases they generate
> constitute a Superpanopticon, a system of surveillance without walls,
> windows, towers or guards. The quantitative advances in the technolo-
> gies of surveillance result in a qualitative change in the microphysics of
> power. (Poster, 1990: 93)

Oscar Gandy argues that information age capitalism operates through
a panoptic sort (the processes by which people are categorized and
valued on the basis of information contained in databases), claiming:

> it is only the locational constraints, the notion of separation by space,
> occasioned by the initial conceptualisation of the panoptic system as a
> building and by the surveillance as visual that limits Foucault's
> construct. But in an age of electronic networks, virtual memory, and
> remote access to distributed intelligence and data, disciplinary surveil-
> lance is no longer limited to single buildings, and observations no
> longer limited to line of sight. (Gandy, 1993: 23)

Digital sorting results in the creation of subjects through databases
that do not replicate or imitate the original subject, but create a

multiplicity of selves that may be acted upon without the knowledge of the original. These 'dividuals' (Deleuze, 1992) – or data subjects – are increasingly more important for social identity than bodily selves (Lyon, 2001; van der Ploeg, 1999, 2002).

The obvious differences between digital surveillance and analogue surveillance are quantitative: computer hard drives can store far more information more conveniently and faster than analogue systems. However, the fundamental differences lie in what can be done with the information gathered. There are two basic processes.

Norris and Armstrong (1999), in their study of closed circuit television (CCTV) in Britain, argue that what is of most concern is the linking of cameras to databases and the integration of different databases. Digitization facilitates interconnection within and between surveillance points and systems. To be truly effective, linkage is often *required* so that captured and stored data can be compared. Technological reasons will always be found to integrate. However, political and economic arguments are not always either presented, heard or assigned equivalent importance, and thus a covert process of 'surveillance creep' (Marx, 1988: 2) occurs, whereby integration is presented as necessary or inevitable.

Importantly, digital systems also allow the application of automated processes: algorithmic surveillance. An algorithm is a mathematical term for a set of instructions:[2] algorithms are the foundation of mathematics and computing. However, algorithms need to be translated into a form that computers are programmed to understand, namely software – essentially many coded algorithms linked together. Algorithmic surveillance refers to surveillance systems using software to extend raw data: from classification (sensor + database 1); through comparison (sensor + database 1 + software + database 2); to prediction or even reaction (sensor + database 1 + software + database 2 + alarm/weapon).

Many of the latest surveillance technologies have embedded digital and algorithmic features. A city centre CCTV system providing images that are watched and analysed by human operators may be digitally recorded and stored, but is not algorithmic. If the system includes software that compares the faces of the people observed with those in a database of suspects, it becomes algorithmic. Patient records in a health service computer are digital and are algorithmic to the extent that software determines the format of the information entered. However, the process becomes algorithmic surveillance when, for example, software compares patient records against signs of particular disease risk factors and categorizes patients automatically.

Some have claimed that algorithmic systems improve on conventional systems. Marx argues that algorithmic surveillance provides the possibility of eliminating the potential for corruption and discrimination (1995: 238). For example, a racist police officer cannot decide to arrest any black male when a facial recognition system can decide categorically whether a particular individual is the wanted man. However, algorithmic surveillance can also intensify problems of conventional surveillance and of computerization. Already, in social policy processes, 'the perceived objectivity of computers is used to validate statistics which support partisan views' (Henman, 1997: 335). Algorithmic systems also pose new questions, particularly relating to the removal of human discretion. In the most extreme cases, such as the development of movement recognition software linked to an automatic lethal response in certain commercially available perimeter defence systems (see Doucet and Lloyd, 2001; Wright, 1998), this can lead to death without explanation or appeal. Even in less immediately vital situations, for example one person's Internet traffic secretly bypassing another's because of algorithmic prioritization, the consequences can nevertheless be serious and exclusionary.

It is critical to stress here the subtle and stealthy quality of the ongoing social prioritizations and judgements that digital surveillance systems make possible. This means that critical social policy research must work to expose the ways in which these systems are being used to prioritize certain people's mobilities, service quality and life chances, while simultaneously reducing those of less favoured groups. Importantly, both beneficiaries and losers may, in practice, be utterly unaware that digital prioritization has actually occurred. This gives many of these crucial processes a curiously invisible and opaque quality that is a major challenge to researchers and policy makers alike.

Digital surveillance and the changing political economies of the city

As Thrift and French (2002) have shown, there are now so many software-based surveillance and IT systems embedded in the infrastructure of cities that even the UK Audit Commission had enormous difficulties finding them all when trying to ensure that they would all function in the new millennium. They were often unable to discover who was responsible for them and how they could be checked and reprogrammed. Thrift and French (2002) claim that the ubiquity of such systems in the modern city is leading to the automatic production of space.

This opacity and ubiquity mean that it is hard to identify how the shift to automated, digital and algorithmic surveillance practices relates to current radical shifts in the political economies of welfare states, governance, punishment and urban space. Richard Jones (2001), following Deleuze (1992), argues that, as at-a-distance monitoring systems become intelligent and immanent within the city, so notions of traditional disciplinary control are replaced by the continuous electronic disciplining of subjects against redefined norms across time and space (see Graham, 1998).

Social, commercial and state definitions of norms of behaviour within the various contexts of the city are thus increasingly automatically policed by assemblages of digital technology and software. These are less and less mediated by human discretion (Lianos and Douglas, 2000). Normative notions of good behaviour and transgression within the complex space–time fabrics of cities are embedded into software codes. So, increasingly, are stipulations and punishments (for example, electronic tagging).

Increasingly, the encoding of software to automatically stipulate eligibility of access, entitlement of service or punishment is often done far away in time and space from the point of application (see Lessig, 1999). Software is coded across the world: call centres that monitor the gaze of automated cameras of electronic tags are switched to low-cost labour locations. Digital surveillance therefore promotes a new round of space–time distanciation, which moves us ever further from modern notions of discipline based on the gaze of supervisors within the same space–time as the disciplined subject (McCahill, 2002). Efforts are then made to enforce such norms and boundaries on the ground on a continuing, real-time basis through the withdrawal of electronic or physical access privileges, the detailed stipulation and monitoring of acceptable behaviours and the automated tracking of individuals' space–time paths.

Within contemporary political-economic contexts marked by privatization and consumerization, this proliferation of automatic systems raises clear concerns that social exclusion itself will be automated. Rather than being based exclusively on uneven access to the Internet, the digital divide in contemporary societies is based on the broader disconnections of certain groups from IT hardware *and* the growing use of automated surveillance and information systems to digitally red-line their life chances within automated regimes of service provision (Jupp, 2001). Such systems actively facilitate mobility, access, services and life chances for those judged electronically to have the correct credentials and exclude or relationally push away others (Norris, 2002). They thereby accelerate the trend away from persons towards data subjects. As Norris et al. suggest, the problem with automated systems is that 'they aim to facilitate exclusionary rather than inclusionary goals' (1998: 271). Algorithmic systems thus have a strong potential to fix identities as deviant and criminal – what Norris calls the technological mediation of suspicion (Norris, 2002). Lianos and Douglas note that this also means that challenging these identifications becomes harder because what they term 'Automated Socio-Technical Environments' (ASTEs) 'radically transform the cultural register of the societies in which they operate by introducing non-negotiable contexts of interaction' (2000: 265).

Digital surveillance techniques therefore make possible the widening commodification of urban space and the erection within cities of myriad exclusionary boundaries and access controls. These range from the electronic tagging of offenders within their defined space–time domains to gated communities with pin number entry systems and shopping malls with intense video surveillance (Davis, 1990; Flusty, 1997). Digital surveillance systems also provide essential supports to the electronically priced commodification of road spaces; to digitally mediated consumption systems; and to smartcard-based public services – all of which allow user behaviours to be closely scrutinized. Crucially, the new digital surveillance assemblage is being shaped in a biased way to neatly dovetail with and support a new political economy of consumer citizenship and individualized mobility and consumption which would otherwise not be possible (Garland, 2001).

This is especially important within a context marked by the increasing privatization of public services, infrastructures and domains (with a growing emphasis on treating users differently based on assessments of their direct profitability). Digital surveillance also provides a new range of management techniques to address the widening fear of crime and the entrenchment of entrepreneurial efforts to make (certain parts of) towns and city spaces more competitive in attracting investors and (selected) consumers.

Digital surveillance and the city: three examples

After this broad examination of the connections between digital surveillance techniques and the changing political economies of cities, we are in a position to examine the links between digital surveillance, exclusion and urban space in more detail. We do this via three examples: first, algorithmic CCTV; second, information, communication and mobility spaces; and, finally, genetic surveillance.

Algorithmic CCTV

Many systems of sorting and analysis can be linked to video surveillance, two examples being facial recognition and movement recognition. These are both *biometric* technologies, basing their categorization upon human bodily characteristics or traces (van der Ploeg, 1999, 2002).

In the UK, facial recognition software is being piloted in three metropolitan areas: Newham in London, Birmingham and Manchester (Meek, 2002). This technology is designed to compare the faces of individuals on the street with those of known offenders in databases. In both cases, the system used is FaceIt ARGUS, one of the most widespread of all facial recognition systems, produced by the US-based Identix Corporation (formerly Visionics).

FaceIt generates a 'faceprint', supposedly unique to each individual (see: http://www.visionics.com/faceit/whatis.html; no longer accessible). Using a series of different algorithms, it draws on relatively simple pattern matching to detect whether a face-like object is present and then whether the object is actually a face. Further algorithms create a normalized face, stripped of place- and time-specific light and shade, and so on. More complex algorithmic processes known as Local Feature Analysis are then used to create the 84-bit faceprint, a set of codes that can be stored in a database or matched against existing stored codes.

Identix says that FaceIt maps the intrinsic shape and features of the face and that the faceprint contains enough information to accurately distinguish an individual among millions of people (see:

http://www.identix.com/products/pro_faceit.html). This can then be used in many ways, from simple verification (checking that an individual is who they say they are) to real-time surveillance. According to previous Visionics publicity, 'FaceIt can find human faces anywhere in the field of view and at any distance, and it can continuously track them and crop them out of the scene, matching the face against a watch list' (see: http://www.visionics.com/faceit/tech/verif.html; no longer accessible).

Another developing area is movement recognition. Systems in use to detect motion and movement tend to be relatively simple, based on blobs of particular colours that remain constant in sampled frames of a CCTV image, such as the EU funded Cromatica project at King's College, London (see: http://www.research.eee.kcl.ac.uk/vrl/#cromatica). This was designed for crowd flow management but, when piloted on the London Underground, attracted attention for its potential to help reduce the number of suicides, as it had been observed that the suicidal 'tend to wait for at least ten minutes on the platform, missing trains, before taking their last few tragic steps' (Graham-Rowe, 1999: 25, cited in Norris, 2002). In Orlando, Florida, another experimental system in a high crime neighbourhood claims to 'detect . . . fires, or unusual body movements' (*Business Week*, 2000: 16).

Gait recognition has also attracted significant media attention. Headlines like 'The way you walk pins down who you are' imply a reversion to Victorian notions of a visible criminal character (see: http://www.isis.ecs.soton.ac.uk/image/gait/press/). The reality is more prosaic, if still technically impressive. Researchers at the University of Southampton have been developing algorithms for the individual human gait. These (like faceprints) have the potential to be stored as information to be compared with existing images. It is perhaps even more complex than facial recognition, but, according to group leader Mark Nixon, 'a distant silhouette will provide enough data to make a positive recognition once we get the system working properly' (McKie, 1999). However, despite the publicity, the systems being developed have not progressed to the point of commercial use at this stage.

Certainty about identity is crucial to the argument for algorithmic CCTV: as was argued earlier, one of the main reasons for its increasing popularity is to counter arguments about human fallibility. But there are allegations that the technologies (and FaceIt in particular) simply do not work. Research by Norris and others (cited in Rosen, 2001) and by the *Guardian* newspaper (Meek, 2002) shows that not a single arrest has been made as a result of the use of FaceIt in Newham and that the authorities overstated both the technological capability of the system and the size of their database of suspects. Until recently, it was relatively unusual for FaceIt to be used in live CCTV systems monitoring people moving freely in urban environments. By far its most common usage remains where movement is spatially restricted and a throughput of well-lit, similarly angled faces is guaranteed (entry systems, airport check-in areas, and so on).[3] However, even in controlled conditions, failure rates of 53 percent have been identified at Palm Beach International Airport (Scheers, 2002). Justification for facial recognition has to fall back on arguments about deterrence that are dominant in UK policy discourses promoting CCTV (Norris and Armstrong, 1999). Such technical arguments should not, however, detract from fundamental questions about categorization and bypass. As described earlier, there are significant concerns about the way in which such systems rely on and reinforce the categorization of certain sociospatial risk categories: high crime neighbourhoods, known criminals or dangerous socioeconomic groups (Lianos and Douglas, 2000).

Information, communication and mobility services in the city

Our second range of examples involves the use of new information and communication technologies (ICTs) and digital surveillance to subtly differentiate consumers within transport, communications or service provision. Here, algorithms are being used at the interface of databases and telecommunications networks to allocate different levels of service to different users on an increasingly automated basis. This is done to overcome problems of congestion, queuing and service quality and to maximize the quality of service for the most profitable users. Examples include Internet prioritization, electronic road pricing, call centre call queuing and the use of biometrics to bypass international passport and immigration controls (see Graham and Marvin, 2001).

When the Internet first became a mass medium in the late 1990s it was impossible to give one user a priority service over another. All packets of data on the Internet were queued when there was congestion. However, on the commercialized Internet, dominated by transnational media conglomerates, new software protocols are being embedded into the routers that switch Internet traffic. These smart routers automatically and actively discriminate between different users' packets, especially in times of congestion. They can sift priority packets, allowing them passage, while automatically blocking those from non-premium users (Schiller, 1999).

Thus, high quality Internet and e-commerce services can now be guaranteed to premium users irrespective of wider conditions, while non-premium users simultaneously experience 'website not available' signals. This further supports the unbundling of Internet and e-commerce services, as different qualities can be packaged and sold at different rates to different markets (Graham and Marvin, 2001). As Emily Tseng suggests, 'the ability to discriminate and prioritize data traffic is now being built into the [Internet] system. Therefore economics can shape the way packets flow through the networks and therefore whose content is more important' (2000: 12).

The integration of customer databases within call centres provides another example of digital discrimination. Initially, call centres operated through the judgement and discretion of call centre operators. One system installed at South West Water in the UK in the mid-1990s, for example, meant that:

> when a customer rings, just the giving of their name and postcode to the member of staff [a practice often now automated through call-line identification] allows all account details, including records of past telephone calls, billing dates and payments, even scanned images of letters, to be displayed. This amount of information enables staff to deal with different customers in different ways. A customer who repeatedly defaults with payment will be treated completely differently from one who has only defaulted once. (*Utility Week*, 1995: 12)

Now that call centres are equipped with Call Line Identification (CLI) allowing operators to detect the phone numbers of incoming calls, such practices are being automated. Automated surveillance systems are emerging that can differentially queue calls according to algorithmic judgements of the profits the company makes from them. 'Good' customers are thus answered quickly, while 'bad' ones are put on hold. As with Internet prioritization, neither user is likely to know that such prioritization and distancing are occurring.

New algorithmic techniques are also being used to reduce road congestion, while improving the mobilities of privileged drivers. With road space increasingly congested, electronic road pricing is an increasingly popular political choice. A range of governments have brought in private or public/private regimes to either electronically price entry into existing city centres (for example, Singapore and, from February 2003, London) or build new private premium highways that are only accessible to drivers with in-car electronic transponders (including Toronto, Los Angeles, San Diego, Melbourne and Manila).

In both cases, road space becomes a priced commodity dependent on users having the appropriate onboard technology and resources – and often bank accounts – to pay bills. In some cases, systems allow traffic flow to be guaranteed whatever the level of external traffic congestion. On the San Diego I-15 highway, for example, software monitoring congestion levels on the premium-priced highway can signal real-time price increases when congestion causes the flow to decrease. Communicated to drivers, this reduces demand and reinstates free flowing conditions.

While such systems have environmental benefits, it can also be argued that their implementation is closely related to the changing political economy of cities. This is because, like Internet prioritization and call centre queuing, they facilitate the removal of what might be called cash-poor/time-rich users from the congested mobility network, in the process facilitating premium network conditions for cash-rich/time-poor users (Graham and Marvin, 2001). The Hong Kong government, for example, recently discussed implementing a city centre road pricing system like that in Singapore. This was not to reduce greenhouse gas emissions; rather, it was a direct response to the lobbying of corporate CEOs who were sick of having to walk the last half mile to meetings in hot, humid conditions because of gridlock. These executives had grown used to a seamless door-to-door service, uninhibited by traffic in Singapore's pricey central business district.

Finally, algorithmic surveillance now allows highly mobile, affluent business travellers to directly bypass normal immigration and ticketing at major international airports. This allows them to move seamlessly and speedily through the architectural and technological systems designed to separate airsides and groundsides within major international airports (Virilio, 1991: 10). For example, handscans for the most frequent business travellers are now in operation in major airports linking the US, the Netherlands, Canada and Germany and other OECD nations under the Immigration and Naturalization Service Passenger Accelerated Service System (INSPASS). Selected premium travellers are issued with a smartcard that records their hand geometry: 'Each time the traveller passes through customs, they present the card and place their hand in a reader that verifies their identity and links into international databases', allowing them instant progress (Banisar, 1999: 67). By 1999, the scheme had 70,000 participants and the INS was planning to extend the system globally. Such systems extend the infrastructure of highly luxurious airport lounges and facilities only accessible to identified elite passengers.[4] ICT surveillance assemblages privilege some users, while those deemed to warrant less (or no) mobility (especially illegal immigrants and refugees) face ever increasing efforts to make international boundaries less permeable through new border control systems.

Genetics and medical surveillance

Medicine, particularly public health and epidemiology, has a long history of surveillant practices, largely in the notification and monitoring of outbreaks of infectious disease (Declich and Carter, 1994; Foucault, 1973, 1975; Mooney, 1999). However, digitization is transforming these practices. Two linked cases will be mentioned here: first, electronic patient records (EPRs); and, second, research into genetics. As van der Ploeg (2002: 62) writes:

> Health care systems throughout the Western countries are moving towards on-line accessible EPRs into which all data on medical history, medication, test results from a broad variety of diagnostic (often already computer based) techniques, and therapies belonging to a particular individual's medical biography are accumulated, and can be accessed by relevant care givers.

EPRs are convenient and contribute to quick and accurate diagnosis of illness and, therefore, patient welfare and public health. However, they also gradually accumulate a mass of personal information, most of which has no direct relevance to any particular medical condition. Such records are protected by law and medical ethics but, as Mooney (1999) has shown in his analysis of debates about public health and privacy in the 18th and 19th centuries, personal rights can lose out to what is considered to be the public good – a slippery and amorphous notion. Regarding CCTV, the media outrage around the Jamie Bulger murder case in the UK led to a massive expansion of video surveillance without much public debate (Norris and Armstrong, 1999), and one can easily imagine external issues like international terrorism or preventative genetics forcing a reconsideration of civil rights versus the public good. The pressure to integrate, for example, medical and police databases for law enforcement purposes will become more and more intense as forensic science improves and with the increasing popularity of biocriminology and the pressure for pre-emptive law enforcement policies such as DNA screening (Rose, 2000).

But it is not *1984*-style fears of state surveillance that give most cause for concern; it is the increasing influence of the private sector in health care provision. The relationship between public database holders and the private sector is a key issue, one that is again complicated by digitization. Modern medical research, and in particular genetics, depends increasingly on high-powered computing. As Moor remarks, 'it is . . . only through the eyes of computers that we can hope to map and sequence the human genome in a practical period of time' (1999: 257).

Genetic records are also so readily digitizable that Nelkin and Andrews (1999) can give several examples of scientists predicting that smartcards with an encoded personal genome will soon replace current methods of personal identification. Progress towards the convergence of EPRs, personal genome records and private financial interests is already well underway. For example, leaked minutes of a high-level advisory group working towards a new health Green Paper by the UK Labour government show that the group proposes making the results of DNA sampling in NHS hospitals available to pharmaceutical companies (Barnett and Hinsliff, 2001). Iceland has licensed its entire national medical database to the American genetics company deCODE for research and commercial purposes (Rose, 2001) and Estonia is also planning a genetic database of its citizens (Pollack, 2000).

Once state EPRs are commodified, so prospects for democratic control over personal information decrease and the discriminatory potential multiplies. The insurance industry is just one domain that is being transformed by this increasing commodification (Cook, 1999; Pokorski, 1997). Insurance has serious implications for personal wellbeing when individuals are increasingly forced to find private health care and retirement solutions and rely less upon decreasing state provision. Those whose genetic records make them too financially risky for insurance companies could find themselves bypassed by neoliberal health policies. Moreover, mutualized life and health insurance systems, built up over centuries and based on the social

pooling of aggregate risks, threaten to be dismantled and individualized in the same ways as are the physical infrastructures of
cities. Users defined through their genetic profiles as low-risk/high-
profit could secede from generalized rates and gain low-cost cover,
whereas those with high risks of long-term costly illness or early
death could be excluded from cover (Graham and Marvin, 2001).

Conclusions: research, policy and resistance

As digital surveillance proliferates, the politics of surveillance are
increasingly the politics of code. The processes through which algorithms and software are constructed are often now the only parts of
the disciplinary chain completely open to human discretion and
shaping. Once switched on, many digital systems become supervised
agents that continually help to determine ongoing social outcomes in
space and time (Lianos and Douglas, 2000).

The research challenges raised here are clear. Software for surveillance is often bought off the shelf from transnational suppliers. Critical
researchers into digital algorithmic systems practices face an imperative
to 'get inside' the production and implementation of code (Thrift and
French, 2002). This might mean switching the focus of research to the
social and political assumptions that software producers embed (unconsciously or consciously) into their algorithms years before and thousands of miles away from the site of application. Research is required to
systematically track the sourcing, implementation and implications of
digital surveillance in practice, across multiple spaces, as the code
moves from inception to application. Such research also needs to
address time, as another implication of digital surveillance is its use in
decreasing the ability of people to escape deemed offences in the distant
past (Blanchette and Johnson, 2002).

The policy implications of such research are complex and problematic. Digital surveillance systems tend to be developed, designed
and deployed in ways that hide the social judgements that such
systems perpetuate. Rates of technological innovation are rapid and
policy makers face serious problems in simply understanding the
esoteric and technical worlds of the new surveillance. Policy makers
also face geographical and jurisdictional problems. Efforts to regulate
and control digital surveillance are necessarily bound by the geographical jurisdictions that give them political legitimacy and power.

But social assumptions embedded in surveillance software in one context can have major ramifications in distant times and places. The practices of digitally sorting and sifting societies occur through globally stretched sociotechnical relations (Lyon, 2001).

Another major problem concerns the dominant policy approach to surveillance: the concept of privacy. Privacy is fundamentally embedded both in the Lockean notion of property and in the patriarchal dynamics of the household (Lyon, 1994). Its current politics are also dominated by the discourse of individualist, libertarian 'cyberliberties', which renders it inadequate to deal with complex sociogeographical polarization.

We believe that a strong regulatory approach, based on the principle of the mutual transparency of state and individual (see Brin, 1999), could simultaneously work at the many geographical scales at which social and economic regulation occurs. However, two current trajectories make this transparent society less than likely. The first is the post-9/11 climate. Currently, many western policy makers would consider such transparency politically unacceptable, particularly as pressures increase from the Right for *decreasing* civil liberties in the name of security (see Huber and Mills, 2002).

The second is that the new digital surveillance systems are being used to support the dominant neoliberal economic agenda (for example, the generalized privatization envisaged by the proposed General Agreement on Trade in Services) because they can allow the 'unbundling' of previously public infrastructures and spaces and support 'pay per use' and sophisticated consumer monitoring. As public, welfare and social service regimes restructure and are privatized or remodelled through various forms of 'partnership', the automated control and sifting capabilities of digital surveillance techniques are increasingly being utilized to support differentiated service regimes. These practices are closely modelled on those in the private sector; in many cases, private sector firms are colonizing public and welfare service regimes with precisely such practices.

Does this mean that the choice is for a critical response to digital surveillance to be bound by either cyberliberties, resistance to the 'war on terrorism' or anti-globalization struggles? Not necessarily – although placing the spread of digital surveillance within a wider political-economic critique is crucial. People do 'refuse to disappear beneath the imperatives of spatial regulation that favors select target markets' (Flusty, 2000: 156). Resistance exists in many forms, from the playful guerrilla art of the Surveillance Camera Players (see: http://www.notbored.org/the-scp.html), the systematic anti-panopticism of the i-SEE project in New York, calculating 'paths of least surveillance' (Schenke and IAA, 2002; see: http://www.appliedautonomy.com/isee/), to the everyday practices of the targeted. In British towns, young black men have been shown to develop elaborate practices to exploit CCTV system 'blindspots' (Norris and Armstrong, 1999; Toon, 2000). Similarly, Flusty has shown how the excluded in LA work to exploit the gaps. One busker, for example, says he 'knows where to find every security camera on Bunker Hill' (Flusty, 2000: 152).

Resistance varies across policy domains; in health, outside professional disquiet, it has been minimal. While Iceland has at least provided mechanisms for public consultation on the role of deCODE (Rose, 2001), the UK government has shown no such inclination. The practices of insurance companies and health providers are similarly opaque, and, unlike the case of CCTV, there seems little space for individual acts of subversion.

Finally, we must stress that digital surveillance systems do have real limits. While the technologies are rapidly increasing their capabilities, they are often still not as reliable as their proponents claim. For example, facial recognition is still prone to misidentification, although the nature of these errors is in itself a matter of concern. In addition, the sheer diversity of identities, social worlds and political pressures in contemporary cities can quickly swamp crude efforts to impose simplistic notions of exclusion and purified urban order. Contemporary cities remain sites of jumbled, superimposed and contested orderings and meanings; they are 'points of interconnection, not hermetically sealed objects' (Thrift, 1997: 143). Multiple 'spillovers' can easily saturate and overwhelm simple attempts at establishing and maintaining 'hard' disciplinary boundaries. Virtually all boundaries remain to some extent porous and perfect control strategies are never possible.

Notes

1. Panopticism derives from Jeremy Bentham's reformatory design, the panopticon, in which prisoners never knew whether or not they were being watched and would therefore modify their behaviour as if the surveillance was constant.

2. The word algorithm derives from the 9th-century Muslim mathematician Muhammed ibn Mūsā al-Khwārizmī. 12th-century Christian scholars used al-Khwārizmī's name, latinized as Algorismus, to differentiate his method of calculation from commonly used methods like the abacus or counting tables. For more on the history of algorithms, see Chabert (1999).
3. This is changing, particularly since 9/11 (see Rosen, 2001).
4. As with facial recognition, such schemes are proliferating in the wake of 9/11, despite having no direct connection with the prevention of terrorism.

References

Banisar, D. (1999) 'Big Brother Goes High Tech', *Covert Action Quarterly* 67: 6.

Barnett, A. and G. Hinsliff (2001) 'Fury at Plan to Sell off DNA Secrets', *Observer* (23 Sept.). [http://www.guardian.co.uk/Archive/Article/0,4273, 4262710,00.html] Accessed 1 November 2002.

Blanchette, J. -F. and Johnson, D. (2002) 'Data Retention and the Panoptic Society: The Social Benefits of Forgetfulness', *The Information Society* 18(1): 33–45.

Business Week (2000) 'Nobody's Watching Your Every Move', 3707 (13 Nov): 16.

Brin, D. (1999) *The Transparent Society*. New York: Perseus.

Chabert, J. (ed.) (1999) *A History of Algorithms*. Berlin: Springer-Verlag.

Cook, E. D. (1999) 'Genetics and the British Insurance Industry', *Journal of Medical Ethics* 25(2): 157–62.

Davis, M. (1990) *City of Quartz*. London: Verso.

Declich, S. and Carter, A. O. (1994) 'Public Health Surveillance: Historical Origins, Methods and Evaluation', *Bulletin of the World Health Organization* 72(2): 285–304.

Deleuze, G. (1992) 'Postscript on the Societies of Control', *October* 59: 3–7.

Doucet, I. and Lloyd, R. (eds) (2001) *Alternative Anti-personnel Mines*. London and Berlin: Landmine Action/German Initiative to Ban Landmines.

Flusty, S. (1997) 'Building Paranoia', pp. 47–60 in N. Ellin (ed.) *Architecture of Fear*. New York: Princeton Architectural Press.

Flusty, S. (2000) 'Thrashing Downtown: Play as Resistance to the Spatial and Representational Regulation of Los Angeles', *Cities* 17(2): 149–58.

Foucault, M. (1973) *The Birth of the Clinic*. London: Tavistock.

Foucault, M. (1975) *Discipline and Punish*. New York: Vintage.

Gandy Jr, O. H. (1993) *The Panoptic Sort*. Boulder, CO: Westview Press.

Garland, D. (2001) *The Culture of Control*. Oxford: Oxford University Press.

Graham, S. (1998) 'Spaces of Surveillant-simulation: New Technologies, Digital Representations, and Material Geographies', *Environment and Planning D: Society and Space* 16: 483–504.

Graham, S. and Marvin, S. (2001) *Splintering Urbanism*. London: Routledge.

Graham-Rowe, D. (1999) 'Warning! Strange Behaviour', *New Scientist* 2216 (11 Dec.): 25–8.

Henman, P. (1997) 'Computer Technology: A Political Player in Social Policy Processes', *Journal of Social Policy* 26(3): 323–40.

Huber, P. and Mills, M. P. (2002) 'How Technology Will Defeat Terrorism', *City Journal* 12(1). [http://www.city-journal.org/html/12_1_how_tech.html] Accessed 1 November 2002.

Jones, R. (2001) 'Digital Rule: Punishment, Control and Technology', *Punishment and Society* 2(1): 5–22.

Jupp, B. (2001) *Divided by Information?* London: Demos.

Lessig, L. (1999) *Code – and Other Laws of Cyberspace*. New York: Basic Books.

Lianos, M. (2001) *Le Nouveau contrôle social*. Paris: L'Harmattan.

Lianos, M. and Douglas, M. (2000) 'Dangerization and the End of Deviance: The Institutional Environment', *British Journal of Criminology* 40(3): 264–78.

Lyon, D. (1994) *The Electronic Eye*. Cambridge: Polity Press/Blackwell.

Lyon, D. (2001) *Surveillance Society*. Buckingham: Open University Press.

McCahill, M. (2002) *The Surveillance Web*. Cullompton, Devon: Willan.

McKie, R. (1999) 'The Way You Walk Pins down Who You Are', *Observer* (12 Dec.). [http://www.guardian.co.uk/Archive/Article/o,4273,3941021 00.html] Accessed 1 November 2002.

Marx, G. T. (1988) *Undercover*. Berkeley: University of California Press.

Marx, G. T. (1995) 'The Engineering of Social Control: The Search for the Silver Bullet', pp. 225–46 in J. Hagan and R. Peterson (eds) *Crime and Inequality*. Stanford, CA: Stanford University Press.

Marx, G. T. (2002) 'What's New about the "New Surveillance"? Classifying for Change and Continuity', *Surveillance & Society* 1(1): 9–29. [http://www.surveillance-and-society.org]

Meek, J. (2002) 'Robo-cop', *Guardian* (13 June). [http://www.guardian.co.uk/Archive/Article/0,4273,4432506,00.html] Accessed 1 November 2002.

Mooney, G. (1999) 'Public Health Versus Private Practice: The Contested Development of Compulsory Disease Notification in Late Nineteenth Century Britain', *Bulletin of the History of Medicine* 73(2): 238–67.

Moor, J. H. (1999) 'Using Genetic Information while Protecting the Privacy of the Soul', *Ethics and Information Technology* 1(4): 257–63.

Nelkin, D. and Andrews, L. (1999) 'DNA Identification and Surveillance Creep', *Sociology of Health and Illness* 21(5): 689–706.

Norris, C. (2002) 'From Personal to Digital: CCTV, the Panopticon and the Technological Mediation of Suspicion and Social Control', pp. 249–81 in D. Lyon (ed.) *Surveillance as Social Sorting*. London: Routledge.

Norris, C. and Armstrong, G. (1999) *The Maximum Surveillance Society*. Oxford: Berg.

Norris, C., Moran, J. and Armstrong, G. (eds) (1998) 'Algorithmic Surveillance: The Future of Automated Visual Surveillance', pp. 255–76 in *Surveillance, Closed Circuit Television and Social Control*. Aldershot: Ashgate.

Pokorski, R. J. (1997) 'Insurance Underwriting in the Genetic Era' (workshop on heritable cancer syndromes and genetic testing), *Cancer* 80(3): 587–99.

Pollack, A. (2000) 'Gene Hunters Say Patients Are a Bankable Asset', *Guardian* (2 Aug.). [http://www.guardian.co.uk/Archive/Article/0,4273,4046698,00.html] Accessed 1 November 2002.

Poster, M. (1990) *The Mode of Information*. Cambridge: Polity Press.

Rose, H. (2001) *The Commodification of Bioinformation*. London: Wellcome Trust. [http://www.wellcome.ac.uk/en/images/hilaryrose1_3975.pdf] Accessed 1 November 2002.

Rose, N. (2000) 'The Biology of Culpability: Pathological Identity and Crime Control in a Biological Culture', *Theoretical Criminology* 4(1): 5–34.

Rosen, J. (2001) 'A Watchful State', *New York Times* (7 Oct.). [http://query.nytimes.com/search/article-page.html?res = 69505E4DE123DF 934A35753C1A9679C8B63] Accessed 1 November 2002.

Scheers, J. (2002) 'Airport Face Scanner Failed', *Wired News* (16 May). [http://www.wired.com/news/privacy/0,1848,52563,00.html] Accessed 1 November 2002.

Schenke, E. and IAA (2002) 'On the Outside Looking out: An Interview with the Institute for Applied Autonomy (IAA)', *Surveillance & Society* 1(1): 102–19. [http://www.surveillance-and-society.org]

Schiller, D. (1999) *Digital Capitalism: Networking the Global Market System*. Cambridge, MA: MIT Press.

Thrift, N. (1997) 'Cities without Modernity, Cities with Magic', *Scottish Geographical Magazine* 113(3): 138–49.

Thrift, N. and French, S. (2002) 'The Automatic Production of Space', *Transactions of the Institute of British Geographers* 27(4): 309–35.

Surveillance, Crime and Social Control

Toon, I. (2000) ' "Finding a Place on the Street": CCTV Surveillance and Young People's Use of Urban Public Space', pp. 141–65 in D. Bell and A. Haddour (eds) *City Visions*. London: Longman.

Tseng, E. (2000) 'The Geography of Cyberspace' (mimeo).

Utility Week (1995) Special issue: 'IT in Utilities' (19 Nov.).

van der Ploeg, I. (1999) 'Written on the Body: Biometrics and Identity', *Computers and Society* 29(1): 37–44.

van der Ploeg, I. (2002) 'Biometrics and the Body as Information: Normative Issues of the Socio-technical Coding of the Body', pp. 57–73 in D. Lyon (ed.) *Surveillance as Social Sorting*. London: Routledge.

Virilio, P. (1991) *The Lost Dimension*. New York: Semiotext(e).

Wright, S. (1998) *An Appraisal of the Technologies of Political Control*. Luxembourg: European Parliament (STOA programme).

❏ Stephen Graham is professor of urban technology at the University of Newcastle's school of architecture, planning and landscape (SAPL) in the UK. His research interests centre on: the relationships between society and new technologies; urban and social theory; telecommunications and information technologies and cities; surveillance and the city; networked infrastructure, mobility and urban change; urban planning and strategy making; and the links between cities and warfare. His books include *Telecommunications and the City: Electronic Spaces, Urban Places* (with Simon Marvin; Routledge, 1996) and *Splintering Urbanism: Technological Mobilities, Networked Infrastructures and the Urban Condition* (with Simon Marvin; Routledge, 2001). *Address*: School of Architecture Planning and Landscape, University of Newcastle, Newcastle-upon-Tyne NE1 7RU, UK. email: s.d.n.graham@ncl.ac.uk ❏

❏ David Wood is Earl Grey postdoctoral research fellow at the University of Newcastle's school of architecture, planning and landscape (SAPL) in the UK. His current project, 'The Evolution of Algorithmic Surveillance and the Potential for Social Exclusion', looks at the sociotechnical history and development of computer-mediated surveillance technologies. His other research interests include: geographies of military intelligence and orbital space; virtual spaces; and social theory. He is also the founder and managing editor of the new international journal of surveillance studies, *Surveillance & Society* (see: http://www.surveillance-and-society.org), part of a project to provide online surveillance studies resources. email: d.f.j.wood@ncl.ac.uk ❏

[26]

Globalizing Surveillance

Comparative and Sociological Perspectives

David Lyon

Queen's University, Ontario

abstract: If surveillance was once thought of as primarily the domain of the nation-state, or of organizations such as firms within the nation-state, in the 21st century it must be considered in a broader context. Surveillance has to do with the rationalized control of information within modern organizations, and involves in particular processing personal data for the purposes of influence, management, or control. It also depends for its success on the involvement of its 'data-subjects'. In countries of the global north, surveillance expanded with increasing rapidity after computerization from the 1970s onwards, a process that also enabled it to spread more readily to other areas, especially from workers and citizens to consumers and travellers. Since the 1980s, surveillance has become increasingly globalized, as populations become more mobile, and as social relations and transactions have stretched more elastically over time and space. Globalizing surveillance was also catalyzed by the events of 11 September 2001. However, surveillance processes occur differently in different cultural contexts, as do responses to them. Understanding comparatively the various modes of surveillance, understood sociologically, helps us grasp one of the key features of today's world and also to see political and policy responses to it in perspective.

keywords: globalization ✦ late modernity ✦ risk ✦ surveillance

Modernity, Surveillance and Risk

Surveillance comes to light, as it were, when people realize that they are being 'watched'. The 'watching' may be almost literal, as in the case of closed circuit television surveillance (CCTV) or much more metaphorical

International Sociology Vol. 19 No. 2

(though no less real) in the case of airport check-ins, supermarket check-outs, Internet cookies, driver's licence production for police, employee cards in the workplace and so on. Surveillance has also become much more visible following the dramatic and disastrous events of 11 September 2001 (hereafter, 9/11). High-tech companies are wooing willing governments with their security and surveillance products, designed to detect 'terrorists' and also other miscreants who may be found in cities or in airports and at borders. In this case, particularly in the USA, much public opinion seems to be tipped in support of surveillance (Lyon, 2003b).

Already, from the reference to 9/11, one may sense the ways that surveillance practices are spreading around the world. If local moral panics produce public interest in video surveillance in streets deemed to be dangerous at night, or on a national level, attacks such as the sarin gas assault on the Tokyo subway in 1995 lead to surveillance crack-downs, then global panic regimes such as that generated by the attacks on the World Trade Center and the Pentagon will have similar effects (Lyon, 2001a). The time-honoured technological fix is invoked once more to combat guerrilla activities (often called 'terrorism') wherever they may appear. This is not for a moment to deny the understandable desire for safe streets, or to underplay the risks of terrorism in the 21st century. It is simply to acknowledge that where older moral markers have vanished, where nation-states experience a reduction of their role to maintaining law and order, where capitalist restructuring is occurring and where technique has a culturally privileged position (Ellul, 1964), technological solutions will readily be sought. It does not follow, however, that 'technology' is privileged in this account.

Surveillance is not new, or a new technological phenomenon, or a response to external threats, or even a product simply of modernity. In its ancient forms, it was relatively simple, having to do with taxation records or the census, or perhaps with the apprehension of criminals or spies. The 'information state' could be said to have appeared in England, for example, from 1500. Edward Higgs (2001) argues that English central state surveillance arose first as a means of shoring up state power itself, over against other states, and not primarily as a means of social control. The census and civil registration helped to create sets of circumscribed rights but at the same time, it has to be said, provided the means for social control, if circumstances seemed to require or invite it.

This paradox of surveillance is noted by Nicholas Abercrombie et al. (1983), in which the means of granting civil rights was at the same time a potential means for states to gain informational power over citizens. This means, importantly, that at least in this case – and, I would argue, in almost all cases – surveillance is an ambiguous process (Lyon, 1994). Even in a globalizing context, I argue, surveillance retains this paradoxical,

Lyon *Globalizing Surveillance*

ambiguous character. Even though alliances of nation-states now boast tremendous surveillance power, using satellite tracking stations and super-computer message filtering devices, and although corporations also have access to international flows of personal data, this does not translate automatically into crude control.

In its modern forms surveillance is both entwined with capitalist production and consumption as well as state-oriented bureaucracies and international military affairs, and has become highly sophisticated. But surveillance is also routine, an aspect of daily life that increasingly involves everyone. In addition, surveillance has become increasingly bound up with the mediation of risk. For Ulrich Beck, what he calls the risk society appears as an outcome of industrial society when the 'social, political, ecological, and individual risks created by the momentum of innovation increasingly elude the control and protective institutions of industrial society' (Beck, 1996: 27). Beck now argues that 'world risk society' has emerged (Beck, 1999) in which uninsurable risks – including 'terrorism' – have become prominent. In the present case, we could argue that the pace of surveillance growth, enabled by commercial pressure, technological innovation and cultural commitments to 'techniques-as-solutions', far outstrips the capacity of analysis and policy to understand and cope with it. Such surveillance both addresses risks and produces others.

Pre-industrial society had incalculable hazards, in the shape of famine, storms, plagues and wars, but in modernity these became calculable, insurable risks, in which the growing state – and eventually the 'welfare state' – played a large part. But whereas Durkheim, Weber and Simmel saw people being 'released' from corporate transcendental securities into industrial society, now individuals are being 'released' from industrial society into Beck's 'world risk society' (Beck, 1996: 29). Risks, in short, are being individualized, and the old provident state is less and less willing to bear their cost. In order to calculate risks, insurance companies need information, and they need standards of judgement by which to determine insurability (Ericson and Doyle, 2003). That information, as it pertains to individuals, is part of what we know as surveillance today.

But at the same time, risks may be reproduced, in a cycle of risk production. The development of risk technologies, and of their associated surveillance systems, may itself be viewed as risky by those who are its data subjects. Thus a further paradox appears, that in order to cope with the rising tide of risks, practices emerge – processing personal data with inadequate safeguards – that are themselves deemed by many to be risky. This has become increasingly clear since 9/11, as civil liberties groups and privacy lobbies have raised a chorus of complaints about personal data abuses and intrusions resulting from new security laws and 'anti-terrorist' measures. Public opinion in the USA may accept in a general sense the surveillance demands of increased security, but opposition groups are becoming increasingly vocal, such that certain measures (air passenger checks, for example; Wald, 2003) are being mitigated.

Late Modernity, Surveillance and Globalization

Surveillance experienced some important changes during the last part of the 20th century. It began to morph from its erstwhile character as a centralized and hierarchical 'apparatus' of the state or of capitalistic corporations and started to take on a different character as a decentralized and rhizomic 'assemblage' (Haggerty and Ericson, 2000). Fragments of data are extracted from bodies (biometrics does this literally; other forms of surveillance rely on behavioural traces) by a variety of agencies to be processed and often profiled to create data images or 'virtual selves'. These are used as the basis of discrimination between one category and another, and to facilitate differential treatment. While some forms of surveillance retain their face-to-face frame, others have become increasingly dependent on software codes and algorithmic methods (Graham and Marvin, 2001). And as a concomitant of these, surveillance is also being globalized in unprecedented ways. Before examining this more closely, it is worth noting some definitional matters.

Surveillance is here thought of as a product of modernity. That said, it may also display 'postmodern' features. While it is important not to give the impression that somehow modernity has been superseded or left behind, it is of little consequence whether one refers to 'late' or 'post' modernity in this context. The former term is preferred by Anthony Giddens (1990), and many have followed his lead, no doubt because it helps to distinguish sociological analysis from the more cultural studies of postmodern*ism* (Lyon, 1999). The latter term, proposed as a sociological category by Zygmunt Bauman (1992), suggests that in several important ways new social formations appear to be in the making, which may be thought of as having integrity in their own right, and not merely as geriatric stages of some previous form. However these changes are designated, it is important to note that modernity has been undergoing some very significant alterations over the past 30 years. Surveillance is implicated in these changes.

'Late modernity' is used here to refer to the general political, economic and cultural transformations that occurred in the last third of the 20th century. For the purposes of understanding surveillance better, my use of 'late modernity' refers especially to the shift to a *consumer* capitalist phase (this is actually what Bauman emphasizes in his treatment of *post*modernity!), alongside a decided *post-welfarist* tilt in social policy and

Lyon *Globalizing Surveillance*

crime control (Garland, 2001). The kinds of information control involved in consumer data management produce the detailed profiling and data mining on customers that make up commercial surveillance today, while that involved in crime control and security measures contributes to the algorithmic surveillance and actuarial justice that has become equally prevalent. Other sorts of surveillance, notably in government administration and the workplace, continue to be highly significant, but in late modernity they are supplemented, and sometimes interfaced or integrated, with the newer kinds. In all cases, 'social sorting' has become more significant (Lyon, 2002, 2003c).

Another feature or cognate aspect of late modernity is globalization. Again, this term is fraught with controversy. Globalization is characterized by action at a distance, such that social relations and transactions are stretched across time–space (Giddens, 1990); the speed, intensity, reach and impact of communications increase globally; networks and nodes become structurally more important (Castells, 1996) depending on information and generating risks; and the global is mediated by the local, such that it makes sense to talk of 'glocalization' (Robertson, 1992, 1995). Globalization has economic, social, cultural and political dimensions, each of which has ramifications for surveillance. These have to do with the political-economic restructuring that began in earnest in the 1970s.

The globalization of surveillance is directly connected with doing things at a distance. We no longer see, let alone know, many with whom we make exchanges or interact. They are geographically apart from us. As social relations are stretched, courtesy of the new communication technologies, so more and more interactions and transactions become abstract and disembodied, which jeopardizes the sorts of trust that once depended upon the face-to-face and the co-present. Some kinds of trust may be reestablished, however, by the use of tokens – such as ID cards, PIN sequences, photo cards, telephone numbers and drivers' licences – all of which now involve searchable databases (see Lessig, 1999). Electronic commerce or air travel are obvious examples of how such systems transcend national boundaries in new nodes and networks, yet different surveillance regimes associated with these have different characteristics in different countries.

In the later 20th century, surveillance underwent certain changes that relate to new technologies. Computers were used to compile personal databases, which became increasingly searchable. As new telecommunications and eventually the Internet and other networks became available, so personal databases became remotely searchable. This is the infrastructural basis of contemporary surveillance, and it also makes it, in principle at least, an international phenomenon. Today's machine-readable passports are a good example of an older administrative scheme that has been upgraded using new technologies (Torpey, 2001; Salter, 2003). Airline passenger data are another example, and in this case, commercial trans-actions are involved in security surveillance. It is also a case that, like passports, requires some international harmonization. To an extent, what happens in one country has to be matched in others.

As noted already, although technological developments facilitate globalized surveillance, it is a big mistake to imagine that the changes taking place have to do merely with new technologies. Communication and information technologies may *enable* aspects of globalization and global surveillance to occur, but they certainly do not *cause* them to do so. Those new technologies are themselves the product of a quest for ever-increasing mobility and speed dating back before the Second World War, but which was galvanized decisively in the economic and technological boom that followed the war. On the one hand, in the commercial sphere, consumer data were increasingly valued and sought as a means of creating customers for products in the lean, just-in-time approach of the so-called new economy. And on the other hand, in the realm of crime control, *potential* suspect data were sought as a means of anticipating and pre-empting illegal activities, many of which were created by the oppor-tunities appearing in dispersed, mobile, affluent societies.

In the 21st century, it is no accident that some of the key surveillance measures are ones that either relate back to earlier quests for geopolitical power, or to the new contexts created by economic restructuring in the 1980s and 1990s. As to the first, security regimes which since the Second World War have become international alliances now boast complex satel-lite tracking systems such as 'Echelon'. This spans several continents, although it is the outcome of a so-called UK–USA agreement, and filters messages from many different media – email, telephone, fax and telex – through a device known as a 'dictionary'. Although military concerns prompted this system in the first place, it is also now used for industrial and commercial intelligence as well.

The latter kinds of surveillance, relating to economic restructuring, also require the processing of large amounts of personal data, but this time in the context of either the control of the drug trade, or in electronic commerce transactions. International trade in illicit drugs has spurred extensive policing and surveillance measures in the past 20–30 years. As for elec-tronic commerce, its practices are both for verifying identities but also for profiling consumers, such that their details too can be filtered, sorting them into various categories of consumption. Policing across borders involves cross-border data flow, as does e-commerce across borders.

So far I have commented on the ways that surveillance is similarly enabled by new technologies, wherever it is found, and on some of the social pressures leading to the development of those systems in an

Lyon *Globalizing Surveillance*

international context. But just as technology does not determine outcomes in a single national context, so does it not do so in a global one either. Globalization is often thought of in primarily economic terms, and this dimension of globalization is certainly significant for surveillance. The flexible labour regimes required for contemporary capitalism entail the extensive use of mobile workers, whose activities are tracked across distance and borders. And more and more commercial activity also occurs in direct ways, courtesy of computer networks, such that personal data flow across national divides as well (Bennett and Raab, 2003).

At the same time, globalization also relates to other entities and processes, notably the activities of the nation-state. Personal data have been flowing over national borders for many years in relation to personal travel, in the systems of customs, immigration and citizenship. The passport is a vital document in this regard (Torpey, 2001). Such data also travel courtesy of policing and intelligence services, and this has only intensified since the attacks of 9/11 (Ball and Webster, 2003). Indeed, as guerrilla warfare has grown as a global phenomenon since the last decades of the 20th century so, paradoxically, high technology surveillance methods have been reinforced (Downey and Murdock, 2003). This in turn is not unconnected with the progressive militarization of policing (Haggerty and Ericson, 2001), and of urban life (Graham and Marvin, 2001), again, as globalized phenomena.

Not only are different social sectors drivers of particular kinds of surveillance, but it is also the case that receptivity to surveillance differs depending on cultural and national contexts. New methods may be acceptable in one context and not another. Thus, for instance, national electronic ID card systems may be found already in use in Thailand, Malaysia and Singapore, but they have been rejected in Korea, and are only at a preliminary planning stage in Canada, the UK and the USA. In another example, the electronic monitoring of offenders, which began in the USA, was slow to find such acceptance in Europe. As Gary T. Marx points out in his comparative study of undercover police methods, it is 'premature to conclude that a standard, technocratic, anticipatory, velvet glove, paradigmatic American social control model is taking over the western democratic world' (Marx and Fijnaut, 1995: 324).

It is true that some structural similarities and the common problems facing (late) modern states may produce similar techniques in different places. Airport security systems are an obvious case in point. Equally, the same transnational corporations are trying to sell their equipment across the world, so, again, the chances are strong of similar solutions appearing in quite distant places (see Zureik, 2003). Sun Microsystems, for instance, a US-based company, provides the equipment, software and support for the national electronic ID system of Thailand. Some countries

141

International Sociology Vol. 19 No. 2

will also want to demonstrate their technical prowess using their surveillance systems – it is arguable that both Spain and Malaysia have developed their new smart ID cards at least in part for this reason (Stalder and Lyon, 2002).

It is also true that local and regional social, political and cultural contexts will experience surveillance in different ways. Some devices with high-level locational surveillance capacities, such as cellphones, are more suited to densely populated areas and thus will increase tracking in cities, but not necessarily in rural areas. Over time, the use of radio-frequency identification devices (RDIFs) and satellite tracking may change this, too. But technological capacities never operate alone. In North America, while commercial interests and government agencies such as the Department of Homeland Security give those technologies their chance, they are also opposed by civil liberties and consumer groups. In South-East Asia, on the other hand, where more authoritarian and less democratic governments are able to mount systems with little public consultation or approval, it is possible to establish large-scale surveillance systems against a backdrop of much more muted dissent.

One of the most striking developments since the 1990s has been that Britain emerged as the clear world leader in CCTV deployment. That country has a far more comprehensive system of urban, public space cameras than any other in the world. This may be explained by the presence of dramatic events (the murder of a small boy whose assailants were caught in the lens of a construction site camera) or long-term problems (such as IRA terrorism) (Norris and Armstrong, 1999). But if one considers the electronic tagging of offenders, it is clear that the USA (where the technique originated) is far more likely to deploy this method than its European counterparts (although there is evidence that this is now changing; Nellis 2000). The mere existence of new technologies is far from a sufficient reason for them to be used.

Wherever they exist, however, and for whatever reasons they have been established, surveillance systems do tend to depend increasingly on searchable databases. This means that they are used for 'social sorting', for the classification of populations as a precursor to differential treatment (Lyon, 2002). In the realm of crime control they display the character of 'categorical suspicion' (Marx, 1988), whereas in the commercial realm they involve 'categorical seduction' (Lyon, 2001b). In the latter case, consumers are sorted and sifted for their relative worth to marketing companies in a form of discrimination that creams some off for special treatment and cuts others off from consuming opportunities altogether (Gandy, 1995).

Social sorting is also a crucially important activity of nation-states, often achieved by means of the census, and of border controls, but also in welfare administration. Comparative studies are very valuable at this

Lyon *Globalizing Surveillance*

level, too. How ID classifications work at borders in Israel is not dissimilar from the ways in which they operated in South Africa under apartheid (Zureik, 2001). Similarly, the categories operated by welfare professionals serve to produce populations for certain purposes, a practice that would bear comparisons across different national jurisdictions (Gilliom, 2001). Beyond this, one could examine fruitfully the ways in which Internet surveillance sorts populations by income, gender and 'race', how CCTV does something similar with less high-tech methods (Norris, 2002), and how this, too, differs from place to place.

Two things have to be recalled about these social sorting processes, particularly in comparative perspective. One is that the systems themselves are not technically foolproof; they may not function in the ways intended (and of course, they may also have unintended consequences). The other is that the success of surveillance systems always depends upon the collusion (however weak or even unconscious) of their subjects. Some will comply willingly, others will negotiate, and yet others may actively resist. This also means that the same technological systems may be used on occasion for quite varying and even contradictory purposes.

This latter point returns us to a consideration of the inherent ambiguity of surveillance processes. The same technologies may be used for highly repressive surveillance purposes and simultaneously for the purposes of counter-surveillance or resistance. Some interesting comparative work could be done in this area. In China, for instance, western corporations have been sought for advice and equipment to bolster the surveillance capacities of a very undemocratic state (Greg, 2001). At the same time, the Internet and email are used in China as a means of operating beyond the reach of the state, by democratic dissidents, Falun Gong members and so on. In Singapore, too, several 'sites of resistance' may be found on the Internet, despite stringent efforts to circumscribe it (Ho et al., 2001).

One of the most striking events for the globalization of surveillance is the aftermath of the attacks of 9/11. This may be seen in two related surveillance areas. One is the ways in which several governments in different countries have proposed new measures for dealing with the 'terrorist' threat (Ball and Webster, 2003). These include 'smart' ID card systems to try to determine who is and is not a legitimate resident or visitor in a given country, CCTV systems with facial recognition capacities in airports and elsewhere, to check against database images of known terrorists, and various other biometric devices to verify identities more satisfactorily (Lyon, 2003d). A considerable amount of research is called for to determine which country adopts which technologies and why. How far does the experience of one country encourage or discourage another?

International Sociology Vol. 19 No. 2

The other surveillance consequence of 9/11 is the proliferation of anti-terrorist legislation in several countries. These tend to relax the limitations on previously stricter laws, such as those to do with wiretapping or indeed any message interception. Few modern western countries have not altered their laws in some respect, or passed new ones, and in East and South-East Asia, new measures have also been adopted. Already existing systems of cross-border policing have been considerably expanded, with long-term consequences for globalized surveillance (Bigo, 2002). Again, comparative investigation to determine the extent of mutual influence between countries will make a vital contribution to social and political understanding.

Globalized Surveillance and its Consequences

I have argued that both for ordinary and extraordinary reasons, surveillance is an increasingly globalized phenomenon. The ordinary reasons are that, just as growing surveillance may be explained in terms of the overall structural developments of the western world since the Second World War (and not as sinister attempts at social control), so now, as modernity globalizes, surveillance globalizes along with it. Electronic commerce, increased geographical mobility, the 'war against drugs' and other such processes bring enhanced personal and population surveillance along with them. The extraordinary reasons relate to the events and consequences of 9/11, that are catalyzing surveillance developments in several countries simultaneously, and, importantly, are permitting further convergence of different kinds (state, commercial) of surveillance. Several consequences may be traced from this.

First, whether for the purposes of commerce or policing, networked surveillance blurs the old borders (and the old boundaries) of surveillance. Standards are developed between countries for electronic transactions and identity verification, for example, but also for the detection and apprehension of offenders or suspects. The use of searchable databases and of remote checking makes possible surveillance across borders, as for instance in the case of airline ticketing and security measures. Unfamiliar methods of checking may appear in airports, and some of them – for example biometric checks in Keflavik Airport, Iceland – may appear unusually stringent given the size or remoteness of the country.

Second, certain surveillance trends may be accelerated in a global context in response to 9/11. Policing offers some good examples. Two trends have emerged in greater strength in recent years – the privatization and the militarization of police. More and more private police forces, often referred to as 'security' agencies or similar, complement public policing in the 21st century. But they also seek, and use, the same kinds of personal data as their public counterparts (Ericson and Haggerty, 1997),

144

Lyon *Globalizing Surveillance*

and they do so according to similar standards (of insurance risk assessment). The other trend is the militarization of the police, which is in one respect a domestication of armed forces once used primarily against external aggressors. Both these trends fit well with the shifts taking place since 9/11, however, in that private police and more military methods are appropriate for the settings in which the new surveillance is required – borders, airports, central urban areas and so on.

Third, in the area of policy, new initiatives are appearing (and others are demanded) in relation to the globalization of surveillance, especially in the commercial realm. As Colin Bennett and Rebecca Grant say, globalization means that personal 'data on individual customers, employees, suppliers, investors, competitors, and so on' are transferred instantaneously around the world, and this traffic 'has the potential to undermine national efforts to protect the privacy of citizens' (Bennett and Grant, 1999: 12). The European Directive on Data Protection has already had extensive influence in Canada and the USA, and this kind of country-to-country or region-to-region transfer of experience on policies and standards is likely to increase. How it occurs, though, is an empirical question, that bears further examination.

Fourth, one can hardly look at the globalization of surveillance, especially within a framework that acknowledges the active role of 'data subjects', without looking at the globalization of resistance. Resistance to surveillance, whether by consumer groups, computer professionals, or civil rights activists (especially after 9/11), is increasingly known about in different countries. Webcams may be used effectively in this regard, for example. The New York Players, who offer dramatic presentations in front of urban video cameras, are known about in other parts of the world. The websites of groups such as Privacy International or the Electronic Privacy Information Center may also be used in a networking fashion for groups that question the existence or extent of surveillance to network with each other. Interestingly, a new body, the Asia-Pacific Privacy Charter Council (www.BakerCyberLawCentre.org/appcc) came into existence in 2003, with the potential to draw many countries beyond Europe and North America into debates over surveillance and privacy.

Fifth, academically, and in relation to policy studies, interest in surveillance and privacy has increased considerably since the 1980s. A number of now classic studies appeared from the mid-1970s (Rule, 1974; Giddens, 1985; Marx, 1988; Flaherty, 1989; Dandeker, 1990; Bennett, 1992; Regan, 1995; inter alia). During the 1990s, a number of more general treatments appeared (e.g. Whitaker, 1999; Staples, 1998), along with further studies of data protection and privacy policy (e.g. Bennett and Grant, 1999; Agre and Rotenberg, 1997) as well as further more theoretically informed studies (e.g. Bogard, 1996; Norris and Armstrong, 1999).

145

International Sociology Vol. 19 No. 2

This accounts for the emergence of 'surveillance studies' as a cross-disciplinary field for research. The disciplines represented include geography, history, information and computing sciences, political science, sociology and policy studies. Although this convergence is mainly evident in Europe and North America, interest is also growing in Pacific Asia and elsewhere (Lyon, 2003a). Comparative studies are becoming increasingly important (such as the European Community initiative on closed circuit television in cities, called the 'Urban Eye' project). A new online journal, *Surveillance-and-Society* (www.surveillance-and-society.org), is helping to crystallize some of these strands of interest.

At present, however, there is arguably a lot more interest in the globalization of legislation relating to surveillance (privacy, data protection) than in the globalization of surveillance itself. This represents a major challenge for sociologists and other social scientists, not least because a crucial first step in considering legal changes is to understand analytically the conditions that gave rise to them in the first place. Three items in particular require careful research.

One task is to discover exactly what happens to personal data when they are extracted from or submitted by individuals. All too often, the existence of a personal database (technology) or a data-processing agency (institution) is taken to be evidence of personal data flows of particular kinds, and with predictable effects. But as we have observed, mere software and hardware, or mere institutional resources do not on their own produce specific kinds of surveillance. They may, however, induce certain kinds of determinisms in researchers. Mapping the trajectories of personal data will take place in largely untouched terrain.

A second task is to find out exactly how people respond to and interact with systems that automate their transactions and handle their data. Again, surprisingly little is known in many cases (with some notable exceptions, e.g. Norris and Armstrong, 1999). Yet so-called data-subjects – agents, embodied persons – actually engage extensive repertoires of response, depending on timing, social context, location and so on (Ball, 2002). This may be simple, unthought compliance, through to skilful negotiation and active resistance. Knowing what occurs, in which contexts, and why, will be an immensely constructive task for surveillance studies.

A third task is to explore the consequences of surveillance – especially in its rapidly globalizing varieties – for governance (Rose, 1999). Understanding surveillance in the 21st century also entails an analytic move beyond the conventional loci of power – the state or the corporation – to discover ways in which all sorts of processes, procedures, strategies and tactics help to shape relations and enable or constrain activities touched by globalized flows of personal data, from international to local community

Lyon *Globalizing Surveillance*

levels. Emergent power relationships, relating to surveillance, and within self-organizing networks, cry out for serious and subtle analysis.

References

Abercrombie, N. et al. (1983) *Sovereign Individuals of Capitalism*. London: Allen and Unwin.

Agre, P. and Rotenberg, M., eds (1997) *Technology and Privacy: The New Landscape*. Cambridge, MA: MIT Press.

Ball, K. (2002) 'Power, Control, and Computer-based Performance Monitoring: Repertoires, Resistance, and Subjectivities', in D. Lyon (ed.) *Surveillance as Social Sorting: Privacy, Risk, and Digital Discrimination*, pp. 210–25. London and New York: Routledge.

Ball, K. and Webster, F. (2003) *The Intensification of Surveillance*. London: Pluto Press.

Bauman, Z. (1992) *Intimations of Postmodernity*. London and New York: Routledge.

Beck, U. (1996) 'Risk Society and the Provident State', in S. Lash, B. Szerszynski and B. Wynne (eds) *Risk, Environment, and Modernity*. London: Sage.

Beck, U. (1999) *World Risk Society*. Cambridge: Polity Press/Malden, MA: Blackwell.

Bennett, C. J. (1992) *Regulating Privacy: Data Protection and Public Policy in Europe and the United States*. Ithaca, NY: Cornell University Press.

Bennett, C. J. (1997) 'Convergence Re-Visited: Towards a Global Policy for the Protection of Personal Data?', in P. Agre and M. Rotenberg (eds) *Technology and Privacy: The New Landscape*, pp. 99–123. Cambridge, MA: MIT Press.

Bennett, C. J. and Grant, R., eds (1999) *Visions of Privacy: Policy Choices for the Digital Age*. Toronto: University of Toronto Press.

Bennett, C. J. and Raab, C. (2003) *The Governance of Privacy: Policy Instruments in a Global Perspective*. Aldershot: Ashgate.

Bigo, D. (2002) 'To Reassure and Protect, after September 11', at: www.ssrc.org/september11/essays/bigo.htm/

Bogard, W. (1996) *The Simulation of Surveillance*. New York: Cambridge University Press.

Castells, M. (1996) *The Rise of the Network Society*. Oxford and Malden, MA: Blackwell.

Dandeker, C. (1990) *Surveillance, Power, and Modernity*. Cambridge: Polity Press.

Downey, J. and Murdock, G. (2003) 'The Counter-Revolution in Military Affairs: The Globalization of Guerilla Warfare', in D. Thussu and D. Freedman (eds) *War and the Media: Reporting on Conflict*. London: Sage.

Ellul, J. (1964) *The Technological Society*. New York: Vintage.

Ericson, R. and Doyle, A., eds (2003) *Insurance and Morality*. Toronto: University of Toronto Press.

Ericson, R. and Haggerty, K. (1997) *Policing the Risk Society*. Toronto: University of Toronto Press.

Flaherty, D. (1989) *Protecting Privacy in Surveillance Societies*. Chapel Hill: University of North Carolina Press.

147

International Sociology Vol. 19 No. 2

Gandy, O. (1995) 'It's Discrimination, Stupid!', in J. Boal and I. A. Brooks (eds) *Resisting the Virtual Life*, pp. 35–48. San Francisco, CA: City Lights.

Garland, D. (2001) *The Culture of Control: Crime and Social Order in Contemporary Society*. Oxford: Oxford University Press/Chicago, IL: University of Chicago Press.

Giddens, A. (1985) *The Nation-State and Violence*. Cambridge: Polity Press.

Giddens, A. (1990) *The Consequences of Modernity*. Cambridge: Polity Press.

Gilliom, J. (2001) *Overseers of the Poor: Surveillance, Resistance, and the Limits of Privacy*. Chicago, IL: University of Chicago Press.

Graham, S. and Marvin, S. (2001) *Splintering Urbanism: Networked Infrastructures, Technological Mobilities, and the Urban Condition*. London and New York: Routledge.

Greg, W. (2001) *The Golden Shield: Corporations and the Development of Surveillance Technology in the People's Republic of China*. Montreal: International Centre for Human Rights and Democratic Development; at: http://go.openflows.org/CGS_ENG.PDF

Haggerty, K. and Ericson, R. V. (2000) 'The Surveillant Assemblage', *British Journal of Sociology* 51(4): 605–22.

Haggerty, K. and Ericson, R. (2001) 'The Militarization of Policing in an Information Age', *Journal of Political and Military Policing* 27: 233–55.

Higgs, E. (2001) 'The Rise of the Information State: The Development of Central State Surveillance of the Citizen in England, 1500–2000', *Journal of Historical Sociology* 14(2): 175–97.

Ho, K. C. and Kluver, R., eds (2003) *Asia.Com*. London and New York: Routledge.

Ho, K. C., Baber, Z. and Khondker, H. (2001) ' "Sites" of Resistance: Alternatives Websites and State–Society Relations in Singapore', *British Journal of Sociology* 53(1).

Lessig, L. (1999) *Code and other Laws of Cyberspace*. New York: Basic Books.

Lyon, D. (1994) *The Electronic Eye: The Rise of Surveillance Society*. Cambridge: Polity Press/Malden, MA: Blackwell.

Lyon, D. (1999) *Postmodernity*. Buckingham: Open University Press.

Lyon, D. (2001a) 'Surveillance after September 11', *Sociological Research Online* 6(3); at: www.socresonline.org.uk/6/3/lyon

Lyon, D. (2001b) *Surveillance Society: Monitoring Everyday Life*. Buckingham: Open University Press.

Lyon, D. (2002) 'Everyday Surveillance: Personal Data and Social Classification', *Information, Communication, and Society* 5(1): 1–16.

Lyon, D. (2003a) 'Cyberspace, Surveillance, and Social Control: The Hidden Face of the Internet in Asia', in K. C. Ho and R. Kluver (eds) *Asia.Com*, pp. 67–82. London and New York: Routledge.

Lyon, D. (2003b) *Surveillance after September 11*. Cambridge: Polity Press/Malden, MA: Blackwell.

Lyon, D., ed. (2003c) *Surveillance as Social Sorting: Privacy, Risk, and Digital Discrimination*. London and New York: Routledge.

Lyon, D. (2003d) 'Technology vs "Terrorism": ID Cards, Biometric Surveillance and CCTV in the City', paper for RC21,14. ISA World Congress, Brisbane, 12 July 2002, *The International Journal of Urban and Regional Research* 27(3): 666–78.

Lyon *Globalizing Surveillance*

Marx, G. T. (1988) *Undercover: Police Surveillance in America*. Berkeley: University of California Press.

Marx, G. T. and Fijnaut, C., eds (1995) *Police Surveillance in Comparative Perspective*. The Hague: Kluwer.

Nellis, M. (2000) 'Law and Order: The Electronic Monitoring of Offenders', in D. Dolowitz et al. (eds) *Policy Transfer and British Social Policy: Learning from the USA?* Buckingham: Open University Press.

Norris, C. (2002) 'From Personal to Digital: CCTV, the Panopticon, and the Technological Mediation of Suspicion and Social Control', in D. Lyon (ed.) *Surveillance as Social Sorting: Privacy, Risk, and Digital Discrimination*, pp. 249–81. London and New York: Routledge.

Norris, C. and Armstrong, G. (1999) *The Maximum Surveillance Society: The Rise of CCTV*. Oxford and New York: Berg.

Regan, P. (1993) 'The Globalization of Privacy: Implications of Recent Changes in Europe', *The American Journal of Economics and Sociology* 52(3): 257–74.

Regan, P. (1995) *Legislating Privacy: Technology, Social Values, and Public Policy*. Chapel Hill: University of North Carolina Press.

Robertson, R. (1992) *Globalization: Social Theory and Global Culture*. London: Sage.

Robertson, R. (1995) 'Globalization: Time–Space and Homogeneity–Heterogeneity', in M. Featherstone et al. (eds) *Global Modernities*. London: Sage.

Rose, N. (1999) *Powers of Freedom*. Cambridge: Cambridge University Press.

Rule, J. (1974) *Private Lives and Public Surveillance*. London: Allen-Lane.

Salter, M. (2003) *The Passport in International Relations*. London: Lynne Rienner

Stalder, F. and Lyon, D. (2002) 'ID Cards and Social Classification', in D. Lyon (ed.) *Surveillance as Social Sorting: Privacy, Risk, and Digital Discrimination*, pp. 77–93. London and New York: Routledge.

Staples, W. (1998) *The Culture of Surveillance*. Boston, MA: Rowman and Littlefield. (Reprinted 2001 as *Everyday Surveillance*.)

Torpey, J. (2001) *The Invention of the Passport: Surveillance, Citizenship and the State*. Cambridge: Cambridge University Press.

Wald, M. (2003) 'US Agency Scales Back Data Required on Air Travel', *The New York Times* 31 July.

Whitaker, J. (1999) *The End of Privacy*. New York: The New Press.

Zureik, E. (2001) 'Constructing Palestine through Surveillance Practices', *British Journal of Middle Eastern Studies* 28(2): 205–27.

Zureik, E. (2003) 'Governance, Security, and Technology: The Case of Biometrics', Surveillance Project/ Sociology Department paper, Queen's University, March. (Forthcoming in *Studies in Political Economy*.)

Biographical Note: David Lyon is director of the Surveillance Project and professor of sociology at Queen's University, Kingston, Ontario, Canada. His latest book is *Surveillance after September 11* (Polity Press/Blackwell, 2003).

Address: Department of Sociology, Queen's University, Kingston, Ontario, Canada K793N6. [email: lyond@post.queensu.ca]

Name Index